Nuns' Priests' Tales

THE MIDDLE AGES SERIES

Ruth Mazo Karras, Series Editor
Edward Peters, Founding Editor

A complete list of books in the series
is available from the publisher.

Nuns' Priests' Tales

Men and Salvation
in Medieval Women's
Monastic Life

Fiona J. Griffiths

PENN

UNIVERSITY OF PENNSYLVANIA PRESS

PHILADELPHIA

Published by
University of Pennsylvania Press
Philadelphia, Pennsylvania 19104-4112
www.upenn.edu/pennpress

Printed in the United States of America on acid-free paper
1 3 5 7 9 10 8 6 4 2

Library of Congress Cataloging-in-Publication Data

Names: Griffiths, Fiona J., author.
Title: Nuns' priests' tales: men and salvation in medieval women's
    monastic life / Fiona J. Griffiths.
Other titles: Middle Ages series.
Description: 1st edition. | Philadelphia : University of Pennsylvania
    Press, [2018] | Series: The Middle Ages series
Identifiers: LCCN 2017027111 | ISBN 9780812249750 (hardcover:
    alk. paper)
Subjects: LCSH: Monastic and religious life of women—History—
    Middle Ages, 600-1500. | Pastoral care—History—To 1500. |
    Catholic Church—Clergy—History—To 1500.
Classification: LCC BX4210 .G754 2018 | DDC 271/.9000902—dc23
LC record available at https://lccn.loc.gov/2017027111

To my parents, with love and gratitude

CONTENTS

LIST OF ABBREVIATIONS

AA SS
Acta sanctorum quotquot toto orbe coluntur. Ed. Johannes Bollandus et al. Editio novissima. Paris: Victor Palmé, 1863– .

BHL
Bibliotheca hagiographica latina antiquae et mediae aetatis, 2 vols., with supplements. Subsidia Hagiographica 6. Brussels: Société de Bollandistes, 1898–1901.

CCCM
Corpus christianorum: continuatio medievalis.

CCSL
Corpus christianorum: series latina.

CSEL
Corpus scriptorum ecclesiasticorum latinorum.

Deux vies
Les deux vies de Robert d'Arbrissel, fondateur de Fontevraud: légendes, écrits et témoignages. Eds. Jacques Dalarun, Geneviève Giordanego, Armelle Le Huërou, Jean Longère, Dominique Poirel, and Bruce L. Venarde. Disciplina monastica 4. Turnhout: Brepols, 2006.

Lacomblet
Urkundenbuch für die Geschichte des Niederrheins. Ed. Theodor Joseph Lacomblet. 4 vols. Düsseldorf: J. Wolf, 1840–1858.

Lambert
Bernard Lambert. *Bibliotheca Hieronymiana Manuscripta.* Instrumenta Patristica IV. 4 vols. in 5. Steenbrugge: Abbatia S. Petri, 1969–72.

The Letter Collection	*The Letter Collection of Peter Abelard and Heloise.* Ed. David Luscombe, trans. Betty Radice, and rev. David Luscombe. Oxford Medieval Texts. Oxford: Clarendon Press, 2013.
Mansi	*Sacrorum conciliorum, nova et amplissima collectio.* Ed. Joannes Dominicus Mansi. 54 vols. Florence, 1759–98. Paris: H. Welter, 1901–1927 (repr. and continuation). Repr. Graz: Akademische Druck- u. Verlagsanstalt, 1960–1962.
MGH	*Monumenta Germaniae Historica.*

Auct. ant.	*Auctores antiquissimi.*
Briefe d. dt. Kaiserzeit	*Die Briefe der deutschen Kaiserzeit.*
Capit.	*Capitularia regum Francorum.*
Capit. episc.	*Capitula episcoporum.*
Conc.	*Concilia.*
DD	*Diplomata.*
Epp. sel.	*Epistolae selectae.*
Epp.	*Epistolae.*
LL	*Leges.*
Poetae	*Poetae Latini medii aevi.*
SS	*Scriptores.*
SS rer. Germ.	*Scriptores rerum Germanicarum.*
SS rer. Merov.	*Scriptores rerum Merovingicarum.*

PL	*Patrologiae cursus completus: series latina.* Ed. J.-P. Migne. 221 vols. Paris: Migne, 1841–1864.

NOTES TO CITATIONS

Biblical citations refer to the Vulgate.

Prologue

It is a curious fact of medieval religious history that the nuns' priest best known to modern audiences is a fictional character: the Nun's Priest of Chaucer's *Canterbury Tales*. In the fourteenth century, when Chaucer wrote his *Tales*, nuns' priests would have been as familiar in England as the other figures he imagined as pilgrims on the road to Canterbury, no more remarkable than, for instance, a knight, a friar, a wife, a monk, or a merchant—characters who also feature in the *Tales*. As Chaucer knew, every female monastery had at least one priest (and often several) who saw to the nuns' spiritual needs, hearing their confessions, ministering the sacraments to them, and sometimes aiding in the management of their affairs. The Nun's Priest of the *Canterbury Tales* was such a figure, who appeared first in the General Prologue to the poem as one of three unnamed priests (all of them, technically, "nuns' priests") accompanying the Prioress, Madame Eglentyne, as she journeyed with her nun-secretary to Canterbury.[1]

The appearance of the Nun's Priest in *The Canterbury Tales* offers an important reminder of the generally routine presence of ordained men alongside nuns within the medieval religious life. For much of the medieval period, nuns across Europe heard the Mass regularly from the lips of priests, whose ties to women's monasteries were embedded within a series of local, institutional, and familial networks. Nuns required priests, as Chaucer implicitly recognized. Yet, at some point between his day and ours, the nuns' priest ceased to be so plainly acknowledged and slipped quietly from historical view. Other figures among the pilgrims—knights, nuns, monks, clerks, lawyers, millers, and friars—appear in modern scholarly accounts of the Middle Ages. The nuns' priest does not. He is absent from most studies of the secular clergy and also from those of male religious life, although it was often ordained monks or friars who ministered to nuns in nearby women's communities. Even histories of female monasticism have often passed over the nuns' priest in silence, preferring to cast the female monastery as a space for women's governance and autonomy.

Nuns' Priests' Tales seeks to restore nuns' priests to discussions of medieval religious life, recognizing that these men were more common and more integral to medieval society than recent accounts have typically allowed. Nuns' priests existed, in large numbers, and they supported female religious life in women's monasteries across Europe throughout the medieval period. They served nuns spiritually as confessors and pastors and often materially as well, attending to the practical needs of women's communities. In certain cases, priests developed deep and cherished friendships with nuns, whom they admired. They lived near, and sometimes with, women, challenging ideas concerning the segregation of the sexes within the religious life. Some men were even buried at female monasteries, extending their spiritual relationship with religious women beyond the grave. Their service to women was crucial to female religious life, but it could be equally central—as I argue in this book—to male spirituality and devotion as well.

The chronological focus of this book—*pace* Chaucer—is the late eleventh and twelfth centuries, a period of tremendous spiritual enthusiasm marked by church reform, the development of new forms of devotion and pious practice, the expansion of the monastic life, and—significantly, for the purposes of this study—the campaign for clerical celibacy.[2] Ecclesiastical rulings during the eleventh century against clerical marriage signaled the beginnings of a "social revolution," as Christopher Brooke argued.[3] The families of priests were dissolved and delegitimized, with catastrophic effects: clerical wives found that their marriages were declared invalid and their children illegitimate, causing them to forfeit dowries and inheritances.[4] The eradication of clerical marriage was the primary concern of church reformers; even so, the disruptive implications of the celibacy movement extended beyond married priests and their families. Secular priests and ordained monks who served among nuns faced a context in which any contact between priests and women might be deemed suspect. As the celibacy movement spread through dioceses in Italy, Germany, northern France, and into England, anxiety concerning relations between the sexes grew—even for men and women in the monastic life, whose vows had long included chastity.

Given the intensity of arguments against clerical marriage during the late eleventh and twelfth centuries, historians have often assumed that priests at this time began to avoid women altogether. Yet this period of tremendous social change was equally marked by the dramatic expansion of female monasticism—an expansion that would not have been possible without the support of ordained men. The resulting contradiction, between the presumed rejection of women by churchmen and the concurrent expansion of female religious life, forms the starting point of my study and is the focus of my first chapter, which examines the nuns' priest as an ambivalent figure in medieval religious life and modern scholarship. Despite the ubiquity of nuns' priests, medieval clerical and monastic sources mention them only infrequently and usually with a mixture of concern, suspicion, and distrust. Modern scholars, guided by the anxieties of the medieval texts, assume a monastic experience defined by the segregation of the sexes and, in effect, by male monastic rejection of women. For both groups—medieval and modern—the nuns' priest has posed problems of categorization and interpretation that obscure the reality of men's spiritual service to religious women. So while historians have tended to accept that nuns had (and, indeed, *needed*) priests, their assumption that male spirituality required separation from women has simultaneously rendered nuns' priests unthinkable as serious religious figures. In this first chapter, I trace medieval and modern perceptions of nuns' priests as contradictory and problematic, showing why these men have been absent from studies of the medieval religious life, and arguing for the need to move beyond fixed assumptions concerning male spirituality in order to bring them back into historical view.

In subsequent chapters, I consider nuns' priests from both a spiritual and an intellectual standpoint, tracing these men's ideas about religious women and their spiritual motivations in ministering to them. What interests me most is not *how* priests provided religious women with pastoral care—that is to say, the practical details that governed their service to nuns—but rather *why* they did so, risking the alleged dangers and temptations of contact with women in order to provide nuns with spiritual care and support. A significant challenge in studying nuns' priests is that few are known by name and fewer still recorded their thoughts and experiences in writing (even Chaucer's Nun's Priest is "strangely unknowable," as Marilyn Oliva has observed).[5] My examination of nuns' priests thus involves two parallel and complementary quests: first, to broaden the scope of enquiry, claiming as "nuns' priests" men who ministered to women, but whose lives and writings have been deemed unrepresentative of mainstream medieval life and thought (notably, but not exclusively, the controversial philosopher and theologian Peter Abelard); and second, to explore nuns' priests in aggregate, focusing less on individual men than on the set of ideas that they held in common, their "tales" as these ideas are invoked in the book's title. Exploring the ideas that nuns' priests shared about service to religious women—the motifs that appear in scattered sermons, letters, wall paintings, manuscript images, biblical commentaries, and the liturgy—allows a more complete sense of how these men, broadly, viewed their spiritual role in relation to nuns, revealing the contours of a clerical counter-discourse in which spiritual care for women was understood as a holy service and an act of devotion and obedience to Christ.

Chapters 2 through 4 treat several of the most prominent motifs embraced by nuns' priests during the eleventh and twelfth centuries, showing how examples and ideas concerning men's spiritual involvement with women drawn from the Bible (Chapter 2), the Church Fathers (Chapter 3), and the heroes of early medieval monasticism (Chapter 4) were adopted and repurposed by these men to explain and defend their spiritual service to nuns. The willingness of nuns' priests to minister to women was not an isolated phenomenon of the central or later Middle Ages, as these examples show, but formed part of a venerable tradition of men's care for pious women that stretched back to the origins of Christianity.

The most compelling model for the spiritual involvement of medieval men with religious women was provided by Jesus himself, as I show in Chapter 2. Not only was Jesus born of a woman, but he surrounded himself both in life and in death with women and revealed himself first to women following his resurrection. Medieval men were well aware of Jesus's close friendships with women and of the spiritual dignity that he accorded them, citing both of these in defending their own service to nuns. They also particularly noted Jesus's concern to arrange for the care of his mother after his death: as he hung on the cross, Jesus commended Mary to his disciple John, entrusting him with her care (John 19:27). Some early exegetes interpreted the commendation as a divine command that all men should provide spiritual care for women. Drawing on this interpretation, certain medieval monks and priests came to view their care for women as a powerful form of Christian devotion—an act of obedience and love for Jesus that was performed through spiritual service to nuns, characterized as Christ's "brides." In serving religious women, these men imagined themselves as emulating John, Jesus's friend and beloved disciple, whose care for Mary had been Jesus's dying command.

In the third chapter, I turn to Jerome (d. 420), the theologian, exegete, and saint who devoted himself to the spiritual guidance of devout Roman noblewomen. For medieval men, whose relationships with religious women were often subject to criticism and distrust, Jerome's example was especially appealing. Unlike John (whose chastity was never called into question), Jerome's relationships with women were widely disparaged during his lifetime, and may even have led to his exile from the city of Rome. Nevertheless, Jerome emerged during the Middle Ages as a model for the chaste spiritual involvement of pious men with women; his relationship with the wealthy widow Paula—which likely formed the source of his troubles in Rome— became a byword for innocent spiritual friendship between the sexes. Nuns' priests regularly cited Jerome as the saintly figure whose involvement with women had inspired their own care for nuns and whose trials demonstrated that even saintly male-female pairs might be maligned. Nuns' priests found further encouragement in Jerome's writings, seizing on his characterization of religious women as *dominae*—"ladies" or "female lords"—a status rooted in women's presumed role as brides of Christ.[6] If nuns were brides of Christ, it followed that priests were their servants, as some men argued, since priests were servants of Christ. According to this logic, providing support for religious women was fundamentally an extension of men's existing service to Christ and a further way to please him.

My fourth chapter examines the most common, and yet least controversial, bond joining chaste men and women within the religious life: the sibling bond between biological brothers and sisters. Although medieval churchmen warned against opposite-sex relations, kinship bonds were generally deemed innocent and "safe" within the early medieval monastic life. My purpose in this chapter is to understand how this became so, particularly given the explicit rejection of biological family in the teachings of the New Testament. As I show, biological kinship emerged within the early monastic life as a legitimate, and even holy, context for engagement between the sexes. Stories of monks who provided spiritual care and attention to a pious sister bolstered the perception that care for a man's sister was not simply acceptable, but might actually form part of his saintly profile. The example of Benedict of Nursia (d. c. 550), the sixth-century abbot whose sister Scholastica supposedly lived near his monastery at Monte Cassino, is a case in point: Benedict and Scholastica were celebrated in medieval legend as saintly twins (despite meager evidence for Scholastica's existence), providing a virtually unimpeachable model of spiritual intimacy between siblings. During the central Middle Ages, men's closest connections to religious women were often founded on concern for a sister in the religious life: the brothers of Christina of Markyate (d. after 1155), Elisabeth of Schönau (d. 1164), and Hildegard of Bingen (d. 1179), for instance, provided spiritual service for nuns in their sisters' communities. Fraternal care was so widely accepted by this time that defensive measures were rarely necessary: few ordained men saw the need to defend, or even explain, their spiritual involvement with a professed sister—a striking exception to the more usually defensive discussions of male pastoral care that appear in other contexts.

In the fifth and final chapter, I turn from models of care that medieval men adopted from past examples and adapted to fit new circumstances in order to explore some of the period's more innovative topoi. In particular, the chapter traces the idea that women's prayers were more efficacious than those of men, a function of the increasingly widespread identification of religious women as brides of Christ. Scholars have for some time recognized that religious men were drawn to holy women whom they viewed as visionaries and prophets. As Caroline Walker Bynum observed some thirty years ago, holy women were sought by men as both a "standard of piety and a window open to the divine."[7] In this chapter, I show that religious women generally—and not only mystics and visionaries—could be viewed as powerful intercessors on men's behalf, a view founded on their presumed and gendered intimacy with Christ. Drawing on a late antique vocabulary, medieval men approached nuns as "brides" (*sponsae*) and "ladies" (*dominae*), whose intercession with the "bridegroom" would be more effective than the intercession of any man— regardless of his purity, devotion, or priestly standing. Evidence from letters, necrologies, and burial records indicates that the promise of intercession by Christ's brides served as a strong incentive to medieval priests, who hoped that women's prayers would accompany them in death, as in life, and bring them ultimately to heaven. Serving as a priest to nuns was no distraction for ordained men, as these examples show, but could be understood as spiritually beneficial and even critical to men's salvation.

*   *   *

In an important study published some years ago, Alcuin Blamires traced what he called the medieval "case" for women, naming both Abelard and Chaucer among the primarily male medieval figures who wrote about women in positive terms, thereby contributing to what Blamires described as a "long-standing medieval tradition in defence of women."[8] However, as Blamires acknowledged, that literature was, by and large, theoretical: the arguments in favor of "woman" that some medieval men developed were not intended to have real implications for actual women, nor, typically, did they. In his

Conclusion, Blamires regretted the fact that the medieval case for women, although it reached "epic proportions" and incorporated a wide range of pro-feminine models, ultimately made very little practical difference.[9]

In this book, I contend that the ideas, motifs, and rhetorical strategies adopted by nuns' priests—their "tales"—*did* make a difference. Like the men whose case for women Blamires so richly explored, nuns' priests knew how to defend women, drawing on classical, biblical, and early Christian profeminine examples. But unlike male proponents of the case for women, nuns' priests were not primarily concerned with women's spiritual dignity or even with their place in the church (although they did tend to exalt women spiritually). They were concerned rather with defending and legitimizing their own position as ordained men whose spiritual role involved supporting and serving female religious life. Nuns' priests faced ridicule, censure, skepticism, and accusations of wrong doing in their spiritual service to women, as I explain in Chapter 1. Their reflections concerning women's place within the religious life had critical implications for their sense of their own spiritual involvement with nuns and for the separate roles, and reciprocal obligations, that they believed bound ordained men to professed women. Studying the "tales" embraced and perpetuated by nuns' priests adds immeasurably to our understanding of male spirituality during the central Middle Ages, broadening our perception of religious men and of their devotional practices beyond the reductionist assumption that celibacy defined male spirituality in the age of reform. At the same time, men's narratives have important implications for the history of women, since priests who found a way to justify men's spiritual involvement with women were more likely to serve willingly in female monasteries, facilitating the liturgical lives of nuns and therefore also the expansion of female monasticism. Such men were critical to female religious life. They, no less than the women they served, deserve our attention.

CHAPTER I

The Puzzle of the Nuns' Priest

Why does anyone who disdains marriage approach a woman?
—Marbode of Rennes, *Epistola ad Robertum*

It is always men's duty to provide for women's needs.
—Abelard, *Institutio*

This chapter addresses a puzzle central to the history of female monasticism, and of male spirituality, in the high Middle Ages. The puzzle is in many ways a simple one, but with considerable implications for our understanding of medieval religious life, for both women and men. Beginning in the late eleventh century, women were drawn in record numbers to the spiritual life, ultimately prompting a surge of monastic foundations that attracted widespread and usually admiring contemporary commentary. In Germany, France, and England, observers noted with wonder the conversion of women across the social spectrum, from noblewomen to farmers' daughters, who dedicated themselves to a religious life inspired by the examples of the apostles and of the early church.[1] Yet the emphasis that medieval observers placed on women's attraction to the religious life at this time was not matched by a parallel or positive discussion of the priests whose work among women was necessary to support the dramatic expansion of female monasticism. Other groups—monks, canons, recluses, hermits, and lay converts—garnered approval and praise from their medieval contemporaries. By contrast, priests ministering to religious women appear only rarely as topics of discussion. When they do, it is primarily as the objects of suspicion and opprobrium.

The relative silence in the medieval sources regarding nuns' priests is remarkable, especially when we consider how many ordained men were needed within female monastic communities at any one time. Nuns, like all women, were barred from ordination to the priesthood.[2] Female monasteries therefore relied on ordained men to provide for certain aspects of their spiritual care: chiefly to celebrate Mass in their chapels, but also to give last rites to their sick and dying and often to hear their confessions as well. The arrangements governing the provision of care by these men could vary considerably.[3] Priests ministering to religious women might be drawn from the local secular clergy, they might be canons attached to the female house, or they might be ordained monks or canons from neighboring, and often affiliated, male communities.[4] Their sacramental service to women might be occasional, or it might be regularized and long-term (even multi-year).[5] But whatever the shifting circumstances of priestly involvement with religious women, the essential fact of male spiritual care remained a constant of female religious life throughout the period. Without exception, nuns required priests to consecrate the Mass for them.[6] The upsurge in female monastic foundations during the late eleventh and twelfth centuries (as many as 50 new foundations in some decades, as Bruce Venarde has shown for France and England) thus required a parallel expansion in the numbers of ordained men who were needed to meet women's sacramental needs.[7]

The significance of these men to the history of female monasticism is vast: they supported female religious life in a period now often seen as its zenith. Yet despite their importance, they have been an enigma to modern scholars, just as they were for medieval observers. As celibate men who engaged in regular and often spiritually intimate contact with women, nuns' priests present a series of apparent contradictions. They alone were permitted to enter a monastic space ostensibly defined as female and to engage spiritually with nuns, whose purity depended paradoxically on their isolation from men. Institutionally, too, they blur distinctions in the religious life, being not fully members of the female house, but also not quite separate from it.[8] Although priests held spiritual power over religious women, they could nevertheless be subject to the temporal authority of the abbess, to whom (depending on local arrangements and the status of the female house) they might even vow obedience.[9] Some priests were selected by women; in cases of abuse or negligence, they could be dismissed by them too, further unsettling hierarchies of authority based on gender and ecclesiastical office.[10] Nuns' priests were, in short, figures of paradox and contradiction. Although widely recognized by their contemporaries as necessary to female religious life, they were consistently troubling to clerical observers, who worried about the potential challenges to ecclesiastical authority as well as the dangers to chastity and propriety inherent in the proximity of women to men within the religious life.

Anxiety and Oversight: The Medieval Sources

Dangers and troubles feature prominently in the few medieval sources that discuss men's spiritual care for religious women, creating the impression that the provision of care for nuns was primarily a "problem" for priests. Churchmen agreed that nuns required the services of one or more priests, as well as the material support of various canons or brothers, and—by the twelfth century—the oversight of a provost, prior, or spiritual father, who held ultimate authority over the women (generally with the help of a prioress or *magistra*).[11] As the twelfth-century monk Idung of Prüfening noted, reflecting a trend toward male supervision of women in material as well as spiritual matters: "it is not expedient for that sex to enjoy the freedom of having its own governance."[12] Yet despite widespread agreement that nuns needed men's services (and that female monasteries should not be allowed to function without them), the means by which such services should be provided had been topics of anxious commentary from the very origins of monasticism. From the standpoint of male spirituality, the most pressing problem lay in the contact with women that men's provision of pastoral care required. Already in the third century, sexual renunciation was a hallmark of the religious life, with many of the desert fathers famed for their total avoidance of women. "A woman's body is fire," one brother had declared, explaining his refusal to touch even his own mother: "simply because I was touching you, the memory of other women might come into my mind."[13]

In keeping with the idea that contact with women was spiritually dangerous for men, rules and prescriptive texts from the earliest centuries of monasticism depict the provision of care for nuns as a perilous assignment, one that was most appropriate for men whose age and reputation signaled their likelihood to withstand temptation. As Basil of Caesarea (d. 379) advised in the fourth century, men chosen to care for women should be "of mature years and reverent in their comportment and character," advice that was repeated (although not always followed) throughout the medieval period.[14] But even advanced age could not fully prevent temptation, as churchmen feared.[15] Accounts of men like the sixth-century monk Equitius, who was (miraculously) made a eunuch in order to safeguard his chastity among nuns, reinforced the sense that temptation for priests serving among women was inevitable (the story of Origen's auto-castration, although deplored, underscored the presumption that only a eunuch could serve safely among women).[16] Limitations were therefore put in place to guard further against both sin and—perhaps just as important—the suspicion of sin. Private conversations with women were to be avoided, as a succession of early rulings advised, recommending that no meeting take place without witnesses to guarantee its blamelessness.[17] According to the seventh-century Council of Seville, which was known and cited during the twelfth century, even the abbot was prohibited from talking with nuns of an affiliated monastery. As a practical matter, he was permitted to speak with the abbess—but only "with two or three sisters for witness."[18] The early ninth-century *Institutio sanctimonialium* likewise ruled that a priest serving in a female house should bring a deacon and a subdeacon with him as witnesses. The men were to enter the inner spaces of the women's cloister only to visit the sick and to celebrate the Mass (which the women were to observe from behind a curtain); once their purpose had been fulfilled, they were to leave.[19] Lingering in the women's cloister was expressly forbidden.[20]

    Sources from the eleventh and twelfth centuries—the particular focus of this book—reflect the mix of anxiety and oversight that had characterized early medieval discussions of pastoral care for women. Stories of religious men who succumbed to sexual temptation while serving women spiritually (or of nuns who became infatuated with their priests) stoked fears that the pastoral relationship could provide an opening for sin. The *Speculum virginum* (c. 1140), written as a model dialogue for monks engaged in the spiritual care of nuns, recounted the fate of one unhappy cleric who fell in love with the prioress of the monastery where he served. Having broken into the women's dormitory to wait in the prioress's bed for her return, the "insolent madman" was "strangled by the very angel who had tempted him." The prioress, coming back from Lauds, was horrified to discover his corpse.[21] Even more worrying than stories of sexual temptation was the fear that men's licit, spiritual admiration of devout women could give way to sin. Writing for a male audience, the abbot Aelred of Rievaulx (d. 1167) explained the insinuation of vice this way: "someone's interest is aroused by hearing about a nun extolled for her holiness of body and spirit, her sincere faith, her outstanding discretion, her rock-solid virtue of humility . . . , her remarkable abstinence, her excellent obedience." Admiration turns to "dutiful" attachment, which leads to "dear" attachment, and then, inexorably, to "vice-prone" attachment.[22] According to this line of reasoning, the most pious women and men were, paradoxically, the most susceptible to temptation.

Concerns relating to the potential for sexual sin in the pastoral relationship had a long lineage within the monastic life. Even so, there were fresh challenges in the eleventh and twelfth centuries. The church reform movement, with its campaign for clerical celibacy, warned secular priests explicitly against marriage, but implicitly against any involvement with women.[23] As R. I. Moore has noted, reform was—at its heart—a project to sharpen the distinction between the spiritual and the secular and to exalt the clergy over the laity.[24] Although women may not have been a direct or intentional target of reform, as some scholars have suggested, they nevertheless became a fault line separating clerical from lay men. Marriage, the production of heirs, and (therefore) women were essential to the fulfillment of the secular roles assigned to laymen. For the clergy, however, women were deemed superfluous, and even dangerous.[25] Priests were urged to keep themselves distant not just from their own one-time wives (whom Peter Damian famously vilified as "hoopoes, screech owls, nighthawks, she-wolves, leeches . . . strumpets, [and] prostitutes"),[26] but from women in general, who were associated in the rhetoric of reform with sexuality, pollution, and sin, as Jo Ann McNamara and Dyan Elliott have shown.[27]

Within the context of reform in the late eleventh and twelfth centuries, some male religious communities withdrew not just from women, but even from nuns, and from the spiritual and material care that women's houses required. The Templar Rule (c. 1129), deciding against female members, declared the "company of women" to be "a dangerous thing, for by it the old devil has led many from the straight path to Paradise."[28] The slightly later Rule of Grandmont (c. 1140–1150) likewise invoked women's "snares" as a danger to men, which justified male monastic separation from them: "If the most mild David, the most wise Solomon, and the most strong Samson, were captured by feminine snares, who will not fall to their charms?"[29] Men in communities such as these found nothing in the Benedictine Rule to require their engagement with women, even in the essential role as priests for nuns. Indeed, the Rule, which had been recognized as the principal guide for the monastic life since the Carolingian reforms, had nothing whatsoever to say on the subjects of women's receipt of care or men's provision of it.[30] More strikingly, since Benedict had written his Rule explicitly for men, it neglected to mention nuns at all, suggesting that the religious life—for monks, at least—could be an entirely single-sex experience.[31]

Nuns, Their Priests, and the Single-Sex Monastic Ideal

The presumption that male monasticism was a single-sex experience has had a formative influence on scholarship, reinforcing the sense of the nuns' priest as a spiritual and institutional anomaly. Admittedly, some monks did refuse all contact with women, barring women from their churches and shrines.[32] However, for women, the monastic life consistently and necessarily included men, contributing to the puzzle I mentioned above.[33] In addition to the priest who celebrated the Mass, and the deacons and subdeacons who were to accompany him as witnesses and helpers, other men were regularly present within the female monastery, even before the reforms of the eleventh and twelfth centuries and the introduction into many houses of a spiritual "father." These men—whether monks, canons, or lay brothers—attended to the women's material needs, overseeing the community's buildings, witnessing its charters, aiding in the management of its finances and estates, and representing the community in its public dealings.[34] Some women's houses—chiefly the aristocratic *Frauenstifte*—had communities of clerics attached to them.[35] These male communities served both the spiritual and the material needs of the women and were often sizeable: during the early ninth century, the women's monastery of Sainte-Croix at Poitiers had the resources to support up to 30 clerics, alongside 100 women.[36] Although early medieval rules required that clerics lived outside the women's enclosure, entering it only when necessary, men associated with houses like Sainte-Croix could nevertheless develop close friendships with the women, as Venantius Fortunatus, possibly chaplain at Sainte-Croix (and later bishop of Poitiers), did in the late sixth century.[37]

As female monasticism expanded during the eleventh and twelfth centuries, men continued to be present in women's communities, and even—in some cases—to live in them. The late twelfth-century necrology of Obermünster in Regensburg, a community of canonesses founded in the ninth century, included the names of sixty-six priests as well as sixty-nine canons, pastors, deacons, and hermits. These men are identified as "brothers living in the upper monastery" (Figure 1).[38] Newer women's communities, too,

Figure 1. Brothers Living in the Upper Monastery. Obermünster Necrology,
BayHStA, KL Regensburg-Obermünster 1, fol. 67v.

included an often sizeable male presence. The Cluniac community of Marcigny, founded in 1055 by Hugh of Cluny (d. 1109) with his brother Geoffrey II of Semur, included between 10 and 20 monk-priests, and by 1117 had almost 100 women.[39] Renco, an older monk who was described as a "wise teacher" and "true philosopher of God," served as the community's first prior.[40] A charter from 1088 mentions brothers of Cluny who lived at the women's house; other documents referred more specifically to brothers and sisters "of Marcigny," implying the men's primary association with Marcigny.[41]

The presence of men in communities typically viewed as "women's" houses was, in fact, not unusual during the late eleventh and twelfth centuries. As Sharon Elkins has shown, a significant number of houses that were founded ostensibly for women during this period actually housed both women and men.[42] Her findings were confirmed by Sally Thompson, whose detailed study of individual women's monasteries revealed a significant number of men.[43] Both studies focused on England, but similar patterns can be seen elsewhere. Indeed, some men actually made their professions at so-called "women's" houses—at communities like Fontevraud in the Loire Valley, which contemporaries consistently viewed as a female house despite its sizeable male community (but which historians now often characterize as a "double" community);[44] Sigena, the Aragonese community founded by Sancha of Léon-Castile (d. 1208), where a significant men's community was subordinated to the prioress's authority; and, until the Premonstratensian General Chapter ruled against the practice in the early thirteenth century, the women's community of Füssenich in the archdiocese of Cologne, where the brothers had their own dormitory.[45] A good number of these men would have served the material needs of the women's community, but those who were ordained would have taken turns ministering to the women's spiritual needs as well.

For the women of these communities, a single-sex life was neither practical nor desirable: without the regular ministrations of a priest, the spiritual life of any female monastery (or, indeed, any grouping of religious women) could be thrown into jeopardy.[46] Modern scholars, like medieval observers, have therefore tended to accept women's interactions with ordained men as necessary and "normal," the consequence of women's exclusion from ordination and dependence on priests for sacramental services. Yet—and here is the crux of the puzzle that this chapter addresses—men's contact with women within the religious life appears in both medieval and modern accounts as dangerous, controversial, suspect, and fraught. Restrictions on the types of men who could theoretically be chosen to care for women (old men, and of good repute) and on their access to the female cloister (limited, and in the company of witnesses) suggest a medieval climate of suspicion and anxiety concerning contact between the sexes within the religious life. As Jerome had written to the priest Nepotian in the late fourth century, cautioning him against contact even with "Christ's virgins," danger lay not just in the sexual temptation posed by women, but also in women's presumed likeness to Eve and their connection to sin. It was Eve who "caused the tiller of paradise to be expelled from his home," Jerome reminded Nepotian, a warning that the twelfth-century bishop Marbode of Rennes (d. 1123) reprised in his disapproving letter to the wandering preacher Robert of Arbrissel (d. 1116): "the beginning of sin was caused by a woman and through her we all die, so if we want to avoid sin, we must cut the cause of sin away from us."[47] Modern scholars have taken exhortations like these as evidence that religious men preferred to avoid contact with women, whom they viewed, with Marbode, as "the cause of sin." So while scholars have accepted and even normalized the presence of men as necessary figures of ecclesiastical authority in women's houses, they nevertheless assume that the ideal religious life for men was one from which women were absent—literally, as Marbode advised, "cut away."

The tendency to assume a single-sex religious ideal for monastic men (and for all priests), but not for professed women (who were, in any case, always "married" to Christ), has left nuns' priests in a curious position: the pastoral care they provided for nuns is thought to have been necessary and even critical to female religious life, yet at the same time to have been a distraction and potential danger to their own male spirituality.[48] According to Herbert Grundmann, whose 1935 study of medieval religious movements remains enormously influential, the obligation for ordained men to provide for women's spiritual and material care was a "trouble and responsibility," which prompted several of the new religious orders of the central Middle Ages to reject women altogether.[49] More recent scholars have largely agreed with Grundmann, assuming that the relationship between nuns and priests (whether these men were ordained monks or, later, friars) was defined by a fundamental, gendered imbalance: nuns needed priests and could not manage without them, while priests, who did not need nuns, avoided them as much as possible—with the exception of holy women, who were celebrated for being "unlike" other women.[50] The assumption of imbalance pervades even the language used to describe the range of services provided by men for religious women: *cura monialium*, or care of nuns. Unlike the gender neutral *cura animarum*, or care of souls, the term *cura monialium* tends to imply, as Brian Patrick McGuire has observed, that "women are a burden, the weaker sex, the dependents who need to be cared for."[51] For Jo Ann McNamara, the *cura mulierum* was the "clergyman's burden"—an unwelcome obligation that priests sought to avoid, and from which they derived no tangible benefit.[52]

The idea that involvement with women was unnecessary and even detrimental to religious men has shaped perceptions of nuns' priests, casting them as fundamentally problematic and even implausible figures: men whose practical circumstances and spiritual vocation (providing sacramental care for women) directly compromised a supposedly fundamental precondition for male spirituality (separation from women). The characterization of nuns' priests as odd and contradictory has meant that they remain largely absent from studies of the monastic "mainstream." Obscured both by medieval rhetoric warning against men's contact with women and by modern assumptions concerning male religious life and spirituality, the men who provided nuns with care, and who thus helped to make possible the dramatic expansion of female monasticism during the eleventh and twelfth centuries, disappear from view. Their near invisibility is exacerbated by the fact that few of these men left any written account of their experiences; even their names are often unknown.

Rhetorical Contests and the Nuns' Priest

A central purpose of this book is to restore these men to view, and to explore the meaning of their spiritual work among women, as they understood and valued it, within the context of eleventh- and twelfth-century male, primarily monastic, spirituality. In so doing, the book offers an expanded understanding of male spirituality, one that moves beyond the presumption of sex segregation in order to accept the sacramental services of nuns' priests as legitimate and spiritually valuable. Historians of masculinity (whether medieval or modern) have typically focused on how masculinity was forged in all-male environments, depicting it as a contest that was waged, first and foremost, between men.[53] Within medieval scholarship, clerical celibacy has served as a primary focal point for the examination of masculinity, with scholars exploring the competing claims to manliness of clerics and laymen.[54] My purpose is rather to show how male spirituality could be forged through men's contact with pious women—that is to say, how priests evolved spiritually through their service to nuns. The involvement of ordained men with religious women was a regular and spiritually significant part of the medieval monastic life—for women, to be sure, but also for a considerable number of men.[55] Throughout the central Middle Ages, growing numbers of religious men (some who are known, but many more who are not) chose to involve themselves with religious women, despite a prevailing climate in which contact between religious men and women was strongly discouraged. These men engaged with women as bishops, priests, provosts, priors, and lay brothers. They founded monasteries for women, and even governed them, as in the case of Bishop Gundulf of Rochester (d. 1108), who ruled Malling for some sixteen years before appointing an abbess, Avice, on his deathbed.[56] If they were monks themselves, they might welcome women into their own religious communities (sometimes warmly, and sometimes temporarily); some, like the Gilbertines, placed their material resources in women's hands, subordinating the men's material needs to female authority.[57] Certain men lived in close quarters with women, testing the limits of chastity and propriety. Establishing spiritual friendships with women whom they embraced as "sisters," "mothers," and *dominae* (a term that could be translated as "ladies" or "female lords," but that specifically invoked the privileged position of the religious woman as a bride of Christ),[58] they sought to explore a version of the religious life in which sexual difference was not so much transcended as it was put to a new, spiritual purpose. As certain medieval sources suggest, these men viewed contact with women as a spiritual opportunity, and not—as many scholars have assumed—as a distraction: according to the *vita* of Abbot Theoger of Saint-Georgen (d. 1120), it was among women that "the highest perfection" was to be found.[59]

These men were, admittedly, swimming against a rhetorical tide. Many medieval monastic texts from the period present the renunciation of sexuality, and therefore the avoidance of women, as a male monastic virtue. Like Benedict of Nursia, who had reputedly plunged himself naked into nettles and briars when tempted by the mere recollection of a woman "he had once seen,"[60] the twelfth-century hermit Godric of Finchale (d. 1170) was celebrated for having thrown "his naked body among the prickly spurs of thorns and brambles" to extinguish carnal desire; his biographer commented that the "old enemy" made images of women appear to him (which he rejected "manfully").[61] Godric's near contemporary, the monk-turned-hermit Aybert of Crépin (d. 1141), reportedly avoided women so completely that when the Virgin Mary appeared in his cell "in the form of a beautiful woman," he recoiled at first and rebuked her.[62] Whereas these men were viewed as saints, the close involvement of men with women within a religious life was often seen as a marker of heresy.[63] At best, it was foolish and spiritually pointless, as several critics warned. Geoffrey of Vendôme (d. 1132) scoffed that Robert of Arbrissel had "discovered a new and unheard of but fruitless kind of martyrdom," through his close involvement with women and the sexual temptations to which he exposed himself.[64] The cautionary tale of Enoc, a Welsh abbot who had reputedly "gathered together . . . a group of virgins for the service of Christ" served as a salutary warning against men's too close spiritual engagement with women. As Gerald of Wales (d. c. 1223) reported, Enoc's spiritual community ended dramatically and in failure: "at length [Enoc] succumbed to temptations and made many of the virgins in the convent pregnant. Finally, he ran around in a comical manner, throwing off the religious habit, and fled with one of the nuns."[65]

The story of Enoc's brief yet disastrous career as a spiritual guide for women appears in the *Gemma ecclesiastica*, a work that Gerald composed as a guide for the clergy of his archdeaconry.[66] Gerald's decision to include Enoc in the text reflects his skepticism concerning men's purportedly spiritual involvement with women.[67] But it can serve equally as an indication that men *were* engaging spiritually with women during the period; this engagement is precisely what Gerald sought to prevent. Viewed in this way (and not as an account of the dangers of involvement with women and Enoc's alleged inability to resist them), Enoc's story confirms what is known from other, scattered, sources: during the eleventh and twelfth centuries, certain monks and priests across Europe were turning their attention to the spiritual lives of women, founding communities for women (and men) that were probably very much like his, or variations on it.[68] These men attracted criticism and suspicions. Goscelin of St. Bertin (d. c. 1107) acknowledged that his "pure encounter" with Eve of Wilton would draw vulgar speculation from critics whom he disparaged as "lecherous" and "dirty"; he defended his relationship with her against "the whisperer of scandal, the lecherous eye, the pointing finger, the spewer of hot air and the dirty snickerer."[69] The Norman abbot of Saint Albans, Geoffrey de Gorron (d. 1146), was "slandered as a seducer" as a result of his spiritual friendship with Christina of Markyate (while she was maligned as "a whore").[70] Attacks like these did not stop men from engaging spiritually with women, and may even have fueled their sense that service to nuns (and the persecution that often followed) was a central part of the male religious life. Most important, such attacks prompted men to develop a defensive vocabulary—which I explore in subsequent chapters—that drew on the examples of Christ, the apostles, and the church fathers: men who had also involved themselves spiritually, and blamelessly, with pious women.

Some of the men who engaged spiritually with women during the eleventh and twelfth centuries are well known: Robert of Arbrissel, a wandering preacher who attracted a motley following of women and men and who promoted chaste, spiritually inspired cohabitation before settling his mixed group of disciples at Fontevraud in 1101;[71] Norbert of Xanten (d. 1134), the radical hermit preacher and later archbishop of Magdeburg, who had accepted both women and men at his foundation at Prémontré;[72] and Gilbert, the priest of Sempringham (d. 1189), who established a community for seven women alongside his parish church, which later grew into "a kind of double monastery" (a "*monasteria duplicia*," in Gerald of Wales's words) that included both women and men.[73] Others are less well known: figures like Gaucher of Aureil (d. 1140), who, "seeking to build the heavenly Jerusalem with walls of both sexes, built a dwelling for women a stone's throw from his own cell";[74] Godwyn (d. c. 1130), an English hermit who provided pastoral care to three women—Emma, Gunilda, and Christina—at his hermitage in Kilburn, which later developed into a monastery for women;[75] Ekkehard of Halberstadt (d. 1084), who served as spiritual father for the recluse Bia from Quedlinburg ("lest the divine service should be lacking"), attracting other monks and female recluses to a small community that formed the basis for the mixed monastery of Huysburg;[76] Betto, a canon from Hildesheim whose "true love of holy virgins and widows" prompted his sponsorship of religious women at Lippoldsberg at the turn of the twelfth century;[77] Theoger of Saint-Georgen, who served as spiritual father for women at the priory of Amtenhausen;[78] Robert, who lived together with a group of women, possibly near the male monastery of Bury St. Edmunds, bestowing "care and love . . . on these handmaidens of God for God's sake," as Anselm of Canterbury (d. 1109) wrote approvingly to him;[79] Richard of Springiersbach (d. 1158), who founded Andernach for his sister Tenxwind and provided a priest, Conrad, for her spiritual guidance;[80] and others, including many whose names and activities either have not survived or were never recorded. Several of these men founded monastic communities in which women and men lived side by side (although often physically separated, as many sources were quick to note), establishing what scholars and some contemporaries recognized as "double" houses.[81] Such communities were common among groups professing a reformed religious life, as Stephanie Haarländer has shown.[82] Monasteries affiliated with the Black Forest reform community of Hirsau, or reformed according to Hirsau customs, almost invariably included women together with men, as at Zwiefalten, where the chronicler Ortlieb commented on the "irreprehensible life" of the nun Hadewic, which he presented as an example "not only for women, but also for men."[83]

The emergence in reforming circles of "double" monasteries demonstrates that the single-sex religious life was not necessarily a spiritual goal for monks, any more than it was a practical option for nuns. Indeed, even before the resurgence of double houses, many men's monasteries had included devout women in their spiritual circles, just as men had lived in and alongside women's houses.[84] The presence of women was often welcomed, as at Bury St. Edmunds, where, according to the Domesday Book, some twenty-eight *nonnae* lived in the late eleventh century, praying "daily for the King and for all Christian people."[85] One of these women, Seitha, met often for spiritual conversation with the sacrist, Toli, and was a regular presence within the monastic church, to which she was sometimes allowed special access.[86] At the Norman monastery of Bec during the late eleventh century, resident women were hailed as "mothers" of the monks.[87] Among them was the founder's mother, Heloise, on whose dower lands Bec had been established.[88] Kinship ties played a role in facilitating women's acceptance at men's communities elsewhere, too. At Cantimpré in the late twelfth century, Abbot John welcomed his widowed mother into the monastery, sparking the growth of a women's community, which later moved to Prémy (where John died and was buried).[89] In the early twelfth century, Guibert of Nogent (d. c. 1124) reported that his mother became a recluse in a cell attached to the abbey church of Saint-Germer-de-Fly, joining "an old woman dressed in monastic habit," who was the sister of the prior, Suger.[90] At Cluny, too, women were received, together with their male relatives, long before the foundation of Marcigny.[91] The presence at "men's" monasteries of these women—and others, like Jutta (d. 1136) and Hildegard at Disibodenberg,[92] Diemut (d. c. 1130–1150) the famous scribe and recluse at Wessobrunn,[93] or Herluca of Epfach (d. 1127/8) who spent the last years of her life at the male Augustinian community of Bernried[94]—significantly blurs the line between "male" and "female" houses, indicating that total segregation by sex may have been less important in practice than it was in theory—and, certainly, less important than it appears in monastic rhetoric.[95]

Monks and priests who welcomed devout women into their communities believed that the ideal religious life could include both sexes. When Gaucher

of Aureil's biographer characterized the presence of women in the saint's monastic vision as part of his attempt to build the "heavenly Jerusalem" with
"walls of both sexes," his language was intentional and significant: the "heavenly Jerusalem" was a model for the monastic life and a metaphor for the monastery itself.[96] Gaucher's sense that the heavenly Jerusalem comprised women
as well as men is echoed in the early thirteenth-century description of the
Gilbertine order as "Peter's vessel let down from heaven on four ropes," or as
a "chariot of Aminadab," with men constituting the wheels on one side and
women the wheels on the other.[97] According to Habakkuk 3:8, the chariot
(*quadriga*) represented salvation; it was consequently often invoked as a symbol of the church. At St. Denis at the mid-twelfth century, the Chariot of Aminadab was shown together with the crucified Christ; the four wheels of the
chariot represented the four gospels.[98] At Sempringham, the same image was
invoked to underscore the salvation shared by both sexes. The biography of
Hugh of Cluny likewise employed biblical language in order to present the
foundation of the women's house at Marcigny as central to the Cluniac
mission: Hugh's biographer, Gilo, likened his inclusion of women in the "ship
of Saint Peter" to Noah's work in selecting two of each kind of animal to
enter into the ark.[99] Hugh himself commented directly on the spiritual implications of supporting women in the religious life, noting in a letter to his
successors that the foundation of Marcigny seemed not to "displease" God, but
rather to obey him.[100]

The appearance of biblical language in accounts of the mixed-sex religious
life suggests that women's presence was perceived as legitimate and spiritually
meaningful in some cases. Biblical examples offered further inspiration for
men's spiritual interactions with women. The mid-twelfth-century chronicle
of Petershausen, a monastery in Switzerland that included both women and
men, explained the presence of women as a function of the monks' larger
attempt to emulate the life of apostles (an attempt that included their asceticism and renunciation of material possessions). As the chronicler wrote,
invoking the presence of women alongside Jesus's disciples,

> It must be noted that pious women served God together with the
> holy disciples; according to this example, it is not blameworthy, but
> greatly worthy of praise, if women are received in monasteries as
> nuns in the service of God, so that each sex, although separated
> one from the other, may be saved in one place.[101]

Monks at the Swiss double monastery of Muri claimed the "life of the holy fathers" (*vita sanctorum patrum*) as a model for the substantial presence of women there; the *Acta Murensia* (c. 1160) noted that the fathers had "also gathered women to themselves for love of God."[102] At Rolduc (Klosterrath), too, the abbot Erpo turned to the apostolic example in order to claim the legitimacy of women's presence among religious men. Since the apostles had had women among them to provide for their material needs (a topic discussed in Chapter 2), Erpo found cause to allow eight women to serve in a domestic capacity at the monastery, despite local opposition.[103] Other sources hint at the idea that the mixed religious life had a spiritual purpose. The *Little Book on the Various Orders and Callings that Exist in the Church*, a mid-twelfth-century polemical text advocating for reform, mentions women's spiritual involvement alongside men, promising a section (now lost) on women who "sweetly take up Christ's yoke with holy men or under their guidance."[104] According to Anselm of Canterbury, female recluses living chastely under male guidance approximated not just the *vita apostolica*, the apostolic life, but the *vita angelica*, the life of the angels living with God.[105]

Certain male monastic reformers viewed the presence of women in the religious life—and men's care for them—as an occasion for spiritual advancement. The early thirteenth-century *Book of St Gilbert*—although not effusive about Gilbert of Sempringham's care for women—nevertheless presented concern for devout women as serving a spiritual purpose.[106] In the first instance, the *Book*'s author argued that care for women was necessary, since women need men's help and the "fathers" required that men provide it: "it is essential that communities of maidens be controlled through the support and administration of monks and clerks," he observed.[107] But it was also "natural," given women's innate weakness, as he explained: the "natural law of pity instructs us, and divine counsel urges us, to do good without stinting to weaker folk." For this, the author observed, "a richer reward is to be expected." In Gilbert's case, the reward was explicitly gendered: "Because the fruit of virgins is one hundredfold, when he [Gilbert] abandoned his own possessions in order to preserve their virgin status he received a hundredfold and possesses eternal life."[108]

Clues that religious men expected a spiritual reward from their spiritual attention to professed women appear elsewhere, as in Anselm of Canterbury's letter to Robert, thanking him for his attention to women and promising him that "a great reward from God awaits you for this holy zeal."[109] Idung of Prüfening, too, observed that a "not insignificant spiritual profit can be produced" through the spiritual direction of nuns.[110] The late twelfth-century foundation charter for the Cistercian monastery of Las Huelgas explained that "especially great merit is obtained from God by establishing monastic communities for women."[111] A similar assumption may have inspired the comments of Herman of Tournai (d. c. 1147) regarding Norbert of Xanten's mixed-sex foundation at Prémontré. Presenting Norbert's ministry to women as especially virtuous, Herman asked: "if . . . Norbert had done nothing else . . . but attract so many women to God's service by his exhortation, would he not have been worthy of the greatest praise?" Tying Norbert's ministry to the example of the apostles, Herman went on to comment that "there has been no one since the time of the apostles who in such a brief space of time has acquired for Christ so many imitators of the perfect life."[112]

The idea that men would be divinely rewarded for their spiritual care of women cuts against the grain of much medieval monastic and clerical polemic concerning the dangers that were supposedly inherent in men's involvement with women. The examples offered here, of men like Gaucher, Gilbert, Hugh, and Norbert (as well as monks at such communities as Muri, Rolduc, and Petershausen), hint at a rich and vibrant male monastic culture in which spiritual service to nuns was accepted and valued—a culture that existed alongside the more widely known context of male monastic reluctance to engage with women. Still, this was not a culture that exalted women unreservedly, or that made arguments we might now recognize as feminist. The male-authored sources give little sense in most cases of the women's own spiritual lives, or of their claims to self-governance or autonomy (even as women's own writings reveal them to have been curious and engaged interlocutors on spiritual matters, often challenging their male advisors, both intellectually and spiritually). Nuns and even holy women are typically depicted as reliant on the help of men, as the *Book of St Gilbert* commented dismissively, "women's efforts achieve little without help from men."[113] Moreover, men serving the needs of religious women sometimes conceived of their service as a form of spiritually inspired submission: an act of voluntary humility that would be rewarded in heaven and that was predicated on the assumption of women's "natural" inferiority.[114] Peter Abelard (d. 1142) commented more than once on this aspect of men's service to women, promising in his monastic *Rule* for women that "the more a man has humbled himself before God, the higher he will certainly be exalted."[115] These men did not argue for structural changes to the gendered hierarchy of the medieval church. However, they did engage voluntarily in service to religious women, dignifying female religious life and often presenting that service as part of the larger quest to achieve a spiritually authentic *vita apostolica*. Religious women needed men's pastoral care, as both women and men assumed. The sources I have presented here, and those that I explore in the following chapters, suggest that some men felt that they would do very well, spiritually, to provide it.

Sources and Interpretations

This book is concerned primarily with ideas and rhetoric relating to men's spiritual care for women, and less with the provision of care itself. For the most part, ordained men provided religious women with spiritual care, free from either scandal or hostility—even though it is primarily in the context of scandal and hostility that these men come into view. Of course, there were instances in which men refused women spiritual care, or mistreated them.[116] Some priests stole from female monasteries; others usurped women's properties.[117] Some were negligent and failed to provide adequate spiritual service.[118] Some preyed on the women, abusing their privileged access to the female monastery to force themselves sexually on the nuns—realizing the worst fears of churchmen. The male author of the *Speculum virginum* warned his female audience against false pastors, men who he claimed were "wolves rapacious for souls, slaying with the swords of incontinence those whom they feed with the word of truth."[119] Writing in the thirteenth century, the Dominican Thomas of Cantimpré (d. c. 1270) advocated a firm response to predatory men (including clerics), advising religious women that "if anyone wishes to solicit you as it were to a holy kiss, if anyone tries to put his hand on your breast, your bosom, or any other part of your body, give him spittle instead of a kiss and let your fist meet his groping hand."[120] These are vivid warnings, to be sure, but there are few indications that they reflect common or recurrent dangers. The general silence of monastic charters and other documents of practice concerning exploitation or scandal reflects the likelihood that, in most cases, the provision of care was routine and, if not always perfect, at least relatively trouble-free.

The puzzle at the heart of this chapter is not that priests failed to provide pastoral care, but that medieval observers generally failed to discuss it in a positive way, even as most acknowledged its necessity: it is a puzzle of language and representation, rather than reality. As I have shown, references to nuns' priests, or to men who served as confessors or spiritual friends to women (and who were usually also ordained), are mired in anxiety, suspicion, and ambivalence. The prevalence and rhetorical force of these sources maligning nuns' priests have led historians to imagine danger, sexual scandal, and hostility in the relationship of priests to nuns—a relationship that is consequently depicted as one of male volition, control, and sometimes even resentment or outright antagonism.[121] The one-sidedness of the sources is exacerbated by the fact that even men who did engage spiritually with women, and who recorded that engagement in writing, tended to deny or downplay the extent of their interaction, further obscuring what was in most cases likely an innocent and even humdrum reality.

Irimbert of Admont (d. 1176) offers a case in point. Admont in Styria is distinct as one of the most long-lasting of the double monasteries founded during the reform period, and also one with the richest extant resources: Admont's medieval library, replete with twelfth-century manuscripts, has survived largely intact.[122] Irimbert was abbot of Admont for several years before his death in 1176. However, before becoming abbot, he had served as spiritual tutor to the nuns of the community, and to nuns at Admont's daughter house, Sankt Georgen am Längsee in Carinthia.[123] As spiritual tutor, Irimbert reported that he had preached to the nuns, although not—as he was careful to point out—face-to-face. Instead, he preached through a window, a circumstance that made it possible, so he claimed, for certain nuns to record his sermons in writing, without his knowledge.[124] Irimbert's emphasis on the strict physical separation of the Admont nuns is confirmed by his now famous account of the 1152 fire that almost destroyed the women's community.[125] As Irimbert reported, when fire swept the monastic compound, the nuns were locked in the women's cloister. As disaster loomed, none of the monks could find the keys to the single door that led to the women's part of the monastery. If Irimbert is to be believed, the keys were difficult to find because they were rarely used: the door between the two parts of the community was opened only for a nun to enter at the moment of her profession or to exit when her body was carried out for burial, or for a priest to give last rites to the dying.[126] Apart from this door, only a single small window in the women's chapter house provided a means for communication with the world beyond the women's cloister. As Irimbert presumably wished to show, the separation of the sexes at Admont was so strict that access to the female community was practically impossible, even in cases of imminent danger.[127]

Evidence from other monastic communities indicates that direct contact between women and men in the religious life was more common than Irimbert's carefully crafted and clearly polemical account implies, suggesting the need to deal carefully with medieval sources that deny or downplay the interaction of the sexes. Some of this evidence is fragmentary, preserved by chance rather than intention. Yet it reflects the practical reality of interaction between monastic men and women more than defensive reports of windows, curtains, grilles, doors, and keys, which often appear in texts intended for a public audience (as, for instance, the *life* of Stephen of Obazine, which detailed elaborate safeguards against contact between the men and women at Obazine/Coyroux).[128] The *Guta-Sintram Codex* (c. 1154), a manuscript produced through the collaboration of a female scribe and a male artist, reveals, for instance, the interchange of scribal hands on a single line, suggesting the close working conditions of the two, likely within a single monastic scriptorium.[129] The collaboration of Guta and Sintram is commemorated in an image showing them both before the Virgin Mary (Figure 2). Likewise, Herman of Tournai's account of the monastery of Saint Martin reports in passing the conversation of a monk with a nun, as he brought linen to the women's convent to be spun—an indication that monks and nuns could speak together during the course of the monastic day.[130]

Other evidence is more fulsome. Goscelin of St. Bertin, who may have been chaplain at Wilton for some time,[131] recalled a feast that he had attended with Eve of Wilton—his spiritual friend and *domina*.[132] Goscelin's memory of the feast suggests that he was sitting beside her: he recalled passing her the roast fish while commenting on its spiritual significance: the roast fish symbolized the suffering of Christ crucified, *"Piscis assus, Christus passus."*[133] In a letter regretting Eve's subsequent departure from Wilton (to live as a hermit in Angers, in a chaste relationship with the male hermit Hervé), Goscelin invoked the power of the written word to restore his presence to her, reminding her of happy times at Wilton: "you will believe me with you at Wilton, before our holy Lady Edith, sitting chastely by your side, speaking with you, admonishing you, consoling you."[134] Eve and Goscelin had evidently shared in many direct conversations. "Do you remember when you told me your dream?" Goscelin asked her. They exchanged gifts (a "common custom" among male and female religious, as Aelred observed, disapprovingly),[135] and attended the dedications of two churches together.[136] At Rupertsberg, the priest Guibert of Gembloux (d. 1213/14) also enjoyed happy relations with the nuns, writing

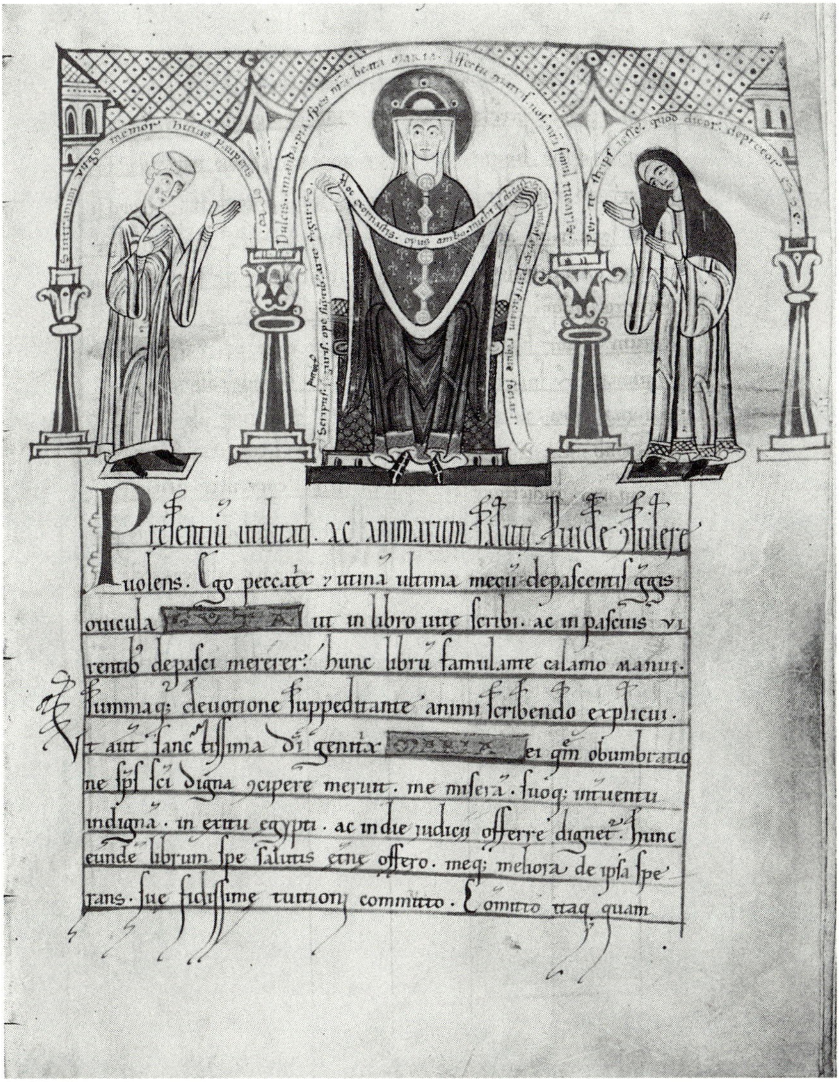

Figure 2. Guta and Sintram with the Virgin Mary. Detail, *Guta-Sintram Codex*, Bibliothèque du Grand Séminaire de Strasbourg, MS 37, p. 9. © Rheinisches Bildarchiv Köln, rba_c004307.

that he was "refreshed" by daily conversation with Hildegard. He reports having exchanged gifts with at least one nun, Gertrude, with whom he was particularly close.[137] Of course, different communities had different practices governing women's enclosure, and so it is not surprising to find variations, even significant ones. Nevertheless, the expectation that women and men could meet within the context of spiritual instruction was foundational to medieval religious life, despite the rhetorical posturing of defensive sources. The *Speculum virginum* assumed that virgins would "see and converse with the male sex," even as it warned against the exchange of "glances, conversations, and little gifts."[138] The text itself was intended for the use of priests who assumed the spiritual care of nuns, and was designed as a model dialogue to guide discussions between a male pastor and his female disciple.[139]

Despite evidence for routine, quotidian interactions between certain monastic men and religious women, defensive accounts like Irimbert's (and, more sensationally, stories of sexual misadventures such as the infamous "nun of Watton"[140]) have attracted disproportionate attention among scholars, contributing to the sense that the separation of men from women must have been the default position for medieval religious life, and that communities like Fontevraud, Prémontré, and a host of other houses that included women alongside men were "experiments" that would inevitably come to an end: the men would withdraw from the women, and both parts would establish primarily single-sex communities, significantly compromising women's ability to secure pastoral care.[141] Accordingly, accounts of the eleventh and twelfth centuries often acknowledge the mixing of the sexes within some monasteries and the flourishing of spiritual friendships between individual men and women ("chaste rhetorical romances," as Jo Ann McNamara termed them, or "heteroasceticism" in Dyan Elliott's terminology), yet depict both as temporary, contingent, and exceptional.[142] For McNamara, the efforts of men like Robert of Arbrissel to forge a new gender order at the turn of the twelfth century were quickly blocked by a clerical hierarchy dominated by celibate men, who vigorously, and even violently, opposed contact with women. As she wrote, "There was a moment in the early twelfth century when they might have led the way to a new and more equitable partnership that narrowed the social effects of biological differences and favored a wider development of the ungendered aspects of the individual personality."[143] However, the "gender crisis" that McNamara argued was prompted by the celibacy movement, and that briefly allowed syneisaktic experiments, was short-lived.[144] Within a short time, as McNamara observed, monastic men were once again firmly separated from women, who were consigned to "fanatic claustration," while a celibate clergy regained its grip on ecclesiastical authority.[145]

Beyond the Single-Sex Model: Symbiosis and Male Spirituality

While recognizing the force and pervasiveness of medieval clerical misogyny, my purpose in this book is to take seriously an alternate possibility: that the symbiosis of male and female within the religious life could be a spiritually meaningful and long term phenomenon, as Kaspar Elm suggested—and not merely a temporary curiosity.[146] Men did not uniformly reject contact with women within the religious life. Many double communities outlasted the spiritual enthusiasm and so-called "experimentation" of the early twelfth century, thriving even after the Second Lateran Council (1139) prohibited the co-celebration of the liturgy, forbidding nuns to "come together with canons or monks in choir for the singing of the office."[147] Some continued into the fifteenth century and beyond, calling into question the assumption that such forms of organization were intrinsically temporary and problematic: the women's communities of Engelberg and Interlaken, for instance, reached their height in the first half of the fourteenth century.[148] An image from the Register-book of Abbot Otto II (1375–1414) from the Petersfrauen at Salzburg shows Benedict instructing monks and nuns together, reflecting the continued dual sex organization of the house in the early fifteenth century.[149] At Schönau, the women's community survived until the early seventeenth century. Meanwhile, in England, only the Dissolution put an end to the involvement of both sexes in the religious life at Sempringham.[150] The establishment of new double houses, like those associated with the Brigittine order, even centuries after the supposed "gender crisis" of the eleventh century, confirms that symbiosis was neither a temporary nor an experimental stage of monastic life, but rather that it held real spiritual meaning for women and men.[151]

Although many mixed communities did physically separate after some period of time, separation was neither inevitable nor was it always the result of men's rejection of women.[152] At the monastery of Saint Martin of Tournai, for instance, separation occurred when the women's community grew too large to be housed together with the men: it was a sign that women's religious life at Saint Martin was thriving.[153] At Disibodenberg, the women chose to separate from the men, despite the men's resistance. The prior Adelbert later admitted to Hildegard that "God took you away from us against our will. . . . We cannot fathom why God did this. . . . For we had hoped that the salvation of our monastery rested with you."[154] When physical separation did occur, for practical or other reasons, the spiritual bond between the women and men often remained in place: after the relocation of the women from Muri to Hermetschwil in 1200, to give one example, a shared necrology continued to report the deaths of both monks and nuns, indicating that the community continued to function as a single, spiritual unit.[155] At Obazine/Coyroux, physical separation had no effect on the men's spiritual and material care for the women. According to the *vita* of Stephen of Obazine, the women continued to be "served each day by the monks, under the direction of the abbot, in divine offices, in holding chapter meetings, in hearing confessions and enjoining penances, in carrying out and burying the dead, or in providing other spiritual benefits."[156] In several instances, physical separation was minimal, as at Rommersdorf/Wülfersberg, where the women moved a mere 800 meters away from the previous double house.[157]

These examples highlight the need to deal carefully with medieval sources, which have often been read to reinforce scholarly presumptions, rather than to challenge them. Like nuns' priests, who have been defined as odd and irregular, double houses are typically characterized as exceptional, experimental, and temporary. The presumption that such houses could not last, because men could not want to share in a religious life with women, mirrors the consensus that priests largely avoided the "burdens" of the *cura monialium* because they had no reason to engage spiritually with nuns. And yet, as the expansion of female monasticism implies and as many sources confirm, priests continued to care for and support religious women, even in the face of a reforming rhetoric that denigrated marriage and women.

Narratives of gender crisis and temporary experimentation cannot account for the structural fact of men's continued care for women. Instead, studies of women and men within the medieval religious life have tended to focus on individual relationships and circumstances, and above all on the appeal of female saints to their male admirers. That men could admire and even idealize individual women is clear from the secular literature of the late eleventh and early twelfth centuries. As C. Stephen Jaeger and Gerald Bond have shown, Latin poems and verse epistles from elite cathedral and court circles increasingly featured praise and admiration of women at this time.[158] Bishops and schoolmen celebrated individual nuns and noblewomen, giving rise to what Bond terms "dominism"—the ritual praise of the lady as superior in virtue.[159] According to Jaeger, women began to be seen as a potentially "positive moral force" and "tutor in ethics" for men—marking a new and unprecedented development in his view.[160] Within the religious life, too, men often held individual women in high regard, as John Coakley has shown in a series of important studies focusing on monastic and mendicant men. These men were drawn to individual holy women, viewing them as spiritual superiors and serving them as scribes, confessors, and often biographers.[161] Since these holy women were extraordinary, by definition, the attraction of their male admirers has also been viewed as extraordinary.[162] Like the relationships explored by Bond and Jaeger, which were playful and rhetorical, but had no practical effect on attitudes toward women, there has been little sense that the admiration of religious men for holy women extended beyond the specific circumstances of the individual male-female relationship, or, indeed, beyond the exceptionality of the female saint.

Women in monastic communities were not, as a group, extraordinary. Occasionally a nun was recognized for her saintliness, but most religious women were not: they were ordinary figures, neither charismatic nor visionary. Even so, scores of equally ordinary ordained men ministered to them, subjecting themselves to gossip and accusations of wrong-doing. Studying these men presents significant challenges, since—unlike the men discussed by Coakley—most monks and priests did not leave written accounts of their involvement with women or explain their motivations for serving them.[163] Other sources are not more forthcoming. Few *vitae* were produced within the context of the pastoral relationship as it developed within the monastery, and narrative sources seldom mention either the men or the care that they provided.[164] These gaps and silences make it all the more difficult to identify and understand nuns' priests. Although they existed, and were vital to female religious life, nuns' priests rarely left a mark on the historic record, appearing primarily as caricatures in the insinuations and accusations of their critics. Bringing these men into view thus requires a new approach to existing sources and a willingness to expand and even redefine the category of nuns' priest to include men who have more typically been viewed as exceptional or unusual—emblematic of medieval monastic "experimentation," but not of the mainstream.

Peter Abelard and Robert of Arbrissel: Exceptionalism and Nuns' Priests

Despite the prevailing silence of the sources, some monks and priests did address the question of pastoral care for women in their lives and writings. One figure who was particularly vocal in acknowledging and defending men's provision of pastoral care to women is the controversial monk-priest Peter Abelard.[165] A philosopher, theologian, and monastic reformer, Abelard was also the most prolific author of guidance literature for religious women during the twelfth century, producing sermons, hymns, letters, exegesis, theological commentary, and advice—including, notably, his *Rule* for nuns and treatise *On the Origin of Nuns*.[166] Abelard was co-founder of the Paraclete, a monastery for women in Champagne, and sometime priest there as well, despite being abbot for several years at St. Gildas in Brittany, some 350 miles away. He was evidently present at the Paraclete enough to attract unpleasant insinuations, including the suggestion that he was sexually enthralled with the Paraclete's abbess, his former wife, Heloise (d. 1164).[167]

Abelard was, without question, an unusual figure with a complicated personal history. He was arrogant at times and intellectually combative: his conflicts with Bernard of Clairvaux (d. 1153) fairly leap off the pages of medieval textbooks. His affair with Heloise, their marriage, and its dramatic conclusion are the stuff of legend. But Abelard was equally a monastic reformer, a man who—like Robert of Arbrissel, whom he admired—devoted many years to the religious life, to preaching, and to the care and support of professed women.[168] In his *Rule* for nuns, Abelard advanced a model of the professed religious life that embraced both women and men—a model founded on his belief in the spiritual complementarity of the sexes. As he argued, female monasteries should not be separate from male ones, but should be paired spiritually and geographically and bound by an "affection of charity" that could be strengthened by bonds of kinship between individual monks and nuns (as, indeed, he was bound to Heloise).[169]

Most striking about Abelard's monastic plan is the fact that women were at its center; men appear in his *Rule* chiefly in order to meet the women's material and spiritual needs (although Abelard envisioned ultimate authority as resting in the hands of an abbot, who was to oversee both the male and the female house).[170] As Abelard wrote, highlighting men's obligation to support religious women, "it is always men's duty to provide for women's needs."[171] In itself, this is not a radical claim: churchmen from the earliest centuries of monasticism had recognized women's reliance on male spiritual support and had assumed that men had some obligation to provide it—even as they worried about potential dangers. What Abelard explored more extensively than any previous writer was the idea that men's service to religious women, even ordinary nuns, had inherent spiritual value: that men could benefit spiritually from it. In Abelard's view, men's ministry to religious women, whom he increasingly came to understand as brides of Christ and therefore men's *dominae*, was an opportunity to be embraced, and not a danger to be avoided.

Abelard's attention to the spiritual care of women, his arguments in favor of their spiritual "dignity" (a topic first explored by Mary Martin McLaughlin in a trailblazing article), and his engagement with women in the face of often vicious criticism, mark him as similar in several ways to Robert of Arbrissel (to whom he may have been connected through Robert's spiritual friend, Hersende—who may have been Heloise's mother).[172] However, one similarity is particularly salient here: both men have been depicted in scholarship on the medieval religious life as "exceptional" and therefore unrepresentative either of medieval monasticism or of medieval religious men. Robert has been viewed as "strange" or "idiosyncratic" (albeit "delightfully so," as Bruce Venarde has observed), and his foundation at Fontevraud as an anomaly—an experiment that attracted more critics than imitators.[173] In the same way, Abelard's personal and intellectual history has traditionally marked him as exceptional and even *avant garde*. To be sure, the circumstances under which Abelard entered the religious life and his admittedly complicated relationship with Heloise make him unusual among nuns' priests, as do his status as a foremost theologian and philosopher and his self-conscious presentation of himself as an outsider and a rebel.[174] Yet the opinion that Abelard was unusual is based not only on his personal circumstances, but also on his voluminous writings for women and his claims regarding women's place in religious life. Like Robert, who is viewed as odd precisely *because* of his involvement with women, Abelard's writings concerning women's place within the religious life have been deemed extraordinary and radical—"the period's most exciting revisionist raids on dominant gender assumptions," as Alcuin Blamires observed in his discussion of Abelard's letter *On the Origin of Nuns*.[175] Abelard's belief in the "supreme importance of women in religious history" was nevertheless exceptional for the twelfth century, as Blamires concluded: Abelard was "ahead of his time," with Christine de Pizan, some three centuries later, as his "closest successor."[176] The assumption that Abelard's ideas about women and men within the religious life had no contemporary impact or resonance has seemed to justify his exclusion from scholarly discussions of men's pastoral care of women, confirming his status as an ultimately atypical figure. Although we now know that men in certain double communities read Abelard's writings about women and implemented some of his ideas (notably at the Augustinian community of Marbach, as I have shown elsewhere),[177] the monastic model he outlined in his *Rule* was never put into practice—not even at the Paraclete, where Heloise had specifically commissioned the work.[178] On this basis, some historians have dismissed the entire project as a half-hearted attempt on Abelard's part to ingratiate himself with Heloise—the fruit of "much dreary toil," as Sir Richard Southern judged Abelard's monastic letters in 1970.[179]

A central argument of this book is that Abelard (like Robert of Arbrissel) was more representative than scholars have typically allowed—perhaps not of medieval monasticism as a whole, but certainly of a subset of ordained men who included women in their vision of the apostolic life and who saw spiritual advantages in their sacramental service to them. While most of these men are unknown, some left writings in which they advanced arguments similar to those made by Abelard, suggesting the contours of a clerical culture in which ordained men engaged willingly in the spiritual care of women. Abelard made his case for men's spiritual support of women with unusual force and clarity. Even so, his ideas were hardly unique.[180]

Abelard's stance on religious women is most closely approximated in the writings of Guibert of Gembloux, the Flemish monk who served as Hildegard of Bingen's secretary from 1177 and then also as priest for the nuns at Rupertsberg.[181] Like Abelard, Guibert enjoyed his service to women and found comfort in the female monastery. As he wrote, life at Rupertsberg was more orderly, more congenial, and more spiritually rewarding than at his home monastery of Gembloux. He described his move to the women's community in terms of Jacob's two marriages: having been delivered from what he characterized as "servitude of bleary-eyed Leah" at Gembloux, he luxuriated at Rupertsberg in the "delightful embraces of comely Rachel."[182] Guibert's long sojourn among the nuns at Rupertsberg was resented by his fellow monks at Gembloux, who demanded his return (implying, as Guibert reported, that he spent his time at Rupertsberg, "lusting with girls in the recesses of the cloister").[183] In response, Guibert defended his work among women in several long letters, which invoke many of the ideas that had appeared in Abelard's writings about men's spiritual care for women: Jesus's care for his female disciples, the example of John the Evangelist's care for Mary at the cross, the "sister women" of the apostles, and Jerome's devotion to Paula and Eustochium (themes I explore in the following chapters).[184] Exalting professed women and presenting their special status as brides of Christ, Guibert effused that "holy virgins are the temple of God the father, the spouses of his son Jesus Christ, [and] the sanctuary of the holy Spirit."[185]

The similarities between Guibert's defense and Abelard's writings are striking. Yet more striking still is the fact that Guibert seems not to have read, or indeed even to have known of Abelard, who died a generation before Guibert began his stint as a nuns' priest. Nevertheless, both men produced parallel and often overlapping arguments in favor of men's involvement with religious women. The similarities between them suggest that by the middle of the twelfth century, if not before, a culture of support for the involvement of men with religious women had developed, a culture that had a distinctive vocabulary and rhetoric.

Abelard did not create this rhetoric, although he might be considered the foremost practitioner of it. Indeed, arguments concerning men's obligation to care for women had circulated in male monastic circles already in the early Middle Ages. During the seventh century, an unnamed abbot composed a rule for the guidance of monks under his authority in which he reasoned that monks should provide religious women with material and spiritual care, since "they are members of Christ, and mothers of the Lord, and through a virgin Christ redeemed us."[186] In the early eleventh century, before the so-called experiments in syneisaktism that McNamara identified as a temporary component of reform, certain churchmen had defended close friendships with religious women, drawing on ideas that Abelard and others would later also adopt. In a letter to an unidentified nun, Bishop Azecho of Worms (d. 1044) admitted that "there are . . . those who say that close friendships and conversations with women must be avoided." Contesting this view, Azecho turned to biblical and early Christian models of male-female spiritual involvement, invoking John's care for the Virgin Mary, as well as Jerome's care for the Roman matron Paula and her daughter Eustochium, as evidence that spiritual friendships with women could be blameless and, in the case of the Virgin, even divinely ordained. Azecho concluded his discussion with a daring modification of Psalm 132:1: "Boldly therefore I say: Behold, how good and how pleasant it is that brothers dwell, *and also the sisters dwell*, in unity."[187] Not everyone agreed with Azecho, of course, and some used Psalm 132 to argue against the spiritual involvement of women with men. During the thirteenth century, Thomas of Cantimpré invoked Psalm 132:1 to explain Abbot John's decision to move women away from the men's monastery at Cantimpré. As Thomas noted, "the prophet says 'it is good and pleasing for brothers'—*not brothers and sisters*—to dwell together in unity.'"[188]

Thomas's invocation of Psalm 132 stands as a reminder that there were two consistently divergent rhetorical positions available to medieval churchmen on the question of spiritual engagement with women, just as there were on "woman" generally.[189] On the one hand, men like Marbode of Rennes and Bernard of Clairvaux sometimes opposed what they saw as the dangerous mixing of the sexes, drawing on a shared vocabulary invoking Eve, Delilah, and other infamous women of the Old Testament to warn monks and priests against contact with women.[190] On the other hand, men like Abelard and Guibert defended the legitimacy of men's involvement with religious women, citing Jesus's care for women, the constancy of the women at the tomb, the apostles' care for widows, Jerome's friendship with Eustochium, and the examples of early medieval men, like Saint Equitius, whose care for women was pure.[191] The more generally positive positions adopted by these men, and others like them (including Marbode, who could also praise women when he wished),[192] have until now been characterized as personal, contingent, exceptional, and sometimes insincere. They have rarely found a place in mainstream monastic or medieval histories.[193]

Viewed in isolation, men in this latter group might well seem exceptional. To be fair, they were often charismatic figures. Whether as monastic founders, itinerant preachers, spiritual gurus, or intellectuals and writers, these men were on a spiritual quest that necessarily involved behaviors beyond the "ordinary." However, they also formed part of a tangible and legitimate religious context, and must be viewed—as Bruce Venarde has rightfully argued for Robert of Arbrissel—within "the contemporary mainstream, in which new opportunities for women's religious life were a significant feature."[194] It is this vision of a "contemporary mainstream" with its new opportunities for women that the following chapters seek to chart, tracing ideas about men's service to women that circulated during the eleventh and twelfth centuries. Men like Abelard and Guibert (as well as Robert, Norbert, Gilbert, and others) were active in supporting the religious life for women, to various degrees and with differing intentionality and success. The biographies of these men are well known. But they shared something in common that has until now escaped scholarly attention: a sophisticated vocabulary drawn from early Christian and patristic sources to defend and explain their spiritual care of women. This vocabulary was broadly known and used by religious men who ministered to pious women, even by those whose names are not known to us. In tracing this vocabulary, the following chapters turn away from a primary emphasis on individual men, focusing rather on the ideas that they held in common, and above all the motifs that they adopted in defending and discussing their pastoral care of women. Drawing evidence from a range of sources—including letters, chronicles, *vitae*, monastic rules, advice literature, and sermons, as well as manuscript illuminations, liturgical drama, and wall paintings—these chapters reveal the contours of a medieval clerical culture in which spiritual service to women was carefully theorized and vigorously defended.

CHAPTER 2

Biblical Models: Women and
Men in the Apostolic Life

The Lord himself did not reject the companionship of women.
                                        —Guibert of Gembloux, Epist. 26

During the late eleventh and early twelfth centuries, churchmen across a broad spectrum imagined and discussed contemporary religious life in terms inspired by the New Testament. Despite some differences, these men were motivated by a shared set of desires: to follow the example of Christ, to live in accordance with gospel accounts of Christ's earliest and closest followers, and to bring into being a renewed and purified church modeled on the community of believers described in the Acts of the Apostles. Such concerns were particularly prominent among men promoting a reform agenda. As Giles Constable observed, "no conscious aspect of the reform movement was more important than the desire to imitate Christ and live the life of the Gospel."[1] In keeping with this desire, the vocabulary adopted by reformers hearkened back to gospel accounts of Christ and of his disciples, and to the model of the early church: the imitation of Christ (*imitatio Christi*), apostolic life (*vita apostolica*), and primitive church (*ecclesia primitiva*) were catchphrases that were deployed regularly in the polemical literature of the period.[2]

For some, the *ecclesia primitiva* was a reflexively male church, a model for male monastics and celibate churchmen who sought to build a heavenly Jerusalem in cloisters and cathedral chapters from which women were actively excluded. However, the biblical account offered significant material to inspire an alternate view, as we began to see in the last chapter. Rather than finding confirmation in the New Testament of men's compulsory separation from women, some monks and churchmen during the eleventh and twelfth centuries identified a biblical model of men's spiritual concern for women and their legitimate involvement with them. As these men recognized, Jesus himself had welcomed women and included them in his ministry. Women had been among Jesus's disciples, following him, supporting him financially, and ultimately forming the core of early house churches. Women were central, too, to the narrative of the passion and resurrection: it was women who remained faithful as Jesus hung on the cross and who were the first to see him after the resurrection. It was a woman—Mary, Jesus's mother—who was the subject of Jesus's last words from the cross to any disciple, and another woman—Mary Magdalene—who announced the news of the resurrection to the apostles, earning recognition among certain exegetes as the *apostola apostolorum*: the apostle of the apostles.

For medieval priests and monks who involved themselves spiritually with nuns, the biblical account offered clear authorization for spiritual contact between the sexes, offsetting persistent anxieties concerning the potential for scandal and sin. Yet the gospel also offered more, as some men argued: a divine command that men care for women, expressed in Jesus's commendation of the Virgin Mary to John the Evangelist at the crucifixion (John 19:25–27). Religious men who practiced new models of syneisaktism during the central Middle Ages saw themselves as acting in direct obedience to this command and in emulation of the apostles, who had cared for widows and virgins in the early church. For these men, the vocabulary of reform—the *ecclesia primitiva* and the *vita apostolica*—conjured a religious community in which the sexes were joined together, chastely and legitimately, in a divinely ordained spiritual quest.

The "Special Favour of His Humility": Dignifying Women in the Gospels

Medieval exegetes did not need to look far for examples of Jesus's attention to women or for the dignity that had been conferred on women through their association with him: the gospels provide ample evidence of Jesus's relations with women. According to Luke's gospel, women accompanied Jesus on his preaching journeys and supported him financially. Luke mentions Mary Magdalene, Joanna the wife of Chuza (Herod's steward), and Susanna, as well as "many others" (Luke 8:2–3). The gospels of Matthew and Mark observed that several women "followed Jesus from Galilee, ministering unto him" and were subsequently present at the crucifixion (Matt. 27:55–56; cf. Mark 15:41, Luke 23:55). All of the gospels report that women stood by Jesus as he died, providing evidence—as medieval exegetes saw it—of women's spiritual fortitude and constancy. Women were the first to see the risen Christ, displacing the disciples who had fled the cross in fear, as numerous commentators pointed out. In the book of Acts, Jesus's women followers appear with the apostles after the ascension, praying together in an upper room (Acts 1:14).

In addition to the women who followed Jesus, provided for his needs, and witnessed his death and resurrection, there were others for whom he performed miracles, or to whom he showed special care and understanding. One of Jesus's most significant miracles was performed in response to the petitions of women: his close friends, the sisters Mary and Martha of Bethany. Jesus's affection for Mary and Martha prompted him to raise their brother Lazarus from the dead, a miracle understood by medieval exegetes to foreshadow his own salvific death and resurrection (John 11:17–44). The gospels describe Mary as having been particularly close to Jesus: it was she who listened eagerly to his teaching (Luke 10:39) and anointed his feet with precious perfume, drying them with her hair (John 12:3; cf. Mark 14:3, where the woman is unnamed). The gospels of John and Mark report that the disciples criticized Mary for her extravagance, but Jesus defended her, declaring that, "She hath wrought a good work upon me" (Mark 14:6).

Jesus's defense of Mary is paralleled in the gospels by his advocacy of other women who were marginal or outcast. John's gospel tells, in particular, of Jesus's mercy to an unnamed woman who had been caught in adultery.[3] While the Pharisees were prepared to have the woman stoned to death, Jesus refused to condemn her, inviting anyone who was without sin to "cast a stone at her" (John 8:7). Jesus's encounter with a further "sinful" woman during a dinner at the home of Simon the Pharisee is reminiscent of the story of Mary of Bethany's anointing of his feet (Luke 7:36–50). Like Mary, this woman bathed Jesus's feet with an alabaster jar of perfume. Sensing the displeasure of his host Simon, Jesus defended the woman's actions, telling her, "Thy faith hath made thee safe. Go in peace." Luke does not name this woman, yet from the sixth century on, she was conflated with the biblical figures Mary of Bethany and Mary Magdalene, producing a composite woman—known to medieval audiences as "Mary Magdalene"—whose chaste love for Jesus was celebrated as having eclipsed the tepid affections of the male disciples.[4]

Medieval exegetes and theologians commented regularly on the spiritual significance of Jesus's attention to women. Their comments were frequently designed to shame contemporary men, showcasing the spiritual potential of purportedly weak women and urging men to emulate (or, better, surpass) them.[5] However, a further strain of exegesis explored the gospels for evidence of women's spiritual dignity, clues that Jesus had especially honored women, redeeming them through his birth (by which female genitalia had been "hallowed," according to Peter Abelard) and in his life: his miracles, his friendships, and his mercy to female sinners.[6] The argument that Jesus had particularly exalted women appeared often in the context of the "case" for women identified by Alcuin Blamires. In Blamires's view, the medieval pro-feminine discourse was exemplified in Abelard's letter *On the Origin of Nuns*, a work that drew heavily on the gospels and the book of Acts to establish the central place held by women within the early church.[7] As Abelard noted in that letter, women (and *only* women) had ministered to Jesus financially. It was a woman who was permitted to wash Jesus's feet—a service that he had provided for his disciples, but that only a woman had the honor of providing for him.[8] Even more strikingly, Jesus allowed himself to be anointed by a woman, an act that Abelard claimed was like "consecrating him king and priest with bodily sacraments."[9] Following Jesus's death, women went to the tomb to prepare his body with spices—ready to "anoint" him once again, as Jesus had implied in his defense of Mary of Bethany (John 12:7; cf. Mark 14:8).[10] Finally, not to overlook the obvious fact of Jesus's birth from a woman, Abelard argued that it had been his deliberate decision to receive flesh from a woman; although he "could have taken his body from a man," Abelard enthused that, "he transferred this special favour of his humility to honour the weaker sex."[11]

Abelard's arguments for women's spiritual dignity in his letter *On the Origin of Nuns* were extensive, and remarkable in that regard. However, they were neither unique nor fully unprecedented: other late antique and medieval men had made similar gospel-based arguments for women's spiritual dignity. Several men highlighted Jesus's decision to enter the world through a woman, for instance. Goscelin of St. Bertin, writing a full generation before Abelard, had noted the significance of Jesus's birth from a woman in the *Liber confortatorius* that he composed for Eve of Wilton: "the Lord Jesus, the morning star . . . chose to rise in the world through a woman."[12] Hugh of Fleury (d. c. 1130), too, had argued for the salvific implications of Jesus's decision to be born of a woman in his *Historia ecclesiastica*, which he dedicated to

Adela of Blois in 1109. As he wrote, by being "born of a woman" Jesus showed "the great benevolence of his graciousness and the immeasurable example of his humility."[13] Writing at the end of the twelfth century (later than Abelard, but with evidently no knowledge of his writings), Guibert of Gembloux likewise commented that, through his birth, Christ honored and strengthened the female sex.[14] Similar ideas had appeared among patristic writers: during the fourth century, Jerome reported a woman's comment to the male saint Hilarion that "it was my sex that bore the savior" (a comment that Abelard repeated).[15]

Blamires identifies the gender polemic of Abelard's letter *On the Origin of Nuns* as "daring," particularly in his claim that a woman had consecrated Christ.[16] Yet Abelard was, if anything, more daring in the case that he made for the legitimacy and spiritual significance of nuns' priests. While drawing on biblical examples of Jesus's attention to women in order to demonstrate the dignity of female religious life, Abelard also claimed a spiritual role for the men who ministered to religious women, invoking Jesus as their ultimate and perfect model. In his letter of consolation to a friend, Abelard hinted at this use of the gospel, commenting on the injustice of accusations against him stemming from his spiritual involvement with nuns. Citing Jesus's care for women as a model for the legitimate engagement of contemporary men with religious women, Abelard asked: "What would my enemies in their malice have said to Christ himself and his followers, the prophets and apostles and other holy fathers, had they lived in their times when these men, pure in body, were seen to enjoy such friendly feminine company?"[17]

Even in this, however, Abelard was hardly unique. Other men also invoked Jesus's friendships with women to justify the spiritually necessary service of ordained men among women. Augustine (d. 430), writing in the fourth century, had commented on Jesus's care for women, noting that the apostles had taken women with them wherever they preached, and that they had done so "by the example of our Lord Himself."[18] In the twelfth century, Sigeboto (a Hirsau monk and author of the *Vita Paulinae*) noted that married women and widows had been among Jesus's entourage.[19] Guibert of Gembloux likewise turned to Jesus's example as he defended his role as priest at Rupertsberg, commenting that "The Lord himself did not reject the companionship of women," but defended female sinners and did not scorn "to have them following him in his company."[20] As Guibert argued, the steadfast presence of women at the cross and the tomb was evidence of Jesus's close ties to women and of their spiritual worthiness: "To whom did the victor rising from the dead first deign to show himself and the triumph of death defeated and the glory of his resurrection, if not to women?" he asked.[21] For Guibert (as for other men), biblical accounts of women's constancy and spiritual fortitude, and of Jesus's example of care and attention for them, were relevant as models for nuns' priests. Conflating contemporary and biblical women, Guibert asked if men should "refuse either society or services" to women, noting that they had been "preferred to the apostles in many things."[22]

Men like these shared Abelard's sense that nuns' priests had biblical authorization for their care for women. Where Abelard was unusual was in the distinctive language he used to describe relations between Christ and holy women. In his letter of consolation to a friend, Abelard commented that women had not only followed Christ and the apostles, but had also "stuck fast" (*adhesisse*) to them as their "inseparable companions."[23] Some years later, in his letter *On the Origin of Nuns*, Abelard extended this motif, attributing to Christ the initiative in forging relationships with women (and not the other way around). As Abelard explained, Christ joined the women to himself as his "inseparable companions"; in so doing he had treated them "equally with the apostles" (*pariter cum apostolis*).[24] As remarkable as this claim was, it was nevertheless eclipsed by Abelard's application of this vocabulary to his own relationship with Heloise. In his second letter, in which he exhorted Heloise to turn herself wholly to religion and to renounce nostalgia for their past, Abelard addressed his former wife as *his* "inseparable companion," seeming to suggest that the spiritual intimacy he shared with Heloise might parallel Jesus's friendships with women.[25]

"Behold Your Mother": The Commendation to John

Abelard's use of the language of "inseparable companionship" to describe both Jesus's relations to women and his own spiritualized relationship to Heloise was unquestionably daring, and probably too daring for most medieval nuns' priests. These men were already subject to suspicions and allegations of misbehavior without proposing to model themselves on Jesus in their relationships with women. As nuns were increasingly characterized as brides of Christ, it would, in any case, have been awkward for priests to claim him as a primary exemplar—implying, as that would, their own status as potential bridegrooms. Abelard appears to have been alone in his use of this particular motif; I find no other examples of ordained men who described religious women as their "inseparable companions," nor, in fact, of similar language in reference to Jesus's relations with women. Jesus had dignified women, traveled with them, healed them, accepted their hospitality and support, and been "anointed" by a woman on several occasions. That much is clear in the biblical account, and it certainly inspired medieval men to see spiritual involvement with women as legitimate. But Jesus's potential as a direct model for men's priestly care of religious women—women increasingly identified as his "brides"—was deeply fraught.

In seeking biblical models for their own spiritual care of women, medieval monks and priests turned more often to the example of John the Evangelist, whose care for the Virgin Mary they understood to have been Jesus's final command from the cross.[26] According to John's gospel (John 19.26–27), Jesus's last thoughts were for his mother, whose comfort and care he was concerned to ensure after his death. As he saw Mary standing at the foot of the cross with the disciple "whom he loved" (and who is thought to have been John), Jesus entrusted Mary to John's care, presenting John as her adoptive son and Mary as John's adoptive mother.[27] "Behold your son," Jesus said to Mary, indicating John as her adoptive child; "Behold your mother," he said to John. Traditional depictions of the crucifixion often highlight this moment, presenting John and Mary as the sole figures flanking the cross, and glossing the entire scene with Jesus's words: "*Ecce filius tuus*" and "*Ecce mater tua*"—reinforcing for medieval audiences the creation of a new family unit, one based on the gendered provision of care. At the cross, John became Mary's "son" and caretaker, while Mary became his "mother."[28]

According to John's gospel, John took Mary to live with him in his own home after the crucifixion (*accepit eam discipulus in sua*) (John 19:27). The biblical text offers nothing further; it does not specify the nature of the living arrangements in John's home, nor does it emphasize the innocence of John's relationship to Mary, which Christians simply assumed had been pure and blameless. Indeed, John's purity was axiomatic to late antique and medieval audiences, who celebrated him not only as Jesus's favorite disciple, but also as the only certain virgin among Jesus's followers.[29] As Jerome had taught, underscoring the physical purity that Jesus, John, and Mary held in common: "the Virgin Mother was entrusted by the Virgin Lord to the Virgin disciple."[30] For medieval nuns' priests, John offered proof that relations between the sexes could be fully chaste. Abelard, for one, invoked John in this way: to shame critics who persisted in seeing scandal where there was none, accusing him of sexual motivation in his care for nuns despite his physical incapacity.

Defending himself through allusion to John's pure and holy example, Abelard pointed out the ridiculousness of accusations against him (as a eunuch, although not a virgin): "anyone who saw the Lord's mother entrusted to the care of a young man . . . would entertain far more probable suspicions."[31]

Like Abelard, medieval men sometimes cited John's relationship to Mary defensively—to shield themselves from accusations of wrongdoing. However, they more often invoked John's guardianship of Mary in a positive and constructive sense: to claim their own care for women as a devotional act motivated by obedience to Christ's dying command. According to certain interpretations of John 19:27, Jesus's commendation of Mary to John at the cross implied an obligation for all religious men to care for religious women, as John had cared for Mary. To be sure, this was a controversial interpretation.[32] Already during the fourth century, Epiphanius of Salamis had warned that the biblical text "must not be twisted to the harm of any who suppose that, by a clumsy conjecture, they can find an excuse here to invent their so-called 'adoptive wives' and 'beloved friends.'"[33] Subsequent exegetes often emphasized allegorical interpretations of the commendation scene that intentionally precluded syneisaktism. For Ambrose, Mary was simply a figure of the church and Jesus's commendation of her a symbolic act, whereby the apostle was entrusted figuratively with the care of all Christ's followers.[34] In his view, the commendation also offered a model of filial piety.[35] Other exegetes cited the commendation as proof of Mary's perpetual virginity: since Jesus had commended her to John, some concluded that she could not have had other children to care for her.[36] Jerome, treading a middle ground, allowed that the commendation offered a model for men's spiritual care, but only of holy women. Interpreting John as a symbol of the apostles and Mary as a symbol of the female saints, Jerome advanced a reading of the scene that emphasized the care that the apostles had provided for holy women.[37]

Despite these cautious readings, some men and women throughout the medieval period nevertheless interpreted the commendation scene as a sign of Christ's dying concern not just for Mary, but for all women. In their view, John's care for Mary served as an example of the sort of care that men ought to provide for religious women.[38] So, for instance, the eighth-century Anglo-Saxon missionary Boniface (d. 754) commended the abbess Leoba to his successor Lull, as he prepared to preach in Frisia, where he would ultimately be martyred.[39] The scene, described in the *Life* of Leoba, is clearly reminiscent of Jesus's commendation of Mary to John: Boniface, facing death, gave Leoba into Lull's care, for him to look after in Boniface's absence. Goscelin of

St. Bertin similarly implied a connection to John 19:26–27 in his eleventh-century *Life* of Edith of Wilton (d. c. 984), describing the reformer and archbishop Dunstan as the "friend of the bridegroom" (*amicus sponsi*) who brought Edith to Jesus and was joined to her as John was to Mary.[40] Bishop Azecho of Worms was explicit in claiming the commendation as a model for men's relations with women, writing a letter to an unnamed nun in which he cited John's care for Mary as evidence that relationships between the sexes were not only permissible, but could even be wholly pleasing to God.[41]

Churchmen at the heart of the ecclesiastical reform movement during the late eleventh century also invoked the commendation as a model for male-female spiritual relations. Pope Gregory VII (d. 1085) maintained a warm spiritual friendship with the countess Matilda of Tuscany, a woman who supported him in all his endeavors, even traveling with him throughout Italy "like another Martha"—an allusion to Jesus's friendship with Mary and Martha.[42] The friendship between the two attracted unsavory gossip and insinuations, likely prompting Gregory to deliver Matilda into the care of Anselm of Lucca, one of his staunch allies in the difficult years after his meeting with Henry IV at Canossa.[43] According to Anselm's biographer, he did this "just as Christ on the cross entrusted his virgin mother to his virgin disciple: saying, 'Mother, behold your son,' and to the disciple: 'Behold your mother.' "[44] The *Vita Mathildis* likewise emphasized Jesus' commendation as the model for Gregory's decision to entrust her into Anselm's care, observing that, "Like Jesus, who, dying on the cross, gave his mother to his disciple, so Gregory, the bishop of Rome, entrusted the lady countess to Anselm."[45] The complications of Gregory's position and the attacks of his critics may have given urgency to the association of Gregory and Anselm with Christ and John in their dealings with Matilda, stressing the chastity and holiness of their relations.

By the twelfth century, Christ's commendation of Mary to John was well established as a common justification for men's spiritual care of women. The *Life* of Christina of Markyate, who was aided in her religious journey by some twenty men, chief among them the abbot Geoffrey of Saint Albans (Geoffrey de Gorron), reports that she had a vision in which she saw herself and Geoffrey flanking Jesus at the altar, just as Mary and John had at the foot of the cross.[46] If the *Life* was composed for the male community at Saint Albans, as Rachel Koopmans suggests, then the inclusion of this scene may have been designed to remind the men, who were sometimes critical of Geoffrey's intimacy with Christina, of the divine injunction that religious men care for women.[47] Similarly, Guibert of Gembloux, whose service as priest to the nuns of Rupertsberg drew the ire of his monastic confrères, defended his spiritual relations with women through reference to John. "With Christ himself commanding from the cross," Guibert wrote, "John . . . undertook to protect the mother of the Lord, and he clung to her until the end of life, and served her in chaste obedience."[48]

In the same way, the early thirteenth-century *Book of St. Gilbert* invoked John's care for Mary in describing Gilbert of Sempringham's care for the women of his community: "Do you not know what happened to St. John the Evangelist? Just as he received our Lord's mother in his home, so this man [Gilbert] took into his charge those women who followed her example."[49] Also writing in the early thirteenth century, Thomas of Cantimpré described how Abbot John had taken his widowed mother into his house, intentionally adopting language that was reminiscent of John 19.27: *suscepit in sua*.[50] At Prémy, the connection to John the Evangelist as a custodian for religious women was strengthened by the fact that the nuns claimed John as their official patron. As Thomas commented, "it was surely fitting and right for the blessed evangelist John to defend the chaste community of virgins," since he had "protected Christ's virgin mother."[51]

Women too recognized the importance of the commendation scene and cited it when reminding men of their spiritual obligations to help and support them. In the sixth century, when Radegund (d. 587) wrote to the Merovingian bishops to appeal for episcopal protection for her foundation at Poitiers, she pointedly reminded them of John's obedient care for Mary. Making her request to the bishops, "in the name of Him who from the Cross did commend His own Mother, the Blessed Virgin, to Saint John," Radegund urged the churchmen to respond favorably, offering John as a model: "Just as the Apostle John fulfilled our Lord's request, so may you fulfil all that which, humble and unworthy though I be, I commend to you."[52] Heloise, too, proposed the commendation to John as a model for Abelard, arguing that men should support religious women financially, as Paul had suggested in his letter to Timothy (1 Tim. 5:16).[53] A woman was equally the source of the identification of Gilbert of Sempringham with John the Evangelist that appeared in the *Book of St. Gilbert*: the image stemmed from a vision received by Agnes, the Cistercian prioress of Nun Appleton.[54] During the late twelfth century, Herrad of Hohenbourg emphasized the centrality of the commendation to the proper interpretation of the crucifixion, glossing her depiction of the crucifixion (fol. 150r of the *Hortus deliciarum*) twice with Jesus's words: "Mother, behold your son," and to John: "Behold your mother"—a scene that is evoked elsewhere in the manuscript where John and Mary are shown together and John is identified as the guardian of virgins (*custos virginum*) (fol. 176v).[55]

As these examples indicate, providing spiritual care for religious women was understood by many—both women and men—as an act of direct obedience to Christ that was modeled on John's obedience to his dying command.[56] This interpretation is most clear in the evidence from Fontevraud, the Loire Valley monastery founded in 1101 by Robert of Arbrissel and typically characterized by historians as "exceptional" (together with Robert himself). As we have seen, Fontevraud included both men and women within a single, spiritual community. However, at Fontevraud ultimate authority lay not in the hands of a male abbot (as at most contemporary double houses), but in those of an abbess: the men were explicitly subjected to female authority.[57] Indeed, Robert's intention was for the women to be dominant, as he declared at the end of his life: "everything I have built anywhere, with God's help, I have placed under [the] dominion and rule" of women. According to his biographer Andrew (likely his chaplain, and therefore a priest of Fontevraud), the Fontevraud men embraced their service and subordination to the women, viewing it in spiritual terms. When Robert asked the men, from his deathbed, "whether you wish to persist in your purpose, that is, obey the command of Christ's handmaids for the salvation of your souls," they responded almost in unison: "God forbid, dearest father, that we ever abandon the sisters since, as you yourself attest, we can in no way do better anywhere else."[58]

The confidence of the Fontevraud men that serving women would advance their own salvation is significant, indicating that men did see spiritual benefits in their care for women, as I argued in Chapter 1. Even more significant is the fact that this confidence was founded on the men's identification with John the Evangelist, whose model of service to Mary was incorporated into the very structure of monastic governance at Fontevraud. As the order grew from a single house to a confederation with some two or three thousand members,[59] we are told that Robert modeled each new house on the special relationship between John and Mary. As Robert's biographer wrote: "because St. John the Evangelist, at Christ's command, unfailingly served . . . [the] Virgin Mother as a devoted minister . . . , wise Robert decreed that the brothers' oratories should be dedicated in John's honor. . . . This must have been done with divine inspiration so that the brothers would rejoice to have as patron of their church the one they regarded as an example of service owed to the brides of Christ."[60] At Fontevraud, and communities associated with it, nuns lived in houses dedicated to "Holy Mary, ever virgin," while men's houses were dedicated to John. The point of the association is clear: the tender concern shown by John for Mary at the crucifixion was to be a model for the care and attentive service of the men to the women at Fontevraud.[61]

The decision to dedicate the men's and women's communities at Fontevraud to John and Mary respectively (with a third house for women devoted to Mary Magdalene) demonstrates the force of the commendation scene as a model for twelfth-century relations between the sexes: some men within the religious life were inspired to serve women precisely because John, in obedience to Christ, had served Mary. Abelard, too, invoked John's model of care for Mary in his *Rule* for the Paraclete, noting that "the Lord himself at his death chose for his mother a second son who should take care of her in material things."[62] Like Robert's biographer, who commented that it was "at Christ's command" that John "unfailingly served . . . [the] Virgin Mother," Abelard emphasized Christ's role in arranging care for Mary, "at his death."

Given the suspicions to which nuns' priests were subject, it was important for them to locate models of holy men whose relationships with women had been pure and blameless and who were themselves beyond reproach. John the Evangelist provided the most compelling human example. His care for Mary was chaste, it was biblical, and it was divinely ordained: men who followed John's example could claim that they did so in obedience to Jesus's direct command. But emulating John could also be understood as a form of devotion. John was regularly depicted in medieval texts and images as Jesus's closest and most cherished disciple; this closeness was often understood as the reason for Jesus's decision to entrust Mary specifically to John, rather than any other disciple.[63] In his Sermon 26, Abelard commented that at the cross John became not only the adopted son of Mary, but also the spiritual brother of Christ (an idea that Anselm had expressed, too).[64] For medieval men to imagine themselves as emulating John in their care for women was, therefore, to imagine themselves approximating John's closeness to Christ as well—a compelling image of male spiritual intimacy with Christ.

A final connection strengthens the suggestion that men's care for women could be perceived as a form of devotion to Christ. According to the biblical account, the relationship of John to Mary was orchestrated by Jesus: he was the son (of Mary) and the friend (of John) who brought the pair together. In the same way, the relationship of priests to nuns was one in which Christ—although physically absent—was consistently rhetorically present as the bridegroom to whom nuns were espoused. The characterization of nuns as brides of Christ was founded on the assumed centrality to female religious life of only one male figure: Christ, the bridegroom. Priests serving women did not imagine themselves as the bridegroom.[65] Rather, they pictured themselves as the "friend of the bridegroom", the *paranymphus*, who assisted at the marriage and brought the bride to her groom.[66] By adopting this identity, men who engaged in spiritual service to women were able to conceive of their care for Christ's "brides" as an important manifestation of their friendship with Christ himself.

Men caring spiritually for women regularly described their service in terms that invoked John's care for Mary, or in the language of "friendship" to Christ the bridegroom, or both. Sympathetic contemporary observers adopted these motifs, too. As we saw above, Goscelin of St. Bertin presented Dunstan as the "friend of the bridegroom," who brought Edith to Jesus. In his *Vita Wulsini*, Goscelin described Wulfsige as bringing the virgin Juthwara to the Lord, "like the friend of the bridegroom and the bridesman of the bride" (*ut amicus sponsi et paranimphus sponse*).[67] At Fontevraud, John the Evangelist was invoked as an "example of service owed to the brides of Christ," implying that men in the community were to serve as caretakers of nuns as Christ's "brides". Similarly, William de Montibus, writing to the nuns at Sempringham after 1202, described Gilbert of Sempringham as "a prudent and provident attendant of the bridegroom" (*paranimphus sponsi*).[68] The language that men adopted in describing their care for religious women reflects their clear understanding that spiritual involvement with women was significant first and foremost within the context of their own relationship (as men) to Christ. As Robert of Arbrissel reminded the men at Fontevraud, they were to serve the women "out of love of their bridegroom Jesus"; for this, they would be "rewarded . . . in the blessed realm of Paradise."[69] By caring for religious women, men felt that they could transcend mere obedience to Christ, establishing themselves as his friends. Viewed in this way, care for women could actually be conceived of as integral to male spirituality, and not—as modern scholars and medieval critics routinely assume—tangential, or even inimical, to it.

John and Mary at Schwarzrheindorf: Arnold von Wied and Female Monasticism

Evidence for John's importance as a model for medieval men in their service to women is most clear in the narrative texts examined above—in the chronicles, *vitae*, and letters, for instance, which explicitly claim him as an exemplar for individual men like Robert, Abelard, Goscelin, Guibert, and Gilbert. That John inspired other men—the mostly unnamed nuns' priests who ministered faithfully to women, yet left little mark on the written record—is implied in monastic records, chiefly dedications. At Fontevraud, as we have seen, the male and female houses were dedicated to John and Mary; Robert's biographer explained that the dedication was intentionally modeled on the commendation of Mary to John, implying that it was intended to inspire at Fontevraud the sort of care for nuns that John had provided for Mary. In other monastic houses that included both women and men, and that had been founded on apostolic ideals, altars or chapels were also dedicated to John and Mary together, suggesting a similar inspiration and intention. Gaucher of Aureil's community, with its "walls of both sexes," included a men's house dedicated to John and a women's house dedicated to Mary.[70] At Zwiefalten, a Hirsau reform monastery founded in 1089, a chapel was dedicated jointly to Mary and John, her "most holy protector."[71] Although no extant narrative text explains the rationale for this dedication, it seems likely that John's service to Mary inspired men at Zwiefalten, just as it had at Fontevraud.

Premonstratensian communities, too, were often dedicated to John and Mary, or to John alone, reflecting his medieval reputation as a protector not only of the Virgin Mary, but of virgins generally. The high altar at Cappenberg, founded near Cologne as a double monastery in 1122, was dedicated to John and Mary; John was featured on the community's seal.[72] The female communities of Gommersheim, Rumbeck, and Keppel were likewise dedicated to Mary and John.[73] Communities at Mariengaarde, Parc-le-Duc, and Gramzow counted John and Mary as their patrons.[74] Other women seem to have identified strongly with John—solidifying the perception of John as a guardian of virgins (as he appears in the female-authored *Hortus deliciarum*).[75] Paulina (d. 1107), founder of Paulinzella, built a chapel dedicated to John the Evangelist, probably at the Peterskloster in Merseburg.[76] Her community at Paulinzella (known as Mariazell before her death) was dedicated to John and Mary when it received papal confirmation.[77] The timing of these dedications (late eleventh and twelfth centuries), and their association with reform communities that included women alongside men, confirm John's importance as a model for monks and priests who welcomed engagement with women in the religious life.

Attention to John's medieval cult may help us to expand our understanding of the many churchmen and monks who provided spiritual support for religious women, but whose involvement with women is never clearly addressed in the sources. The twelfth-century church at Schwarzrheindorf, just across the Rhine river from Bonn, offers a useful example.[78] Built in the mid-twelfth century as a private family chapel by Arnold von Wied (d. 1156), the Schwarzrheindorf church has a complicated and, in many ways, obscure history. It seems likely that the church incorporated a female religious community from the time of its foundation, although the sources are silent on this point. Certainly by 1172, some twenty years after the church's dedication in 1151, an organized women's monastery was in place; it remained until the early nineteenth century.[79] Despite the longevity of its women's community, Schwarzrheindorf is rarely remembered as a female monastery, but is instead celebrated for its elaborate design: its unusual double story construction and its wall paintings, which are hailed as some of the most extraordinary extant Romanesque frescoes in Germany.[80]

Like Schwarzrheindorf, which is known for its art and architecture but not for its female monastic community, Arnold von Wied is rarely remembered in terms of his support for women's religious life. By the time that the church was dedicated,[81] Arnold had served for more than a decade as chancellor to the emperor Conrad III, and had recently been chosen Archbishop of Cologne.[82] He is typically famed for his achievements in traditional spheres of activity: his renewal of the Cologne church, reported by Otto of Freising, and his service to Frederick Barbarossa, whom he crowned emperor at Aachen in 1152.[83] Arnold's role in the founding of a female monastery at Schwarzrheindorf has attracted comparatively little attention. To be fair, the sources are unclear on the nature and extent of his involvement. A series of charters from the 1170s report only that, some point before his unexpected death in 1156, Arnold handed the Schwarzrheindorf church over to his sister Hadwig, an influential woman who served as abbess of both St. Hippolyt in Gerresheim and the imperial foundation at Essen.[84] According to Archbishop Philip I of Cologne, Arnold trusted Hadwig (a "strong woman") more than anyone else after God; for her part, she "did not disappoint" her brother in his expectations.[85]

The dearth of early sources makes it impossible to determine whether the female community was already in place when Arnold handed the church to his sister, or if she established it later herself (perhaps even in accordance with his plans).[86] What is clear is that contemporaries perceived Arnold and Hadwig as having acted together in the foundation of the community. A monumental fresco in the apse of the upper church commemorates their

Figure 3. Arnold and Hadwig at the Feet of Christ in Majesty. Apse,
Doppelkirche, Schwarzrheindorf, Germany. Photograph: Foto Marburg /
Art Resource, N.Y.

partnership, showing Arnold and Hadwig at the feet of the enthroned Christ as
co-founders and co-supplicants, suggesting that Arnold was remembered
within the women's community not only as the community's founder, but
more familiarly as a brother in spiritual partnership with his sister (Figure 3).[87]
A second fresco hints that Arnold may have imagined himself relating to
religious women in another, even more powerful way: as a spiritual son inspired by what he understood as Christ's dying command. A depiction of the
crucifixion (Figure 4) in the northern conch of the lower church suggests an
interpretation of the passion narrative that highlighted John's adoptive care
for Mary. Although much of the image is conventional, John and Mary
appear disproportionately large compared to other figures and are shown
together and not, as is more common, flanking the cross.[88] The commendation,
which thus emerges as the focal point of the Passion scene, is depicted as a moment of extreme tenderness. Mary, turning away from the cross, buries her
head in John's shoulder, while John embraces her, inclining his head toward
her own.[89]

Figure 4. Mary and John at the Crucifixion. Northern conch,
Doppelkirche, Schwarzrheindorf, Germany. Photograph: Foto Marburg /
Art Resource, N.Y.

While depictions of the crucifixion routinely include John and Mary, the
Schwarzrheindorf fresco is unusual in featuring them so prominently, suggesting that the commendation scene may have held particular meaning for
Arnold—as it so clearly did for other men. Further evidence from the church
strengthens this suggestion: an inscription recording the 1151 consecration reports that the altar in the upper church was dedicated to the Virgin and
John.[90] Although we still cannot be certain that Arnold intended to promote
female religious life through his foundation at Schwarzrheindorf, the crucifixion image, together with the dedication to John and Mary, is strongly suggestive. As we have seen, attention to the commendation often appears in
contexts marked by men's concern for the spiritual lives of women. Arnold
himself was evidently drawn by the spiritual potential of religious women: he
wrote to Hildegard of Bingen, addressing her as "a blazing lantern in the house
of the Lord," requesting a copy of her visionary work *Scivias*, and indicating
that he had planned to visit her at Rupertsberg.[91] He may also have known of
Hildegard's younger protégée, Elisabeth of Schönau, whose visions concerning

the Cologne relics of St. Ursula and the 11,000 virgin martyrs were dissemi-
nated in 1156, just shortly after his death in that same year.[92] Arnold certainly
knew Elisabeth's maternal great-uncle, Bishop Ekbert of Münster (1127–1132),
and possibly also her brother, Ekbert (d. 1184), who left a promising ecclesiastical career at Saint Cassius in Bonn (across the Rhine from Schwarzrheindorf)
in 1155 to support her at Schönau.[93]

The strongest evidence that Arnold was motivated by concern for female religious life comes from his own family. Arnold had at least three
brothers, and four sisters—three of whom were, or became, abbesses.[94] In
addition to Hadwig (who was abbess of Essen and Gerresheim), Hizecha was
abbess of Vilich, while Sophia ultimately became abbess of Schwarzrheindorf. A fourth sister, Siburgis, served as deaconess at the new community. As
we shall see in Chapter 4, it was not unusual for men to partner with their
devout sisters in order to found female monastic houses, or to support their
sisters' spiritual lives in other ways (sometimes by serving as their priests). It
is entirely possible that Arnold wished to promote the spiritual lives of his
sisters, and so worked with Hadwig to found a religious community for Sophia
and Siburgis.[95] The possibility that Arnold intended Schwarzrheindorf to be
a house for women is particularly intriguing, given that he founded it as a
burial chapel. When Arnold died in 1156, he was buried there himself.[96] This
is no incidental detail: as I argue in Chapter 5, men who chose burial among
religious women believed that the prayers and intercessions of women were
more powerful than those of men, and more likely, ultimately, to secure their
salvation.[97] The decision to convert the Wied family chapel into a female monastery meant that Arnold's soul (when he died) would be commemorated primarily by religious women—a situation that contemporary men sought, and
that may have motivated Arnold, too.

Widows and "Sister Women": The Apostles and Women

The questions and uncertainties surrounding the women's community at
Schwarzrheindorf are by no means unusual: many women's houses are
poorly documented, and men's spiritual involvement with women, as I noted
in Chapter 1, is reported only vaguely—if at all. Still, if Arnold had indeed
sought to support women through his foundation at Schwarzrheindorf, his
actions would have been fully in accordance with the spiritual climate of the

time. Women's religious life was thriving in Cologne in the mid-twelfth century. New houses for religious women were founded in and around the city, many of them in association with reform movements that included both sexes— chiefly the Premonstratensians and the reform congregation associated with Siegburg (with which Schwarzrheindorf was associated).[98] The example of John the Evangelist inspired some men in these communities, as we have seen. However, John was not the only New Testament figure to whom they could turn as a model for the care of women. According to Acts, in the period after the resurrection, as the church began to organize itself, care for women (mostly widows) emerged as an urgent matter. In response, the disciples authorized the community to choose seven deacons, who were tasked with the women's material care (Acts 6:1–5). Among them was Stephen, "a man full of faith and of the Holy Spirit," who—having taken on the care of widows—quickly emerged as an evangelist who performed "great wonders and signs" and spoke with the "wisdom of the Spirit." Stephen's public ministry provoked swift opposition, and he was stoned to death.

As a proto-martyr, Stephen was a figure of enormous spiritual significance for late antique Christians. After his body was discovered near Jerusalem in 415, Stephen's cult developed rapidly, especially in the East, where it was promoted by the empresses Pulcheria and Eudocia.[99] In the West, Augustine reported the miracles wrought by Stephen's relics in his *City of God*.[100] Stephen's developing cult focused on his public ministry and death; even so, his care for women was well known and was even seen by some as providing a rationale for his evangelism. In a sermon for Stephen's feast day, Abelard observed that Stephen had begun to minister through the Spirit, to preach, and to perform wonders only *after* he had been commissioned by the laying on of hands to care for widows. For Abelard, the connection was plain: Stephen had received merit because he served women, since God rewards those who "humiliate" themselves in service to the "weaker sex."[101]

The election of deacons to serve women's needs within the early church suggested, as the commendation scene had also, that providing care for women in the spiritual life was a valid service for religious men.[102] A further example of apostolic involvement with women was still more compelling for nuns' priests—even as it was more consistently controversial. Like the women who had followed Jesus, and supported him financially, there were women among the apostles, as Paul noted in his letter to the Corinthians. Claiming that it was an apostolic "right" to "lead around a sister woman (*adelphēn gynaika*),"

Paul observed that the "rest of the apostles and the brothers of the Lord and Cephas" were accompanied by "sister women" (I Cor. 9:5).[103]

Paul's reference to the sister women of the apostles raised significant interpretive problems for late antique exegetes. The possibility that these women had been wives—the now standard Protestant interpretation—was foreclosed by the Latin fathers in the fourth century.[104] Jerome argued vigorously against the idea in his *Adversus Jovinianum*, acknowledging that the Greek term Paul had used—*gynaika*—could mean either woman or wife, but affirming that "we must understand, not wives, but those women who ministered of their substance."[105] Augustine, too, noted that some had been "deceived" by the obscurity of the Greek word, concluding that Paul had meant to refer to the apostolic right of being supported materially by women—a privilege he had denied himself in deference to the moral sensibilities of the Gentiles. As Augustine argued, the "sister women" should be understood in conjunction with the women who followed Jesus: both provided financial support for male preaching and teaching.[106] The presence of women among the apostles had been authorized by Jesus's blameless example, Augustine wrote, declaring that: "if anyone believes that the Apostles did not bring women of holy life with them wherever they preached the Gospel . . . let him hear the Gospel and realize that the Apostle did this by the example of our Lord Himself."[107]

The patristic interpretation of Paul's "*adelphēn gynaika*" as "sister women" (and not "sister wives") came to dominate medieval Latin exegesis. However, the assumption that the women had been present only in a financial capacity, to support the apostles materially, did not always hold sway. Eastern exegetes had emphasized Paul's identification of the women as "sister" as well as "woman," arguing that the term "sister" suggested their status as co-workers. In the early third century, Clement of Alexandria (d. c. 215) argued that the sister women were ministers of the gospel, who introduced the gospel to other women, working alongside the male apostles. As Clement wrote, "They [the Apostles], in conformity with their ministry, concentrated without distraction on preaching, and took their women as sisters, not as wives, to be their fellow-ministers for house-wives, through whom the teaching about the Lord penetrated into the women's quarters without scandal."[108] John Chrysostom (d. 407) modified Clement's argument, maintaining that the women merely followed the apostles, although he allowed that they sought instruction from them as well.[109]

Medieval Latin theologians also puzzled over the role of the women among the apostles, generally concluding that there were spiritual, as well as financial, reasons for their presence. The ninth-century theologian Walafrid Strabo (d. 849) explained the presence of "sister women" in his commentary on I Corinthians, noting that: "The Lord in his company had women lest they should seem to be disconnected from salvation."[110] Haimo of Auxerre (d. c. 855) reinforced Jerome's interpretation of the "sister women," noting the ambiguity of the Greek phrase, but affirming the interpretation of the women as faithful helpers and patrons, rather than wives.[111] Like Jerome and Augustine, Haimo associated Paul's "sister women" with the women who had supported Jesus on his travels, cautioning that Paul had refused the support of women in order to avoid causing scandal among the Gentiles. Hervé de Bourg-Dieu (d. 1149/50), the twelfth-century Benedictine exegete, emphasized material reasons for the presence of the sister women, although (like Chrysostom) he assumed that the women were motivated by the desire to learn (*desiderio doctrinae coelestis*).[112]

Despite differences in interpretation, one thing was clear to medieval churchmen: the apostles had female associates. Given that late antique exegetes had foreclosed the possibility that the "sister women" were (or ever had been) wives, medieval men simply accepted that the apostles had maintained close relations with women to whom they were neither married nor otherwise related—in short, that the apostles had shared in spiritual friendships with women. Not all men concluded that biblical evidence for Paul's "sister women" therefore justified close interactions between medieval religious men and women—but some did.[113] They found the apostolic model useful in two regards: first, and most obvious, it allowed nuns' priests to identify themselves with the apostles; and second, it provided a powerful negative association for their critics, whom they likened to the enemies of the early church. During the twelfth century, Christina of Markyate's biographer scorned what he referred to as a "depraved and perverse generation . . . which despised the disciples of Christ because they took women about with them," in a bid to demonstrate the wickedness of attacks on Christina and Abbot Geoffrey.[114] Similarly, Guibert of Gembloux invoked the apostles' relations with women in the context of a lengthy recitation of holy men who had involved themselves with women. Commenting that the disciples had accepted the companionship of women, in keeping with the example of Christ, Guibert remarked that Peter's wife had accompanied him on preaching trips—an anecdote taken from the pseudo-Clementine *Recognitiones*, which Guibert explained with reference to the "sister women" of I Corinthians.[115] Most striking is the claim advanced by Sigeboto that Paulina herself belonged among the women who had followed the apostles: in his view, Paulina was a true daughter of Paul.[116]

Women's Spiritual Constancy: Remembering the Cross and the Tomb

Women's place in the gospels and in the apostolic church, as supporters and companions of Jesus and the disciples, was widely recognized by medieval churchmen, who accepted that men's care for them had been divinely authorized: John the Evangelist, Stephen, and the apostles with their "sister wives" were examples to which nuns' priests could turn in order to justify and explain their own spiritual service among women. However, with the exception of the Virgin, the women who received diaconal care or who accompanied the apostles were peripheral or anonymous figures. By contrast, the New Testament women who appeared in the narrative of the crucifixion and resurrection were central to Christianity. They featured prominently in medieval exegesis, and in art, music, and the liturgy, showcasing the spiritual potential of women, as well as their deep intimacy with Christ—an intimacy that was deeper, according to many exegetes, than even that of the apostles. For Gregory the Great (d. 604), the constancy of the women at the cross served to explain Job's comment that his flesh had been consumed while his skin clung to his bones (Job 19:20): women had clung to Christ like skin to bone when the apostles (likened to the "flesh") had fled, an analogy that subsequently became the standard interpretation of Job, disrupting the more typical association of women with the flesh, as Blamires has shown.[117]

Gregory's unusual characterization of the apostles as "carnal" or "fleshly" in their desertion of Jesus at the crucifixion was founded on the idea that holy women had shown themselves superior to the male disciples in love and faithfulness at the cross. Textual support for such a view was plentiful. All four of the gospels report women's presence at the crucifixion and their steadfast vigil near the cross until Jesus died.[118] The male disciples, by contrast, were conspicuous in their absence. With the exception of John's reference to "the disciple whom [Jesus] loved," no gospel account places any disciple at the cross. Peter (the "Rock") had even denied Jesus three times after he was arrested (Matt. 26:69–75)—a fact that Abelard emphasized in his letter *On the Origin of Nuns*, noting that "the women were not parted from him either in mind or in body even in death."[119] The constancy of the women—and the absence of the men—continued beyond the cross. The gospels report that women followed Jesus's body to the tomb and returned on Easter morning with spices and perfumes to prepare it for burial. Finding the tomb empty, the women became the first to learn of the resurrection, which they subsequently announced to the apostles, at the command—according to some accounts—of the angels, and even of Christ himself. Of these women, Mary Magdalene emerged in the lead role. All four gospels name her as having been at the tomb on Easter morning; John goes further, identifying her as the sole woman at the tomb (John 20:1). As John reported, the risen Christ appeared only to Mary Magdalene, charging her with announcing the good news to the male apostles (John 20:17; cf. Mark 16:9–11).

The centrality of women to accounts of the first Easter fueled early criticism of the new religion. During the second century, the Greek philosopher Celsus mocked the faith for its reliance on female witnesses, noting derisively that only a "hysterical female" had reported the resurrection—the event on which claims to Jesus's divinity rested.[120] Yet despite criticisms like these, Christians across the centuries celebrated the presence of women at the empty tomb on Easter morning, imagining the resurrection as a drama in which the human figures were exclusively female. Women's prominence during the first Easter was underscored, for instance, in the early eleventh-century Bernward Gospels, which present women as the only witnesses to the crucifixion, effacing the other figures at the cross and seemingly eliding the crucifixion and resurrection: while the cross is foregrounded, the background displays the empty tomb and abandoned grave clothes, traditionally invoked as evidence that Christ had indeed risen (Figure 5).[121] The resurrection was featured as an exclusive encounter between the women and the angel at the empty tomb in other manuscripts, too: the eleventh-century Glazier Evangelistary, likely from Salzburg (Figure 6),[122] the roughly contemporary Benedictional of Bishop Engilmar of Parenzo (Figure 7),[123] and the twelfth-century St. Albans Psalter (Figure 8).[124]

The perception of the resurrection as a drama featuring female players was reinforced in the liturgy. From the beginning of the tenth century, the biblical account of women's presence at the tomb had been extended and elaborated in the Easter trope *Quem quaeritis*, which—although inspired by the biblical text (particularly Luke)—marked a new and spiritually significant development. The trope appeared first in the early tenth century, and was widely known throughout Europe by about 1000.[125] In its simplest form, *Quem quaeritis*

Figure 5. Crucifixion. *Bernward Gospels*, Hildesheim, Domschatz Nr. 18
Fol. 175r. © Dommuseum Hildesheim.

Figure 6. Resurrection. *Glazier Evangelistary*, The Morgan Library
and Museum. MS G.44, fol. 86r. Gift of the Trustees of the William S.
Glazier Collection, 1984.

Figure 7. The Women at the Tomb. *Benedictional of Bishop Engilmar of Parenzo*, The J. Paul Getty Museum, Los Angeles, Ms. Ludwig VII 1, fol. 40v.

presented the angels at the tomb in dialogue with the women, who had come with spices to honor the body of the crucified Christ. "Whom do you seek in the tomb, Christians?" the angels asked, while the women responded, "Jesus, the crucified Nazarene." The trope concluded with the angels announcing the resurrection ("He is not here, he has risen as he foretold") and charging the women to spread the good news: "Go, announce that he has risen from the tomb."[126]

Within a century of its appearance, *Quem quaeritis* was incorporated into an Easter play, the *Visitatio sepulchri*, which dramatized the women's arrival

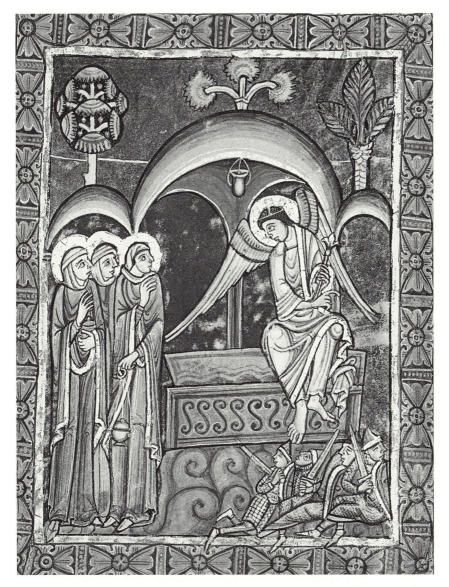

Figure 8. Resurrection. *St. Albans Psalter. Dombibliothek Hildesheim, HS St. God. 1* (Property of the Basilica of St. Godehard, Hildesheim), p. 50.

at the tomb and their encounter with the angels.[127] The earliest *Visitatio sepulchri* appears in the Winchester *Regularis Concordia*, a late tenth-century guide for Benedictine monasteries in England. According to the text, four monks were to perform the events of Easter morning during the course of Easter Matins, before the *Te Deum*.[128] One brother, wearing an alb, was to position himself as the angel before the "sepulcher," while the other three, wearing copes and carrying thuribles, were to represent the women who came to the tomb on Easter morning. After singing the *Quem quaeritis*, and once the "angel" had announced the resurrection, all four were to take up and display the empty linens of the tomb, "as though showing that the Lord was risen."[129]

As effective as manuscript images were in underscoring the constancy of women at the cross and tomb, the *Visitatio sepulchri* was even more powerful. In men's monasteries, performance of the *Visitatio sepulchri* required that monks act the parts of the women at the tomb; these men could not have failed to notice the absence of the male disciples from the biblical account. The discrepancy between the men's absence from the tomb and the women's presence would have been even more striking in women's communities, where nuns could assume the roles of the faithful women, performing women's biblical constancy for audiences that included, in many cases, not only other nuns, but also their priests and male personnel. At the monastery of Sainte-Croix at Poitiers, for instance, one of the community's clerics played the angel, while a nun acted the role of Mary Magdalene.[130] Even in cases where the entire community (nuns and their clerics) participated in the performance of the *Visitatio sepulchri*, women held a position of spiritual prominence. At Barking, according to an early fifteenth-century ordinal, the nuns and clerics processed together from the chapel of Mary Magdalene to the high altar, yet at the altar only nuns ("dressed in dazzling surplices") were selected to play the three Marys at the tomb.[131] Even more surprising is the depiction of these nuns as performing a priestly role through the drama. In the ordinal, as Yardley and Mann have shown, the Marys are described as *sacerdotes*.[132]

The events of Easter weekend provided a tangible opportunity for medieval monks and churchmen to acknowledge the spiritual priority of the biblical women. As Abelard had noted, praising the holy women in contrast to the absent and fearful male disciples, "The rams, or rather the shepherds, of the Lord's flock ran off, but the ewes remained unafraid."[133] In a letter to the nun "Idonea" written from exile in 1170, Thomas Becket (d. 1170) offered a similar account of the apostles' "faithlessness" as a foil to the spiritual strength of the women at the cross and tomb:

When the apostles wavered, fled, and what is worse fell into
faithlessness, women followed the Lord as he went forth to his
passion, and which is a clear sign of greater faith, they followed
him even when dead, and deserved to be encouraged by the vision
and speech of angels, and to receive the first fruits of the Lord's
resurrection and, when the apostles hid themselves, almost overwhelmed by despair, they announced the glory of the Redeemer
and the grace of the Gospel.[134]

Concluding that women had "deserved" to be the first to learn of the resurrection by virtue of their loyalty at the passion, Thomas implied that Jesus
had deliberately chosen to honor them in his resurrection.[135] That women
subsequently announced the resurrection to the apostles—who reportedly
refused to believe them (Luke 24:11; Mark 16: 11)—suggested a further honor:
apostolic status. Since the term "apostle" literally meant "one who is sent," desig-
nating those who spread the message of Jesus's teaching, several exegetes
claimed that the women at the tomb had been apostles in announcing the resurrection. As the author of the *Sermo in veneratione sanctae Mariae Magdalenae* reasoned, "if the disciples were called 'apostles' because they were sent by
the Lord to preach the gospel to everyone, no less was the blessed Mary Magdalene dispatched by him to the apostles, in order that any doubt or incredu-
lity about his Resurrection might be removed from their hearts."[136] In fact, a
number of exegetes commented pointedly that the women had served as "apostles to the apostles," underscoring once again the inferior faith of the male
apostles. Already in the third century, Hippolytus of Rome had identified the
women at the tomb as being like apostles, commenting that they had announced the resurrection, as apostles to the apostles (*quae apostoli ad apostolos
fiebant*).[137] By the fourth century, Jerome extended the claim beyond similarity, arguing that the women at the tomb had served as "apostles to the apostles" (*apostolas apostolorum*).[138]

By the late eleventh and early twelfth centuries, comparisons between the
disciples (who had abandoned Jesus) and the women (who had remained faithful) came to focus on the figure of Mary Magdalene, who was identified as a
particular friend and beloved of Christ, a woman who had "attained such
friendship and intimacy with the Lord that she could salve even his head with
sweet ointments," as Goscelin of St. Bertin wrote (contrasting her to John the
Baptist, who "trembled and did not dare to touch Christ's sacred head").[139]
Mary's love for Christ was her distinguishing characteristic, as male exegetes

consistently noted. "Loving much, the saint deserved to be loved much and she was the first to see the risen Lord," an early eleventh-century psalter from Christ Church, Canterbury, explained.[140] Several writers noted Mary's love for Christ and her individual priority at the tomb (by which she eclipsed the other women, at least according to John's gospel) and began to identify her, specifically and exclusively, as *the* "apostle to the apostles" (*apostola apostolorum*).[141] A twelfth-century Cistercian *life* commented that Mary "was glorified by his first appearance; raised up to the honor of an apostle; instituted as the evangelist of the resurrection of Christ; and designated the prophet of his ascension to the apostles."[142] The St. Albans Psalter took the unusual step of featuring Mary Magdalene alone announcing the news of the resurrection to the gathered apostles (Figure 9), visually reinforcing her priority among the women and her elevation over the male disciples, as well as her singular role in spreading the news of the resurrection.[143] The placement of this image, facing the women at the tomb in a single opening, provided a powerful message of women's devotion and spiritual authority—a message that was especially powerful given the manuscript's male patronage and production and its likely female ownership.[144]

The depiction of Mary Magdalene in the St. Albans Psalter raises an important point: texts and images exalting Mary and emphasizing her apostolic status often appear in works written by men and either to or about contemporary women. Medieval religious men evidently saw Mary Magdalene as relevant to women in their own time. Hugh of Cluny, for instance, argued for Mary Magdalene's apostolic role as apostle to the apostles (*apostola apostolorum*) in a letter to his successors at Cluny, urging their continued support for the nuns at Marcigny.[145] Abelard, too, invoked the Magdalene in his writings for and about women, commenting in his Easter Sermon that the Magdalene was unequivocally the apostle to the apostles, since Christ had enjoined her to announce the good news to them.[146] The author of the *Liber de modo bene vivendi, ad sororem* commented that, although she was not a nun, Mary Magdalene "saw the risen Christ and deserved to be an apostle to the apostles (*apostolorum apostola*)."[147] So, too, Peter of Blois (d. 1211/1212), writing to a group of unidentified nuns, commented that "she who had been a sinner in the city, with love and tears, not only deserved to be liberated from sin, but to be made an apostle and evangelist (*apostola et evangelista*), indeed (what is more), she was made apostle to the apostles (*apostolorum apostola*), hurrying to announce the resurrection of the Lord to the apostles."[148]

Figure 9. Mary Magdalene Announcing the Resurrection. *St. Albans Psalter. Dombibliothek Hildesheim, HS St. God. 1* (Property of the Basilica of St. Godehard, Hildesheim), p. 51.

Devotion to Mary Magdalene intensified during the course of the twelfth century, as the number of foundations dedicated to her, her mounting presence in the liturgy, and the growing cult centered at Vézelay demonstrated.[149] Central to Mary's cult was her role as a figure superior in love and devotion to the apostles. Drawing on the tradition of praising holy women at the expense of the disciples, medieval exegetes typically contrasted Mary's devotion to the faithlessness of Jesus's closest male followers, as Geoffrey of Vendôme did, commenting that "Peter denies that thing which the woman [Mary] preaches."[150] The sermon *In veneratione sanctae Mariae Magdalenae* similarly noted that Mary had watched as Christ was arrested, beaten, mocked, and crucified, while the apostles—who had earlier professed their desire to die with him (John 11:16)—fled in fear. Mary remained with Christ, according to the sermon, since she loved him "more closely" and "more fervently."[151] Her reward, according to Peter the Venerable (d. 1156), was that "Christ joins her to himself."[152]

Mary's loving devotion to Christ fascinated medieval audiences, prompting elaborations of her role in the Easter story that far exceeded the slender biblical evidence. Most exegetes agreed that Mary had been the first to see the risen Christ since she had persevered in seeking him.[153] To churchmen, Mary's devotion was implicitly gendered, calling to mind the bride of the Song of Songs, who had sought her bridegroom in the garden just as Mary sought Jesus. It was a short leap to identify Mary directly with the bride, an idea that had its roots in the third century with Hippolytus's suggestion that the bride prefigured the sisters Mary and Martha. Gregory the Great developed this association in the sixth century, and his ideas were picked up in the sermon *In veneratione sanctae Mariae Magdalenae*, which presented Mary Magdalene explicitly as a bride.[154] At the Paraclete during the twelfth century, Mary Magdalene took center stage as the bride searching for her lost Bridegroom in the Easter sequence *Epithalamica*.[155] Bridal imagery drawn from the Song of Songs infused the Paraclete liturgy for Easter. As Chrysogonus Waddell has observed, for Abelard, the Song of Songs was "preeminently a paschal canticle": it formed the basis for the Easter hymns that Abelard composed for the Paraclete, was featured prominently in the Easter Sunday office, and was read in refectory during Easter week.[156]

Reconfiguring the drama of the women at the tomb as a specifically bridal performance meant that interpretations of women's biblical devotion to Christ became even more markedly gendered: Mary Magdalene in the garden was not simply a woman, but a bride, and implicitly the bride of Christ—a role that churchmen typically assigned to religious women, but that they rarely applied to other men before Bernard of Clairvaux's sermons on the Song with their allowance for a male bride.[157] Elevating Mary as the "apostola" and bride focused the events of Easter on a relationship of intimacy and fervent devotion from which men generally felt themselves to be excluded. A collection of prayers that Anselm of Canterbury sent to Matilda of Tuscany, in around 1104, included a prayer to Christ, in which Anselm specifically lamented his absence from the tomb:

> Would that with that blessed band of women
> I might have trembled at the vision of angels
> and have heard the news of the Lord's Resurrection,
> news of my consolation,
> so much looked for, so much desired.[158]

Although Sarah McNamer cautions against a reading that conflates the "I" of Anselm's prayers with Anselm himself, it is hard to imagine, as Barbara Newman has observed, that Anselm could pen such prayers without praying as he advised others to do.[159] Anselm may have wished he had been at the tomb, but he—like many men—imagined that women could more easily picture themselves there. Just as Abelard advised Heloise to "be always present at his tomb, weep and wail with the faithful women. . . . Prepare with them the perfumes for his burial," Aelred of Rievaulx encouraged his sister to identify directly with the Magdalene, laying out a series of affective meditations on the life of Christ for her spiritual exercise.[160] With the sinful woman she was to wash Christ's feet, with Mary of Bethany to anoint his head, and with Mary Magdalene to "keep company" at the tomb, "taking with you the perfumes she has prepared."[161]

The willingness of men such as these to emphasize Mary's incomparable devotion to Christ had real implications for contemporary medieval women, and for men's involvement with them. To some men, the spiritual fortitude and constancy of the women at the cross implied a similar spiritual potential among contemporary women. Like Thomas Becket, who sought Idonea's help in preventing the coronation of the young prince Henry, men invoked the women at the tomb in works of exhortation and spiritual encouragement for female friends and correspondents. Writing almost a century before Thomas, Gregory VII praised the empress Agnes of Poitou for her spiritual fortitude, likening her to the women at the tomb: "For just as they came before all the disciples to the tomb of the Lord with amazing love and charity, so you, in devout love, have visited the church of Christ . . . before many or rather before almost all of the princes of the earth."[162] Peter Damian (d. 1072), also writing to Agnes, described her as having come to Rome with her sister-in-law Ermensinde like Mary Magdalene and the other Mary, "not to anoint with aromatic oil the body of Jesus, but to wash his feet with their tears."[163] Hildebert of Lavardin (d. 1133), writing to thank Matilda of Scotland, Queen of England, for the gift of a candelabrum, compared her, too, to the holy women who came "to the cross with tears and to the tomb with spices."[164]

Praising Mary and the women at the tomb, these men exalted their female friends and correspondents, yet in so doing they also exalted themselves by association.[165] The events of Easter weekend allowed men (should they wish) to view women as having been central to the narrative of salvation and uniquely faithful to Christ. As Abelard noted in his letter *On the Origin of Nuns*, the holy women at the tomb had been "set over the apostles."[166] The spiritual implications of women's biblical constancy were enormous, overturning even the curse of Eve, as Hippolytus implied in the third century: "Christ himself came to them so that the women would be apostles of Christ and by their obedience rectify the sin of the ancient Eve."[167] Contrasting Mary Magdalene with Eve, the Cistercian *life* of Mary noted that, "Just as Eve in Paradise had once given her husband a poisoned draught to drink, so now the Magdalene presented to the apostles the chalice of eternal life."[168] The exaltation of biblical women emboldened medieval men to defend their spiritual attention to contemporary women. As Hugh of Fleury declared, defending his writing for Adela of Blois through reference to Mary, since "a woman sitting at the Lord's feet" learned "better" and "more devoutly" than pious men, "the feminine sex does not lack understanding of profound matters."[169] Some seven hundred years before Hugh, Jerome had also anticipated the attacks of critics who might question his praise for the Roman widow Marcella. In his defense, Jerome invoked the holy women "who followed our Lord and Savior and ministered to him of their substance," the women at the cross, and Mary Magdalene as examples of women's spiritual strength, claiming to "judge of people's virtue not by their sex but by their character."[170]

For the most part, as I argued at the outset of this chapter, medieval men did not invoke Jesus as a model for their involvement with women, choosing instead the less controversial example of John the Evangelist. However, there was one gospel account of Jesus's concern for women to which they did turn for inspiration: his defense of Mary of Bethany, whose anointing of his feet with perfume had met with accusations of wastefulness.[171] Jesus's defense furnished proof not only that he tolerated women followers, but that he would support and protect them. In a prayer to Mary Magdalene, Anselm of Canterbury remembered:

> How he defended you
> when the proud Pharisee was indignant,
> how he excused you, when your sister complained[172]

When Aelred urged his sister to identify with the woman who had anointed Christ, he reminded her that Christ had defended Mary, saying, "Let her be, she did well to treat me so."[173] Abelard and Guibert, too, noted Jesus's defense of the anointing woman.[174] In the St. Albans Psalter, Jesus's defense is represented visually: Jesus is shown engaged in lively conversation with Simon the Pharisee, while a woman cradles his feet, drying them with her unbound hair (Figure 10).[175] Gesturing to her, and clearly addressing the Pharisee, Jesus defends her from the Pharisee's criticism.

Interpretations of the passion that emphasized women's spiritual leadership and that featured Mary Magdalene either as the bride or as the new Eve, who ministered "the chalice of eternal life," furnished men with an intellectual rationale for their spiritual involvement with women: as Hugh of Fleury noted, women were not lacking in devotion or understanding. The fact that Jesus himself had defended his women followers publicly energized these men still further, strengthening their belief in women's spiritual dignity. An episode in the *life* of Robert of Arbrissel highlights the practical implications of these ideas for women. According to his biographer, Robert came one day to preach at the church of Menelay l'Abbaye with his customary entourage of women. The group was met at the door by a group of local countrymen who declared that women were forbidden to enter the sanctuary, threatening that "if any one of them presumed to enter, she would die at once." Refusing to be stopped, Robert led the women into the church, presenting them as "brides of Christ" and citing Jesus's treatment of the sinful woman of Luke 7 as evidence that Jesus had accepted and even favored women. Observing that Jesus had not prevented women from touching his physical body (and had even allowed a woman to anoint him), Robert asked the doorkeepers: "Which is the greater thing, God's material temple or the spiritual temple in which God lives?"[176] Robert's actions at Menelay l'Abbaye mark an important moment at which men's devotion to the Magdalene had a

Figure 10. Jesus Defending Mary. *St. Albans Psalter. Dombibliothek Hildesheim, HS St. God. 1* (Property of the Basilica of St. Godehard, Hildesheim), p. 36.

measurable impact on the lives of contemporary women, as Jacques Dalarun has observed.[177] Robert's reference to Jesus's treatment of the sinful woman as an example of how men ought to treat women meant that his own female companions were ultimately allowed access to the church.

Conclusion

The presence of women at the cross and tomb during the first Easter provided an important precedent for medieval women and men, confirming not only women's centrality to salvation history, but also their potential for discipleship and even spiritual superiority. Although women's biblical priority was sometimes used to shame contemporary men, their centrality to the Easter narrative—which was celebrated in hymns, sermons, and *vitae*, in the visual record, the liturgy, and the earliest church dramas—was more often deployed to promote women's religious life, to establish their spiritual authority, and to justify their relations with ordained men. Women, too, understood the powerful message of female apostolicity that was embedded in the Easter narrative. According to Goscelin of St. Bertin, Edith of Wilton embroidered an alb on which she depicted herself as Mary Magdalene kissing the footprints of Jesus.[178] If Goscelin's report is accurate, Edith's choice of subject was particularly significant. By imagining herself as Mary Magdalene, a woman closer to Christ even than the apostles, Edith powerfully asserted the potential for women's spiritual authority.[179] In recounting the story, Goscelin reinforced the implied message of women's spiritual intimacy with Christ, exalting both the Wilton women and himself as their hagiographer, and perhaps also as their chaplain.

By the twelfth century, the gospel example was so well established as a justification for close contacts between the sexes that churchmen worried more about its potential for abuse than about its legitimacy (which they simply assumed). In a letter to Bernard of Clairvaux, the Premonstratensian provost Eberwin of Steinfeld observed that heretics claimed apostolic models to defend their relationships with women. As he wrote: "These apostles of Satan had among them continent women (so they say)—widows, virgins, their wives, some among the elect, some among the believing; in the guise of [real] apostles who had been given the power to surround themselves with women."[180] Eberwin's alarm at the misuse of the apostolic example is echoed in Hugh of

Rouen's report that heretics "say they lead a common life in their houses and have women with them just like the apostles."[181]

Neither Eberwin nor Hugh denied the validity of the apostolic example, even as they worried about its misapplication. Like other medieval men and women, they recognized that the New Testament offered important models for the blameless and irreproachable spiritual involvement of men with women. Some monks and churchmen adopted these models in their own lives and in their service to nuns. Inspired by Christ's healing miracles for women, his friendship with Mary and Martha of Bethany, his defense of the sinful woman, and his concern for his mother Mary, these men sought to honor Christ in their relations with women. As they did, they often fashioned themselves after the example of John the Evangelist, approaching religious women as brides of Christ and imagining themselves as Christ's friend and *paranymphus*.

CHAPTER 3

Jerome and the Noble Women of Rome

The blessed priest Jerome often honored holy Paula and her
daughter Eustochium with many writings.
—Hugh of Fleury, *Historia ecclesiastica*

Medieval men searching the Scriptures for models of licit spiritual involvement with women found rich material in the life of Christ, whose concern for
women and inclusion of them among his closest supporters offered clear
authorization for women's participation—alongside men—in the religious
life. Exegetes cited Jesus's involvement with women as an example of his "benevolence" and "humility," as Hugh of Fleury did in his writings for Adela of
Blois.[1] Yet, as we saw in the previous chapter, priests and monks who engaged
directly with religious women rarely depicted themselves as emulating Christ,
invoking him more often as the absent bridegroom of professed women than
as their own exemplar. Such men found a more fitting model in John the Evangelist, who, acting in obedience to Christ's dying command, had taken the
virgin mother of Christ to live with him, *in sua*.

John's care for Mary was accepted through the ages as having been spiritually inspired and wholly blameless. As Jesus's favored disciple and a presumed
virgin, his innocence was never in doubt. Even so, John's example was wanting
in one important respect: very little was known of his care for Mary beyond
the fact of Christ's commendation of Mary to him and his apparent acceptance. The biblical record is silent concerning the practical details of their
relationship—how the two interacted, what support John provided, and the
ways in which they were perceived by their contemporaries. A second saintly
figure offered a more richly textured, yet still supposedly virtuous, model of

care for women: the fourth-century church father Jerome.[2] In contrast to John, Jerome's relations with noble Christian women in Rome were abundantly documented, allowing medieval men a deeper understanding of how, and why, he had engaged spiritually with women. The fact that Jerome's friendships with women had prompted significant controversy during his own lifetime made him all the more relevant as a model for medieval men, who often faced criticism. Jerome chronicled these controversies in various letters and other texts, turning to biblical examples as he defended himself. His writings are littered with references to John the Evangelist, the apostles with their "sister" women, and the holy women at the tomb—subjects explored in the previous chapter.

By the eleventh and twelfth centuries, Jerome's relations with women were celebrated as blameless and pure, despite the scandal they had provoked in his own day. To medieval men, Jerome therefore offered a saintly model of male spiritual care for women that, in their view, closely paralleled their own: his involvement with women was presumed to have been chaste and spiritually inspired, yet he had nevertheless been attacked by critics, who accused him (unfairly, as medieval audiences believed) of base motives. For modern scholars, Jerome's example is instructive for a further reason: unlike John the Evangelist, who was consistently viewed as pure, Jerome's reputation for pious involvement with women had developed over time—from the fourth century, when his friendships with women had been denounced as improper (and probably immoral), to the twelfth century, by which time they were accepted, and even celebrated, as a central component of his saintly reputation. The evolution of Jerome's reputation, which I trace in this chapter, demonstrates the lengths to which medieval men went to find, and to fashion, appropriate models for their involvement with women. As I show here, Jerome was adopted as a model largely because he had been ostracized for his friendships with women—an experience that John the Evangelist (so far as we know) did not share, but that medieval men knew all too well.

Reginald's *Life of Malchus*: Jerome's Virgin Saint Reimagined

An important indication of Jerome's growing centrality to eleventh- and twelfth-century ideas about women and men in the religious life can be found in the writings of Reginald of Canterbury (d. c.1109), a Benedictine monk from France, possibly Poitou, who came to England in the late eleventh century and became abbey poet at St. Augustine's in Canterbury. Reginald was the author of an epic verse *Life* of Malchus, the fourth-century Syrian saint whom Jerome had celebrated for his lifelong dedication to chastity.[3] According to Jerome's telling of the *Life*, Malchus had fled his family as a young man in order to avoid marriage and had adopted the monastic life in the desert. After some years, he left the monastery to visit his mother, was captured by Saracens, and was taken into slavery. Forced by his master into marriage and, facing yet again the dreaded prospect of losing his virginity, the unhappy Malchus despaired: only his wife's suggestion that they pursue a chaste marriage dissuaded him from suicide. After some years of chaste cohabitation, the two escaped. Malchus returned to the monastic life and placed his wife in the spiritual care of devout virgins.[4]

Reginald's retelling of the *Life* of Malchus, some seven hundred years after Jerome, added significantly to Jerome's short prose text. Most interesting for the purposes of this study are the additions that appear in the third book of the *Life*, which opens as Malchus and his wife—identified by Reginald as Malcha—return to Malchus's cell as a newly married couple. As in Jerome's *Life*, Malchus threatens suicide, and is dissuaded by Malcha. However, in Reginald's account this episode is significantly amplified. Although Jerome had described in brief the chaste life of the two, whom he claimed to have met in the Syrian desert (the woman "very withered" and "already close to death"), Reginald added specific details concerning the organization of their domestic and spiritual life.[5] Malcha plays a new and larger role, in keeping with Reginald's decision to identify her by name. In Jerome's *life*, she had been the one to suggest chaste marriage (offering that Malchus should "take me as your partner in chastity").[6] Reginald expanded Malcha's proposal in his version. Inviting Malchus to make her his partner in a spiritual union, Reginald's Malcha declared, "I shrink from a carnal association with you, I wish a spiritual one, without the squalor and pestilence of filth."[7] In Jerome's account, Malchus had accepted the suggestion of chaste marriage and little more was said.[8] Reginald's Malchus, by contrast, overwhelmed at his narrow escape from death, praises Malcha enthusiastically, calling her his "savior" (*salvatrix*) and "enlivener" (*vivificatrix*) and thanking God for her:

O happy woman, your prudence and clever speech,
Saved me and prepared for you a companion and a husband.
I count myself happy and you my mother,
You are my savior, you my hope, you my enlivener,
You my sister and mother, my spouse, I your brotherly husband.[9]

Not content with praising Malcha directly, Malchus then turns to thank Christ for having provided such a companion:

> Christ, I give you thanks for the many advantages
> Which you gave to a wretch by the merits of this woman.[10]

As Reginald's third book draws to a close, Malchus and Malcha live chastely together. Malchus becomes Malcha's spiritual guide and teacher, familiarizing her with the monastic life and instructing her in the psalms while she, in turn, teaches him the domestic arts. In describing Malchus and Malcha in the period after their marriage, Reginald went so far as to adopt monastic terminology: in his account, the married-yet-chaste Malchus is a monk (*monachus*) and his wife, Malcha, a nun (*monacha*).[11]

Reginald's depiction of Malchus as a saint who, although he would rather die than lose his virginity, "did not shrink to live with a nun" was evidently not controversial at the turn of the twelfth century.[12] Once he had completed his reworked *Life* of Malchus, with its new emphasis on Malcha and her role in Malchus's spiritual life, Reginald circulated the poem to a number of friends in England and northern France, monks and churchmen like himself.[13] Among the men who received his text were the monk and hagiographer, Goscelin of St. Bertin (who was also resident at St. Augustine's, Canterbury in the 1090s), the poet and cleric Hildebert of Lavardin (bishop of Le Mans from 1096–1125, but in exile in England between 1099–1100; archbishop of Tours from 1125–1133), and Anselm, abbot of Bec and then archbishop of Canterbury from 1093—men who were likely to be sympathetic to his positive portrayal of Malcha as *salvatrix*.[14] Each of these men was involved spiritually with women in some way. Goscelin had served as spiritual advisor and tutor to the recluse Eve of Wilton, devoting himself to her spiritual instruction, composing the *Liber confortatorius* for her, and—significantly—depicting her as his spiritual superior. Echoing Malchus's spiritual esteem for Malcha, Goscelin wrote to Eve: "I have the building materials of comfort in you, which I do not find in myself."[15] Hildebert, too, corresponded with several religious women, and was the author of (among other things) a *Life* of Mary of Egypt, a fourth-century prostitute saint who had retreated into the deserts of Egypt to atone for her life of sin.[16] Hildebert's *Life* tells of Mary's encounter with the monk Zosimus, a man well advanced in holiness, who, despite the apparent spiritual disparity between them, found in her a source of inspiration and even spiritual superiority. According to Hildebert, Zosimus praised the former prostitute to Christ, describing her as: "the woman whom I wish for, whom I seek, [and] in whose heavenly prayer I hope."[17] Anselm of Canterbury, a third recipient of Reginald's *Life* of Malchus, may also have been receptive to Reginald's optimism concerning the possibilities of chaste spiritual friendships between the sexes, despite his role in enforcing clerical celibacy in England. Before becoming archbishop, Anselm had been abbot of the Norman monastery of Bec, a male community that included several women. As archbishop, he maintained close epistolary friendships with a number of women and composed spiritual works for them.[18] He also founded a house for women in honor of Mary Magdalene, and clearly approved of other men who devoted themselves to women's spiritual care.[19]

Jerome as Spiritual Advisor and Friend to Women

Reginald's carefully orchestrated circulation of the *Life* of Malchus suggests a context quite unlike the one normally associated with clerical celibacy and reform, one in which ideas concerning the licit involvement of men with women within the religious life could be shared between like-minded churchmen and in which a common language was developed, which argued for the blamelessness and, importantly, the spiritual merit of contact between the sexes within the religious life. Yet Reginald's *Life* of Malchus does more than simply indicate a literary vogue for heroic tales of chastity preserved, or even for saintly relations between holy men and women. By choosing Jerome's *Life* of Malchus as his subject, Reginald participated in a trend that had begun in the ninth century and that gained considerable momentum during the eleventh and twelfth centuries, a trend that consistently highlighted Jerome's relations with women and depicted him as a model for men's spiritual attention to women.[20]

Evidence of Jerome's concern for women was not hard to find: more than any other late antique Christian author he had devoted himself to the spiritual care of pious women.[21] Indeed, from the moment of his arrival in Rome in 382, Jerome had been at the center of a circle of pious noblewomen who had abandoned lives of comfort in favor of ascetic renunciation. These women sought him as a teacher and ascetic exemplar; Jerome, in turn, embraced these roles, lavishing attention on his female disciples, showering them with spiritual advice, and addressing their theological questions in lengthy letters.

Jerome's spiritual involvement with women left a significant impression on his writings, a fact that made him particularly accessible as a model for medieval men.[22] In his translations, biblical commentaries, and even in the

Vulgate itself, Jerome acknowledged the intellectual acuity and spiritual inspiration of his women friends—above all, the mother-daughter pair, Paula and Eustochium. Many of his works were written either for women or at their instigation. Of Jerome's twenty-three extant biblical commentaries, for instance, twelve were dedicated to women; of the ten he wrote in Bethlehem between 386 and 393, nine were dedicated to Paula and Eustochium.[23] Jerome's *Life* of the desert saint Hilarion may have been dedicated to the consecrated virgin, Asella.[24] Some of his works were composed in response to women's requests. Paula's daughter Blesilla commissioned his commentary on Ecclesiastes, while Hedibia and Algasia, two women from Gaul, each sent him a series of knotty theological problems, to which he responded in long letters (Epist. 120 and 121).[25] Marcella, Jerome's closest and most scholarly disciple in Rome, inundated him with theological questions, leading him to call her his "slave driver."[26] Altogether, women requested from Jerome many more works than he could possibly produce: in the preface to his translation of Origen's commentary on Luke, which he undertook at the express request of Paula and Eustochium, he recalled how Blesilla had pressed him to undertake the translation of Origen's twenty-five volumes on Matthew, five on Luke, and thirty-two on John, a task that he admitted was "beyond my powers, my leisure, and my energy."[27]

Jerome's theological writings and translations showcase his commitment to providing women with religious instruction and guidance. However, the spiritual intimacy of his friendships with women is most clear in his surviving letters. Almost a third of these were addressed to women, and many more were certainly written, but lost.[28] Indeed, Jerome reports that he wrote to Paula and Eustochium every day in Bethlehem; only a small number of these letters have survived.[29] He wrote so often to Marcella (his most frequent addressee of either sex) that he seems to have intended that his letters to her constitute a work of their own. In *De viris illustribus*, Jerome listed among his writings "one book of Epistles to Marcella," suggesting that his letters to her were meant to be read together.[30] Some of Jerome's letters to women must be considered as works of spiritual guidance in their own right, notably his famous Epist. 22 on virginity, which he addressed to Eustochium.[31] Others are quasi-hagiographic, praising the lives of holy women: Paula (Epist. 108 to Eustochium),[32] Marcella (Epist. 127 to Principia), Asella (Epist. 24 to Marcella),[33] Lea (Epist. 23 to Marcella), Blesilla (Epist. 38 and 39 to Marcella and Paula respectively), and Paulina (Epist. 66 to her widower, Pammachius). These texts reflect not only Jerome's friendships and fascination with pious women, but also his clear desire to be remembered in conjunction with them. As Andrew

Cain has argued, Jerome intentionally presented himself as the spiritual guide and trusted friend of the Christian noblewomen of Rome in a bid to establish his reputation as an exegete and ascetic—to position himself, so Cain writes, as a "figure of virtually apostolic proportions."[34]

Jerome's writings for women were extensive, comprising a significant portion of his oeuvre. Yet his friendships with women were rarely discussed in the period after his death. In the *Lausiac History*, Palladius praised Paula as a "woman highly distinguished in the spiritual life," but dismissed Jerome as envious, bad tempered, and a hindrance to her.[35] Some three centuries later, the biographer of St. Sadalberga (c. 605–670), abbess of Laon, invoked Jerome's portraits of holy women, but commented only on Sadalberga's imitation of Melania and Paula (and not directly on Jerome's relations with these women).[36] Only in the late seventh century did Jerome's dedication to women begin to attract positive attention.[37] In a treatise on virginity composed for the nuns of Barking, Aldhelm (d. 709) remarked on the many commentaries that Jerome, "driven on by the intelligence of the mother (Paula) and the diligence of the daughter (Eustochium), laboriously produced." (Like Jerome, Aldhelm was later remembered for his writings for women: a late tenth-century image shows him presenting *De virginitate* to the abbess Hildelith of Barking, together with a group of nuns).[38] The *Life* of the Frankish saint Hiltrude (d. c. 785) commented that she and her brother Guntard were "another Jerome and Eustochium," with Hiltrude living in a cell adjoining the monastery where Guntard was abbot.[39] However, apart from these few and scattered references, Jerome's involvement with women was rarely mentioned before the ninth century. Indeed, the two earliest biographies of Jerome—*Plerosque nimirum*, dating to the second half of the sixth century, and *Hieronymus noster*, written between the sixth and the eighth centuries—are silent on the subject.[40] Jerome's many friendships with women are also absent from early depictions, which tended to present him as a biblical scholar and ascetic, but never alongside women. The earliest image of Jerome, produced at Corbie in the seventh or eighth century, shows him as an old bearded man, in Byzantine dress, holding a stylus and wax tablet.[41]

Jerome in the Ninth Century: Alcuin, Paschasius, and the Nuns of Chelles and Soissons

It was not until the middle of the ninth century that Jerome's connections with women began to feature in texts and images from the Continent, a development linked to the intellectual renaissance in which his translations and other writings figured prominently.[42] At that time, several things happened. First, Jerome's letters to women were mined for inclusion in the *Institutio sanctimonialium*, the rule for women promulgated by Louis the Pious at the Synod of Aachen in 816.[43] The *Institutio* drew so prominently on Jerome that it was sometimes later referred to as the rule of Jerome (as at Lippoldsberg in the twelfth century, where the women promised to fulfill "St. Jerome's instructions for nuns").[44] Second, Paschasius Radbertus, abbot of Corbie (abbot 843/4–849/53, d. c. 860), adopted Jerome's relationships with women as a framing device for his sermon on the assumption of the Virgin. This text, which Paschasius composed for the nuns of Soissons at their request, was written in Jerome's voice and addressed to "Paula" and "Eustochium," reinforcing Jerome's model as a provider of spiritual care to women.[45] Finally, the makers of the First Bible of Charles the Bald, a manuscript produced at St-Martin, Tours and possibly presented to Charles the Bald in 845, took the unprecedented step of featuring Jerome as a teacher of women in one of the manuscript's frontispieces (Figure 11).[46] The image narrates Jerome's life following his flight from Rome to Bethlehem in 385 and shows him teaching Paula and Eustochium (identified in a titulus) alongside two other women, one of whom appears to be transcribing his words onto a scroll on her lap.[47] A second monumental Bible, the Bible of San Paolo fuori le mura (c. 870), probably from Reims, also shows Jerome addressing two women, one of whom holds an open book, the other a scroll (Figure 12).[48] A monk hovers behind them, and a third woman stands just beyond the door.[49]

The emphasis on Jerome as a teacher of women in these two Bibles marks an important departure from earlier traditions, which had tended to favor images of Jerome as a scholar, monk, or ascetic. Their appearance—at this precise point in the ninth century—has puzzled scholars. As Herbert Kessler declared, "These are among the most enigmatic ninth-century paintings."[50] No pictorial precedents have been found, despite the best efforts of art historians, and the precise subjects and sources of the two images remain unknown.[51] According to Rosamond McKitterick, it is likely that the images were, in fact, entirely new compositions that were designed to reflect the cultural context in which they were created: one marked by the engagement of Carolingian noblewomen in learned spiritual discourse with leading theologians and scholars—men like Alcuin of York (d. 804) and Paschasius Radbertus.[52] These women were sometimes explicitly compared with Jerome's circle of

Figure 11. Scene from the Life of Jerome. *First Bible of Charles the Bald,*
Bibliothèque nationale de France, Lat. 1, fol. 3v.

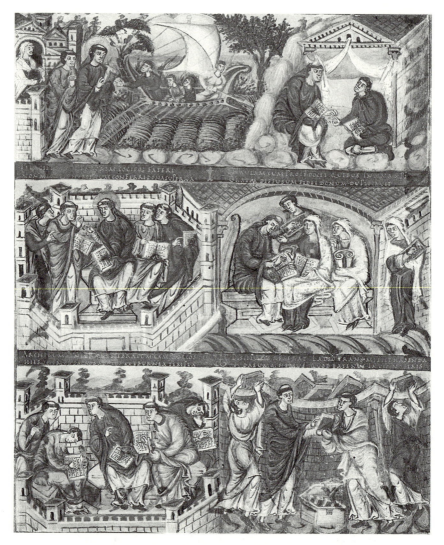

Figure 12. Scene from the Life of Jerome. *Bible of San Paolo fuori le mura*, Abbazia di San Paolo fuori le mura, s.n., fol. 2v.

female friends, while the men, whether explicitly or implicitly, often modeled themselves after the example of Jerome.

Alcuin's friendships with religious women at the turn of the ninth century would have been known to the scribes and copyists at St-Martin and may have played some role in inspiring their depiction of Jerome. An Anglo-Saxon scholar trained at York, Alcuin had been the leader of Charlemagne's court school in Aachen and the emperor's trusted advisor before retiring to St-Martin, where he served as abbot from 796 until his death in 804.[53] Alcuin's friendship with Charlemagne was close: he addressed the emperor playfully as "David." He was on familiar terms, too, with Charlemagne's sister, Gisela ("Lucia"), and his daughter, Rotrude ("Columba").[54] Gisela (d. 810) was abbess at Chelles, a sixth-century foundation that, at least in its early years, had housed both men and women.[55] By the time that Gisela was abbess, Chelles had become an important intellectual center with an active scriptorium in which texts were not only copied but also composed.[56] Rotrude (d. 810) was a nun at Notre Dame, Soissons, having previously been kept by Charlemagne at court for many years, with certain unfortunate consequences, as Einhard noted.[57] Both Rotrude and her sister, Bertha (who later became a nun at Chelles), took lovers by whom they had children, before entering the monastery.[58]

Alcuin's relationship with Gisela and Rotrude was similar in many respects to Jerome's friendship with Paula and Eustochium. Like Paula and Eustochium, Gisela and Rotrude were powerful noblewomen who had chosen to pursue the religious life. Both sets of women were, moreover, socially superior to their male teacher.[59] Both were learned, and both were praised for their learning. Jerome wrote that Paula had learned Hebrew so well that she could "enunciate her words without the faintest trace of a Latin accent"—a facility that he attributed to Eustochium as well.[60] The theological questions that Eustochium sent Jerome struck him like a fist, he wrote, leaving him regretting his own stupidity.[61] Although Alcuin was less effusive than Jerome, he honored Gisela as a *femina verbipotens* in an early verse addressed to her and her brother Pippin ("Julius") and, like Jerome, wrote a series of letters to Gisela and Rotrude.[62] Finally, just as Jerome had dedicated many of his theological and exegetical works to women, Alcuin addressed his commentary on John to Gisela and Rotrude, at their request.

Alcuin knew Jerome's work and was influenced by it. His quest to secure a corrected text of the Bible meant that he engaged deeply with Jerome's scholarly writings and, of course, with his Vulgate.[63] The library at St-Martin included many of Jerome's works, among them copies of his letters and the

Commentariorum in Esaiam, a work that Jerome dedicated to Eustochium and in which he defended women, commenting famously that "in the service of Christ it is not the difference of sexes but the difference of minds that matters."[64] Jerome's influence can be seen in Alcuin's writings.[65] Alcuin's commentary on Ecclesiastes, in particular, is heavily reliant on Jerome's commentary, which he wrote in Bethlehem and dedicated to Paula and Eustochium. In his preface, Jerome recalled how Blesilla had asked him to produce the commentary after they had studied Ecclesiastes together.[66] Although she died before he began the work, Jerome memorialized her—in part—through the text.

It is possible that Alcuin's involvement with Gisela and Rotrude influenced the Tours artists in their depictions of Jerome, inspiring the new attention to Jerome's relations with women that the Bible images showcased. Yet despite similarities between the two men, Alcuin never cited Jerome as his model in writing to women; instead, it was Gisela and Rotrude who invoked Jerome, encouraging Alcuin to answer their theological questions just as Jerome had devoted himself to the pious women in Rome. When Gisela and Rotrude asked Alcuin to compose a commentary for them on John, they reminded him that "most blessed Jerome did not spurn the prayers of noble women by any means, but dedicated many works . . . to them."[67] Copies of Alcuin's commentary on John often circulated with Gisela and Rotrude's letter of request as a preface, making Jerome's model of writing for women (and Alcuin's implicit adoption of that model) part of the textual tradition. Subsequent men, too, may have taken Gisela and Rotrude's request as a prompt: an early ninth-century copy of Alcuin's commentary, prefaced by both the women's letter (fol. 1r-2r) and Alcuin's response (fol. 2r-5r),[68] was given to the female community at Essen by a certain Liudo.[69] Although Liudo's identity remains unknown, his gift of the manuscript placed Gisela and Rotrude's appeal to Alcuin in the hands of the Essen women, furnishing them with an explicit claim to male spiritual care based not only on Jerome's original example, but implicitly also on Alcuin's emulation of him. It is tempting to imagine that Liudo, too, sought to identify himself with Jerome, as a man who supported the religious lives of women. Liudo may even have been one of the many priests and laymen who served the women at Essen; however, on this question the sources are silent.[70]

Gisela and Rotrude's invocation of Jerome offers evidence of the growing willingness during the period to acknowledge Jerome's relationships with women, and even to view these as exemplary: the two women approached Alcuin in some measure as their own "Jerome." As with the Essen copy of Alcuin's commentary, manuscript evidence confirms the association of

Jerome with women. During Gisela's abbacy, Chelles owned a manuscript containing more than one hundred of Jerome's letters, the largest extant Carolingian collection of his correspondence.[71] The structure and organization of the manuscript suggest that Jerome was thought to be especially relevant to women readers. Almost one-third of the letters included in the manuscript were addressed to women. These were grouped together at the end of the manuscript, beginning with letter 22 to Eustochium and emphasizing, above all, Jerome's correspondence with Marcella. The later history of the collection confirms the connection to women. At some point, probably in the tenth century, the manuscript passed to the canonesses at Quedlinburg, a community that (like Essen) housed noble and highly educated women, many of them linked to the Ottonian dynasty.[72]

Alongside Alcuin's example of care and involvement with women, there were other sources of inspiration that may have motivated the Tours artists in their depiction of Jerome. Around the time that the Tours artists were completing the First Bible of Charles the Bald, Paschasius Radbertus adopted both Jerome's voice and his persona in a sermon that he wrote for the nuns of Soissons, a community with close institutional and familial ties to Corbie (and where, according to Engelmodus of Soissons, Paschasius had been raised from babyhood).[73] The sermon, known by its incipit "Cogitis me," was addressed to "Paula" and "Eustochium," and provided material to be read, both in the chapel and the refectory, for the Feast for the Assumption of the Virgin.[74] Paschasius's decision to write as "Jerome" was probably inspired, at least in part, by the traditional use of nicknames at the Carolingian court: "Paula" and "Eustochium," the recipients of the letter, have been identified as Theodrada, abbess of Notre Dame at Soissons, and her daughter Imma, a virgin living in the same community.[75] The mother-daughter pairing naturally called to mind Paula and Eustochium. Even so, Paschasius's decision to present himself as "Jerome" in writing to these women is significant, indicating once again the growing association of Jerome with the spiritual care and encouragement of religious women and his importance as an exemplar for medieval men.

Unlike Alcuin, whose association with Jerome had been prompted by Gisela and Rotrude, Paschasius explicitly identified himself with Jerome and was deeply influenced by him.[76] As we saw above, Jerome had often written in direct response to the requests of his female correspondents, acknowledging the forcefulness of their requests: "cogis me" (you compel me), he wrote to Eustochium in his commentary on Isaiah, as elsewhere.[77] In the same way, Paschasius noted the entreaties of the women of Soissons as the inspiration for his work. His sermon on the Assumption begins in typical Jeromian style, "Cogitis me, o Paula et Eustochium" (you compel me, o Paula and Eustochium), highlighting his relationship with the women. Jerome's influence is clear, too, in Paschasius's choice of the Assumption of the Virgin as his subject for the sermon. Emphasizing physical purity and encouraging the Virgin as a model for Theodrada and Imma, Paschasius advocated a celibate life of prayer for women, much like that which Jerome had prescribed for Eustochium in his famous letter 22.[78]

Paschasius's imitation of Jerome was so convincing that his sermon "Cogitis me" was accepted as authentic even during his own lifetime.[79] In subsequent centuries, the sermon's popularity contributed significantly to Jerome's reputation as a spiritual guide for women. Bishop Hincmar of Reims (d. 882) had a deluxe copy of the work made, despite the protestations of Ratramnus of Corbie that Paschasius was its true author.[80] The sermon was incorporated quickly into the liturgy of the Feast of the Assumption, with excerpts read during Matins.[81] It was known in the eleventh century at Monte Cassino and at Cluny, where it formed the basis for lessons. In fact, the customs of Cluny require that the sermon be read for the Vigil of the Assumption, in place of the gospel.[82] Odilo of Cluny (d. 1049) referred directly to "Cogitis me" in his own sermon on the Assumption, which was preached to a mixed audience of women and men.[83] At Farfa, it provided all of the readings for nocturns for the Feast of the Assumption.[84]

During the twelfth century, "Cogitis me" was read and cited as an authentic part of Jerome's oeuvre. It was known as the work of Jerome to Rupert of Deutz (d. 1129) and William of Newburgh (d. c. 1201), authors who offered Marian interpretations of the Song of Songs.[85] Gerhoch of Reichersberg (d. 1169) allowed that "Cogitis me" might be read for the Feast of the Assumption of the Virgin (in a letter responding to the query of an unidentified community of women, possibly at Admont).[86] Gerhoch also cited the text in his own commentary on the Psalms, specifically noting "Jerome's" writing for women.[87] For Abelard, Paschasius's text was proof that "Jerome" had never been able to refuse the requests of women.[88]

Making Jerome Blameless

Jerome's fourth-century contemporaries would have been more than a little bit surprised by his emergence in the ninth century as a model for the legitimate interaction of religious men with women. During his own lifetime, Jerome's relationships with Roman noblewomen had been viewed with a mixture of suspicion and anger. At best, he was seen to have encouraged for these women a dangerous form of asceticism, which in the case of Blesilla was thought to have led to her death.[89] At worst, he was blamed for discrediting Christians through his stinging caricatures of priests who frequented the homes of women, particularly in his letter to Eustochium (Epist. 22), which caused an uproar.[90] In later years, Jerome referred to this upset in derisive terms, commenting to Marcella that, "the one thing that I have unfortunately said has been that virgins ought to live more in the company of women than of men, and by this I have made the whole city look scandalized and caused everyone to point at me the finger of scorn."[91]

In fact, Jerome drastically underestimated the outrage that his writings had provoked. His criticisms of worldly priests, "who seek the presbyterate and the diaconate simply that they may be able to see women with less restraint," was met with horror by Christians who thought he had provided an opening for pagan critics of the faith. Jerome's gift for satire is most clear in his denunciation of these men, whom he urged Eustochium to avoid:

> Such men think of nothing but their dress; they use perfumes
> freely, and see that there are no creases in their leather shoes. Their
> curling hair shows traces of the tongs; their fingers glisten with
> rings; they walk on tiptoe across a damp road, not to splash their
> feet. When you see men acting in this way, think of them rather as
> bridegrooms than as clerics.[92]

The irony, of course, is that while Jerome warned both men and women against contact with the opposite sex, he did not practice what he preached, but maintained close relations with a tight circle of female friends in Rome. That irony was not lost on Jerome's clerical contemporaries, who found themselves on the receiving end of his biting criticisms, while watching in astonishment as his familiarity with women deepened. It may not have mattered to them that Jerome's contact with women took place in the context of shared Bible study and prayer, and never at the dinner table (or worse).[93] In 385, the third year of his residence in Rome, matters came to a head: Jerome was forced to leave the city for the Holy Land, never to return.[94] Details concerning the circumstances under which he left are unclear (although some years later, Rufinus threatened to make public an account of the verdict against him). Jerome himself chose not to elaborate on the reasons for his departure, reporting in a letter to Asella only that, "men have laid to my charge a crime of which I am not guilty."[95] The tone of his letter nevertheless hints at allegations of a sexual sort. Defending his behavior—and particularly his relationship with Paula—he protested: "If they have ever seen anything in my conduct unbecoming a Christian let them say so. . . . Has my language been equivocal, or my eye wanton? No; my sex is my one crime, and even on this score I am not assailed, save when there is a talk of Paula going to Jerusalem."[96]

Of all Jerome's relationships, it was evidently his intimacy with Paula, a widow with five children, which attracted the malicious attention of gossipmongers (indeed, Jerome may have written the *life* of Malchus to defend his spiritual intimacy with her).[97] As Jerome later remembered: "Before I became acquainted with the family of the saintly Paula, all Rome resounded with my praises. . . . But when I began to revere, respect, and venerate her as her conspicuous chastity deserved, all my former virtues forsook me on the spot."[98] Still, Jerome refused to deny his fascination with Paula, freely admitting that "Of all the ladies in Rome but one had power to subdue me, and that one was Paula." Asceticism was the basis of her appeal, as he wrote: "She mourned and fasted, she was squalid with dirt, her eyes were dim from weeping. For whole nights she would pray to the Lord for mercy, and often the rising sun found her still at her prayers. The psalms were her only songs, the Gospel her whole speech, continence her one indulgence, fasting the staple of her life."[99]

Jerome's critics might have found it difficult to accept his protestations of innocence, given that Paula and Eustochium left Rome in his wake, joining him in Cyprus and continuing with him to the Holy Land, where they founded a community for women alongside his house for men (anticipating the sort of monastic organization that Abelard, for instance, would later recommend).[100] When Paula died, Jerome chose to bury her beneath the Church of the Nativity in Bethlehem, identifying her with one of the holiest places of Christianity and launching what he must have hoped would be a saint's cult—one that would be directly associated with his own activities as Paula's spiritual director and friend.[101] At his death in 420, Jerome's body, too, was laid beneath the Church of the Nativity, near the graves of both Paula and Eustochium.[102] Although his relics were later moved to the Basilica of Santa Maria Maggiore in Rome, the connection to Paula and Eustochium remained: a thirteenth-century mosaic in the apsidal arch of the basilica depicts Jerome, clad as a bishop, reading to Paula and Eustochium.[103] The incipit of the open book from which he reads is clearly visible in the mosaic: "Cogitis me," the beginning of Paschasius's pseudo-Jeromian sermon for "Paula" and "Eustochium" (Figure 13).

In the centuries immediately after his death, Jerome's terse comment that he had been charged with a crime of which he was innocent attracted little attention. The biography *Hieronymus noster* reported simply that Jerome's enemies—men whose own lax behavior he had criticized—had left a trap for him, without mentioning the nature of the trap, Jerome's controversial relations with women, or the suspicions that these relations had raised.[104] By the

Figure 13. Jerome with Paula and Eustochium.
Basilica of Santa Maria Maggiore, Rome.

twelfth century, however, Jerome's relations with women were highlighted in accounts of his exile from Rome—albeit to emphasize his innocence: the "trap" was identified as a "woman's garment," as the twelfth-century French theologian and liturgist Johannes Beleth reported.[105] The thirteenth-century *Golden Legend* of Jacobus de Voragine offered still greater detail, noting that Jerome's enemies had placed a woman's garment near his bed in the night. Waking for Matins, "as was his custom," he put the garment on and proceeded to church (a comical scene reproduced in the *Belles Heures* of Jean, Duc de Berry; Figure 14).[106] As Jacobus explained, "His adversaries, of course, had done this in order to make it look as if he had a woman in his room." For Jacobus de Voragine, as for other men during the central Middle Ages, the legend confirmed two central assumptions: first, that Jerome was innocent of all charges; and second, that the allegation of sexual misconduct—the "trap" that had been set for him—was the work of malicious men. Jacobus commented that Jerome "had denounced some monks and clerics for their lascivious lives, and they were so resentful that they began to lay snares for him."[107]

Jerome's trials did nothing to detract from his medieval appeal. If anything, they recommended him still more to men during the central Middle Ages, who saw in him not only a model of men's legitimate spiritual care for religious women, but also one of innocence accused. Since Jerome's virtue was unquestioned during the medieval period, the accusations against him were understood to have been fully unjust. Suffering them patiently, Jerome therefore exemplified the spiritual ideal of Christian sacrifice: his example suggested that service to women, and the malicious accusations that such service almost always provoked, could be spiritual ends in themselves for medieval religious men, whose endurance of false accusations might be interpreted as a form of *imitatio Christi*. Jerome himself had suggested the connection. Invoking John 15:18—in which Jesus had comforted his disciples that "If the world hate you, know that it hated me before you."—Jerome declared as he left Rome: "I thank my God that I am counted worthy of the world's hatred."[108] A decade later, in a letter to Furia, he associated himself once again with Christ in his experience of unjust accusations: "Men . . . will cry out that I am a sorcerer and a seducer; and that I should be transported to the ends of the earth. They may add, if they will, the title of Samaritan; for in it I shall but recognize a name given to my Lord."[109] By highlighting the innocent suffering of Christ, Jerome at once defended himself and painted his accusers as corrupt and wicked men. Medieval men who invoked Jerome as a model for their spiritual involvement with women achieved something similar: by invoking Jerome,

they underscored the purity of their relations with women, the injustice of accusations against them, and the wickedness of those who attacked them.

Jerome in the Eleventh and Twelfth Centuries

Jerome's reputation for licit spiritual involvement with women was considerably advanced in the late eleventh and twelfth centuries as his works received renewed attention and were copied, read, and studied widely. As in the ninth century, interest in Jerome as a translator and interpreter of sacred scripture grew in conjunction with intellectual renaissance and concern for the reform of the religious life.[110] Around the time that Reginald of Canterbury produced his poetic rewriting of Jerome's *Life* of Malchus, Guigues de Châtel (1083–1136), the fifth prior of the Grande Chartreuse, produced a new edition of Jerome's letters.[111] Some years later, Nicolò Maniacutia, a Cistercian monk at the abbey of Trois Fontaines near Rome, produced a new *Life* of Jerome, in which he highlighted Jerome's friendship with Paula and Eustochium and reported the trap laid for him by his enemies (identified as pseudo-clerics and—monks), who tricked him into wearing a woman's garment.[112] Women, too, were engaged in reading, copying, and transmitting Jerome's works. At the Bavarian monastery of Wessobrunn, the female recluse and scribe Diemut copied several works of Jerome, including a substantial collection of his letters, his *Contra Vigilantium*, and his *De hebraicis questionibus*.[113] Manuscripts of Jerome also feature in the twelfth-century collection of Zwiefalten, another Hirsau reform monastery that included both a female community and female scribes.[114] Alongside the many works of Jerome in the Zwiefalten collection was a copy of the *Institutio canonum Aquisgranesium*, which included, appropriately enough, both the *Institutio canonicorum* and the *Institutio sanctimonialium*, with its extensive prefatory excerpts from Jerome.[115] At Lamspringe, female scribes copied "Cogitis me" alongside Bede's commentaries on Ezra and Nehemiah, toward the end of the century.[116]

At Corbie, too, Jerome's works received new attention during the twelfth century. Indeed, it may be no coincidence that Jerome and Paschasius were both copied and read at Corbie at this time. In each case, the monks chose to highlight the men's relations with women. The monk artists who copied Paschasius's commentary on Psalm 44 prefaced the commentary with a remarkable image of Paschasius presenting the work to a group of five canonesses—suggesting a willingness at Corbie to remember, and perhaps also to celebrate, Paschasius as a man who had devoted himself to religious women (Figure 15).[117] At around the same time, Corbie scribes and artists collaborated in the production of a manuscript that included Jerome's commentary on Ecclesiastes, a work that had been commissioned by Blesilla, but was dedicated to Paula and Eustochium. The Corbie artists privileged Jerome's relationships with these three women, depicting Jerome at his desk, flanked by Paula and Eustochium (Figure 16).[118] A titulus identifies the patron or scribe of the book as the priest Ivo.[119]

Religious men during the central Middle Ages invoked Jerome's example of relations with women in several different ways. Some referenced him to explain and exalt their own writing for women. In his epitaph for the empress Adelheid, Odilo of Cluny commented that, had Jerome been alive during Adelheid's lifetime, he would have commended her just as he had "Paula and Eustochium, Marcella and Melania, Fabiola and Blesilla, Leta and Demetrias."[120] Although Odilo intended to pay tribute primarily to Adelheid by this reference, placing her among the company of women whose sanctity had captured Jerome's attention, he also implicitly identified himself with Jerome as a man who eulogized holy women. Other men cited Jerome to justify their decision to write for women in the first place, often noting—as Bishop Azecho of Worms did—that Jerome had preferred to write to women, rather than to men.[121] Abelard also made this point. Noting that Jerome had responded with alacrity to the requests of Paula and Eustochium, while he neglected to write to Augustine, Abelard commented: "we know that Jerome toiled over the copying or composition of so many lengthy volumes at the request of the women we mentioned, showing them far more respect in this than he showed a bishop."[122] In dedicating the *Historia ecclesiastica* to Adela of Blois, Hugh of Fleury likewise defended his work with reference to Jerome: "To those who will take it amiss that I have dedicated this work to you, I answer: the blessed priest Jerome often honored holy Paula and her daughter Eustochium with many writings."[123] In the latter part of the twelfth century, Gerhoch of Reichersberg similarly claimed Jerome as a model, likening his writing for women to Jerome's compositions for Paula and Eustochium.[124]

Jerome's appeal to men such as these, who wrote theological and other texts for women, lay not only in his saintly example of literary attention to women, but also in his defense of men's writing for women. Jerome's letter 65 to Principia (a commentary on Psalm 44, written at her request) included a prologue in praise of holy women, which functioned equally as a vigorous defense of his writings to women. "I am blamed by many," Jerome commented,

Inhoc opere quod ultra uires elaboraui
quia me ipse ad id impuli dum caritas
id coegit. Cuius adeuntis uel abeun-
tis causa sicut saluator ait. ipsius e
inspirantis uoluntate. quamuis eius
nesciatur aduentus. uel recessus dum
replet omnia. Propterea recte nemo e
qui prohibeat ei loqui p quem uult. cui
sub est posse docere & aspirare omnia
que uult. Sine quo recte sapio. nec
ipsi angeli qui uirtutes sunt. unquam
possunt aut sapiunt quin uerba ca-
nit. uerbo dm celi firmati sunt. & spu
oris eius omnis uirtus eorum. Quod
si eorum. proculdubio & scorum.

...um sollicitudi-
ne pastoralis of-
ficii curisq re-
giminis. & ne-
gotiis actionu
essem tandem
preoccupatus. di-
uino dispensante
iudicio. reculi
que ad ea studia
que prefecto recenti animo. remis-
sa temporibus uarios rerum secularu
anfractus abieceram. Sicq longo int
uallo intermissa reuocaui. Hinc uter
altera cordis silentia. int amenos scriptura-
rum scarum recessus. recensui in mente
quod tam sce matri olim. qm tibi ex uob
deuoueram scribere. Sed quia illa iam
legit in libro uite inestimabilia. que hu-
mani sermo non capit. uobis que filie
estis debui reddere quod decreueram.
Q mia sicut inuerecundi debitoris est.
pmissa denegare. ita honesti & libati
sine mora. ultroneum offerre. Preser-
tim quia ado heres constituta est matri
beate hereditatis. que erat filia caris-
sima matris. cui totum me deuoui
fore presens quod sum. & quod debue-
ram in xpo dilectionis. ut exsoluerem.
Qm a fenus caritatis tunc bene debetur cum exsoluitur. & soluendo
semp iure debetur. In hoc ipso nego-
tio completa e prophetia psentis psalmi
cum dicitur. pro patribus tuis nati
sunt e filii constitues eos principes.
Constituta e g a do dilectissime.
& que sunt filia beate matri facta e op-
tima nutrix cui totum debemus

Figure 15. Paschasius with Canonesses. Bibliothèque nationale de France,
Lat. 12298, fol. 177v.

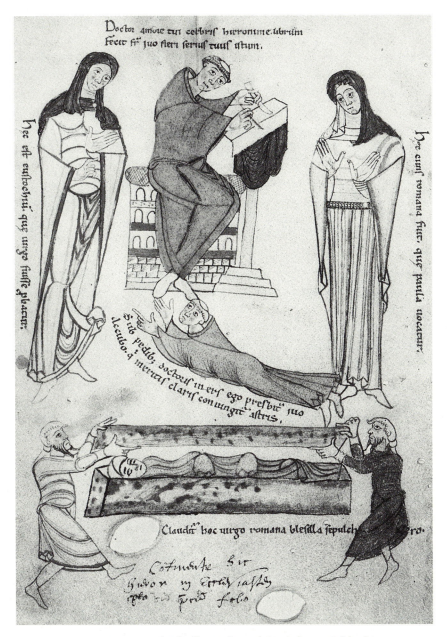

Figure 16. Jerome with Blesilla, Paula, and Eustochium. Bibliothèque nationale de France, Lat. 13350, fol. Bv.

"since now and then I write to women and prefer the more fragile sex to the manly one."[125] Defending himself, Jerome noted the biblical precedence of women over men: Deborah went into battle because Barak refused to go alone (Judges 4:8); Hulda was prophetess while Jeremiah was in jail (IV Kings 22:14); and Mary Magdalene had faith, while the apostles doubted. Adding to these examples a catalogue of notable women from the Old Testament (Sara, Rebecca, Miriam, Rachel, Ruth, Esther, Judith, Hannah, and others), Jerome also noted Jesus's attention to women: "Women followed the Lord and ministered to him from their resources. He who from five loaves, fed five thousand men, excluding women and children, did not refuse to receive the food of holy women." Continuing, Jerome observed that Priscilla and Aquila had taught the apostle Apollos (Acts 18:26), prompting him to ask: "If it was not disgraceful for an apostle to be taught by a woman, why should it be disgraceful to me to teach women after men?"[126] A similar defense of writing to women appears in the prologue to Jerome's commentary on Sophonia (Zephaniah), a work dedicated to Paula and Eustochium. Writing that "it seems necessary to respond to those who judge me worthy of mockery, because omitting men, I should write especially to you, o Paula and Eustochium," Jerome noted the various holy women of the Old and New Testaments, as well as examples of the Greek and Roman women with whom ancient philosophers had contact—proof that "philosophers of the world sought differences in souls not bodies," a claim Jerome had made, too, in his *Commentariorum in Esaiam*.[127] Turning, finally, to the example of Christ, whose attention to women would inspire men throughout the medieval period, Jerome noted simply that "the Lord at his resurrection appeared first to women and . . . they were the apostles of the apostles."[128] In his letter 127 to Principia (written in praise of Marcella), Jerome revisited the theme: "The unbelieving reader may perhaps laugh at me for dwelling so long on the praises of mere women; yet if he will but remember how holy women followed our Lord and Savior and ministered to Him of their substance, and how the three Marys stood before the cross and especially how Mary Magdalen— called the tower from the earnestness and glow of her faith—was privileged to see the rising Christ first of all before the very apostles, he will convict himself of pride sooner than me of folly. For we judge of people's virtue not by their sex but by their character (*non sexu sed animo*)."[129] As we saw in the previous chapter, medieval men drew on many of these same biblical models in defending themselves, sometimes citing Jerome directly as they did so.

During the central Middle Ages, Peter Abelard found particular solace in Jerome's example, celebrating him as "the greatest doctor of the Church and glory of the monastic profession" and styling himself in large measure as a "second Jerome."[130] Abelard cited Jerome repeatedly in his writings for the women of the Paraclete, finding key justifications for his own involvement with women in Jerome's letters and commentaries. Abelard's letter 9, sometimes called *De studio litterarum*, is so rife with excerpts from Jerome (drawn chiefly from his letter 107 on the education of Paula) that Jean Leclercq dismissed it as a mere florilegium of extracts.[131] But Abelard did not simply copy Jerome's advice on education, he also rehearsed several of the arguments that Jerome advanced for writing to women in the first place. As Abelard reminded readers of his letter *On the Origin of Nuns*: "Everyone knows too that St. Jerome harvested a great number of holy books which he left to the Church at the request of Paula and Eustochium."[132] Abelard was clearly familiar with that harvest, citing in his own writings Jerome's Epist. 39 (to Paula, after Blesilla's death), Epist. 108 (to Eustochium, after death of Paula), Epist. 127 (to Principia about Marcella), Epist. 45 (to Asella), Epist. 46 (from "Paula and Eustochium" to Marcella), Epist. 130 (to Demetrias), Epist. 54 (to Furia), and two letters to Eustochium—Epist. 31 and Epist. 22—as well as Epist. 107 and Epist. 65.

Abelard's affinity for Jerome is not surprising: both men were divisive figures, intellectually arrogant, and controversial. Hounded by their enemies (real and imagined), both men found comfort in the company of religious women—Abelard at the Paraclete, which he described once as a "haven of peace away from raging storms," and Jerome in the friendship of wealthy Roman women.[133] Both men wrote substantial texts for women, with whom they shared close, spiritual friendships: Abelard for Heloise and the nuns under her authority, and Jerome—as we have seen—for Paula, Eustochium, and Marcella, as well as others. Both men, moreover, faced opposition to their involvement with women. While Jerome was expelled from Rome, Abelard's relations with Heloise were mired in scandal: their affair, their botched marriage, and Abelard's castration. By the time that he wrote his *Historia calamitatum*, sometime around 1132, Abelard was deeply embittered by the continued accusations that his involvement with women provoked. In frustration and anger at the false charges hurled against him—that he continued to be "in the grip of the pleasures of carnal concupiscence"[134]—Abelard turned to Jerome, "whose heir I consider myself as regards slanders and false accusations."[135] Finding particular solace in Jerome's letter to Asella (Epist. 45)—written as he left Rome, in disgrace—Abelard recalled Jerome's complaint that he had been praised throughout Rome before he knew Paula. "Often I repeated to myself St. Jerome's lament in his letter to Asella about false friends," Abelard remembered, quoting Jerome: "The only fault found in me is my sex, and that only when Paula comes to Jerusalem."[136]

Abelard cited Jerome to comfort himself, but also to underscore his innocence, to defame his accusers (whom he depicted as jealous and evil men), and to claim the virtue that was to be found in suffering unjust accusations. In his *Historia calamitatum*, Abelard cited Jerome's self-justificatory comments to Nepotian ("if I still sought men's favor . . . I should be no servant of Christ") and to Asella ("Thank God I have deserved the hatred of the world").[137] Of course, Jerome also offered a rich example of men's pious devotion to women—one to which Abelard, and other men, could turn in justifying their involvement with women as "saintly" and theologically sound. Jerome's writings, too, shaped Abelard's sense of his role at the Paraclete, as a monk ministering to nuns—one of whom was his former wife. Jerome's *life* of the saintly and chaste Malchus was evidence, in Abelard's view, that holy men could involve themselves in pure relations with women. "What would my detractors have said," Abelard asked, "if they had seen Malchus, the captive monk of whom St. Jerome writes, living together with his wife? In their eyes it would have been a great crime, though the splendid doctor had nothing but high praise for what he saw."[138] For Abelard (as also for Reginald, whom Abelard does not appear to have known), Malchus's example of chaste marriage was a sign that such pure spiritual relationships between the sexes were possible and that they had been approved by no less a figure than St. Jerome, the "famous doctor."

A central argument of this book is that Abelard was not alone among medieval men either in his attention to women or in the arguments that he made concerning men's spiritual involvement with women. Others, too, invoked Jerome in situations where accusations of wrongdoing might be leveled. A generation before Abelard, Goscelin of St. Bertin had cited Jerome's relationship with Paula and Eustochium in order to defend the spiritual companionship of saint Edith of Wilton and her mother Wulfthryth with their chaplain Benno of Trier (just as he had invoked the example of John the Evangelist in characterizing the relationship of Dunstan and Edith): in Benno, Goscelin wrote, the mother-daughter pair Edith and Wulfthryth (whom he likened to Paula and Eustochium) "had as it were their own Jerome."[139] Goscelin may have found personal validation in Jerome's example, styling himself as a "Jerome" in his relationship to Eve of Wilton. In the *Liber confor-*

tatorius, which Goscelin wrote for Eve following her decision to become an anchorite in Angers, Goscelin encouraged Eve to model herself on the examples of Paula and Eustochium, implicitly suggesting himself as her "Jerome."[140] Similarly, Christina of Markyate's mid-twelfth-century biographer described Christina as Paula to Geoffrey's Jerome, in a move that was designed to cast them both as innocent victims of scandalmongers. Referring to the rumors and "fictitious tales" that circulated concerning their friendship, Christina's biographer wrote that "listening to them you might think that one was Jerome, the other Paula."[141] Directly echoing Jerome's complaint to Asella that his reputation had been secure before he met Paula (a complaint adopted by Abelard as well), Christina's biographer continued: "Before they had come to love each other in Christ, the abbot's well-known integrity and the virgin's holy chastity had been praised in many parts of England. But when their mutual affection in Christ inspired them to greater good, then the abbot was slandered as a seducer and the maiden as a whore."[142] As Dyan Elliott rightly notes, the identification of contemporary men with Jerome in these cases seems to have been founded on "scandal, not sanctity."[143]

The Bride of Christ as *"Domina"*

Jerome's model offered medieval men much-needed comfort, helping them to understand why the care for women that they believed had been divinely ordained (based on the commendation to John) could nevertheless provoke vicious attacks. Yet Jerome also offered more, presenting in his writings a compelling case for women's spiritual superiority founded on his identification of devout women as brides of Christ. As I argued in the previous chapter, when men wrote to and about religious women during the eleventh and twelfth centuries, they stressed their chastity and the innocence of their intentions. But they did not dwell long on their earthly relationships to women. Instead, they focused attention away from themselves as potential lovers, embracing the traditional characterization of religious women as brides of Christ. Of course, the bridal motif was not invented by reformist ideology, but had a long history, stretching back at least to the second century when Tertullian had applied the metaphor to consecrated virgins in North Africa.[144] However, it gained significant early traction through the writings of Jerome, who adopted the idea in his letter to Eustochium, both to exalt her and to stress her spiritual intimacy with Christ.

In his famous letter 22, Jerome addressed Eustochium as his *domina* (his "lady," or literally, his female "lord"), commenting by way of explanation that "I am bound to call my Lord's bride 'Lady.'"[145] Later in the same letter, he elaborated on Eustochium's "rank" in relation to his own, addressing her as his *domina* once again: "my Eustochium, daughter, *domina*, fellow-servant, sister (*germana*)—these names refer the first to your age, the second to your rank, the third to your religious vocation, the last to the place which you hold in my affection."[146] Of all the ways that Jerome felt himself bound to Eustochium, it was this second, her "rank," that most influenced him. Since Eustochium was Christ's "bride," she was logically Jerome's *domina*, given that he imagined himself primarily as Christ's "servant." Addressing Eustochium as his *domina* was one way in which Jerome could articulate his primary relationship of servitude to Christ, and thereby remove both Eustochium and himself from suspicion of wrong-doing.

The spiritual love triangle that Jerome imagined bound him to Eustochium, and both of them to Christ, was deeply compelling for religious men during the late eleventh and early twelfth centuries.[147] The fiery reformer Peter Damian adopted the idea in his letters for the countess-turned-nun Blanche of Milan. Addressing Blanche as *domina mea*, Peter explained: "I call you my *domina*, or better, my queen, espoused to my Lord, the king of heaven."[148] Hildebert of Lavardin, a recipient of Reginald's *life* of Malchus, echoed Jerome's subordination to Eustochium in writing to the countess-turned-nun Adela of Blois: "The bride of my lord is my *domina*."[149] So, too, Goscelin of St. Bertin addressed Eve as *domina mea*, calling to mind Jerome's positioning of himself in relation to Eustochium. Like Jerome, Goscelin linked his description of Eve as his *domina* to her relationship with Christ, "for whom alone," as he wrote to her, "you have gone into enclosure."[150]

Abelard, too, refusing Heloise's post-conversion claims on him as her husband, situated himself rather as her servant, writing to her in the 1130s: "you must realize that you became my superior from the day when you began to be my lady (*domina mea*) on becoming the bride of my Lord."[151] In his letter *On the Origin of Nuns*, Abelard once again invoked Jerome's rhetorical subordination to Eustochium, presenting biblical women as mothers and *dominae* of the apostles.[152] However, his most far-reaching application of Jerome's model of religious women as *dominae* appeared in a sermon (Sermon 30) that he preached for the Paraclete in its early years.[153] At this time, Heloise's community of religious women was newly established at the Paraclete, under circumstances that were evidently austere. Seeking to raise much-needed funds for the new community, Abelard addressed himself to an audience of potential donors, encouraging them to view the nuns as their *dominae*—women who not only deserved their support, but whose heavenly bridegroom would ensure that earthly supporters were amply rewarded. Citing Jerome's subordination to Eustochium as his *domina*, Abelard explained to his audience that all nuns were brides of Christ, and were therefore superior to all men (who could, at best, be "servants," but never brides). Advising that nuns "join themselves to a heavenly bridegroom and, made brides of the highest king, become ladies (*dominae*) of all his servants," Abelard urged that "You should not delay in assisting their poverty." A reward would be waiting for donors in heaven, where they would "reap eternal rewards through those women who here receive temporal goods from you, by the gift of their bridegroom, the Lord Jesus Christ."[154] As we shall see in Chapter 5, the privileged spiritual status of nuns as brides of Christ had important implications for perceptions of their efficacy in prayer, since the prayers of nuns were—literally, as Abelard and others believed—the prayers of brides. Begging Heloise's "bridal" prayers, Abelard wrote explicitly of the vicarious salvation that he expected to gain through her: "Whatever is yours cannot, I think, fail to be mine, and Christ is yours, because you have become his bride."[155] In Abelard's view, even salvation could come to him through Heloise—a spiritual benefit that he promised to male donors who supported the female religious life.

Abelard's ideas about religious women have typically been thought of as "daring," yet ultimately irrelevant in his own time. However, Abelard's fundraising sermon for the Paraclete, with its claims to women's spiritual superiority as brides of Christ and *dominae* of men (an idea inspired by Jerome), was known and read by other religious men within a few decades of its composition in the early 1130s.[156] The sermon survives now in a single manuscript from the second half of the twelfth century: Colmar, Bibliothèque municipale, MS 128.[157] The manuscript's provenance gives a valuable indication of Abelard's readership, hinting at the reception of his ideas concerning men's support for women's religious life. Colmar MS 128 was preserved in the library of Marbach, an Augustinian reform monastery that seems to have been a double community at some point (possibly even from its foundation in the late eleventh century). By the middle of the twelfth century, Marbach supported a female daughter house at nearby Schwarzenthann, where several of the Marbach canons served as priests.

The presence of Abelard's sermons in the collection at Marbach is suggestive of Abelard's twelfth-century influence and appeal: like Reginald's *Malchus*,

Abelard's sermons seem to have circulated among communities of like-minded men. Concrete evidence that the Marbach canons found Abelard's ideas concerning women compelling, and that they worked to implement his model of mutuality between the sexes in the religious life, is provided in the mid-twelfth-century *Guta-Sintram Codex*, a manuscript that was produced through the joint efforts of Guta, a canoness at Schwarzenthann, and Sintram, a canon of Marbach. The codex is known primarily for its depiction of Guta and Sintram paying homage to the Virgin Mary, with Sintram to the Virgin's right and Guta to her left (Figure 2).[158] In a text on the dedication page, Guta claims responsibility for the writing of the manuscript and reports that Sintram was the author of its miniatures.[159] However, Sintram also seems to have served in a scribal capacity: it is likely his hand—Hand "B"—that appears alongside Guta's at times, suggesting that their cooperation involved close working conditions, possibly even in the same room.[160] Most interesting is Sintram's presumed role (as Hand "B") in copying several selections from Abelard's Sermon 30 (with the incipit *Beati pauperes*) into the codex—placing them prominently on the folio facing the dedication to the Virgin (Figure 17).[161] The idea that pious women were brides of Christ, and therefore *dominae* of men, features prominently in the selections from Abelard's sermon that Sintram chose to copy. As brides, *Beati pauperes* claims that nuns deserve men's care; yet the text also offers the assurance that nuns can reward men through their intimacy with the bridegroom and the gendered efficacy of their prayers.

The appearance of *Beati pauperes* in the *Guta-Sintram Codex* indicates not just that Abelard's monastic writings were known and read, but also that Jerome's ideas about men's rhetorical subordination to nuns, as brides and *dominae*, had a role in shaping relations between religious women and men in German-speaking lands, even some eight hundred years after his death.

A final example from the turn of the twelfth century offers a slightly different vantage point from which to consider Jerome's influence, showing how women may have viewed the bridal motif. Baudri of Bourgueil (d. 1130) (author of the first *Life* of Robert of Arbrissel) wrote to Constance, likely a nun at Le Ronceray, sometime around 1096–1106, addressing her as "the bride of my Lord" (*sponsa mei domini*).[162] In her response, Constance initially resisted Baudri's overtures of friendship, only to convince herself—on the basis of Jerome's bridal motif—of her obligation, as a nun, to love religious men, whom she characterized as "servants of the bridegroom," or "friends of the bridegroom" (language that might be seen to invoke John's service to Mary at the cross):

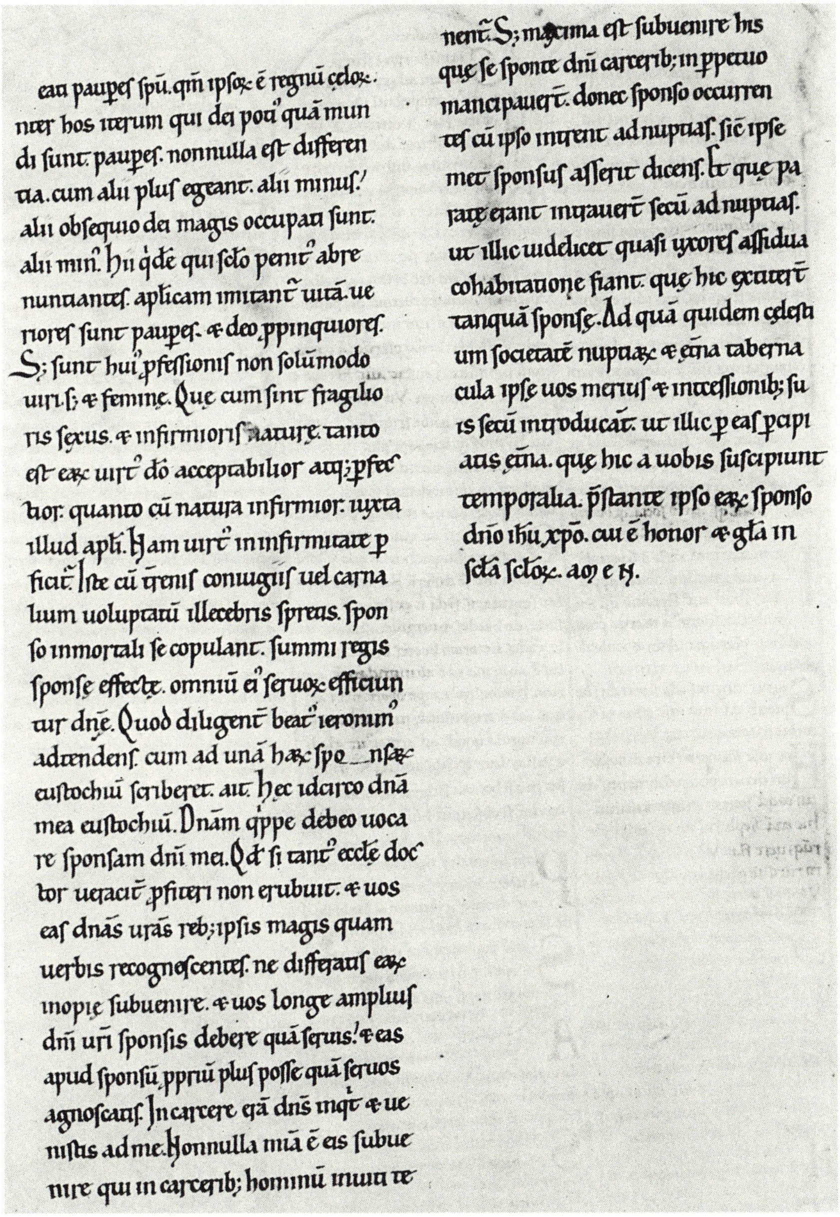

eam paupes spu. qm ipsox e regnu celox.
nter hos iterum qui dei pou qua mun
di sunt paupes. nonnulla est differen
tia. cum alii plus egeant. alii minus.
alii obsequio dei magis occupati sunt.
alii min. hii qde qui scto penit abre
nuntiantes. aplicam imitant uita. ue
riores sunt paupes. & deo ppinquiores.
S; sunt hui pfessionis non solumodo
uiris; & femine. Que cum sint fragilio
ris sexus. & infirmioris nature. tanto
est eax uirt do acceptabilior atq; pfec
tior. quanto cu natura infirmior. iuxta
illud apli. Ham uirt in infirmitate p
ficit. Iste cu ternis coniugiis uel carna
lium uoluptatu illecebris spreis. spon
so inmortali se copulant. summi regis
sponse effectx. omniu ei seruox efficiun
tur dne. Quod diligent beat ieronim
adtendens. cum ad una hax spo nse
eustochiu scriberet. ait. hec idcirco dna
mea eustochiu. Dnam qppe debeo uoca
re sponsam dni mei. Qd si tant ecce doc
tor ueracit pfiteri non erubuit. & uos
eas dnas uras reb; ipsis magis quam
uerbis recognoscentes. ne differatis eax
inopie subuenire. & uos longe ampluis
dni uri sponsis debere qua seruis. & eas
apud sponsu pprium plus posse qua seruos
agnoscatis. In carcere qa dns inqt & ue
nistis ad me. Honnulla mia e eas subue
nire qui in carcerib; hominu inuita re

nent. S; maxima est subuenire his
que se sponte dni carcerib; in ppetuo
mancipauert. donec sponso occurren
tes cu ipso intrent ad nuptias. sic ipse
met sponsus asserit dicens. Et que pa
rate erant intrauert secu ad nuptias.
ut illic uidelicet quasi uxores assidua
cohabitatione fiant. que hic exutert
tanqua sponse. Ad qua quidem celesti
um societate nuptiax & etiam taberna
cula ipse uos meruis & intcessionib; su
is secu introducat. ut illic p eas papi
atis etiam. que hic a uobis suscipiunt
temporalia. pstante ipso eax sponso
dno ihu xpo. cui e honor & gla in
scta sctox. aoj e ij.

Figure 17. *Beati pauperes.* Guta-Sintram Codex, p. 8. Strasbourg,
Bibliothèque du Grand séminaire, MS 37, fol. 3v. 1154.

The bride of God should love God's servants.
You are a servant of the bridegroom, you are brother and co-heir;
You, too, you are worthy by my bridegroom's love.
The bride should respect the friends of her bridegroom.
Therefore I respect you, I love you vigilantly.[163]

Although the attribution of this poem to Constance is contested, these lines confirm the importance of the bridal motif as a way for men and women to characterize relations between the sexes in the religious life and to emphasize their purity and saintly motivation.[164] Presenting women as brides of Christ and men as his servants or friends underscored the centrality of Christ to these relations; women (like men) could imagine their relations with opposite-sex religious figures as mediated through their primary allegiance and loyalty to Christ. Religious women could justify their affection for monks and priests on the basis that brides should love their bridegroom's servants. Viewing each other through the lens of the bridal relationship, both men and women found cause to admire and support each other—in service, ultimately, to Christ.

Conclusion

Reference to Jerome in the context of men's spiritual involvement with women was never just a trope.[165] Men who invoked Jerome as a model did so consciously and intentionally, in a bid to defend their involvement with women, linking themselves to a tradition of innocent, and even saintly, relations between religious men and women. As a respected theologian, biblical commentator, and translator, Jerome offered a model of men's care for women that was beyond suspicion—if not during his own lifetime, then certainly by the ninth century, when his saintly reputation was firmly established. His depiction in both the First Bible of Charles the Bald and the Bible of San Paolo fuori le mura, his prominence in the *Institutio sanctimonialium*, and his association with Paschasius's widely known sermon "Cogitis me" confirm his ninth-century reputation for chaste, spiritual involvement with women, as does the manuscript witness of the Chelles letter collection. By the twelfth century, Jerome's reputation for the spiritual guidance of women was secure; allegations of impropriety in his relations with women were firmly understood (and dismissed) as the machinations of jealous and evil men.

Women, too, recognized the usefulness of Jerome's model, invoking him in order to prompt contemporary men to engage spiritually and intellectually with them. As we saw, it was Gisela and Rotrude who encouraged Alcuin to view himself as Jerome's heir, consciously fashioning themselves as the spiritual and intellectual successors to Jerome's female disciples. In the twelfth century, too, Heloise claimed Jerome as a model of men's care for women. While Abelard may have pictured himself as Jerome's heir in "slanders and false accusations," a persecuted genius like the famous church father, it was Heloise who encouraged him to consider himself as Jerome's heir in his role as the author of spiritual works for women. References to Jerome appear in her letters first in letter 6, in which—putting aside reflections on the past— she asked Abelard to write both a Rule for the Paraclete and a history of the order of nuns.[166] From that point on, Heloise referred increasingly to Jerome, although perhaps not as Abelard intended. Where Abelard encouraged the Paraclete women to model themselves on "the blessed disciples of St. Jerome, Paula and Eustochium,"[167] Heloise evidently preferred Marcella as her spiritual and intellectual ideal.[168] The distinction is important. Paula and Eustochium received Jerome's dictates with unquestioning devotion, following him to the Holy Land and even dying there with him. Meanwhile, Marcella had remained in Rome, where she maintained her own spiritual circle, interacting with Jerome regularly, but at arm's length. Marcella was, moreover, the most scholarly and even critical of Jerome's female friends. Jerome remembered her intellectual acuity, commenting in a letter to Principia that "she never came to see me that she did not ask me some question concerning them [the scriptures], nor would she at once acquiesce in my explanations but on the contrary would dispute them."[169] In a letter complaining of enemies who attacked him for altering the biblical text, Jerome anticipated Marcella's concerned response: "I know that as you read these words you will knit your brows, and fear that my freedom of speech is sowing the seeds of fresh quarrels; and that, if you could, you would gladly put your finger on my mouth to prevent me from even speaking of things which others do not blush to do."[170]

Heloise saw herself more in the mode of Marcella than of Eustochium and Paula, whose main advantage was their fierce asceticism rather than their intellectual agility. Abelard, too, may have recognized that Marcella was a more fitting model for Heloise than either Paula or Eustochium. In his letter 9, on the education of women, he noted the consolation that Jerome had taken in his exchange of letters with Marcella—the sort of epistolary consolation

that he had once considered as one of Heloise's chief attractions as his prospective lover.[171] Even so, in writing to Heloise, Abelard tended to emphasize
Marcella's humility more than her intelligence. Although Marcella was often
called upon to settle theological disputes after Jerome's departure from Rome,
Abelard noted that she never took credit for her answers, but—in obedience
to Paul's prohibition of women's teaching—attributed them either to Jerome,
or to some other male teacher.[172]

Heloise's Marcella was less demure than Abelard's. If Abelard's Marcella
refused credit for teaching men, Heloise's Marcella refused to be taught without engaging in debate; like Heloise herself, her Marcella continually questioned her male teacher. In the preface to the *Problemata*, the series of questions
that she sent Abelard, Heloise invoked Marcella, reminding Abelard of
Jerome's many letters to her, often written in response to Marcella's theological
questions. Still, it was not Marcella's questions that Heloise emphasized, but
rather Jerome's praise for her, which—as Heloise commented to Abelard—
"your wisdom knows better than my simplicity."[173] In fact, Heloise cited
Marcella not primarily as a questioning woman, but rather as one who could
scarcely be satisfied with the answer she was given. Remembering Jerome's
commentary on Galatians, Heloise noted Jerome's recollection of Marcella
as his intellectual counterpart: as Heloise reported, Jerome had written that
Marcella did not "accept whatever I may answer as correct. . . . Instead, she
investigates everything, and weighs it all in her sagacious mind, and so she
makes me feel that I have not so much a pupil as a judge."[174]

In the final analysis, Heloise cited Marcella primarily in order to goad
Abelard into action. If Jerome had written for women, and if Abelard fancied
himself a second Jerome, then, as Heloise hinted broadly, he should answer
her questions. "To what purpose then are these things, O dear to many, but
dearest to us?" she asked, once she had rehearsed Jerome's praises for Marcella.
"They are not mere testimonies; they are admonitions, reminding you of your
debt to us, which you should not delay in paying."[175] Heloise's strategy—of
using Jerome's dedication to women to shame Abelard into taking her requests
more seriously—is one that Gisela and Rotrude had used to good effect. Abelard,
like Alcuin, may have seen himself as Jerome's intellectual heir. Heloise, like
women before her, reminded Abelard that concern for women, and engagement with them, had been a hallmark of Jerome's spiritual life—providing a
saintly model that medieval churchmen would do well to emulate.

CHAPTER 4

Brothers, Sons, and Uncles: Nuns' Priests and Family Ties

You are my shelter in Christ;
you, dearest sister, are my security.
                    —Leander of Seville, *De institutione virginum*

She led me to the intimate ministry of Jesus my Lord.
                    —Ekbert of Schönau, *De obitu domine Elisabeth*

Medieval men who engaged spiritually with religious women found comfort and encouragement in the saintly examples of John the Evangelist and Jerome, whose models of involvement with the Virgin Mary and the pious noblewomen of Rome, respectively, offered them two basic assurances: first, that men's care for women was divinely ordained; and second, that criticism was inevitable (even if it was wholly unjust). As we saw in Chapters 2 and 3, men who turned to John and Jerome for inspiration and justification were often those who were already involved with religious women, whether directly as priests or indirectly as founders of monasteries for women, as women's correspondents, or as authors of spiritual guides for them. These men sought to defend themselves against public skepticism, insinuations of wrongdoing, and occasional hostility. At the same time, they worked to fashion a spiritual identity for themselves, as religious men, in which service to women played a central role.

A further group of men—the subjects of this chapter—were equally engaged with religious women, yet they were, relatively speaking, little concerned with either justifying that involvement or explaining it. Like the ordained men who invoked John and Jerome, this group, too, had time-honored and pious exemplars to whom they could turn—early medieval figures like Caesarius of Arles (d. 542), Benedict of Nursia, and Leander of Seville (d. c. 600), each of whom was strongly associated in the medieval imagination with one woman in particular: a devout sister. Like Caesarius, Benedict, and Leander, the men considered in this chapter provided spiritual care for their own biological kin—chiefly their sisters, but also their mothers, nieces, and cousins. Yet despite the shared familial circumstances of their spiritual involvement with women, these ordained kinsmen (as I shall call them) rarely, if ever, invoked early medieval exemplars of men's spiritual involvement with female kin.

The lack of defensive rhetoric among ordained kinsmen during the central Middle Ages marks a significant exception to the more general pattern of cynicism and distrust of nuns' priests that I outlined in Chapter 1. The present chapter therefore adopts a different approach from the previous two, taking as its subject not the construction of a defensive rhetoric over time, but rather its absence. As I argue, ordained kinsmen rarely defended themselves because they rarely needed to: by the central Middle Ages, kinship ties between professed men and women were typically spared the sorts of suspicions and criticisms that were directed at nuns' priests generally. A central concern of this chapter is to explore why that was the case—why family ties between professed men and women (notably brothers and sisters) were so often exempt from criticism, while relations between unrelated nuns and priests attracted anxious and disapproving commentary. Kinship was not automatically sanctioned within early Christian communities, making the medieval acceptance of sibling pairs in the religious life all the more remarkable. Indeed, early Christians were wary of the distractions of family life. As Jesus had announced to his crowds of followers, "if any man come to me, and hate not his father, and mother, and wife, and children . . . he cannot be my disciple" (Luke 14:26; cf. Mark 10:29, Matt. 19:29).[1] In keeping with this teaching, late antique and early medieval saints were famed for their rejection of kin ties and their absorption into a new "family" defined by spiritual rather than biological bonds. However, by the eleventh and twelfth centuries, as I show in this chapter, biological family had gained prominence as the default context for spiritual relations between the sexes—a stunning reversal of early Christian teaching and opinion. Most striking, it was increasingly assumed not simply that a religious man *could* legitimately provide spiritual care for his female kin (and above all, for his biological sister—his *germana*), but that he *should* do so.[2] Care for a pious sister emerged as an almost essential element of male sanctity.

Saintly Siblings at the Mid-Twelfth Century

Of all the ways in which individual monks and priests engaged with religious women during the eleventh and twelfth centuries, the most consistent and widely accepted was as kinsmen providing spiritual care for female family members, especially devout sisters.[3] Ordained brothers wrote to their professed sisters, advised them on spiritual matters, devised rules for their religious lives, founded monasteries for them (often paired with their own "male" houses), and sometimes served directly as their priests or confessors.[4] In some cases, sisters lived with or near their monastic brothers, as the sister of the prior at Saint-Germer-de-Fly evidently did, according to Guibert of Nogent.[5] Some sisters traveled with brothers as they moved from one house to another: the recluse Mechthild moved with her brother Bernhelm to Sponheim when he was made abbot there, while the sister of Ludolf came with him to St. Lawrence in Oostbroek, where he became abbot.[6] Even hermits sometimes lived in close proximity to their pious sisters: Burchwine, the sister of Godric of Finchale, lived in a secret cell not far from his own oratory. Godric advised Burchwine on the religious life (albeit "from a distance"), perhaps inspiring Aelred of Rievaulx, who visited Godric at his hermitage and also supported his own sister in her religious life, writing a rule (*De institutione inclusarum*) for her.[7] As we saw in Chapter 2, members of the secular clergy, too, could maintain warm ties with professed sisters: the archbishop of Cologne, Arnold von Wied, had several sisters in the religious life whom he may have wished to support through his foundation at Schwarzrheindorf. Indeed, it was through his partnership with his sister Hadwig that the community was established.

The involvement of these, and many other eleventh- and twelfth-century men, with devout sisters occasioned surprisingly little commentary among their contemporaries—and, specifically, little negative commentary. Observers typically report the presence of a man's sister in his religious life incidentally, without commenting on the propriety or even the spiritual purpose of the relationship. Guibert of Nogent, for instance, registered no surprise that the sister of Suger, the prior at Saint-Germer-de-Fly, could be found "dressed in monastic habit" and living near her brother's monastery. Even the arrival of a new abbot with his sister in tow seems to have been accepted as unremarkable: no evidence of astonishment, discomfort, or criticism appears in the extant sources that describe such an event. In some cases, the sibling bond was a subject of praise, as with Arnold von Wied: Archbishop Philip I of Cologne marveled that Arnold trusted his sister Hadwig more than anyone else after God.

One effect of this lack of censure is that sibling relations in the religious life can be difficult to trace. Of course, a man's spiritual involvement with his sister did sometimes result in the production of texts—letters, a rule, or a *vita*, for instance. Men who produced texts, for or about their sisters, often reflected on the specific spiritual dynamics of the sibling relationship, as we shall see. But in most cases, the sibling bond elicited little explicit or self-conscious commentary. Occasional references to sisters (or, indeed, to brothers) in the religious life allow historians a glimpse of kinship ties, but no clear understanding of how they were perceived by contemporaries, or why they were generally accepted. No descriptive source reports, for instance, that the chastity of a monk, hermit, or priest was deemed to be "safe" in the presence of his female relatives, although medieval observers seem to have accepted that this was the case—that is to say, that a chaste man who avoided "women" was nevertheless safe in the presence of his sister, mother, or aunt (and the corollary: that a chaste woman would remain chaste in the company of a male relative).

Amid this general silence, one work stands out for its reflection on the spiritual role of family ties, as well as their presumptive chastity and legitimacy: the mid-twelfth-century *Liber revelationum* of Elisabeth of Schönau.[8] Kin ties were not the subject of Elisabeth's visions, yet kinship came into focus as she considered a seemingly separate question: the authenticity of a trove of relics that had been discovered outside the Cologne city walls and identified with the legendary virgin martyr Saint Ursula and her eleven thousand female companions. This question of authenticity was critical to the spiritual identity of Cologne in the mid-twelfth century. Virgin martyrs, who had "poured out their blood for Christ," had been associated with the city of Cologne from at least the early fifth century.[9] However, the link between these unnamed early medieval women and Ursula, who was celebrated as the Christian daughter of a British king, was tenuous at best. According to legend, Ursula had been returning from a pilgrimage to Rome with a group of female companions when the women were martyred by pagan Huns near Cologne. Until the early twelfth century, only this legendary association linked Ursula to the city. However, in 1106, excavations in a Roman cemetery outside the city walls uncovered a mass of bones, which supporters of Ursula's cult quickly identified with the band of martyred virgins. Skeptics, meanwhile, questioned the association, doubting the authenticity of the relics.

For Elisabeth, the authenticity question hinged on the spiritual status of opposite-sex relations within the religious life. As she reported, her revelations were prompted by the arrival at the monastery of Schönau of two sets of bones from the Cologne cemetery—one set those of a woman, and the other those of a man. The presence of men's bones among the relics came as a surprise, Elisabeth admitted, causing her to doubt their connection with Saint Ursula and her troop of female virgins. Confessing her doubts, she wrote that, "like others who read the history of the British virgins, I thought that that blessed society made their pilgrimage without the escort of any men."[10] Elisabeth's concerns were soon put to rest in a revelation from the two saints whose bones had arrived at Schönau: Verena and Caesarius. Admitting that men had indeed accompanied the virginal women, Verena and Caesarius explained to Elisabeth that they had done so primarily as members of the women's families. Caesarius, for instance, was Verena's cousin. Another male martyr, Saint Adrian, had been martyred alongside four of his sisters: Babila, Juliana, Aurea, and Victoria.[11] Others among the men were clerics who had accompanied their virginal nieces, as in the cases of James, the archbishop of Antioch, and the bishops Maurisus and Marculus.[12] The familial connection allayed Elisabeth's doubts concerning the men's presence among the virgins, and she acknowledged the relics as authentic.

Spiritual Versus Biological Kinship in Early Christianity

Elisabeth's revelations are valuable for the light that they shed on male-female interactions within the religious life in the mid-twelfth century, suggesting, more than any other contemporary source, that opposite-sex spiritual relationships could be legitimized through blood ties. The contrast with biblical Christianity, with its ambivalence concerning natural kinship, is remarkable. As we saw above, early Christians had been more likely to reject biological ties than to celebrate them. Accepting Jesus's directive that a true disciple must "hate" his family, early Christians had fled wives, parents, and children, embracing a new, spiritual "family" in which men and women were bound together as metaphorical "brothers" and "sisters" in Christ.[13] Although this fictive family was created—in many cases—at the expense of biological kinship, the vision of the early church as a "family" nevertheless provided an important framework within which unrelated men and women could interact on the basis of pure and disinterested familial affection, rather than potentially sexual love. Within the biblical context, fictive kinship promoted an egalitarian spirit in which opposite-sex relations were (initially, at least) exempt from suspicion or concern. The apostle Paul referred consistently to Christian believers in kinship terms, addressing them individually and corporately as "brothers" and "sisters," and Jesus taught that all believers were joined to him, and thus to each other, by ties of spiritual kinship: as his brother, sister, and mother.[14]

Despite its early promise, fictive kinship as a new model for Christian community proved to be relatively short-lived. Spiritual kinship could not guarantee the purity of relations between the sexes, nor could it dispel persistent concerns regarding the conduct of spiritual siblings. Spiritual "brothers" and "sisters" were soon advised to maintain a certain distance from each other, loving each other as family—yet from afar. Even the kiss of peace could be suspect, as the second-century writings of Clement of Alexandria indicate. Sensing the potential for temptation and wrongdoing, Clement urged believers to exercise moderation in their enthusiasm for the ritual kiss, cautioning that it could cause "shameful suspicions and slanders" through "unrestrained use."[15]

Clement did not comment explicitly on the limits of spiritual kinship in guarding purity, even as he argued that men and women should exercise caution in their interactions with each other. However, the roughly contemporary *Shepherd of Hermas* reflected more directly on the ideal relationship of chaste opposite-sex believers, proposing biological rather than spiritual kinship as the appropriate model for pure and selfless Christian affection. The text reported how an angel had instructed the visionary to treat his wife henceforth as a "sister," an injunction presumably to refuse sexual relations with her.[16] The implication of the passage is clear: treating one's wife as a "sister" meant treating her, in sexual terms, as a biological brother treated his blood sister—that is, chastely. The slippage between spiritual and biological models of kinship in this short report is telling. Although the New Testament had taught that spiritual kinship was superior to its biological counterpart, biological kinship nevertheless quickly crept back into Christian usage as a model for the ideal interactions of unrelated men and women. Loving one's spouse as a "sister" became a byword for chaste marriage, as Gregory the Great implied some centuries later, writing in laudatory terms of a priest who "loved his wife as a brother loves his sister," although he avoided her.[17] During the fourth century, Jerome had argued a similar point in his *life* of Malchus, presenting Malchus's chaste marriage as the equivalent of a sibling relationship. As Malchus's wife commented of their decision to remain chaste, "Let the masters think you my husband, Christ will know that you are my brother."[18]

In these cases, admittedly, kin relations between biological siblings were not directly celebrated. There is no talk in these texts of actual blood brothers and sisters (or cousins and uncles), as there would be in Elisabeth of Schönau's revelations many centuries later. Nevertheless, there was a growing sense already in the second century that behaving "like" blood siblings (chiefly, it seems, by refraining from sexual relations) was desirable for opposite-sex Christians. By the early fourth century, the tide of Christian opinion had moved even further away from metaphorical kinship and towards the biological relationship. Spiritual kinship was no longer sufficient to shield opposite-sex ascetics from scrutiny, as the Council of Ancyra (314) ruled: "We prohibit those virgins, who live together with men *as if* they were their brothers, from doing so" (my italics).[19] By this time, behaving like siblings was not an accepted practice for unrelated women and men, draining spiritual kinship of at least some of its force and meaning. Jerome, notably, presented Malchus's spiritual cohabitation with his wife as short-lived. As Malchus commented when he placed her in the company of devout virgins, "I handed [her] over to the virgins, loving her as a sister but not entrusting myself to her as to a sister."[20]

Meanwhile, early fourth-century texts began to hail blood kinship as legitimate, spiritually inspired, and presumptively chaste. While the Council of Ancyra warned against couples who lived together like siblings, the slightly earlier Synod of Elvira (c. 306) had ruled in favor of churchmen who did, in fact, live with female relatives. Almost anticipating the familial tableau that would enliven Elisabeth of Schönau's twelfth-century visions, the Synod allowed that bishops and other clerics should permit their daughters and sisters to live with them, provided that these women had vowed themselves to God.[21] Confirming the openness to family reflected in this ruling, the church leaders at Nicaea (325) declared that, while clerics were to refrain from entertaining unrelated women in their homes, they might continue to welcome their "mother or sister or aunt," explicitly claiming that these women were above suspicion.[22]

Patristic and Early Medieval Churchmen as Brothers

The opening to biological family that began to appear in ecclesiastical legislation during the early fourth century was reflected in the lives and writings of contemporary churchmen. In the city of Rome, where noblewomen were increasingly attracted to the ascetic life, ties between pious women and their male kin were strong. Several men encouraged their sisters in the religious life, modeling a form of male spirituality that was, significantly, entirely without biblical precedent. Pope Damasus I (366–384), for whom Jerome served as secretary upon his arrival in Rome in 382, memorialized his sister Irene, who had adopted the ascetic life in Rome probably around 360. In an epitaph that he composed for her tombstone, Damasus identified Irene as his *germana* or "blood sister," writing that "I did not fear her death, since she approached heaven freely / but I confess that I was pained to lose the companionship of her life."[23] The *Liber pontificalis* reports that Damasus was reunited with Irene in death: he was buried "close to his mother and sister."[24] Ambrose (d. 397), the future bishop of Milan, also maintained close ties to a sister, Marcellina, who was consecrated as a virgin by Pope Liberius in Rome sometime around 353. Ambrose offered Marcellina advice on the religious life, penning a text *On Virgins* (*De virginibus*) for her;[25] he also praised her in his funeral oration for their brother, Satyrus.[26] When Ambrose died, it was Marcellina who provided information concerning her brother's life to his biographer, Paulinus of Milan.[27] Ambrose was buried in the basilica in Milan; when Marcellina died a year later, she was buried there as well. Augustine of Hippo, Ambrose's younger contemporary, likewise offered some support for his sister's religious life, taking an interest in the community of women of which she was head and addressing a letter to the women after her death, a text often hailed as Augustine's "rule" for the female monastic life.[28]

The extant sources show that these men engaged spiritually with their pious sisters, yet they do not generally comment on the legitimacy of that engagement. Instead, it was Jerome—a man who had a sister, but was not particularly close to her spiritually—who offered one of the earliest and most extensive validations of family ties between opposite-sex kin.[29] Purporting to write to a mother and daughter in Gaul at the urging of the mother's concerned son, Jerome expressed considerable unease at the women's living arrangements (Epist. 117).[30] As he explained in a prefatory note to his letter, "A certain brother from Gaul has told me that his virgin-sister and widowed mother, though living in the same city, have separate abodes and have taken to themselves clerical protectors either as guests or stewards; and that by thus associating with strangers they have caused more scandal than by living apart."[31] In the letter that followed, Jerome urged a reconciliation between the two women, underscoring the importance and spiritual value of kinship and commenting on the "natural ties and reciprocal duties" that should rightfully bind a daughter to her mother. Addressing himself first to the daughter (whose disregard for her mother he deplored), Jerome invoked the Christian obligation to obey parents, an obligation he located in the New Testament and, above all, in the (somewhat equivocal) example of Jesus. As Jerome commented, "The Lord Jesus was subject to His parents." Noting Jesus's dying concern for Mary, Jerome reminded the women that "when [Jesus] hung upon the cross He commended to His disciple the mother whom He had never before His passion parted from Himself."[32]

If the daughter's separation from her mother was troubling to Jerome, even more disturbing were her current living conditions: in the company of a so-called "monk" whom she presented as her partner in the religious life (but who was more likely her paramour, as Jerome hinted broadly). Explaining that kin ties should be the first and most natural context for the pursuit of the religious life, Jerome allowed the rejection of family only when a convert wished to pursue a communal religious life specifically among virgins: in this context alone he invoked Jesus's command that believers "hate" their families (Luke 14:26). Of course, it was appropriate, Jerome noted, for the daughter to prefer Jesus to her own mother, since "you are bidden to prefer [Him] to your own soul." But it was not appropriate for her to prefer a cleric to her own biological family. Privileging biological kinship over the implicit claims of "spiritual" brotherhood (and thereby inverting the New Testament model), Jerome fumed against the clerical interloper: "what excuse has a stranger for thrusting himself in where there are both a mother and a brother, the one a widow and the other a monk?"[33] Jerome's advice to the daughter was emphatic. Her cohabitation with an unrelated man, even if it was chaste and spiritually motivated, was dangerous; she should return to her blood brother and mother, who were better able to support and encourage her in the religious life.[34]

Brothers and Sisters in the Early Monastic Life

The privileging of familial relations that characterized Jerome's letter 117 confirms the evidence of brotherly attention to sisters that marked the lives of his contemporaries, churchmen like Damasus, Ambrose, and Augustine. But Jerome's letter also sheds light on a further aspect of relations between biological brothers and sisters: the shared involvement of opposite-sex family members in the early monastic life, a phenomenon that would become increasingly important in subsequent centuries. The mother and daughter to whom Jerome addressed his letter had—as he reminded them—a spiritual caregiver in their kinsman, a monk: "Your son is a monk," Jerome wrote to the mother, "if he were to live with you, he would strengthen you in your religious profession and in your vow of widowhood."[35]

In writing this letter, Jerome promoted a religious life for women that was based in the family and that had its place in the home where (as he argued) male relatives could provide spiritual support and protection. As Susanna Elm has shown, this sort of familial arrangement was characteristic of late antique monasticism, which had its base in the household.[36] Evidence for the structure and organization of household monasticism is most clear in the fourth-century *life* of Macrina (d. 379), a text written by her brother, Gregory of Nyssa. According to the *life*, Macrina had adopted the religious life at the age of twelve when, having been bereaved of her fiancé, she claimed the dignity of widowhood and shut herself up in her family's villa at Annisa.[37] Macrina was soon joined by her mother, and then others, until the household had developed into a small religious community. It was in this household community that Macrina raised her youngest brother Peter. As Gregory comments admiringly, she "became everything for the little boy: father, teacher, tutor, mother, counsellor in all that was good."[38]

Peter's presence among the women of Macrina's household community indicates that there was initially no segregation of the sexes in life at Annisa.[39] Although the community was divided into groupings based on age and sex as it grew, in keeping with its domestic roots, both women and men continued to have a place: there was a house for virgins, one for monks, a third for children, and a fourth for guests.[40] The mixed religious life of Macrina's community likely inspired a further brother, Basil of Caesarea, in the monastic life that he promoted at his foundation, which was not far from Macrina's house at Annisa. Basil's monastic complex also included both men and women, as well as children, in separate houses.[41] A theologian and defender of the Eastern Church against heresy, Basil is typically famed for his role in the development of Eastern monasticism. However, in Gregory's eyes, it was Macrina who was the spiritual leader in the family.[42] It was she, he notes, who provided Basil with spiritual encouragement when he returned from his studies "puffed up with pride," ultimately prompting him to reject "worldly fame."[43]

Macrina's example, in conjunction with Jerome's advice to the women in Gaul, indicates the importance of the family, and the home, as an accepted mixed-sex environment for the early pursuit of the religious life. A further set of texts dating to the second half of the fourth century indicates that family bonds were not limited to settings that were either home-based or overtly familial. Supportive spiritual bonds between opposite-sex siblings were also evident among the earliest monastic communities in the deserts and valleys of Egypt. Indeed, alongside the well-known male ascetics who withdrew to the wilderness during the early fourth century were their equally devout (although less well known) sisters. The pious aspirations of these women do not typically feature in the *vitae* of their more celebrated brothers. Still, it is intriguing that hagiographers mentioned them at all. Rather than denying or ignoring the presence of a holy man's sister, biographers of the desert fathers began specifically to mention such women in the context of the male saint's pious life, in the process fashioning a new topos of male sanctity: fraternal spiritual care for a pious sister.

The attention of the male saint to the spiritual life of his sister is underscored in the *lives* of both Antony (d. 356) and Pachomius (d. c. 346), men who are typically hailed as founding fathers of monasticism. Accounts of their involvement with their sisters are brief, yet meaningful in the context of the broader fourth-century opening to family within the religious life. Antony's biographer, the bishop Athanasius of Alexandria, reported that before Antony adopted the religious life, he ensured his sister's future, placing her with a group of religious women.[44] Pachomius's biographer provides more details concerning the saint's spiritual concern for his sister, who was identified in the *Bohairic Life* as Maria. Although Pachomius refused to see Maria when she first visited him in the desert, he later installed her as the head of a female community that was twinned with his male one.[45] Guaranteeing the viability of the new female community, he sent brothers to build a women's monastery across the river from the men's house, selected an old man named Apa Peter to provide for the women's spiritual needs, and furnished them with a copy of his *Rule* for monks, providing the earliest evidence of men's spiritual and material care for women in the monastic life.[46] Pachomius's community maintained close ties with Maria's foundation, although the two were physically separate: according to Palladius, when one of the women died, her body was brought to the male house and buried in the men's own tombs.[47]

The presence of sisters alongside brothers in these early monastic accounts was not coincidental, but should be seen as intrinsic to the rise of monasticism. Indeed, when monasticism was carried to the West during the early fifth century, the association of brothers and sisters went too. John Cassian (d. 430/435), who introduced monasticism to southern Gaul, devoted attention to both sexes, establishing a monastery for men as well as one for women—reputedly for his sister—near Marseilles.[48] During the following century, Caesarius of Arles likewise founded communities for both women and men, placing his sister, Caesaria, as abbess over the female house.[49] Caesarius's involvement with his sister is well documented, and formed a central part of his own spiritual life. In addition to writing a letter to her on the religious life (*Vereor*), Caesarius penned a rule for the women of her community (*Regula sanctarum virginum*).[50] His connection to the female house was strong, despite the physical separation that he required between men and women.[51] Indeed, Caesarius envisioned himself in death not among the men, but among the women. When he died, he was buried in the women's basilica, alongside Caesaria.[52]

Further to the west, in Spain, the brothers Leander and Isidore (d. 636)—both bishops of Seville—maintained similarly warm relations with their sister, Florentina, a woman professed to the religious life in North Africa. Leander, who had been a monk before being elevated to the bishopric, composed a rule to guide Florentina in her religious life (*De institutione virginum et contemptu mundi*), while Isidore dedicated his *De fide catholica contra Judaeos* to her.[53] A Carolingian manuscript of Isidore's work, possibly from Corbie, includes a depiction of him presenting the text to Florentina. An inscription records his dedication: "My sister Florentina, accept the codex that I have happily composed for you. Amen."[54] An early ninth-century epitaph notes that Isidore was buried with Florentina and Leander, a detail that—although it cannot be confirmed from contemporary sources—conforms to the example of shared burial offered by Caesarius (and many others).[55]

Benedict of Nursia and Scholastica

The presence of sisters alongside holy men within the early monastic life is remarkable, given the early Christian repudiation of family. There was, as we have seen, little biblical precedent for close ties with biological kin within early Christianity, which privileged spiritual over biological kinship.[56] Admittedly, in many of the instances discussed above, the sister of a holy man was a shadowy figure—present in the sources, yet rarely richly drawn (Macrina, who was a saint in her own right, is a notable exception). But this fact, too, is interesting and suggests that biographers went to considerable efforts to emphasize a male saint's fraternal care for his sister, mentioning it even when the evidence was thin, or lacking. Unlike other male-female relationships in the religious life, which were consistently problematic for observers, the sibling bond emerges as one that biographers intentionally and repeatedly promoted.[57] Of course, not all male saints were associated with a sister (even a shadowy one), and some holy men avoided their female relatives, like the novice who refused to touch even his own mother.[58] Yet the persistence with which sisters appear in the recorded *lives* of early monastic men is indicative of the role of family in the construction of male spirituality and the evolution of monastic life. The fact that evidence for a sister's very existence is often thin raises the interesting possibility that she may even have been fabricated.[59] If that was so, we must ask why men would have invented pious sisters, when medieval sources generally deny the interaction of holy men with women altogether.

The example of St. Benedict of Nursia is instructive in considering these questions. Like many of the male heroes of early monasticism, Benedict was associated with a sister, Scholastica, from the late sixth century. However, evidence for Scholastica's life is thin: she appears only in Gregory the Great's *life* of Benedict, and then in only two of its chapters. Still, her presence in the *life* launched Scholastica to sainthood and provided the basis for the belief, current by the ninth century, that she and Benedict had been twins.[60] By the central Middle Ages, Scholastica was celebrated as a saint in her own right and was depicted alongside Benedict, both as his partner in the religious life and as the patron of female monasticism. The *Codex Benedictus*, produced at Monte Cassino in the eleventh century, commemorated Scholastica (together with Benedict and Maurus) as a saint of the community.[61]

According to Gregory's short account, Scholastica had been dedicated to the religious life as a child, yet maintained contact with her famous brother, visiting him once a year at a house not far from Monte Cassino. On the particular occasion that Gregory reported, Scholastica and Benedict had spent a day together in holy conversation when dusk began to fall. Realizing that Benedict would soon leave her, Scholastica begged him to stay the night. When he refused, Scholastica began to pray, weeping as she did. As though mirroring her tears, the skies burst open with a torrential rain, preventing Benedict from returning to his monastery (a scene depicted in the *Codex Benedictus*; Figure 18). He chastised her, but Scholastica defended herself, invoking God as her advocate: "When I appealed to you, you would not listen to me. So I turned to my God and He heard my prayer. Leave now if you can. Leave me here and go back to your monastery." Resigning himself to the delay, Benedict spent the night in a holy vigil with his sister. Three days later, Scholastica died, and Benedict sent for her body, which he put in his own tomb at Monte

Figure 18. Scholastica and Benedict. *Codex Benedictus*, Biblioteca Apostolica
Vaticana, Vat. lat. 1202, fol. 72v.

Cassino. As Gregory concluded, "The bodies of these two were now to share
a common resting place, just as in life their souls had always been one in
God."[62]

The formulaic nature of Gregory's account—the brother momentarily
rejecting the sister (as Pachomius had initially rejected Maria) and the burial
in a shared tomb (Damasus and Caesarius, as well as hints of Pachomius and
Ambrose)—call into question the story's authenticity. To be sure, medieval

hagiography was a formulaic enterprise, in which past exemplars were routinely repurposed. However, the possibility that Benedict did not have a sister or, more to the point, that Scholastica (if she existed) was not his biological sister,[63] raises some important questions. First, if Benedict did not have a blood sister, and there was no historical person named Scholastica, why did Gregory see the need to invent her? Second, if Scholastica did exist, as a companion, or spiritual "sister," but not as a biological sister to Benedict, why did Gregory imply that she was his blood sister—and why was she later revered as his twin?[64]

Answers to these questions point to the centrality of the sibling bond as an established and clearly privileged form of engagement between men and women within the medieval religious life by the late sixth century. The second question is straightforward enough: as we have already seen, relationships between brothers and sisters who were blood relatives were permissible within the early monastic life, even as relationships between unrelated men and women were typically suspect. In a letter to a local magistrate, Symmachus, Gregory himself advised that priests should not live with women "except of course a mother, sister, or wife, whose chastity should be preserved."[65] If Benedict had maintained a close friendship with a pious but unrelated woman, Gregory may have chosen to describe her as his sister (his *soror*) in order to emphasize the closeness and the blamelessness of their bond.

The answer to the first question is more complex. If Benedict had neither a sister nor a close female spiritual companion, why might Gregory have chosen to depict him with one? One answer may be that by the time Gregory was writing carefully prescribed contact with a holy woman—ideally a sister—had become an important element in the spiritual portfolio of a holy man. By this time, many families were Christianized, and therefore less likely to distract or dissuade believers, as they may have done in the early church. Indeed, promoting biological family in the medieval religious life may have served to strengthen and expand the faith, encouraging family sponsorship of monasteries and churches. As Jane Tibbetts Schulenburg has proposed, the presence of a sister added "gender symmetry" to the male religious life, an idea that underscores the importance of both male and female elements within religion.[66] Gregory's emphasis on Scholastica as a spiritual leader may have been inspired by Leander of Seville, whose close relationship with his sister, Florentina, was likely known to Gregory. Leander was Gregory's direct contemporary and close friend; the two met in Constantinople in around 580, and maintained contact in the years following, exchanging long letters and sometimes gifts.[67] Gregory certainly knew Leander's spiritual writings, and he may have adopted from Leander a sense of the spiritual value and legitimacy of brother-sister spiritual relations.

Gregory's decision to feature Scholastica in his account of Benedict's *life*, and to paint her, at least temporarily, as the spiritual superior in the relationship, perpetuated the ideal of the brother-sister bond, mediating the late antique paradigm of sibling intimacy to later medieval audiences. Although Scholastica is only briefly attested in Gregory's *life* of Benedict, her fame grew in concert with that of her saintly brother, whose *Rule* ensured that he was known, and venerated, throughout Western Christendom. Scholastica, too, became widely known in the century after Gregory's death. Her cult spread, and her relics even became the goal of acquisitive monks. Sometime between 690 and 707, monks from the French monastery of Fleury reportedly traveled to Monte Cassino, uncovered the tomb shared by Benedict and Scholastica, and retrieved the relics of both.[68] A mid-ninth-century account written by Adrevald of Fleury adds that the Fleury group had been accompanied by monks from Le Mans, whose specific goal was to recover Scholastica's relics. Although the Fleury monks succeeded in retrieving the relics of both saints, the Le Mans contingent ultimately secured some relics of Scholastica and founded a new monastery in her honor to house them—solidifying her medieval cult.[69]

Gregory's *life* of Benedict, with its account of the saint's close spiritual relationship with Scholastica, was "one of the most widely read and remembered books in monastic culture," as Mary Carruthers comments.[70] The model of sibling engagement that Gregory promoted in this work proved enormously influential, expanding upon earlier models of saintly siblings (like Pachomius and Maria, Caesarius and Caesaria, and Leander and Florentina), while also establishing a pattern of brother-sister spiritual care and devotion that placed sibling relations at the heart of the monastic life—a striking achievement, given that Benedict's *Rule* made no mention of women.[71] Through Gregory's *life*, Scholastica became known and venerated as a saint in her own right, a woman whose loving and tearful prayers were viewed as spiritually decisive, overcoming even the wishes of her pious brother. Writers in the centuries after Gregory—men like Aldhelm, Bede (d. 735), Paul the Deacon (who spent the decade before his death in 799 as a monk at Monte Cassino), Bertharius (abbot of Monte Cassino, d. c. 883), and Alberic of Monte Cassino (fl. 1065–1100)—composed texts celebrating Scholastica.[72] A further measure of Scholastica's expanding cult is the adoption of her name by nuns at their profession, as at

Barking in the seventh century.[73] By the later Middle Ages, Scholastica was venerated in her own right; an independent *life* appears in the late thirteenth-century South English Legendary.[74]

As paradigmatic saintly siblings, Benedict and Scholastica were celebrated for their close spiritual ties, both in life and in death. Sermons, hymns, and poems presented them together as models of holiness in the monastic life. Given their spiritual prominence, it is surprising how little evidence exists for their exemplarity in later centuries as authorization for other opposite-sex pious siblings. Some pious siblings were likened to Benedict and Scholastica, such as the eighth-century saint Hiltrude, who lived in a cell attached to the monastery where her brother Guntard was abbot. Hiltrude's biographer described the two as another Scholastica and Benedict—and also, notably, as another Jerome and Eustochium.[75] However, for the most part, Benedict and Scholastica were not cited as models, whether in a defensive mode or as positive exemplars for pious siblings. The contrast with both John and Mary, and Jerome and Eustochium, pairs who were regularly invoked when questions concerning the propriety of a man's spiritual relationship with religious women were raised, is notable. Benedict was central to medieval religious life; his absence from the rhetorical arsenal of nuns' priests demands explanation. It cannot be that his relationship with Scholastica was unknown or irrelevant, but rather the opposite: the model that these two encapsulated—of pious opposite-sex siblings interacting in a chaste, shared religious life—had gained such swift and wide acceptance in the centuries after Gregory's death that it was not necessary to invoke them explicitly.

The success of the saintly sibling model meant that both criticism and defense were rare. Medieval audiences assumed that Benedict's relationship with Scholastica had been pure and spiritually motivated as a function of their kinship—an assumption that was tacitly extended to include other brothers and sisters in the religious life. But the effect of Benedict's model went beyond the presumption that kin relations were pure. Medieval audiences also came to assume that providing spiritual care for pious female kin (and above all, a man's sister) was a marker of male sanctity: Benedict's relationship with Scholastica solidified the expectation that fraternal care could (and should) form part of the male religious life. Indeed, Benedict's care for Scholastica was often embellished beyond the bare bones of what Gregory had reported, broadening the spiritual implications of their relationship. According to Abelard, who cited Benedict and Scholastica as a model for monastic organization (and not, notably, as a defense against critics), Benedict's fraternal concern for

Scholastica shaped relations between their two monasteries, which Abelard then claimed were linked by spiritual care and oversight.[76] In Abelard's view, men's provision of spiritual care for women was one manifestation of the pious sibling relationship, in which not just individuals, but ultimately also male and female houses, could be joined by kinship ties.

Mutual Advantage in the Spiritual Life: The Twelfth Century

By the middle of the twelfth century, when Elisabeth of Schönau recorded her visions concerning St. Ursula and the virgin martyrs, the idea that men in the religious life (both monks and secular priests) could interact blame-lessly with female kin was firmly established. In 1123, the First Lateran Coun-cil forbad priests to live with wives or concubines, but nevertheless allowed them to live with female kin, explicitly invoking the precedent set at Nicaea.[77] Elisabeth herself maintained a close relationship with her brother Ekbert, even prompting him to join her in the religious life at the double monastery of Schönau, where he served as her secretary and aide until her death.[78] Indeed, Ekbert's arrival at Schönau in 1155 may have had some role in spurring Elisabeth's interest in the spiritual legitimacy of kinship. Ekbert certainly worked with her on the textual shaping and publication of the *Liber revelationum*, with its assumption that male-female kinship was a legitimate basis for spiritual com-panionship.[79] The larger context of Elisabeth's visions—Cologne at the mid-twelfth century—suggests a further potential influence on the work. As we saw in Chapter 2, the archbishop of Cologne, Arnold von Wied, maintained close ties with his sisters in the religious life, partnering with Hadwig in the foundation at Schwarzrheindorf. Ekbert had been a canon at Saint Cassius in Bonn—directly across the Rhine from Arnold von Wied's chapel at Schwarzrheindorf—before joining Elisabeth at Schönau. Arnold's close ties with his sisters in the religious life, which were showcased at the dedication of Schwarzrheindorf in 1151 and in the fresco of Arnold with Hadwig in the apse of the upper church (Figure 3), may have influenced Ekbert's decision to support Elisabeth—a decision that meant abandoning an almost certain path to ecclesiastical advancement in the footsteps of his maternal great-uncle Ekbert, bishop of Münster.[80]

The sibling model was forged during the formative centuries of Chris-tianity and of monasticism in the West.[81] It is therefore not surprising that when Elisabeth reflected on the role of kinship in the religious life, she did so in relation to St. Ursula, a woman whose martyrdom was located in the legendary past, before the full Christianization of Germany. In Elisabeth's imagining, the mixed-sex group that comprised the martyrs of Cologne— brothers and sisters, cousins of both sexes, and uncles with their nieces—was bound together by kinship. Elisabeth may have been inspired by the texts of early monasticism and the prevalence in them of sisters, yet she added significantly to existing motifs, reporting the mutual spiritual advantage that the martyrs derived from their shared religious life.[82] Many of the male martyrs had been bishops, as Elisabeth's saintly visitors told her. These men had furnished the virgin martyrs with the sacraments during the course of their travels, providing a central justification for their presence: women needed priests to celebrate the Mass for them.[83] Yet, as Elisabeth noted, the women were not alone in profiting from the arrangement: the men, too, benefited from their proximity to holy women, drawing inspiration from their courage and devotion, and ultimately earning sainthood alongside them. As Caesarius explained, Verena "strengthened me to undergo martyrdom and I, seeing her steadfastness in agony, suffered together with her."[84] In Elisabeth's visions, it was Verena and not Caesarius who was the spiritual leader in the relationship.

The presumption that the kin relationship could be mutually advantageous marks an important development in relations between religious women and ordained men. As we saw in previous chapters, some ordained men—inspired by John the Evangelist and Jerome—came to see the provision of spiritual care for women as a legitimate spiritual service, one that could even draw them closer to Christ as his "friends." Yet the rhetorical models that they adopted—which were centered on Christ as the bridegroom and nuns as his brides—did not acknowledge that the male-female relationship could be intrinsically spiritually beneficial. However, the sibling relationship, as it evolved over the course of the centuries, provided just such a possibility: a model of spiritual engagement from which both a sister and her brother were seen to benefit.

The spiritual advantages of the sibling relationship are, to be sure, most readily apparent from the standpoint of religious women. Ordained brothers contributed to the spiritual lives of their sisters, providing material support, advice, and also priestly services. Indeed, the earliest textual evidence for the provision of pastoral care to monastic women appeared in the context of the sibling relationship: Pachomius's provision of Apa Peter to care for the women of his sister's community, to be their "father," and to "preach frequently to them on the Scriptures for their soul's salvation."[85] As the *Bohairic Life* reports, Apa Peter took up residence on the women's side of the river, becoming the

earliest known resident male spiritual guide and guardian for nuns. During
the eleventh and twelfth centuries, religious women found that ordained male
relatives were often the most consistent and reliable source for spiritual care.
Elisabeth of Schönau's situation—living in a double monastery alongside a
brother who supported her religious life and sometimes celebrated the Mass
for her—was not, in fact, unusual.[86] Elisabeth's contemporary, Hildegard of
Bingen, also relied for a time on ordained kinsmen to provide care in the religious life. When she experienced difficulties in securing priests from Disibodenberg, Hildegard appealed to Pope Alexander III, who assigned her nephew
Wezelin (then provost of St. Andrew in Cologne) to resolve the matter.[87] Some
years later, facing renewed difficulties, Hildegard received support from her
brother Hugo, a canon from Mainz who came to Rupertsberg to provide care
for the nuns (among them another one of his sisters, Clementia).[88]

While women often looked to ordained kinsmen for spiritual support,
the benefits of the sibling relationship were not one-sided. Sisters provided
brothers with spiritual encouragement, often serving as the spiritual leader in
the relationship—as Scholastica had in Gregory the Great's brief account, or
Macrina in Gregory of Nyssa's *life*.[89] Men in turn recognized deep piety in
their sisters, often admitting a spiritual imbalance in the relationship from
which they felt that they stood to benefit. Leander of Seville, for instance,
described himself as spiritually dependent on Florentina. Encouraging her to
maintain a life of sexual purity, Leander made clear his expectation that he
would receive an eternal reward through her. "Although I do not have within
myself what I wish you to achieve," Leander wrote, praising Florentina's
virginity and hinting at his own unchasteness, "You are my shelter in Christ;
you, dearest sister, are my security." In Leander's view, Florentina's power
derived from her status as the bride of Christ—a status in which he could not
share, except vicariously. Placing his whole confidence in Florentina, Leander
urged her to intercede on his behalf with her heavenly bridegroom. As he
wrote, laying bare his own hope for salvation through Florentina, Christ would
not "allow to perish a brother whose sister He has espoused."[90]

Even more than their early monastic counterparts, men who provided for
their sisters' material and spiritual needs during the twelfth century expected
to benefit from the relationship. This sort of spiritual exchange is clear in
Ekbert's relationship with Elisabeth. Although he was her superior in ecclesiastical matters, having been educated in Paris and ordained to the priesthood,
Elisabeth was unquestionably the spiritual leader in the relationship. It was
Elisabeth's visionary gift that prompted Ekbert's move from Saint Cassius

to Schönau, where he served as Elisabeth's secretary and aide, recording her visions (a task he executed with some editorial license). Ekbert's oversight may have provided Elisabeth with a degree of protection from potential critics. For Ekbert, however, the advantages of the relationship were equally, if not more, significant. Through Elisabeth, Ekbert believed that he had access to theological truths, which she obtained in visionary dialogues, primarily with the Virgin Mary. Ekbert turned Elisabeth's visionary experiences to his own advantage, priming her with questions on delicate doctrinal matters, which he then encouraged her to present to her heavenly visitors.[91] Indeed, Ekbert was so fascinated by Elisabeth's visionary spirituality that he sought similar religious expression himself, asking his sister on her deathbed to intercede on his behalf so that he could inherit her visionary gift.[92]

In addition to these tangible benefits, Ekbert profited from Elisabeth's spiritual advice. It was most likely she who had prompted him to enter the religious life and who encouraged him to seek ordination.[93] On one occasion, Elisabeth comforted a priest (possibly Ekbert) who had accidentally spilled the consecrated wine at the Eucharist.[94] After her death, Ekbert (who became abbot of Schönau in 1166) described Elisabeth as "that chosen lamp of heavenly light, that virgin outstanding and honored by the abundant grace of God, that splendid gem of our monastery, the leader of our virginal company." Reflecting on her spiritual influence on him, Ekbert effused that "She bought me forth into the light of untried newness; she led me to the intimate ministry of Jesus my Lord; with her honeyed mouth she used to offer me divine consolation and instruction from heaven and made my heart taste the first fruits of the sweetness hidden from the saints in heaven."[95]

Ekbert's sense of his sister's spiritual superiority is echoed in the contemporary writings of Aelred of Rievaulx. In the *Rule* that Aelred penned for his sister's religious life, he recalled their youth together, bemoaning his past sins and reminding her of her spiritual care for him: "you mourned for me and upbraided me often when we were young and after we had grown up."[96] Even though Aelred had attained the abbatial dignity by the time of writing, he nonetheless continued to depict his sister as his spiritual superior. Commenting that "we have run the same course, we were alike in everything: the same father begot us, the same womb bore us and gave us birth," Aelred contrasted his own life of sin to the holy example of his sister, who had remained continent while he "freely abandoned [himself] to all that is base."[97] "O sister," he wrote: "How much more happy is the man whose ship, full of merchandise and loaded with riches, is brought to a safe homecoming by favorable winds than he who suffers shipwreck and barely escapes death with the loss of all?"[98]

The belief that women had the potential to surpass men in their piety and the intimacy of their relationship to Christ shaped the interactions of ordained men with pious kinswomen, adding to the idea that brothers *ought* to attend to their sisters' needs a sense of the real benefits to men in providing care. Leander and Aelred were explicit about their sense of their sisters' spiritual superiority. For Leander, Florentina was his "safety" and his "security"; for Aelred, his sister was a spiritual support, who remained pure as he wallowed in sin. Peter Damian (who had been orphaned and was raised by his beloved sister, Rodelinda) wrote in a similar vein to his sisters, Rodelinda and Sufficia, expressing his confidence in their spiritual power: "I have every confidence that through your merits . . . I too will be absolved from my sins and restored to innocence of life."[99] In a rare biblical reference to the spiritual potential of the sibling bond, Peter reminded the women that Lazarus had been brought back to life by the prayers of his sisters, suggesting that they, too, should devote themselves to prayer. Men such as these celebrated their sisters as spiritual superiors, despite the fact that these women could never attain the priesthood, as the men themselves, despite their admitted flaws, could. To modern ears, the praises of these men may ring hollow, offering rhetorically what was not possible practically: ecclesiastically sanctioned authority in the religious life. Yet men's spiritual esteem for their pious sisters is equally evident in the actions of monks and priests who served their sisters spiritually without either reporting their experiences in writing, or lavishing their sisters with praise.

Gregory, an ordained monk at Saint Albans and the brother of Christina of Markyate, is a good example. Like early monastic sisters of pious men, Gregory appears only as a shadowy figure in the *life* of his more celebrated saintly sibling. Even so, Christina's relationship with Gregory was close; her biographer comments that she "cherished" him "with extraordinary affection."[100] Gregory returned her affection; it was his practice to visit Christina at Markyate, to stay with her, and, while he was there, to say Mass for her community. As an ordained monk, Gregory held ecclesiastical authority, yet there is no question that Christina was the spiritual superior in their relationship, interceding for her brother and mediating heavenly messages to him. Christina's intercession for Gregory, and also for another brother named Simon, who appears as a witness to a Markyate charter, is implied in the St. Albans Psalter, which includes obits for both men.[101]

Gregory's cameo appearance in Christina's *life* confirms both the potential benefits that a brother in the religious life could derive from his saintly sister and the very real concern of a brother to provide for his sister's spiritual needs. Though less spiritually mature than Christina, Gregory was nonetheless able to furnish her with a central spiritual benefit: the Mass. As his example suggests, the pastoral care of a woman by a man related to her—here a brother, although elsewhere a nephew or uncle—raised few suspicions of wrongdoing. Christina's biographer reports Gregory's involvement with his sister openly and with none of the defensive language that he marshaled elsewhere in connection with Christina's friendship with Abbot Geoffrey. With permission from his abbot, Gregory even stayed overnight at Markyate, a feat that few monks would have dared (and that even Benedict had resisted initially).

The catalogue of eleventh- and twelfth-century brothers and sisters is lengthy. It includes, among others, Burchard of Worms (d. 1025), who nourished his sister with "brotherly love" and prompted her conversion to the religious life;[102] Hugh of Cluny, who founded Marcigny with his brother Geoffrey II of Semur, no doubt with his mother, Aremburgis, and his sister, Ermengardis, in mind;[103] the reformer Vital of Savigny (d. 1122), who, with his brother, founded Abbaye Blanche, where their sister Adelina would become abbess;[104] Anselm of Canterbury, who guided and supported his sister Richeza in her marriage and, later, widowhood;[105] Bernard of Clairvaux, who encouraged his sister Humbeline to adopt the religious life as a nun at Jully;[106] Richard of Springiersbach, who founded the Augustinian community at Andernach for his sister Tenxwind;[107] the brother of Abbot Gervase of Arrouaise, who served as prior at his sisters' community of Harrold in England;[108] and possibly also Peter of Blois, who wrote a letter of spiritual advice to his *dilectissima soror* (although not *germana*), Christiana.[109] In each case, the brother provided care for his sister, whether by founding a monastery for her, serving as her priest or as provost of her community, or writing letters or other texts to guide her in the religious life. Often, concern for a sister formed part of a larger phenomenon that included a man's entire family—as with Bernard of Clairvaux, whose conversion was a family affair involving several of his brothers and kinsmen. The conversion of so many men could have serious implications for their wives; indeed, when Bernard's kinsmen converted, many of their wives entered the religious life at Jully, alongside his sister Humbeline. The history of Jully confirms the significance of family ties in the religious life: before Jully came into being as a priory associated with the "men's" house at Molesmes, the Jully women had simply lived at Molesmes. Notable among them was the sister of the reforming abbot, Robert of Molesmes (d. 1111), a woman by the name of Odelina.[110]

Families in the Religious Life

Thus far, this chapter has focused primarily on sibling relations. Yet spiritual relationships between uncles and nieces, cousins, sons and mothers, fathers and daughters, and even (former) husbands and wives were also common. Indeed, as Bernard of Clairvaux's example suggests, entire families sometimes converted to the religious life as a group, entering neighboring communities. Women who converted individually might even live alongside kinsmen in communities generally designated as "male." As we saw in Chapter 1, women could be present near (if not "in") men's houses as relatives of the monks. At Bec in the late eleventh century, the founder's mother, Heloise, lived along-side the men.[111] During Anselm's time at Bec, several other women joined the community when their husbands became monks. The monastery's chronicle reports that "in the time of Abbot Anselm three noble matrons gave them-selves in subjection to Bec: Basilia wife of Hugh of Gournay, her niece Amfrida, and Eva wife of William Crispin."[112] These women were venerated as "mothers" within the community. According to Herman of Tournai, a similar situation unfolded at the monastery of Saint Martin in the late elev-enth century, where both of his parents and at least one of his brothers made their profession.[113] Nor was Herman's family unique: he reports that "Henry, an extremely wealthy man, together with his wife, Bertha, his as-yet unweaned son, John, and two daughters, Trasberga and Iulitta, entered the monastic life in almost the same fashion."[114] Ultimately the number of women who con-verted at Saint Martin meant that they required their own community, which the abbot Odo of Orléans founded and placed under the authority of a woman named Eremburg—his sister.[115]

Families during the central Middle Ages could embrace the religious life together, entering monasteries either as nuclear families with small children or as kin groupings comprised of adult children, extending the kinship ties that existed between professed siblings to encompass entire kin groups.[116] Although saints' *lives* from the period sometimes present family ties as an obstacle to the religious life (in keeping with early hagiographic models), the reality was that family became more, and not less, important with the late eleventh- and twelfth-century shift away from child oblation toward adult conversion.[117] This shift meant that new recruits to the religious life had lived many years in the world and so brought with them into the monastery not just strong ties to family members, but also related obligations. From the cloister, monks and nuns continued to concern themselves with their families—with their mothers and fathers, brothers and sisters, husbands and wives, and even children.

Narrative sources provide a number of examples of monks and nuns who maintained close ties to family members, both within the monastery and beyond it. Elisabeth of Schönau was close with several siblings, in addition to Ekbert. When she died, she was surrounded by what may have been the last remaining members of her nuclear family, two of them at least "from afar."[118] Likewise, Christina of Markyate recreated at Markyate and Saint Albans a household in miniature, in which at least two of her siblings shared the religious life she had chosen. When her brother Gregory died, both Christina and her sister Margaret, who was also a nun at Markyate, were present at the burial.[119] As we have already seen, Hildegard had at least one sister with her at Rupertsberg; their brother Hugo served for a time as the women's provost. At Sempringham, Sharon Elkins comments that "three nuns were sisters, their uncle was a member of the monastery, and their parents were affiliated, as part of the 'fraternity.'"[120] Based on her study of nuns who had relatives within the religious life in the later Middle Ages, Marilyn Oliva similarly notes that several brothers "remembered their sisters in their wills, which indicates at the very least that the male clerics had not forgotten about their monastic sisters."[121] Far from renouncing family and the purported dangers of the flesh, these examples demonstrate that medieval monastic men and women maintained close ties with blood kin, despite their entrance into the new, spiritualized "family" of the monastery. The blurring of spiritual and biological kin that resulted is most clear in a comment made by Bernard of Clairvaux's biographer that Humbeline "proved to be a true sister of the holy monks of Clairvaux not only in the flesh but also in the spirit."[122] Richard of Springiersbach's sister Tenxwind of Andernach was similarly described as his sister (*germana*) both "in the flesh and in the spirit."[123]

Elisabeth of Schönau's Cologne vision, with its abundance of episcopal uncles providing spiritual care for their saintly nieces, underscores the fact that contact between male and female family members in the religious life quite often occurred within the context of pastoral care. Indeed, some of the period's most interesting literature of spiritual advice for women was composed by male relatives, as in the cases of Peter the Venerable and Osbert of Clare

(d. c. 1158), who wrote for their nieces, Margaret and Pontia, and Margaret and Cecilia, respectively.[124] Peter extended the spiritual reach of kinship beyond the avuncular relationship, encouraging his nieces to remember the "great faith" and "unimaginable fervour of love" of their grandmother (his mother), Raingard, a nun at Marcigny.[125]

One kin relationship did not feature in Elisabeth's visions: that of husband and wife. For obvious reasons, the nuptial relationship was more complicated than relationships based on biological kinship ties. While ties between blood kin were presumed to be sexually pure, married partners were expected to be (or to have been) sexually active. Although many husbands and wives embraced the religious life late in life and renounced married sex, the relationship remained sexually charged for onlookers, who typically doubted that chastity could so neatly displace desire. When Abelard wrote to Heloise, he therefore addressed her almost exclusively in kinship terms that denied or minimized his marriage to her: in his letters, Heloise appears more often as his "sister" and the "bride" of Christ, than as his former wife. For Heloise, such kinship metaphors lacked force. When she claimed Abelard's spiritual and material support, she did so on the basis of their earthly marriage bond and the obligation it had created. "Consider the close tie by which you have bound yourself to me," she wrote, "and repay the debt you owe a whole community of devoted women by discharging it the more devotedly to her who is yours alone."[126] In her view, the marriage bond joined her to Abelard, and would continue to join them even from within the cloister.

Of the many reasons for which Abelard has been deemed "unique" and "exceptional" in his writings about religious women, his marriage to Heloise is surely the most significant. The idea that a priest who served women spiritually and was the effective founder of their community could previously have been sexually involved with one of the nuns (let alone the abbess) has struck modern readers as improbable, confirming Abelard's presumed exceptionality. And yet, the medieval evidence shows that husbands and wives did embrace the religious life together, sometimes entering the same monastery, or houses that were closely associated and geographically proximate. In his *Rule*, Abelard actively encouraged this sort of pairing of male and female houses. As he wrote, "whoever wishes to be converted along with a mother, sister, daughter, or any other woman for whom he is responsible will be able to find complete consolation there, and the two monasteries should be joined by a greater affection of charity and a concern for each other the more closely their members are united by some kinship or affinity."[127]

Although Abelard did not directly acknowledge the possibility that husbands and wives might embrace religion together, they often did. Examples like Ralph and Mainsendis, and Henry and Bertha, couples who converted at Tournai, show that husbands and wives could remake themselves as chaste spiritual "brothers" and "sisters." According to Gilo's *life* of Hugh of Cluny, former husbands and wives who entered Cluny/Marcigny played "twin" roles, implying that former spouses could assume the spiritual privileges of blood kinship.[128] Like Abelard, some husbands were founders of communities for their wives, and some even served as priests—becoming spiritual "fathers" to their former wives. Jerome's *life* of Malchus had allowed for this possibility, presenting Malchus as his wife's guide in the religious life. Reginald's twelfth-century rewriting of the *life* highlighted this point, presenting the two explicitly as a "monk" and a "nun."

To be sure, Malchus was a legendary (and chaste) figure, whose example serves as an indication of what was deemed praiseworthy in the religious life, rather than as evidence of religious practice or experience. Yet there were medieval men who entered the religious life with wives, who subsequently became their spiritual "sisters." Eckenbert of Worms (d. 1132) offers one example.[129] Eckenbert was married when he converted to the religious life; he renounced the world together with his wife, Richlindis.[130] The two began by embracing charity and asceticism, but ultimately left their home in Worms for a place outside the city, where Eckenbert built "a few little houses made of rods and mud." Most interesting for the purposes of this book is the fact that this early religious community was centered on Richlindis and the women who joined her. According to his biographer, Eckenbert lived nearby, "in a little house set apart from the habitations of the women," devoting himself to prayer, reading, and contemplation.[131] After some while, Eckenbert secured a place to found a community for men, at Frankenthal. Yet he remained close to Richlindis for some time, delegating the task of building the new male community to trusted helpers.[132] When the two houses were at last established, the women's community—which remained linked to the men's house—became known as "lesser Frankenthal." Richlindis, who outlived Eckenbert by some years, served as *magistra* of the women's community.

Eckenbert's case was not so very unusual, especially among noble converts who often embraced the religious life as a kin group.[133] The foundation of Arnstein, a Premonstratensian community on the Lahn, also had its origins in the joint conversion of a husband and wife.[134] In 1139, Count Ludwig III of Arnstein transformed his castle into a religious community; his wife

Guda became a hermit nearby. Both Ludwig and Guda died at Arnstein. At Cluny/Marcigny, the conversion of Hugh's family during the latter part of the eleventh century fueled the growth of the community. Following the entrance of Hugh's mother, Aremburgis, his three sisters, and several of his nieces, Hugh's brother Geoffrey II of Semur also embraced the religious life. Some years later, Geoffrey III of Semur followed, adopting the religious life at Cluny/Marcigny together with his wife Ermengard and their three daughters: Adelaide, Agnès, and Cécile. While Geoffrey's son, Renaud, later became abbot of Vézelay, Geoffrey himself was made prior of Marcigny—putting him in a position of leadership over his own former wife and daughters.[135]

Conclusion: The Dangers of Family Life

In this chapter, I have argued that relationships between biologically related women and men were typically exempt from suspicion within the medieval religious life, despite early Christian warnings against biological family and consistent anxieties regarding relations between the sexes. While the evidence points overwhelmingly to the acceptance of kin bonds, a current of suspicion nevertheless remained. Elisabeth of Schönau's otherworldly visitor Verena was quick to point out that among the 11,000 virgin martyrs of Cologne the men had kept apart from the saintly women, joining them only on Sundays, and then for the sole purpose of providing pastoral care.[136] The eighth-century Anglo-Saxon saint Guthlac was famed for having refused physical contact with his sister, Pega, explaining on his deathbed that "I have in this life avoided her presence so that in eternity we may see one another in the presence of our Father amid eternal joys."[137] The twelfth-century *Guthlac Roll* shows Pega as being present only after Guthlac's death, reinforcing his celebrated purity and separation from her in life.[138] The desire to escape temptation by avoiding even a beloved sister was shared by other men, who chose not to have contact with female family members. Temptation was real, as Jean Gerson (d. 1429) would acknowledge several centuries later. Having composed a series of letters and treatises for his six sisters, in which he encouraged them spiritually and provided guidelines for their religious lives, Gerson nevertheless admitted that he had suffered from carnal thoughts in their presence.[139]

The danger that even relations between brothers and sisters could be tainted by sexual scandal was underlined in the biblical story of Amnon and Thamar, who were half-siblings through their father, King David (2 Samuel

13:7–16). Amnon, burning with illicit desire for his sister Thamar, feigned illness in order to lure her into his bedchamber, where he raped her before throwing her out of his house in disgust. The story of Amnon and Thamar was not lost on medieval audiences, who recognized that any relationship could be polluted with unchastity. Thus although Jerome had encouraged the mother and daughter in Gaul to look to their kinsman for spiritual support, he warned Eustochium that "near relationship is no safeguard," reminding her that "Amnon burned with illicit passion for his sister Tamar."[140] The seventh-century Spanish abbot and, later, archbishop, Fructuosus of Braga likewise invoked Amnon and Thamar, warning his monastic audience against contact with women, even those women related to them: "That none may assume that his chastity is safe in the presence of a woman related to him, let him remember how Thamar was corrupted by her brother Amnon when he pretended to be ill."[141] In the ninth century, Pope Nicholas I cited Amnon and Thamar as evidence that the cohabitation of women and men—even those related by blood— could give rise to lechery.[142] In the early thirteenth century, Gerald of Wales reiterated this caution, reminding his clerical audience that, although men vowed to continence were permitted to live with female relatives, they should avoid temptation, since "Thamar was corrupted by her own brother Aman." As Gerald wrote, "We have even heard of certain priests who, at the instigation of the ancient enemy and because of the occasion and convenience afforded by living together, have indulged in detestable concubinage with their nieces, their sisters, and even with their own mothers!"[143] Recognizing the danger, several early medieval church councils had warned priests not to welcome female family members in their homes, even though the tradition established at Nicaea explicitly allowed familial cohabitation.[144]

Incest fears were evidently real enough, yet interpretations of Amnon and Thamar did not always emphasize sexual temptation between biological siblings. Other interpretations were possible. An early thirteenth-century moralized Bible highlights the contemporary concern with clerical immorality, presenting Amnon not as a lecherous brother intent on the seduction of his sister, but rather as a corrupt churchman violating a female member of his flock.[145] Interpretative texts make clear the threat posed to female congregants by immoral churchmen. "That Moab [sic: Amnon] feigns sickness to deceive his sister signifies the rich clerics who feign sickness to deceive the good virgins," notes one commentary, while another observes: "That Moab lies with his sister Thamar by force and takes her virginity signifies those bad clerics who take the good virgins and force them and deceive them with gifts and with promises and take their virginity and their goodness."[146] As these texts indicate, concern with the dangers of biological incest could be eclipsed by concern with the more immediate reality of spiritual incest, defined as intercourse between an unchaste churchman and his spiritual child. As Peter Damian had argued, any ordained minister who had sex with a woman committed incest, since "all the children of the church are undoubtedly your children."[147] Given the very real dangers of spiritual incest, the manuscript seems to imply that a woman could be secure in her relationship with her priest *only* if he was, in fact, her biological brother.

The scale of change traced in this chapter from the fourth century (when kin relations first began to be accepted in ascetic circles) to the twelfth century (by which time they were omnipresent) is dramatic. A marker of that change can be seen in legends about St. Augustine. Whereas in his own lifetime Augustine had refused to allow either his sister or any other female relative to stay at his house, by the twelfth century, his relationship with his saintly mother Monica was celebrated as a model of purity.[148] An account of the translation of Monica's relics dating to about 1162 underscores the presumed purity of Augustine's relations with his mother, echoing the confidence that appeared in Elisabeth's visions a decade earlier concerning the purity of opposite-sex kin relations. The account is provided by Walther of Arrouaise, an Augustinian canon who had retrieved the relics from Ostia and brought them to his monastery. Walther reports how Augustine had appeared to the travelers, dressed in episcopal garb and accompanied by a beautiful woman. Recognizing that the presence of his female companion might scandalize his audience, Augustine hastily identified the woman as Monica, claiming his blood ties to her as the reason for his devotion: "Do not be amazed that I love her and honor her, since she is my mother."[149] For Walther, Augustine's appearance served to verify the authenticity of the relics associated with him. Yet, for modern readers the account confirms the central place of kin relations in twelfth-century religious life as a blameless venue for male-female interaction. Augustine's care for Monica was not to amaze or trouble anyone, Walther reported, since (as the saint himself announced), "she is my mother." Of course, as we saw in Chapter 2, the presumed blamelessness of the mother-son bond was central to medieval understandings of John the Evangelist's care for Mary—an important legitimizing motif for nuns' priests. John cared for Mary because Christ had asked him to, but also because both men saw her as their "mother."

CHAPTER 5

Speaking to the Bridegroom: Women and the Power of Prayer

Mercifully spare your monks, I beseech you, O Jesus
—*St. Albans Psalter*

Monks and priests who involved themselves with religious women during the central Middle Ages drew on a rich and well-established rhetoric in order to defend the propriety and legitimacy of relations between the sexes within the religious life. Whether as reformers embracing the *vita apostolica*, as pastors in the tradition of Jerome, or as brothers providing support for their biological sisters, such men found in biblical texts, patristic writings, and early monastic *lives* endorsement for their spiritual involvement with women (as well, on occasion, as the opposite). What may sometimes be less clear is *why* they chose to involve themselves with women to begin with. Why—given the unpleasant suspicions that they faced, the vicious hints of wrongdoing, the inevitable damage to reputation, and the palpable temptations to which they occasionally admit—did men engage spiritually with women? In the case of men who provided care for their biological sisters, a mixture of familial obligation and affection likely provided the initial context and motivation for their spiritual service (although not all brothers were devoted to their sisters, obviously, and some mistreated, avoided, or ignored them). Yet even when brothers devoted themselves to the spiritual care of a religious sister, affection was enhanced by something more compelling: the belief that men, even ordained men, could best access God through a religious woman and that a man's salvation could be gained through her intercession. As Leander of Seville wrote to his sister Florentina in the sixth century, linking her physical purity and intimate relationship to Christ to her presumed intercessory power: "If you are acceptable to God, if you shall lie with Christ upon the chaste couch, if you shall cling to the embrace of Christ with the most fragrant odor of virginity, surely, when you recall your brother's sins, you will obtain the indulgence which you request for that brother's guilt."[1]

The idea that a pious man—and, in Leander's case, one who would later become an archbishop[2]—could benefit through the intercession of a religious woman is striking. By the central Middle Ages, to be sure, individual holy women were often acknowledged as visionaries or prophets whose purportedly unique and direct access to God might be harnessed for the benefit of Christian society broadly.[3] Visionary women like Hildegard of Bingen and Elisabeth of Schönau were approached by men who sought answers to theological or doctrinal questions. However, in Leander's account, it is neither Florentina's saintliness nor her visionary experiences that set her apart. Instead, the presumed efficacy of her prayers was based on Leander's sense of her spiritual potential, rooted in her sex and specifically in her gendered physical purity and status as a bride of Christ. Leander assumed that, as a woman and as a virgin, Florentina was more perfectly positioned to plead with Christ than he (or, frankly, any man, whether virgin or not, ordained or not) could be.

"Spare your monks": Christina of Markyate as Intercessor

An example of female prayerfulness from the middle of the twelfth century confirms this reading of Leander and extends the implications of his confidence in women's prayer beyond the immediate context of the sibling relationship, and, in fact, beyond the explicit context of either virginity or the religious woman as bride of Christ. In Chapters 2 and 3, we saw how men invoked the examples of John the Evangelist and Jerome in order to defend their involvement with women. One woman who appeared in this context was the twelfth-century English holy woman, Christina of Markyate.[4] Christina's friendship with the Benedictine abbot of Saint Albans, Geoffrey de Gorron, exemplifies many of the themes that I explore in this book. Christina and Geoffrey maintained a close spiritual relationship over the course of several years, despite insinuations of wrongdoing and the ever-present threat of scandal. An anonymous *vita* of Christina composed during the 1130s—possibly by Geoffrey's nephew, Robert de Gorron (d. 1166), the sacristan and later abbot of Saint Albans—defines their relationship in by-now familiar terms:

Christina is depicted as Paula to Geoffrey's Jerome, their detractors are likened to critics of the apostles' relations with women, and Christina is reported as having seen herself in a vision, together with Geoffrey, at the foot of the cross, much like Mary and John in the commendation scene.[5] Most important, like many of the men and women examined here, Christina's friendship with Geoffrey inverted traditional and gendered ecclesiastical hierarchies: Geoffrey—an abbot and priest—looked to Christina for spiritual guidance and supported her in the religious life, while Christina—a recluse and later nun—provided Geoffrey with advice and intercession.

Evidence for Christina's prayerful reputation appears in two roughly contemporary sources: first, her *vita*; and second, the St. Albans Psalter.[6] This richly illuminated composite manuscript was produced at Saint Albans between about 1125 and 1140 and is now sometimes known as the Psalter of Christina of Markyate, in recognition of her likely ownership of it.[7] Of the two, Christina's *vita* offers the more direct evidence for her spiritual standing, showcasing her role as an adviser to Geoffrey and a spiritual intermediary between him and God. Indeed, according to her biographer, Christina first came to know Geoffrey through a vision in which she learned that he was about to embark on a course of action that was offensive to God. Although Geoffrey refused to listen when she urged him to abandon his plan, he later relented and subsequently obeyed her in everything. Christina's *vita* located Geoffrey's "true" conversion to the religious life in this moment. As her biographer wrote, Geoffrey "promised to give up everything unlawful, to fulfil her commands, and that he would himself be the patron of her hermitage." In return, Geoffrey earned "her intercession with God."[8] Christina's intercession for Geoffrey subsequently became the thread that drew the *vita* together: prayer was the currency that bound Geoffrey to Christina, and by which she gained his support and obedience. According to the *vita*, she prayed "for him with tears almost all the time," and "in God's presence she would often put him before herself."[9] Twice Christina's prayers delivered Geoffrey from grave illness, and on more than one occasion she advised him on matters related to his abbatial office, even providing him with financial advice.[10]

Like the *vita*, the Psalter features the intercession of a woman, twice showcasing a praying nun (possibly Christina herself, as I explain below). In the first instance, a nun is shown leading four monks to Christ within a capital "C", the initial to Psalm 105 ("Confitemini domino") (Figure 19).[11] In the margin above the initial, a rubric records the woman's intercessory prayer:

Parce tuis queso
monachis clementia ihu;

ONFITEMINI
dno quoniam bonus:
qm in sclm miscdiaci:
Quis loquetur poten
tias dni.auditas
faciet omis laudeses.
Beati qui custodiunt
iudicium:& faciunt
iusticiam in omni tempore.
Memento nri dne inbeneplacito populi tui:
uisita nos insalutari tuo.
Aduidendum inbonitate electors tuors:
adletandum inletitia gentis tue:
ut lauderis cum hereditate tua.
Peccauim' cum patribus nris:
iniuste egim' iniquitatem fecim'.
Patres nri inegypto n intellexerunt
mirabilia tua.nonfuerunt memores
multitudinis miscdie tue.
Et irritauert ascendentes inmare mare
rubru:& saluauit eos ppt nom suum:

Figure 19. Initial, Psalm 105. *St. Albans Psalter. Dombibliothek Hildesheim,
HS St. God. 1* (Property of the Basilica of St. Godehard, Hildesheim), p. 285.

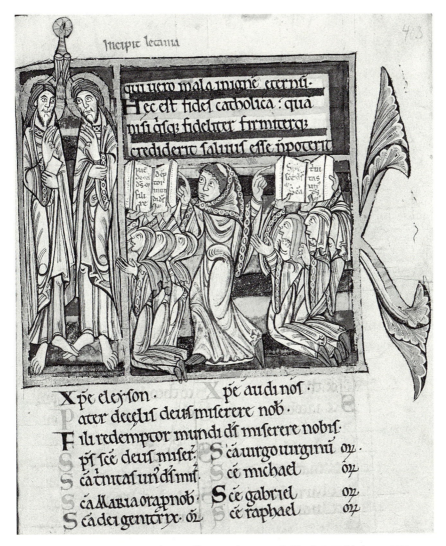

Figure 20. Litany Initial. *St. Albans Psalter. Dombibliothek Hildesheim, HS St. God. 1* (Property of the Basilica of St. Godehard, Hildesheim), p. 403.

"Mercifully spare your monks, I beseech you, O Jesus" (*Parce tuis queso monachis clementia IHY*). In the image, Jesus, standing to the right, stretches out to touch the woman, whose hand crosses the boundary between earth and heaven. Meanwhile, a monk (possibly Geoffrey), stands just behind the woman, seeming to urge her into Christ's presence.[12] A second initial features a group of nuns in prayer before the Trinity, depicted as two young men together with a dove (Figure 20).[13] This second initial—a "K" (for *Kyrie eleison*, "Lord have mercy")—marks the beginning of the Litany, a subject appropriate to the depiction of prayer. Of the praying nuns, one again appears to cross the boundary between heaven and earth, stretching her hand into the heavenly realm defined by the Trinity. Behind her an oversized monk appears to orchestrate the women's prayers: he does not pray but rather points to the text of the women's prayers, inscribed on books that they hold above their heads.[14]

These two images are remarkable as indications of the presumed prayerfulness of women: they suggest that women could be viewed as powerful intercessors for men, even for religious men. The circumstances of the manuscript's production, and the placement of these images in it, extend its clearly gendered presentation of prayer. Most scholars agree that the Psalter was owned by Christina and likely also produced for her.[15] The fact that it was written and illustrated at the male monastery of Saint Albans means that its celebration of women's intercession was the work of monks, who may have intended the book for the use of a religious woman. The chronology of the Psalter's production suggests, moreover, that its emphasis on female prayerfulness was not coincidental, but intentional and personally motivated. Production of the Psalter was a long and complex process that involved compilation, adaptation of existing components, and new composition over the course of some fifteen years. According to the scenario proposed by Morgan Powell, this process took place in conjunction with Christina's evolving devotional practices and as a result of her spiritual discussions with Geoffrey, whom Powell identified not only as the manuscript's patron, but also as the mastermind behind the project.[16]

Production of the Psalter was already underway by the time that the author of the *vita* began to record his account of Christina's spiritual life. Given that several elements in the *vita* echo episodes and spiritual emphases from the Psalter, it seems likely that the Psalter (which Christina may have been using as it was revised and completed) exerted some influence on her spiritual experience.[17] Two exceptions nevertheless suggest that influence could flow in the opposite direction as well—that the Psalter could be used to commemorate Christina's spiritual life and experiences, as they were reported in the *vita*. These two exceptions correspond precisely with those places in the Psalter in which women's prayerfulness is emphasized: the Psalm 105 initial and the Litany initial. Significantly, both images were the result of late revision or addition to the Psalter and were finalized after the main work on the manuscript had been completed. The Litany initial is the more radically revised of the two. The original, a more clearly defined "K," was expanded to include the woman, the monk, and the praying nuns—an expansion that almost completely obscured the "K" and left no room for the word (*Kyrie*) that the initial introduced.[18] Modification of the Psalm 105 initial was also dramatic, although instead of expanding an existing image, the manuscript's makers pasted the "C", featuring the interceding nun, into the manuscript.[19]

The deliberate, and even awkward, nature of these alterations underscores the importance to the Psalter's makers of their subjects: women and prayer. The fact that the initials seem to have been modified in light of events described in Christina's *vita* suggests that the changes were intended specifically to commemorate Christina as an intercessor. In the case of the Psalm 105 initial, the image seems to reflect a vision, reported in the *vita*, in which Christina saw herself facing Christ with Geoffrey on her right.[20] According to her biographer, Christina was initially disturbed: she wished that Geoffrey, and not she, might have the more prominent position. However, she soon came to understand that the "right hand" (which Christ extends to her in the Psalter initial) "was indeed hers."[21] This episode was important to Christina: her biographer reports that she discussed it often with Geoffrey. The deliberate placement of this initial in the Psalter implies that the vision was important to Geoffrey as well, and to the monks of Saint Albans. Modifications to the Psalm 105 initial make little sense unless it is Christina who is shown. Female intercession is not relevant to Psalm 105, but seems to have been shown here due to the coincidence that the psalm begins with a "C"—for "Confitemini," but also for "Christina."[22]

Modifications to the Litany initial seem also to have been inspired by the *vita*. According to Christina's biographer, on one occasion as she prayed for Geoffrey's salvation Christina received a vision in which she saw herself in a room with two handsome men clothed in white, on whose shoulders a dove was resting. In the vision, Geoffrey, whom she saw standing outside, "humbly begged her to introduce him to the people standing in the divine presence at her side." As Christina's biographer writes: "with all the energy of which she was capable, with all the love she could pour out, with all of the devotion she knew, she pleaded with the Lord to have mercy on her beloved."[23] The original Litany initial showed two men in white in the ascender of the "K," with a dove hovering above them (the Trinity). As with the Psalm 105 initial, modifications to the Litany initial seem to have been designed to bring it more closely into alignment with the description from the *vita*, strengthening the argument that the *vita* served as its source. Whereas the original initial "K" had featured only the Trinity, the modifications introduced a nun (probably Christina), a monk (possibly Geoffrey), and a group of praying nuns. Although the resulting initial is not a direct illustration of the episode from the *vita* (in her vision, Christina saw herself in the presence of the Trinity, with Geoffrey outside, while in the initial, both the nun and the monk appear outside the heavenly realm), it does approximate it. One seemingly minor modification to the initial strengthens the suggestion that the *vita* was its source. In the original initial, the dove of the Holy Spirit had been depicted with its wings spread above the heads of the Father and Son (as they are still faintly visible); in the revised initial, the spread wings were replaced by the folded wings of the resting dove as it is described in Christina's vision—a modification that serves little apparent purpose other than to conform to the text.[24]

These images, and their placement in the Psalter, solidify the connection between women and prayer that had been suggested centuries earlier in Leander's writing for Florentina, reaffirming his expectation of the spiritual benefits that he might gain through his sister and demonstrating their continued relevance for religious men. Like Florentina (whom Leander imagined praying for him), Christina is depicted both in her *vita* and in the Psalter as praying for religious men. As we have seen, the *vita* reported a vision in which Christina saw herself between Christ and Geoffrey, with Christ's right hand in "her possession." The vision is revealing. Like monks in many monastic communities during the twelfth century, Geoffrey was ordained.[25] And yet it is Christina, a religious woman, rather than an ordained member of the clergy, who is imagined introducing Geoffrey to the Trinity. Given that the role of the priest was to mediate between God and man, to link heaven and earth, the relationship should logically have been reversed, with Christina seeking the divine through Geoffrey, a priest. Of course, the inclusion of this episode in the *vita*, which was likely composed for a male audience, may have been calculated to deflect criticism of Geoffrey's relationship with Christina: by emphasizing Christina's prayerfulness, the author of the *vita* may have hoped to underscore for the Saint Albans monks the tangible spiritual benefits that could be gained through men's support of religious women.[26] It is possible, too, that the men involved in making the Psalter may have seen themselves as more closely connected to Christ (as his "friends") through their support of Christina, who is consistently described as Christ's bride in the *vita*.

Yet the emphasis on Christina's intercession in the Psalter—a book that was likely kept at Markyate and used by the women there—suggests that the manuscript's patron (Geoffrey) and its makers (the scribes and artists at Saint Albans) had a further goal in mind. The intentional inclusion in the Psalter of initials commemorating Christina's exemplary intercession suggests that their purpose was not simply to record Christina's prayerfulness (which had, in any case, already been reported in the *vita*), but to encourage intercessory prayer as a spiritual vocation among the Markyate women.[27] Nowhere is this more clear than in the Litany initial, with its depiction of women praying as a group. In modifying the initial, the manuscript's makers expanded the depiction of prayer beyond the specific context of Christina's special relationship with Geoffrey (which had been the focus of the vision in the *vita*), in order to present religious women in general as intercessors. While the Psalm 105 initial had celebrated Christina alone, the Litany initial transcended the individual. In it, prayer is not depicted as the particular preserve of the saint, something that only Christina could do (as only Hildegard of Bingen could receive visions, for instance), but as an activity in which all of the women of her community were encouraged to join. As such, the Litany initial was not merely commemorative, but may even have been prescriptive, providing a model for the spiritual practice of intercessory prayer among the women at Markyate.[28] If the Psalter was kept at Markyate, then the nuns who turned to the Litany to script their prayer would have found in the initial a powerful reminder of the prayerfulness of their local saint, Christina, and of her spiritual friendship with Geoffrey. But they would also have found a clear case for the importance of their own intercession and, by implication, an indication of the intended beneficiaries of their prayers: the monks of Saint Albans.[29]

Women, Men, and Prayer: Abelard and Heloise

Together, the *vita* of Christina of Markyate and the St. Albans Psalter offer compelling evidence for the association of women with prayer during the twelfth century—above all, with prayer for religious men.[30] Yet they do not explain how this connection came about, on what foundation it was based, or why it was often advanced by the very men, who—as priests—could legitimately claim privileged access to God themselves. A more complete discussion of the gendered efficacy of women's prayer appears in the roughly contemporary letters of Abelard and Heloise. Unlike Christina, whose intercessions on Geoffrey's behalf are described at length in her *vita*, little is known of Heloise's piety or devotional experience beyond her own repeated protestations of spiritual inadequacy. As far as we know, Heloise received no visions, had no mystical experiences, and was viewed by her contemporaries neither as a holy woman nor as a saint, although she was widely respected as an abbess. She was not a virgin and, in fact, admitted to vivid and ongoing sexual temptation. Nevertheless, Abelard repeatedly cast Heloise as his intercessor, begging her prayers on his behalf, and offering a fulsome explanation of her qualifications for prayer—both as his wife (a status that she repeatedly claimed, but that he usually worked hard to deny) and, more importantly, as a religious woman and bride of Christ.

Abelard's first request for women's prayer appears in his earliest extant letter to Heloise following their entrance into the religious life. Responding to Heloise's request for "some word of comfort" to strengthen her in her service to God, Abelard countered with a request of his own: that Heloise and the nuns at the Paraclete pray for him.[31] By his own admission, the Paraclete women were already in the habit of praying for him during his visits to the community. "O God," they would pray together, "who through thy servant"—meaning, of course, Abelard—"hast been pleased to gather together thy handmaidens in thy name, we beseech thee to grant both to him and to us that we persevere in thy will." In his letter, Abelard suggested a revised version of this prayer, tailored to his evidently perilous position at St. Gildas, where he served as abbot. According to his suggestion, the leader should pray:

Save thy servant, O my God, whose hope is in thee. Send him help, O Lord, from thy holy place, and watch over him from Zion. Be a tower of strength to him, O Lord, in the face of his enemy.

The women were then to respond:

O God, who through thy servant hast been pleased to gather together thy handmaidens in thy name, we beseech thee to protect him in all adversity and restore him in safety to thy handmaidens.[32]

Ever the optimist, Abelard went on to note that should he "enter upon the way of all flesh," he should be buried at the Paraclete in the women's burial ground, where his tomb would serve as a visual reminder for them to continue in their prayers for him. Admitting that his choice was deeply gendered, Abelard offered the remarkable explanation that no place is "more fitting for Christian burial among the faithful than one among women dedicated to Christ."[33]

Abelard's request for the prayers of the Paraclete nuns—in life and in death—appears at the end of a letter in which he made a case for the gendered efficacy of women's prayer.[34] Although he had begun by requesting Heloise's prayers—specifically reminding her of her obligation, as his wife, to pray for him—he ultimately advanced an argument for the efficacy of her prayers that rested more on Heloise's sex and religious status than on her relationship to him. Indeed, Abelard argued that Heloise's prayers were particularly pleasing to God because she was a woman and a nun. As he explained, women's prayers are effective as a function of their place within the family: women pray for their "dear ones," and wives for their husbands.[35] Biblical miracles in which the dead had been brought back to life were, Abelard reminded Heloise, performed largely for women in their roles as mothers and sisters: Lazarus was raised because of the prayers of his sisters Mary and Martha; the widow of Nain received her son from the dead; and mothers saw their children raised from the dead through the Old Testament prophets Elisha and Elijah.[36] Given that the prayers of these laywomen found favor with God, Abelard reasoned that the prayers of nuns would be all the more effective, since, as he observed, they are "bound to God by the profession of holy devotion."[37] Women's chastity was integral to the efficacy of their prayers. Carefully sidestepping the question of virginity, he observed that "The more God is pleased by the abstinence and continence which women have dedicated to him, the more willing he will be to grant their prayers."[38] Finally, he allowed that, as his wife, Heloise's prayers should be especially effective on his behalf. To drive this point home, he offered the example of Queen Clothilda, whose prayers had reputedly brought about the conversion of her husband Clovis, the first Christian king of France.[39]

Drawing on late antique and medieval traditions that associated women with the conversion of their male kin, Abelard presented all women as natural intercessors, whose prayer on behalf of their families was particularly efficacious. Although he mentioned only Clovis's wife Clothilda, he could well have included the early seventh-century queens Bertha, wife of Æthelberht, king of Kent, and Æthelburh, wife of Edwin, king of Northumbria—both of whom were remembered by medieval audiences as having influenced the conversion of their husbands (in Æthelburh's case, the obligation to aid in her husband's conversion had been underscored by Pope Boniface, who urged her to "kindle a spark of the true religion in your husband").[40] Abelard might also have mentioned the late antique saints Thecla, who was sought by Tryphaena to pray for her dead daughter Falconilla; Perpetua, whose prayers from prison reportedly delivered her dead brother Dinocrates from torment; and Monica, who by her prayers secured the conversion of both her husband and her saintly son—Augustine of Hippo.[41]

Abelard's arguments for women's prayerfulness provide a useful parallel to Christina's *vita* and the Psalter. In Abelard's view, prayer was the spiritual work of women as a group, and not the exclusive purview of holy women as individuals. Like the unnamed praying women featured in the Litany initial, the Paraclete nuns to whom he ultimately addressed himself had no particular claim to efficacy in prayer beyond their religious profession, and their dedication as women to lives of chastity. Yet Abelard extended his requests for prayer beyond Heloise to include her entire community, who were to pray on his behalf during his life and to receive his body in death. As in Christina's *vita* and Psalter, Abelard assumed that men were the logical beneficiaries of women's prayer. At no point did he encourage the women of the Paraclete to pray for each other, or to support Heloise, their abbess, in prayer. Rather, he consistently depicted women as intercessors on men's behalf. He even—somewhat bizarrely—noted the intercession of Abigail with King David (1 Samuel 25:23–33), highlighting Abigail's success in diverting David from his plan to punish her husband Nabal. Although Abigail went to David without Nabal's knowledge (actually declaring that her husband was a "wicked man"), and although Nabal was struck dead some days later, freeing Abigail to marry David (which she did), Abelard presented the story to Heloise as an example of "how much your prayers for me may prevail on God, if this woman's did so much for her husband."[42] The key point for Abelard lay in the fact that "the man's wrongdoing was wiped away by the entreaties of his wife"—an observation that echoed the pious hope of other religious men during the period, that salvation might come to them through a woman's prayer.

Women, Prayer, and the Bridal Metaphor

The association of women with prayer, and especially prayer for men, had a long history already by the eleventh and twelfth centuries. Late antique and early medieval men had sought women's prayers, emphasizing prayer and intercession as central spiritual functions for them. Like Monica, whom Augustine mentions chiefly in terms of her prayerfulness (and whose relics, as we saw in the last chapter, prompted a renewal of her cult in the twelfth century), other late antique women were celebrated by male admirers for their faithfulness in prayer. Jerome, whose friendships with women deeply influenced medieval men (not least Abelard himself), wrote time and again of the prayer-fulness of the Roman women of his circle—of Lea, who "passed sleepless nights in prayer"; Asella, whose "holy knees hardened like those of a camel from the frequency of her prayers"; Blesilla, whose sincerity in prayer Jerome recalled admiringly ("Who can recall without a sigh the earnestness of her prayers?"); and Paula, whose night-time prayers were interrupted only by the rising sun.[43]

Within early Christian communities, too, women had been closely associated with prayer. Indeed, prayer itself was often gendered female: catacomb paintings from the second century depict the praying figure of the *orans* almost exclusively as a woman.[44] As a spiritual vocation, prayer was primarily associated with a subset of women: virgins and widows, women whose lives were marked by chastity and spiritual devotion. On the one hand, the connection was practical. Prayer was a demanding task, which was often seen as incompatible with the obligations and distractions of marriage. So when Jerome wrote to Laeta on the education of her daughter, Paula, he proposed a rigorous schedule of prayer and psalms appropriate to her unmarried state, advising that she ought to "rise at night to recite prayers and psalms; to sing hymns in the morning; at the third, sixth, and ninth hours to take her place in the line to do battle for Christ; and, lastly, to kindle her lamp and to offer her evening sacrifice."[45] On the other hand, the connection was cultic, since marriage (and, more particularly, sexual intercourse) was thought to preclude effective prayer, a fact that shaped Jerome's insistence on clerical celibacy. As he opined, "A layman, or any believer, cannot pray unless he abstain from sexual intercourse."[46]

As Jerome's comment indicates, chastity was valued in both men and women and was typically a prerequisite for prayer in both sexes. However, for women, chastity held particular spiritual meaning. From at least the early third century, female virgins had been characterized as brides of Christ, a motif that Dyan Elliott argues originated as a disciplinary tactic. Fearing that sexual abstinence might produce a form of angelic androgyny in women, the Carthaginian theologian Tertullian (d. c. 220) had promoted the idea that consecrated virginity constituted a form of spiritual marriage—albeit to a heavenly, rather than an earthly, bridegroom. As Elliott notes, the effect was to bind female virgins to their sexed bodies (foreclosing the possibility of virginal androgyny), while also subjecting them to a firmly gendered hierarchy: would-be virgins found themselves paradoxically defined by the very institution they had rejected.[47]

Being a bride of Christ involved practical limitations: churchmen warned that Christ's brides should keep themselves veiled and secluded, fearing that virgins might even cuckold their heavenly spouse. These fears led, as Elliott shows, to scrutiny, suspicion, and even denunciation of religious women during the later Middle Ages.[48] Yet despite the potential for danger, bridal status held significant possibilities for religious women, as we saw in Chapters 2 and 3. Religious men were often deeply respectful of women whose spiritual nuptials were presumed to qualify them for special intimacy with the bridegroom. Leander, imagining Florentina with Christ on the "chaste couch," conjured an intimate and affectionate scene from which he, as a man, expected to be excluded. Male admirers who construed women as "brides of Christ" viewed them (like Jerome) as their *dominae*, implying women's superiority and their own spiritually ordained subservience. As Abelard explained more than once, monks and priests were merely servants of Christ, whereas professed women were his brides. Offering spiritual service to the bride thus became—for some men—a way of serving the bridegroom, providing a potent justification for men's spiritual care of religious women.

The bridal motif provided grounds for a further justification for men's care, based on the intersection of ideas concerning women's prayer and their privileged intimacy with the bridegroom. Men hoped that Christ might be pleased at the services they provided for religious women, and that by serving as *paranymphus* to the bride, they might also draw closer to the bridegroom. At the same time, they hoped that, as brides, religious women might request and receive rewards for them from the bridegroom. Religious men who sought women's prayers and intercession believed not just that women were well suited to prayer, but that the intercession of a wife with her husband (and, specifically, of a bride with her heavenly bridegroom) was uniquely powerful. In their discussions of women's prayerfulness, men therefore consistently evoked the connection between the prayers of religious women and their bridal intimacy with Christ: prayer *was* intimacy, as far as many male observers were concerned. Jerome was most clear in characterizing prayer as the conversation of a chaste woman with her heavenly bridegroom. Of Lea, for instance, he wrote: "To the Bridegroom she spoke constantly in prayer and psalmody."[49] In his hugely influential letter 22 to Eustochium, Jerome asked, "Do you pray?," advising her that in prayer, "You speak to the Bridegroom."[50]

Jerome's letter to Eustochium has rightly been characterized as a panegyric on virginity. When Jerome spoke of Eustochium in prayer, he gave his imagination free rein: picturing Eustochium praying in the privacy of her chamber, he described a suggestive scene in which Christ would put "his hand through the hole of the door" wakening her with love.[51] But virginity per se was neither a requirement for prayer, nor—more significantly—for bridal status. Widows as well as virgins could claim bridal status, since the Christian conception of spiritual marriage did not require technical virginity of the religious woman who was to be presented as a spiritual "bride." Indeed, Tertullian (the "father of the bride," as Elliott calls him for his role in originating the motif) had explicitly allowed that chaste widows might consider themselves brides of God, writing that widows who had rejected remarriage "prefer[red] to be wedded to God."[52]

Jerome, too, specifically encouraged devout widows to consider themselves as brides of Christ, writing to the widow Salvina that she owed her chastity "not to one who is dead but to one with whom she shall reign in heaven."[53] Even Paula—a widow who had been a mother several times over—was depicted as a spiritual bride. In a letter from Bethlehem (likely ghost written by Jerome), Paula and Eustochium urged Marcella to join them, promising her that "we shall weep copiously, we shall pray unceasingly [and] wounded with the Saviour's shaft, we shall say one to another: 'I have found Him whom my soul loveth; I will hold Him and will not let Him go.'"[54] The idea that widows were legitimately brides of Christ was reinforced by the developing characterization of *Ecclesia* as a widow who had refused to take another spouse after the death of Christ. As Caesarius of Arles asked in the sixth century, making the connection explicit: "Why is the church considered as a widow unless it is because her husband, Christ, appears to be absent?"[55]

The Intercession of Wives

Abelard's expressed confidence in the superiority of women's prayer must be understood against a late antique background in which chaste women had been associated with prayer and their prayers recognized as the prayers of brides. Like late antique men, Abelard viewed praying women as brides "speaking" to their bridegroom. However, in his hands the bridal motif also became a way to argue for the particular efficacy of nuns' prayers, since he imagined nuns as having a distinctive and powerful influence on their "husband." Offering the secular parallel of wives who interceded with noble husbands on behalf of their friends and supplicants, Abelard suggested that nuns were uniquely positioned to pray and to receive answers to their prayer from their heavenly bridegroom. In writing to Heloise, he made this point clear, commenting that "in common law it is accepted that wives are better able than their households to intercede with their husbands, being ladies rather than servants." "So," he explained, "you should not be surprised if I commend myself in life as in death to the prayers of your community."[56]

Abelard's faith in the intercession of religious women as brides with their heavenly bridegroom was built on a late antique spiritual foundation, but also on long-standing assumptions concerning the ability of secular women to exert a positive influence on their husbands. By the eleventh century, the wives of powerful men had emerged as the most common and most widely recognized secular intercessors.[57] More than anyone else, a man's wife was thought to be able exert a positive influence on him. According to Anselm, intervening with her husband was part of a wife's duties: she "should diligently encourage him [her husband] in well-doing, and calm his spirit with her mildness if he were perchance unjustly stirred up against anyone."[58] As Sharon Farmer has noted, a woman's influence with her husband was thought to exceed even that of his priest. In his early thirteenth-century *Manual for Confessors*, Thomas of Chobham therefore encouraged priests to approach women as vehicles through which they might shape the behaviors of men. As he advised, "no priest is able to soften the heart of a man the way his wife can." "Even in the bedroom," Thomas wrote, "In the midst of their embraces, a wife should speak alluringly to her husband, and if he is hard and unmerciful, and an oppressor of the poor, she should invite him to be merciful; if he is a plunderer, she should denounce plundering; if he is avaricious, she should arouse generosity in him."[59]

Medieval queens were expected to use their position of influence and intimacy with their royal husbands in order to intercede on behalf of their households, their extended families, and the kingdom generally.[60] Early medieval churchmen highlighted the intercessory obligations of contemporary queens, offering the Old Testament Queen Esther as a model; Esther had saved the Jewish people from certain death through her intercession with King Ahasuerus.[61] During the ninth century (876), Pope John VIII wrote to Richildis, second wife of Charles the Bald, encouraging her to support the church and likening her to Esther: "you will be for the Church of Christ near [your] pious husband in the way of that holy Esther who was near her husband on behalf of the Israelite people."[62] The slightly earlier coronation *ordo* (856) for Judith, Charles the Bald's eldest daughter and wife of Æthelwulf, also highlighted Esther's intercessory role: through Esther, God "inclined the savage heart of the king toward mercy and salvation."[63] Also in the ninth century, Hrabanus Maurus sent a commentary on the Book of Esther to the empress Judith of Bavaria, second wife of Louis the Pious, and then also to Ermengard, the wife of Lothar I.[64] According to the Anglo-Saxon exegete Aelfric (d. c. 1025),

Esther did not stop at intercession, but also brought about the King's conversion: as he wrote, "the king was corrected through the belief of the queen to worship God who controls all things."[65] Esther was equally relevant for nuns, who were not just royal brides, but brides of the "highest king," as Peter of Blois wrote in a letter to the abbess Matilda of Wherwell. Calling to mind Ahasuerus's plan to kill the Israelites, and Esther's prayers and tears, by which she "recalled the king to mercy," Peter encouraged Matilda to "Be wakeful and pray, bride of the highest king."[66]

While Esther was a favorite exemplar for medieval queens, queenly intercession was most perfectly demonstrated in the Virgin Mary. As queen of heaven, Mary interceded with her son on behalf of all Christians, offering the ultimate model for women's prayerful intercession with their heavenly king.[67] Of course, religious women could not replicate Mary's influence with Christ. Nevertheless, holy women as intercessors had long been associated with the Virgin through medieval litanies, which from the Carolingian period onward had lumped all women into a single category: "virgo."[68] Unlike holy men, who appeared in litanies according to a variety of types—apostles, martyrs, evangelists, prophets, patriarchs, confessors, and monks, for instance—all holy women, whether technically virgins or not, were presented in litanies as *virgines*, a term that Felice Lifshitz argues represented a spiritual, rather than a corporeal category.[69] The grouping of female intercessors together as *virgines* underscored their similarity to Mary, the "holy virgin of virgins."[70] It also implied that chaste women in prayer were to be considered as both brides of Christ and liturgical "virgins."

The appearance of the liturgical "virgo" in Carolingian litanies, and the resulting association of female intercessors as *virgines* with the Virgin Mary, provided the backdrop to men's developing sense of women's gendered qualification for prayer. Medieval supplicants (male and female) assumed as a matter of course that Mary's prayers would be effective; a prayer to the Virgin in the ninth-century *Book of Cerne* exemplified this confidence, proclaiming that "we believe and know for certain that everything you wish for you are able to obtain from your son, Our Lord Jesus Christ."[71] An eleventh-century poem from northern France expressed a comparable sense of Mary's influence with Christ:

Whatever you wish
Your only son will give you.
For whomever you seek
You will have pardon and glory.[72]

For Anselm of Canterbury, it was Mary's physical connection to Christ that undergirded her intercession.

> Who can more easily gain pardon for the accused
> by her intercession,
> than she who gave milk to him
> who justly punishes or mercifully pardons all and each one?[73]

In the same way, men who begged the prayers of religious women emphasized women's bridal relationship to Christ. If Christ would give his mother "everything" she wished for, men hoped and believed that he would not deny his "bride" her requests on their behalf. Moreover, if men pleaded that Christ would "spare the servant of your mother" (as Anselm did), stressing their relationship to the Virgin as a justification for their claim to Christ's mercy, they also seem to have imagined that Christ might spare the "servant" of his "bride"— that is to say, that he would look favorably on the prayers of men who had served religious women, and whose petitions were brought by nuns, as brides, before the heavenly throne.[74] As I argued in Chapter 2, men who served women spiritually often conceived of their service as being that of the *paranymphus*, the friend of the bridegroom, a role that they construed as bringing them closer to Christ, but that they may also have viewed as strengthening their claims to women's bridal intercession.

The Gender of Prayer

Accounts of women's prayerfulness have this in common: they come primarily from the pens of men, and most often from the pens of men who were the admirers, spiritual friends, or disciples of the women they celebrated as "prayerful."[75] Whether the women themselves were especially devoted to prayer is largely unknowable, since most women left no account of their spiritual lives. Rather, it was men who imagined a female religious life centered on prayer, which they then advocated in their letters, rules, biographies of holy women, and histories. The early emphasis on prayerfulness for women, evident in the writings of Jerome, for instance, was amplified in early monastic texts, which deepened the association of religious women, as nuns, with prayer. By the sixth century, as Gisela Muschiol has noted, prayer was established as a central spiritual function for nuns.[76] Subsequent accounts of saintly nuns routinely emphasize their prayerfulness. The biography of the Merovingian holy woman, Monegund (d. 570), reported that she achieved healing for those who visited her through intercessory prayer; the community of women that gathered around her was dedicated to prayer.[77] Rusticula, abbess of St. Jean in Arles (d. c. 632), is described by her biographer, Florentius, as an *advocatrix*, whose prayers saved many.[78] Gertrude of Nivelles's (d. 659) biographer presented the strength of her prayers as a function of her virtuous life.[79] Balthild of Chelles (d. c. 680) healed many from illnesses through her "holy intercession."[80] The "monacha" queen, Radegund, scorned the royal marriage bed, devoting herself to prayer throughout the night, according to her biographer, Venantius Fortunatus.[81] Radegund's devotion to prayer is celebrated in an eleventh-century illustrated *life*, in which she is shown prostrate on the floor in prayer as Clothar sleeps (Figure 21).[82]

Women's prayerfulness within the monastic life was considered as a spiritual service to society broadly. According to his biographer, Caesarius of Arles established his monastic foundation for women at St. Jean in order to ensure the defense of the city through prayer: "The man of God formulated the idea by divine inspiration from the ever-reigning Lord that the church of Arles should be adorned and the city protected not only with countless troops of clergy but also by choirs of virgins."[83] Significantly, Caesarius's *rule* for women placed a greater emphasis on prayer than did his *rule* for men, leading Albrecht Diem to conclude that the rise of intercessory prayer was linked to the emergence, specifically, of female monasticism.[84] Prayer for the good of society was also part of the spiritual service provided by nuns at the community of Sainte-Croix at Poitiers during the sixth century. As Baudonivia remembered, Radegund "taught us also to pray incessantly for their [all the kings'] stability. . . . She imposed assiduous vigils on her flock tearfully teaching them to pray incessantly for the kings."[85] Confirmation that women's prayer could be viewed as protective of the Christian community is found in the biography of the Merovingian holy woman, Genovefa of Paris (c. 420–509). When Paris was threatened by Attila's advancing army in 451, the saint roused the "the matrons of the city" to prayer, persuading them to "undertake a series of fasts, prayers, and vigils in order to ward off the threatening disaster, as Esther and Judith had done in the past." Although the men had been ready to flee the city, the women remained and "gave themselves up to God and labored for days in the baptistery—fasting, praying, and keeping watch as she [Genovefa] directed."[86] As a result of their prayers, the city was saved.

Figure 21. Radegund in Prayer. Bibliothèque municipale de Poitiers
MS 250, fol. 24r.

Not surprisingly, prayer played a central part in men's spiritual friendships with women throughout the medieval period. Some men emphasized prayer as an exchange or "counter-gift" to be offered in return for spiritual service.[87] So, for instance, Donatus of Besançon (d. c. 660) had begged the prayers of the women in return for his *Regula ad virgines*, first in life ("while I abide in this vile body") and then also in death ("when at the Lord's bidding I migrate").[88] Aldhelm, likewise, requested women's prayers in return for his writing for them: "Let the welcome reward for my present little work be the frequently conferred exchange of your prayers, and let the mainstay of my sweat and labour be the support (given by) your intercession."[89] Of course, prayer could also be central to men's relations with religious women even when the men offered nothing by way of exchange. Writing to Abbess Ethelburga of Fladbury, Alcuin simply asked her to "remember my name faithfully in your prayers with all your people." Just as Abelard later would, Alcuin provided explicit instructions on how he wished Ethelburga to pray: "I have sent you a flask and plate to make offerings to the Lord God with your own hands. When you look at them say: 'Christ, have mercy on thy poor servant Alcuin.'"[90]

Alcuin's letters offer an opportunity to examine the gendering of prayer in a comparative context. In a letter to Fredegisus, an Anglo-Saxon monk and teacher at Aachen, Alcuin mentioned prayer, but only to ask that Fredegisus secure the prayers of Gisela and Rotrude; he made no mention of the fact that Fredegisus (his previous pupil and eventual successor as abbot of St-Martin, Tours) might also pray for him. Admittedly, Alcuin enjoyed a close friendship with Gisela and Rotrude, and so it may have been natural for him to focus on their prayers, rather than those of Fredegisus. However, there was clearly a gendered element to his request. Advising Fredegisus to "Beg them to remember my old age in their prayers," Alcuin went on to imagine Gisela and Rotrude as brides of Christ, invoking the Song of Songs as he did: "They should hold fast to him till they are led into the treasuries of the king's glory, there to rest in love on flowers of eternal joy, with the Bridegroom from his bedchamber putting his left arm of present good beneath their heads and embracing them with the right arm of eternal joy."[91]

The bridal relationship that Alcuin imagined bound Gisela and Rotrude, respectively, to Christ may explain his failure to beg Fredegisus's prayers: in Alcuin's view, Fredegisus was not a bride, nor would he ever become one. Although Alcuin wrote some forty-five letters to male religious, he never described a monk or abbot as a "bride" of Christ—reserving such language exclusively for nuns.[92] By contrast, the women he approached for prayer are repeatedly characterized in his letters as spiritual brides (even if, like Rotrude, they were neither virgins nor widows). Alcuin encouraged Ethelburga, for instance, to view herself as the bride of Christ, writing that she would "sing an everlasting song of praise in the presence of her bridegroom" after her death.[93] In another letter to Ethelburga, Alcuin encouraged her to be a "worthy bride" for God.[94] Gisela, too, he addressed as a "virgin most beloved in Christ" (*dilectissimae in Christo virgini*) and a "noble handmaid of God" (*clarissima Dei famula*), declaring himself "lucky to enjoy the protection of your most holy prayer as you promised."[95] Almost directly anticipating the language that Abelard would adopt many centuries later in his exhortations to Heloise, Alcuin asked, "What glory could be greater for you or honor more lofty than to be the bride of the king who is above all kings?"[96]

To be sure, religious men also begged the prayers of their monastic confrères and of other holy men; the exchange of prayer was, after all, a mainstay of the religious life for men as well as for women. However, when men wrote to women, their vocabulary typically shifted to reflect a gendered understanding of women's spiritual standing and of their particular bridal relationship to Christ.[97] With the exception of the "matrons" who prayed alongside Genovefa, praying women are most frequently approached rhetorically as "virgins" or "brides," emphasizing their chastity and sexual status. Many of the men who begged women's prayers invoked their assumed future status in heaven ("when you happily enter the kingdom with the holy and wise virgins," as Caesarius wrote, invoking the Parable of the Wise and Foolish Virgins; or "when you are granted the blessed palm of virginity in the choir of worshippers and holy virgins," as Donatus effused), or their priority as brides of the heavenly king ("if you shall lie with Christ upon the chaste couch," Leander imagined, picturing his sister in Christ's pure embrace). In these instances, men clearly assumed the gendered superiority of women's prayers. They implied, too, that women's prayers would not just be heard by Christ, but also answered by him, as Paschasius Radbertus did in addressing himself to Theodrada and Imma: "you whose prayers our God sometimes appears to obey."[98]

The appeal of women's prayers was predicated on a number of related factors, which are nicely expressed in Paschasius's confidence that God sometimes appears to "obey" the prayers of Theodrada and Imma. Religious men who sought women's prayers seem to have believed that religious women could achieve through their prayers what men were unable to achieve for themselves.

They believed that the prayers of professed women were qualitatively different from the prayers of men (whether the men in question were ordained or not, holy or not). In fact, they seem to have believed that women's prayers were better than men's prayers—which is to say, they believed that women's prayers were both more likely to be heard by Christ and more likely to be answered by him. They believed these things because they imagined that religious women enjoyed a particular relationship with Christ—a relationship based on women's bridal potential, and one that men across the centuries (like Alcuin, Paschasius, and Abelard, as well as others) believed was not fully available to them. Abelard was explicit on this point, approaching Heloise as Christ's bride, yet repeatedly styling himself (and all monks) only as Christ's servant. Although he briefly acknowledged Heloise's special obligation as his wife to pray for him, Abelard was much more comfortable imagining Heloise in prayer as Christ's bride. Similarly, in Paschasius's view, all nuns were betrothed to Christ and could be brides; all monks could not.[99] During the twelfth century, Bernard of Clairvaux's sermons on the Song of Songs encouraged Cistercian monks to imagine themselves as brides, thereby bypassing the religious women who had functioned as intercessors for earlier medieval men and who continued to function in that capacity for contemporary Benedictines, like Abelard.[100] Nevertheless, for many men during the twelfth century and beyond, the prospect of women's bridal intercession continued to be gender-specific: for such men, only women could be brides, and therefore only women could pray as brides speaking to their husband.

In keeping with the idea that the prayers of women as brides were different, and better, than men's, early medieval male authors frequently praised women's power of prayer, while lamenting their own seeming inability to pray effectively. The priest Florentius, biographer of Rusticula, offers one example. Florentius begged the prayers of the women of St. Jean in Arles, stressing their chaste devotion to Christ and implying his own spiritual insufficiency. As he wrote: "I beseech you to pray, virgins of Christ, that while I submit to your authority, I may, by your intercession, deserve the help which I cannot obtain for myself."[101] The women he addressed were not saints—as he believed Rusticula was—but simply nuns who had professed the religious life. A similar contrast between the assumed spiritual power of the women and the helplessness of the man is implied in the writings of Caesarius of Arles, who compared the salvation of the nuns of St. Jean (whom he characterized as "wise" virgins) to his own exile among the ranks of the spiritually "foolish"—the virgins who, according to Jesus's parable, would be excluded from the celestial marriage feast.[102] Donatus, likewise, stressed his own spiritual inadequacy, begging the women that "you will make holy offerings to the Lord for me so that, when you are granted the blessed palm of virginity in the choir of worshippers and holy virgins, I will at least be granted forgiveness for my sins and offenses."[103]

Ambivalent Models

The foundational importance of the bridal model to perceptions of women's prayers may be most clear in its absence, that is to say, when women's prayerfulness did not involve a bridal element (or, indeed, when it could not). The Old Testament matron Hannah, who prayed for a son and was delivered of a child, Samuel, offers a biblical example of female prayerfulness that did not fit the model presented thus far of bridal, intercessory prayer. Hannah's prayerfulness is reported twice in the Vulgate: first, when she prayed for a son at Shiloh (1 Samuel 1:10–11); and second, in her song of thanksgiving after she had presented Samuel as an offering to God (1 Samuel 2:1–10). Hannah's song was incorporated into the liturgy as one of the canticles for Lauds in the Roman breviary and was widely recognized as an important model for the *Magnificat*, Mary's canticle of praise at the Visitation (Luke 1:46–55).[104] Nevertheless, as a model for women's prayerfulness, Hannah posed certain problems. Although she offered an example of answered prayer, many men cautioned that she was no intercessor, since she had not prayed for others, but only for herself. Exegetes worried, moreover, that fertility and motherhood were not appropriate contexts within which to encourage female prayerfulness. Augustine was especially concerned that the objects of Hannah's prayerfulness (pregnancy, childbirth, and motherhood) disqualified her as a model of prayer for devout women, who had vowed themselves to lives of chastity. Writing in response to Proba's request for advice on prayer, Augustine cautioned against adopting Hannah's prayer as a model, noting its deviation from the structure provided in the Lord's Prayer: prayer for a child could hardly be considered "deliverance from evil," he opined.[105] More worryingly, as a sexually active married woman who had prayed to become pregnant, Hannah was directly at odds with the model of the prayerful woman as chaste that Jerome and Augustine encouraged among their female friends and disciples. So although medieval men praised Hannah as a selfless

Figure 22. Four Scenes from the First Book of Samuel. Washington, D.C., National Gallery of Art. B-17, 714.

mother and as a prophetess (based on her perceived role in foretelling the birth of Christ), few offered her as a model of female prayerfulness.

Medieval ambivalence concerning Hannah's prayerfulness is underscored in a leaf from a late eleventh-century Italian Bible, in which her prayer is subordinated to that of her husband, Elkanah (Figure 22).[106] Although the Vulgate reported that Hannah had prayed alone at Shiloh, and later that she gave Samuel to Eli as an offering to God, the makers of this manuscript inserted Elkanah into both episodes, prioritizing his prayer at Shiloh (with Hannah shown praying behind him), and privileging him holding the baby Samuel at the presentation to Eli. The impulse to insert Elkanah into both scenes suggests an unwillingness to recognize Hannah in prayer as independent of her husband, or to accept that her prayers—the prayers of a married laywoman—could have been effective.[107]

Accounts of saintly women's prayerfulness could also sometimes be minimized, suggesting that some medieval audiences balked at attributing too much power to female prayer. As we saw above, Gregory praised Scholastica as being "mightier than her brother" through prayer, yet subsequent writers nevertheless questioned the efficacy of her prayers.[108] Writing in the ninth century, Bertharius of Monte Cassino shifted attention away from Scholastica: "Surely she did not do this herself?" he asked, attributing the miracle to Benedict: "for if [he] had not refused her, the miracle would not have happened."[109] Similarly, a sermon by Alberic of Monte Cassino presented Scholastica in terms of eleventh-century asceticism (rather than prayerfulness per se), emphasizing her vigils and her tears ("each night she drenched her bed and flooded the covers with tears").[110] Both texts were included in the eleventh-century *Codex Benedictus*, in which Scholastica is shown praying, while Benedict is caught, seemingly surprised by the efficacy of her prayers (Figure 18).[111]

Despite certain concerns about Scholastica's prayerfulness, she was often celebrated in later centuries as a prayerful model for saintly women. Goscelin of St. Bertin adopted Scholastica's model in his *life* of Seaxburh, the seventh-century queen and later abbess of Ely. Recounting how Seaxburh had invited Archbishop Theodore of Canterbury to her new monastic foundation on the Isle of Sheppey (which he described as a "private site for prayer"), Goscelin reported that the archbishop was forced to stay with Seaxburh to "exchange words . . . about the sweetness of eternal life." According to Goscelin, Theodore had initially refused to remain with Seaxburh (as Benedict had refused to stay with Scholastica), but he was "outdone by her prayers."[112] Illustrating many of the themes discussed in this book, Goscelin's *life* of Seaxburh depicts the saint as having close spiritual ties to both Theodore and the abbot Hadrian, religious men to whom she was bound "in the ardor of her faith and in true love of God."[113] For their part, these men imagined Seaxburh as a bride of Christ. When Theodore arrived at Sheppey, he was prepared—in Goscelin's words—to "unite a new bride to Him in a new marriage."[114] Goscelin's familiarity with the story of Scholastica and Benedict, and his willingness to apply it to his account of Seaxburh's relationship to Theodore of Canterbury, shows— once again—how ideas and motifs justifying men's involvement with women in the religious life could be deployed by monks and priests who were inclined to support women. Goscelin's invocation of Scholastica as a model for Seaxburh exonerated Theodore from criticism: like Benedict, Theodore's prolonged presence at Sheppey was presented as a function of a woman's prayerfulness and, most important, of divine intervention favoring her request.

Women's Prayer as Counter-payment for Men's Support

Monks and priests who valued women's prayers and believed that women enjoyed enhanced influence with Christ were often also spiritually involved with women. These men praised women's prayers as special and different from their own, they imagined women praying for themselves and other men, and they assumed that women's prayer would be the reward for their spiritual service to female monasteries. As Abelard proposed, sending a book of hymns to the Paraclete women, the nuns should offer prayers for him in return: "And so, as you entreat me in this, brides and handmaids of Christ, we too in return entreat you to lift up with the hands of your prayers the burden you have placed on our shoulders."[115]

The expectation that women would pray in return for men's guidance, protection, and support is clear in an early twelfth-century charter recording the relationship between the women of Fontevraud and Bishop Peter of Poitiers. "In exchange for . . . protection," the charter reports that "the handmaids of Christ who are or will be in the Church of Fontevraud will pray for you daily while you live, and when one of you dies, they will render the same service to the Lord for the soul of the deceased brother as they would for the soul of a nun of their own congregation who left this world."[116] The emphasis on women's prayer in this charter reflects the broader organization of the community at Fontevraud; as Robert of Arbrissel's biographer reported, Robert had separated the men from the women, dedicating the women to prayer in the cloister and the men to the physical labors necessary to support the community.

Although the division was described in terms of women's "weakness" (the *vita* reports that he "committed the gentler and weaker sex to psalm-singing and contemplation and the stronger sex to the duties of the active life"),[117] the women's prayers were evidently a source of power for the community. When the Fontevraud women faced opposition from the archbishop of Bourges over Robert of Arbrissel's burial place (with the archbishop wishing to keep Robert's body at Orsan, where he planned to be buried at Robert's feet), they threatened to withhold their prayers. As they wrote to the archbishop: "we will no longer be your daughters and we will no longer pray for you and yours until you return our good father to us."[118] The nuns were successful: Robert's body (minus his heart, which was given to the priory at Berry) was returned to Fontevraud.[119]

Prayer as a form of exchange was also central to the relationship between Christina of Markyate and Geoffrey de Gorron, abbot of Saint Albans, as we saw at the beginning of this chapter. From the outset, Christina's biographer presented the relationship between the two as mutually beneficial: Christina prayed for the abbot, while he supported her financially. He was "her beloved friend" (*delecti ac familiaris sui*); she was his "faithful protectress" (*probate patrone*).[120] A passage from the *Lives of the Abbots of St. Albans* reports that Geoffrey had even "constructed" the house at Markyate, "giving to it rents and tolls from various places for the sustenance of Christina, his beloved, and her congregation of sisters there." Christina, in turn, served as Geoffrey's spiritual advocate, pleading with God on his behalf. Yet Geoffrey's support for the women was evidently resented by many of the Saint Albans monks, who "murmured" over the gifts he gave the women.[121] His intimacy with Christina came under attack too: her biographer mentions the "spiteful gossip" and, more specifically, rumors that Christina was "bound to the abbot by ties of carnal love."[122]

The decision to commission a biography of Christina may have been intended to counter these sorts of rumors, defending the spiritual merits of Geoffrey's special relationship with her, and, in particular, justifying the financial support that the abbot gave the women at Markyate.[123] Christina's biographer emphasizes time and time again the reciprocal element in her relationship with him, commenting on several occasions that what Christina gained in material assistance, Geoffrey gained in spiritual sustenance: "God decided to provide for the needs of his virgin through this man and through her to bring the man back to the fullness of his vocation," he noted on one occasion.[124] "In this way, your virgin was relieved of anxiety about material concerns, while the abbot through the virgin was freed from spiritual anguish," he observed on another.[125] And again: "While he [Geoffrey] busied himself in supplying the maiden's needs, she [Christina] strove to enrich the man in virtue."[126] These were not incidental comments. Christina emerges from the pages of the *vita* as a valuable resource, whose intercession for Geoffrey was a form of return on his financial investment in her community. This image of Christina was confirmed in the Psalter, which encouraged her to remember that her role was to pray for the monks of Saint Albans, that prayer was the currency with which she (and all the women at Markyate) was to repay Geoffrey's support.[127]

The idea that women's prayer could be a counter-payment for men's spiritual and material care for them—that women's intercession could in some sense be "bought" by men—is most clearly expressed in Abelard's Sermon 30, the fundraising sermon for the Paraclete that he delivered in the early 1130s.[128] The sermon functioned on two levels, presenting an argument for the spiritual value of donations generally, followed by a gendered case for the particular value of donations to women. In making the first argument, Abelard invoked the parable of the shrewd manager, in which Jesus had taught that men should use their worldly wealth to gain "friends" who would help them when the money was gone (Luke 16:1–13). Men who use worldly wealth to gain friends will be welcomed into "eternal dwellings," Jesus promised (Luke 16:9). Abelard's gendered interpretation of the text featured religious women as the archetypal "friends" of the parable—friends who were uniquely positioned as brides of Christ to help men spiritually. In the sermon, Abelard therefore offered his audience a tidy exchange between men's financial gifts and women's intercession: "there (in heaven)" he promised his male audience, "you may reap eternal rewards through those women who here receive temporal goods from you."[129]

The survival of the sermon in Colmar MS 128, and the textual reuse of certain selections in the *Guta-Sintram Codex* (copied by Sintram with the incipit *Beati pauperes*), allow some sense of how Abelard's audience may have responded to his arguments in favor of donations to women. At Marbach, where male members of the community did serve women spiritually (as priests at Schwarzenthann), the spiritual appeal of women's prayers was evidently strong. The selections from Abelard's sermon that Sintram chose to copy into the *Guta-Sintram Codex* showcase Abelard's confidence in the spiritual value of service to, and support for, women in the religious life. Claiming religious women as the "poor" of the beatitudes, Sintram's excerpted text encouraged its implied male audience to come to women's aid: "you should not delay in assisting their poverty, recognizing them as your ladies (*dominae*) by your actions more than by your words. Acknowledge that you owe more by far to the spouses of your Lord than to his servants and that they have greater influence with their own Spouse than do his servants." Having presented religious women as brides of Christ (invoking Jerome's elevation of Eustochium as his *domina*), the text repeats Abelard's claim that men should expect to benefit spiritually through women's bridal intercession: "May those very brides, through their merits and prayers, lead you with them to that fellowship of the celestial marriage feast and to the eternal tabernacles, so that there you may reap eternal rewards through those women who here receive temporal goods from you, by the gift of their bridegroom, the Lord Jesus Christ."[130]

The textual reuse of Abelard's Sermon 30 in the *Guta-Sintram Codex* provides compelling evidence for the appeal of Abelard's ideas concerning men's "obligation" to serve women within the religious life, as well as their relatively quick circulation beyond the Paraclete: the sermon, delivered in the early 1130s, was copied into the *Guta-Sintram Codex* at around the mid-twelfth century. At Marbach and Schwarzenthann, Abelard's ideas concerning relations between religious men and women were known and adopted in the very way that he might most have hoped: to structure a mutually beneficial relationship between two opposite-sex religious communities. Like Robert of Arbrissel, who encouraged the men at Fontevraud to imagine that they could gain salvation through their service to women, Abelard (and also Sintram) taught that men would be led to the "fellowship of the celestial marriage feast" by women, who, as brides, had a guaranteed spot at the wedding banquet.[131] Charter evidence reveals that the men at Marbach had not only read Abelard and copied him, but that they actually structured their involvement with women on the basis of his promise of a spiritual reward: charters on page 2 of the *Guta-Sintram Codex* record that the canons provided the women of Schwarzenthann with material support. The women, meanwhile, functioned as intercessors for the two communities, providing in return for the men's material support prayers by which the men might ultimately be welcomed into "eternal dwellings" as Abelard (and Jesus, through the parable) had promised.[132]

Wise Virgins at the Judgment

Abelard's reference to the "celestial marriage feast" in Sermon 30 (and Sintram's adoption of the motif in the *Guta-Sintram Codex*) adds a final dimension to discussions of women's bridal intercession, implying the high spiritual stakes of women's prayers. Although the parable of the shrewd manager in Luke 16 formed the basis of Abelard's sermon, providing a generic argument for the benefits of almsgiving, Abelard turned to the parable of the Wise and Foolish Virgins (Matt. 25:1–13) to deepen his argument for the spiritual benefits of giving specifically to religious women, whom he characterized as brides and implicitly also as "wise" virgins. As Abelard wrote, these women were waiting—with lamps at the ready—in the cloister for the arrival of the bridegroom: at his coming they would go together to celebrate the marriage. "Those who were ready entered with him into the nuptials," he remarked in the sermon, citing Matt. 25:10.

By the twelfth century, when Abelard delivered his sermon and Sintram copied it, the Wise and the Foolish Virgins were often depicted on the west façade of cathedrals, reflecting the understanding of the bridegroom's arrival as the moment of judgment (Figure 23).[133] As in these depictions, which accentuate the dismay of the foolish virgins, the happy prospect of the wise virgins in Abelard's sermon conjured up an opposing and significantly less rosy image. Lurking just behind the sermon text—with its chaste brides and celestial feasts—was the specter of those women who would never be brides: the foolish women of the parable, whose lamps were not ready when the bridegroom arrived. "I know you not," the bridegroom declared when they came knocking at the closed door of the marriage celebration, with their oil lamps belatedly filled. These foolish virgins were not the focus of Abelard's sermon, yet they hover at the margins of his text, a salient reminder of the fate awaiting the spiritually unprepared at the judgment. Hell was hardly the subject of Abelard's sermon, but it was an important sub-text, and a warning: choosing intercessors was a serious task, Abelard warned, with eternal implications.

In Abelard's view, the Paraclete nuns were the "wise virgins" whose intercession would be most effective on his (and other men's) behalf. The identification drew on several metaphors at once: the religious woman as bride of Christ and liturgical *virgo*, and the consecrated virgin as a "wise virgin" (an identification confirmed in ceremonies for the consecration of virgins, which incorporated elements inspired by the parable).[134] In texts from the early Middle Ages, praying women were described both as wise virgins and as brides. In the sixth century, Caesarius of Arles had grasped the dual significance of women's prayers, begging the intercession of the women at St. Jean, "so that when you happily enter the kingdom with the holy and wise virgins, you may, by your suffrages, obtain for me that I remain not outside with the foolish."[135] Abelard's innovation was to unite ideas concerning women's bridal prayerfulness

Figure 23. Wise and Foolish Virgins. Basilica of Saint-Denis.
Central portal, west façade.

with those reflecting their spiritual privilege as "wise virgins," presenting
both as inducements to prospective donors. To patrons and supporters of religious women, he offered the chance to be led by Christ's brides "to that
fellowship of the celestial marriage feast and to the eternal tabernacles," there
to "reap eternal rewards." Sintram's decision to copy this section of the sermon indicates that Abelard's message was heard and clearly understood by

contemporary religious men. The prayers of nuns were not just desirable; they were spiritually decisive.

Abelard's emphasis in Sermon 30 on nuns as wise virgins may explain, finally, his decision to be buried at the Paraclete, and his claim that no place was more "fitting" for Christian burial "than one amongst women dedicated to Christ." Abelard chose burial among nuns since he believed that, as brides, nuns were the most effective as intercessors and that, as wise virgins, they were guaranteed a place at the "celestial marriage feast." Evidence from the *Guta-Sintram Codex* suggests that other men found Abelard's reasoning compelling in this regard, too. The *Guta-Sintram Codex* included a number of texts that were central to monastic life at Marbach, among them a homiliary, the Rule of Saint Augustine (and a commentary on the rule), and the famous Customs of Marbach.[136] However, the bulk of the manuscript (almost half of its current 163 folio pages) was given over to the shared necrology of Schwarzenthann and Marbach, which, despite the loss of its last three months, lists in excess of 4000 names. The fact that the necrology was kept at Schwarzenthann indicates that it was the women who were tasked with the job of remembering and praying for the dead. The prayers of the Schwarzenthann canonesses were sought and valued, and may even have augmented the appeal of the Schwarzenthann cemetery as a burial place: entries in the necrology make special mention of those who were buried "here." Among those mentioned were donors to the community, and, significantly, several priests from Marbach—presumably men who had provided spiritual service to the Schwarzenthann women and who then chose to be buried in the women's cemetery.[137] As these men seem to have assumed, women's prayers were fundamentally, and most powerfully, prayers for the dead—the prayers that would aid their souls in the interim between death and resurrection and, crucially, at the final Judgment.

Conclusion

When Abelard died in 1142, his body was transferred from the Cluniac priory of St. Marcel-sur-Saône to the Paraclete nuns' cemetery, where, as he hoped, the nuns would offer prayers for him, remembering him regularly and interceding on his behalf.[138] Abelard's request for burial among women, and his justification for the excellence of women's prayers, are, admittedly, unusual: no other monk or priest that we know of made quite such an extensive case for women's prayers. Yet, as we have seen in this chapter, the constituent elements of Abelard's case were present in medieval culture, both secular and religious. His arguments for women's prayerfulness drew on widely held ideas concerning the obligations of wives and queens to intercede with (and for) their husbands, as well as long-standing Christian traditions emphasizing women's prayerfulness as both brides of Christ and "wise virgins." Although Abelard presented his case for women's prayers more explicitly than other men, his confidence in women's intercession was clearly shared by his contemporaries—most obviously at Marbach, where his ideas were directly embraced through *Beati pauperes*, and at Saint Albans, where Abbot Geoffrey supported Christina as his own personal intercessor.

Further evidence for men's confidence in women's prayerfulness can be found in non-narrative sources, chiefly charters of donation, testaments, and burials. The many donors who supported female religious life as it expanded during the twelfth century hoped for a spiritual reward in return, most likely (as Abelard promised donors to the Paraclete) women's prayers—in life and in death.[139] At Rupertsberg, burial emerged as a critical source of income soon after the community's foundation: the *life* of Hildegard reports how the monastery's financial difficulties were alleviated through the favor of "many wealthy families" who "gave their dead an honorable burial with us."[140] The connection between donors, burial, and women's prayer that is implicit in this account is explicit elsewhere. Charters of gifts to the monastery of Saint-Antoine-des-Champs, a Parisian house founded in the late twelfth century in response to the preaching of Fulk of Neuilly, show clearly the value to donors of women's prayers. As Constance Berman observes, charters that record "the establishment of anniversary masses, the erection of chapels and chaplaincies, and gifts for prayers or for burial . . . make it clear that it was the intercessory function of these religious women which was most important."[141] Evidence that donors favored female houses for burial (and commemorative prayer) is clear among Cistercian abbey churches in the Low Countries, too, according to Thomas Coomans, whose study of princely burials shows a marked preference for female houses: of 86 princely burials in 16 Cistercian abbeys, Coomans finds 18 burials at five men's houses and 68 burials at 11 women's houses.[142] These findings corroborate those of Erin Jordan, whose study of patronage of men's and women's Cistercian houses in Flanders and Hainaut during the thirteenth century shows that men's houses did not "outpace" women's houses in donor preference or requests for prayer.[143] While many scholars have assumed that donors preferred the Masses of ordained monks to the prayers of nuns, the dramatic growth of Cistercian houses for women in the early thirteenth century suggests that donors were not in short supply—and that women's prayers were not a debased coin in the later period.

The Cistercian evidence leads beyond the temporal focus of this book, into the thirteenth century, when new devotional and theological trends opened up more opportunities for prayerful women. The emerging concept of purgatory created a "new sphere of influence" for women, as Barbara Newman has argued: women performed what she calls an "apostolate to the dead," offering prayers and assuming penitential suffering in order to deliver souls from purgatory.[144] The intensity and manifestation of women's prayers for the dead evolved during the course of the later Middle Ages, but the fundamental association of women as intercessors remained in place, as it had been through the central Middle Ages when communities like Quedlinburg and Gandersheim in the tenth century, Niedermünster and Obermünster in the tenth and eleventh centuries, and Fontevraud and Las Huelgas in the twelfth century, had emerged as dynastic mausoleums.[145] Abelard's claims that burial among religious women was the ideal goal for Christian death hardly seem unusual in this context. In the first century, Christianity had emerged as a religion centered on the death of one man—Christ—who had been mourned first and foremost by women. The medieval tradition of Christian mourning and intercessory prayer implicitly perpetuated this gendered relationship: women mourned and prayed for men.[146]

In the context of this book, what is most interesting is the possibility that priests and monks may have viewed women's prayers and commemoration as a spiritually decisive reward for their sacramental service. At Marbach, we know that this was so: priests were buried at Schwarzenthann, where they were prayed for by the nuns and their names recorded in the community's necrology. At the Paraclete, where Abelard was buried in 1142, other men sought burial as well: in 1156, Heloise gained papal permission for lay brothers to be buried in the nuns' cemetery.[147] Priests were subsequently buried in the Paraclete cemetery, as well as elsewhere in the monastery, including the chapter room, where at least one priest—Hato—was buried. Chrysogonus Waddell notes that twenty-seven priests were buried at the Paraclete in less than ninety years.[148] At Obermünster in Regensburg during the last quarter of the twelfth century the community produced a luxurious illustrated necrology, which included some 1300 names—among them a substantial number of priests, canons, pastors, deacons, and hermits.[149] These men are commemorated across several folio openings: for clerics (fols. 65v-67r) and brothers (fols. 67v-68r). The priest who celebrated Mass for the women may have seen in this necrology an implicit promise of future prayers for his soul; he may even have imagined himself as one of the officiating priests memorialized on fol. 67v (Figure 1).[150] Other pieces of evidence—taken together—add to the presumption that women's prayers continued to exert spiritual appeal, even after the widespread ordination of monks meant that male monasteries could more easily offer Masses for donors' souls. As we saw in Chapter 2, Arnold von Wied was buried in a chapel that ultimately became a women's monastic community (if it was not already one at the time of his death); could it be that the hope of women's commemoration inspired him in the foundation? The sources do not say. Yet it is clear that men routinely associated women with prayer for the dead. Goscelin of St. Bertin reported how women at Barking had commemorated the dead (especially dead brothers): the abbess Ethelburga (a seventh-century figure) reportedly "held it a very sweet thing after lauds and vigils to lead the choir not to their beds but to the tombs of the brothers and to commend the souls of the dead to God in sacred hymns."[151] Christina of Markyate, too, may have had a particular dedication to prayer for the dead. Her biographer reports that she preferred Saint Albans to other monasteries for her profession, since, among other reasons, Roger's body was buried there.[152] It is possible that Christina assumed that, in staying, she could intercede more effectively on Roger's behalf. The St. Albans Psalter suggests that she did: Roger's *obit* in the Psalter reminded its owner to remember Roger in prayer.[153]

Men who supported religious women spiritually—serving as their priests, confessors, or spiritual friends—faced accusations and insinuations of wrongdoing, as I have noted throughout this book. These accusations would someday come to an end. However, the spiritual rewards that some religious men believed they might earn through their service to pious women were eternal and would easily outlast earthly criticisms and suspicion. Men who served as nuns' priests believed that they would thereby secure women's bridal prayers on their behalf, until—in Abelard's language—they would be led by Christ's brides "to that fellowship of the celestial marriage feast and to the eternal tabernacles"—literally to their "eternal rewards." Salvation was, of course, the reward that these men sought, and that many believed they would achieve through women's prayerfulness and bridal privilege.

Conclusion

A certain set of voices has been largely absent from my discussion in this book, which has focused—as the title makes clear—on the "tales" of nuns' priests. As I have argued, nuns' priests found ample justification for their spiritual service to religious women in early Christian exemplars, claiming John the Evangelist and Jerome as primary models for their pure, yet often maligned, involvement with women. John's example was especially compelling to nuns' priests, since he had been commanded from the cross by Christ himself to take Mary into his protective, familial care. As a symbol of men's obligation to guard and support women spiritually, there could hardly be a more powerful image than Mary and John, standing together as "mother" and "son" at the foot of the cross, beneath the dying Christ.

Men's ideas and voices have been most prominent in this book, and by design: my purpose has been to show how men's support and care for religious women could form a central part of male spirituality and pious practice during the reform period—a period that has most often been associated with celibacy and the presumption of men's withdrawal from women within the religious life. As I have shown, there was another path for religious men, one that did not require separation from women, but that instead prompted intensive, yet chaste, spiritual involvement with them. While recognizing the pervasive and destructive force of medieval misogyny (and its effects within the religious life), I have worked to present a view of the period that acknowledges the voluntary spiritual service that some men provided for religious women. The men whose voices have featured in the preceding chapters advanced a form of male spirituality that included, and even embraced women—albeit primarily as vehicles for male spiritual experience and expression. Sincere and lasting friendships between the sexes certainly developed; however, the ideas relating to "woman" that I have outlined here were relevant in the first instance to men, who could more readily picture themselves as the *paranymphus* (the bridesman and friend of the bridegroom) if they first cast nuns as Christ's brides.

While my primary purpose has been to explore the spiritual outlook of nuns' priests, an underlying goal of this book has been to add to our knowledge of nuns—the professed women to whom these men ministered and who played such a vital role, symbolically, in men's spiritual lives. By highlighting the positive ways in which men perceived their spiritual service to women, I have sought to show that the pastoral relationship could be fulfilling and spiritually prized by both nuns and their priests. That nuns needed priests has long been recognized, and sometimes bemoaned as one consequence of women's "sacramental disability."[1] That priests needed women, too, or thought they did, has rarely been suggested, except in cases of men's attraction to individual, holy women—visionaries and saints, whose spiritual virtuosity made them expressly "unlike" other women. My argument in this book has been that ordinary priests, who served ordinary nuns, could see in these women a gendered spiritual power from which they felt that they could benefit: nuns could be approached as brides of Christ, a status to which no monk or priest, before the twelfth century, imagined he might have personal or direct access.[2]

The voices that are largely absent from this book are, of course, the voices of the nuns themselves. The omission has been intentional, yet I am conscious of the danger that, by focusing on men, I might seem to perpetuate a set of traditional assumptions: first, that women were passive recipients of men's care; and second, that the spiritual care of women was a topic that was discussed primarily between men, and that was governed exclusively by men's interests, availability, and volition. A further concern is related: that by tracing and reproducing men's ideas about women, I might seem to imply that women shared men's gendered spiritual ideas, or that they participated in their creation. By way of conclusion, then, I would like to turn to the question of how nuns interacted with their priests, particularly with regard to the celebration of the Mass (the moment at which priestly authority in the female monastery was made most visible) and the characterization of the nun as a "bride" of Christ—a characterization that appears first and most often in the writings of men and that often privileged women, but that also had the capacity, as Dyan Elliott has shown, to expose them to significant limitations and ultimately also to real danger.[3]

Claiming Care: Nuns and the Bridal Metaphor

The most direct witness to women's interactions with priests regarding provision of pastoral care during the twelfth century comes from the writings of Heloise, whose dialogue with Abelard about the religious life for women inspired much of Abelard's writing on the subject.[4] Two of Abelard's most important works for women, his *Rule* and his letter *On the Origin of Nuns*, were written at Heloise's express request and according to guidelines that she proposed. But Heloise did not simply ask Abelard to write for her and for the nuns of the Paraclete; she also argued that he ought to do so, offering evidence that women saw the provision of care for women as a duty for men and that they took an active role in urging men to provide it. In letter 6, Heloise reminded Abelard of his various obligations to support the Paraclete, peppering her text with the language of duty and commitment. If he worried that he was wasting his time in the wilds of Brittany amongst murderous and immoral monks, she offered the nuns of the Paraclete as willing alternatives: "While you spend so much on the stubborn, consider what you owe to the obedient; you are so generous to your enemies but should reflect on what you owe to your daughters."[5] If he was anxious for the future of the Paraclete as a place of worship, and for his own reputation as its founder, she reminded him of the special obligation that bound him to the Paraclete community as its creator: "It is for you then, my lord, while you live, to establish for us what we are to adhere to for all time, for after God you are the founder of this place, through God you are the planter of our community, with God you should be the instructor of our religious life."[6]

Above all, however, Heloise reminded Abelard of the biblical command that men should support holy women, transcending the language of personal and even corporate obligation that most clearly bound him to both Heloise and the Paraclete in order to focus on what men, as a group, owed religious women. Turning to the question of material care, Heloise noted that "apostolic authority" had granted devout women the "special concession . . . of being supported by services provided by others rather than by their own labor." Invoking Paul's remarks concerning church support for widows (1 Tim. 5:16), she concluded that, "It is right and proper that [nuns] should be supported from the funds of the Church as if from the personal resources of their husbands."[7] In the context of Heloise's other writings, this might seem an unusual claim, since she generally avoided the language of spiritual marriage that Abelard repeatedly and enthusiastically encouraged for her: Heloise never embraced the exalted status that he promised she would enjoy as a bride of Christ, maintaining instead her marital claims on Abelard as her husband.[8] Her claim to church support, while it might seem to imply a willingness to acknowledge nuns as brides whose husband (Christ) had died, more likely reflects Heloise's desire to dignify professed women as "widows" in an early Christian sense, that is, as an "order" for women within the church.[9]

In this book, I have argued that the characterization of nuns as brides of Christ significantly motivated men's willingness to provide spiritual care for them. Given the importance of the bridal motif, it is striking how little evidence there is for bridal language in negotiations of pastoral care by women in the period before 1200. To be sure, the sources that typically governed the practice of pastoral care, and that do sometimes include women's communal claims on men, were generally legal texts, which tend to be functional, rather than justificatory or explanatory. Charters detailing the practical arrangements between nuns and the local male communities that often provided priests shed light on women's networks and connections, demonstrating, for instance, that nuns sought out and successfully maintained several sets of relationships at one time, receiving pastoral care from priests at various houses in a series of overlapping and carefully choreographed relationships. At Hohenbourg, for example, care was provided during the last quarter of the twelfth century by priests drawn from at least three male communities, two of which were founded by the abbess specifically to ensure a steady stream of priests. These charters showcase the active role that women took in securing and negotiating pastoral care, giving lie to the notion that they were passive recipients of men's care. Yet, bridal language does not figure into the documented, legal arrangements of these women with religious men (nor, as I have shown elsewhere, did bridal motifs play a particular role in the women's spiritual formation at Hohenbourg).[10]

A second series of charters governing arrangements between monks and nuns survives from Rupertsberg, the monastery founded by Hildegard of Bingen at the mid-twelfth century. Like the Hohenbourg materials, these show women claiming care, although in circumstances that were hotly contested: Disibodenberg (the "male" monastery to which Hildegard had been given as a child, but from which she had separated when she founded Rupertsberg) had repeatedly failed to provide Rupertsberg with priests. The Rupertsberg charters insist on the men's obligation to provide care, marking a stark contrast to the persuasive approach that Heloise had adopted in her letters to Abelard. Where Heloise had sought to encourage Abelard's care, invoking the same saintly and apostolic examples that he (and other men) would also reference in their own writings, Hildegard's tack was less conciliatory: first, she chastised the monks of Disibodenberg for threatening to disrupt the spiritual life at Rupertsberg (writing sternly in the voice of "I who am"),[11] and then she turned to legal measures, securing a charter from Archbishop Arnold of Mainz requiring Disibodenberg's provision of priests.[12] As at Hohenbourg, bridal language had no place in letters or charters relating to priestly care at Rupertsberg.

The absence of bridal language from Hildegard's legal wranglings with the monks of Disibodenberg is consistent with her other writings: Hildegard generally shied away from the insistent bridal language that many men used to describe the piety of women, and which Hildegard's own biographer, Theoderic of Echternach, applied to her.[13] For Hildegard, it was not a human figure, but rather *Ecclesia*, the Church, who was the archetypal bride of Christ.[14] Nevertheless, she celebrated "woman" in her visionary texts and viewed religious women (especially virgins) as spiritually distinctive and exalted, even going so far as to allow virgins at Rupertsberg to dress in white garments and to ornament themselves with crowns and rings on feast days. Word of these unusual practices spread, prompting a disapproving letter from the *magistra* Tenxwind of Andernach. As Tenxwind wrote to Hildegard:

> They say that on feast days your virgins stand in the church with
> unbound hair when singing the psalms and that as part of their
> dress they wear white, silk veils, so long that they touch the floor.
> Moreover, it is said that they wear crowns of gold filigree, into
> which are inserted crosses on both sides and the back, with a figure
> of the Lamb on the front, and that they adorn their fingers with
> golden rings.[15]

In her response, Hildegard explained that nuns—because of their virginal status—were exempt from the limitations placed on other women. The female virgin, Hildegard declared, "stands in the unsullied purity of paradise, lovely and unwithering," an idea that she expressed, too, in her antiphon for virgins.[16]

In Hildegard's view, the virgins at Rupertsberg claimed a prelapsarian femininity that justified their sumptuous ornamentation on feast days.[17] Bridal symbolism featured in this context, although as a seemingly secondary matter: the virgin's "white vestment," Hildegard claimed, was a "lucent symbol of her betrothal to Christ."[18]

Beyond Texts: Women and Liturgical Textiles

Tenxwind's elaborate descriptions of the women's clothing at Rupertsberg, and Hildegard's explanation, offer an important viewpoint from which to consider the self-image of medieval nuns, hinting at the women's perception of themselves first and foremost as virgins, and only secondarily as brides.[19] Hildegard's writings confirm such a view: her virgins had more in common with the one hundred and forty-four thousand virgins of the Apocalypse (Apoc. 14:1–5) than with the veiled virgins of Tertullian's anxious imagination, whose spiritual nuptials left them perpetually in danger of cuckolding Christ (or, in fact, with the would-be "brides" whose purported desire for legal marriage to Christ prompted men to produce affective scripts for them, as McNamer argued).[20] As Hildegard explained to Tenxwind, the nuns' crowns were a means for the women to have the Lamb's name "written on their foreheads" (Apoc. 14:1)—a "shocking claim for the eschatological quality of the liturgical celebration in her church at Rupertsberg," as Felix Heinzer has commented.[21] The contrast between virginal nuns and religious men (whether monks or priests) is clear in Hildegard's writing, which consistently locates virginity in the female body, relegating men—even virginal men—to the category of the merely chaste.[22]

Hildegard's elitist views on virginity and her elaborate, even theatrical, celebration of the nuns' prelapsarian claims within the church itself could not have gone unnoticed by the priests at Rupertsberg. The effect on these men of the Rupertsberg nuns, gloriously attired in silks and gold, with long flowing robes and unbound hair, must have been quite striking. Unfortunately, no textual account reports their reactions, although Guibert of Gembloux—like Hildegard—repeatedly acknowledged the special spiritual status of virgins, commenting that "holy virgins are the temple of God the father, the spouses of his son Jesus Christ, and the sanctuary of the holy Spirit."[23] Still, the spectacle that Tenxwind's letter describes raises the question of how nuns and priests interacted in the physical space of the church, and how nuns responded to the authority of their priests and the exclusive access of these men not only to the altar, but to the very body and blood of Christ through the Mass. At Rupertsberg, priests who celebrated the Mass would have been confronted by a dramatic performance of the nuns' gendered spiritual priority as "virgins"— a status that (at least according to Hildegard) was exclusive to women. Only women could be virgins, as Hildegard taught. Moreover, as virgins, the Rupertsberg nuns escaped the spiritual limitations—stemming from the fall— that were typically invoked to justify women's exclusion from the altar and the priesthood.

Liturgical textiles offer a further perspective on women's sense of their role in the liturgy and their relationship with Christ and, by implication, also with their priests.[24] Women were barred from consecrating the Mass, as we know, but they were also prohibited from touching (or even approaching) the altar—a fact that most historians have assumed rendered them passive observers rather than participants in the Mass. Women were equally prohibited from touching liturgical textiles except when laundering them, a point that church councils reiterated and that Abelard incorporated into his *Rule* for the Paraclete.[25] Even so, it was often the case that women had made these same liturgical textiles, or that they had commissioned and given them as patrons.[26] Indeed, more than any other type of liturgical gift (except perhaps candles), textiles were likely to have been made by women. Not only was textile work seen as uniquely appropriate for women,[27] but—possibly in keeping with the apocryphal story of Mary spinning thread for the production of the temple curtain—the production of ecclesiastical linens was especially encouraged for them.[28] Like Christina of Markyate, who sent slippers and three miters she had embroidered as a gift for Pope Adrian IV, monastic women made and gave textile gifts to ordained men for them to wear as they served at the altar.[29]

In Chapter 2, we saw how Edith of Wilton was famed for having embroidered an alb on which she depicted herself as Mary Magdalene kissing the footprints of Jesus. According to Goscelin of St. Bertin's biography of Edith, the alb was "made out of the whitest linen (*ex bisso candidissimo*)" and was "a symbol of her innocence." Embellished with "gold, gems, pearls, and little English pearls, woven around the yoke" it featured a depiction of the apostles gathered around Christ on its lower border. As Goscelin reported, Edith embroidered "around the feet, the golden images of the Apostles surrounding the Lord, the Lord sitting in the midst, and Edith herself prostrated in the place of Mary the supplicant, kissing the Lord's footprints."[30]

Edith's decoration of the alb was significant not only for the evidence it provides for her spiritual identification with Mary Magdalene, but also for its implications concerning liturgical display and priestly authority at Wilton. A white linen, fitted tunic that reached to the ankles, the alb was the basic vestment worn by all clerics before the twelfth century.[31] Decoration of albs was not uncommon: decorative borders could be embroidered along the lower edge of the alb, or around the wrist or neck opening. In the context of female monastic life, however, the iconographic program of Edith's alb was spiritually assertive, to say the least: by depicting herself on an alb as Mary Magdalene—the "most blessed lover of Christ"—Edith not only placed herself directly at the altar (assuming that the alb was worn by the officiating priest at Wilton), but also pictured herself within salvation history and even implied that she outranked the priest spiritually, associating herself with the one woman who had displaced the male apostles at the moment of Christ's death and resurrection. Like the priests at Rupertsberg, who ministered to nuns whose virginal priority was announced through their extravagant feast-day attire, the Wilton priest could hardly have escaped the implications of Edith's alb, which not only invoked women's historical priority at the cross and tomb, but also claimed the gendered spiritual superiority of monastic women and their privileged intimacy with Christ.

Edith's alb survives only in the written record—through Goscelin's description of it. Yet extant liturgical textiles produced by women confirm that women did, indeed, picture themselves at the altar, or in a special relationship with Christ (or with Mary)—despite their exclusion from the priesthood. A set of priestly vestments produced during the mid-thirteenth century by nuns at the Benedictine monastery of Göß featured female figures, chiefly the Virgin Mary, but also Abbess Chunegunde II (before 1239-after 1269), who had commissioned the vestments, and Adala, a patron of the monastery.[32] The Göß vestments constitute one of the most remarkable and intact ensembles of medieval liturgical textiles; they include a cope, a chasuble, a dalmatic, a tunic, and an antependium, now in Vienna, as well as further items in Cologne and London.[33] Though designed for use by some of the men who ministered to the Göß community and its parish,[34] the vestments were conceived of as gifts to the Virgin Mary.[35] The Virgin figures prominently on several of the pieces, notably on the cope (Figure 24), where she appears in a central medallion, nursing the infant Christ child, and on the antependium (Figure 25).

While emphasizing the Virgin as patron of the women's church, the Göß vestments also highlighted the role of contemporary women as patrons of the

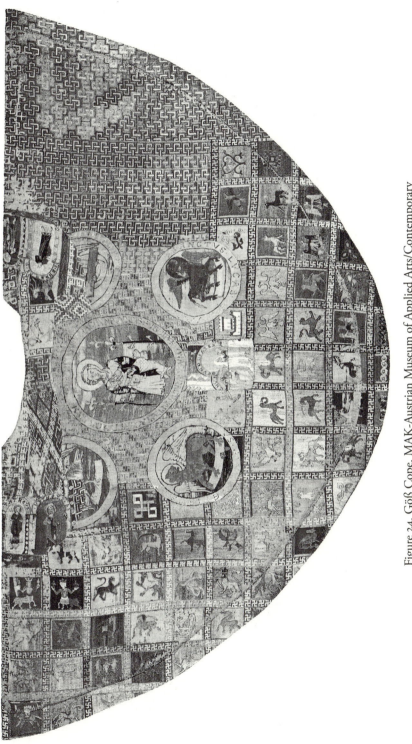

Figure 24. Göß Cope. MAK-Austrian Museum of Applied Arts/Contemporary Art, Vienna, T 6903/1908. Photograph: © MAK/Ingrid Schindler.

Figure 25. Göß Antependium. MAK-Austrian Museum of Applied Arts/Contemporary Art, Vienna, T 6902/1908. Photograph: © MAK/Ingrid Schindler.

Figure 26. Chunegunde. Detail, Göß Cope, MAK-Austrian Museum
of Applied Arts/Contemporary Art, Vienna, T 6903/1908.
Photograph: © MAK/Ingrid Schindler.

church, reminding the priests who wore the cope and chasuble of women's
place in salvation history. The inscription around the central medallion on the
cope identifies Chunegunde as its donor.[36] Below the medallion, Chunegunde
appears with a nun, who is identified by a partial inscription (Figure 26).[37] A
further image of the abbess appears on the antependium, the textile hanging
designed to ornament the front of the main altar at Göß. Here, Chunegunde
is depicted to the lower left of the Virgin, who is shown in a central medallion, enthroned and holding the Christ child. Two additional medallions flank
this central one, depicting the Annunciation and the Three Magi respectively.
Chunegunde, shown outside the medallions, to the lower left of the Virgin, is
paralleled to the lower right of the Virgin by an image of Adala, who, with
her son Aribo (later bishop of Mainz), had founded the monastery in the early
eleventh century.[38] The central focus of the antependium—a cover for the altar that women were normally forbidden even to touch—is thus comprised
exclusively of female figures: the Virgin, Chunegunde, and Adala. In total,
Chunegunde is named five times on the Göß pieces.

A second antependium, dating from the early thirteenth century, also features contemporary women, locating them at the altar even more powerfully
than the Göß vestments would (Figure 27).[39] Produced at Rupertsberg some

Figure 27. Rupertsberg Antependium. Musées Royaux d'Art et d'Histoire, Brussels, Inv.-Nr. Tx.1784. © RMAH, Brussels.

fifty years after Hildegard's death, the antependium is an impressive piece of work, with embroidery in various colors, and gold and silver thread on purple silk, possibly from Byzantium; pearls may once have adorned the scene, but are now lost.[40] Christ appears at the center of the antependium in a mandorla, surrounded by the four evangelist symbols; around this central image are a series of further figures, among them Martin of Tours and Rupert (two patron saints of the monastery), Hildegard (holding a model of the church), Adelheid (possibly the second abbess of monastery, 1179–1210), Agnes, Duchess of Nancy and Lothringia (patroness of the monastery), Conrad (possibly Conrad of Münster), and Godefridus (presumably the procurator of the monastery).[41] However, the most remarkable aspect of this scene is the series of ten nuns shown along the lower border of the antependium. These women, with their hands and faces raised in adoration to Christ, were members of the Rupertsberg community and likely had a role in making the altar hanging. They are identified on the piece by name: Guda, Sophia, Ida, Agnes, D(omi) na Elis(b) (abbess from 1210–1235), Ida, Sophia, Mehtild, Adelhedis, and Gerdrudis.[42] The decision to feature these women on the antependium—women who were living and named members of the community—intensifies the association of women with the altar, in this case the high altar of the convent church at Rupertsberg.[43] By depicting themselves on a hanging designed for the high altar, the women suggested not just their participation in the Mass, but also their special access to Christ—unmediated by a priest.

A final antependium, produced during the later Middle Ages (and thus well beyond the period that has occupied me here), confirms women's sense of their special access to Christ, and their public claims—through liturgical textiles—to spiritual priority. The antependium, known as the Wichmanns-burger antependium, was produced at the Cistercian monastery of Medingen, one of the Heideklöster, a group of five female houses near Lüneburg, not far from Hamburg.[44] During the late fifteenth century, these communities formed the center of a monastic reform movement that ushered in new forms of artistic expression, principally manuscript production and textile work. The Wichmannsburger antependium offers a rich example of the incorporation of liturgical texts within a textile piece: it is ornamented with no fewer than 89 figures and 55 inscriptions, in both German and Latin (Figure 28).[45] Although designed and produced at Medingen, the antependium was displayed in the parish church of Wichmannsburg, a church that had belonged to the women's house since 1339.[46] As Henrike Lähnemann shows, the inscriptions, taken largely from Medingen manuscripts, provide the key to understanding the

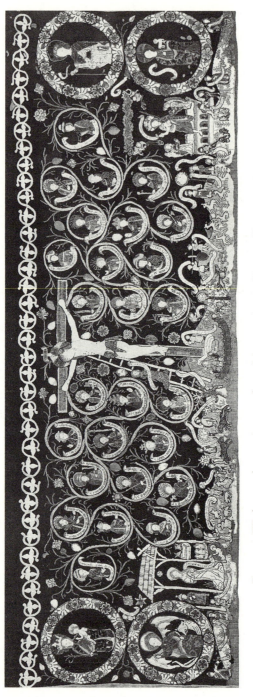

Figure 28. Wichmannsburger Antependium. Museum August Kestner, Hannover, W.M. XXII 8. Photograph: © Museum August Kestner.

iconographic program of the piece, which—as she argues—was intended to provide spiritual instruction to a lay population.[47]

Most interesting, in light of the concerns of this book, is the centrality to the antependium of the moment of transubstantiation, the moment when the bread and wine become—in the hands of the priest—the body and blood of Christ. This moment is highlighted through the organization of the antependium around the central image of Christ crucified, a towering depiction that bisects the cloth and easily overshadows two other half-size scenes from the life of Christ: the nativity and the resurrection. From the cross, Christ's nailed hands drip blood, which sustains the grapevines on which various biblical, apostolic, and holy figures are represented as half-figures. The eucharistic emphasis of the whole is underscored through depictions of a woman gathering roses beneath the cross, one of Joshua's scouts carrying grapes from the Promised Land, and a man praying on bended knee. Among these figures, the viewer's eye is drawn to the image of a single woman ascending the ladder leading to the pierced side of the dying Lord. A demon below aims an arrow at her, in a bid to prevent her from reaching her goal. In her hands, the woman holds a text band with the inscription: "An desse(n) bom wil ik stighe(n). un(d) de vruch" (Auf diesen Baum werde ich steigen und die Fruch[t nehmen]", a paraphrase of Song of Songs 7:8: "I will climb the palm tree and gather its fruit").[48] The centrality of the female figure underscores the confidence that nuns had in their gendered access to the crucified Christ, despite their official prohibition from the priesthood. It is a woman (not a priest) who ascends the ladder, approaching the dying Christ.

Further instances could be adduced in which women's liturgical textiles implied their participation at the altar or their spiritual priority at the cross and tomb. Nuns—like the monks and priests discussed in Chapter 2—were well aware of the historical priority of women in the gospel accounts of the passion and resurrection. They identified themselves, at times, with Jesus's female followers and supporters, women whose faith had so manifestly eclipsed that of the male disciples at the first Easter. Through their patronage and textile production, professed women put these ideas into action, claiming a place at the contemporary altar—the most potent physical symbol of their exclusion from the priesthood and their reliance on ordained men. Viewing women's textile gifts in this way has profound implications for how we understand the ministrations of priests in female monastic communities, since both the altar and the priest himself were often quite literally "dressed" in textiles that had been commissioned, given, and often even designed and produced by women.

These textiles provided a visual context for the performance of the Mass, some-times asserting women's spiritual primacy, as the feast-day dress of nuns at Rupertsberg evidently did. It is certainly worth considering the effect of women's decoration of their altars (at Göß, Rupertsberg, or Wichmannsburg) and their clothing of the priest himself (at Göß and also Wilton, if it was a priest who wore Edith's alb): did women's textiles curb or mitigate the author-ity of the priest? Assuming, as I do, that women intended to speak through their textile gifts, what significance can we attach to the visual programs of the textiles they made for the ornamentation of their churches, and their priests?

Letters from churchmen to secular women suggest that women's liturgi-cal gifts did serve to "place" women at the altar, allowing them a liturgical role that church councils explicitly and repeatedly refused. In a letter to Queen Matilda of England (d. 1118), Ivo of Chartres (d. 1115/1116), for instance, thanked the queen for a gift of bells to his church and assured her that the sound of the bells would prompt thoughts of her at the altar as the priests consecrated the host. Ivo promised that, through her gift, Matilda would be a participant with the priest in "these [spiritual] goods."[49] Hildebert of Lavardin was even more explicit in claiming the spiritual significance of a liturgical gift that Matilda had given, a precious candelabrum. Noting the queen's disqualifica-tion from the priesthood, based on her sex, Hildebert argued that Matilda had become like the holy women of the gospels through her gift. Just as those women had ministered to Christ's lifeless body through the spices they brought to the tomb, Hildebert wrote that Matilda took an active role in the ritual of the Mass by means of the candelabrum she gave. This gift, he told her, served as a proxy for her presence at the altar: "You also are present when Christ is sacrificed and when he is delivered to the grave; neither is celebrated without your services, since you prepare the lights in that place, where we believe in our hearts and confess with our mouths that the author of light is present."[50]

Claims that women could participate in the Mass through their liturgi-cal gifts are less explicit in the monastic setting than they are in relation to noble patrons like Matilda. However, it is clear from secular texts that women knew and shared ideas concerning the spiritual implications of their church patronage. Sending a chasuble to the dean of Amiens, the displaced French queen Ingeborg of Denmark (d. c. 1237) expressed her desire to participate in the Mass, commenting: "we have sent a chasuble, asking that you include us in your prayers, and . . . that you should make us participants in the offices and benefices that are held [in your church]."[51] While less direct, the monastic evidence indicates that nuns, too, saw spiritual meaning in their textile gifts, and, like Ingeborg, sought to participate by their gifts in the liturgical offices celebrated by their priests. According to Goscelin of St. Bertin, the spiritual significance of women's production and ornamentation of liturgical textiles extended beyond their proxy participation at the altar, allowing them even to shape clerical virtue. In describing Edith's needlework, Goscelin adopted language from Exodus 28, directly associating her with the sisters of Old Testament priests. As he wrote,

> Like the sister of Aaron and the sister of the priests of God, she embroidered with flowers the pontifical vestments of Christ with all her skill and capacity to make splendid. Here purple, dyed with Punic red, with murex and Sidonian shellfish, and twice-dipped scarlet were interwoven with gold; chrysolite, topaz, onyx, and beryl and precious stones were intertwined with gold; union pearls, the shells' treasure, which only India produces in the east and Britain, the land of the English, in the west, were set like stars in gold; the golden insignia of the cross, the golden images of the saints were outlined with a surround of pearls.[52]

Allegorical interpretations of Exodus 28 had traditionally emphasized the components of priestly vestments as markers of virtue, ideas that are reflected in medieval vesting prayers.[53] Goscelin's implied claim—that Edith contributed to clerical virtue through her needlework—indicates that churchmen could view religious women as having an influence on the spiritual authority of the priesthood through their production and donation of liturgical textiles.

Women were not fully excluded from the liturgy, even though they were not ordained to the priesthood. Secular women were lavish patrons of the church, whose gifts underscored the historical centrality of women to the unfolding of salvation history. Religious women, too, frequently featured themselves on the liturgical textiles that they made and gave, suggesting their sense that the possibilities for women's sacramental participation had not been foreclosed.[54] Like the sisters of Aaron, the Old Testament High Priest, women made and produced the cloths that priests used at the altar. For Abelard, writing to Heloise, the "daughters of Aaron" shared equally with their brothers in the Levite inheritance[55]—a claim that may have inspired more than a few female monastic needle-workers as they imagined an altar that, although officially off limits to women, they might nevertheless approach through their embroidered images.

Women and Priests: "Less Readily Heard"

Attending to women's liturgical textiles, made to clothe both the altar and the body of their priest, allows us insight into an implicit dialogue between women and their priests that is rarely explicit in textual records. Through nuns' liturgical textiles, we can glimpse women's perceptions of themselves as spiritual actors vis à vis Christ, the altar, and their priests. The prevalence of women's liturgical gifts, their tendency to focus on the altar, and their iconographic programs (which often highlighted themselves or other women), together suggest women's deep devotion to the Mass and their sense of themselves as centrally involved in the liturgy—regardless of ecclesiastical prohibitions.[56] Women's textiles hint, moreover, at their claims to a gendered spiritual priority, even over and above their priests.

A fifteenth-century textile strip, now at Gandersheim, confirms that liturgical textiles could be used by women to assert themselves spiritually, making an argument about female sanctity to their own priests, much as Edith's alb may have done.[57] The Gandersheim strip probably served originally as the border for a cope, or pluvial, the outermost vestment worn by a cantor, by priests under certain circumstances, and by clergy during liturgical processions or synods.[58] In its present state, the strip features five figures, all of them female. Mary is at its center, receiving news of the incarnation from the angel Gabriel. To her left and right a further four women are shown, three of them early Christian virgin martyrs: saints Barbara, Catharine, and Apollonia. In emphasizing these women—first, the mother of Christ, and then other saintly women who had suffered violently for their faith—the makers of the textile may have wished to remind the priests who would ultimately wear it of the central role played by female saints and martyrs in Christian history. Yet, like Edith depicting herself as Mary Magdalene on the alb she embroidered, the women who likely produced this textile also included a contemporary image: the fifth figure featured on the textile is an unidentified canoness (Figure 29). By including this woman among the identifiable saints depicted on the border, the makers suggested the ongoing potential for female sanctity among the women to whom the intended recipient—a priest—presumably

Figure 29. Canoness. Detail, Gandersheim Textile. Portal zur Geschichte, Inv. Nr. 84.

ministered. Although this priest held spiritual authority over the women in his care, the visual program of the strip seemingly claimed for women the potential for spiritual superiority: these women could join in the blessed congregation of female saints and virgin martyrs, and so transcend priestly oversight.

The Gandersheim strip postdates the period addressed in this book by several centuries, and yet it is worth considering that eleventh- and twelfth-century women might also have cautioned their priests against wielding their power indiscriminately—even as they relied on them for the sacraments. Once again, Heloise offers an apposite example. As abbess, she knew that male support was necessary to the survival of the Paraclete, and she knew how to induce Abelard to provide it. She was familiar with the biblical examples of John the Evangelist and of the seven deacons chosen to minister to devout women in the early church, both of which she cited in writing to him. She knew, too, of Jerome's devoted care for the women of Rome, and urged Abelard to adopt Jerome as a model, reminding him of Jerome's saintly care and concern for Paula, Eustochium, and Marcella (whose example of questioning engagement she adopted for herself). However, Heloise also recognized that not every priest would share Abelard's ideas concerning the spiritual value of service among women, and she worried that a future priest might be less motivated to support the women, or less able to do so. Underscoring the very real possibility that the Paraclete nuns might have difficulty securing a sympathetic and competent priest after Abelard's death, Heloise confessed to him her concern that "After you we may perhaps have another to guide us, one who will build something upon another's foundation, and so, we fear, he may be less likely to feel concern for us, or be less readily heard by us (*a nobis minus audiendus*); or indeed, he may be no less willing, but less able."[59]

Heloise's comment that a future priest might be "less readily heard" by the Paraclete women is telling, hinting at the complex dynamics that governed relations between nuns and their priests: evidently not all priests were "heard" by the nuns under their spiritual supervision, just as Heloise chose not always to "hear" Abelard, departing from his advice on several points. As Heloise herself reveals, religious women were not unquestioning and passive recipients of male pastoral care, but were engaged and sometimes critical in assessing the morality, theological training, and even the ability of their priests. That women could be critical of their priests is equally clear from the *Hortus deliciarum*, in which priests and monks are regularly depicted in scenes of sin, judgment, and hell: a monk clutching his moneybag is shown being led into hell, a priest tempts a nun with coins as she seeks to climb the ladder of virtue, and avarice is identified as a uniquely priestly sin.[60] Notably, it is religious men—and not women—who feature as sources of sin and temptation in these images. Religious women were clearly capable of criticizing their priests, whom they might sometimes choose not to "hear."

*   *   *

Almost two decades ago, Joan Ferrante cautioned against an overly negative interpretation of the possibilities available to medieval women, commenting that "to concentrate too much on the negative is to play into the hands of the patriarchal view that women were able to do little, therefore they did nothing valuable, therefore we do not need to include them in our studies."[61] Much has changed since Ferrante's plea for greater attention to "what medieval women could and did do"—a subject whose richness and depth she explored in her work on women's participation in medieval textual production. Recent work on queenship, power, militancy, holiness, authorship, artistry, patronage, gender and sexuality—as well as a host of other topics—has dramatically expanded our sense of women's spheres of activity and influence. But a further aspect of Ferrante's study has attracted less attention. Commenting on the collaboration of men with women in the production of medieval texts, Ferrante noted that it was often clerics who worked together with individual women (generally secular women) to produce histories that not infrequently featured women as subjects of praise. "There is no small irony," she observed, "in the fact that the same institution that produced such virulent misogyny, the church, also produced some very strong propaganda for women's claims."[62]

In this book, I have tried to heed Ferrante's call to balance theory and practice—positive and negative—as I focused on medieval priests and their relations with women. Like Ferrante, I acknowledge misogyny, but I have been cautious not to let the presumption that misogyny was dominant and universal obscure the productive ways in which women and men nevertheless interacted, and the positive views of "woman" that some religious men held.[63] Instead of focusing on "virulent misogyny," I have emphasized the "strong propaganda for women's claims" that emerged from the pens of individual religious men, whether monks or secular priests. In so doing, I have drawn on the work of such scholars as Alcuin Blamires, John Coakley, Julie Hotchin, Mary Martin McLaughlin, Constant Mews, Barbara Newman, Bruce

Venarde, and of course Joan Ferrante herself—all of whom have explored the productive possibilities of women's relations with religious men, and vice versa.

For the most part, however, I have let the medieval sources guide me—drawing me into a world of spiritual symbolism, ambivalence, enthusiasm, and sometimes gender inversion. Women were subject to their priests, but they also warned the men that they might not always be "heard." Men ministered the sacraments to nuns, controlling a central spiritual symbol and experience, but they also imagined women at the cross and tomb, touching Christ's body, anointing his head and washing his feet, and witnessing his resurrection. Medieval nuns stood at a distance from the altar (sometimes behind a screen or in a segregated nuns' choir), yet they placed themselves on it figuratively through their textile gifts, often richly embroidered with images of female saints, of women at the cross, and of themselves, as named individuals, adoring Christ. Men imagined nuns as brides of Christ, attributing a spiritually intimate role to women, while picturing themselves as mere servants and nuns as their *dominae*. These ideas may never have become dominant in medieval religion, but they were consistently present and consistently known—both to women and to the men whose spiritual services supported and enabled female religious life. My account of these men and of their spiritual and intellectual networks offers a counter to narratives of decline for women and mounting misogyny, while proposing a new way of considering male spirituality—one that recognizes men's confidence in religious women, who, as brides and "wise virgins", might guide them, at the last, to the heavenly wedding feast.

Beati pauperes

"Beati pauperes spiritu quoniam ipsorum est regnum celorum."[1] Inter hos iterum qui Dei potius quam mundi sunt pauperes, nonnulla est differentia, cum alii plus egeant, alii minus! Alii obsequio Dei magis occupati sunt, alii minus.[2] Hii quidem qui, seculo penitus abrenunciantes, apostolicam imitantur vitam, veriores sunt pauperes et Deo propinquiores. Sed sunt hujus professionis non solummodo viri, sed et feminę. Quę cum sint fragilioris sexus et infirmioris naturę, tanto est earum virtus Domino acceptabilior atque perfectior, quanto cum natura infirmior, juxta illud apostoli: "Nam virtus in infirmitate perficitur."[3] Iste cum terrenis conjugiis vel carnalium voluptatum illecebris spretis, sponso immortali se copulant, summi regis sponsę effectę, omnium ejus servorum efficiuntur dominę. Quod diligenter beatus Hieronimus adtendens, cum ad unam harum sponsarum. Eustochium scriberet, ait: "Hęc idcirco domina mea Eustochium, Dominam quippe debeo vocare sponsam Domini mei."[4] Quod si tantus ecclesię doctor veraciter profiteri non erubuit, et vos eas dominas vestras rebus ipsis magis quam verbis recognoscentes, ne differatis earum inopie subvenire, et vos longe amplius Domini vestri sponsis debere quam servis! Et eas apud sponsum proprium plus posse quam servos agnoscatis.[5] "In carcere eram, Dominus inquit, et venistis ad me."[6] Nonnulla misericordia est eis subvenire, qui in carceribus hominum inviti tenentur. Sed maxima est subvenire his, quę se sponte Domini carceribus in perpetuo mancipaverunt, donec sponso occurrentes cum ipso intrent ad nuptias, sicut ipse met sponsus asserit dicens: "Et quę paratę erant intraverunt secum ad nuptias."[7] Ut illic videlicet quasi uxores assidua cohabitatione fiant, quę hic extiterunt tanquam sponsę. Ad quam quidem celestium societatem nuptiarum et ęterna tabernacula,[8] ipsę vos meritis et intercessionibus suis, secum introducant, ut illic per eas percipiatis ęterna, quę hic a vobis suscipiunt temporalia, prestante ipso earum sponso Domino Jesu Christo, cui est honor et gloria, in sęcula sęculorum. Amen.

Translation

Blessed are the poor in spirit for theirs is the kingdom of heaven. Again, among the poor who belong to God rather than to the world, there is a difference, because some are more in need and others less! Some are occupied more in the service of God, others less. Those who imitate the apostolic life, renouncing the world utterly, are more authentically poor and closer to God. To this profession belong not only men, but also women. Because these women are of the more fragile sex and a more infirm nature, their virtue is all the more gratifying and perfect to God as their nature is weaker, as the apostle writes: "For virtue is made perfect in weakness." These women have rejected earthly unions and the enticements of carnal pleasures. They join themselves to a heavenly bridegroom and, made brides of the highest king, become mistresses (*dominae*) of all his servants. Blessed Jerome noted this, when he wrote to Eustochium, one of these brides, saying: "For this reason is this woman Eustochium my mistress, because I am duty bound to call the bride of my Lord 'mistress.'" But if the great doctor of the church was not embarrassed to profess this truly, you should not delay in assisting their poverty, recognizing them as your mistresses by your actions more than by your words. Acknowledge that you owe more by far to the spouses of your Lord than to his servants and that they have greater influence with their own Spouse than do his servants. "For I was in prison," the Lord says, "and you came to me." It is a mercy to assist them who are held in prisons of men against their wishes, but it is most merciful to succour these who have voluntarily surrendered themselves in perpetuity to the cloisters of God, until meeting the Groom they enter into marriage with him, just as the Bridegroom himself confirms, saying, "And those who were ready entered with him into the nuptials." Thus those they who have lived here as brides shall become, as it were, wives in that place, dwelling together always. May those very brides, through their merits and prayers, lead you with them to that fellowship of the celestial marriage feast and to the eternal tabernacles, so that there you may reap eternal rewards through those women who here receive temporal goods from you, by the gift of their bridegroom, the Lord Jesus Christ, to whom be honor and glory, for ever. Amen.

NOTES

PROLOGUE

1. Chaucer, *The Canterbury Tales*; ed. Benson, 26.

2. For a detailed discussion of the spiritual enthusiasm and religious renewal that marked the late eleventh and twelfth centuries, see Constable, *Reformation*. On clerical celibacy, see Parish, *Clerical Celibacy*; Barstow, *Married Priests*; Thibodeaux, *Manly Priest*; and the essays in Frassetto, ed., *Medieval Purity and Piety*.

3. Brooke, "Gregorian Reform in Action," 18.

4. For the effects of the celibacy campaign on the families of priests, see van Houts, "The Fate of the Priests' Sons"; Thibodeaux, *Manly Priest*, 64–85; Taglia, "'On Account of Scandal . . .'"; and Elliott, "The Priest's Wife."

5. Oliva, "The Nun's Priest," 115.

6. For discussion of the term *domina*, and its semantic range, see Chapter 1, n. 58.

7. Bynum, *Holy Feast*, 229.

8. Blamires, *Case*, 1. Blamires describes the "case for women" as "a corpus of ideas about how to fashion a commendation of women explicitly or implicitly retaliating against misogyny." Blamires, *Case*, 2.

9. Blamires, *Case*, 230.

CHAPTER I

Notes to epigraphs: Marbode, *Epistola ad Robertum*, 14; *Deux vies*, 538–539.
Abelard, *Institutio*, 40; *The Letter Collection*, 406–407.

1. Bernold of Constance (d. 1100) commented specifically on the numbers of women adopting the religious life, writing in 1091 that "an innumerable multitude not only of men, but even of women, adopted such a life in these times, in order to live in obedience to clerics or monks." Bernold of Constance, *Chronicon*; ed. Robinson, 382–384. Guibert of Nogent (d. c. 1124) commented on the "crowds" of converts—both women and men—joining those who "ushered in a new season of religious conversion." Guibert of Nogent, *Monodiae*, I, 11; ed. Labande, 72; trans. Archambault, 33. Herman of Tournai (d. c. 1147) wrote of a similar scene, noting the "youths and maidens, old men and youngsters, abandoning the world and coming from all over the province to convert." Herman explicitly linked the conversions to the apostolic example, commenting that "it was like that which one reads in the *Acts of the Apostles*." Herman of Tournai, *Liber de restauratione*, 66; ed. Waitz, MGH SS 14, 305; trans. Nelson, 96. The *life*

of Stephen of Obazine (d. 1159), too, reports on the striking conversions of women. Noting that "nobles and lowborn persons, men as well as women, began to leave the world," the *life* particularly emphasized the "wondrous change" embraced by noblewomen, who "converted to this poverty and humility." *Vita S. Stephani Obazinensis*, I, 29 and I, 30; ed. Aubrun, 86–88; trans. Feiss, O'Brien, and Pepin, 158, 159.

2. Gary Macy has shown that abbesses (like abbots) were "ordained" to their ministry in the early Middle Ages, and were recognized as such by their contemporaries. It was only toward the end of the twelfth century that "the concentration of sacramental power into the hands of the priest" took place, and with it the redefinition of ordination to focus on "the power to consecrate the bread and wine during the liturgy of the Mass." Macy, *Hidden History*, 47, 110. On the ordination rites and significant liturgical roles of abbesses in the early medieval period, see Macy, *Hidden History*, 80–86. For the exclusion of women from all forms of ordination during the twelfth and thirteenth centuries, see Macy, *Hidden History*, 89–110. For the continued involvement of religious women in various forms of ministry, see Bugyis, *In Christ's Stead*.

3. On the variety of arrangements between women's monasteries and their priests, see the essays in Griffiths and Hotchin, eds., *Partners in Spirit*. On men's provision of pastoral care for women, see Griffiths and Hotchin, "Women and Men in the Medieval Religious Landscape"; Schreiner, "Seelsorge in Frauenklöstern"; Bouter, ed., *Les religieuses dans le cloître et dans le monde*, 331–391; Johnson, *Equal in Monastic Profession*, 180–191; Parisse, *Les nonnes au Moyen Age*, 134–140; Golding, *Gilbert*, 71–137; and, focusing on Fontevraud, Gold, *The Lady and the Virgin*, 76–115. For women's perspectives on pastoral care, see Griffiths, "'Men's Duty,'" 15–19; Lewis, *By Women*, 176–199; and Hotchin, "Abbot as Guardian," 59–63.

4. From the ninth century on, monks in many communities were ordained. On the increasing ordination of monks, see Constable, "Religious Communities, 1024–1215," 351–352.

5. Seguin served some twenty-five years as prior at Marcigny during the early twelfth century. Wollasch, "Frauen in der Cluniacensis ecclesia," 105; and Wischermann, *Marcigny-sur-Loire*, 98–102. Gunther served as provost of Lippoldsberg for some twenty years, from c. 1138/9 until 1161. Hotchin, "Women's Reading and Monastic Reform," 148. The chaplain Walter is listed as a witness in charters from the English community of Godstow for some 15 years. Elkins, *Holy Women of Twelfth-Century England*, 64. Similarly long service can be seen in the fourteenth century. Peter, the chaplain at Kirschgarten in Worms, served from 1315–1331. Kleinjung, *Frauenklöster als Kommunikationszentren*, 91.

6. For the increasing emphasis on the Mass in monastic life from c. 400–c. 1200, with particular attention to relations between nuns and ordained men, see Griffiths, "The Mass in Monastic Practice." As Gisela Muschiol has shown, early medieval nuns were less reliant on ordained men than religious women in the later period, a function of the more frequent celebration of the Mass in monastic communities after the eighth century. Muschiol, "Zeit und Raum"; and Muschiol, "Men, Women, and Liturgical Practice." By the early thirteenth century, ordained men were required not only to consecrate the Mass, but for a variety of pastoral tasks, as abbesses were prohibited from hearing their nuns' confessions, blessing them, and preaching within their own communities. Macy, *Hidden History*, 102–103. Despite women's exclusion from ordination, nuns could sometimes communicate in the absence of a priest, distributing the *eulogia* or bread that had already been blessed. See Macy, *Hidden History*, 63–64; Leclercq, "Eucharistic Celebrations Without Priests"; Leclercq, "Prières médiévales pour recevoir l'Eucharistie," 329–331; and Lauwers, "Les femmes et l'eucharistie."

7. Venarde, *Women's Monasticism*, 54. For the expansion of women's monasticism in Germany, see Felten, "Frauenklöster"; Bönnen, Haverkamp, and Hirschmann, "Religiöse

Frauengemeinschaften," 412–414; Röckelein, "Frauen im Umkreis der benediktinischen Reformen"; Parisse, *Religieux et religieuses*; and Wilms, *Amatrices ecclesiarum*, 21–24, 54–55. For expansion in England, see Elkins; and Thompson, *Women Religious*. Urban Küsters showed that women's religious enthusiasm and conversion at this time prompted developments in men's provision of spiritual care for them; Küsters focuses on the *St. Trudperter Hohelied*, a vernacular text written for nuns in the second quarter of the twelfth century. Küsters, *Der verschlossene Garten*.

8. Some priests came from male communities, to which they would return after a period of service among women. Others were permanently attached to women's communities, living in houses founded by powerful nuns to ensure their access to spiritual care as, for instance, at St. Gorgon and Truttenhausen (founded in 1178 and 1180, respectively, by Herrad, abbess of Hohenbourg). Griffiths, *Garden of Delights*, 43–47.

9. Canons at Sainte-Radegonde in Poitiers, a community dependent on the abbey of Sainte-Croix, vowed obedience to the abbess and were required to perform regular sacramental services for the women. A ninth-century capitulary of Louis the Pious reports that the clerics were to be obedient to the women in all things. "Ipsi per omnia ad dictam congregationem sanctae crucis honeste et perfecte obedientes sint atque subiecti." *Capitulare de monasterio S. Crucis Pictavensi* (822–824), cap. 7; ed. Boretius, MGH Capit. 1, 302. For a discussion of relations between the canons at Sainte-Radegonde and the abbess of Sainte-Croix from the sixth to the fifteenth century, see Edwards, "'Man Can be Subject to Woman'"; and (although in less detail) Favreau, "Le culte de Sainte Radegonde à Poitiers."

10. Although the choice of a priest was not official until it had been confirmed by the bishop, nuns and canonesses could often secure the right to choose their priest, as Caesarius of Arles advocated for the women at Arles during the early sixth century: Caesarius of Arles, *Testamentum*, 5; ed. and trans. de Vogüé and Courreau, 387; trans. Klingshirn, 73. Augustine assumed that monastic women could request the "transfer" of their male *praepositus* if he was not satisfactory. Augustine of Hippo, Epist. 211 (*Obiurgatio*, 4); trans. Lawless, 106. During the central Middle Ages, the right to choose a priest or provost was often negotiated by the women, and confirmed in foundation charters. At Ichtershausen, the earliest Cistercian house for women in northern Germany, the nuns secured a charter in 1147 from Bishop Heinrich of Metz stipulating that any provost who lived "freely and reprehensibly," or who misappropriated the monastery's property, should be dismissed from his position. *Mainzer Urkundenbuch. II*, ed. Acht, no. 98.

11. For discussion of the provost and his role in women's monasteries, see Schlotheuber, "The 'Freedom of Their Own Rule.'" In Parisse's view, the office of the provost enabled male control and surveillance over nuns in reformed communities. Parisse, *Religieux et religieuses*, 167.

12. Idung of Prüfening, *Argumentum super quatuor questionibus*, 7; ed. Huygens, 75; trans. Leahey, 176.

13. *The Desert Fathers*, trans. Ward, 31. In his *life* of Gregory VII (c. 1128), Paul of Bernried reports how Gregory had touched his niece's necklace while discussing her desire to practice a life of chastity—a transgression for which he was punished. As Paul wrote, "This reminds us of the saying, 'It is well for a man not to touch a woman.'" Paul of Bernried, *Vita Gregorii*, 32; trans. Robinson, 280–281.

14. Basil of Caesarea, *The Longer Responses*, 33; trans. Silvas, 236. Jerome wrote to Eustochium that she should "ask one whose life commends him, whose age puts him above suspicion, whose reputation does not belie him." Jerome, Epist. 22.29; ed. Hilberg, I, CSEL 54, 187; trans. Fremantle, 34. In the twelfth century, Aelred of Rievaulx advised his sister

that the priest provided for her should be "an elderly man of mature character and good reputation." Aelred of Rievaulx, *De institutione inclusarum*, 6; ed. Hoste and Talbot, 642; trans. Macpherson, 51.

15. Aelred of Rievaulx warned that "the evil in our very bodies is always to be feared; it can . . . arouse and unman even the oldest." Aelred of Rievaulx, *De institutione inclusarum*, 6; ed. Hoste and Talbot, 642; trans. Macpherson, 52.

16. In his *Dialogues*, Gregory the Great reported that, as Equitius was praying one night, he saw himself made a eunuch "while an angel stood by"; thereafter, he felt secure enough in his God-given virtue to take on the care of women, although he warned others "not to be too eager to follow his example." Gregory the Great, *Dialogues*, I, 4, 1–2; ed. de Vogüé, II, 38; trans. Zimmerman, 16. Gerald of Wales reported the story of a late antique monk named Eliah, who acted as chaplain and steward for some three hundred women. Experiencing "carnal desires," Eliah withdrew into the desert and was visited by angels, who delivered him from temptation: one "held him by the hands and another by the feet; the third hastily seized a sharp knife and cut off his testicles." (As Gerald clarified, "he did not really do so; it only seemed that he did"). Gerald of Wales, *Gemma ecclesiastica*, II, 17; ed. Brewer, 246; trans. Hagen, 187. For discussion, see Murray, "Sexual Mutilation and Castration Anxiety"; Kuefler, "Castration and Eunuchism in the Middle Ages"; and the essays in Tracy, ed., *Castration and Culture*. Origen's auto-castration is reported by Eusebius: Eusebius of Caesarea, *Ecclesiastical History*, 6.8.1–2; trans. Oulton and Lake, II, 28–29. For "physical and spiritual castration" among early Christians, see Kuefler, *Manly Eunuch*, 260–273. On Origen's context and legacy, see Finn, *Asceticism in the Graeco-Roman World*, 100–130.

17. Penalties for infractions could be severe: Fructuosus of Braga (d. 665) declared that any monk speaking to a nun alone "shall be publicly stretched out and flogged with one hundred blows of the lash." Fructuosus of Braga, *Regula monastica communis*, 15; PL 87: 1123; trans. Barlow, 199.

18. Second Council of Seville (619), canon 11; ed. Mansi, 10: 560–561. This ruling was well known: Gratian cited it in his *Decretum*: Gratian, *Decretum*, C.18 q.2 c.24; ed. Friedberg, 1, 835–836. Abelard referred to it in his *Rule* for the Paraclete: Abelard, *Institutio*, 42; *The Letter Collection*, 408–409.

19. *Institutio sanctimonialium*, 27; ed. Werminghoff, MGH Conc. 2.1, 455. For discussion, see Schilp, *Norm und Wirklichkeit*; Muschiol, "Liturgie und Klausur," 129–135; and Muschiol, "Das 'gebrechlichere Geschlecht,'" 24–27. As a further precaution, the *Institutio* required that the women make their confession in church and in view of the other sisters.

20. An early ninth-century capitulary noted that no man could enter the female monastery except the priest, who was permitted to enter with a witness to visit the sick or to say Mass for the nuns; he was to leave immediately having fulfilled his spiritual purpose. *Capitulare ecclesiastica ad Salz data a. 803–4*, c. 5; ed. Boretius, MGH Capit. 1, 119. See also *Capitulare missorum generale*, c. 18; ed. Boretius, MGH Capit. 1, 95.

21. *Speculum virginum*, 2.260–302; ed. Seyfarth, 50–51; trans. Newman, 276–277. For discussion of the *Speculum*, see the essays in Mews, ed., *Listen Daughter*; and Powell, "The Mirror and the Woman." The *life* of Christina of Markyate tells of a cleric who took Christina into his care, only to be tormented by desire until he was driven to present himself naked before her. *De S. Theodora*, 43; ed. Talbot, 114; rev. trans. Fanous and Leyser, 46. Women, too, could fall in love with their priests, as Ivo of Chartres (d. 1115/16) recognized, reminding the nuns at St. Avit that they had vowed to marry Christ, not clerics. Ivo of Chartres, Epist. 10; ed. Leclercq,

42–43. Gerald of Wales reported the story of a Gilbertine nun who became infatuated with Gilbert of Sempringham. To quell the woman's desire, Gilbert allegedly presented himself naked at the chapter meeting—a "horrid sight" as Gerald commented. Gerald of Wales, *Gemma ecclesiastica*, II, 17; ed. Brewer, 247–248; trans. Hagen, 188. For a discussion of love between nuns and monks, see Schmidt, "Amor in claustro."

22. Aelred of Rievaulx, *Speculum caritatis*, 3.66–68; ed. Hoste and Talbot, 136–137; trans. Connor, 266–267. Aelred's fear that temptation could strike even the most pious was confirmed in Jacques de Vitry's (d. 1240) report of a man (possibly Jacques himself), who grasped a holy woman's hand "from an excess of spiritual affection" and became sexually aroused: the man "felt the first masculine stirrings rising in him." The woman, Marie d'Oignies, knew nothing of the priest's arousal, but heard a voice from heaven, commanding, "Do not touch me." Jacques de Vitry, *Vita B. Mariae Oigniacensis*, VIII, 75; *AA SS*, June, 4: 656; trans. King, 102. This episode is discussed in Brown, "The Chaste Erotics." The *life* of Abundus (d. 1239) also reported that temptation befell a "certain devout man" who "had a caring love for a girl living a dedicated religious life." As Abundus's biographer Goswin of Bossut commented, "the spiritual love he had been showing the girl turned into a fleshly love." Goswin of Bossut, *Vita Abundi*, 17; ed. Frenken, 29; trans. Cawley, 239. Similarly, Thomas of Cantimpré bemoaned the fact that "religious men are copulating with religious women," commenting that "what certain men began in the spirit is consummated in the flesh." Thomas of Cantimpré, *Bonum de universale de apibus*, 2.30.19; cited in Elliott, *Bride*, 174.

23. For a discussion of the historiography of "reform" as it relates to women, see Griffiths, "Women and Reform"; and Griffiths, "The Cross and the *Cura monialium*." Beatrix Wilms offered an early corrective to the tendency to focus on women as objects of male control in studies of the reform period. As she showed, women were actively involved in reform and were often reformers themselves; they were, moreover, often admired by religious men, whose spiritual lives were re-energized through them. Wilms, 204.

24. Moore, "Family, Community, and Cult."

25. On clerical celibacy and reform, see the essays in Frassetto, ed., *Medieval Purity and Piety*; Barstow, 47–104; McLaughlin, *Sex, Gender, and Episcopal Authority*, 31–36; Thomas, *The Secular Clergy*, 154–189. Jennifer Thibodeaux explores the implications for clerical masculinity of the imposition of celibacy on the clergy: Thibodeaux, *Manly Priest* (see also n. 54, below). For medieval arguments in defense of clerical marriage, see Frauenknecht, *Der Verteidigung der Priesterehe*; Barstow, 105–73; Melve, "The Public Debate on Clerical Marriage"; Thibodeaux, *Manly Priest*, 86–111; van Houts, "The Fate of the Priests' Sons"; and Meijns, "Opposition to Clerical Continence."

26. Peter Damian, Epist. 112.34; ed. Reindel, MGH Briefe d. dt. Kaiserzeit 4.3, 278; trans. Blum, 4, 276. See Leclercq, "S. Pierre Damien et les femmes;" Elliott, "The Priest's Wife," 100–106. On the concern of reformers like Peter Damian to ensure the purity of the priesthood as an order "set apart" from secular society, see Fulton, *From Judgment to Passion*, 106–118. Fulton notes that "Peter was afraid, not of women, or money, or food as such, but of hell" (114).

27. McNamara, "Herrenfrage"; Elliott, "The Priest's Wife," 81–85. For a similar interpretation, see Macy, *Hidden History*, 111–127. Other scholars, notably Conrad Leyser and Maureen Miller, have cautioned against a literal interpretation of reforming rhetoric, arguing that "woman" served a symbolic function for reformers, providing a means for elite men to discuss and negotiate power among themselves. As Leyser and Miller argue, reformers were more concerned with notions of masculinity, and its gradations among ordained and secular men, than

with vilifying women. Leyser, "Custom, Truth, and Gender"; Miller, "Masculinity, Reform, and Clerical Culture." See also McLaughlin, *Sex, Gender, and Episcopal Authority*. Drawing attention to the sexualized language of reform, McLaughlin argues that institutions, and not individuals, were the primary focus of reforming concerns.

28. "Sorores quidem amplius periculosum est coadunare, quia antiquus hostis femineo consorcio complures expulit a recto tramite Paradisi." *La règle du temple*, 70; ed. Curzon, 69; trans. Upton-Ward, 36. For discussion, see Bom, *Women in the Military Orders of the Crusades*, 23–27; Nicholson, "Templar Attitudes"; and Forey, "Women and the Military Orders." Bom and Nicholson note that women continued to be accepted to the Temple even after 1129.

29. "Si David mansuetissimus, Salomon sapientissimus, Samson quoque fortissimus, muliebri laqueo capti sunt, quis eius blanditiis non cedet?" Stephen of Muret, *Regula*, 39; ed. Becquet, 86. For discussion of the *Rule*, see Becquet, "La règle." The inevitability of sexual temptation was underscored, too, by the Cistercian abbot Bernard of Clairvaux, who cautioned his monks against contact with women, noting that "To be always in a woman's company without having carnal knowledge of her .. [is] .. a greater miracle than raising the dead." Bernard of Clairvaux, *Sermo* 65.4; ed. Leclercq, Talbot, and Rochais, *Sancti Bernardi Opera*, 2, 175; trans. Walsh and Edmonds, *On the Song of Songs*, 3, 184. See Berman's interpretation of this sermon as dealing with "heretics, not syneisacticism." Berman, "Were There Twelfth-Century Cistercian Nuns?" 847, n. 60.

30. The Mass was not a central focus of monastic life (either for men or for women) when Benedict wrote his *Rule*. He therefore offered no explicit guidance concerning celebration of the Mass, and envisioned a monastic community of laymen (indeed, he advised caution regarding the acceptance of priests into the community). Griffiths, "The Mass in Monastic Practice."

31. Heloise criticized Benedict's inattention to the needs of women in the monastic life. Heloise, Epist. 6.4; *The Letter Collection*, 220–221. See Georgianna, "In Any Corner of Heaven." According to Idung of Prüfening, Benedict's silence on the topic of women indicated not that monasticism was a male phenomenon, but that religious women needed no rule of their own, since men routinely exercised spiritual oversight over them ("in those times monasteries of virgins existed only under the guardianship of abbots"). Idung of Prüfening, *Argumentum super quatuor questionibus*, 7; ed. Huygens, 75; trans. Leahey, 176. In his *Dialogus duorum monachorum*, Idung noted Benedict's failure to discuss male supervision of female religious life, concluding that, since Basil had addressed the question, "abbots may, if they wish, act as spiritual guides to nuns." Idung of Prüfening, *Dialogus duorum monachorum*, 3, 12; ed. Huygens, 159; trans. O'Sullivan, 107.

32. Gerald of Wales reports, for instance, the refusal of a group of male hermits to allow women access to the island on which they lived. Gerald of Wales, *Itinerarium Kambriae*, II, 7; ed. Dimock, 131; trans. Thorpe, 190. For spatial restrictions on women's access to male saints' shrines, or monastic churches, see Schulenburg, "Gender, Celibacy, and Proscriptions of Sacred Space."

33. As Jo Ann McNamara writes, "It is probable that there were establishments of men which effectively barred all women from the cloistered precincts. But there was no known community of nuns without some considerable detachment of men who came and went freely and their regulation was one of the problems confronting every abbess and her subordinate officials." McNamara, *Ordeal of Community*, 10. Bönnen, Haverkamp, and Hirschmann similarly observed that: "ausschließlich von Frauen bewohnte Klöster hat es wohl nie gegeben." Bönnen, Haverkamp, and Hirschmann, 379. On the challenges to female enclosure posed by male staff in women's houses, see Hicks, *Religious Life in Normandy*, 122–126.

34. The sixth-century *Rule* of Caesarius of Arles allowed that churchmen were permitted to enter the "cloistered part of the monastery and the oratories." Skilled workmen were also allowed occasional admittance, to perform necessary repairs. Caesarius of Arles, *Regula sanctarum virginum*, 36; ed. de Vogüé and Courreau, 218–219; trans. McCarthy, 182–183.

35. Schäfer, *Die Kanonissenstifter*, 95–114. On arrangements between canons and canonesses, see Schilp, ". . . *sorores et fratres*"; Schilp, "Der Kanonikerkonvent"; Klapp, "Negotiating Autonomy"; and Andermann, "Zur Erforschung mittelalterlicher Kanonissenstifte," 26–29. Penny Gold explores the charters from Le Ronceray d'Angers for evidence of relations between the nuns and their male personnel. As she comments, "the canons were not just 'employees' but members of the community—not in the same way the nuns were, yet they were more integrally involved in community identity and community affairs than one might suspect." Gold, "The Charters of Le Ronceray d'Angers," 127.

36. *Capitulare de monasterio S. Crucis Pictavensi* (822–824), cap. 6–7; ed. Boretius, MGH Capit. 1, 302. Gerbstedt, founded in 985, housed an abbess and twenty-four sisters, and had income sufficient to allow for six priests, a deacon, and a subdeacon. *Urkundenbuch der Klöster der Grafschaft Mansfeld*, ed. Krühne, 9. The community of St. Stephan in Strasbourg, founded in the eighth century, included some 30 women, 4 canons or priests, and (during the later Middle Ages) as many as 18 other clerics. Klapp, "Negotiating Autonomy," 376. The size of male communities at select women's houses can be found in Parisse, *Les nonnes*, 136–137; and Schäfer, *Die Kanonissenstifter*, 97–100.

37. Koebner, *Venantius Fortunatus*, 39–66. Fortunatus wrote a biography of the Frankish queen and nun, Radegund (*De vita sanctae Radegundis*), as well as several poems for women at Sainte-Croix, in which he thanked them for gifts and expressed his affection: *Venantius Fortunatus: Personal and Political Poems*, trans. George. On Fortunatus's poems to Radegund and Agnes, see George, *Venantius Fortunatus*, 161–177. On his relationships with these women against the frame of "ennobling love," see Jaeger, *Ennobling Love*, 34–35; and, with reference to the medieval tradition of *courtoisie*, see Dronke, *Medieval Latin*, I, 200–209. Fortunatus's background and biography are discussed in George, *Venantius Fortunatus*, 18–34 (see 212–214 for evidence concerning the date of his ordination as priest).

38. Obermünster necrology, BayHStA, KL Regensburg-Obermünster 1, fol. 67v. On the Obermünster necrology, see Edwards, *Noblewomen of Prayer*, 160–165. Edwards comments that "the nuns are described in exactly these terms, merely substituting 'sororum.'" (164, n. 309)

39. For the size of the men's community, see Wischermann, *Marcigny-sur-Loire*, 143. See also Wollasch, "Frauen in der Cluniacensis ecclesia," 102–103; and Röckelein, "Die Auswirkung der Kanonikerreform des 12. Jahrhunderts," 282–291.

40. Gilo, *Vita sancti Hugonis abbatis*, I, 12; ed. Cowdrey, 61–63. For discussion of pastoral care at Marcigny, see Hunt, *Cluny*, 186–194. For the priors of Marcigny, see Wischermann, *Marcigny-sur-Loire*, 93–110. Wollasch comments that the monks Hugh sent to Marcigny were old and sick. Wollasch, "Frauen in der Cluniacensis ecclesia," 102. On Cluniac monasteries for women in England, and their ties to men's houses, see Thompson, *Women Religious*, 83–93.

41. *Le cartulaire de Marcigny-sur-Loire*, I, nos. 13, 31, 72, and II, no. 164; ed. Richard, 13, 29, 54, 97. On men at Marcigny, see Wischermann, *Marcigny-sur-Loire*, 83–87, 93–110, 139–143.

42. Sharon Elkins comments that "approximately one quarter of all the new foundations for women were actually for women and men." Elkins, xvii. Penny Johnson notes that there were "variations" on the "theme of isolation of one sex within the cloister." Johnson, 30.

43. Thompson, *Women Religious*, 70–73. As Thompson noted, "the association of men and women following a religious life was more prevalent than has hitherto been recognized." Thompson, *Women Religious*, 72–73. See also Bönnen, Haverkamp, and Hirschmann, 374.

44. The literature on Fontevraud is extensive. Parisse, "Fontevraud, monastère double" (on the question of Fontevraud as a "double" monastery); Dalarun, "Pouvoir et autorité"; Kerr, *Religious Life for Women*; Müller, *Forming and Re-Forming Fontevraud*; and Venarde, *Women's Monasticism*, 57–66. With particular attention to relations between the women and men (which, as Bienvenu and Simmons note, could be problematic), see Bienvenu, "Origines et évolution"; Gold, "Male/Female Cooperation"; Simmons, "The Abbey Church at Fontevraud;" and Thompson, *Women Religious*, 113–132. The desertion of men from Fontevraud is attested in sources from the mid-twelfth century: Bienvenu, "Origines et évolution," 73–75.

45. For Sigena, see García-Guijarro Ramos, "The Aragonese Hospitaller Monastery of Sigena"; and Bom, 82–85. For Füssenich, see Wolbrink, "Necessary Priests and Brothers." Men in "women's" houses of the Premonstratensian order in Cologne are listed in Ehlers-Kisseler, *Die Anfänge der Prämonstratenser*, 519–565.

46. Hildegard of Bingen expressed the real concern that, without a priest to serve at Rupertsberg, "spiritual religion will be totally destroyed among us." Hildegard of Bingen, Epist. 10; ed. Van Acker, CCCM 91, 24; trans. Baird and Ehrman, I, 45–46. For discussion, see Griffiths, "Monks and Nuns at Rupertsberg" and this book's Conclusion.

47. Jerome, Epist. 52; ed. and trans. Cain, 40–41. Marbode, *Epistola ad Robertum*, 9; *Deux vies*, 532–533.

48. On the characterization of religious women as brides of Christ, see Elliott, *Bride*. Elliott traces the metaphor of marriage to Christ in the lives of religious women across more than a millennium—from late antiquity, when the bridal metaphor was first applied to the individual female virgin, to the fifteenth century, when anxieties concerning the bride's potential for adultery coincided with gendered and erotically inflected charges of witchcraft.

49. Grundmann, *Religious Movements in the Middle Ages*, 91 (referring here to the order of Cîteaux). Grundmann outlined Franciscan and Dominican efforts to avoid the pastoral care of women during the thirteenth century, establishing a model of male opposition to the care of women that has been widely accepted. Grundmann, 89–137. Sally Thompson, too, sees the "provision of masculine support" as a significant problem for religious women, with the new orders ultimately rejecting female members. Thompson, *Women Religious*, 212–213. The assumption that male monastic and mendicant orders rejected female members, and the pastoral obligations they represented, was based largely on Cistercian and Premonstratensian examples. Joseph Greven highlighted the supposed Premonstratensian rejection of women in Greven, *Die Anfänge der Beginen*. For a revision of Greven's thesis, see Freed, "Urban Development and the 'Cura monialium.'" Bruno Krings and Shelley Amiste Wolbrink offer revised accounts of women's involvement with the Premonstratensian Order: Krings, "Die Prämonstratenser und ihr weiblicher Zweig"; and Wolbrink, "Women in the Premonstratensian Order." Concerning the Cistercian response to women, see Thompson, "The Problem of the Cistercian Nuns"; and the revision of early Cistercian women's history provided by Berman, "Were There Twelfth-Century Cistercian Nuns?"; Berman, *Cistercian Evolution*, 39–45; Felten, "Der Zisterzienserorden und die Frauen"; and Felten, "Zisterzienserinnen in Deutschland." See also Barrière and Henneau, eds., *Cîteaux et les femmes*; Lester, *Creating Cistercian Nuns*; and Freeman, "Nuns." Martha Newman explores the "anxieties and contradictions" for some Cistercian monks in response to the spiritual proximity of women: Newman, "Real Men and Imaginary Women."

50. On men's attraction to holy women, see McGuire, "Holy Women and Monks"; Coakley, *Women, Men, and Spiritual Power*; and the essays in Mooney, ed., *Gendered Voices*. See also below, n. 161. For the contrary argument that women were more emotionally and spiritually invested in their male spiritual guides than these men were in them, see Elliott, *Bride*, 163–164.

51. McGuire, "Holy Women and Monks," 347–348.

52. McNamara, *Sisters in Arms*, 220. In his discussion of the *cura monialium*, Brian Golding comments that "the authority exercised over female communities by male clerics . . . was often autocratic and often resented, both by the nuns themselves and also by those who exercised it, as inappropriate activity." Golding, "Bishops and Nuns," 97. For a brief discussion of the historiography of the pastoral care of nuns, see Griffiths, " 'Men's Duty.' " For a significant exception to the assumption that the care of women was a "burden" for men, see Hotchin, "Female Religious Life and the *Cura monialium*"; and Hotchin, "Abbot as Guardian." Hotchin comments that the presence of women alongside religious men "could provide a significant outlet for male spiritual expression." Hotchin, "Abbot as Guardian," 59. For a similar view, see Wilms. Barbara Newman notes how "close spiritual bonds between male and female religious, coupled with increasing demands for physical distance, gave rise to the problem (and opportunity) of the *cura monialium*." Newman, "Liminalities," 380.

53. Toby Ditz draws attention to the pitfalls of men's history as a unilateral enterprise from which women—and the effects of men's gendered power—are absent. Ditz, "The New Men's History," 2.

54. The literature on medieval masculinity as it relates to clerical celibacy is large. See McNamara, "Herrenfrage"; Thibodeaux, *Manly Priest*; Arnold, "The Labour of Continence"; Miller, "Masculinity, Reform, and Clerical Culture"; Swanson, "Angels Incarnate"; Elliott, "Pollution, Illusion, and Masculine Disarray"; and the essays in Cullum and Lewis, eds., *Religious Men and Masculine Identity* and Thibodeaux, ed., *Negotiating Clerical Identities* (especially Part II, "Priestly Masculinity: Reconciling Celibacy and Sexuality").

55. I have benefited enormously in my thinking on this issue from the work of John Coakley, Julie Hotchin, Constant Mews, and Bruce Venarde.

56. Gundulf was loved by both men and women, according to his biographer, who reports that he devoted himself to the religious lives of both sexes: *Vita Gundulfi*, 34; ed. Thomson, 58. Gundulf was especially revered by Matilda of Scotland, who sought his guidance. *Vita Gundulfi*, 37; ed. Thomson, 61. For a discussion of Gundulf's foundation in light of episcopal oversight of nuns in twelfth- and thirteenth-century England, see Golding, "Bishops and Nuns," 100–102. Concerning the historical context of the *Vita Gundulfi*, see Potter, "The *Vita Gundulfi* in its Historical Context."

57. As Brian Golding observes, "everything, including gold and silver and all receipts from lands and sales of produce, was in the custody of the nuns." Golding, *Gilbert*, 110.

58. Sean Gilsdorf argues for a translation of *domina* that maintains the origins of the word in the Latin verb, *dominare*, to rule. "Lady" is not an accurate translation, he contends, since that word refers not to a female ruler, but to the consort of a male lord. Gilsdorf, *Queenship and Sanctity*, 66. Barbara Newman comments that *domina* was "the most common devotional title" for the Virgin Mary. Newman, *Frauenlob's Song of Songs*, 176. In the context of men's spiritual care for women, the title *domina* implied the superior status of the religious woman, by virtue of her spousal relationship to Christ. As Jerome wrote to Eustochium, whom he addressed as "mi domina Eustochium", "I am bound to call my Lord's bride 'Lady.' " Jerome, Epist. 22.2; ed. Hilberg, I, CSEL 54, 145; trans. Fremantle, 23. For the influence of Jerome's model of religious women as *dominae*, see Chapter 3. Gerald Bond identifies a "nexus of ritual

praise, feminine image, and ideology," which he calls "dominism," and which shaped "the various cults of the lady as a being of superior goodness and beauty." Bond's focus is primarily on secular women; however, his comments are relevant, too, for the religious context. Bond, *Loving Subject*, 136. For the construct of the *domina* in Roman elegy, see Fulkerson, "*Servitium amoris*," 182–188. Fulkerson, too, notes that *domina* is the "female version of 'master.' " (180).

59. "Immo vero in feminis ea maxima inventa perfectio est." Wolfger of Prüfening, *Vita Theogeri*, I, 25; ed. Jaffé, MGH SS 12, 459. A number of men identified an immediacy and simplicity in women's spirituality that they feared was lacking among male religious: as Osbert of Clare wrote to Matilda of Darenth: "holy men wish to enjoy in this world the intimacy of your sanctity." Matilda was probably a nun at Malling. Osbert of Clare, Epist. 41; ed. Williamson, 140–153. On men who defended the spiritual strength of women, see Wilms, 201–217.

60. Gregory the Great, *Dialogues*, II, 2, 1–3; ed. de Vogüé, II, 136–139; trans. Zimmerman, 59–60.

61. "Quod si adhuc aculeus ardentis libidinis desaeviret, nudum corpus inter spinarum et veprium hirsuta acumina solebat ingerere; et sic toto dilaceratus corpore, ex vulnerum multitudine voluptatem in dolorem convertere. Nec tamen sic antiquus hostis exsuperari potuit, sed species mulierum quandoque visibiles, modo spirituales, ei frequenter opposuit. Quae omnia tyrunculus Christi constanter respuit, et omnes suggestionum illius versutias vel illecebras viriliter edomando calcavit." Reginald of Durham, *Libellus de vita et miraculis S. Godrici*, 27; ed. Stevenson, 76. Despite avoiding women, Godric nevertheless oversaw the spiritual life of his sister, Burchwine. Reginald of Durham, *Libellus de vita et miraculis S. Godrici*, 61–63; ed. Stevenson, 140–145. Gerald of Wales reported both the story of Benedict's temptation and that of Godric's in his *Gemma ecclesiastica*: Gerald of Wales, *Gemma ecclesiastica*, II, 10; ed. Brewer, 212–216; trans. Hagen, 163–164.

62. "Sancta vero Dei Genitrix Virgo illico in forma pulcherrimæ mulieris, cum multitudine puellarum inferioris staturæ, per visum, Dei famulo apparuit: quas cum vidisset, visus est dixisse: Si pridem feminas in claustro vidissem, utique eas inde expulissem, Quare igitur huc accedere præsumpsistis? Ad hæc Virgo sancta: Tace, Frater, ego sum Virgo Maria, quam tam dulciter invocasti." Robert of Ostrevand, *Vita s. Ayberti*, 12; *AA SS*, April, 1: 676. Caesarius of Heisterbach told a parallel story of a nun who came across a man in the cloister (actually a demon in disguise); she fainted from the shock. Caesarius of Heisterbach, *Dialogus miraculorum*, 5.45; ed. Strange, I, 330–331; trans. Scott and Bland, I, 380. Cited in McGuire, "Friends and Tales," 237.

63. Guibert of Nogent wrote of mixed communities as being potentially heretical. Guibert of Nogent, *Monodiae*, 3.17; ed. Labande, 428–434; trans. Archambault, 195–198. See the edition and interpretation of this passage offered by Mews, "Guibert of Nogent's *Monodiae*." For male-female spiritual engagement as a possible sign of heresy, see Simons, *Cities of Ladies*, 19–24; Berman, "Were There Twelfth-Century Cistercian Nuns?" 847, n. 60; and Chapter 2, n. 181.

64. Geoffrey of Vendôme, *Epistola ad Robertum*, 4; *Deux vies*, 570–571. For Robert's habit of sleeping among women, see Jaeger, *Ennobling Love*, 129–130. Iogna-Prat argues that contact with women (and intentional exposure to sexual temptation) could serve as a form of "ordeal" in male penitential spirituality: Iogna-Prat, "La femme dans la perspective pénitentielle." Geoffrey's opposition to Robert's practices did not mean that he opposed all close friendships between the sexes: he wrote to the hermit Hervé of Vendôme and the recluse Eve of Wilton ("servo et ancillae Dei Herveo et Evae"), making no mention of the scandals that their friendship might provoke. Geoffroy de Vendôme, Epist. 27; ed. Giordanengo, 46–51.

65. "Demum temptationibus succumbens, plures illic praegnantes effecit. Demumque cum una habitu rejecto joculariter discurrens, aufugit." Gerald of Wales, *Gemma ecclesiastica*, II, 17; ed. Brewer, 248; trans. Hagen, 188–189.

66. Gerald reported Enoc's misdeeds in no less than three separate works. For discussion, see Cartwright, *Feminine Sanctity*, 178–181.

67. See above, n. 21, for Gerald's report of a nun, who became infatuated with Gilbert of Sempringham.

68. For a brief overview of women's involvement in the religious life of the period, alongside men and with their encouragement, see Constable, *Reformation*, 65–74. Constance Berman has challenged the presumption of sex-segregation within the medieval monastic life, highlighting the deep ties that bound reform houses for women and for men. Berman, "Men's Houses, Women's Houses." In an important essay on twelfth-century women as "readers, writers, and participants in literate culture," Barbara Newman argues that "twelfth-century reform fostered new styles of relations between religious men and women." These relations, as she shows, were frequently collaborative and mutually beneficial. Newman, "Liminalities," 354. Constant Mews surveys the implications of this culture for women and men in religious life in: Mews, "Negotiating the Boundaries of Gender."

69. Goscelin of St. Bertin, *Liber confortatorius, prologus*; ed. Talbot, 26; trans. Otter, 19. For discussion of Goscelin's relationship with Eve as "deep, intimate, and mutually beneficial," see Canatella, "Long-Distance Love" (here 36). See also O'Brien O'Keeffe, "Goscelin and the Consecration of Eve"; and Hayward, "Spiritual Friendship and Gender Difference." For Goscelin's activities at Wilton, see Bugyis, "Recovering the Histories of Women Religious."

70. *De S. Theodora*, 76; ed. Talbot, 174; rev. trans. Fanous and Leyser, 79. For discussion of Christina's life and context, including her relationship with Geoffrey, see Chapter 5.

71. According to a biography written by Baudri of Bourgueil, Robert sought a place where women and men "could live and share communal life without concern for scandal." Baudri of Bourgueil, *Historia magistri Roberti*, 3; *Deux vies*, 160–161. Robert's life is reported in two *vitae*: the first, written by Baudri (who was abbot of Bourgueil until 1107, when he became bishop of Dol), is traditionally known as the *Vita prima*, but appears in the manuscript sources as *Historia magistri Roberti fundatoris Fontis-Ebraudi*; a second anonymous text, most likely written by Robert's chaplain, Andrew, is often known as the *Vita altera* but was designated in the earliest manuscript as the *Supplementum historiae vitae Roberti*. For an edition and translation of both *lives*, see *Deux vies*, 125–300. Concerning Robert, see Dalarun, *Robert of Arbrissel*; Bienvenu, *L'étonnant fondateur de Fontevraud*; and the essays in Dalarun, ed., *Robert d'Arbrissel et la vie religieuse*. Bruce Venarde surveys scholarly interpretations of Robert and his legacy: Venarde, "Robert of Arbrissel and his Historians." Concerning Robert's spiritual care for women, see Griffiths, "The Cross and the *Cura monialium*."

72. Felten, "Norbert von Xanten." On the Premonstratensians and women, see Wolbrink, "Women in the Premonstratensian Order"; Wolbrink, "Necessary Priests and Lay Brothers"; Krings, "Die Prämonstratenser und ihr weiblicher Zweig"; and Ehlers-Kisseler, 249–279. Although earlier scholarship assumed that Premonstratensians rejected the incorporation of women within a generation of Norbert's death (based on a Chapter decision c. 1198 for which no document is now extant), more recent accounts have shown that women continued to be accepted in Premonstratensian communities. See above, n. 49. On Premonstratensian houses for women in England, see Thompson, *Women Religious*, 133–145.

73. *The Book of St. Gilbert*, 9; ed. and trans. Foreville and Keir, 30–35. Gerald of Wales, *Gemma ecclesiastica*, II, 17; ed. Brewer, 247; trans. Hagen, 188. Brian Golding's study of

Gilbert and his order is essential reading: Golding, *Gilbert*. For discussion of contemporary perceptions of Sempringham as "double", see Sykes, "*Canonici Albi et Moniales*." For debates concerning Gilbert's intentions regarding women, see below n. 106. The *Book of St. Gilbert* (presenting an "argument against detractors") commented that "this devising of a new type of religious life does not damage the Universal Church," observing that the order was both accepted by bishops and confirmed by the papacy. *The Book of St. Gilbert*, 20; ed. and trans. Foreville and Keir, 56–57.

74. "Quare ex utroque pariete, virorum scilicet ac mulierum, celestem nitens edificare Iehrusalem, quantum iactus est lapidis a cella sua habitaculum feminarum construxerat." *Vita S. Gaucherii*, 12; ed. Becquet, 52. The women's house was at Bos-las-Mongeas. Gaucher's *vita* included a section, now lost, entitled *De institutione sanctimonialium*. *Vita S. Gaucherii*, *prologus*; ed. Becquet, 44. Gaucher's promotion of female religious life was not universally welcomed: one of his disciples, Stephen of Muret (d. 1124), chose to move away from the community, fearing that contact with women posed a danger to his soul. After his death, Stephen's followers founded the Order of Grandmont.

75. *Westminster Abbey Charters,* ed. Mason, no. 249. Discussed in Thompson, *Women Religious*, 25; and Elkins, 48. For other examples of spiritual friendships between eremitic women and men in twelfth-century England, see Elkins, 38–42.

76. "Eodem anno Burchardus Halberstadensis episcopus, animarum cure deditus, quandam Dei famulam nomine Biam, enutritam in monasterio a Dei genitricis quod situm est ad occidentem civitatis Quidelingeburh, solitariam vitam desiderare intelligens, in loco competenti Huiusburh nomine fecit includi. Cui ne divinum servicium deesset, Ekkehardum canonicum Sancti Stephani in Halberstad, quem ipsa secreti sui desiderii antea conscium fecerat, presbiterum ibidem constituit." *Annalista Saxo*, a. 1070; ed. Waitz MGH SS 6, 697–698. The women were removed from Huysburg in 1156, but returned some thirty years later. Huysburg continued to include both men and women until 1411. Bogumil, *Das Bistum Halberstadt im 12. Jahrhundert*, 67–69. See also Parisse, *Religieux et religieuses*, 162.

77. "Casto sanctarum virginum viduarumque amore devinctus." *Chronicon Lippoldesbergense*, 5; ed. Arndt, MGH SS 20, 548. Julie Hotchin explores the history of Lippoldsberg, the women's ties to their male spiritual directors, and the intellectual climate of the community, as reflected in its library catalogue: Hotchin, "Women's Reading and Monastic Reform." On Lippoldsberg within the context of female monasticism in Saxony (with particular attention to the role of "spiritual father"), see Parisse, *Religieux et religieuses*, 158–162; and Schlotheuber, "The 'Freedom of Their Own Rule.'" Nuns at Lippoldsberg maintained warm relations with monks at nearby Reinhardsbrunn; Sindold, the librarian at Reinhardsbrunn, described the prioress Margaret as his "spiritual mother." *Die Reinhardsbrunner Briefsammlung*, 35; ed. Peeck, MGH Epp. sel. 5, 35. See the important essay on Reinhardsbrunn and the *cura monialium* by Julie Hotchin: Hotchin, "Abbot as Guardian."

78. Wolfger of Prüfening, *Vita Theogeri*, I, 25–26; ed. Jaffé, MGH SS 12, 459–462. Theoger also served as an advisor to Herluca of Epfach. Paul of Bernried, *Vita b. Herlucae*, 11; *AA SS*, April, 2: 553. See Küsters, *Der verschlossene Garten*, 147–150; and, on St. Georgen, Bauerreiß, "St. Georgen im Schwarzwald."

79. Anselm of Canterbury, Epist. 414; ed. Schmitt, *Opera*, V, 361–362; trans. Fröhlich, 3, 186. Cf. Anselm of Canterbury, Epist. 230; ed. Schmitt, *Opera*, IV, 134–135; trans. Fröhlich, 3, 199–200.

80. *Fundatio monasterii sanctae Mariae Andernacensis*; ed. Holder-Egger, MGH SS 15.2, 968–970. Andernach was founded in 1128 by Richard and Tenxwind, and settled with

women who had previously been living at Springiersbach—a community founded by their mother, Benigna. Springiersbach included numerous double monasteries and women's houses in its ambit. *Speculum virginum*, ed. Seyfarth, 45*-48*; Haverkamp, "Tenxwind von Andernach und Hildegard von Bingen." Men, as well as women, lived at Andernach until at least 1197. Bönnen, Haverkamp, and Hirschmann, 397.

81. On double monasteries, see Hilpisch, *Die Doppelklöster*; Elm and Parisse, eds., *Doppelklöster*; Peyroux, "Abbess and Cloister"; Haarländer, "'Schlangen unter den Fischen'"; Marti, "Einleitung: Doppelklöster"; de Kegel, "'Vom ordnungswidrigen Übelstand'?" and Küsters, *Der verschlossene Garten*, 142–155 (with double houses grouped according to congregation). On the difficulties associated with identifying double houses, see Haarländer, "Doppelklöster und ihre Forschungsgeschichte"; Gilomen-Schenkel, "Das Doppelkloster–eine verschwiegene Institution"; and Gilomen-Schenkel, "Engelberg, Interlaken und andere autonome Doppelklöster." Although Sharon Elkins rejected the term "double monastery" as inaccurate (as she argued, all women's houses included a male element to some extent, and so were implicitly "double" houses), other scholars have defended its usefulness. Katharine Sykes has shown that the perception of some houses as "double" was indeed medieval. Elkins, xvii–xviii; Sykes, "*Canonici Albi et Moniales*." Gratian referred to the "duplex monasterium": Gratian, *Decretum*, C.18 q.2 c.21; ed. Friedberg, 1, 834. For Gerald of Wales's description of the Gilbertine Order as a "monasteria duplicia", see above, n. 73.

82. Stephanie Haarländer identifies double houses as a feature of Augustinian reform communities (including Prémontré (1120/1121), Klosterrath/Rolduc (1104), and Springiersbach (c. 1107)), Benedictine reform communities (among them those founded by Vital of Savigny (d. 1122), Stephen of Obazine (d. 1159), Gilbert of Sempringham (d. 1189), and Robert of Arbrissel (d. 1116)), military and hospital orders, and charismatic groups. Haarländer, "'Schlangen unter den Fischen,'" 58–59. Hedwig Röckelein highlights the involvement of women in reform during the twelfth century, noting the emergence of close ties with men's houses and the "rich spiritual and cultural fruit" that resulted. Röckelein, "Die Auswirkung der Kanonikerreform des 12. Jahrhunderts," 65.

83. "Eius irreprehensibilis vita non solum feminis, set etiam viris possit exemplo fore." Ortlieb, *De fundatione monasterii Zwivildensis*, 20; ed. Abel, MGH SS 10, 85. Ortlieb mentioned 67 monks, 130 lay brothers, and 60 sisters at Zwiefalten. Ortlieb, *De fundatione monasterii Zwivildensis*, 18; ed. Abel, MGH SS 10, 83. Founded as a daughter house of Hirsau in 1089, Zwiefalten had established a female community by 1100. The women were separated from the men and settled in their own house east of the men's house, encircled by a wall. Constable, *Reformation*, 69–70. On Hirsau and women, see Küsters, *Der verschlossene Garten*; Küsters, "Formen und Modelle religiöser Frauengemeinschaften"; Röckelein, "Die Auswirkung der Kanonikerreform des 12. Jahrhunderts," 292–296; and Roitner, "*Sorores inclusae*," 73–77. For the dedication of Hirsau monks to the spiritual care of women, see Hotchin, "Female Religious Life and the *Cura monialium*"; and Hotchin, "Abbot as Guardian." Elsanne Gilomen-Schenkel emphasizes the involvement of Hirsau communities with women in her study of Benedictine houses in the diocese of Constance: Gilomen-Schenkel, "'Officium paterne providentie' ou 'Supercilium noxie dominationis,'" 368. On reformed monks and women, see Schreiner, "Mönchtum zwischen asketischem Anspruch und gesellschaftlicher Wirklichkeit," 273–277.

84. Foot, *Veiled Women*, I, 172–179; Magnani, "L'ascétisme domestique féminin (IVe-XIIe siècle)"; Signori, "Anchorites in German-Speaking Regions"; Bönnen, Haverkamp, and Hirschmann, 376–379; Huyghebaert, "Les femmes laïques dans la vie religieuse"; and Lutter,

Geschlecht und Wissen, 55. Küsters notes that female recluses living alongside men's houses often formed the nucleus of emerging women's communities. Küsters, "Formen und Modelle religiöser Frauengemeinschaften," 209.

85. Foot, *Veiled Women*, II, 49–50. For a more detailed discussion of "nonnae" at Bury St. Edmunds, see van Houts, "The Women of Bury St. Edmunds," 62–69. Women also lived near or at St. Albans and Evesham. Thompson, *Women Religious*, 47; and Hollis and Wogan-Browne, "St. Albans and Women's Monasticism." See also L'Hermite-Leclercq, "Incertitudes et contingences aux origines des monastères féminins," 125–128.

86. On one occasion Seitha remained in the monastic church after Matins to pray; on another, she found relief from a sore finger by touching the shrine of St. Edmund. Seitha was the source for four miracles that were added to Herman the Archdeacon's *Miracula sancti Eadmundi* by Goscelin of St. Bertin sometime around the turn of the twelfth century. For discussion, see van Houts, "The Women of Bury St. Edmunds," 64–66; and Licence, "History and Hagiography," 526–531.

87. For women at Bec, see Vaughn, *St. Anselm and the Handmaidens of God*, 67–115.

88. Gilbert Crispin noted that Heloise "performed the duty of a handmaid, washing the garments of God's servants and doing most scrupulously all the extremely hard work imposed upon her." Gilbert Crispin, *Vita Herluini*, 42; ed. Abulafia and Evans, 193; trans. Vaughn, 73. On women (particularly widows) in men's monasteries, see Hicks, 136–140. Women were also accommodated at Tiron. According to Bernard of Tiron's biographer, Beatrix, countess of Perche, "lived at Tiron . . . and built the large basilica church with many cash outlays." Geoffrey Grossus, *Vita Beati Bernardi Fundatoris Congregationis de Tironio*, 81; PL 172: 1416; trans. Cline, 87.

89. Thomas of Cantimpré, *Vita Ioannis Cantipratensis*, I, 6 and II, 3; ed. Godding, 262, 279; trans. Newman, 63 and 82. The prioress of Prémy, Iueta, was a widow of Douai, who had "abandoned her worldly goods because of the blessed John's teaching." Thomas of Cantimpré, *Vita Ioannis Cantipratensis*, I, 12; ed. Godding, 266; trans. Newman, 67. On Prémy, see Felten, "Verbandsbildung von Frauenklöstern," 302–306. A number of men who engaged spiritually with women died and were buried in female houses. For further discussion, see Chapter 5.

90. Guibert of Nogent, *Monodiae*, 1.14; ed. Labande, 102; trans. Archambault, 46. Constant Mews comments that "such arrangements did not necessarily provoke controversy." Mews, "Negotiating the Boundaries of Gender," 120. For the identification of the "old woman" as Suger's sister, see Guibert of Nogent, *Monodiae* 1.20; ed. Labande, 170; trans. Archambault, 74. On Guibert's mother, and her spiritual ambitions, see Mulder-Bakker, *Lives of the Anchoresses*, 24–50; and Elliott, *Bride*, 121–125.

91. Wollasch, "Parenté noble," 7. Wollasch comments that women lived at an *oratorium* near Cluny in the first half of the tenth century. Wollasch, "Frauen in der Cluniacensis ecclesia," 97.

92. *Vita domnae Juttae inclusae*; ed. Staab; trans. Silvas. For discussion, see Felten, "What Do We Know About the Life of Jutta and Hildegard"; Felten, "Hildegard von Bingen zwischen Reformaufbruch und Bewahrung des Althergebrachten," 143–149; Felten, "*Noui esse volunt . . . deserentes bene contritam uiam . . .* ," 37–51; Nikitsch, "Wo lebte die heilige Hildegard wirklich?"; and Mews, "Hildegard of Bingen and the Hirsau Reform."

93. Beach, *Women as Scribes*, 32–64.

94. Herluca may have been drawn to Bernried when her friend, Sigeboto, a priest at Epfach where she lived for 36 years, became provost at the community. Robinson, "*Conversio* and

conversatio," 185–187. Herluca's *vita,* composed by her friend Paul of Bernried, was dedicated to the canons at Bernried who had accepted and clearly admired her. Paul describes the circumstances under which Herluca came to Bernried: Paul of Bernried, *Vita b. Herlucae,* 44; *AA SS,* April, 2: 556. On Herluca, see Maier, "Ein schwäbisch-bayerischer Freundskreis Gregors VII"; Schnitzer, *Die Vita B. Herlucae Pauls von Bernried*; Küsters, *Der verschlossene Garten,* 114–121; Robinson, "*Conversio* and *conversatio*"; Griffiths, "Women and Reform"; Küsters, "Formen und Modelle religiöser Frauengemeinschaften," 197–200; and Signori, "Eine Biographie als Freundschaftsbeweis." Evidence that Herluca and Diemut of Wessobrunn were known to each other, and indeed corresponded, is presented in Bodarwé, "Verlorene Zeugnisse einer Frauenfreundschaft." Herluca was encouraged in her religious life by the abbot William of Hirsau (d. 1091), as well as Theoger of St. Georgen: Paul of Bernried, *Vita b. Herlucae,* 11; *AA SS,* April, 2: 553. William's support for all those seeking the religious life (including rich and poor, men and women) is reported in Haimo, *Vita Willihelmi,* 6; ed. Wattenbach, MGH SS 12, 213.

95. Of course, even in cases where we know that women lived in or alongside men's houses, the sources are often silent. The *Annales* of Disibodenberg, to give one example, first acknowledged the presence of women only at the death of the *magistra* Jutta—who was revered as a local holy person and had, by the time she died, lived for almost a quarter century at the "men's" house. "Ianuarii obiit divae memoriae domna Iudda, 24 annis in monte sancti Dysibodi inclusa, soror Megenhardi comitis de Spanheim. Haec sancta mulier inclusa est Kalend. Novembris, et aliae tres cum ea, scilicet Hyldegardis et suimet vocabuli duae; quas etiam, quoad vixit, sanctis virtutibus imbuere studuit." *Annales Sancti Disibodi,* a. 1136; ed. Waitz, MGH SS 17, 25. The silence of the sources regarding the presence of women at Disibodenberg is discussed in Felten "Frauenklöster," 213. For further discussion of the challenges involved in "finding" women in monastic sources, see below, n. 152.

96. Jennifer Harris explores the language of the heavenly Jerusalem in liturgies for church dedications, focusing on Cluny as a "locus sanctissimus." Harris, "Building Heaven on Earth."

97. *The Book of St. Gilbert,* 19; ed. and trans. Foreville and Keir, 50–53. Burton explores the metaphor of the "chariot" in the context of the female priory of Swine during the later Middle Ages: Burton, "The 'Chariot of Aminadab.'"

98. *The Royal Abbey of Saint-Denis in the Time of Abbot Suger,* ed. Crosby, Hayward, Little, and Wixom, no. 16, p. 86.

99. Gilo, *Vita sancti Hugonis abbatis,* I, 12; ed. Cowdrey, 62–63.

100. "Visum est nobis Deo non displicere, imo eius voluntati obedire." Hugh of Cluny, *Scriptum quoddam commonitorium sive deprecatorium ad successores suos pro sanctimonialibus Marciniacensibus*; ed. Cowdrey, 171.

101. "Ubi hoc quoque notandum, quod devote mulieres pariter cum sanctis discipulis Deo militabant, et ideo hoc exemplo non est vituperabile, set magis laudabile, si sanctimoniales feminae in servorum Dei monasteriis recipiantur, ut uterque sexus, ab invicem tamen sequestratus, uno in loco salvetur." *Casus monasterii Petrishusensis,* 9; ed. Pertz, MGH SS, 20, 625. Gilomen-Schenkel stresses the importance of the Petershausen chronicle, which presents the only "programmatic" defense of the double monastery known to her: Gilomen-Schenkel, "Engelberg, Interlaken und andere autonome Doppelklöster," 123. On Petershausen in the context of Hirsau reform, see Küsters, *Der verschlossene Garten,* 150–151; Küsters, "Formen und Modelle religiöser Frauengemeinschaften," 210. See also Schreiner, "Mönchtum zwischen asketischem Anspruch und gesellschaftlicher Wirklichkeit," 273–277. Monasteries founded or reformed by Petershausen frequently adopted the double house organization. Gilomen-Schenkel, "Double

Monasteries in the South-Western Empire," 53–54. For Premonstratensian double monasteries in western Switzerland in the twelfth century, see Tremp, "Chorfrauen im Schatten der
Männer."

102. "Nobis est exemplum vita sanctorum patrum, qui et ipsi feminas congregaverunt ob
amorem Dei." *Acta Murensia*; ed. Kiem, 60–61. The "fathers" were also invoked as an example
in the *migravit* of Robert of Arbrissel, which noted that Robert joined women with men in his
communities "with God's inspiration" and "according to the example, rules, and all sound
teaching of the holy Fathers." *Migravit*, 2; *Deux vies*, 636–637.

103. "Arbitrabatur Erpo, qui illius subrogatus est loco, aliquas hic esse recipiendas, ad vestes
universorum conficiendas, et quod eodem et diverso illarum ministerio non posset aecclesia
carere, cum etiam in apostolorum obsequio religiosae secundi sexus personae legantur minis-
trasse." *Annales Rodenses*, a. 1141; ed. Pertz, MGH SS 16, 715. Rolduc (Klosterrath) had been
founded in 1104 by Ailbert (d. 1122), together with two of his brothers, seeking the *vita apostolica*. Other men, and women, soon joined them. However, the presence of women was a point
of contention, and Ailbert left in 1111. The women remained, but were relocated to Kerkrade in
1126. The *Annales Rodenses*, which report on the community's early years and on the presence
of women, were written c. 1155/60. Dereine, *Les Chanoines*, 169–217; Deutz, "Die Frauen im
Regularkanonikerstift Klosterrath"; Deutz, *Geistliches und geistiges Leben*; Gärtner, "Das Chorherrenstift Klosterrath"; and Felten, "Frauenklöster," 243–244.

104. *Libellus de diversis ordinibus et professionibus qui sunt in aecclesia*; ed. Constable and
Smith, 4–5.

105. Anselm of Canterbury, Epist. 230; ed. Schmitt, *Opera*, IV, 134–135; trans. Fröhlich,
2: 199–200. As Anselm advised Robert, Seitha, and Edith, "take the example for your lives
from the angels in heaven."

106. The *Book of St. Gilbert* presented Gilbert's involvement with women as a derivative
interest: when Gilbert could not find men "willing to lead such strict lives for God's sake," he
gave his attention to women instead. *The Book of St. Gilbert*, 9; ed. and trans. Foreville and
Keir, 30–31. Golding cautions that empathy for women was "not apparent" in Gilbert, who
gave little indication that he "believed himself to have a vocation for the *cura monialium*." Golding, "Authority and Discipline," 110. Sykes maintains that Gilbert's intention had been to
found a house for men, not women. Sykes, *Inventing Sempringham*, 46–47. The common explanation that men's involvement with women was accidental rather than intentional is addressed in n. 181 below.

107. *The Book of St. Gilbert*, 15; ed. and trans. Foreville and Keir, 46–47.

108. *The Book of St. Gilbert*, 9; ed. and trans. Foreville and Keir, 30–31. The assumption
that men serving women would receive a reward was shared by the men at Fontevraud; see
Chapter 2, n. 58.

109. Anselm of Canterbury, Epist. 414; ed. Schmitt, *Opera*, V, 361–362; trans. Fröhlich,
3, 186. The *vita Theogeri* comments that Theoger of St. Georgen "turned the convent of women
to his profit (*in suum verterit lucrum*)," suggesting that attention to religious women was
perceived to be spiritually advantageous to men. Wolfger of Prüfening, *Vita Theogeri*, I, 25;
ed. Jaffé, MGH SS 12, 459. Robert of Arbrissel noted that "he alone had gotten praise" for the
religious life of the women at Fontevraud. Andrew, *Supplementum*, 41; *Deux vies*, 266–267.

110. Idung of Prüfening, *Dialogus duorum monachorum*, 3, 13; ed. Huygens, 159; trans.
O'Sullivan, 107. In Idung's dialogue, the Cistercian remarked that "not insignificant spiritual
injury" can also result from the spiritual direction of nuns.

111. Foundation Charter for Las Huelgas (June 1, 1187); trans. Berman in *Women and Monasticism*, 21.

112. "Si ergo nihil aliud domnus Norbertus fecisset, sed, omissa conversione virorum, tot feminas servitio divino sua exhortatione attraxisset, nonne maxima laude dignus fuisset? . . . Mihi videtur verum esse, quod plurimi asserunt, a tempore apostolorum nullum fuisse qui tam brevi temporis spatio sua institutione tot perfectae vitae imitatores Christo acquisierit." Herman of Tournai, *De miraculis S. Mariae Laudunensis*, III, 7; PL 156: 996–997; trans. Antry and Neel, 80. Herman was nevertheless clear that the women accepted at Premonstratensian monasteries were strictly cloistered and separated from worldly influences.

113. *The Book of St. Gilbert*, 11; ed. and trans. Foreville and Keir, 36–37.

114. Submission could be a spiritual goal, as Jacques Dalarun observed in his study of Fontevraud. Dalarun, "Pouvoir et autorité," 346; and Dalarun, "Robert d'Arbrissel et les femmes," 1149. The spiritual appeal of submission and the paradox of Christian inversions of power are the subjects of Dalarun's study, *Gouverner c'est servir*, in which he revisits the organizational structure of Fontevraud and the Paraclete: Dalarun, *Gouverner c'est servir*, 139–173.

115. Abelard, *Institutio*, 50; *The Letter Collection*, 414–415.

116. Hildegard's difficulties in securing pastoral care at Rupertsberg are a case in point. See above, n. 46, and this book's Conclusion. Wolbrink discusses "controversies" between men and women in Premonstratensian monasteries: Wolbrink, "Women in the Premonstratensian Order," 400–405. See also the challenges faced by women at Steinbach: Griffiths, "Brides and *dominae*," 68.

117. Griffiths, *Garden of Delights*, 40–42. Conflict over resources is evident, too, in the case of Le Ronceray d'Angers: Gold, "The Charters of Le Ronceray d'Angers," 128–129.

118. Medieval nuns often complained when priestly behavior was found wanting. See, for instance, the efforts of Ivetta of Huy (d. 1228) to have unworthy priests removed and replaced by those more acceptable to the women. Mulder-Bakker, "Ivetta of Huy," 241. Canonesses in Strasbourg also complained about abusive and predatory priests: Hirbodian, "Pastors and Seducers."

119. "Woe is me!" the *Speculum* author writes, "how many monasteries of virgins in our times do we see plagued by this evil. . . . Holy virgins . . . win everlasting reproach and punishment through the very men whose teaching and example should have given them hope of gracious light and glory." *Speculum virginum*, 5.1029–1031 and 5.1057–1062; ed. Seyfarth, 149–150; trans. Newman, 291–292. The late twelfth-century female-authored *Hortus deliciarum*, too, acknowledged the dangers to women of immoral priests, offering its female audience the image of a priest tempting a nun—with the promise of money—away from her pursuit of the "crown of life" (*Hortus deliciarum*, fol. 215v). *Hortus deliciarum*, ed. Green, Evans, Bischoff, and Curschmann, II, Pl. 124.

120. Thomas of Cantimpré, *Vita Lutgardis Aquiriensis*, 1.21; *AA SS*, June, 3: 241; trans. King and Newman, 236. On Thomas's concerns regarding the dangers of intimacy between nuns and their male spiritual guides, see Elliott, *Bride*, 204–213.

121. Jo Ann McNamara describes the pastoral care of women, the *cura mulierum*, as the "care (and control) of women." McNamara, *Sisters in Arms*, 5.

122. On Admont, see Lutter, 52–125; Beach, *Women as Scribes*, 65–103; Roitner, "Das Admonter Frauenkloster im zwölften Jahrhundert"; Seeberg, "Spuren der Nonnen"; Seeberg, *Die Illustrationen im Admonter Nonnenbrevier von 1180*; and Hamburger, "Art, Enclosure, and the Pastoral Care of Nuns."

123. Tomaschek, "Carinthischer Sommer 1151"; Lutter, 59, 69–75. Tomaschek considers the significance of Irimbert's commentaries for nuns.

124. On Irimbert's collaboration with female scribes, see Marti, "Double Monasteries in Images," 82–86; Beach, *Women as Scribes*, 85–103; and Beach, "Claustration and Collaboration Between the Sexes," 60–67.

125. Irimbert of Admont, *De incendio monasterii sui*. For discussion of the fire and its implications for women's religious life at Admont, see Lutter, 69–71; and Roitner, "*Sorores inclusae*," 88–94.

126. Irimbert reports that the door was locked with three locks ("clavibus tribus obseratur"). Irimbert of Admont, *De incendio monasterii sui*; in Lutter, 224. According to the *vita Theogeri*, professed women did not exit the cloister except when they were "carried out dead for burial": "A viris tanta separatio fuit, ut monasterium quae semel fuisset ingressa, raro ulterius, nisi mortua efferretur, exiret." Wolfger of Prüfening, *Vita Theogeri*, I, 25; ed. Jaffé, MGH SS 12, 460. For the rather different circumstances in which the door between the men's and the women's communities in Salzburg was periodically opened, see Klueting, "Die Petersfrauen im Doppelkonvent an St. Peter in Salzburg."

127. Jeffrey Hamburger cautions that "Irimbert's account offers not so much a description as an exemplum of enclosure." Hamburger, "Art, Enclosure, and the Pastoral Care of Nuns," 38. Christine Lutter, too, concludes that Irimbert's account of the fire at Admont may have been a topos. Lutter, 86. Beach comments that, "Irimbert may well have exaggerated the drama of the rescue or the confusion of the released nuns in the interest of emphasizing the separateness of the sexes." However, she maintains that "the monastery's nuns and monks did not interact freely." Beach, *Women as Scribes*, 69.

128. Stephen of Obazine's biographer commented on the tremendous care that he took to ensure the security of the women, writing of a system of double doors that allowed the women to receive goods without being seen by the monks, or seeing them. *Vita S. Stephani Obazinensis*, II, 3; ed. Aubrun, 98–101; trans. Feiss, O'Brien, Pepin, 165–166. Coyroux and Obazine were separated by a distance of about 600 to 700 meters. For discussion, see Barrière, "The Cistercian Convent of Coyroux." The *Book of St. Gilbert* comments that "the canons lived a long way distant from the women and had no access to them except for administering some divine sacrament when there were many witnesses present. Only the church where divine service is celebrated is common to all, but then only for the solemn rite of the Mass, once or twice a day, and there is a wall which blocks it throughout so that the men cannot be seen or the women heard." *The Book of St. Gilbert*, 16; ed. and trans. Foreville, 46–47. For discussion of the liturgical implications of the presence of both women and men at Gilbertine houses, see Sorrentino, "'In Houses of Nuns, in Houses of Canons'"; and Golding, *Gilbert*, 126–132. At Fontevraud, Loraine Simmons identifies a pervasive "proximity anxiety" that "test[ed] and strengthen[ed] resistance to the temptations of sex." Simmons, 106.

129. *Guta-Sintram Codex*, Bibliothèque du Grand Séminaire de Strasbourg, MS 37. See the facsimile and commentary: *Le Codex Guta-Sintram*, ed. Weis. On p. 4 of the *Codex*, hand A (which belonged to Guta) was replaced by hand B (which most likely belonged to Sintram) in the middle of a line. After switching, hand B continued to write until p. 9, at which point hand A appeared again. On the possibilities for collaboration between religious men and women within the scriptorium, see Beach, "Claustration and Collaboration Between the Sexes." Where paleographical evidence points to the presence of both men's and women's hands within the same folio, and even within a single line, Beach assumes collaboration within a single scriptorium. On the *Guta-Sintram Codex* as evidence for the spiritual and practical involvement of

religious men with women, see Griffiths, "Brides and *dominae*." Gilomen-Schenkel considers the *Guta-Sintram Codex* as evidence for the dissolution of a double monastery: Gilomen-Schenkel, "Der Guta-Sintram-Codex als Zeugnis eines Doppelklosters."

130. Herman of Tournai, *Liber de restauratione*, 69; ed. Waitz, MGH SS 14, 307; trans. Nelson, 101. For an important discussion of conversation between the sexes in the religious life, see van Houts, "Conversations"; and, in the early thirteenth-century Cistercian milieu, McGuire, "Friends and Tales," 200. Wolbrink shows that "practical interaction between male and female Premonstratensians was a part of daily monastic life in northwestern Germany." Wolbrink, "Women in the Premonstratensian Order."

131. Hollis, "Goscelin's Writings and the Wilton Women," 219–220. On Goscelin's reference to priests at Wilton during the time of Abbess Wulfthryth, see Hollis, "Goscelin's Writings and the Wilton Women," 226. On the spiritual and textual context within which Goscelin was active, see Bugyis, "Recovering the Histories of Women Religious"; and Leyser, "C. 1080–1215: Texts."

132. Goscelin described Eve as his "lady" (*domina mea*): Goscelin of St. Bertin, *Liber confortatorius*, I; ed. Talbot, 33; trans. Otter, 31. O'Brien O'Keeffe argues that Eve was not a nun at Wilton (although she had been consecrated there), and proposes that she was older when she met Goscelin than previous scholars assumed. O'Brien O'Keeffe, "Goscelin and the Consecration of Eve." Christina of Markyate's biographer also reports "sitting at table with the handmaid of Christ." For discussion, see Koopmans, "Dining at Markyate."

133. Goscelin of St. Bertin, *Liber confortatorius*, I; ed. Talbot, 28; trans. Otter, 25. The episode is discussed in van Houts, "Conversations," 278–279.

134. Goscelin of St. Bertin, *Liber confortatorius*, I; ed. Talbot, 27; trans. Otter, 21–22. On Goscelin as Eve's teacher, see Hollis, "Wilton as a Centre of Learning."

135. Aelred warned his sister against the giving of such gifts as "a belt [or] a gaily embroidered purse" to young monks or priests. Aelred of Rievaulx, *De institutione inclusarum*, 7; ed. Hoste and Talbot, 643; trans. Macpherson, 53. Christina of Markyate gave gifts to the abbot Geoffrey of St. Albans ("two undergarments", which he requested "not for pleasure"). *De S. Theodora,* 71; ed. Talbot, 160; rev. trans Fanous and Leyser, 71. Geoffrey is often credited with giving Christina a magnificent illuminated psalter. See Chapter 5 for discussion.

136. O'Brien O'Keeffe, "Goscelin and the Consecration of Eve," 263–264.

137. Guibert of Gembloux, Epist. 38, l. 35; ed. Derolez, CCCM 66A, 368; trans. Silvas in *Jutta and Hildegard*, 100. Guibert's letters to and from Gertrude appear in his letter collection: Guibert of Gembloux, Epist. 34–5, 37; ed. Derolez, CCCM 66A, 346–351, 360–365. For discussion, see Griffiths, "Monks and Nuns at Rupertsberg." Although Guibert reports his own close ties to the Rupertsberg nuns, he nevertheless emphasized the strict enclosure of Hildegard and Jutta at Disibodenberg, perhaps in response to increasing anxieties concerning contact between the sexes, as Felten suggests. Felten, "What Do We Know About the Life of Jutta and Hildegard," 30–32.

138. *Speculum virginum* 2.256–257 and 2.461; ed. Seyfarth, 50, 57; trans. Newman, 276, 280. The expectation that nuns would meet with men for spiritual conversation is evident, too, in the statutes from Fontevraud: "Sisters should never speak to any man without a guardian who should sit between them, hearing what is said and if it is useful." *Additions to the Statutes*, 4; *Deux vies*, 428–429.

139. Mews, "Virginity, Theology, and Pedagogy"; Powell, "The *Speculum virginum*"; and Powell, "The Mirror and the Woman," 133–173. Latin manuscripts of the *Speculum virginum* survive predominantly from male rather than female religious houses, a fact that has

sometimes been interpreted as evidence that men, like women, read it for spiritual formation. Newman, "Flaws in the Golden Bowl," 22.

140. Aelred of Rievaulx, *De Sanctimoniali de Wattun*; PL 195: 789–796. For discussion of this incident, see Golding, *Gilbert*, 33–38; Constable, "Aelred of Rievaulx and the Nun of Watton"; Freeman, "Nuns in the Public Sphere"; and Sykes, *Inventing Sempringham*, 51–57. In fact, contemporary criticism of the Gilbertines was fairly minimal, even in the wake of the scandal at Watton. Golding, *Gilbert*, 168–170. Letters of support for the order, following the lay brothers' revolt, are included in the *Book of St. Gilbert*; ed. and trans. Foreville and Keir, 134–167. The bishop of Winchester wrote to the pope that "The whole kingdom of England approves and admires the fact that the virgins are enclosed on their own, while the canons who administer the sacraments to them live apart, and that access to the nuns is not allowed except under the pressure of extreme need and then only when witnessed by both sexes." *The Book of St. Gilbert*, Epist. 4; ed. and trans. Foreville and Keir, 146–147.

141. De Kegel identifies various phases in the development of double monasteries, in which dissolution is the presumed end point. De Kegel, "'Vom ordnungswidrigen Übelstand'?" Elkins commented that although double monasteries appear in scholarly discussion, they are typically treated as a "peripheral phenomenon." Elkins, xvii.

142. McNamara, "Herrenfrage," 11. Elliott, *Bride*, 150–171; and Elliott, "Alternative Intimacies." Writing from the perspective of monastic history (rather than women's history), Giles Constable noted that "openness to women" was "one of the most striking features of religious life in the eleventh and twelfth centuries"; however, he cautioned that it emerged "against a background of general suspicion and distrust" and ultimately gave way to "the old dislike and fear of women." Constable, "Religious Communities," 344, 347; and Constable, *Reformation*, 73. Brian Golding locates Gilbert of Sempringham's foundation for women within a "framework of experimentation and radical reform, which paradoxically both appealed to women and sought to distance itself from them." Golding, *Gilbert*, 77.

143. McNamara, "Herrenfrage," 12. In Elliott's view, the intimate spiritual and emotional bonds that could develop between holy women and clerics were not disruptive of gender roles, but were quasi-conjugal (and ultimately temporary). Elliott, *Bride*, 155.

144. On the practice of syneisaktism (close ties between a celibate man and an unmarried woman, a *syneisaktes*) in early Christianity, see Achelis, *Virgines subintroductae*; Clark, "John Chrysostom and the 'Subintroductae'"; Elm, "*Virgins of God*", 47–51; and Elliott, *Spiritual Marriage*, 32–38. Syneisaktism was condemned at the Council of Nicaea (325), although it continued in various forms.

145. McNamara, "Herrenfrage," 18.

146. Elm, "Le personnel masculin," 331.

147. Second Lateran Council (1139), canon 27; *Decrees of the Ecumenical Councils*, ed. and trans. Tanner, I, 203.

148. Engelberg remained a double community until the early seventeenth century. De Kegel, "'Monasterium, quod duplices [. . .] habet conventus,'" 201; Gilomen-Schenkel, "Engelberg, Interlaken und andere autonome Doppelklöster." Marti discusses manuscript production within the double monastery at Engelberg: Marti, *Malen, Schreiben und Beten*.

149. Registerbook of Abbot Otto II (1375–1414), Salzburg, Stiftsarchiv der Erzabtei St. Peter, Hs. A 7, fol. 1r. For discussion, see Klueting, 414. The women's house at the Frauenberg existed until 1583. At Schiffenberg (founded c. 1129), too, men and women continued to live in close association until the end of the Middle Ages. Bönnen, Haverkamp, and Hirschmann,

398. The women at Zwiefalten were not moved to Mariaberg until 1349. Küsters, "Formen und Modelle religiöser Frauengemeinschaften," 214.

150. For Schönau, see Kemper, "Das benediktinische Doppelkloster Schönau," 56; for Sempringham, see Sykes, "*Canonici Albi et Moniales*," 245. Sykes comments that "arrangements at the houses of Sempringham persisted until the Dissolution." Golding takes a dimmer view, declaring that "by 1300 the Gilbertine experiment was largely dead." Golding, *Gilbert*, 4. In his view, the status of the Gilbertine women deteriorated relative to that of the canons during the thirteenth century. Golding, *Gilbert*, 133–135.

151. For monastic foundations of the Brigittine order, see Nyberg, *Birgittinische Klostergründungen*. Nyberg prefers to describe the Brigittine monastery as a "Gesamtkloster" rather than a "double monastery."

152. Separation itself requires careful interpretation, since many double communities appear in the sources only at the moment of separation, giving a false sense of the frequency with which double monasteries separated. Double communities that did not separate may be more difficult to detect in narrative or other written sources, since even male monasteries that welcomed women tended not to highlight their presence. Bönner, Haverkamp, and Hirschmann, 377–378. Stephanie Haarländer and Franz Felten have both observed that narrative sources tend to engage in "circumlocution" where the presence of women is concerned. Haarländer, "Doppelklöster und ihre Forschungsgeschichte," 35–40; Felten, "Frauenklöster." For the silences of the sources concerning the presence of women alongside men in the religious life, see also Gilomen-Schenkel, "Das Doppelkloster."

153. Herman of Tournai, *Liber de restauratione*, 69; ed. Waitz, MGH SS 14, 307; trans. Nelson, 99.

154. Hildegard of Bingen, Epist. 78; ed. Van Acker, CCCM 91, 175; trans. Baird and Ehrman, I, 173. For discussion, see Griffiths, "Monks and Nuns at Rupertsberg."

155. 117 monks and 144 nuns are listed in the necrology in the sixty years after the women's relocation (between 1200 and 1260). Gilomen-Schenkel, "Double Monasteries in the Southwestern Empire," 62. Necrologies are rich sources for monastic community and often reveal the existence of a double monastery when other sources are silent. See Gilomen-Schenkel, "Nekrologien als Quellen für Doppelklöster"; Gilomen-Schenkel, "Das Doppelkloster," 204–206; and Gilomen-Schenkel, "Engelberg, Interlaken und andere autonome Doppelklöster," 123–127. Axel Müssigbrod cautions that not all women named in necrologies from men's houses—even in terms suggestive of a religious profession (*sanctimonialis*, *devota*, or *monacha*)—were members of the male house or professed women at all. Müssigbrod, "Frauenkonversionen in Moissac."

156. *Vita S. Stephani Obazinensis*, II, 3; ed. Aubrun, 98–99; trans. Feiss, O'Brien, and Pepin, 165. Nevertheless, the author of the *life* noted that the women's move was prompted by Stephen's realization that "women could not long dwell virtuously among men." *Vita S. Stephani Obazinensis*, I, 30; ed. Aubrun, 90–91; trans. Feiss, O'Brien, and Pepin, 160

157. Felten, "Frauenklöster," 264–5; Bönnen, Haverkamp, and Hirschmann, 402–403. Krings notes that Maisental was separated from Weißenau by 500 meters. Krings, "Die Prämonstratenser und ihr weiblicher Zweig," 98.

158. Bond; Jaeger, *Ennobling Love*. Essential reading is provided in Dronke, *Medieval Latin*, I, 210–238.

159. On Bond's concept of "dominism", see Bond, 136–137.

160. Jaeger, *Ennobling Love*, 90, 105. In fact, as we shall see, Jerome and other religious men of the late antique and early medieval centuries were equally capable of admiring and exalting individual women.

161. Coakley, *Women, Men, and Spiritual Power*; Coakley, "Friars, Sanctity, and Gender"; Coakley, "Gender and the Authority of Friars." For the related argument that holy women "had something that devout men sought and needed: the immediacy of contact with the divine, as well as the language in which to convey this presence," see McGuire, "Holy Women and Monks," 357. McGuire commented on the potential mutuality of the relationship between holy women and monks, observing that "just as much as the women were made to need them in economic and social terms, they as men needed women in personal and emotional terms." (352)

162. The attention to "exceptional" religious women in much existing scholarship is discussed in Griffiths and Hotchin, "Women and Men"; and Coakley, "Afterword." Barbara Newman makes a case for the importance of studying "the ordinary religious woman" in Newman, "Flaws in the Golden Bowl," 20.

163. Evidence for men's spiritual attention to women can be found in the "literature of formation" examined by Newman. Of forty-five texts that she identifies as having been composed between 1075 and 1225, fourteen were addressed to women (although not necessarily by their priests). Newman, "Flaws in the Golden Bowl," 21.

164. Some female saints' *vitae* were written by men who knew their female subjects as members of the same monastic order, as founders of the man's monastery, or as recluses living close to his community. Wilms, 202–204, and 29–30 (for a listing of twelfth-century female saints).

165. The literature on Abelard is vast, and growing. See, in particular, Mews, *Abelard and Heloise*; Mews, *Abelard and his Legacy*; Clanchy, *Abelard*; Marenbon, *Abelard in Four Dimensions*; Marenbon, *The Philosophy of Peter Abelard*; and Ruys, *The Repentant Abelard*. New approaches to Abelard's life and legacy appear in the essays gathered in Brower and Guilfoy, eds., *The Cambridge Companion to Abelard*; and Hellemans, ed., *Rethinking Abelard*. Still foundational are the essays in *Pierre Abélard - Pierre le Vénérable*; Thomas, ed., *Petrus Abaelardus*; and Jolivet and Habrias, eds., *Pierre Abélard*. Debate concerning the "lost love letters" of Abelard and Heloise has generated a tremendous body of scholarship in recent years. For attribution of the *Epistolae duorum amantium* to Abelard and Heloise, see Mews, *Lost Love Letters*; and Newman, *Making Love* (with an important review of the debate).

166. As Clanchy observes, "Abelard was the greatest provider of devotional literature for nuns in the twelfth century." Clanchy, *Abelard*, 153. Mary Martin McLaughlin commented that Abelard's writings for the Paraclete comprised "the most comprehensive response of the early twelfth century to the problems of women and their religious life." McLaughlin, "Peter Abelard and the Dignity of Women," 292–293.

167. Abelard wrote that "my detractors, with their usual perverseness, had the effrontery to accuse me of most shamefully doing what genuine charity prompted; they said that I was still in the grip of the pleasures of carnal concupiscence and could rarely or never bear the absence of the woman I had once loved." Abelard, Epist. 1.65; *The Letter Collection*, 102–103. On Abelard's involvement at the Paraclete, see Mews, *Abelard and Heloise*, 145–173. On Heloise, see Bourgain, "Héloïse, vie et œuvres"; Mews, "Heloise"; and the essays in Wheeler, ed., *Listening to Heloise*. On the expulsion of the nuns from Argenteuil, which prompted the establishment of the women's community at the Paraclete, see Waldman, "Abbot Suger and the Nuns of Argenteuil."

168. Abelard praised Robert in a letter to the bishop of Paris as an "outstanding herald of Christ." Abelard, Epist. 14; ed. Smits, 280; trans. Ziolkowski, 195. For Abelard as a monastic reformer and founder, see Luscombe, "Monasticism in the Lives and Writings of Heloise and

Abelard"; Marenbon, "Life, Milieu, and Intellectual Contexts," 25–26; and von Moos, "Abaelard, Heloise und ihr Paraklet." For similarities between Abelard and Robert, see below, n. 172. Mary Martin McLaughlin highlights Abelard's role as monastic reformer, noting that "by replacing his deserted students with Heloise and her nuns, he joined the company of monastic founders and reformers, becoming himself one of the 'new apostles' who were in this period reinvigorating the spiritual life of Christendom." McLaughlin, "Abelard as Autobiographer," 480.

169. Abelard, *Institutio*, 43; *The Letter Collection*, 410–411.

170. Abelard, *Institutio*, 44; *The Letter Collection*, 410–411. McLaughlin noted that Abelard's *Rule* emphasized "masculine supervision rather than feminine subordination." McLaughlin, "Peter Abelard and the Dignity of Women," 324. Despite Abelard's plan for ultimate male authority at the Paraclete, in the *Institutiones nostrae*, as Golding observed, "the abbot/provost has disappeared", leaving the abbess in complete authority over the community. Golding, "Authority and Discipline," 97. See below, n. 178.

171. Abelard, *Institutio*, 40; *The Letter Collection*, 406–407. For discussion, see Griffiths, "'Men's Duty'"; and, on structures of authority at the Paraclete (with reference to those at Fontevraud and Sempringham), Golding, "Authority and Discipline," 93–98. On Abelard's model for relations between monastic women and men, see McLaughlin, "Peter Abelard and the Dignity of Women," 322–327. In his earlier writings, Abelard had argued for men's care for women on the basis that "the weaker sex needs the help of the stronger." Abelard, Epist. 1.68; *The Letter Collection*, 110–111.

172. McLaughlin, "Peter Abelard and the Dignity of Women." For discussions of Abelard's defense of women, see also Blamires, *"Caput a femina, membra a viris"*; Blamires, *Case*, 199–207; and Griffiths, "'Men's Duty.'" Similarities between Abelard and Robert have been noted by a number of scholars, notably: Mews, "Negotiating the Boundaries of Gender," 143–146; Venarde, "Robert of Arbrissel and Women's *Vita religiosa*"; Dalarun, *"Capitula regularia magistri Roberti"*; Dalarun, "Nouveaux aperçus"; Felten, "Verbandsbildung von Frauenklöstern"; Golding, "Authority and Discipline"; and Elliott, *Bride*, 154. For the identification of Hersende as Heloise's mother, see Robl, *Heloisas Herkunft*. Mews describes the identification as "quite plausible": Mews, "Negotiating the Boundaries of Gender," 147, 125–129. In a later essay, he suggests that Heloise's father may have died in the First Crusade, leaving her widowed mother to enter a monastery. Mews, "Heloise," 269.

173. Bruce Venarde discussed the idea of Robert's "strangeness or marginality" in an important essay: Venarde, "Robert of Arbrissel and Women's *Vita religiosa*," 329.

174. Mews comments that Abelard "is often perceived as a quintessential rebel." As he writes, "there is a long tradition of bracketing together both Abelard and Heloise as fundamentally secular figures, at odds with the dominant religious traditions of their day, as represented by Bernard of Clairvaux." Mews, *Abelard and Heloise*, 19. On Abelard's self-conscious self-representation, see Verbaal, "Trapping the Future"; and McLaughlin, "Abelard as Autobiographer."

175. Blamires, *"Caput a femina, membra a viris,"* 56. Elsewhere, Blamires refers to it as a "zealously pugnacious piece." Blamires, *Case*, 202. Mary Martin McLaughlin described *On the Origin of Nuns* as the "most lavish encomium of holy women." McLaughlin, "Peter Abelard and the Dignity of Women," 295. Abelard's letter *On the Origin of Nuns* is Epist. 7; *The Letter Collection*, 260–351.

176. Blamires, *Case*, 199, 207.

177. At the Augustinian community of Marbach/Schwarzenthann, Abelard's writings directly affected male monastic attitudes toward religious women and men's role in providing for their needs. See Griffiths, "Brides and *dominae*"; and below, Chapter 3. For Abelard's sermons at Einsiedeln and Engelberg, see de Santis, *I Sermoni*, 54–55. Further attention to manuscripts of Abelard's writings may yield other instances in which Abelard's readership and impact can more clearly be traced. Luscombe draws particular attention to **T**, which he notes "is unique among the surviving MSS of the letter collection and best among them reflects the history and aims of the founders and the foundation of the Paraclete, for **T** alone presents the entire collection with the full text of the Rule." Luscombe, *The Letter Collection*, lxxxi. See also McLaughlin and Wheeler, "MS T (Troyes Bibliothèque Municipale, MS 802)"; and Dalarun, "Nouveaux aperçus."

178. Most striking is Heloise's decision to ignore Abelard's requirement of male authority at the Paraclete. The *Institutiones nostrae* neglect the position of the male abbot and declare instead, "soli abbatisse et priorisse debitum exhibetur obedientie." *Institutiones nostrae* "De obedientia," VI; *The Paraclete Statutes: Institutiones nostrae*, ed. Waddell, 10 (and Waddell's discussion, pp. 99–102). As David Luscombe observes, the *Institutiones* "set Abelard aright on matters of diet and authority: his most unconventional ideas, such as the allowance of meat and the provision of a male superior, are not taken up." Luscombe, "From Paris to the Paraclete," 272. On the failure of the Paraclete to adopt Abelard's *Rule*, see *The Paraclete Statutes. Institutiones nostrae*, ed. Waddell, 28–61; and Waddell, "Heloise and the Abbey of the Paraclete," 111–115. Luscombe argues that failure to adopt Abelard's *Rule* was no sign of disrespect to Abelard: Luscombe, "Pierre Abélard et l'abbaye du Paraclet."

179. Southern, *Medieval Humanism*, 101. Mary Martin McLaughlin challenged Southern's assumption that Abelard found his work "dreary," arguing that he forged a spiritual role for himself through his spiritual direction of nuns. McLaughlin, "Peter Abelard and the Dignity of Women," 331, 316–317. Blamires, too, defended Abelard's letter against charges that it was "conscientious hack work", arguing that it was "not drudgery but committed polemic." Blamires, "*Caput a femina, membra a viris*," 62. Arguments for the integrity of the letter collection and its relevance to the entire Paraclete community have been widely accepted. See, for instance, Powell, "Listening to Heloise."

180. Mary Martin McLaughlin commented that Abelard "was far from unique among his contemporaries in his concern for women, and particularly for their religious life," even though no other contemporary figure wrote as much for, or about, women as he did. His fellow reformers were "similarly, if not so articulately" concerned with problems relating to female religious life. McLaughlin, "Peter Abelard and the Dignity of Women," 291, 332.

181. On Guibert, see Coakley, *Women, Men, and Spiritual Power*, 45–67; and Griffiths, "Monks and Nuns at Rupertsberg." Like Abelard, Guibert reported that he had adopted the spiritual care of nuns by chance, rather than design: he first came to Rupertsberg, so he wrote, only to serve Hildegard, but soon found himself as the sole priest for all the nuns. For the circumstances that led to Guibert's installation as priest at Rupertsberg, see Griffiths, "Monks and Nuns at Rupertsberg," 157–160. Priests serving among nuns often described their spiritual involvement with women as an unintentional or chance development, a rhetorical strategy likely intended to deflect criticism. Accounts of Norbert, Gilbert, Abelard, and Guibert all present their attention to women as the result of circumstances, rather than volition. See above, n. 106; for the idea that "a number of the celebrated founders of various female communities . . . stumbled upon their destinies by accident," see Elliott, *Bride*, 163.

182. Guibert of Gembloux, Epist. 38, ll. 16–18; ed. Derolez, CCCM 66A, 367; trans. Silvas in *Jutta and Hildegard*, 99. Abelard, too, had preferred life among religious women to that among men: while he had experienced suffering and persecution at his home monastery of St. Gildas, Abelard reports that he found in the Paraclete "a haven of peace away from raging storms." Abelard, Epist. 1.70; *The Letter Collection*, 112–113.

183. Guibert of Gembloux, Epist. 26, ll. 470–74; ed. Derolez, CCCM 66A, 283; trans. Coakley in *Women, Men, and Spiritual Power*, 60. Coakley suggests that Guibert may be quoting from his attackers here.

184. Guibert's most sustained discussion of the spiritual involvement of men with women appears in a letter that he wrote sometime in 1178 or 1179 and addressed to his friend Ralph, a monk at the Cistercian monastery of Villers in Brabant. Guibert of Gembloux, Epist. 26; ed. Derolez, CCCM 66A, 270–294. See also Guibert's letter to Bovo: Epist. 38; ed. Derolez, CCCM 66A, 366–379; trans. Silvas in *Jutta and Hildegard*, 99–117.

185. Guibert of Gembloux, Epist. 26, ll. 553–554; ed. Derolez, CCCM 66A, 285.

186. "Sunt membra Christi, et matres Domini; et per virginem nos redemit Christus." *Regula cujusdam patris*, 18; PL 66: 991.

187. "Licenter igitur dicam: Ecce quam bonum et quam iocundum habitare fratres, habitare etiam sorores in unum." *Die Ältere Wormser Briefsammlung*, 45; ed. Bulst, MGH Briefe d. dt. Kaiserzeit 3, 82 [emphasis mine]. Azecho showed particular kindness to Gunnhild of Denmark (the daughter of Cnut and Emma), when she arrived as a young girl to marry Conrad II's son, Henry (later Henry III). Azecho would visit Gunnhild, bringing her almonds and offering kind words to comfort her. Tyler, "Crossing Conquests," 181. Gunnhild's daughter, Beatrix (d. 1061), became abbess at Gandersheim and Quedlinburg.

188. Thomas of Cantimpré, *Vita Ioannis Cantipratensis*, II, 3; ed. Godding, 279; trans. Newman, 81 [emphasis mine]. By contrast, the *Book of St. Gilbert* explained the peacefulness with which different groups—including women and men—could coexist within the religious life, citing the Psalm: "charity overcomes envy and a delight in their fellowship makes them live in unity as brothers." *The Book of St. Gilbert*, 19; ed. and trans. Foreville and Keir, 52–53.

189. For a selection of medieval texts, both celebrating and denigrating women, see *Woman Defamed and Woman Defended*, ed. Blamires. Jaeger traces the "double image of women," contrasting medieval ideas of "bad and dangerous" women with "virtuous women": Jaeger, *Ennobling Love*, 83–101.

190. Marbode advised his male audience to "beware the honied poisons, the sweet songs, and the pull of the dark depths," counseling flight from the attractions of women: Marbode of Rennes, *Liber decem capitulorum*, 3, ll. 71–72; ed. Leotta, 108; trans. Blamires in *Woman Defamed*, 102.

191. Guibert cited Equitius as an example of spiritual castration parallel to his own, claiming to have been delivered from what he described as "the tearing to pieces of unclean spirits" (*a dilaceratione tamen spirituum immundorum*) or, more graphically, as "the furnace of foul smelling and sulphureous wanton flesh" (*a camino fetentis et sulphuree carnalis petulantie*). Guibert of Gembloux, Epist. 26, ll. 424–425 and 428; ed. Derolez, CCCM 66A, 282. Guibert of Gembloux, Epist. 26, ll. 492–498, 614–616; ed. Derolez, CCCM 66A, 284, 287.

192. Marbode and Baudri of Bourgueil engaged in playful literary friendships with women in which they sometimes explored the idea of women's virtue and potential moral superiority. On these friendships, see Bond; Jaeger, *Ennobling Love*, 91–101; and Newman, *Making Love*,

4–24. Because these men did not support female religious life generally, or serve women in a spiritual capacity, I have not focused on them in this study.

193. Brian Golding acknowledged instances in which men engaged spiritually with women, yet cautioned that "it remains to be demonstrated that these [examples—like Abelard's—of men's care for women] were the norm, rather than the exceptions." Golding, "Authority and Discipline," 109.

194. Venarde, "Robert of Arbrissel and Women's *Vita religiosa*," 329. As Venarde notes, "Despite Robert's reputation for eccentricity, his activities were not unique and he was never an isolated figure." Venarde, "Introduction: Robert of Arbrissel's World," xxiv. Fontevraud received significant support from contemporaries and was much admired: the archbishop of Bourges vied to have a monastery of Fontevraud nuns within his province. Andrew, *Supplementum*, 31; *Deux vies*, 248–249. Constant Mews argues for the need to situate both Abelard and Robert in their spiritual and historical context. As he writes, "While Robert and Abelard have both tended to attract attention as charismatic personalities, it may be more useful to see their lives within the context of a broader questioning of roles of both women and men in the late eleventh and early twelfth centuries." Mews, "Negotiating the Boundaries of Gender," 113.

CHAPTER 2

Note to epigraph: Guibert of Gembloux, Epist. 26, ll. 521–522; ed. Derolez, CCCM 66A, 285.

1. Constable, *Reformation*, 153.

2. Constable, "Renewal and Reform"; Constable, *Reformation*, 125–167; McDonnell, "The 'Vita apostolica'"; Constable, *Three Studies*, 143–248; Olsen, "The Idea of the *Ecclesia primitiva*"; Dereine, "La 'Vita Apostolica.'" On the varieties of medieval reform, and the language used to describe it, see Barrow, "Ideas and Applications."

3. On the complicated textual history of the *pericope adulterae*, see Knust, "Early Christian Re-Writing."

4. For the medieval identification of Mary Magdalene with the sinful woman who "loved much" and with Mary of Bethany, who anointed Jesus's head and was credited by him with having chosen "the better part," see Jansen, *Making of the Magdalen*, 18–46; and Mulder-Bakker, "Was Mary Magdalen a Magdalen?" Devotion to the cult of Mary Magdalene intensified in the eleventh and twelfth centuries, as Victor Saxer has shown: Saxer, *Le culte de Marie Madeleine en Occident*.

5. On the trope of pious women shaming men, see Clark, "Sex, Shame, and Rhetoric"; and Brakke, "The Lady Appears." In his *Life and Passion of Christina* (composed for a male audience), Alfanus of Salerno (d. 1085) commented that "The Lord has offered us a model in the feminine sex, so that, challenged by the virtue of women, we may regain the toughness of the virile soul which we have lost through sinful living." Discussed in McLaughlin, *Sex, Gender, and Episcopal Authority*, 170.

6. Abelard, Epist. 7.31; *The Letter Collection*, 318–319.

7. Blamires calls this letter Abelard's most "zealously pugnacious piece." Blamires, *Case*, 202. On Abelard's "gender polemic" in this letter, see Blamires, "*Caput a femina, membra a viris*". Abelard argued that the *ordo* of holy women was part of the original church, established by Jesus himself, as Gary Macy observes. Macy, *Hidden History*, 93–96.

8. Abelard, Epist. 7.3; *The Letter Collection*, 262–263.

9. Abelard, Epist. 7.4; *The Letter Collection*, 264–265. Referring to the anointing of medieval kings and priests, Abelard drew a clear, and spiritually meaningful, distinction: "Christ himself was anointed by a woman as Christians by men; that is to say, the head itself by a woman, the members by men." Abelard, Epist. 7.5; *The Letter Collection*, 266–267. Cf. Abelard, *Sic et non*, 105; PL 178: 1494–1495 and Abelard, *Sermo* 11 (*De Rebus Gestis in Diebus Passionis*); PL 178: 455. For discussion, see Blamires, "*Caput a femina, membra a viris,*" 64–65.

10. Abelard, Epist. 7.6; *The Letter Collection*, 268–269.

11. Abelard, Epist. 7.31; *The Letter Collection*, 318–319. On the paradox of Christ's birth from a woman, and gender paradox in Christianity generally, see McLaughlin, "Gender Paradox."

12. Goscelin of St. Bertin, *Liber confortatorius*, II; ed. Talbot, 64; trans. Otter, 74.

13. "Quod autem de femina nasci voluit, magnum nobis benignitatis suae beneficium ostendit et immensum humilitatis exemplum." Hugh of Fleury, *Ex historia ecclesiastica*; ed. Waitz, MGH SS 9, 350. On Adela, see LoPrete, *Adela of Blois*; and Bond, 129–157.

14. Guibert of Gembloux, Epist. 26, ll. 706–707; ed. Derolez, CCCM 66A, 290.

15. Jerome, *Vita Hilarionis*, 7.2; ed. Morales, 232–233; trans. Fremantle, 305. Cf. Abelard, Epist. 7.31; *The Letter Collection*, 318–319.

16. Blamires, *Case*, 206.

17. Abelard, Epist. 1.67; *The Letter Collection*, 106–107.

18. Augustine of Hippo, *De opera monachorum*, 5.6; ed. Zycha, CSEL 41, 539; trans. Muldowney, 338. Augustine commented that "faithful women, possessing the goods of this world, went along with the Apostles and ministered to them from their own supplies so that the servants of God might lack none of those commodities which constitute the necessities of life." Augustine, *De opere monachorum*, 4.5; ed. Zycha, CSEL 41, 538–9; trans. Muldowney, 338.

19. Sigeboto, *Vita Paulinae*, *prefatio*; ed. Dieterich, MGH SS 30.2, 911; trans. Badstübner-Kizik, 92. On Sigeboto's *life* of Paulina in the context of the Hirsau reform, see Badstübner-Kizik, *Die Gründungs- und Frühgeschichte des Klosters Paulinzella und die Lebensbeschreibung der Stifterin Paulina*; Küsters, "Formen und Modelle religiöser Frauengemeinschaften," 200–203; and Küsters, *Der verschlossene Garten*, 121–130.

20. Guibert of Gembloux, Epist. 26, ll. 521–529; ed. Derolez, CCCM 66A, 285.

21. Guibert of Gembloux, Epist. 26, ll. 544–546; ed. Derolez, CCCM 66A, 285.

22. Guibert of Gembloux, Epist. 26, ll. 550–552; ed. Derolez, CCCM 66A, 285.

23. Abelard, Epist. 1.67; *The Letter Collection*, 106–107. Mary Martin McLaughlin highlighted the importance of Christ's "teachings and actions" in Abelard's conception of women's "dignity" in the religious life. McLaughlin, "Peter Abelard and the Dignity of Women," 301–303.

24. Abelard, Epist. 7.12; *The Letter Collection*, 280–281. My reading here differs from that of Luscombe.

25. Abelard, Epist. 5.23; *The Letter Collection*, 202–203. Abelard employed the concept of the "inseparable companion" in certain other contexts, too. In his *Introductio ad Theologiam*, he wrote that the soul is the "inseparable companion of corporal entities" (*anima inseparabilis comes est corporum*). Abelard, *Introductio ad Theologiam*, I, 17; PL 178: 1014. In his sermon 26, *De Sancto Iohanne Evangelista*, Abelard described Peter, James, and John as "inseparabiles comites." Abelard, *Sermo* 26 (*De Sancto Iohanne Evangelista*), ll. 12–13; ed. de Santis, 235. Finally, in his answer to one of Heloise's questions about the Beatitudes in the *Problemata*, Abelard described justice and mercy as the "inseparable companions" of Jesus. Heloise and Abelard, *Problemata*, 14; PL 178: 701; trans. McLaughlin with Wheeler, 237. On Christ as a model for

Abelard, see Frank, "Abelard as Imitator of Christ." On the language of "inseparable" companionship, see Valentine, "'Inseparable Companions.'"

26. See my discussion of John's exemplarity in Griffiths, "The Cross and the *Cura monialium.*"

27. Concerning Mary's role at the crucifixion, see Neff, "The Pain of *Compassio.*"

28. For the importance of John's status as Mary's adopted son, see Hamburger, *St. John the Divine*, 165–178.

29. The commendation contributed to the growing cult of St. John the Evangelist, offering further proof of John's status as the most beloved of the disciples. Together with the favor shown John when he rested on the breast of Christ, the care of Christ's mother was one of the principal privileges accorded him, solidifying his place in medieval theology and art. For John's presumed virginity, see Hamburger, "Brother, Bride, and *alter Christus.*" According to early legends, John had intended to marry, but had been called away by Christ from the actual wedding. Some medieval commentators identified John with the bridegroom at the wedding at Cana, and Mary Magdalene as the bride whom he had abandoned. Volfing, *John the Evangelist*, 27–31.

30. Jerome, *Adversus Jovinianum*, I, 26; PL 23: 248; trans. Fremantle, 366. Volfing observes that some commentators, among them Rupert of Deutz, characterized John as a "eunuch" on the basis of his celibacy. Volfing, 33–36.

31. Abelard, Epist. 1.67; *The Letter Collection*, 108–109.

32. For late antique and medieval interpretations of the commendation to John, see Koehler, "Les principales interprétations traditionnelles de Jn. 19, 25–27"; and Kneller, "Joh 19, 26–27 bei den Kirchenvätern."

33. Epiphanius of Salamis, *The Panarion of Epiphanius of Salamis*; trans. Williams, II, 609.

34. Ambrose, *Expositio Evangelii secundum Lucam*, 10.134; ed. Adriaen, CCSL 14, 384; trans. Ní Riain, 353. Ambrose warned that no woman should interpret the commendation as license to "live at her ease" or to leave an old husband in order to marry a younger one. Instead, as he noted, "what we have here is a mystery of the Church."

35. Ambrose, *Expositio Evangelii secundum Lucam*, 10.132; ed. Adriaen, CCSL 14, 383–384; trans. Ní Riain, 353.

36. Athanasius made this argument. Brakke, *Athanasius and the Politics of Asceticism*, 277.

37. Jerome, *Adversus Vigilantium*, 12; ed. Feiertag, CCSL 79C, 24; trans. Fremantle, 422.

38. Lifshitz notes that, already in the eighth century, John's cult was used as a "prop to syneisactism." However, in the area of Lifshitz's study, it was not the Virgin who was imagined as John's companion, but rather his female follower, Drusiana. Lifshitz, *Religious Women*, 117.

39. Rudolf of Fulda, *Vita Leobae abbatissae Biscofesheimensis*, 17; ed. Waitz, MGH SS 15.1, 129; trans. Talbot, 221–222.

40. Goscelin of St. Bertin, *Vita s. Edithae*, 21; ed. Wilmart, 88; trans. Wright and Loncar, 53–54. For discussion of Goscelin's *Vita s. Edithae*, its composition, and its reception at Wilton, see Bugyis, "Recovering the Histories of Women Religious." See also O'Brien O'Keeffe, "Edith's Choice."

41. "Iohannis certe et Marię in spiritalis contemplacionis dilectione cohabitatio magna fuit et mirifica." *Die Ältere Wormser Briefsammlung*, 45; ed. Bulst, MGH Briefe d. dt. Kaiserzeit 3, 82.

42. Cowdrey, *Pope Gregory VII,* 301. On Mary and Martha in medieval thought, see Constable, *Three Studies,* 1–141. For a reevaluation of Gregory's role in the campaign for clerical celibacy, see Cowdrey, "Pope Gregory VII and the Chastity of the Clergy"; and Blumenthal, "Pope Gregory VII and the Prohibition of Nicolaitism."

43. Cowdrey discusses Gregory's relationship with Matilda, and the scandal it provoked: Cowdrey, *Pope Gregory VII,* 300–301.

44. "Sicut in cruce Christus matrem virginem virgini discipulo commendavit: Mater, inquiens, ecce filius tuus; ad discipulum autem: Ecce mater tua." *Vita Anselmi episcopi Lucensis,* 12; ed. Wilmans, MGH SS 12, 17.

45. Gregorius presul Romanus, ut aegit Iesus

In cruce qui moriens dat discipulo genitricem,

Commisit dominam sic Anselmo Comitissam

Donizone, *Vita Mathildis,* II, 2, ll. 284–286; ed. Golinelli, 144–146.

46. *De S. Theodora,* 79; ed. Talbot, 180–182; rev. trans. Fanous and Leyser, 82–83. Concerning Christina's relationships with men, see Elliott, "Alternative Intimacies"; and Jaeger, *Ennobling Love,* 174–183. Christina's relationship to Geoffrey is discussed in greater detail in Chapter 5.

47. Koopmans, "Dining at Markyate"; and Koopmans, "The Conclusion of Christina of Markyate's *Vita.*"

48. Guibert of Gembloux, Epist. 26, ll. 579–81; ed. Derolez, CCCM 66A, 286. For discussion of Guibert's service among women, see Griffiths, "Monks and Nuns at Rupertsberg."

49. *The Book of St. Gilbert,* 53; ed. and trans. Foreville and Keir, 124–125.

50. Thomas of Cantimpré, *Vita Ioannis Cantipratensis,* I, 6; ed. Godding, 262; trans. Newman, 63. Similarly suggestive language had already appeared in the twelfth-century *life* of Christina of Markyate, to describe the patronage that Christina received from Archbishop Thurstan of York (*ex illa hora accepit eam in sua*). *De S. Theodora,* 43; ed. Talbot, 112; rev. trans. Fanous and Leyser, 45.

51. Thomas of Cantimpré, *Vita Ioannis Cantipratensis,* II, 5; ed. Godding, 281; trans Newman, 83.

52. Gregory of Tours, *Decem libri Historiarum,* 9.42; ed. Krusch and Levison, MGH SS rer. Merov. 1.1, 474; trans. Thorpe, 538.

53. Heloise, Epist. 6.28; *The Letter Collection,* 254–255.

54. See above, n. 49.

55. Herrad of Hohenbourg, *Hortus deliciarum,* ed. Green, Evans, Bischoff, and Curschmann, I, Nos. 212, 235. On the spiritual and intellectual contexts of the *Hortus deliciarum,* see Griffiths, *Garden of Delights.*

56. It may have been with a well-developed sense of irony, then, that Judith, wife of Earl Tostig, commissioned a crucifix together with representations of John and Mary for the cathedral at Durham. Simeon of Durham records that she arranged for the gift in an attempt to atone for her unsuccessful attempt to enter St. Cuthbert's church, from which women were barred entry. Judith's gift may in fact have been intended as a rebuke to the monks of Durham, who upheld the prohibition on women's entry into the church in direct opposition to the evangelist's example. Simeon of Durham, *History of the Church of Durham,* 46; trans. Stevenson, 682–683; discussed in Schulenburg, "Gender, Celibacy, and Proscriptions of Sacred Space," 190.

57. At Fontevraud, the abbess held ultimate authority—both spiritual and material—over the entire community. Dalarun, "Pouvoir et autorité"; and Golding, "Authority and Discipline."

Robert's emphasis on the spiritual and material priority of the women is reflected in the popular understanding of the community not as a double monastery, but as a female monastery, with a staff of priests and laybrothers attached. Parisse, "Fontevraud, monastère double." At St-Sulpice la Forêt, too, the abbess held authority over both the women and the men of the community. Guillotel, "Les premiers temps de l'abbaye de St-Sulpice la Forêt"; and Everard, "The Abbey of Saint-Sulpice la Forêt," 110.

58. Andrew, *Supplementum*, 3; *Deux vies*, 192–195. The men's oath to serve the women was also recorded in the earliest statutes of Fontevraud. A text of these statutes, dating from the period 1106–1112, has been identified by Dalarun in a manuscript from the sixteenth century: *The Original Statutes*; *Deux vies*, 388–405. For discussion, see Dalarun, "Les plus anciens statuts"; and *Deux vies*, 329–387. See also Dalarun, "*Capitula regularia magistri Roberti*." Annalena Müller cautions that aristocratic abbesses of Fontevraud during the early modern period manipulated existing documents and authorized the writing of new histories in order to further their claims to female abbatial power over ordained men within the order. Müller, *Forming and Re-Forming Fontevraud*.

59. For these numbers, see Baudri of Bourgueil, *Historia*, 23; *Deux vies*, 180–181.

60. Andrew, *Supplementum*, 11; *Deux vies*, 210–211. Andrew commented that when Robert founded a new house for women, he appointed brothers to "serve" them ("ad earum servitium").

61. The care for women that was provided by men at Fontevraud continued to be associated with the commendation scene long after Robert's death. A Latin libellus devoted to St. John and St. James the Greater connects Robert of Arbrissel's foundation at Fontevraud to the commendation scene: Gotha, Universitäts- und Forschungsbibliothek Erfurt-Gotha, MS Membr. I 68, fol. 123v. In the same way, a Middle High German libellus (Bamberg, Staatsbibliothek, Cod. hist. 153, fols. 134r–135r) commented that the community was "founded in the memory and in the love of our beloved Lord Jesus Christ who on the Holy Cross commended his beloved mother to the apostle and disciple St. John." However, the libellus inverted the structure of authority established by Robert, noting that "the canons should come before the three hundred women": cited in Hamburger, *St. John the Divine*, 166.

62. Abelard, *Institutio*, 40; *The Letter Collection*, 406–407.

63. On the centrality of the commendation to John to medieval conceptions of John's deification, see Hamburger, *St. John the Divine*, 165–178. In his sermon 26, Abelard cited the commendation of Mary to John as evidence of John's preeminence among the disciples. Abelard, *Sermo 26 (De Sancto Iohanne Evangelista)*, ll. 23–33; ed. de Santis, 236.

64. Abelard, *Sermo 26 (De Sancto Iohanne Evangelista)*, ll. 56–7; ed. de Santis, 237. As Anselm wrote:

Mary, how much we owe you, Mother and Lady,
by whom we have such a brother!
What thanks and praise can we return to you?

Anselm of Canterbury, *Oratio 7*; ed. Schmitt, *Opera*, III, 24; trans. Ward, 124.

65. Dyan Elliott offers a different interpretation, in which women and their priests engaged in a form of "heteroasceticism" that was "quasi-conjugal," and in which priests ultimately came to serve as a "proxy" for women's affection for Christ, the heavenly bridegroom. Elliott, *Bride*, 150, 155, 167–171. In her view, Robert of Arbrissel was assuming the persona of the celestial bridegroom through his controversial practice of sleeping (chastely) among women. Elliott, *Bride*, 170.

66. The *paranymphus* assisted at weddings in the ancient world, serving as a go-between between the bride and bridegroom before the wedding, and bringing the bride to the groom for the wedding ceremony. According to the *Hortus deliciarum*, care for the bride was explicitly part of the *paranymphus*'s job: "paranimphus amicus sponsi et sponse, vel brutebote. Item paranimphi custodes sive servatores sponse." Herrad of Hohenbourg, *Hortus deliciarum*, ed. Green, Evans, Bischoff, and Curschmann, II, No. 791 n. 21, marginal note. For Aelred of Rievaulx, the angel Gabriel served as a *paranymphus* at the annunciation, which Aelred described as the marriage of the Virgin to God. Aelred of Rievaulx, *Sermo* 9, 15; ed. Raciti, CCCM 2A, 74. As Megan McLaughlin notes, male ecclesiastics had long imagined themselves as serving as *paranymphus* at the mystical marriage of Christ and the Church. In this marriage, bishops could play the role of bridegroom, being joined to their churches in unions governed by sacred laws. McLaughlin, *Sex, Gender, and Episcopal Authority*, 56–57.

67. Goscelin of St. Bertin, *Vita sancti Wlsini*, 25; ed. Talbot, 85.

68. The text of the sermon is reproduced in: Goering, *William de Montibus*, 225–226.

69. Andrew, *Supplementum*, 51; *Deux vies*, 278–279.

70. Becquet, ed., "La vie de Saint Gaucher," 42–43.

71. "Fecit unam construi in honore sanctae Dei genetricis et eius sanctissimi tutoris apostoli Iohannis capellam." Ortlieb, *De fundatione monasterii Zwivildensis*, 18; ed. Abel, MGH SS 10, 83. The high altar at Marcigny was dedicated to the Trinity, Mary, and John the Evangelist. Wollasch, "Frauen in der Cluniacensis ecclesia," 103.

72. Schreiber, "Die Prämonstratenser und der Kult," 9, 7.

73. Schreiber, 8.

74. Schreiber, 7, 9.

75. It may have been in his role as guardian of virgins that John appeared at Jutta's side as she died, protecting her from the assaults of demons. *Vita domnae Juttae inclusae*, 9; ed. Staab, 186; trans. Silvas, 82.

76. Sigeboto, *Vita Paulinae*, 12; ed. Dieterich, MGH SS 30.2, 916; trans. Badstübner-Kizik, 104.

77. Sigeboto, *Vita Paulinae*, 27; ed. Dieterich, MGH SS 30.2, 922; trans. Badstübner-Kizik, 117.

78. On the history of Schwarzrheindorf, see Frizen, *Die Geschichte des Klosters Schwarzrheindorf*; and Kunisch, *Konrad III., Arnold von Wied und der Kapellenbau von Schwarzrheindorf*.

79. In 1172, Sophia von Wied issued a charter referring to herself as abbess of "Rindorf." Lacomblet, I, no. 444. Semmler argues that an informal women's community was established at Schwarzrheindorf from the church's foundation, although he admits that the monastic history of Schwarzrheindorf is a "puzzle." Semmler, *Die Klosterreform von Siegburg*, 163–165. On Schwarzrheindorf in the context of monastic expansion for women in the twelfth century, see Felten, "Frauenklöster," 249–250.

80. The literature related to the Schwarzrheindorf frescoes is extensive. For a general overview, see Kern, "Das Bildprogramm der Doppelkirche von Schwarzrheindorf"; and Verbeek, *Schwarzrheindorf*. On specific aspects of the visual program, see Odell, "Reading Ezekiel, Seeing Christ"; Esmeijer, "Open Door and the Heavenly Vision"; and Derbes, "The Frescoes of Schwarzrheindorf, Arnold of Wied, and the Second Crusade."

81. An inscription in the church records the 1151 dedication: Ilgen, "Die Weiheinschrift vom Jahre 1151," 36–37. Present at the dedication were Conrad III, Otto of Freising, and Wibald of Stavelot, as well as bishops and churchmen from Cologne and Bonn, the abbot Nicholas of Siegburg, and various nobles and ministerials.

82. On Arnold's career, see Wolter, *Arnold von Wied*. Before being made archbishop, Arnold had served as provost at St. Georg in Limburg an der Lahn, at St. Servatius in Maastricht, and at the cathedral in Cologne (from 1127). Concerning the political role of the archbishopric of Cologne, see Georgi, "*Legatio virum sapientem requirat*."

83. "Arnaldus Coloniensis archiepiscopus, vir honestus suaeque ecclesiae reparator." Otto of Freising and Rahewin, *Gesta Friderici I. imperatoris*, 29; ed. Wilmans, MGH SS 20, 412. Frederick refers to Arnold's "preclara merita." *Die Urkunden Friedrichs I*, no. 150; ed. Appelt, MGH DD F I, 254.

84. Archbishop Philip I of Cologne recorded in an 1176 charter that Arnold had handed the church over to Hadwig while he was still alive. "Soror eius domna Hedewigis Esnidensis abbatissa, cui predictus archiepiscopus, quia nulli post deum melius confidebat, adhuc vivens eandem ecclesiam commiserat." Lacomblet, I, no. 460. Cf. Lacomblet, I, no. 445. On Hadwig, see Buhlmann, "Die Essener Äbtissin Hadwig von Wied."

85. In 1176, Archbishop Philip I of Cologne commented that Arnold trusted Hadwig more than anyone else ("quia nulli post deum melius confidebat"). Lacomblet, I, no. 460. His 1173 charter noted that "Predicto itaque viro a mundi laboribus erepto prenominata soror eius ut mulier fortis operi sibi commisso impigre se succinxit et fratrem a desiderio suo non fraudavit." Lacomblet, I, no. 445. Arnold had trusted Hadwig as his representative some years earlier, leaving her to manage his affairs during his absence on the Second Crusade (1147–1149). Since work on the church at Schwarzrheindorf was likely under way at this time, it is probable that Hadwig's responsibilities during Arnold's absence included oversight of the building project. Frizen, 25–26; Buhlmann, 51.

86. Archbishop Philip I of Cologne notes that Hadwig enlarged the church ("predictam ecclesiam cum magno sumptu amplificavit") and that she built a cloister ("claustrum quoque propriis expensis construxit"). Lacomblet, I, no. 460. Frizen assumes that Hadwig carried out Arnold's wishes in the establishment of the women's community (although she argues that the structural changes that were required indicate that Schwarzrheindorf may not originally have been intended as a monastery). Frizen, 28. As Ilgen notes, there is no reference in the dedication inscription to the church's purpose as a religious community. Ilgen, 38.

87. The painting of the upper church is typically dated to the period after Arnold's death in 1156, while wall paintings in the lower church are generally dated to period before the dedication in 1151. Verbeek associates the upper church paintings with the monastic life at Schwarzrheindorf, suggesting that their visual program was developed in conjunction with the monastic foundation. Verbeek, 55–59. Kern agrees that the upper church was painted some 20 years after the lower church, although he argues that both parts were planned together: Kern, 355, 371. Esmeijer agrees, commenting that the visual program of both parts "must have been planned from the beginning as a whole." Esmeijer, "The Open Door and the Heavenly Vision," 53. Andrea Worm revisits the dating of the wall paintings, suggesting that the upper church was painted between 1166 and 1173, and the lower church "not . . . much earlier": Worm, "A Gospel Book in Cambridge," 24–25.

88. For the iconography of the crucifixion in Western art, see Schiller, *Iconography*, II, 99–117.

89. Neff highlights the salvific implications of Mary's suffering at the foot of the cross: Neff, "The Pain of *Compassio*," 257.

90. Ilgen, "Die Weiheinschrift." This altar, located in what became the nuns' choir, formed the focal point for women's worship at Schwarzrheindorf. At the dedication in 1151, the church had four altars.

91. Hildegard of Bingen, Epist. 14; ed. van Acker, CCCM 91, 31; trans. Baird and Ehrman, I, 52. On Hildegard's visionary reputation, see Newman, "'Sibyl of the Rhine'"; and the essays in Newman, ed., *Voice of the Living Light*. Arnold did visit Hohenbourg, the women's monastery in Alsace in which women's intellectual and spiritual life flourished in the last decades of the twelfth century. His visit in 1153, as part of the entourage of Frederick Barbarossa, predated work on the *Hortus deliciarum*, but may have been linked to the reform of the community, which was later credited to Frederick's support. Griffiths, *Garden of Delights*, 24–25.

92. See below, Chapter 4.

93. Bishop Ekbert of Münster had formerly been provost at Saint Cassius and knew both Arnold of Wied and Rainald of Dassel (who became archbishop of Cologne in 1159). Kunisch assumes that Ekbert of Schönau's criticisms of worldly bishops, with their building projects and monuments, were directed at least in part at Arnold von Wied. Kunisch, 60–61.

94. Arnold's siblings and their families are listed in: Frizen, 10–12. One of Arnold's nieces, Irmgard, was *magistra* at Andernach.

95. A charter from 1173 notes that Hadwig had brought Sophia and Siburgis to Schwarzrheindorf: "in locum predictum duas sorores suas Sophiam er Siburgim devotas deo feminas induxit." Lacomblet, I, no. 445. On the origins of other nuns at Schwarzrheindorf, see Frizen, 48–50.

96. Arnold's burial at Schwarzrheindorf is recorded in a diploma of Frederick Barbarossa from September 17, 1156: *Die Urkunden Friedrichs I*, 150; ed. Appelt, MGH DD F I, 253–254. Kern assumes that Arnold had intended the church as his burial chapel from the outset, although the sources are silent on this point (beyond noting that Arnold built the church "ut anime sue . . . esset remedium"): Kern, 353. Archbishop Philip I of Cologne notes the memorial function of the chapel in his 1173 charter: Lacomblet, I, no. 445.

97. For details concerning burial and memorial practices at Schwarzrheindorf, see Archbishop Philip I of Cologne's 1176 charter: Lacomblet, I, no. 460. The charter indicates that Schwarzrheindorf exercised limited parish rights, including the right to bury and baptize. Canons were present at Schwarzrheindorf from the outset and appear as witnesses in the earliest charter issued by Sophia as abbess in 1172: "Godefridus, Heroldus, Herimannus, sacerdotes et canonici in Rindorf." Lacomblet, I, no. 444. Concerning female monasteries and parish churches, see Röckelein, ed., *Frauenstifte, Frauenklöster und ihre Pfarreien*.

98. For the increase in monasteries for women in the Cologne archdiocese from the ninth through the twelfth century, see Felten, "Frauenklöster," 207–209; and Stein, *Religious Women of Cologne*. On Premonstratensian expansion in Cologne, see Ehlers-Kisseler. The reform congregation associated with Siegburg, a male monastery not far from Bonn, included many new houses for women in Cologne. For female communities associated with Siegburg, see Semmler, 151–169; and Röckelein, "Frauen im Umkreis der benediktinischen Reformen," 299–302.

99. Clark, "Claims on the Bones of Saint Stephen." On the gender politics of early martyr cults, see Lifshitz, "The Martyr, the Tomb, and the Matron," 313.

100. Augustine of Hippo, *De civitate Dei*, 22, 8; ed. Dombart and Kalb, CCSL 48, 821–824; trans. Bettenson, 1041–1043. Orosius brought some relics of Stephen with him from Palestine. See Hunt, *Holy Land Pilgrimage*, 212–220.

101. Abelard, *Sermo 32* (*De Laude Sancti Stephani Protomartyris*); PL 178: 574. In his letter *On the Origin of Nuns* Abelard referred to Stephen as having been appointed to "wait on" women (*ad ministrandum eis*), and for "the ministry and service of holy women" (*ministerio atque obsequio sanctarum feminarum*). Abelard, Epist. 7.12; *The Letter Collection*, 278–281. In a related

sermon (Sermon 31), addressed first to "brothers," Abelard spoke of the women who had joined the apostles and been embraced by them, and of the selection of deacons who had been chosen to care for the material needs of the women, freeing them to delight in the calm of the spiritual marriage bed. Abelard, *Sermo* 31 (*In Natali Sancti Stephani*); PL 178: 570.

102. In his *Rule*, Abelard linked his decision to require monks and lay brothers to provide for the external needs of the nuns, invoking the appointment of the seven deacons in Acts as his "authority." Abelard, *Institutio*, 40; *The Letter Collection*, 406–407. Cf. Abelard, Epist. 1.68; *The Letter Collection*, 110–111. See also Abelard, Epist. 7.12; *The Letter Collection*, 278–279; and *Sermo* 31; PL 178: 569–573.

103. For discussion of this passage, see Cook, "1 Cor 9,5: The Women of the Apostles."

104. Eastern theologians, by contrast, who accepted the idea of apostolic marriage, cited Paul as their authority. As Eusebius wrote, "Paul himself does not hesitate in one of his letters to address his wife, whom he did not take about with him in order to facilitate his mission." Eusebius of Caesarea, *Ecclesiastical History*, 3.30.1–2; trans. Oulton and Lake, I, 268–269. In the twelfth century, Guibert of Nogent reported Eusebius's contention that Paul had been married, reporting that Eusebius "most absurdly called the sister of Paul a wife" (*sororem absurdissime Pauli dixit uxorem*). Guibert of Nogent, *De virginitate*, 5; PL 156: 587.

105. Jerome, *Adversus Jovinianum*, I, 26; PL 23: 245; trans. Fremantle, 365.

106. Augustine, *De opere monachorum*, 4.5; ed. Zycha, CSEL 41, 539; trans. Muldowney, 338.

107. Augustine, *De opere monachorum*, 5.6; ed. Zycha, CSEL 41, 539; trans. Muldowney, 338. Abelard cited this passage twice: Abelard, Epist. 1.67; *The Letter Collection*, 106–107. Abelard, Epist. 7.12; *The Letter Collection*, 280–281.

108. Cited in *First Corinthians*, trans. Fitzmyer, 358.

109. Cook, "1 Cor 9, 5: The Women of the Apostles," 363.

110. "Dominus in comitatu suo mulieres habuit ne viderentur alienae a salute." Walafrid Strabo acknowledged the traditional, material interpretation, noting that "the women also ministered to him; thus also the apostles." Walafrid Strabo, *Glossa ordinaria: Epistola I Ad Corinthios*, 10; PL 114: 533.

111. "Quidam non intelligentes proprietatem Graecae linguae, fefellit eos ambiguitas verbi Graeci, in hoc quod dicit sororem mulierem, quasi uxores habuerint apostoli quas secum ducerent, nam *gyne* utrumque significat et uxorem et mulierem." Haimo of Auxerre, *In Epistolam I Ad Corinthios*; PL 117: 552.

112. Hervé de Bourg-Dieu, *Commentaria in Epistolas divi Pauli: In Epistolam I ad Corinthios*, 9; PL 181: 897.

113. Many theologians stressed Paul's decision *not* to have a sister woman to avoid scandal, suggesting that it was the potential for scandal rather than involvement with women per se that posed a problem. For Jerome, the key point of Paul's text was not so much the presence of "sister women" among the apostles (whatever their capacity) as Paul's decision not to have a sister woman himself. In his Epist. 123 to the widow Ageruchia, Jerome cited Paul's self-sacrifice as he encouraged Ageruchia to avoid the company of young women, whose behavior could prove a source of temptation. Jerome, Epist. 123.14; ed. Hilberg, III, CSEL 56/1, 89; trans. Fremantle, 236.

114. *De S. Theodora*, 76; ed. Talbot, 172; rev. trans. Fanous and Leyser, 78.

115. Guibert of Gembloux, Epist. 26, ll. 564–565, 573–575; ed. Derolez, CCCM 66A, 286. Guibert went on to note Paul's dedication in writing to women, commenting on the zeal with

which he corresponded with women and commended them, although they were separated from him. Guibert of Gembloux, Epist. 26, ll. 576–578; ed. Derolez, CCCM 66A, 286.

116. Sigeboto, *Vita Paulinae, prefatio*; ed. Dieterich, MGH SS 30.2, 911; trans. Badstübner-Kizik, 92.

117. Gregory the Great, *Moralia in Job*, 49, 57; ed. Adriaen, CCSL 143A, 732. For discussion, see Blamires, *Case*, 146–148.

118. Claudia Setzer argues that the gospel authors were ambivalent about the women's presence at the empty tomb, even as they all reported the women's priority. Setzer, "Excellent Women."

119. Abelard, Epist. 7.7; *The Letter Collection*, 274–275.

120. Origen, *Contra Celsum* 2, 55; trans. Chadwick, 109. For discussion, see MacDonald, "Was Celsus Right? The Role of Women in the Expansion of Early Christianity."

121. Dommuseum Hildesheim, Domschatz Nr. 18, fol. 175r.

122. Morgan Library, MS G.44, fol. 86r.

123. The J. Paul Getty Museum, Los Angeles, Ms. Ludwig VII 1, fol. 40v.

124. St. Albans Psalter. Dombibliothek Hildesheim, HS St. God. 1 (Property of the Basilica of St. Godehard, Hildesheim), p. 50. The Psalter was paginated rather than foliated.

125. Bjork, "On the Dissemination of *Quem quaeritis* and the *Visitatio sepulchri*."

126. *Interrogatio*:

Quem quaeritis in sepulchro, Christicolae?

Responsio:

Iesum Nazarenum crucifixum, o caelicolae.

Non est hic, surrexit sicut predixerat; ite, nuntiate quia surrexit de sepulchro.

Young, *The Drama of the Medieval Church*, I, 201.

127. The foundational study is: Young, *Drama*, I, 201–238. Scholarship on the *visitatio* is extensive; for a recent account of the *visitatio* in the Anglo-Saxon context, see Bedingfield, *The Dramatic Liturgy*, 156–170. Carol Symes critiques Young's argument that the tenth-century *visitatio* is "the earliest instance of medieval drama," proposing an earlier and often spontaneous culture of performance that reformers sought to restrain. Symes, "The Medieval Archive and the History of Theatre," 30–34.

128. Although the *Regularis Concordia* was directed to monks and nuns alike, it assumed an exclusively male vocabulary. Joyce Hill examines an eleventh-century adaptation of the *Regularis Concordia*, made for a female audience: Hill, "Making Women Visible."

129. *Regularis Concordia*, 51; ed. and trans. Symons, 50.

130. Favreau, "Heurs et malheurs de l'abbaye," 139–140.

131. The ordinal has survived in a single manuscript: University College, Oxford, MS 169. The liturgical dramas for Easter week are edited and translated in Yardley and Mann, eds. and trans., "The Liturgical Dramas for Holy Week at Barking Abbey." At Notre-Dame-aux-Nonnains, the performance involved the entire community—nuns and clerics, as well as altar boys (who played the angels). For discussion, see Johnson, 139. Pappano comments on the particular spiritual appeal to nuns of the resurrection narrative, in which holy women had played such a central role. As she writes, women's liturgical drama reflects "traditions that contested the male, clerical monopoly of Christ's body." Pappano, "Sister Acts," 48.

132. Yardley and Mann, eds. and trans., "The Liturgical Dramas for Holy Week at Barking Abbey," 31.

133. Abelard, Epist. 7.10; *The Letter Collection*, 274–275.

134. Thomas Becket, Epist. 289; ed. and trans. Duggan, II, 1232–1233. Duggan proposes that "Idonea" may have been Mary of Blois, daughter of King Stephen.

135. According to Abelard, women "were judged worthy to be the first to see the glory of the risen Lord," precisely because of their faithfulness at the cross. Abelard, Epist. 7.10; *The Letter Collection*, 274–275.

136. "Et si discipuli ideo apostoli vocati, quia missi sunt ab ipso ad praedicandum Evangelium omni creaturae, nec minus beata Maria Magdalene ab ipso Domino destinata est ad apostolos, quatenus dubietatem et incredulitatem suae Resurrectionis, ab illorum cordibus removeret." *Sermo in veneratione sanctae Mariae Magdalenae*; PL 133: 721; trans. in Blamires, *Case*, 110.

137. Jansen, "Maria Magdalena," 58.

138. "Mihi tantum, quia aliud operis incumbit, in fine prologi dixisse sufficiat, Dominum resurgentem primum apparuisse mulieribus, et apostolorum illas fuisse apostolas, ut erubescerent viri non quaerere, quem iam fragilior sexus invenerat." Jerome, *Commentariorum in Sophoniam prophetam*, prologus; ed. Adriaen, CCSL 76A, 655.

139. Goscelin of St. Bertin, *Liber confortatorius*, IV; ed. Talbot, 101; trans. Otter, 126. Victor Saxer identified the eleventh and twelfth centuries as a period of "Magdalenian fermentation." Saxer, "Maria Maddalena," 1089.

140. Discussed in Ortenberg, "Le culte de sainte Marie Madeleine," 27. The idea that Mary had been the "the first one to see the resurrected Lord," as Goscelin of St. Bertin also noted, was not universally accepted. In the fourth century, Jerome had commented that Mary Magdalene "was privileged to see the rising Christ first of all before the very apostles." However, Abelard noted opposing views on the question of Mary's priority in his *Sic et non*: "Quod Dominus resurgens primo apparuerit Mariae Magdalenae, et non." Goscelin of St. Bertin, *Liber confortatorius*, III; ed. Talbot, 85; trans. Otter, 103. Jerome, Epist. 127.5; ed. Hilberg, III, CSEL 56/1, 149; trans. Fremantle, 255. Abelard, *Sic et non*, 86; PL 178: 1472.

141. Jansen observes that "the image of the *apostolorum apostola* was ubiquitous, indeed almost inescapable in the Middle Ages." Jansen, "Maria Magdalena," 77. For Bernard of Clairvaux, who deployed the term in the plural—*apostolae apostolorum*—it was not simply the Magdalene, but with her the other women at the tomb, who were deservedly apostles. Bernard of Clairvaux, *Sermo* 75.8; ed. Leclercq, Talbot, and Rochais, *Sancti Bernardi Opera*, 1, 251–252.

142. *De vita beatae Mariae Magdalenae et sororis ejus sanctae Marthae*, 29; PL 112: 1479; trans. Mycoff, 79. The *vita* noted Mary's presence at both the resurrection and ascension: "Just as before he had made her the evangelist of his resurrection, so now he made her the apostle of his ascension to the apostles—a worthy recompense of grace and glory, the first and greatest honor, and a reward commensurate with all her services." *De vita beatae Mariae Magdalenae*, 27; PL 112: 1474; trans. Mycoff, 73.

143. St. Albans Psalter. Dombibliothek Hildesheim, HS St. God. 1 (Property of the Basilica of St. Godehard, Hildesheim), p. 51. Carrasco comments that depictions of Mary Magdalen announcing the resurrection are "so rare as to be almost unique": Carrasco, "The Imagery of the Magdalen in Christina of Markyate's Psalter (St. Albans Psalter)," 69. A further manuscript, the *Gospels of Henry the Lion and Matilda*, also featured Mary Magdalene as the "apostola." For discussion, see Monroe, "Mary Magdalene as a Model of Devotion," 100.

144. On the creation and ownership of the psalter, see Chapter 5.

145. Hugh of Cluny, *Commonitorium ad successores suos pro sanctimonialibus Marciniacensibus*; PL 159: 952. Ortenberg comments on the attention to Mary Magdalene in relation to contemporary women: Ortenberg, 32–34.

146. Abelard, *Sermo* 13; PL 178: 485. On Abelard's devotion to the Magdalene, see Mews, "Heloise, the Paraclete Liturgy, and Mary Magdalen"; Valentine, 155–163; and Mulder-Bakker, "Was Mary Magdalen a Magdalen?" According to Constant Mews, Heloise may have influenced Abelard's thinking concerning Mary's apostolate, since he had not referred to her as "apostola" in the 1120s. Mews, "Heloise and Liturgical Experience," 33.

147. "Maria Magdalena saecularis fuit, sed tamen Christum resurgentem vidit et Apostolorum apostola esse meruit." *Liber de modo bene vivendi, ad sororem*, 65; PL 184: 1240.

148. "Quae ergo fuerat in civitate peccatrix, dilectione et lacrymis, non solum liberari meruit a peccatis, sed fieri apostola et evangelista, imo (quod majus est), apostolorum apostola, festinans ad annuntiandum apostolis resurrectionem Domini." Peter of Blois, Epist. 234; PL 237: 507. On Peter's letters to individual women, see Markowski, "Treatment of Women in Peter of Blois' Letter Collection."

149. Many of these communities were linked to female religious life. The first daughter house of the Paraclete, at Trainel, was dedicated to Mary Magdalene in 1142. Mews, "Heloise, the Paraclete Liturgy, and Mary Magdalene," 103. A house for women at Fontevraud was dedicated to Mary Magdalene (La Madeleine). Paulina's biographer Sigeboto reports that she dedicated a chapel to Mary Magdalene. Sigeboto, *Vita Paulinae*, 18; ed. Dieterich, MGH SS 30.2, 918; trans. Badstübner-Kizik, 108.

150. "Petrus negat quem mulier praedicat." Geoffrey of Vendôme, *Sermo* 9; ed. Giordanengo, 136. Kienzle explores the idea of Magdalene's spiritual priority, particularly in comparison to Peter: Kienzle, "Penitents and Preachers." On the positive potential for women in the cult of Mary Magdalene, see Taylor, "Apostle to the Apostles: The Complexity of Medieval Preaching About Mary Magdalene."

151. "Arctius et ferventius." *Sermo in veneratione sanctae Mariae Magdalenae*; PL 133: 718. On this sermon, see Iogna-Prat, "La Madeleine du *Sermo in veneratione sanctae Mariae Magdalenae*." Iogna-Prat rejects the traditional attribution of the sermon with Odo of Cluny, proposing instead that it may have been composed at Vézelay. Nelson comments on the importance in this sermon of Mary as a woman that was "good to think" for its male contemplative audience. Nelson, "Women and the Word," 59.

152. "Christus eam sibi consociat." Peter the Venerable, *In honore sanctae Mariae Magdalenae hymnus*; PL 189: 1019.

153. "Et quia ab inquisitione non cessavit, prima videre meruit." *Sermo in veneratione sanctae Mariae Magdalenae*; PL 133: 719.

154. Mews and Renkin, "Legacy of Gregory the Great," 329–330. In the late twelfth-century *Gospels of Henry the Lion and Matilda*, the connection between Mary Magdalene and the bride of the Song of Songs is made visually manifest. Monroe, "Mary Magdalene as a Model of Devotion," 108.

155. The *Epithalamica* has been attributed variously to Abelard, to a Paraclete nun, and to Heloise. For the ascription to Abelard, see Waddell, "'Epithalamica'"; and Bell, *Peter Abelard After Marriage*. For arguments in favor of Heloise as the probable author, see Wulstan, "Heloise at Argenteuil and the Paraclete"; Wulstan, "*Novi modulaminis melos*: The Music of Heloise and Abelard"; and Mews, "Heloise and Liturgical Experience at the Paraclete." Barbara Newman writes that the Easter sequence seems "more likely" to be the work of Heloise than of Abelard. Newman, "Liminalities," 375. For a more cautious assessment, see Dronke and Orlandi, "New Works by Abelard and Heloise?" Abelard's argument that female monasticism had its origins in women's ministry to Christ made the Easter liturgy especially relevant to the

Paraclete nuns, as Flynn observes: Flynn, "Letters, Liturgy, and Identity," 331. See also Flynn, "*Ductus figuratus et subtilis.*"

156. Waddell, " 'Epithalamica,' " 247. On Abelard's liturgical corpus, see Waddell, "Peter Abelard as Creator of Liturgical Texts."

157. On Bernard's use of the image of the Bride in his sermons, see Engh, *Gendered Identities*; Krahmer, "The Virile Bride" and Moore, "The Song of Songs in the History of Sexuality." For the appeal of the Song within the male monastic context, see Turner, *Eros and Allegory*. According to Sarah McNamer, who stresses the legal and literal aspects of bridal status for religious women, the bride was merely a "provisional persona" for monks, and never a central identification. McNamer, 28. In her view, marriage to Christ (in a legal, ritualized sense) directly and powerfully influenced women's devotional practice, giving them a "strong legal incentive to cultivate compassion for Christ." McNamer, 16. While I do not find evidence in women's own writings for their strong spiritual identification with the bride (which was more often encouraged for them by male advisors), I agree with Barbara Newman that "playing the bride's role was probably never as easy or straightforward for monks as for religious women." Newman, "Gender," 46.

158. Anselm of Canterbury, *Oratio* 2; ed. Schmitt, *Opera*, III, 8; trans. Ward, 96.

159. McNamer writes that these prayers were scripts to guide prayer and to "elicit feelings," rather than indications of the author's own spiritual state of mind. McNamer, 68–71. As Newman commented in a review of McNamer's book: "I must also ask whether it is possible to script such powerfully moving prayers, so novel in genre and feeling, if one cannot oneself pray in that mode." Newman, Review of *Affective Meditation*, 524.

160. Abelard, Epist. 5.28; *The Letter Collection*, 206–209.

161. Aelred of Rievaulx, *De institutione inclusarum*, 31; ed. Hoste and Talbot, 664–673; trans. Macpherson, 82–92.

162. "Nam sicut ille pre cunctis discipulis ad sepulchrum Domini miro caritatis ardore venerunt, ita vos ecclesiam Christi quasi in sepulchro afflictionis positam pre multis immo pene pre omnibus terrarum principibus pio amore visitatis." *Das Register Gregors VII*, I, 85; ed. Caspar, MGH Epp. sel. 2.1, 122.

163. Peter Damian, Epist. 104.2; ed. Reindel, MGH Briefe d. dt. Kaiserzeit 4.3, 142; trans. Blum, 4, 146. On Peter's involvement with women, see Leclercq, "S. Pierre Damien et les Femmes."

164. "Ad crucem cum lacrymis," "ad monumentum cum aromatibus." Hildebert of Lavardin, Epist. I, 9; PL 171: 161.

165. See, for example, Jerome, *Adversus Vigilantium*, 12; ed. Feiertag, 24; trans. Fremantle, 422. As Jerome wrote, "I am not ashamed of having a faith like that of those who were the first to see the risen Lord; who were sent to the Apostles; who, in the person of the mother of our Lord and Saviour, were commended to the holy Apostles. Belch out your shame, if you will, with men of the world, I will fast with women." Mary Martin McLaughlin noted that Abelard's praise for women also served to "defend and dignify his own role as the founder and guide of a community of women." McLaughlin, "Peter Abelard and the Dignity of Women," 303.

166. Abelard, Epist. 7.11; *The Letter Collection*, 276–277.

167. Cited in Jansen, "Maria Magdalena," 58. Dominique Iogna-Prat comments that Mary Magdalene functioned as a "bridge" between the Virgin and Eve. Iogna-Prat, "La Madeleine," 60.

168. *De vita beatae Mariae Magdalenae*, 27; PL 112: 1475; trans. Mycoff, 73.

169. "Sed et mulier secus pedes Domini sedens audiebat verba oris eius, tanto Phariseis et Saduceis non solummodo sed et ipsis Christi ministris melior. quanto devotior. Sexus enim femineus non privatur rerum profundarum intelligentia, verum, ut in sequenti lectione lucide declarabimus, solet aliquando feminis inesse magna mentis industria et morum probatissimo-

rum elegantia." Hugh of Fleury, *Ex historia ecclesiastica*; ed. Waitz, MGH SS 9, 350; trans. Bond in *Loving Subject*, 155. Bond highlights Hugh's "redemption" of the *domina* in his dedicatory letter to Adela. Bond, 154.

170. Jerome, Epist. 127.5; ed. Hilberg, III, CSEL 56/1, 149; trans. Fremantle, 255.

171. In each of the gospel accounts, those present criticized the woman, either for her sinfulness or for her wastefulness. Yet Jesus defended her, drawing attention to her love for him (Luke), or linking the perfume with preparations for his death and burial (Mark, Matthew, and John).

172. Anselm of Canterbury, *Oratio* 16; ed. Schmitt, *Opera*, III, 65; trans. Ward, 202.

173. Aelred of Rievaulx, *De institutione inclusarum*, 31; ed. Hoste and Talbot, 667; trans. Macpherson, 86.

174. Abelard, Epist. 7.6; *The Letter Collection*, 268–269. Guibert of Gembloux, Epist. 26, ll. 526–527; ed. Derolez, CCCM 66A, 285.

175. St. Albans Psalter. Dombibliothek Hildesheim, HS St. God. 1 (Property of the Basilica of St. Godehard, Hildesheim), p. 36.

176. Andrew, *Supplementum*, 71–72; *Deux vies*, 294–295.

177. Dalarun, "Robert d'Arbrissel et les femmes," 1152–1154; and Dalarun, "La Madeleine dans l'Ouest de la France," 117–118. For a broader discussion of the ways in which religion "became feminine" in the period between the eleventh and the fifteenth centuries, see the essays in Dalarun, *Dieu changea de sexe* (comprising twelve articles originally published between 1985 and 2007).

178. As Goscelin commented, "There is an alb which she made out of the whitest linen (*ex bisso candidissimo albam*), a symbol of her innocence, very striking in its gold, gems, pearls, and little English pearls, woven around the yoke in keeping with her golden faith and gemlike sincerity; around the feet, the golden images of the Apostles surrounding the Lord, the Lord sitting in the midst, and Edith herself prostrated in the place of Mary the supplicant, kissing the Lord's footprints." Goscelin of St. Bertin, *Vita s. Edithae*, 16; ed. Wilmart, 79; trans. Wright and Loncar, 48 (Wright and Loncar translate "bisso" as "cotton").

179. For discussion, see Griffiths, "'Like the Sister of Aaron'"; Bugyis, "Recovering the Histories of Women Religious," 292. Bugyis argues that Edith embroidered the alb for herself, at the point at which she was made abbess. Goscelin included the account of Edith's alb in the recension of her *vita* that he produced for the Wilton women; he offered another version to Lanfranc. On the two versions of the *vita*, see Hollis, "Goscelin and the Wilton Women," 237–241.

180. "Isti apostolici Satanae habent inter se feminas (ut dicunt) continentes, viduas, virgines, uxores suas, quasdam inter electas, quasdam inter credentes; quasi ad formam apostolorum, quibus concessa fuit potestas circumducendi mulieres." Eberwin of Steinfeld, *Epistola ad S. Bernardum* (Epist. 472.6); PL 182: 679–680.

181. "Dicunt se communem in domiciliis suis vitam ducere, et more apostolico secum mulieres habere." Hugh of Rouen, *Contra Haereticos*, 3.4; PL 192: 1289; cited in Constable, *Reformation*, 158–159.

CHAPTER 3

Note to epigraph: Hugh of Fleury, *Ex historia ecclesiastica*, praefatio; ed. Waitz, MGH SS 9, 350.

1. See Chapter 2, n. 13.

2. For accounts of Jerome's life, see Brown, *Through the Eye of a Needle*, 259–288; Rebenich, *Hieronymus und sein Kreis*; Williams, *The Monk and the Book*; and Rice, *Saint Jerome in the Renaissance*, 1–22.

3. Reginald wrote his *Life* sometime between 1082–c.1095/1107. *The Vita sancti Malchi of Reginald of Canterbury*, ed. Lind, 9–11. For discussion of Reginald's method and intention in the *life*, see Heffernan, 132–136. For Jerome's *life* of Malchus, which he wrote in Bethlehem at the end of the fourth century, see Jerome, *Vita Malchi*; ed. and trans. Gray. Manuscripts of Jerome's *Vita Malchi* are listed in Lambert, II, no. 263. See also Jerome, *Vita Malchi*, ed. and trans. Gray, 68–76.

4. In Jerome's account, Malchus explains: "the woman I handed over to the virgins, loving her as a sister but not entrusting myself to her as to a sister." Jerome, *Vita Malchi*, 10.3; ed. and trans. Gray, 90–91.

5. Jerome, *Vita Malchi*, 2.2; ed. and trans. Gray, 80–81. Although the *Life* began with Jerome's claim to have seen a pious old couple living together, he reported later in the text (*Vita Malchi*, 10.3) that Malchus had delivered his "wife" into the care of virgins once he returned to the male religious life, implying that the two separated fairly quickly and seemingly contradicting his earlier claim to have met them as an elderly couple. For discussion of this point, see Burrus, "Queer Lives of Saints," 465. For chaste marriage in the medieval spiritual life, see Elliott, *Spiritual Marriage*.

6. Malchus's wife continues: "Let the masters think you my husband, Christ will know that you are my brother." Jerome, *Vita Malchi*, 6.7; ed. and trans. Gray, 84–87.

7. Horreo carnalem, desidero spiritualem
Iuncturam tecum sine sordibus et lue fęcum.
Reginald of Canterbury, *Vita sancti Malchi*, III, ll. 442–443; ed. Lind, 92.

8. By contrast, in Aldhelm's account of Malchus, Malchus acts without his wife to embrace chastity. Aldhelm, *Prosa de virginitate*, 31; ed. Gwara and Ehwald, CCSL 124A, 393–399; trans. Lapidge and Herren, 91. Jerome's *life* of Malchus was evidently known in Anglo-Saxon England, although no manuscript witness has survived. An Old English version of the *life* was copied at Worcester in the mid-eleventh century. See Beckett, "Worcester Sauce"; and Dendle, "The Old English 'Life of Malchus'" (Part 1 and Part 2).

9. O mulier lęta, ratio tua, lingua faceta,
Me tibi salvavit sociumque virumque paravit.
O me felicem puto teque meam genitricem,
Tu mea salvatrix, tu spes, tu vivificatrix,
Tu soror et mater, coniunx, coniunx ego frater.
Reginald of Canterbury, *Vita sancti Malchi*, III, ll. 467–471; ed. Lind, 93.

10. Christe, tibi grates per tot mihi commoditates
Quas misero dederis meritis huius mulieris.
Reginald of Canterbury, *Vita sancti Malchi*, III, ll. 480–481; ed. Lind, 93.

11. For Malcha as a nun, see Reginald of Canterbury, *Vita sancti Malchi*, III, l. 497; ed. Lind, 94.

12. "Cum monacha monachus non horret vivere Malchus." Reginald of Canterbury, *Vita sancti Malchi*, III, l. 497; ed. Lind, 94.

13. *Vita sancti Malchi of Reginald of Canterbury*, ed. Lind, 11.

14. The appearance of Latin nouns like *salvatrix* and *vivificatrix* in the twelfth century (primarily, although not exclusively, with reference to the Virgin Mary) is an index of the spiritual opening toward women that this book seeks to chart.

15. Goscelin of St. Bertin, *Liber confortatorius*, I; ed, Talbot, 35; trans. Otter, 34. Reginald praised Goscelin in two poems: Liebermann, "Raginald von Canterbury," 542–546.

16. Among Hildebert's female addressees were Cäcilie, abbess of Caen (Poem 46), Muriel of Wilton (Poem 26), Adela of Blois (who became a nun at Marcigny) (Poems 15 and 10, as well as several letters). Hildebert of Lavardin, *Carmina minora*; ed. Scott, 37 (Poem 46), 17–18 (Poem 26), 5 (Poem 15), 4 (Poem 10). Hildebert also wrote to secular women, including Matilda of Scotland and the Empress Matilda. See Dalarun, "Hagiographe et métaphore," 44–46; von Moos, *Hildebert*, 370–371. He may have been the author of an epitaph for Robert of Arbrissel (described as the "sower of God"), although the epitaph does not mention Robert's involvement with women. *Epitaphium Roberti de Arbrissel*; *Deux vies*, 579–607. On Hildebert's exile in England, see von Moos, 8–9. Hildebert's ties to the so-called "Loire Valley school" are discussed in Newman, *Making Love*, 5–10. On the poets of the "Loire school," see also Dalarun, "La Madeleine"; Tilliette, "Hermès amoureux"; Mews, *Lost Love Letters*, 87–101; and Signori, "Muriel und die anderen."

17. "Quam volo, quam quero, cuius prece celica spero." Hildebert of Lavardin, *Vita beate Marie Egiptiace*, l. 799; ed. Larsen, 290; trans. Pepin and Feiss, 109. For the literary influence of Reginald's *Vita Malchi* on Hildebert's *Vita Marie*, see Hildebert of Lavardin, *Vita beate Marie Egiptiace*; ed. Larsen, 323.

18. Vaughn explores Anselm's correspondence with women, noting his attention particularly to "powerful aristocratic married women." Vaughn, *St. Anselm and the Handmaidens of God*, 2. For Anselm's letters to abbesses and nuns, see Vaughn, *St. Anselm and the Handmaidens of God*, 160–202. On Anselm's attention to women, see also Golding, "Bishops and Nuns," 102–108.

19. See Chapter 1, n. 109.

20. For Jerome's reputation and influence in the Middle Ages and Renaissance, see Uttenweiler, "Zur Stellung des hl. Hieronymus im Mittelalter"; Laistner, "The Study of St. Jerome in the Early Middle Ages"; and Rice.

21. On Jerome's relations with women, see Feichtinger, *Apostolae apostolorum*; Krumeich, *Hieronymus und die christlichen feminae clarissimae*; Kelly, *Jerome*, 91–103; and McNamara, "Cornelia's Daughters." Elizabeth Clark examines Jerome's relations with women in the context of classical and Christian approaches to friendship: Clark, *Jerome, Chrysostom, and Friends*, 35–79. See also Clark, "Theory and Practice."

22. Jerome's writings on female piety are addressed in: Laurence, *Jérôme et le nouveau modèle féminin*; and Steininger, *Die ideale christliche Frau*, 65–163. Wiesen explores Jerome's writings on women in his letters, polemical writings, and exegetical works. Wiesen, *St. Jerome as a Satirist*, 113–165.

23. LeMoine, "Jerome's Gift to Women Readers," 231. LeMoine underscores the ambiguity of Jerome's textual "gifts" to women readers, noting his simultaneous praise for women and his denunciation of them. He was, she concludes, an "almost unbelievable paradox" (239).

24. Harvey, "Jerome Dedicates his *Vita Hilarionis*."

25. For discussion, see Cain, "Defending Hedibia."

26. Jerome, Epist. 28.1; ed. Hilberg, I, CSEL 54, 227. Clark calls Marcella "Jerome's most scholarly female friend." Clark, *Jerome, Chrysostom, and Friends*, 65. See also Hinson, "Women Biblical Scholars in the Late Fourth Century."

27. The preface is translated in *Jerome: Letters and Select Works*, trans. Fremantle, 496.

28. Jerome's extant letters, totaling 123, include some forty letters to women. The collection includes only one letter from women: Epist. 46, purportedly from Paula and Eustochium to Marcella, but more likely by Jerome. Adkin, "The Letter of Paula and Eustochium to

Marcella." Cain identifies Jerome's 123 extant letters and classifies them by type: Cain, *Letters of Jerome*, 207–219. Elizabeth Clark shows that Jerome wrote more letters to women, as a percentage of his total epistolary output, than either Chrysostom or Augustine. Clark, "Theory and Practice in Late Ancient Asceticism," 34.

29. "Epistolarum autem ad Paulam et Eustochium, quia quotidie scribuntur, incertus est numerus." Jerome, *De viris illustribus*, 135; PL 23: 719. As Cain notes, only five letters survive from Jerome's early years in Bethlehem (386–93). Cain, *Letters of Jerome*, 220–222.

30. "Ad Marcellam epistularum librum unum." Jerome, *De viris illustribus*, 135; PL 23: 717. For Jerome's letters to Marcella, see Lambert, IA, p. 78. Cain discusses the likely content and intended purpose of the *liber*: Cain, *Letters of Jerome*, 68–98.

31. Jerome, Epist. 22; ed. Hilberg, I, CSEL 54, 143–211; trans. Fremantle, 22–41.

32. Jerome, *Epitaphium Sanctae Paulae*; ed. and trans. Cain. For discussion of Jerome's purpose in this text, see Cain, "Jerome's *Epitaphium Paulae*." On Paula, see Krumeich, *Paula von Rom*. Jerome's portrayal of Paula served as a major source for Geoffrey Grossus's *life* of Bernard of Tiron. Cline, "Literary Borrowing from Jerome's Letter." The letter also served as the basis for portions of the *life* of Theoger of St. Georgen: Wolfger of Prüfening, *Vita Theogeri*, I, 25; ed. Jaffé, MGH SS 12, 459–460. Cf. Jerome, *Epitaphium Sanctae Paulae*, 20; ed. and trans. Cain, 74–79.

33. On letters 127 and 24 (accounts of Marcella and Asella), see Cain, "Rethinking Jerome's Portraits."

34. Cain, "Rethinking Jerome's Portraits," 57; and Cain, *Letters of Jerome*, 89–92. In an autobiographical section of *De viris illustribus*, Jerome emphasized his writings for women, intentionally and explicitly promoting his reputation as a spiritual guide for women. Jerome, *De viris illustribus*, 135; PL 23: 715–719. While Cain argues for the centrality of women to Jerome's presentation of himself as a spiritual guide and exegete, Peter Brown offers a dissenting view, arguing that Jerome "may have approached Paula and other devout ladies as a fallback to his main career in the service of Damasus." Brown, *Through the Eye of a Needle*, 262. See also Brown, *Body and Society*, 366–386.

35. Palladius, *Lausiac History*, 41.2 and 36.6; trans. Meyer, 118, 104.

36. *Vita Sadalbergae*, 25; ed. Krusch, MGH SS rer. Merov. 5, 64; trans. McNamara and Halborg, 192.

37. Caesarius of Arles and Leander of Seville, both authors of monastic rules composed for their sisters, echoed Jerome in their writings for women, but did not explicitly cite him in that context. For details, see Antin, "Jérôme antique et chrétien," 39–40.

38. Aldhelm, *Prosa de virginitate*, 49; ed. Gwara and Ehwald, CCSL 124A, 659–661; trans. Lapidge and Herren, 116. For the image of Aldhelm presenting *De virginitate* to women, see London, Lambeth Palace Library, MS 200, fol. 68v. The Lambeth Palace manuscript is discussed in Kiff-Hooper, "Class Books or Works of Art?" Hollis discusses Aldhelm's writings for the Barking community: Hollis, *Anglo-Saxon Women*, 75–112. Aldhelm praised Eustochium in his *Carmen de virginitate* and mentioned Jerome's writing for her. Aldhelm, *Carmen de virginitate*; ed. Ehwald, MGH Auct. ant. 15, 440; trans. Lapidge and Rosier, 150.

39. "Dum ille huic alterum exhibebat Jheronimum, haec illi alteram Eustochium." *Vita S. Hiltrudis virginis*; *AA SS*, September, 7: 494.

40. For discussion of the *vitae* of Jerome, see Vaccari, "Le antiche vite di S. Girolamo"; and Rice, 23–48. *Plerosque nimirum* appears in two recensions: BHL 3870 and BHL 3871 (PL 22: 201–214). For manuscripts of *Plerosque nimirum*, see Lambert, IIIB, no. 900. Cavallera dates *Plerosque nimirum* to the second half of the sixth century. Cavallera, II, 142. The dating of *Hieronymus noster* (BHL 3869; PL 22: 175–184) is contested. Vaccari dates it to the second half of the eighth century, while

Cavallera proposes a broader range, between the sixth and the eighth centuries. Vaccari, 5–7; Cavallera, II, 140. For manuscripts of *Hieronymus noster*, see Lambert, IIIB, no. 901.

41. Images of Jerome are listed in Lambert, IVA, no. 995. For traditional depictions of Jerome, see Conrads, *Hieronymus*; Jungblut, *Hieronymus*; and "Saint Jérôme dans l'art de l'enluminure," in Lambert, IVA, pp. 69–76.

42. From her study of manuscript production at St. Gall from the middle of the eighth century until the early decades of the tenth century, Bernice Kaczynski has shown that Jerome was the most frequently copied patristic author before 840. Kaczynski, "The Authority of the Fathers," 9–11. On Jerome's popularity during the Carolingian renaissance, see also Kaczynski, "Edition, Translation, and Exegesis."

43. *Institutio sanctimonialium*; ed. Werminghoff, MGH Conc. 2.1, 421–456. Gisela Muschiol notes the strong influence of Jerome on the *Institutio sanctimonialium* (above all in his Epist. 22), especially in comparison with the *Institutio Canonicorum*, which drew from a wider range of sources. Muschiol, *"Hoc dixit Ieronimus,"* 113–114. Concerning the *Institutio*, see Schilp, *Norm und Wirklichkeit*.

44. *Mainzer Urkundenbuch. I*, ed. Stimming, no. 405. Similarly, Adelheid of Vilich (d. 1015) was described as having lived in a community in Cologne "secundum regularem institutionem sancti Iheronimi." Bertha of Vilich, *Vita Adelheidis abbatissae Vilicensis*, 3; ed. Holder-Egger, MGH SS 15.2, 757.

45. Paschasius Radbertus, *De assumptione sanctae Mariae*, 1; ed. Ripberger, CCCM 56C, 109. On the sermon, see Ripberger, *Der Pseudo-Hieronymus-Brief*; and Muehlberger, *Cogitis Me: A Medieval Sermon on the Assumption*. For manuscripts of this work, see Lambert, IIIA, no. 309; and Ripberger, 49–55. Mayke de Jong discusses the difficult political circumstances in which Paschasius became abbot of Corbie, and his retirement sometime between 849 and 853. De Jong, "Jeremiah, Job, Terence."

46. Paris, Bibliothèque nationale de France, Lat. 1, fol. 3v. On this manuscript, see Dutton and Kessler, *The Poetry and Paintings of the First Bible of Charles the Bald*. For discussion of the image, see Kessler, *The Illustrated Bibles from Tours*, 84–95; Ganz, "The Vatican Vergil and the Jerome Page"; and McKitterick, "Women in the Ottonian Church," 82–85.

47. Eustachio nec non Paulae divina salutis
Iura dat altithrono fultus ubique deo.

48. Rome, Abbazia di San Paolo fuori le mura, s.n., fol 3v. For discussion, see Kessler, *Illustrated Bibles*, 84–95; and Gaehde, "The Turonian Sources," 361–365.

49. On the possible identity of this woman, see McKitterick, "Women in the Ottonian Church," 82; and Kessler, *Illustrated Bibles*, 90.

50. Kessler, *Illustrated Bibles*, 84.

51. Kessler (following Nordenfalk) posits a lost fifth-century Italian model, a theory (and approach) that Rosamond McKitterick dismisses. Kessler, *Illustrated Bibles*, 95; McKitterick, "Women in the Ottonian Church," 81, n. 7. Renate Jungblut suggests that inspiration for the images may have come from a lost illustration of Jerome's *vita*, an unlikely scenario given that the earliest *vitae* pass largely in silence over Jerome's relations with women. Jungblut, 8.

52. McKitterick, "Women in the Ottonian Church," 85–86. On the spiritual and intellectual lives of Carolingian women, see Garver, *Women and Aristocratic Culture*, 122–169. The fact that Jerome's reputation for care of women was forged during the ninth century is striking, given that this period is generally thought to have witnessed creeping limitations and restrictions on men's spiritual involvement with women. The willingness of ninth-century men to imagine and celebrate Jerome's relations with women directly contradicts perceptions of the

Carolingian reforms as having been deleterious for women, demonstrating how positive assessments of women's religious life, and men's involvement with them, could coexist with other, less positive judgments.

53. On Alcuin, see Bullough, *Alcuin*; Depreux and Judic, eds., *Alcuin: De York à Tours;* Houwen and MacDonald, eds., *Alcuin of York*; and Bullough, "Charlemagne's 'Men of God.'"

54. Garrison, "The Social World of Alcuin"; and Garrison, "Les correspondants d'Alcuin."

55. Gisela held the abbacy of Notre Dame in Soissons at the same time as that of Chelles. On the early history of Chelles, see Berthelier-Ajot, "Chelles à l'époque mérovingienne"; Bateson, "Origin and Early History of Double Monasteries," 155–156; Hilpisch, 38–39; and McKitterick, "Nuns' Scriptoria," 4.

56. Bischoff, "Die Kölner Nonnenhandschriften und das Skriptorium von Chelles"; McKitterick, "Nuns' Scriptoria," 1–22; and Nelson, "Gender and Genre," 191–194. McKitterick notes that "the role of the convent of Chelles . . . as an alternative sphere of activity and location of female royal presence, and even power, is an intriguing element about which we have only the merest hints." McKitterick, *Charlemagne*, 91.

57. "adversae fortunae malignitatem expertus est." Einhard, *Vita Karoli Magni*, 19; ed. Holder-Egger, MGH SS rer. Germ. 25, 25; trans. Noble, 39. Rotrude had been betrothed as a child to the Byzantine emperor Constantine VI, although no marriage took place. On Charlemagne's relations with his daughters, see Nelson, "Women at the Court of Charlemagne"; and Scharer, "Charlemagne's Daughters." On Rotrude, see Nelson, "La cour impériale de Charlemagne," 185–187.

58. Rotrude had a son, Louis, with Count Rorigo; Louis later became abbot of St. Denis and archchancellor to Charles the Bald. Bertha had two sons, Nithard and Hartnid, with Angilbert, lay abbot of St-Riquier. McKitterick, *Charlemagne*, 92 (Table 4).

59. On the importance of social distinctions in Jerome's friendships with women, see Clark, *Jerome, Chrysostom, and Friends*, 60–70. Clark suggests that Jerome was attracted by the noble lineage and wealth of his female friends, noting that class distinctions were preserved at Paula's monastery in Bethlehem (67). Cain emphasizes Paula's financial support for Jerome's projects: Cain, "Jerome's *Epitaphium Paulae*."

60. Jerome, Epist. 108.26 (*Epitaphium Sanctae Paulae*); ed. and trans. Cain, 88–89. On Paula's trilinguism, see Cain, "Jerome's *Epitaphium Paulae*," 122–123.

61. Jerome, *Commentariorum in Esaiam*, 16, prol.; ed. Adriaen, CCSL 73A, 641.

62. Alcuin, *Carmen* 12; ed. Dümmler, MGH Poetae 1, 237. For discussion of Alcuin's correspondence, see Garrison, "Les correspondants d'Alcuin." As with the letters of Paula and Eustochium, the bulk of the women's letters to Alcuin have not survived. On Gisela as a *femina verbipotens*, see Nelson, "Women and the Word," 64–65.

63. On the Vulgate during the medieval period, see Loewe, "The Medieval History of the Latin Vulgate"; and Linde, *How to Correct the Sacra Scriptura?*. On Carolingian reforms of the biblical text, see Fischer, "Bibeltext und Bibelreform"; and Kaczynski, "Edition, Translation, and Exegesis." On the place of Tours in Carolingian bible production, with a cautious assessment of the influence of Alcuin's bible, see McKitterick, "Carolingian Bible Production."

64. "In servitute Christi nequaquam differentiam sexuum valere, sed mentium." Jerome, *Commentariorum in Esaiam*, 12, prol.; ed. Adriaen, CCSL 73A, 466. In letter 127 to Principia, Jerome made a similar comment. See Chapter 2, n. 170. For a listing of manuscripts of Jerome from St-Martin, Tours, see Lambert IVB, pp. 217–218. See also Rand, *A Survey of the Manuscripts of Tours*.

65. For Jerome as an epistolary model for Alcuin, see Veyrard-Cosme, "Saint Jérôme dans les lettres d'Alcuin."

66. As Jerome wrote, Blesilla "asked me to throw my remarks upon all the more obscure passages into the form of a short commentary, so that, when I was absent, she might still understand what she read." Jerome, *Commentarius in Ecclesiasten*, praefatio; ed. Adriaen, CCSL 72, 249; trans. Fremantle, 487. LeMoine draws attention to the misogynist elements in the *Commentary on Ecclesiastes*: LeMoine, 238.

67. "Beatissimum siquidem Hieronimum, nobilium nullatenus spernere feminarum preces, sed plurima illarum nominibus . . . dedicasse opuscula." *Epistola famularum Gislae et Rectrudis ad Alcuinum* (Epist. 196); ed. Dümmler, MGH Epp. 4, 323–325. For knowledge of Jerome's works in female monastic communities from the eighth to the thirteenth century, see El Kholi, *Lektüre in Frauenkonventen*, 121–129.

68. Alcuin, *Epistola ad Gislam et Rectrudem* (Epist. 213); ed. Dümmler, MGH Epp. 4, 354–357.

69. "Liudo dedit." Düsseldorf, Universitäts- und Landesbibliothek, MS B 4, fol. 2r. The manuscript is described in Bodarwé, *Sanctimoniales litteratae*, 383–384. See also *Krone und Schleier*, cat. no. 97. Bodarwé argues that Liudo (who has not been identified) gave the manuscript sometime before the middle of the tenth century. Bodarwé, *Sanctimoniales litteratae*, 206, n. 76.

70. On men at Essen, see Schilp, "..*sorores et fratres*"; and Schilp, "Der Kanonikerkonvent."

71. Halle, Universitäts- und Landesbibliothek, Qu. Cod. 74. The manuscript is described in Bodarwé, *Sanctimoniales litteratae*, 419–421; and Fliege, *Die Handschriften der ehemaligen Stifts- und Gymnasialbibliothek Quedlinburg*, 33–38. See also *Krone und Schleier*, cat. no. 104. A tenth-century manuscript from Regensburg (most likely from the female house of Niedermünster) also included several of Jerome's letters to women: Wolfenbüttel, Herzog August Bibliothek, 18. 4. Aug. 2° (2210). For discussion, see El Kholi, 123–124. Jerome's letters did not circulate as a single collection during the medieval period. For the transmission history of Jerome's letters, see Cain, *Letters of Jerome*, 223–228.

72. On evidence for women's reading practices in Quedlinburg Codex 74, see Scheck, "Reading Women at the Margins of Quedlinburg Codex 74."

73. Engelmodus wrote that Paschasius had been abandoned as a baby, but was taken in by the nuns of Notre Dame. Engelmodus of Soissons, *Ad Ratbertum Abbatem*; ed. Traube, MGH Poetae 3, 62–66. Paschasius grew up at Soissons (which, like many women's houses, included ordained as well as lay men), gained his early education among the women, and was even tonsured there, before entering Corbie. In the prologue to *De partu virginis*, Paschasius addressed the nuns directly and acknowledged his debt to them. Paschasius Radbertus, *De partu virginis*, praefatio; ed. Matter, CCCM 56C, 47. On Paschasius in his monastic context, see Peltier, *Pascase Radbert*. On Paschasius's relations with Notre Dame du Soissons, see Ripberger, 14–17. At Soissons at this time, 216 nuns were joined by some seventy external sisters and maidservants, 130 men, and 25 priests, deacons, and other clerics. Ripberger, 3, n. 6.

74. Ripberger, 21–22.

75. Theodrada was a cousin of Charlemagne and the sister of Adalard and Wala, half-brothers who had served as abbots of Corbie and for whom Paschasius composed *vitae*. See Paschasius Radbertus, *Charlemagne's Cousins*, trans. Cabaniss.

76. On Paschasius's patristic sources, see Peltier, 132–147; and Ripberger, 30–36. For the influence of Jerome's writings on Paschasius, see Ripberger, 30–31. For manuscripts of Jerome at Corbie, see Lambert IVB, p. 179; and Ganz, *Corbie in the Carolingian Renaissance*, passim.

77. Jerome, *Commentariorum in Esaiam*, prol.; ed. Adriaen, CCSL 73, 1.

78. Paschasius Radbertus, *De assumptione sanctae Mariae*, 101; ed. Ripberger, CCCM 56C, 155. Paschasius's emphasis on Mary as a model for nuns is discussed in: Appleby, " 'Beautiful on the Cross, Beautiful in his Torments,'" 34–39. Paschasius also produced a commentary on Psalm 44 for the nuns of Soissons, and a treatise on Mary's virginity, *De partu virginis*, which he dedicated to Imma. Paschasius Radbertus, *Expositio in Psalmum XLIV*; ed. Paulus CCCM 94. Paschasius Radbertus, *De partu virginis*, ed. Matter CCCM 56C. Jerome had written a commentary on Psalm 44, for Principia (Epist. 65), and had addressed the subject of Mary's virginity in his tract against Helvidius. Paschasius may have written a further three sermons on Mary's assumption as well as *De nativitate s. Mariae*, a pseudo-Jeromian letter addressed to "Paula" (Epist. 50; PL 30: 297–305). The sermons on Mary's assumption circulated as the work of Ildefons of Toledo (*Sermo* 1–3; PL 96: 239–257). On these works, see Peltier, 111–115.

79. Ripberger, 36.

80. Lambot, "L'homélie du Pseudo-Jérôme;" and Barré, "La Lettre du Pseudo-Jérôme sur l'assumption." On contemporary hesitations concerning Jerome's authorship of the letter, see Ripberger, 8–9. As Barré notes, Paschasius was not trying to fool anyone, least of all at Corbie, where his authorship was known. Barré, 224, n. 4.

81. For the incorporation of the sermon into the liturgy, see Ripberger, 36–43; Fulton "*Quae est ista*," 90–100; and Matter, *Voice*, 152–155.

82. "ad nocturnos legitur sermo sancti Hieronymi, Cogitis me, o Paula, qui cum tantae sit excellentiae, ad nonam lectionem nequaquam pronuntiatur Evangelium, sed omnes lectiones de eodem sermone fiunt." *Consuetudines cluniacensis*, 36 ("De Assumptione S. Mariae"); PL 149: 683.

83. "Qui ad plenum vult cognoscere gloriam solemnitatis hodiernae, legat sermonem quem supradictus Pater Hieronymus edidit, et ad sanctam Paulam, et ad Eustochium filiam ejus virginem, et ad caeteras virgines non solum praesentes, sed etiam ad superventuras transmisit." Odilo of Cluny, *Sermo 12. De Assumptione Dei genitricis Mariae*; PL 142: 1028.

84. Ripberger, 39–40.

85. References to "Cogitis me" as the work of Jerome in the writings of William and Rupert are provided in Fulton, *From Judgment to Passion*, 346, 301.

86. The letter is reproduced in Lutter, 230–234. For discussion of the letter, and questions concerning the identification of the women, see Lutter, 115–119; and El Kholi, 96–98. For Gerhoch's other letters to women, see Lutter, 108–115.

87. "Lege Hieronymum ad Paulam et Eustochium de assumptione sanctae Mariae." Gerhoch of Reichersberg, *Commentarius aureus in psalmos et cantica ferialia*; PL 193: 645.

88. Abelard, Epist. 7.48; *The Letter Collection*, 344–345.

89. Cain, *Letters of Jerome*, 102–105.

90. Writing to Demitrias, Jerome claimed that this letter had led to his unpopularity: Jerome, Epist. 130.19; ed. Hilberg, III, CSEL 56/1, 200; trans. Fremantle, 271.

91. Jerome, Epist. 27.2; ed. Hilberg, I, CSEL 54, 225; trans. Fremantle, 44.

92. Jerome, Epist. 22.28; ed. Hilberg, I, CSEL 54, 185; trans. Fremantle, 34. I have altered Fremantle's translation of "clericos."

93. Jerome wrote to Asella that he had never seen Paula at the dinner table. Jerome, Epist. 45.3; ed. Hilberg, I, CSEL 54, 325; trans. Fremantle, 59.

94. For the circumstances of Jerome's departure from Rome, see Cain, *Letters of Jerome*, 99–128. Cain proposes a situation in which Jerome was convicted in an ecclesiastical court of unethical conduct stemming from his relationship to Paula. He notes that Jerome was evasive

when discussing the trial and its outcome, both in his letter to Asella (Epist. 45) and in the preface to his translation of Didymus's *On the Holy Spirit*, where he described having been examined by a "senate of Pharisees." If Jerome had sworn not to take Paula with him, then her separate departure for the East allowed him to maintain the letter, if not the spirit, of his oath (allowing him to avoid perjury, as Rufinus reportedly commented). Cain, *Letters of Jerome*, 121–122. For an interpretation of Jerome's removal from Rome emphasizing financial matters rather than sexual scandal, see Brown, *Through the Eye of a Needle*, 262–263.

95. Jerome, Epist. 45.6; ed. Hilberg, I, CSEL 54, 328; trans. Fremantle, 60.

96. Jerome, Epist. 45.2; ed. Hilberg, I, CSEL 54, 324; trans. Fremantle, 59. In his letter to Furia, Jerome seems to expect that he might be called a seducer: Jerome, Epist. 54.2; ed. Hilberg, I, CSEL 54, 467; trans. Fremantle, 103.

97. Harvey notes similarities between Jerome's relationship with Paula and Malchus's chaste relationship with his wife. Harvey, 287–288.

98. Jerome, Epist. 45.3; ed. Hilberg, I, CSEL 54, 325; trans. Fremantle, 59. Abelard cited this passage: Abelard, Epist. 7.49; *The Letter Collection*, 348–349.

99. Jerome, Epist. 45.3; ed. Hilberg, I, CSEL 54, 325; trans. Fremantle, 59. Years later, Jerome wrote to Eustochium praising Paula's saintly behavior and bemoaning his own inability adequately to record her virtues: "If all the members of my body were transformed into tongues, and if each and every one of my limbs were to resound in a human voice, I could say nothing worthy of the virtues of the holy and venerable Paula." Jerome, Epist. 108.1 (*Epitaphium Sanctae Paulae*); ed. and trans. Cain, 42–43.

100. Jerome reported that Paula left Rome to follow him, leaving behind her young son Toxotius weeping at the pier. Jerome, Epist. 108.6 (*Epitaphium Sanctae Paulae*); ed. and trans. Cain, 48–49. For discussion of the monastic foundation at Bethlehem, which Jerome established for women and men, with Paula's money, see Cain, "Jerome's *Epitaphium Paulae*," 111–112.

101. On Jerome's decision to bury Paula beneath the Church of the Nativity in Bethlehem, see Cain, "Jerome's *Epitaphium Paulae*," 128–129; and Engelbrecht, "S. Paulas Grab."

102. Kelly, 332.

103. For discussion of the mosaic, see Tosti-Croce, "La Basilica tra due e trecento."

104. "Quidam ex Clericorum Monachorum ordinibus pro petulantia proque ingluvie discursantes, ad effugandum Urbe Hieronymum, qui utrorumque eorum vitia scribens deprehenderat, insidias paraverunt." *Hieronymus noster*; PL 22: 178.

105. "Unde cum Romanos de avaritia reprehenderet, derisus est ab eis per vestem muliebrem." Johannes Beleth, *Summa de ecclesiasticis officiis*, 157i; ed. Douteil, CCCM 41A, 301.

106. The Belles Heures of Jean de France, Duc de Berry. The Cloisters Collection, 1954 (54.1.1), fol. 184v.

107. Jacobus de Voragine, *Legenda Aurea*; trans. Ryan, 598.

108. Jerome, Epist. 45.6; ed. Hilberg, I, CSEL 54, 327; trans. Fremantle, 60.

109. Jerome, Epist. 54.2; ed. Hilberg, I, CSEL 54, 467; trans. Fremantle, 103. Cain comments that Jerome "masterfully recast his shameful condemnation after the fact as the exile of a divinely ordained prophet." Cain, *Letters of Jerome*, 10.

110. Constant Mews notes Jerome's significance for reform communities during the period, commenting on the increased textual transmission of his writings at this time, above all among reformers. Mews, "Un lecteur de Jérôme." Gisela Muschiol, too, notes Jerome's importance within the religious life, tracing the monastic reception of his ascetic writings. Muschiol, "*Hoc dixit Ieronimus*."

111. Guigues de Châtel, *Ad Durbonenses fratres*; ed. Laporte, 214–219.

112. BHL 3873. "Unde quidam pseudoclerici ac monachi, quorum scribens vitam deprehenderat, occasione delatrandi accepta, eum infamia subnotare miserrimi homines conabantur. Et quia ipsi vitiis subjacebant carnalibus, ad excusandas excusationes in peccatis, id ipsum Hieronymo imponebant. Denique isti vestem muliebrem prope lectum, qua se indueret surrecturus ad matutinas, imposuerunt." Nicolò Maniacutia, *Sancti Eusebii Hieronymi vita*; PL 22: 186. See Cavallera, II, 143–144; Wilmart, "Nicolas Manjacoria"; Chiesa, "Maniacutia, Nicolò"; and Linde. For manuscripts of Maniacutia's *vita*, see Lambert, IIIB, no. 904.

113. Beach, *Women as Scribes*, 40–42 (# 36, 40, and 43). The manuscripts that Diemut copied formed the basis for the library at Wessobrunn. Beach, *Women as Scribes*, 63–64.

114. On Zwiefalten, see Chapter 1, n. 83. Of the 285 manuscripts that have been identified with the community, some one hundred date from the twelfth century. See the discussion in Mews, "Monastic Educational Culture Revisited." For the activity of female scribes at Zwiefalten (of whom only one, Mathilde von Neuffen, is known by name), see Beach, "'Mathild de Niphin' and the Female Scribes of Twelfth-Century Zwiefalten."

115. Stuttgart, Württembergische Landesbibliothek, Cod. Theol. 4°, 232. Mews, "Monastic Educational Culture Revisited," 188.

116. Wolfenbüttel, Herzog August Bibliothek, Cod. Guelf. 1030 Helmst., fols. 129r-147v. For a description of the manuscript and its contents, see *Geschrieben und gemalt*, ed. Härtel, 93–94.

117. Paris, Bibliothèque nationale de France, Lat. 12298, fol. 177v.

118. Paris, Bibliothèque nationale de France, Lat. 13350, fol. Bv.

119. Doctor amore tui celebris Hieronime librum
Fecit frater Ivo fieri servus tuus istum.
Sub pedibus doctoris iners ego presbiter Ivo
Decubo, qui meritis clarus coniungitur astris.

120. Odilo of Cluny, *Epitaphium Adalheide Imperatricis*; PL 142: 970; trans. Gilsdorf, 129. The *Warenne Chronicle* (c. 1157) equally invoked Jerome's praise of holy women in reference to Matilda of Scotland's epitaph. *The Warenne (Hyde) Chronicle*, 31; ed. and trans. van Houts and Love, 64–65.

121. For Azecho of Worms, see *Die Ältere Wormser Briefsammlung*, 45; ed. Bulst, MGH Briefe d. dt. Kaiserzeit 3, 82.

122. Abelard, Epist. 7.49; *The Letter Collection*, 346–347. The idea that Jerome ignored Augustine's letter was widespread.

123. "His autem qui sinistrorsum suscepturi sunt, quod hoc opus vobis dedicavi, respondeo: beatum Hieronymum presbyterum sanctam Paulam et eius filiam Eustochiam multis scriptis honorasse saepe." Hugh of Fleury, *Ex historia ecclesiastica*, praefatio; ed. Waitz, MGH SS 9, 350. For discussion, see Ferrante, *To the Glory*, 96–98.

124. "Despondi enim vos uni viro virginem castam exhibere Christo, sicut vir illustris Paulam et Eustochium desponderat eidem." Gerhoch of Reichersberg. *Epistola Gerhohi ad quasdam sanctimoniales*; in Lutter, 232.

125. "Scio me, Principia, in Christo filia, a plerisque reprehendi, quod interdum scribam ad mulieres, et fragiliorem sexum maribus praeferam." Jerome, Epist. 65.1; ed. Hilberg, I, CSEL 54, 616. Abelard cited this defense in his Epist. 9; ed. Smits, 225; trans. Ziolkowski, 18.

126. "Si doceri a femina non fuit turpe apostolo, mihi quare turpe sit post viros docere et feminas?" Jerome, Epist. 65.1; ed. Hilberg, I, CSEL 54, 618. On Jerome's letter to Principia,

and his application of bridal imagery to celibate (not necessarily virginal) women, see Hunter, "The Virgin, the Bride, and the Church."

127. See above, n. 64.

128. Jerome, *Commentariorum in Sophoniam prophetam*, prologus; ed. Adriaen, CCSL 76A, 655; trans. Ferrante, *To the Glory*, 48.

129. Jerome, Epist. 127.5; ed. Hilberg, III, CSEL 56/1, 149; trans. Fremantle, 255.

130. Abelard, *Institutio*, 123; *The Letter Collection*, 508–9. For Abelard's identification with Jerome, see Mews, "Un lecteur de Jérôme"; Blamires, "No Outlet for Incontinence"; and Muschiol, "*Hoc dixit Ieronimus*," 116–120. Mary Martin McLaughlin identified Abelard as "in certain respects a 'second Jerome.'" However, as she comments, "the Jerome whom Abelard admired and emulated was not the merciless castigator of feminine uselessness and corruption, but the more benevolent Jerome whose personal life and loyalties centered upon the noble ladies of the Aventine." McLaughlin, "Peter Abelard and the Dignity of Women," 309–310.

131. Leclercq, "'Ad ipsam sophiam Christum,'" 177. Ziolkowski comments that "this denigration of the letter misses the point, since its imposition of Jerome and Marcella upon Abelard and Heloise was deliberate and sophisticated." *Letters of Peter Abelard*, ed. Ziolkowski, 7.

132. Abelard, Epist. 7.48; *The Letter Collection*, 344–5. Elsewhere Abelard noted that it was "mainly at their request that this doctor with so many volumes lit up the Church." Abelard, *Institutio*, 128; *The Letter Collection*, 516–517.

133. Abelard, Epist. 1.70; *The Letter Collection*, 112–113.

134. Abelard, Epist. 1.65; *The Letter Collection*, 102–103.

135. Abelard, Epist. 1.74; *The Letter Collection*, 118–119. Elsewhere Abelard commented that, "When . . . I recalled the injustice of such a calumny against so great a man, I took no small comfort from it." Abelard, Epist. 1.65; *The Letter Collection*, 102–103. Abelard likened his move to St. Gildas to Jerome's exile from Rome: "the jealousy of the French drove me West as that of the Romans drove Jerome East." Epist. 1.60; *The Letter Collection*, 94–95.

136. Abelard, Epist. 1.65; *The Letter Collection*, 102–103. Cf. Abelard, Epist. 7.49; *The Letter Collection*, 348–349. For a similar evocation of Jerome's complaint to Asella, see the *life* of Christina of Markyate: *De S. Theodora*, 76; ed. Talbot, 174; rev. trans. Fanous and Leyser, 79.

137. Abelard, Epist. 1.74; *The Letter Collection*, 118–119.

138. Abelard, Epist. 1.68; *The Letter Collection*, 108–109. Wim Verbaal draws attention to stylistic parallels between Abelard's *Historia calamitatum* and Jerome's *life* of Malchus, arguing that Abelard framed his own history through Jerome's Malchus. Verbaal, 195–196, 200–203.

139. *Vita s. Edithae*, 14; ed. Wilmart, 73; trans. Wright and Loncar, 45.

140. Goscelin of St. Bertin, *Liber confortatorius*, III; ed. Talbot, 81; trans. Otter, 97.

141. *De S. Theodora*, 76; ed. Talbot, 175; rev. trans. Fanous and Leyser, 79.

142. *De S. Theodora*, 76; ed. Talbot, 175; rev. trans. Fanous and Leyser, 79.

143. Elliott "Alternative Intimacies," 173. As Elliott remarks elsewhere, Jerome's relationship with Paula was invoked most often as a model for "transhistorical commiseration over unwarranted slander." Elliott, *Bride*, 156.

144. Elliott, *Bride*, 14–29.

145. "Dominam quippe debeo vocare sponsam domini mei." Jerome, Epist. 22.2; ed. Hilberg, I, CSEL 54, 145; trans. Fremantle, 23.

146. "Mi Eustochia, filia, domina, conserva, germana—aliud enim aetatis, aliud meriti, illud religionis, hoc caritatis est nomen." Jerome, Epist. 22.26; ed. Hilberg, I, CSEL 54, 181; trans. Fremantle, 33.

147. Barbara Newman notes that within the religious context, the "ennobling love" of the twelfth century, so elegantly discussed by C. Stephen Jaeger, "becomes the dynamic of a new kind of triangle, binding a man and a woman in God in precarious *caritas*." Newman, "Liminalities," 362. Goscelin of St. Bertin was explicit in referencing Christ's role in his relationship with Eve of Wilton, describing his letter to her as "sealed with Christ as mediator." Goscelin of St. Bertin, *Liber confortatorius*, prologus; ed. Talbot, 26; trans. Otter, 19.

148. "Domina, inquam, mea, immo et regina, Domino meo caelesti scilicet regi . . . desponsata." Peter Damian, Epist. 66.16; ed. Reindel, MGH Briefe d. dt. Kaiserzeit 4.2, 266; trans. Blum, 3, 57. Peter Damian's adoption of Jerome's language of spiritual "lordship" for women devoted to Christ neatly side-stepped the question of virginity—the context of Jerome's initial use of the bridal motif. Eustochium was Jerome's *domina* because she was a bride of Christ, and a virgin.

149. "Sponsa domini mei domina mea est." Hildebert of Lavardin, Epist. I, 6; PL 171: 149. Jacques Dalarun notes, too, that Hildebert's letter to the recluse Athalise was inspired by Jerome's letter to Eustochium. Dalarun, "Hagiographe et métaphore," 44.

150. Goscelin of St. Bertin, *Liber confortatorius*, I; ed. Talbot, 33; trans. Otter, 31. Robert of Arbrissel addressed Agnes, prioress of Orsan, as "my lady, my daughter, and my disciple" (*dominae meae, filiae atque discipulae*). Andrew, *Supplementum*, 36; *Deux vies*, 258–259.

151. Abelard, Epist. 5.3; *The Letter Collection*, 180–181.

152. Abelard, Epist. 7.23; *The Letter Collection*, 306–307.

153. Abelard, *Sermo* 30; ed. Granata. Sermon 30 was composed after Heloise's move from Argenteuil in 1129, but before Abelard wrote the *Historia calamitatum*, in about 1132. For discussion of the sermon in the context of both monastic prayer and the spiritual involvement of women with men, see Schmid, "Bemerkungen zur Personen- und Memorialforschung," 105–110.

154. "Iste, cum terrenis coniugiis vel carnalium voluptatum illecebris spretis sponso immortali se copulant, summi regis sponse effecte, omnium eius servorum efficiuntur domine." Abelard, *Sermo* 30.4; ed. Granata, 58. "Ut illic per eas percipiatis eterna que hic a vobis suscipiunt temporalia, prestante ipso earum sponso Domino Iesu Christo." Abelard, *Sermo* 30.4; ed. Granata, 59.

155. Abelard, Epist. 5.34; *The Letter Collection*, 212–213.

156. On this point, and for further discussion, see Griffiths, "Brides and *dominae*."

157. For a description of the manuscript, see de Santis, *I Sermoni*, 12–20. Colmar, Bibliothèque municipale, MS 128 offers an important textual witness to Abelard's sermon corpus: it contains four of the nine Abelardian sermons that have survived in manuscript form (a total of thirty-six sermons have been attributed to him and are known from early published editions). In addition to sermon 30, the manuscript contains sermons 2, 4, and a sermon not included in the 1616 *Editio princeps*, the "Adtendite a falsis prophetis," which was identified by L. J. Engels as the work of Abelard. Engels, "*Adtendite a falsis prophetis*." On Abelard's sermon collection and the manuscript witnesses, see de Santis, *I Sermoni*, 1–29.

158. Inscriptions in the arches over their heads identify the two as Guta: "Per te, strips [sic] Jesse, quod dicor deprecor esse" and Sintram: "Sintrammi, Virgo, memor, huius pauperis esto." *Le Codex Guta-Sintram*, ed. Weis, I, p. 9. See Marti, "Double Monasteries in Images," 79–82. Discussion of the codex's miniatures is provided in Walter, "Les miniatures du Codex Guta-Sintram."

159. Guta writes, "Presentium utilitati ac animarum saluti provide consulere volens, ego peccatrix et utinam ultima mecum depascentis gregis ovicula, GUTA, ut in libro vitę scribi, ac in pascuis virentibus depasci mererer, hunc librum famulante calamo manui summaque devotione suppeditante animi scribendo explicui." She further tells us that "Miniatum vero sive illuminatum a quodam humili canonico Marbacensi et indigno presbitero nomine SINTRAMMO et ad finem usque perductum." *Le Codex Guta-Sintram*, ed. Weis, I, p. 9–10.

160. See Chapter 1, n. 129.

161. For the text of *Beati pauperes*, see the Appendix. For the identification of *Beati pauperes* as an excerpt from Abelard's sermon, see Griffiths, "Brides and *dominae*." *Beati pauperes* seems to have been added at some point after the completion of the manuscript in 1154, but nonetheless still during Sintram's lifetime. The text was written in fairly large letters and was evidently to be further distinguished by two capital letters, a "B" for "beati" and an "I" for the "inter hos" of its second sentence. These capitals are unfinished, adding weight to the hypothesis that the text was a later addition to the manuscript and did not form part of the original plan for the codex. *Le Codex Guta-Sintram*, ed. Weis, I, p. 8; and *Le Codex Guta-Sintram*, ed. Weis, II, 54–55. See also Weis, "La prière dans un monastère de femmes."

162. Baudri of Bourgueil, *Carmen* 200, l. 137; ed. Tilliette, II, 129; trans. Bond in *Loving Subject*, 176–177. On Baudri's correspondence with Constance, see Kong, *Lettering the Self*, 15–54.

163. Baudri of Bourgueil, *Carmen* 201, ll. 116–120; ed. Tilliette, 133; trans. Bond in *Loving Subject*, 188–189. For discussion, see Tilliette, "Hermès amoureux." On Baudri and his context, with attention to his correspondence with women, see Tilliette, "La vie culturelle dans l'Ouest de la France au temps de Baudri de Bourgueil."

164. While Dronke attributes the poem to Constance, Tilliette claims Baudri as its author, and Newman agrees. Dronke, *Women Writers*, 84–85; Tilliette, "Hermès amoureux," 140; Newman, *Making Love*, 7–8. Katherine Kong argues that "there is no compelling reason to question Constance's authorship." For her analysis, the presentation of the "female voice" is more significant than the "actual authorship" of the piece (a position that Newman acknowledges, too). Kong, *Lettering the Self*, 28.

165. As Joan Ferrante noted, "Jerome's letters, like his commentaries, so many of them addressed to women, were known and read, and they provided an unimpeachable model for male-female friendship among religious." Ferrante, *To the Glory*, 26. Dyan Elliott identifies Jerome's relationship with Paula as "the orthodox prototype for a type of spiritualized heterosexual intimacy." Elliott, "Alternative Intimacies," 175–176. Jacques Dalarun writes that Jerome's letter to Eustochium was the "modèle obligé de tout clerc s'adressant à une femme." Dalarun, "Hagiographe et métaphore," 44. Jocelyn Wogan-Browne, too, observes that Jerome was "a well-known and often consciously deployed prototype for the relations between clerics and their female patrons and audiences." Wogan-Browne " 'Our Steward, St. Jerome' " 139.

166. Heloise, Epist. 6.3; *The Letter Collection*, 218–221.

167. Abelard, *Institutio*, 128; *The Letter Collection*, 516–517.

168. On Heloise's affinity for Marcella, see Dronke, *Women Writers*, 135; Ferrante, *To the Glory*, 59–60; and Blamires, "No Outlet for Incontinence."

169. Jerome, Epist. 127.7; ed. Hilberg, III, CSEL 56/1, 151; trans. Fremantle, 255.

170. Jerome, Epist. 27.2; ed. Hilberg, I, CSEL 54, 224–225; trans. Fremantle, 44.

171. Abelard, Epist. 9; ed. Smits, 227; trans. Ziolkowski, 20. For Abelard's consideration of letter writing in his relationship with Heloise, see Abelard, Epist. 1.16; *The Letter Collection*,

26–27. In his letter to Principia, Jerome remembered the solace he took in his correspondence with Marcella: "Not much was lost by a separation thus effectually bridged by a constant correspondence." Jerome, Epist. 127.8; ed. Hilberg, III, CSEL 56/1, 152; trans. Fremantle, 256.

172. Abelard, Epist. 9; ed. Smits, 227; trans. Ziolkowski, 20. Abelard quotes here from Jerome's Epist. 127.7 (ed. Hilberg, III, CSEL 56/1, 151; trans. Fremantle, 255): "When she answered questions she gave her opinion not as her own but as from me or some one else."

173. Heloise and Abelard, *Problemata*; PL 178: 677; trans. McLaughlin with Wheeler, 213. On Heloise's learning, as reflected in the *Problemata*, see Mews and Perry, "Peter Abelard, Heloise and Jewish Biblical Exegesis." See also Dronke, "Heloise's *Problemata* and *Letters*."

174. Heloise and Abelard, *Problemata*; PL 178: 677; trans. McLaughlin with Wheeler, 213.

175. Heloise and Abelard, *Problemata*; PL 178: 678; trans. McLaughlin with Wheeler, 213.

CHAPTER 4

Notes to epigraph: Leander of Seville, *De institutione virginum*; PL 72: 878; trans. Barlow, 189; and Ekbert of Schönau, *De obitu*; ed. Roth, 263; trans. Clark, 255.

1. According to Elizabeth Clark, the rise of Christianity was accompanied by a "blow to 'family values,'" as church fathers extolled the ascetic renunciation of both marriage and family. Clark, "Antifamilial Tendencies in Ancient Christianity," 358. For the argument that late antique Christian discourse was not entirely anti-family, see Jacobs, "'Let Him Guard *Pietas*'"; and Krawiec, "'From the Womb of the Church.'" On the centrality of the family to early monasticism, see also Elm, "Formen des Zusammenlebens männlicher und weiblicher Asketen."

2. *Germana* was sometimes used metaphorically among Christians to refer to spiritual kinship, but it more usually referred to blood ties. *Oxford Latin Dictionary*, ed. Glare, sv *germana*.

3. On the importance of sibling relations in the religious life, see Schulenburg, *Forgetful of Their Sex*, 271–305; and Griffiths, "Siblings and the Sexes." For pious brothers and sisters in later periods, see Ray, "Brothers and Sisters in Christ, Brothers and Sisters Indeed"; and Laningham, "Making a Saint out of a Sibling." On ties between brothers and sisters generally, see Larrington, *Brothers and Sisters*; and Lyon, *Princely Brothers and Sisters*.

4. The role of secular brothers (often bishops) in founding monastic houses for their religious sisters has been noted by Hasdenteufel-Röding: Hasdenteufel-Röding, *Studien zur Gründung von Frauenklöstern*, 62–76. As she shows, it was not unusual for sisters to serve as abbesses of houses founded by their brothers.

5. See Chapter 1, n. 90.

6. For Mechthild, see Silvas, *Jutta and Hildegard*, 60, n. 19. Ludolf reported that "electus in abbatem et vocatus a Flandria veni ad locum presentem mecum adducens sororem meam uterinam sed Deo desponsatam, quam in ecclesia nostra sub habitu regulari de consilio fratrum nobiscum habitare permisimus." Ludolf went on to describe how a women's community gathered at Oostbroek, and was eventually settled at the "Nova Curia." Van Heussen, *Historia episcopatuum foederati Belgii*, I, 130.

7. Reginald of Durham, *Libellus de vita et miraculis S. Godrici*, 61–63; ed. Stevenson, 140–145. Aelred of Rievaulx, *De institutione inclusarum*; ed. Hoste and Talbot; trans. Macpherson. Paul of Bernried reported, too, how the hermit Konrad of Beuerberg (founder of the cell

at Beuerberg) had a sister, Gepa, with him in the religious life. Paul of Bernried, *Vita b. Herlucae*, 37; *AA SS*, April, 2: 555.

8. On Elisabeth's life and revelations, see Clark, *Elisabeth of Schönau*. Elisabeth's visions are edited in *Die Visionen der hl. Elisabeth*, ed. Roth; trans. Clark, *Elisabeth of Schönau: The Complete Works*. On the specific revelations discussed here, the *Revelatio de sacro exercitu virginum Coloniensium*, see Clark, *Elisabeth of Schönau*, 37–40. This work, transmitted in seventy medieval manuscripts, was Elisabeth's most popular text.

9. An inscription (c. 400) on the south wall of the church of St. Ursula in Cologne offered the earliest evidence for the cult, referring simply to virgins who had "poured out their blood for Christ." Montgomery, *St. Ursula and the Eleven Thousand Virgins*, 9–12; and Cusack, "Hagiography and History."

10. Elisabeth of Schönau, *Liber revelationum*, 3; ed. Roth, 124; trans. Clark, 215.

11. Elisabeth of Schönau, *Liber revelationum*, 15; ed. Roth, 131; trans. Clark, 223. On witness testimony in the *Revelations* in the context of twelfth-century legal practice, see Campbell, "Sanctity and Identity: The Authentication of the Ursuline Relics and Legal Discourse in Elisabeth von Schönau's *Liber Revelationum*."

12. Elisabeth of Schönau, *Liber revelationum*, 9, 10, 14; ed. Roth, 128, 128, 130; trans. Clark, 218, 219, 221–222.

13. On the concept of fictive, or spiritual, kinship within early Christianity, see the essays in Moxnes, ed., *Constructing Early Christian Families*.

14. As several of the gospels report, Jesus had refused to acknowledge the kinship claims of his mother as she waited on one occasion to speak with him. "Who is my mother?" he asked, declaring that "whosoever shall do the will of my Father, that is in heaven, he is my brother, and sister, and mother" (Matt. 12:46–50; cf. Mark 3:31–35; Luke 8:19–21).

15. Clement of Alexandria, *Paedagogus*, 3.11.81; ed. Mondésert and Matray, 156–157; cited in Penn, *Kissing Christians*, 1. That the fraternity of unrelated "brothers" and "sisters" could be perceived as "promiscuous" is discussed by Brown, *Body and Society*, 140–159. At Fontevraud in the twelfth century, the kiss of peace was given indirectly. According to the community's statutes, "They should never give each other the kiss of peace, but instead all kiss the marble passed to them through the window under the supervision of the sacristan." *The Revised Statutes*, 25; *Deux vies*, 412–413.

16. *The Shepherd of Hermas*, vis. 2.2.3; trans. Lake in *The Apostolic Fathers*, II, 19. Jerome expressed a similar idea, writing that a chaste wife was her husband's "sister," an idea that also appears in the writings of Paulinus of Nola and in Gregory of Tours's account of Riticius, who was buried alongside his virginal spouse. Jerome, Epist. 71.3; ed. Hilberg, II, CSEL 55, 4; trans. Fremantle, 153. Paulinus of Nola, *Carmen* 25; trans. Walsh, 245–253. Gregory of Tours, *Liber in gloria confessorum*, 74; ed. Krusch, MGH SS rer. Merov. 1.2, 341–342.

17. Gregory the Great, *Dialogues*, IV, 12, 2; ed. de Vogüé, III, 48–49; trans. Zimmerman, 203.

18. Jerome, *Vita Malchi*, 6.7; ed. and trans. Gray, 86–87.

19. Council of Ancyra (314), canon 19; ed. Mansi, 2: 519. On the conflation between metaphorical kinship (which was not necessarily chaste) and biological kinship, see Boswell, *Same-sex Unions*, 131–135.

20. Jerome, *Vita Malchi*, 10.3; ed. and trans. Gray, 90–91. On the ambiguity in Jerome's account concerning the length of Malchus's cohabitation with his wife, see Chapter 3, n. 5.

21. Synod of Elvira (305), canon 27; ed. Mansi, 2: 10. For discussion of these rulings and their context, see Elm, "*Virgins of God*," 25–59.

22. First Council of Nicaea (325), canon 3; *Decrees of the Ecumenical Councils*, ed. and trans. Tanner, I, 7. The catalogue of "acceptable" kinswomen published at Nicaea was repeated by many other church councils—East and West—in subsequent years. For a list of councils forbidding clerics to live with women unrelated to them, see de Labriolle, "Le 'mariage spirituel,'" 222.

23. "Non timui mortem caelum quod liber adiret / sed dolui, fateor, consortia perdere vitae." *Epitaphius sororis*: *Epigrammata Damasiana*, ed. Ferrua, 109.

24. *Liber pontificalis*, 39; ed. Mommsen, MGH Gesta pontificum Romanorum I, 84; trans. Davis, 29.

25. Ambrose of Milan, *De virginibus*; ed. Gori; trans. Ramsey.

26. Ambrose of Milan, *De excessu fratris sui Satyri*, I, 76; PL 16: 1313–1314; trans. Bonnot, 53.

27. Paulinus of Milan, *Vita Ambrosii*, 1, 4; PL 14: 27, 28; trans. Ramsey, 196, 197.

28. Augustine of Hippo, Epist. 211; trans. Lawless, 104–118. Lawless presents the letter in two parts: the Reprimand for Quarrelling Nuns (*Obiurgatio*) and the *Rule*. Augustine refers to his sister in *Obiurgatio*, 4; trans. Lawless, 107. Medieval evidence for Augustine's authorship of a monastic rule is discussed in Leyser, "Augustine in the Latin West," 460–464. Despite Augustine's involvement in the religious life of his sister's community, he did not mention his sister in his *Confessions*, as Clark notes. Clark, "Theory and Practice in Late Ancient Asceticism," 28.

29. For references to Jerome's own sister, see Jerome, Epist. 6.2 and 7.4; ed. Hilberg, I, CSEL 54, 25, 29; trans. Fremantle, 8, 9. Jerome credits the deacon Julian with his sister's conversion; in a letter to Julian, he describes his sister as your "daughter in Christ" (*sororem meam, filiam in Christo tuam*). Jerome, Epist. 6.2; ed. Hilberg, I, CSEL 54, 25. On Jerome's relations with his younger brother Paulinian, see Kim, "Jerome and Paulinian, Brothers."

30. Cain argues that the letter was fictional, but nevertheless occupied a "vital place" in Jerome's oeuvre. Cain, "Jerome's *Epistula CXVII* on the *Subintroductae*."

31. Jerome, Epist. 117.1; ed. Hilberg, II, CSEL 55, 422–423; trans. Fremantle, 215.

32. Jerome, Epist. 117.2; ed. Hilberg, II, CSEL 55, 424; trans. Fremantle, 216.

33. Jerome, Epist. 117.5; ed. Hilberg, II, CSEL 55, 428; trans. Fremantle, 217.

34. Jerome's orientation toward biological family is reinforced by his characterization of the daughter's clerical friend, whom he denigrated in terms of failed kinship as "a man who perhaps has left behind him a sister and mother of his own." Jerome, Epist. 117.4; ed. Hilberg, II, CSEL 55, 426; trans. Fremantle, 217. For Jerome's stance on family, see also Epist. 125 to Rusticus; and Epist. 54 to Furia. In his letter 125 to Rusticus, Jerome reinforced his criticisms of priests who sought women's companionship, writing that, "you must not imitate those who leave their own relations and pay court to strange women." Jerome was critical, too, of women who become "spiritual mothers" to younger men: "I know some women of riper years, indeed a good many, who, finding pleasure in their young freedmen, make them their spiritual children and thus, pretending to be mothers to them, gradually overcome their own sense of shame and allow themselves in the licence of marriage." Jerome, Epist. 125.6; ed. Hilberg, III, CSEL 56/1, 123; trans. Fremantle, 246. To Furia, Jerome wrote, "'Honour thy father,' the commandment says, but only if he does not separate you from your true Father. Recognize the tie of blood but only so long as your parent recognizes his Creator." Jerome, Epist. 54.3; ed. Hilberg, I, CSEL 54, 468; trans. Fremantle, 103.

35. Jerome, Epist. 117.11; ed. Hilberg, II, CSEL 55, 433; trans. Fremantle, 219.

36. Elm, "*Virgins of God*"; and Elm, "Formen des Zusammenlebens männlicher und weiblicher Asketen." As Elm comments, "A sizeable proportion of the male ascetics were clerics and lived together with their own sisters of other female relatives." Elm, "*Virgins of God*," 161–162. On late antique household monasticism, see also Brown, *The Body and Society*, 263–265; and, with a particular focus on women, the essays by Kate Cooper in Mulder-Bakker and Wogan-Browne, eds., *Household, Women, and Christianities.*

37. Silvas refers to early monasticism as a "domestic ascetic movement." Silvas, *Macrina the Younger*, 3. According to Rousseau, the community was primarily an "extended family." Rousseau, "The Pious Household and the Virgin Chorus."

38. Gregory of Nyssa, *The Life of Macrina*, 12; ed. and trans. Maraval, 182–183; trans. Petersen, 61.

39. Peter later became head of the male portion of the double community. Gregory of Nyssa, *The Life of Macrina*, 37; ed. and trans. Maraval, 258–259; trans. Petersen, 80.

40. Silvas, *Asketikon*, 20–22.

41. Silvas, *Asketikon*, 23–25. Silvas writes that the example of Macrina's religious life "cannot but have been a material factor in Basil's own turn, or preferably *re*-turn, to Scripture and in the resultant 'Christianization' of his ascetic discourse" (92). Susanna Elm writes that "it is reasonable to suggest that Basil and Macrina developed their ideas in continuous exchanges, although we do not possess a single source by her alone." Indeed, she notes that Basil "seems to have considered Macrina's community as model." Elm, "*Virgins of God*," 102, 104, n. 90. Nevertheless, Basil's rule for monks warns against entanglement with family members who remain in the world and sets forth strict guidelines concerning contact between consecrated men and women. Basil of Caesarea, *The Longer Responses*, 32–33; trans. Silvas, 233–236.

42. Silvas, *Asketikon*, 147–148. For a sketch of Basil's career and thought, see Sterk, *Renouncing the World*, 13–92. See also Stramara, "Double Monasticism in the Greek East."

43. Gregory of Nyssa, *The Life of Macrina*, 6; ed. and trans. Maraval, 162–163; trans. Petersen, 56. Basil does not discuss Macrina's possible influence on him. For one hypothesis concerning the family dynamics, see Meredith, "Gregory of Nazianzus and Gregory of Nyssa on Basil."

44. Athanasius of Alexandria, *The Life of Antony*, 3; ed. and trans. Bartelink, 134–5; trans. Vivian and Athanassakis, 61.

45. *Pachomian Koinonia*, trans. Veilleux, I, 49–51 (*The Bohairic Life of Pachomius*, 27). On Pachomian foundations for women, see Elm, "*Virgins of God*," 289–296. For a discussion of women's involvement in the early monastic life, see Hasdenteufel-Röding, 30–41; McNamara, *Sisters in Arms*, 61–88.

46. Despite his support for his sister's religious life, Pachomius's rule established that no monk should visit the women's community "unless he has there a mother, sister, or daughter, some relatives or cousins, or the mother of his own children" (*Pachomian Rule*, 143). *Pachomian Koinonia*, trans. Veilleux, II, 166. The *Bohairic Life* further notes that only brothers "who had not yet attained perfection" could visit a relative in the women's community (*The Bohairic Life of Pachomius*, 27). *Pachomian Koinonia*, trans. Veilleux, I, 50.

47. Palladius, *Lausiac History*, 33.1; trans. Meyer, 95. The *Bohairic Life* offers a different account, in which the deceased sister was "carried to the mountain" for burial (*The Bohairic Life of Pachomius*, 27). *Pachomian Koinonia*, trans. Veilleux, I, 51.

48. Gennadius of Marseilles noted that Cassian founded two monasteries "id est virorum et mulierum." Gennadius of Marseilles, *De viris inlustribus*, 62; ed. Richardson, 82.

Cassian's relationship with his sister is somewhat obscure; Columba Stewart writes that "of family members he mentions only a sister who remained somehow a part of his monastic life." Stewart, *Cassian the Monk*, 4–5. Although Cassian recognized the tradition that monks were to shun women and bishops, he admits that he had been unable to avoid (*vitare*) his sister. Cassian, *De institutis coenobiorum*, 11.18; ed. and trans. Guy, 444–445.

49. Caesarius initially sent his sister to a monastery in Marseille (presumably Cassian's foundation for women) in order that she might be "a pupil before becoming a teacher." *Vita Caesarii*, I, 35; ed. Morin, 196–197; trans. Klingshirn, 27. On Caesarius, see Klingshirn, *Caesarius of Arles*.

50. Caesarius of Arles, *Vereor* (Epist. 21); ed. de Vogüé and Courreau; trans. Klingshirn. Caesarius of Arles, *Regula sanctarum virginum*; ed. de Vogüé and Courreau; trans. McCarthy.

51. The separation of the two communities was in keeping with canon 28 of the early sixth-century Council of Agde. Council of Agde (506), canon 28; ed. Mansi, 8: 329. Caesarius warned his sister and her companions against the dangers of contact with the opposite sex. Caesarius of Arles, *Vereor* (Epist. 21), 3; ed. de Vogüé and Courreau, 302–311; trans. Klingshirn, 131–133.

52. Caesaria's death and burial are discussed in: *Vita Caesarii*, I, 58; ed. Morin, 228; trans. Klingshirn, 39. Caesarius's death and burial in the basilica of St. Mary are described in: *Vita Caesarii* II, 50; ed. Morin, 308; trans. Klingshirn, 65.

53. Leander of Seville, *De institutione virginum*; PL 72: 873–894; trans. Barlow, 183–228. Isidore of Seville, *De fide catholica contra Judaeos*; PL 83: 449–538.

54. "Soror mea Florentina accipe codicem quem tibi composui feliciter amen." Paris, Bibliothèque Nationale, Cod. lat. 13396, fol. iv.

55. Williams, "León: The Iconography of a Capital," 242.

56. Mary and Martha, with their brother Lazarus, offer one example of New Testament siblings; however, it was the relationship between the sisters that preoccupied medieval exegetes, rather than the sisters' relationship with Lazarus. Constable, *Three Studies*, 1–141.

57. Brother-sister relationships are so prominent within the texts of early monasticism that one scholar remarked: "It was almost as important for these mythological heroes of medieval hagiography to have a sister as it is for the President of the United States to have a wife." Cusack, "St. Scholastica: Myth or Real Person?" 148.

58. Chapter 1, n. 13.

59. Albrecht Diem assumes that these female figures were fabricated. "One of the most persistent (but also misleading) *topoi* in monastic origin myths is that of the 'little sister,' or sometimes niece or cousin," he comments, observing that "if a great monastic founder did not have a 'little sister,' tradition needed to invent one." Diem, "The Gender of the Religious," 435.

60. For various interpretations of Scholastica's significance in the *life*, see Wansbrough, "St. Gregory's Intention"; de Vogüé, "The Meeting of Benedict and Scholastica"; and Cusack, "St. Scholastica: Myth or Real Person?" For a survey of scholarship on Scholastica's identity, see Boo and Braun, "Emerging from the Shadows."

61. Biblioteca Apostolica Vaticana, Vat. lat. 1202.

62. Gregory the Great, *Dialogues*, II, 33, 4, II, 34, 2; ed. de Vogüé, II, 232–233, 234–235; trans. Zimmermann, 103, 104.

63. This is Cusack's conclusion. Cusack, "St. Scholastica: Myth or Real Person?" 159.

64. Gregory's account implied a biological bond, but eschewed the most explicit language of kinship, describing Scholastica as Benedict's *soror*, rather than his *germana* or *soror uterina*.

65. Gregory the Great, Epist. I. 50; ed. Norberg, I, 64; trans. Martyn, I, 175.

66. Schulenburg, *Forgetful of Their Sex*, 283.

67. Gregory the Great (c. 540–604); Leander of Seville (c. 542–600). According to John Martyn, the "longest and by far the most autobiographical" of Gregory's letters was written to Leander. Martyn, *Gregory and Leander*, vii.

68. Walter Goffart cautions that the monks at Fleury and Le Mans were less concerned with Scholastica than with Benedict, whose importance was "overshadowing." Goffart, "Le Mans, St. Scholastica, and the Literary Tradition," 129.

69. Adrevald reports that Scholastica's bones were separated from Benedict's through the prayers of the people. Adrevald of Fleury, *Historia translationis s. Benedicti*, 12–13; ed. de Certain, 10–13.

70. Carruthers, *Craft of Thought*, 184.

71. The paradox between Benedict's silence concerning women in his *Rule* and his famously close relationship with Scholastica was tacitly acknowledged in the late twelfth-century *Exordium magnum* of Conrad of Eberbach. Conrad observed that the Cistercians followed Benedict's example in everything, refusing contact with women and allowing no burials in their monasteries (although he commented that Benedict had allowed his sister to be buried at Monte Cassino). Conrad of Eberbach, *Exordium magnum cisterciense*, I, 20; ed. Griesser, CCCM 138, 42; trans. Ward, 93.

72. Aldhelm, *Carmen de virginitate*; ed. Ehwald, MGH Auct. ant. 15, 436–437; trans. Lapidge and Rosier, 147–148. Bede, *In die festo sanctae Scholasticae virginis*; PL 94: 480–489. Bertharius of Monte Cassino, *Vita s. Scholasticae Virginis*; PL 126: 979–988. Alberic of Monte Cassino, "The Homily of Alberic the Deacon on Saint Scholastica," trans. Coffey. See also Forman, "Three Songs About St. Scholastica by Aldhelm and Paul the Deacon." Although both Bertharius and Alberic celebrated Scholastica, they hesitated to accept that her prayers had been more powerful than Benedict's. See Chapter 5 for discussion.

73. Aldhelm mentions a nun named Scholastica among the women at Barking in his preface to the *De virginitate*. Aldhelm, *Prosa de virginitate, prologus*; eds. Gwara and Ehwald, CCSL 124A, 27; trans. Lapidge and Herren, 59.

74. "The Life of St. Scholastica in the *South English Legendary*," ed. Whatley.

75. "Quasi alter alteri Scholasticae eructabat Benedictus." *Vita S. Hiltrudis virginis*; *AA SS*, September, 7: 494.

76. As Abelard observed, "the convent of St. Scholastica, which was situated on land belonging to the brethren of a monastery, was also under the supervision of one of the brothers, and was given both direction and comfort through frequent visits by him or the other brothers." Abelard, *Institutio*, 41; 406–407.

77. First Lateran Council (1123), canon 7; *Decrees of the Ecumenical Councils*, ed. and trans. Tanner, I, 191.

78. For a discussion of Ekbert's role and his influence in Elisabeth's life and visions, see Coakley, *Women, Men, and Spiritual Power*, 25–44; Clark, "Repression or Collaboration?"; Clark, *Elisabeth of Schönau*, 130–133; and Clark, "Holy Woman or Unworthy Vessel?" Ekbert was at Elisabeth's side when she died, and recorded the details of her death in a quasi-hagiographic text, *De obitu domine Elisabeth*, which he composed for female relatives at the Augustinian community of Andernach. See below n. 118.

79. Coakley, *Women, Men, and Spiritual Power*, 36–38.

80. Bishop Ekbert of Münster, a supporter of the church reform movement, is best known as the bishop at whose court "Herman the Jew" first encountered Christianity and debated the faith with Rupert of Deutz. Clark, *Elisabeth of Schönau*, 11–12.

81. Schulenburg underscores the prevalence of early medieval brother-sister saints and notes, too, the many monastic houses that were established as "cooperative ventures" between siblings. Schulenburg, *Forgetful of Their Sex*, 276. Schulenburg assumes that such opposite-sex sibling relationships fell out of favor as a result of church reforms; however, as I show, evidence for the continued importance of family ties in the religious life during the twelfth century is strong.

82. Barbara Newman writes that Elisabeth's revelations present a "vision of religious life as a glorious, equal-opportunity venture in which women and men could provide mutual aid and comfort." Newman, "Preface," xvii. Franz Felten notes the importance of Elisabeth's visions for the light they shed on life within the double monastery at Schönau: Felten, "Frauen-klöster," 269–270. For a study of Elisabeth's visions against the backdrop of the double monastery, see Kemper, "Das benediktinische Doppelkloster Schönau."

83. According to one explanation, Ursula's father had arranged that bishops from Britain accompany the women on their initial journey in order to provide "comfort" for them. Elisabeth of Schönau, *Liber revelationum*, 6; ed. Roth, 126; trans. Clark, 217. Hildegard also assumed that the presence of "religious and learned" men among the women was due to the need for men's protection and service. Hildegard of Bingen, *In matutinis laudibus*, 3–4; ed. and trans. Newman, *Symphonia*, 236–239.

84. Elisabeth of Schönau, *Liber revelationum*, 3; ed. Roth, 124; trans. Clark, 214.

85. *Pachomian Koinonia*, trans. Veilleux, I, 50. (*The Bohairic Life of Pachomius*, 27).

86. Coakley notes that Ekbert was neither Elisabeth's confessor nor her spiritual adviser; nevertheless, he celebrated Mass for the women on occasion. Coakley, *Women, Men, and Spiritual Power*, 35, 30.

87. For Hildegard's nephew, see Hildegard of Bingen, Epist. 10-10r; ed. Van Acker, CCCM 91, 23–25; trans. Baird and Ehrman, I, 45–47.

88. Guibert of Gembloux reports the presence of Hildegard's brother, Hugo, at Ruperts-berg. Guibert of Gembloux, Epist. 26, ll. 307–308; ed. Derolez, CCCM 66A, 279. Silvas provides a genealogical table listing Hildegard's siblings: Silvas, *Jutta and Hildegard*, 279.

89. In his treatise *De anima et resurrectione*, Gregory referred to Macrina explicitly as "the teacher." Gregory of Nyssa, *De anima et resurrectione*; trans. Moore and Wilson, 430. Elizabeth Clark cautions that accounts of early Christian women were "literary constructions, some of a high rhetorical order." In her view, Macrina was a "tool" that Gregory used to "think through various troubling intellectual and theological problems." Clark, "The Lady Vanishes," 15, 27.

90. Leander of Seville, *De institutione virginum*; PL 72: 878; trans. Barlow, 189–190. The author of the *Liber de modo bene vivendi, ad sororem* (long thought to be the work of Bernard of Clairvaux) makes the same argument, drawing directly on Leander's text, although he removes all reference to biological brotherhood. *Liber de modo bene vivendi, ad sororem*, 73; PL 184: 1306. On the *Liber* and its Middle English translation, see McGovern-Mouron, "'Listen to Me, Daughter, Listen to a Faithful Counsel.'"

91. Coakley writes that Ekbert approached Elisabeth as a "kind of a research assistant," using her to find answers to the questions that interested him. Coakley, *Women, Men, and Spiritual Power*, 28.

92. Ekbert of Schönau, *De obitu*, 2; ed. Roth, 271; trans. Clark, 265. Coakley cautions that Ekbert was hesitant to admit his spiritual attraction to Elisabeth, noting that he did not want to present himself as other than her supervisor. Coakley, *Women, Men, and Spiritual Power*, 35. Still, he did sometimes appear, as Coakley notes, as the "recipient of her graces" (44).

93. Elisabeth of Schönau, *Libri visionum*, 1.59; ed. Roth, 29; trans. Clark, 81. Here Elisabeth records that she prayed to the Virgin "especially" for a certain friend, likely Ekbert, who was a deacon, but whom she had encouraged to seek priestly ordination. See also Emecho of Schönau's record of the event: *Vita Eckeberti*, ed. Widmann, 449–450. I am not persuaded by Coakley's judgment that Ekbert viewed Elisabeth as "naturally subordinate to himself." Coakley, *Women, Men, and Spiritual Power*, 44.

94. Elisabeth of Schönau, *Libri visionum*, 2.25–26; ed. Roth, 51–52; trans. Clark, 113–114.

95. Ekbert of Schönau, *De obitu*; ed. Roth, 263; trans. Clark, 255.

96. Aelred of Rievaulx, *De institutione inclusarum*, 32; ed. Hoste and Talbot, 674; trans. Macpherson, 94.

97. Aelred of Rievaulx, *De institutione inclusarum*, 32; ed. Hoste and Talbot, 673–674; trans. Macpherson, 93–94.

98. Aelred of Rievaulx, *De institutione inclusarum*, 32; ed. Hoste and Talbot, 675; trans. Macpherson, 95.

99. Peter Damian, Epist. 94.27; ed. Reindel, MGH Briefe d. dt. Kaiserzeit 4.3, 41; trans. Blum, 4, 45. Concerning Peter's affection for his sister, Rodelinda, "who had been a second mother" to him, see Peter Damian, Epist. 149.14; ed. Reindel, MGH Briefe d. dt. Kaiserzeit 4.3, 552; trans. Blum, 4, 178. Peter Damian also instructed one of his sisters in theological matters, writing a letter (Epist. 93) about the Last Judgment, at her request. Ferrante describes this letter as a "theological tract," in which he encouraged his sister's "intellectual investigation." Ferrante, *To the Glory*, 27, and 228 n. 43.

100. *De S. Theodora*, 70; ed. Talbot, 156; rev. trans. Fanous and Leyser, 70.

101. Gregory's obit appears on the calendar for February and Simon's for November. *Der Albani-Psalter*, pp. 4, 13.

102. *Vita Burchardi episcopi*, 12; ed. Waitz, MGH SS 4, 837. Burchard directed his sister's education in the religious life, "consecrated" her to the service of God, and later supported her in her role as abbess.

103. The two women appear first in the community's entry list. Wischermann, 39. Two other sisters, Mathilda and Adelheid, subsequently entered the community as well, as did two of Hugh's nieces, Ermengardis and Lucia. Wollasch, "Frauen in der Cluniacensis ecclesia," 99. Other monks at Cluny arranged for their own sisters to enter Marcigny, as did a certain Bernard, who coordinated the transfer of his sister, Anna, from St. Jean, Autun, to Marcigny. *Le cartulaire de Marcigny-sur-Loire*, II, no. 175; ed. Richard, 103–104. Some men, like Peter the Venerable, even had mothers who were "sisters" at Marcigny.

104. Mews, *Lost Love Letters*, 162.

105. Promising his nephew that he would care for Richeza, Anselm wrote, "As far as I am able, I shall not cease to help her in every way as long as I live." Anselm of Canterbury, Epist. 328; ed. Schmitt, *Opera*, II, 260; trans. Fröhlich, III, 45. For Anselm's relations with Richeza, see Vaughn, *St. Anselm and the Handmaidens of God*, 118–124.

106. According to Bernard's biographer, Humbeline came one day to see her brother, magnificently attired and accompanied by a large retinue. Bernard "reviled and cursed her" and refused to see her. Humbeline, struck to the core, called on Bernard to speak with her, lamenting that "if my own brother spurns my body and its appearance, as a servant of God he should not refuse to help my soul." Promising to obey his advice, Humbeline was ultimately received by Bernard, who (in the tradition of Pachomius and Maria) encouraged her to reject worldly enticements. Some years later, she entered the monastery at Jully and was made prioress, succeeding her sister-in-law, Elisabeth. William of St. Thierry, *Vita prima Bernardi*, 6; PL 185: 244;

trans. Webb and Walker, 51. The spiritual importance of the sibling bond is emphasized once more in Bernard's *Life of St. Malachy*, where he records that Malachy encouraged his sister to adopt a more religious life, although in vain. When she died, without having been reconciled to the faith, Malachy's prayers on her behalf secured God's forgiveness for her. Bernard of Clairvaux, *Vita sancti Malachiae*, 5; eds. Leclercq, Talbot, and Rochais, *Sancti Bernardi Opera*, 3, 320.

107. Felten, "Frauenklöster," 257–260. See Chapter 1, n. 80.

108. Elkins, 55–56.

109. Peter of Blois, Epist. 306; PL 207: 114–116. "Charissimae sorori suae Christianae."

110. Bönnen, Haverkamp, and Hirschmann, 377, n. 32. For charters recording the entrance of women at Molesme, see *Women and Monasticism*, trans. Berman, 90–91.

111. See Chapter 1, n. 88. Other mothers who joined communities associated with their sons include Peter the Venerable's mother, who became a nun at Marcigny, and Ediva, founder of Godstow, who moved to Oxford likely to be close to her son, the abbot of Abingdon (possibly Walkelin, formerly a monk at Evesham, as Emilie Amt suggests). Amt, "The Foundation Legend of Godstow Abbey." By contrast, Paulina, founder of Paulinzella, withdrew from her foundation after her son, Werner, converted and joined her. She noted that it was permissible for her to live with Werner (as his mother), but that not all the monks were her biological sons. Citing I Cor. 13:2, Paulina noted that even if their holiness could move mountains, women and men mixing together would attract criticisms. Sigeboto, *Vita Paulinae*, 26; ed. Dieterich, MGH SS 30.2, 922; trans. Badstübner-Kizik, 116. Cf. *Speculum virginum*, 5.1243–1248; ed. Seyfarth, 156.

112. *Chronicon Beccensis*; PL 150: 648; cited in Vaughn, *St. Anselm and the Handmaidens of God*, 91.

113. Herman of Tournai, *Liber de restauratione*, 62–63; ed. Waitz, MGH SS 14, 302–305; trans. Nelson, 89–94.

114. Herman of Tournai, *Liber de restauratione*, 65; ed. Waitz, MGH SS 14, 305; trans. Nelson, 95. The conversion of an entire household is also recounted in the life of Stephen of Obazine: *Vita S. Stephani Obazinensis*, I, 29; ed. Aubrun, 86–89; trans. Feiss, O'Brien, and Pepin, 158–159. For other examples of conversions involving entire families, see documents from Coyroux/Obazine in *Women and Monasticism*, trans. Berman, 79–80. Berman describes such communities as "double-houses or family monasteries," underscoring the extent to which family ties dictated the mixed-sex character of much monastic life in the twelfth century. Berman, *Cistercian Evolution*, 123.

115. Herman of Tournai, *Liber de restauratione*, 69; ed. Waitz, MGH SS 14, 307; trans. Nelson, 99.

116. Even in the early Middle Ages, the entrance of entire family groups was not uncommon. Fructuosus of Braga's seventh-century "General Rule for Monasteries" notes some of the problems that the entrance of families could pose, cautioning that families "may not hold converse together, except with the permission of the prior." Demonstrating that the entrance even of small children was not unusual, Fructuosus nevertheless allowed that exceptions should be made for the "tiniest children . . . who are still in the cradle," who were allowed to go "to their father or mother when they wish." Fructuosus of Braga, *Regula monastica communis*, 6; PL 87: 1115; trans. Barlow, 186.

117. Even so, the incidence of "saintly siblings" declined at this time, as Schulenburg observes: Schulenburg, *Forgetful of Their Sex*, 305.

118. Ekbert reports having summoned Elisabeth's sister to her deathbed, describing her as "a God-fearing woman whom I had called from afar for Elisabeth's funeral." Ekbert of Schönau, *De obitu*, 2; ed. Roth, 273; trans. Clark, 268. For the arrival of Elisabeth's brother,

see *De obitu*, 2; ed. Roth, 276; trans. Clark, 272. Schulenburg notes that saintly siblings were often present at a brother's or sister's death, and often took a leading role in preparing for the burial: Schulenburg, *Forgetful of Their Sex*, 297–303.

119. *De S. Theodora*, 70; ed. Talbot, 160; rev. trans. Fanous and Leyser, 71. Christina nevertheless cited Jesus's exhortation to reject family (Matt. 19:29) in defending her decision to refuse her parents' plan for her marriage. *De S. Theodora*, 16; ed. Talbot, 62; rev. trans. Fanous and Leyser, 18.

120. Elkins, 99.

121. Oliva, "All in the Family?," 164.

122. "Non minus animo quam carne illorum probaretur virorum Dei esse germana." William of St. Thierry, *Vita prima Bernardi*, 6; PL 185: 245; trans. Webb and Walker, 52. Although Humbeline played a relatively small role in Bernard's *life*, she was memorialized alongside him as the founder of the Cistercian tradition for women. For discussion of Humbeline's depiction in art, see France, "The Iconography of Bernard of Clairvaux and his Sister Humbeline"; and France, "Nuns and the Iconography of Bernard," 160–165. France notes that Humbeline is depicted alongside Bernard in a fifteenth-century manuscript of the *Miroir Historial* of Vincent of Beauvais, giving the erroneous impression that she had entered the religious life with him. France, "The Iconography of Bernard of Clairvaux and his Sister Humbeline," 10–12.

123. "Carnis et spiritus germana." *Fundatio monasterii sanctae Mariae Andernacensis*; eds. Holder-Egger, MGH SS 15.2, 969.

124. Peter the Venerable, Epist. 185; ed. Constable, I, 427–434; trans. Morton in *Guidance for Women*, 98–108. Osbert of Clare, Epist. 21–22; ed. Williamson, 89–96; trans. Morton in *Guidance for Women*, 111–120. Osbert was involved in the foundation for women at Kilburn, in his role as prior of Westminster.

125. Peter the Venerable, Epist. 185; ed. Constable, I, 433; trans. Morton in *Guidance for Women*, 106.

126. Heloise, Epist. 2.7; 128–131.

127. Abelard, *Institutio*, 43; 410–411. In fact, as Abelard likely knew, the practice of pairing male and female monasteries had its origins in the very real concern that male monastic founders like Pachomius and Caesarius had in ensuring the spiritual welfare of their kinswomen.

128. Gilo, *Vita sancti Hugonis abbatis*, I, 12; ed. Cowdrey, 63.

129. On Eckenbert, see Schulz, "Das Leben des hl. Eckenbert."

130. Eckenbert's wife had been his former concubine. *Vita S. Eckenberti*, 5, 7; ed. Boos, 132, 133–134; trans. Bachrach, 65, 67. On the separation of married partners and their conversion to the monastic life, see Birkmeyer, *Ehetrennung und monastische Konversion*.

131. *Vita S. Eckenberti*, 10; ed. Boos, 135; trans. Bachrach, 70.

132. *Vita S. Eckenberti*, 11; ed. Boos, 136; trans. Bachrach, 71.

133. On this point, see Wollasch, "Parenté noble."

134. Krings, *Das Prämonstratenserstift Arnstein*, 48–65, 98–101.

135. Wollasch, "Parenté noble," 10. See *Le cartulaire de Marcigny-sur-Loire*; ed. Richard, 240–241 (tableau généalogique); and Wischermann, 355.

136. Elisabeth of Schönau, *Liber revelationum*, 10; ed. Roth, 128; trans. Clark, 219.

137. Felix, *Vita Sancti Guthlaci*, 50; ed. and trans. Colgrave, 154–155.

138. British Library, Harley Roll Y.6, Roundel 16.

139. Discussed in McGuire, "Late Medieval Care and Control of Women," 33, n. 98.

140. Jerome, Epist. 22.12; ed. Hilberg, I, CSEL 54, 159–160; trans. Fremantle, 26–27.

141. Fructuosus of Braga, *Regula monastica communis*, 17; PL 87: 1124; trans. Barlow, 201.

142. "For where a man lives together with a woman, it is difficult for the snares of the ancient enemy to be lacking, snares which, without doubt, were not lacking in that place where a brother and a sister, namely Ammon and Thamar, lived alone together for the briefest of times." Pope Nicholas I, Epist. 99.50; ed. Perels, MGH Epp. 6, 586.

143. Gerald of Wales, *Gemma ecclesiastica*, II, 15; ed. Brewer, 236; trans. Hagen, 180.

144. Referring to instances of priests who had apparently impregnated their sisters, the ninth-century Council of Mainz ruled that women who were blood relations should not be allowed to live with clerics. Council of Mainz (888), 10; ed. Mansi, 18: 67.

145. Vienna, Österreichische Nationalbibliothek, Codex Vindobonensis 2554, fols. 46r–46v. See *Bible moralisée*, ed. Guest. On the basis of internal evidence, Tracy Chapman Hamilton argues that the manuscript was produced for Blanche of Castile: Hamilton, "Queenship and Kinship." On the depiction of Amnon and Thamar in the manuscript, see Guest, "'The Darkness and the Obscurity of Sins,'" 91–95.

146. Trans. in *Bible moralisée*, ed. Guest, 124–125.

147. Peter Damian, Epist. 61.11; ed. Reindel, MGH Briefe d. dt. Kaiserzeit 4.2, 215; trans. Blum, 3, 10. Discussed in McLaughlin, "The Bishop as Bridegroom," 223.

148. On Augustine's deep love and respect for Monica, see Cooper, "Augustine and Monnica." Concerning Augustine's caution regarding his own sister and nieces, Possidius writes:

> No woman ever lived in his house, or stayed there, not even his own sister, who as a widow in the service of God lived for many years, to the very day of her death, as prioress of God's handmaidens. It was the same with his brother's daughters, who were also enrolled in God's service, although the councils of the holy bishops had allowed an exception to be made of them. He used to say that even though no suspicion of evil could arise from his sister or his nieces stopping with him, *they* would have to have other women attending on them and staying with them, and other women would be coming to see them from outside, and all this might give scandal or prove a temptation to the weak.

Possidius, *Vita Augustini*, 26; PL 32: 55; trans. Hoare, 58. A similar reasoning was at work in Theodulf of Orléans's decision to abolish the privilege of clerics to live with female family members: "Let no woman live with a presbyter in a single house. Although the canons permit a priest's mother and sister to live with him, and persons of this kind in whom there is no suspicion, we abolish this privilege for the reason that there may come, out of courtesy to them or to trade with them, other women not at all related to him and offer an enticement for sin to him." McCracken and Cabaniss, ed. and trans., *Early Medieval Theology*, 385.

149. Walther of Arrouaise, *Historia translationis reliquiarum Aroasiam*, 4; *AA SS*, May, 1: 488. "Nolite mirari si eam diligam, & ei honorem deferam, quia ipsa est mater mea." On Arrouaise, see Milis, *L'Ordre des chanoines réguliers d'Arrouaise*.

CHAPTER 5

Note to epigraph: St. Albans Psalter. Dombibliothek Hildesheim, HS St. God. 1 (Property of the Basilica of St. Godehard, Hildesheim), p. 285.

1. Leander of Seville, *De institutione virginum*; PL 72: 878; trans. Barlow, 189.

2. Leander was still a monk when he wrote for Florentina.

3. On this topic see Coakley, *Women, Men, and Spiritual Power.*

4. On Christina, see the essays in Fanous and Leyser, eds., *Christina of Markyate.*

5. *De S. Theodora;* ed. Talbot; rev. trans. Fanous and Leyser. On the case for Robert de Gorron's authorship of the *vita,* see Bugyis, "The Author of the *Life* of Christina of Markyate." For the dating of the *vita* to the 1130s, see L'Hermite-Leclercq, *Vie de Christina de Markyate,* II, 39, 43, 66; and (arguing for a slightly later dating of the text) Koopmans, "The Conclusion of Christina of Markyate's *Vita*"; and Koopmans, "Dining at Markyate." Kathryn Kerby-Fulton suggests that Christina's *life* drew on material "composed not by a man, but by a *woman,* an intimate of Christina's house at Markyate." Kerby-Fulton, "Skepticism, Agnosticism, and Belief," 14. Katie Bugyis suggests that this woman was Christina's own sister, Margaret. Bugyis, "Envisioning Episcopal Exemption," 59.

6. St. Albans Psalter. Dombibliothek Hildesheim, HS St. God. 1 (Property of the Basilica of St. Godehard, Hildesheim). The Psalter is available in facsimile: *Der Albani-Psalter.* See also the marvelous website with full-page images of each folio, produced under the supervision of Jane Geddes and hosted by Aberdeen University: https://www.abdn.ac.uk/stalbanspsalter /english/index.shtml. For a general overview and introduction to the Psalter, see Geddes, *The St. Albans Psalter.* See also the essays in Bepler and Heitzmann, eds., *Der Albani-Psalter. Stand und Perspektiven der Forschung.*

7. Ursula Nilgen proposed renaming the Psalter in order to highlight its connection to Christina: Nilgen, "Psalter der Christina." Morgan Powell discusses the composite nature of the manuscript and the chronology of its production: Powell, "Making the Psalter." In a related article, he places the manuscript in the context of Christina's visionary persona and experience, and her relations with Abbot Geoffrey: Powell, "The Visual, the Visionary, and her Viewer." My argument here is indebted to Powell's analysis of the Psalter in these two articles.

8. *De S. Theodora,* 57; ed. Talbot, 138; rev. trans. Fanous and Leyser, 59.

9. *De S. Theodora,* 60; ed. Talbot, 144; rev. trans. Fanous and Leyser, 62. See also *De S. Theodora,* 59, 74, 78. Koopmans writes notes that "although the author of the *vita* never reports an instance in which he himself benefited from Christina's prayers, he was clearly fascinated by this aspect of her powers, urging her, it appears, to be specific about how they actually worked, and reporting with precision in his text about the kinds of physical and visual signs that Christina received when God decided to answer her prayers." Koopmans, "Dining at Markyate," 146.

10. *De S. Theodora,* 59, 63, 65; ed. Talbot, 140, 146, 150. Koopmans argues that the monks resented Geoffrey's financial support for Markyate, and stopped work on Christina's *vita* as soon as Geoffrey died, leaving it unfinished. Koopmans, "The Conclusion of Christina of Markyate's Vita," 666. For an alternate explanation for the abrupt ending of the *vita,* see Bugyis, "Envisioning Episcopal Exemption."

11. St. Albans Psalter. Dombibliothek Hildesheim, HS St. God. 1 (Property of the Basilica of St. Godehard, Hildesheim), p. 285.

12. Geddes and Powell identify the monk as Geoffrey, based on "textual echoes in the *Vita,*" as Powell writes. Geddes, *The St. Albans Psalter,* 108; Powell, "The Visual, the Visionary, and her Viewer," 353–354.

13. St. Albans Psalter. Dombibliothek Hildesheim, HS St. God. 1 (Property of the Basilica of St. Godehard, Hildesheim), p. 403.

14. Building on the earlier suggestions of Talbot and Swarzenski, Powell identifies Geoffrey as "the monk who directs their [the women's] devotions." Powell, "Making the Psalter," 321.

15. For the argument that the Psalter was constructed for Christina's use, see Nilgen, "Psalter der Christina"; Powell, "Making the Psalter"; Powell, "The Visual, the Visionary, and her Viewer"; and Geddes, *The St. Albans Psalter*. Donald Matthew presents a dissenting view, as does Rodney Thomson: Matthew, "The Incongruities of the St. Albans Psalter;" and Thomson, "The St. Albans Psalter: Abbot Geoffrey's Book?"

16. Powell made a compelling case for Geoffrey's role as the patron and donor of the Psalter, describing him as the "impresario who continuously directed and contributed to its design and production." Powell, "Making the Psalter," 302.

17. Powell particularly notes the parallel between the manuscript's Emmaus cycle and the report in the *vita* of Christina's reception of a pilgrim at Markyate. Powell, "The Visual, the Visionary, and her Viewer," 346–347; and Powell, "Making the Psalter," 314–315. On women's spiritual experiences and the influence of visual imagery, see Hamburger, *The Visual and the Visionary*.

18. For a discussion of modifications to the initial, see Powell, "The Visual, the Visionary, and her Viewer," 350–351; and Powell, "Making the Psalter," 319–321. On the initial, and its appearance in the Psalter, see Nilgen, "Psalter der Christina"; Powell, "The Visual, the Visionary, and her Viewer," 352–354; Geddes, *The St. Albans Psalter*, 94–97, 123; and Geddes, "The St. Albans Psalter," 198–199.

19. Powell concludes that the parchment patch was pasted over an existing initial. Powell, "The Visual, the Visionary, and her Viewer," 352.

20. *De S. Theodora,* 79; ed. Talbot, 182; rev. trans. Fanous and Leyser, 83.

21. The "right hand" of the bridegroom held particular meaning for religious women, to whom it implied the embrace of the beloved. Song of Songs 2:6.

22. The initial could simultaneously depict "Clementia" as Mercy personified. I thank Wim Verbaal for this suggestion.

23. *De S. Theodora,* 69; ed. Talbot, 156; rev. trans. Fanous and Leyser, 69. The connection between the initial and the scene from Christina's *vita* was suggested by Ursula Nilgen; Nilgen, "Psalter der Christina," 163.

24. Powell, "Making the Psalter," 319–321; Powell, "The Visual, the Visionary, and her Viewer," 349–352; Geddes, *The St. Albans Psalter*, 100–101. Haney disagrees: Haney, *The St. Albans Psalter*.

25. *De S. Theodora,* 68; ed. Talbot, 154; rev. trans. Fanous and Leyser, 68. Christina's biographer comments that "she communicated at the table of Christ as often as the abbot celebrated the mysteries of the divine word."

26. Koopmans, "The Conclusion of Christina of Markyate's *Vita*," 680. Bugyis suggests that a further motive for the *vita* lay in St. Albans's bid for episcopal exemption, which she suggests was to be furthered through the remarkable visionary depiction in the *vita* of Christina crowned with a crown from the back of which "hung two white fillets [*albe due uitte*], like a bishop's miter [*instar episcopalis mitre*], descending all the way to her waist." Cited in Bugyis, "Envisioning Episcopal Exemption," 45.

27. Matthew argued that the subject of the initial—a nun interceding for monks—made it impossible for the manuscript to have been owned by women. As he wrote: "a psalter kept at Markyate would surely not present the prioress as interceding for monks." Matthew, 406. Con-

sidered in light of men's interest in women's prayer—indeed, as I argue in this chapter, their *fascination* with women's prayer—the opposite is more likely true: the image would make very little sense unless it was placed in the hands of women—as a potent reminder to them of their spiritual duties to the monks who provided for their spiritual (and often material) care.

28. This suggestion is widely accepted. Powell comments that "several scholars" have seen in this initial "an unmistakable reference to the intended use of the book itself." Powell, "Making the Psalter," 319. See also Powell, "The Visual, the Visionary, and her Viewer," 350, 351. Haney and Matthew reiterate Dodwell's conclusion that the women represent the church, and not a specific female community: Haney, *The St. Albans Psalter*, 335–336; and Matthew, 408. Thomson argues against Markyate ownership of the Psalter, noting among other things that the "Litany suffrages are masculine." Thomson, "The St. Albans Psalter: Abbot Geoffrey's Book?" 61.

29. Despite the emphasis in the Psalter and the *vita* on Christina's prayerful service to the monks of Saint Albans, as Katie Bugyis points out, Markyate was established as a priory independent of Saint Albans when the women's community was dedicated on May 27, 1145. Bugyis, "Envisioning Episcopal Exemption," 60.

30. This argument holds, even if—as Rodney Thomson argues—the Psalter was made and intended as Geoffrey's book, and not Christina's. As Thomson comments, "those features of the Psalter that refer, or have been thought to refer, to the relationship between Geoffrey and Christina, could be seen as representing his side of the relationship rather than Christina's." Thomson, "The St. Albans Psalter: Abbot Geoffrey's Book?" 59. The emphasis on female intercession remains significant, regardless of the intended recipient of the book.

31. Abelard, Epist. 2.16; *The Letter Collection*, 140–141. Abelard, Epist. 3.2; *The Letter Collection*, 142–145.

32. Abelard, Epist. 3.10–11; *The Letter Collection*, 152–155.

33. Abelard, Epist. 3.12; *The Letter Collection*, 154–155.

34. Schmid, "Bemerkungen zur Personen- und Memorialforschung." Matthew Innes also acknowledged Abelard's "theology of female prayer"; however, he characterized Abelard's defense of female prayer as a unique and personal justification of his "deeply felt and long-established belief about the role of women." Innes, "Keeping it in the Family," 26.

35. Abelard, Epist. 3.3; *The Letter Collection*, 144–145.

36. Abelard, Epist. 3.7; *The Letter Collection*, 148–149. Cf. Epist. 7.37; *The Letter Collection*, 328–329.

37. Abelard, Epist. 3.5; *The Letter Collection*, 146–147.

38. Abelard, Epist. 3.7; *The Letter Collection*, 148–149.

39. Abelard, Epist. 3.9; *The Letter Collection*, 150–151. For Clothilda, see Gregory of Tours, *Decem libri Historiarum*, II, 29–31; ed. Krusch and Levison, MGH SS rer. Merov. 1.1, 74–78; trans. Thorpe, 141–145. Clothilda's role in Clovis's conversion was acknowledged in a tenth-century ivory binding, which shows her watching from the background as Bishop Remigius of Reims baptized the king. Schulenburg, *Forgetful of Their Sex*, plate 14.

40. Bede, *Historia ecclesiastica*, I, 25 and II, 9; ed. and trans. Colgrave and Mynors, 72–77, and 162–167. For Pope Boniface's letter to Æthelburh, see Bede, *Historia ecclesiastica*, II, 11; ed. and trans. Colgrave and Mynors, 172–175. On early medieval queens and conversion, see Hollis, *Anglo-Saxon Women*, 208–242; and Nolte, "Gender and Conversion."

41. For Thecla, see *The Acts of Paul and Thecla*, 4.4; ed. Barrier, 149. For Perpetua, see *Passio Sanctarum Perpetuae et Felicitatis*, 7–8; ed. and trans. Heffernan, 109–110, 128–129. For discussion of both women as intercessors, see Trumbower, *Rescue for the Dead*, 56–90. For

Monica as intercessor, see Augustine, *Confessions*, 9, 8; ed. O'Donnell, I, 110–111; trans. Pine-Coffin, 192. Clark cautions that Monica is "a literary representation," and cannot be read as a transparent portrait. Clark, "Rewriting Early Christian History," 10.

42. Abelard, Epist. 3.5; *The Letter Collection*, 146–147.

43. Jerome, Epist. 23.2; ed. Hilberg, I, CSEL 54, 212; trans. Fremantle, 42. Jerome, Epist. 24.5; ed. Hilberg, I, CSEL 54, 216–217; trans. Fremantle, 43. Jerome, Epist. 39.1; ed. Hilberg, I, CSEL 54, 294; trans. Fremantle, 49. Jerome, Epist. 45.3; ed. Hilberg, I, CSEL 54, 325; trans. Fremantle, 59. Of course, Jerome did discuss the prayerfulness of certain men; however, it was the prayers of women that he primarily valued and sought. Jerome advised the married Paulinus to "pray constantly." (Jerome, Epist. 58.6; ed. Hilberg, I, CSEL 54, 535; trans. Fremantle, 121). To Rusticus he wrote: "learn the psalms word for word, pray without ceasing." (Jerome, Epist. 125.11; ed. Hilberg, III, CSEL 56/1, 129–130; trans. Fremantle, 248).

44. Although the *orans* could sometimes be male, and might be interpreted as a symbol (of the soul, or of the church, for instance) rather than a woman, it is nevertheless significant, as Torjesen argues, that the most recognizable visual depiction of early Christian prayer is a female figure. Torjesen, "The Early Christian *Orans*," 45.

45. Jerome, Epist. 107.9; ed. Hilberg, II, CSEL 55, 300; trans. Fremantle, 193. He gave similar advice to the virgin Demetrias, encouraging her to pray and recite the psalms at frequent intervals, day and night (Epist. 130.15; ed. Hilberg, III, CSEL 56/1, 195; trans. Fremantle, 269).

46. Jerome, *Adversus Jovinianum*, I, 34; PL 23: 257; trans. Fremantle, 371. In his letter to Pammachius, Jerome invoked I Cor. 7:5 to claim that devotion to prayer is possible for married couples only if they refrain from intercourse. Jerome, Epist. 48.15; ed. Hilberg, I, CSEL 54, 376; trans. Fremantle, 75. For discussion of Jerome's approach to the prayer of married laymen and women, see Yates, "Weaker Vessels and Hindered Prayers." For interpretations of I Cor. 7:5 in ascetic discourse (with particular attention to Jerome), see Hunter, "Asceticism, Priesthood, and Exegesis."

47. Characterizing the bridal motif as the "ultimate disciplinary tool," Elliott argued that it served to "transform the feisty virgin into a stay-at-home wife." Elliott, *Bride*, 42, 39. Eva Schlotheuber notes that new ideas regarding female religious life during the twelfth century highlighted the role of nun as bride of Christ, but also required strict enclosure and separation from secular affairs. Schlotheuber, "Die gelehrten Bräute Christi," 57–61. On enclosure, particularly in monasteries of the Hirsau reform circle, see Roitner, "*Sorores inclusae.*"

48. Elliott argues that the seeming elevation of the religious woman as a bride of Christ simultaneously raised the specter of her potential faithlessness: the bride was held to be permanently at risk of falling into the arms of the wrong lover. By the later Middle Ages, the bride of Christ was on a downward trajectory, which would lead her directly into Hell, as the title of Elliott's book makes plain (*The Bride of Christ Goes to Hell*). On the later medieval fate of the bride of Christ, see especially Elliott, *Bride*, 233–279. Jerome warned darkly of the evils of virgins who "have prostituted the members of Christ, and have changed the temple of the Holy Ghost into a brothel." Jerome, Epist. 22.6; ed. Hilberg, I, CSEL 54, 150; trans. Fremantle, 24.

49. Jerome, Epist. 24.4; ed. Hilberg, I, CSEL 54, 216; trans. Fremantle, 43.

50. Jerome, Epist. 22.25; ed. Hilberg, I, CSEL 54, 178; trans. Fremantle, 32.

51. Jerome, Epist. 22.25; ed. Hilberg, I, CSEL 54, 178; trans. Fremantle, 32.

52. Elliott, *Bride*, 28. Although widows are characterized here as brides of God (not Christ), non-virgins, too, began to be identified as brides of Christ, marking what Elliott describes as "one of the great sea changes in medieval spirituality." Elliott, *Bride*, 3. Elizabeth Clark

explores the early Christian context of the bridal metaphor, tracing its application to an ever-widening group that included not just virgins, but the faithful married, widows, and even men. As she writes, Christ was imagined by the Church Fathers as an "equal opportunity bridegroom." Clark, "The Celibate Bridegroom," 16.

53. Jerome, Epist. 79.7; ed. Hilberg, II, CSEL 55, 96; trans. Fremantle, 167.

54. Jerome, Epist. 46.13; ed. Hilberg, I, CSEL 54, 344; trans. Fremantle, 65. On the authorship of this letter, see Adkin, "The Letter of Paula and Eustochium to Marcella."

55. "Quare autem ecclesia vidua intellegitur, nisi quia vir eius Christus quasi absens esse videtur?" Caesarius of Arles, Sermo 49.1; ed. Morin, 222.

56. Abelard, Epist. 5.4; The Letter Collection, 180–181. Abelard described himself as Heloise's servant, both in the context of her "marriage" to Christ, of which he was an observer, and on the basis of his monastic ideal, within which the abbot was to regard himself as the nuns' "servant." Abelard, Institutio, 44; The Letter Collection, 410–411.

57. On intercession as "mediation" and "petition," see Gilsdorf, The Favor of Friends.

58. Eadmer, Vita Anselmi; ed. and trans. Southern, 55–56.

59. Cited in Farmer, "Persuasive Voices," 517.

60. On queens as intercessors, see Gilsdorf, The Favor of Friends, 114–124; Parsons, "The Intercessionary Patronage of Queens Margaret and Isabella of France"; Parsons, "The Queen's Intercession"; Huneycutt, "Intercession and the High-Medieval Queen"; and Strohm, "Queens as Intercessors."

61. On Esther and early medieval queens, see Klein, Ruling Women, 165–173; and Huneycutt, "Intercession and the High-Medieval Queen." In the early twelfth century, Robert of Arbrissel offered Esther as a model for Ermengarde of Anjou, countess of Brittany, reminding her how Esther had "greatly benefited God's people" through her marriage to an "infidel prince." Robert of Arbrissel, Sermo Domni Roberti, 6; Deux vies, 464–465.

62. "Eritis pro Ecclesia Christi apud pium conjugem more sanctae illius Esther pro Israelitica plebe apud maritum." Pope John VIII, Ad Richildim Augustam; PL 126: 698; cited in Huneycutt, "Intercession and the High-Medieval Queen," 129.

63. "Efferatum cor regis ad misericordiam et salvationem." Hincmar of Reims, Coronatio Iudithae Karoli II filiae; ed. Pertz, MGH LL I, 450; cited in Huneycutt, "Intercession and the High-Medieval Queen," 129.

64. Hrabanus Maurus, Expositio in Librum Esther; PL 109: 635–670. Hrabanus Maurus, Epistola Rabani in Librum Hester; ed. Dümmler, MGH Poetae, 2, 167–168.

65. Trans. in Klein, Ruling Women, 167–168.

66. Peter of Blois, Epist. 17, 6; ed. Revell, 100. Later medieval texts, too, presented Esther as a model for religious women. The Ancrene Wisse linked women's prayer with the example of Esther interceding on behalf of the Jews with Ahasuerus. "Many would have been lost who are saved through the anchoress's prayers, as they were through Esther's," the author explained, presenting Esther as the "true anchoress" and claiming that Ahasuerus "stands for God." Anchoritic Spirituality, trans. Savage and Watson, 111. Similarly, Humbert of Romans (d. 1277) presented Christ as the "true Asuerus" in his Constitutions, implicitly invoking Esther as a model for Dominican sisters. "What purity, what fragrance should cling to those who wish to enter into the house of the true Asuerus; how becoming it is for those who wish to please such a Spouse to be adorned with virtue and holiness." Cited in Hindsley, The Mystics of Engelthal, 4–5.

67. On Mary as intercessor, see Oakes, Ora pro nobis; Fulton, From Judgment to Passion, 204–243; and Rubin, Mother of God, 130–137.

68. Felice Lifshitz introduces the concept of the "liturgical *virgo*," exploring the implications for women (and for men) of women's reduction to a single category of holiness. Lifshitz, "Gender Trouble in Paradise"; and Lifshitz, "Priestly Women, Virginal Men."

69. Noting the presence of Mary Magdalene among the *virgines* of medieval litanies, Lifshitz wrote that "the category always encompassed women who must have undergone the experience of vaginal penetration." Lifshitz, "Priestly Women, Virginal Men," 89. Elliott talks about the difference between "anatomical virginity" and "virginity as a state of mind." Elliott, *Bride*, 25.

70. In the St. Albans Psalter, Mary is described as "Sancta virgo virginum." St. Albans Psalter. Dombibliothek Hildesheim, HS St. God. 1 (Property of the Basilica of St. Godehard, Hildesheim), p. 403.

71. "Confidimus enim et pro certo scimus quia omne quod vis / potes impetrare a filio tuo domino nostro iesu christo." "Oratio ad sanctam Mariam," *Book of Cerne*, ed. Kuypers, 154; trans. in Oakes, 26.

72. "Quod uoles, unigenitus, / Donabit tibi Filius; / Pro quibus uoles veniam / Impetrabis et gloriam." *Anima mea*, ed. Cottier, 144; trans. in Rubin, 132.

73. Anselm of Canterbury, *Oratio* 6; ed. Schmitt, *Opera*, III, 15; trans. Ward, 110.

74. "Dear Lord, spare the servant of your mother," Anselm wrote. Anselm of Canterbury, *Oratio* 6; ed. Schmitt, *Opera*, III, 16; trans. Ward, 112. Christina of Markyate's biographer noted that she experienced a vision of the "queen of heaven" in which the queen advised an angel to "ask Christina what she wants, because I will give her whatever it is." *De S. Theodora*, 42; ed. Talbot, 110; rev. trans. Fanous and Leyser, 44.

75. For the gendered gaze of male hagiographers, see the essays gathered together in Mooney, ed., *Gendered Voices*.

76. Muschiol, *Famula Die*, 178–191; Muschiol, "Zur Typologie weiblicher Heiliger," 42–43; and Muschiol, "Vorbild und Konkurrenz." See also Hasdenteufel-Röding, 149–158. Peter Brown similarly notes the association of nuns with prayer, commenting that "nuns rather than monks led the way," in the emergence of the medieval monastery as a "powerhouse of prayer." Brown, *The Rise of Western Christendom*, 226.

77. Gregory of Tours, *Liber vitae patrum*, 19; ed. Krusch MGH SS rer. Merov. 1.2, 286–291; trans. James, 118–125.

78. Florentius, *Vita Rusticulae*, 29; ed. Krusch, MGH SS rer. Merov. 4, 351; trans. McNamara and Halborg, 136.

79. *Vita sanctae Geretrudis*, 7; ed. Krusch, MGH SS rer. Merov. 2, 461–64; trans. McNamara and Halborg, 227–228.

80. *Vita sanctae Balthildis*, 16; ed. Krusch, MGH SS rer. Merov. 2, 503; trans. Fouracre and Gerberding, 130.

81. Echoing Jerome's sense of the incompatibility of earthly marriage and prayer, Fortunatus stressed Radegund's rejection of earthly ties, and her preference for a heavenly spouse: "though married to a terrestrial prince, she was not separated from the celestial one. . . . she was more Christ's partner than her husband's companion." Venantius Fortunatus, *De vita sanctae Radegundis*, I, 3; ed. Krusch, MGH SS rer. Merov. 2, 366; trans. McNamara and Halborg, 72. For discussion, see Glenn, "Two Lives of Saint Radegund"; and Elliott, *Bride*, 79–103.

82. Poitiers, Bibliothèque municipale, MS 250, fol. 24r. On this manuscript, see Carrasco, "Spirituality in Context." Carrasco argues for an interpretation of the manuscript's many images as "an interpretation of the saint's hagiographic personality . . . conditioned by the

institutional history of Radegund's foundations, and by the spiritual climate of the late eleventh century" (416).

83. *Vita Caesarii*, I, 28; ed. Morin, 184; trans. Klingshirn, 22.

84. Diem, "The Gender of the Religious," 441.

85. Baudonivia, *De vita sanctae Radegundis*, II, 10; ed. Krusch, MGH SS rer. Merov. 2, 384; trans. McNamara and Halborg, 93.

86. *Vita Genovefae virginis Parisiensis*, 12–13; ed. Krusch, MGH SS rer. Merov. 3, 219–220; trans. McNamara and Halborg, 23. Nelson notes that Genovefa was denounced as a "pseudo-prophet" and almost killed: Nelson, "Women and the Word," 73.

87. See, for instance, the discussion in: Hasdenteufel-Röding, 154–155. On gifts and counter-gifts in the medieval economy, see the essays in Davies and Fouracre, eds., *The Languages of Gift*; Bijsterveld, *Do ut des*; and Curta, "Merovingian and Carolingian Gift Giving."

88. Donatus, formerly a monk at Luxeuil, composed a rule for the women of Jussanensis, a community founded by his mother Flavia and in which his sister Siruda also lived. As he wrote: "To the holy virgins of Christ whom I venerate most highly, Gauthstruda and all her flock whom God's handmaid Flavia gathered into a community, greetings from Donatus, least little servant of all God's bondsmen and women." Donatus, *Regula ad virgines*; ed. De Vogüé, 237; trans. McNamara and Halborg, 32. On the *Regula*, see Diem, "New Ideas Expressed in Old Words."

89. Aldhelm, *Prosa de virginitate*, 60; ed. Gwara and Ehwald, CCSL 124A, 757–759; trans. Lapidge and Herren, 131.

90. Alcuin, Epist. 102; ed. Dümmler, MGH Epp. 4, 149; trans. Allott, 55–56.

91. Alcuin, Epist. 262; ed. Dümmler, MGH Epp. 4, 420; trans. Allott, 89–90.

92. Zola, *Radbertus's Monastic Voice*, 118–121. When Rotrude and Gisela wrote to Alcuin, they suggested singing the marriage song with him, evidence (according to Zola) that they viewed male monastics as brides, even if Alcuin did not share that view. Alcuin, Epist. 196; ed. Dümmler, MGH Epp. 4, 324. Discussed in Zola, 121. Elizabeth Clark shows that patristic writers had been willing to consider Christ's marriage to male brides: Clark, "The Celibate Bridegroom," 17–18. For male brides in early Christian Greek sources, see Kuefler, *Manly Eunuch*, 137–142.

93. Alcuin, Epist. 36; ed. Dümmler, MGH Epp. 4, 78.

94. Alcuin Epist. 300; ed. Dümmler, MGH Epp. 4, 459.

95. Alcuin Epist. 15; ed. Dümmler, MGH Epp. 4, 40–41; trans. Allott, 101. Alcuin also comments on their "pact of love" (*pactum caritatis*).

96. "Quae tibi maior esse gloria poterit vel sublimior honor, quam eius regis esse sponsam, qui super omnes reges est." Alcuin, Epist. 15; ed. Dümmler, MGH Epp. 4, 41.

97. Of course, not all men described praying women in explicitly gendered terms. Rudolph, a monk at Fulda, emphasized the power of prayer in his *life* of Leoba, depicting her as effective and consistent in prayer without presenting her prayerfulness in gendered terms. Rudolf begged the prayers of women in his dedication of the *vita* to Hadamout, although his request was not strongly gendered. Rudolf of Fulda, *Vita Leobae abbatissae Biscofesheimensis*; ed. Waitz, MGH SS 15.1, 122; trans. Talbot, 205.

98. Paschasius Radbertus, *De assumptione sanctae Mariae*, 108–109; ed. Ripberger, CCCM 56C, 158.

99. Paschasius used language drawn from the Song of Songs in his *Life* of Adalhard, but he did not encourage bridal identification in his writings for monks (as he did for nuns). Paschasius

Radbertus, *Charlemagne's Cousins*, trans. Cabaniss, 32. As Zola observed, "the differences between Radbertus's bridal writings for nuns and ones for monks suggest that he may have believed that nuns enjoy a closer relationship to Christ than most monks do." Zola, 104–105.

100. On the male bride in Bernard's sermons, see Chapter 2, n. 157.

101. Florentius, *Vita Rusticulae*, prologue; ed. Krusch, MGH SS rer. Merov. 4, 340; trans. McNamara and Halborg, 122.

102. See below, n. 135.

103. Donatus, *Regula ad virgines*; ed. De Vogüé, 240; trans. McNamara and Halborg, 34.

104. Benko, "The Magnificat." Hannah was consistently identified as a precursor to the Virgin: not only was Hannah's presentation of Samuel to Eli seen as a model for Mary's presentation of Jesus at the temple, but her miraculous pregnancy was also regularly cited as a model for the miraculous pregnancy of Mary's mother, St. Anne. See, for example, Anderson, *St. Anne in Renaissance Music*, 54–55.

105. As Augustine argued, Hannah's prayer could only be seen as conforming to Jesus's instructions that Christians pray for "deliverance" from evil if barrenness within marriage was considered an "evil." Augustine of Hippo, Epist. 130.16.29; ed. Goldbacher, CSEL 44, 74–75; trans. Parsons, II, 399.

106. Washington, D. C., National Gallery of Art. B-17, 714. On medieval depictions of Hannah, see Altvater, "Barren Mother, Dutiful Wife, Church Triumphant."

107. The makers of the St. Albans Psalter expressed greater confidence in Hannah's prayerful efficacy, showing her in an initial to the *Canticum Annae* presenting Samuel as an offering at the temple, thereby confirming the manuscript's tendency to privilege the prayerfulness of women. St. Albans Psalter. Dombibliothek Hildesheim, HS St. God. 1 (Property of the Basilica of St. Godehard, Hildesheim), p. 375.

108. Gregory the Great, *Dialogues*, II, 33, 5; ed. de Vogüé, II, 234–235; trans. Zimmerman, 103.

109. "Nunquid ipsa hoc fecit, quod magis tua sancta negatio fecit: quia si non negasses, miraculum non eveniret." Bertharius of Monte Cassino, *Vita s. Scholasticae Virginis*, 12; PL 126: 984.

110. Alberic of Monte Cassino, "The Homily of Alberic the Deacon on Saint Scholastica," trans. Coffey, 300. Alberic's sermon, composed for Scholastica's feast day, explicated the gospel reading of the day, Matt. 25:1–12, concerning the Wise and Foolish Virgins. Alberic sidesteps questions to do with the efficacy of Scholastica's prayer, locating the source of her miracle rather in her tears.

111. Vatican City, Biblioteca Apostolica Vaticana, Vat. Lat. 1202, fol. 72v.

112. Goscelin of St. Bertin, *Vita beate Sexburge regina*, 11; ed. and trans. Love, 158–159.

113. Goscelin of St. Bertin, *Vita beate Sexburge regina*, 10; ed. and trans. Love, 154–155.

114. Goscelin of St. Bertin, *Vita beate Sexburge regina*, 11; ed. and trans. Love, 156–157.

115. *Hymn Collections from the Paraclete*, ed. Waddell, II, 9; trans. Ziolkowski in *Letters of Peter Abelard*, 46. Elsewhere, Abelard directly linked his skill in composition to the prayerfulness of the women on his behalf: "consider attentively how extraordinary your praying may cause our capability to be." *Hymn Collections from the Paraclete*, ed. Waddell, II, 89; trans. Ziolkowski in *Letters of Peter Abelard*, 50. See also Abelard's dedication to the *Commentary on the Six Days of Creation*, trans. Ziolkowski in *Letters of Peter Abelard*, 60–63.

116. *Deux vies*, 483–486 (at 486).

117. Andrew, *Supplementum*, 16; *Deux vies*, 162–163. Lutter comments on the ways in which women's gendered "weakness" qualified them for prayer, while also fueling arguments concern-

ing their need for "protection" and supporting their claustration. Lutter, 210. For the topos of women's "strength" in "weakness," see Griffiths, "'Men's Duty.'"

118. Andrew, *Supplementum*, 62 ; *Deux vies*, 286. Robert reminds the archbishop of Bourges how he had asked for Fontevrist nuns to settle in his province : "You asked me to give some of my good women to you, and I did so. . . . You made this place ready for them, for the salvation of your soul and the souls of your loved ones." Andrew, *Supplementum*, 31 ; *Deux vies*, 249. Nuns at Admont withdrew their love from one who had been unfaithful to them, an act that, according to Lutter, effectively meant the withdrawal of their prayers. Epist. 2; ed. in Beach, "Voices from a Distant Land," 52; and Lutter, 208–209.

119. Dalarun, *Robert of Arbrissel*, 156–158.

120. *De S. Theodora,* 64, 63; ed. Talbot, 148, 146; rev. trans. Fanous and Leyser, 65, 64. For the reciprocity inherent in their relationship, see *De S. Theodora,* 68; ed. Talbot, 154; rev. trans. Fanous and Leyser, 68.

121. *Gesta abbatum,* as cited in Koopmans, "The Conclusion of Christina of Markyate's *Vita*," 677. The *Gesta abbatum* comments further that Geoffrey transferred to Markyate various rights belonging to St. Albans "without the convent's consent." *Gesta abbatum,* as cited in Koopmans, "The Conclusion of Christina of Markyate's *Vita*," 684.

122. *De S. Theodora,* 64, 76; ed. Talbot, 148, 172; rev. trans. Fanous and Leyser, 65, 78.

123. Koopmans notes that, "writing a *Vita* was the first step in establishing Christina as not only Geoffrey's personal intercessor but as a woman worthy of general reverence as a saintly figure." Koopmans, "The Conclusion of Christina of Markyate's *Vita*," 680.

124. *De S. Theodora,* 55; ed. Talbot, 134; rev. trans. Fanous and Leyser, 57.

125. *De S. Theodora,* 57; ed. Talbot, 138; rev. trans. Fanous and Leyser, 59.

126. *De S. Theodora,* 68; ed. Talbot, 154; rev. trans. Fanous and Leyser, 68.

127. Koopmans makes this point, observing that Christina's biographer "chose to portray [her] past and present life as revolving around his community at St. Albans." Koopmans, "Dining at Markyate," 157, 154.

128. Abelard, *Sermo* 30; ed. Granata.

129. "Ad quam quidem celestium societatem nuptiarum et eterna tabernacula ipse vos meritis et intercessionibus suis, secum introducant, ut illic per eas percipiatis eterna que hic a vobis suscipiunt temporalia, prestante ipso earum sponso Domino Iesu Christo." Abelard, *Sermo* 30; ed. Granata, 59. The author of the early thirteenth-century *vita* of Gilbert of Sempringham also interpreted his foundation for women at Sempringham in light of the parable of Luke 16. *The Book of St. Gilbert,* 9; ed. and trans. Foreville and Keir, 30–31.

130. See the Appendix for the text of *Beati pauperes.*

131. For the idea of salvation through women in the *life* of Robert of Arbrissel, see Griffiths, "The Cross and the *Cura monialium*."

132. Griffiths, "Brides and *dominae*," 74–75.

133. Körkel-Hinkfoth, *Die Parabel von den klugen und törichten Jungfrauen,* 39–47. Körkel-Hinkfoth notes that, in France, the parable of the virgins was overwhelmingly associated with the Judgment. Körkel-Hinkfoth, 41. Elizabeth Clark notes that the "merger of Judgment seat and *thalamos*" took place in patristic exegesis, as hopes for Jesus's immediate return to earth were replaced by the expectation of heavenly union with him after death. Clark, "The Celibate Bridegroom," 12.

134. Consecrated virgins and praying women had long been associated with the "wise virgins" of Matthew 25. Liturgies for the consecration of virgins include consecration ceremonies

in which the consecrands carried candles, evoking the wise virgins with their lamps, while certain prayers for the blessing of the veil expressed the wish that the consecrand "be found worthy to enter. . . . into the nuptials of eternal happiness" with the "prudent virgins." For the textual influence of Matthew 25 in ceremonies for the consecration of virgins, see Borders, "Gender, Performativity, and Allusion" (here at 22). For the early medieval development of the ceremony, see Gussone, "Die Jungfrauenweihe in ottonischer Zeit." Goscelin of St. Bertin describes how he was "struck to the quick" by Eve of Wilton, when he witnessed her "marriage" with God, as she approached the altar with "glittering candles like the stars and constellations above." Goscelin of St. Bertin, *Liber confortatorius*, I; ed. Talbot, 28; trans. Otter, 23. For discussion of this ritual, see O'Brien O'Keeffe, "Goscelin and the Consecration of Eve."

135. Caesarius of Arles, *Regula sanctarum virginum*, 1; ed. de Vogüé and Courreau, 172–173; trans. McCarthy, 170.

136. For a codicological description of the codex, see *Le Codex Guta-Sintram*, ed. Weis, II, 11. The text of the necrology is reproduced in *Le Codex Guta-Sintram*, ed. Weis, II, 78–116.

137. The first column of the necrology listed all ordained priests who were related to Marbach, from the pope to the community's canon-priests. Of this last group, four who were buried at Schwarzenthann before 1158 were presumably men who had provided spiritual service to the women's community. *Le Codex Guta-Sintram*, ed. Weis, II, 145–148. See also Weis, "Die Nekrologien."

138. Vanuxem, "La mort et la sépulture d'Abélard." By arranging for Abelard's body to be brought to the Paraclete, Heloise noted that Peter the Venerable had relinquished the "privilege" (*beneficium*) due to Cluny." Peter the Venerable, Epist. 167 (Heloise, Letter to Peter the Venerable); ed. Constable, I, 400. See also Schmid, "Bemerkungen zur Persona- und Memorial Forschung," 110–117.

139. On women, death, and intercession, see Lauwers, *La mémoire des ancêtres*, 425–459; see also Schilp, "Stiftungen zum Totengedenken."

140. *Vita sanctae Hildegardis*, II, 5; ed. Klaes, CCCM, 126, 29; trans. Silvas, 165.

141. Berman, "Dowries, Private Income, and Anniversary Masses," 4. See also Berman, "How Much Space Did Medieval Nuns Have or Need?" As Berman comments, "leaders of medieval society, even preeminent theologians, supported communities of religious women, often providing property bequests to those nuns in return for anniversary prayers, probably masses, but possibly commemorations during the office." (102)

142. Coomans, "Cistercian Nuns and Princely Memorials," 731.

143. Jordan, "Gender Concerns," 76. Jordan writes that, "men's houses clearly did not have a monopoly on commemoration." "Gender Concerns," 87.

144. Newman notes that purgatory "filled an overwhelming place in the visions, devotions, and works of charity undertaken by religious women." Newman, "On the Threshold of the Dead," 109. On the "birth of purgatory", see Le Goff, *The Birth of Purgatory*.

145. On Ottonian queens and intercession, see Corbet, *Les saints ottoniens*. On Gandersheim, see Althoff, "Unerkannte Zeugnisse." Concerning Quedlinburg, see Leopold, "Damenstiftskirche und Wipertikirche in Quedlinburg." On early medieval women's monasteries as "Begräbnisorte," see Muschiol, *Famula Dei*, 337–343; and Hasdenteufel-Röding, 142–149. For Obermünster and Niedermünster, see Edwards, *Noblewomen of Prayer*. For Fontevraud, see Nolan, *Queens*, 105–114; Nolan, "The Queen's Choice"; and Wood, "Fontevraud." Fontevraud possessed the bodies of Eleanor of Aquitaine (d. 1204) and Henry II (d. 1189), as well as their

son Richard I (d. 1199) and daughter Joan (d. 1199) (all three predeceased Eleanor). For burial at Las Hulegas, see Walker, "Leonor of England"; and Walker, "Images of Royal and Aristocratic Burial," 162–165. On mourning and burial as "political roles played by the queens of Castile," see Shadis, *Berenguela of Castile*, 149–171 (here at 151).

146. Katherine Clark comments on the "asymmetry" in spiritual relations between husbands and wives: "the widow was the partner designated as the active intercessor, but no parallel discourse existed concerning a widower's intercession for his deceased wife." Clark, "Purgatory, Punishment, and the Discourse on Holy Widowhood," 191. Corbet comments, too, on the asymmetry in prayer for the dead, which was a task particularly for widows. Corbet, 199. Maria Hillebrandt notes that women who made donations to Cluny *pro remedio animae* mentioned the salvation of their husbands more frequently than any other relation, yet only infrequently mentioned their own natal families. Men, by contrast, were more likely to give gifts with an eye on their own spiritual benefit. Hillebrandt, "Stiftungen zum Seelenheil durch Frauen," 62.

147. McLaughlin, "Peter Abelard and the Dignity of Women," 326, n. 128; McLaughlin, "Heloise the Abbess," 7.

148. Waddell, "Cistercian Influence on the Abbey of the Paraclete?" 334, 337.

149. Obermünster necrology, BayHStA, KL Regensburg-Obermünster 1.

150. As Carolyn Edwards comments, "commemorative, intercessory prayer was the primary task of the nuns of Niedermünster, and of Obermünster." Edwards, *Noblewomen*, 32.

151. Goscelin of St. Bertin, *Vita et virtutes sanctae Ethelburgae virginis*, 4; ed. Colker, 404–405; trans. Morton in *Guidance for Women*, 145.

152. *De S. Theodora*, 50; ed. Talbot, 126; rev. trans. Fanous and Leyser, 52. Roger died c. 1121/1123 at Markyate, but his body was moved to Saint Albans. Koopmans, "Dining at Markyate," 152.

153. "Obiit Rogeri heremite monachi sancti albani apud quemcumque fuerit hoc psalterium fiat eius memoria maxime hac die." St. Albans Psalter. Dombibliothek Hildesheim, HS St. God. 1 (Property of the Basilica of St. Godehard, Hildesheim), p. 11.

CONCLUSION

1. The term "sacramental disability" was proposed by Penny Johnson, who noted that religious women were financially disadvantaged in that they had to pay priests to serve at altars from which they were excluded. Johnson, 225–226.

2. On the benefits of attending to the "ordinary" in medieval religious life, see Coakley, "Afterword."

3. Elliott, *Bride*.

4. While earlier generations of scholars assumed Abelard's intellectual primacy in his relationship with Heloise, more recent studies have acknowledged her importance as a learned figure of the twelfth century. Peter Dronke argued that Heloise had already established a mature letter-writing style before she met Abelard; indeed, he posited that she may have influenced Abelard stylistically and intellectually. Dronke, *Women Writers*, 112. Constant Mews has argued persuasively for Heloise's intellectual integrity and excellence quite apart from her relationship with Abelard. As Mews has shown, Heloise's literary activity extended well beyond

the letters to Abelard that appear in the collected correspondence and for which she is best known. Indeed, Mews suggests that Heloise may have been the author of some of the sequences generally attributed to Abelard. Mews, "Heloise and the Liturgical Experience." For contemporary evidence for Heloise's renown as a writer, see Mews, "Hugh Metel, Heloise, and Peter Abelard." See also Mews, "The Voice of Heloise," in *Lost Love Letters*, 145–177. For the idea that Heloise and Abelard collaborated in the production of texts for the Paraclete, see Clanchy, *Abelard,* 169–172; and Newman, "Authority, Authenticity, and the Repression of Heloise." Heloise's writings, not only in her letters, but also in the questions presented in the *Problemata*, have been taken as evidence of the high level of scholarship at the Paraclete under her authority. Marenbon comments that the *"Problemata Heloissae* show even more clearly that Heloise and the nuns of the Paraclete were as eager and advanced in their studies of theology as the men Abelard was teaching in Paris." Marenbon, *Philosophy,* 76–77. Barbara Newman argues that Heloise "came to Abelard with not only her mind but her imagination well stocked." Newman, "Authority, Authenticity, and the Repression of Heloise," 70. On the education of Heloise and her interactions with Abelard before their marriage, see Newman, *Making Love.*

    5. Heloise, Epist. 2.7; *The Letter Collection,* 128–129.

    6. Heloise, Epist. 6.33; *The Letter Collection,* 256–259.

    7. Heloise, Epist. 6.28; *The Letter Collection,* 254–255. Material care was a significant source of concern for male houses considering the incorporation of female communities. Lester, *Creating Cistercian Nuns,* 94–107. For financial considerations as a source of conflict at Markyate and Saint Albans, see Koopmans, "The Conclusion of Christina of Markyate's *Vita.*" For financial conflicts between Rupertsberg and Disibodenberg, see Griffiths, "Monks and Nuns at Rupertsberg."

    8. Heloise famously remarked that she would have preferred to be Abelard's "meretrix" than wife of Augustus. Heloise, Epist. 2.10; *The Letter Collection,* 132–133.

    9. Macy, *Hidden History,* 67–68. On nuns as "widows" at the Paraclete, see Flynn, "Abelard and Rhetoric."

    10. For the absence of bridal spirituality and metaphors from the spiritual and intellectual formation of nuns at Hohenbourg, see Griffiths, *Garden of Delights.*

    11. In a prologue to her commentary on the Athanasian Creed, Hildegard records how she had returned to Disibodenberg sometime after the separation to finalize certain financial details. At the same time, she seems to have combated the men's attempts to recall her secretary Volmar—a Disibodenberg monk who had moved with her to Rupertsberg. Speaking in the voice of "I who am" (*ego, qui sum*), Hildegard warned the men: "if [. . .] you try to take the shepherd of spiritual medicine away from them, then again I say, you are like the sons of Belial, and in this do not consider the justice of God." ("Si autem pastorem spiritalis medicinae ipsis abstrahere tentaveritis, tunc iterum dico quod similes sitis filiis Belial, et in hoc justitiam Dei non inspicitis.") *Explanatio symboli sancti Athanasii*; PL 197: 1066.

    12. Arnold's charter was issued in 1158. *Mainzer Urkundenbuch. II,* ed. Acht, no. 231; trans. in Silvas, *Jutta and Hildegard,* 243–246. The obligation was confirmed by Frederick Barbarossa in a charter of 1163, and it appears again in Hildegard's *vita,* which adds that the women should have free choice in selecting their priests. For Frederick Barbarossa's charter of 1163, see *Mainzer Urkundenbuch.* II, ed. Acht, no. 274; trans. in Silvas, *Jutta and Hildgard,* 246–248. For the women's dependence on Disibodenberg and their choice of priests, see *Vita sanctae Hildegar-*

dis, ed. Klaes, 103*-106*. For discussion of pastoral care at Rupertsberg, see Griffiths, "Monks and Nuns at Rupertsberg."

13. For the complex authorship and production of Hildegard's biography, see Newman, "Three-part Invention"; Newman, "Hildegard and Her Hagiographers." Newman comments that Theoderic "casts Hildegard in the bridal role, although she herself—despite her admiration for Bernard—was not especially drawn to that book or the nuptial mysticism it inspired." Newman, "Hildegard and Her Hagiographers," 26.

14. On *Ecclesia* as bride of Christ in Hildegard's thought, see Newman, *Sister of Wisdom*, 196–249. Elsewhere Newman contrasts the bridal spirituality of the *Speculum virginum*, which concludes with an *Epithalamium*, with the closing section of Hildegard's *Scivias*, with its focus on *Ecclesia triumphans*. Newman, "Liminalities," 383.

15. Hildegard of Bingen, Epist. 52; ed. van Acker, CCCM 91, 126; trans. Baird and Ehrman, I, 127. For discussion of Tenxwind's letter, see Haverkamp, "Tenxwind von Andernach und Hildegard von Bingen"; Newman, *Sister of Wisdom*, 221–222; and Flanagan, "'For God Distinguishes the People of Earth as in Heaven.'"

16. Hildegard of Bingen, Epist. 52r; ed. van Acker, CCCM 91, 129; trans. Baird and Ehrman, I, 129. Hildegard's antiphon for virgins is: Hildegard of Bingen, *Symphonia armonie celestium revelationum*, 55 (*O pulcre facies*); ed. and trans. Newman, 218–219.

17. The term "prelapsarian femininity" is Maud Burnett McInerney's. McInerney, "Like a Virgin," 135.

18. Hildegard of Bingen, Epist. 52r; ed. Van Acker, CCCM 91, 127–130; trans. Baird and Ehrman, I, 129. Sabina Flanagan suggests that the practice at Rupertsberg of nuns wearing elaborate festal clothing may have been intended to parallel the rich vestments worn by monastic priests. Flanagan, "Hildegard of Bingen's Social Ideas," 16, n. 5. John van Engen surmises that the festal dress of the nuns at Rupertsberg may have been linked to their reception of the Eucharist. Van Engen, "Abbess: 'Mother and Teacher,'" 37.

19. A significant exception is Christina of Markyate, for whom bridal status offered legal protection against marriage to a human spouse. As Christina warned Beorhtred, "Beware . . . of wanting to take to yourself the Bride of Christ, lest in his anger he slay you." *De S. Theodora*, 22; ed. Talbot, 72; rev. trans. Fanous and Leyser, 23. On the legal implications of Christina's marriage to Christ, see Head, "The Marriages of Christina of Markyate."

20. McNamer, 25–57.

21. On the eschatological implications of Hildegard's liturgical celebrations, see Heinzer, "Unequal Twins," 103–104. I am grateful to Eva Schlotheuber for alerting me to the significance of the nun's crown and for sharing her article on nuns' attire: Eva Schlotheuber, "Best Clothes and Everyday Attire." See also Bynum, "'Crowned with Many Crowns'"; Hotchin, "The Nun's Crown"; Gussone, 35–36; Schlotheuber, *Klostereintritt*, 156–174; Wetter, "Von Bräuten und Vikaren Christi"; and Koslin, "The Robe of Simplicity."

22. Hildegard consistently denied men status as "virgins" (even though the virgins of the Apocalypse are described as those who "cum mulieribus non sunt coinquinati"; Apoc. 14:4). McInerney notes that Hildegard draws a distinction between "female virginity" and "male chastity." McInerney, "Like a Virgin," 145. For the gendering of the "virgo" as female in the context of the litany, see Lifshitz, "Priestly Women, Virginal Men."

23. See Chapter 1, n. 185.

24. For discussion of religious women as makers and donors of liturgical textiles, see Griffiths, " 'Like the Sister of Aaron.' "

25. The Council of Paris prohibited women from the area around the altar and warned that they were not to touch priestly garments. *Concilium Parisiense* (829), c. 45; MGH Conc. 2.2, 639. In the ninth century, Bishop Haito of Basel (d. 836) warned that no women were to be involved in service at the altar, though he allowed that they could launder soiled linens: "When the altar cloths must be washed, they are to be taken by clerics and given to women at the railings and returned to the same place." Haito of Basel, *Capitula*, 16; ed. Brommer, MGH Capit. episc. I, 215. Abelard echoed these guidelines, stipulating that "neither the sacristan nor any of the sisters shall ever be allowed to touch the relics or the altar-vessels, nor even the altar-cloths except when these are given them to be washed." Abelard, *Institutio*, 52; *The Letter Collection*, 414–415. Even so, Abelard noted that the women should "prepare the hosts themselves." For the sacramental ministries of Benedictine nuns in England during the central Middle Ages, and the role of the sacristan, see Bugyis, *In Christ's Stead*.

26. On liturgical textiles, see Braun, *Die liturgische Gewandung*; Walsh, *Mass and Vestments*. On ornamentation of the altar, see Braun, *Der christliche Altar*, II (*Die Ausstattung des Altares*). On clerical vestments, see Miller, *Clothing the Clergy*; and, for a broad overview, Mayo, *A History of Ecclesiastical Dress*. On textiles from female monasteries, see Schilp and Stauffer, eds., *Seide im früh- und hochmittelalterlichen Frauenstift*; and Seeberg, *Textile Bildwerke im Kirchenraum*.

27. For the engagement of Carolingian women in the production and transmission of textiles, see Garver, *Women and Aristocratic Culture*, 224–268; and Garver, "Textiles as a Means of Female Religious Participation." For the involvement of English women with textile work, see Halpin, *The Religious Experience of Women in Anglo-Saxon England*, 47–114. Lynda Coon comments on the spiritual symbolism of women's textile work in late antiquity and the early Middle Ages. Coon, *Sacred Fictions*, 41–44. Jane Tibbetts Schulenburg notes the association between textile work and sanctity for medieval women: Schulenburg, "Holy Women and the Needle Arts." Maureen Miller draws particular attention to the production of clerical clothing by women: Miller, *Clothing the Clergy*, 141–176. As she writes: "if the wearing of vestments was central to a clerical spirituality about the cultivation of virtue, how did collaboration with women to produce these garments figure in this spirituality?" Miller, *Clothing the Clergy*, 148. Her focus is primarily on secular women, who provided churchmen with ornate vestments, but the question is equally valid (if not more so) for the monastic women I examine here.

28. According to the *Protevangelium of James*, Mary was responsible for weaving a cloth for the temple veil. *Protevangelium of James*, 10; ed. Cullmann, 379–380. Depictions of the Annunciation often showed Mary spinning as Gabriel appeared to her. Gibson explores medieval legends of Mary weaving and spinning, tracing them to the eighth-century *Gospel of Pseudo-Matthew*: Gibson, "The Thread of Life in the Hand of the Virgin."

29. *The Life of Christina of Markyate*, trans. Fanous and Leyser, xxv. See also the discussion of Christina's gift in Bugyis, "Envisioning Episcopal Exemption."

30. Goscelin of St. Bertin, *Vita s. Edithae*, 16; ed. Wilmart, 79; trans. Wright and Loncar, 48 (Wright and Loncar translate "bisso" as cotton).

31. Concerning the alb, see Braun, *Die liturgische Gewandung*, 57–101; and Walsh, *Mass and Vestments*, 387–394. On the possibility that Edith made the alb for herself, see Chapter 2, n. 179.

32. Vienna, Österreichisches Museum für angewandte Kunst, Inv.-Nr. T.6902–6906. Concerning the textiles from Göß, see Eggert, "Textile Strategien der Grenzüberschreitung"; Grönwoldt, "Gestickte Dalmatik"; and Schuette and Müller-Christensen, *The Art of Embroidery*, nos. 113–119.

33. A stole is in the Schnütgen-Museum, Cologne, and further pieces in London's Victoria & Albert Museum. Pollak, "The Vienna 'Gösser Ornat.'"

34. Göss was a *Doppelkirche*, which had canons who ministered to the parish of St. Andreas. The vestments were likely only used on the memorial day (September 7th) of the community's founder, Adala. Naschenweng, "Das Profeßbuch und Necrologium."

35. A Middle High German inscription on the dalmatic records: "Deu die himelisch Chuneginne gezieret hat mit der siden wat deu helfe ir unde ir gesinde hinze ir heiligem chinde." Grönwoldt, 633. Eggert discusses the (German) translation of this inscription: Eggert, 285, n. 22.

36. "Celi matrona chunegundis suscipe dona casula cu(m) cappa placeat tibi celica mater" (Mistress of heaven, accept the gifts of Chunegund; may the chasuble with the cope be pleasing to you, heavenly mother). Dreger, "Der Gösser Ornat," 632. The dalmatic also claims Chunegunde as donor (and possibly maker): "Chunigundis abbatissa hoc opus est operata." Grönwoldt, 633.

37. The Chunegunde image had originally appeared on the chasuble, but was sewn onto the cope when both pieces were reworked in the sixteenth century. Schuette and Müller-Christensen, nos. 113 and 119.

38. Hedwig Röckelein discusses the commemoration of monastic patrons on liturgical textiles, particularly antependia: Röckelein, "Gründer, Stifter und Heilige."

39. Musées Royaux d'Art et d'Histoire, Brussels, Inv.-No. Tx.1784. *Krone und Schleier*, no. 202. For discussion of the antependium, see Von Wilckens, "Das goldgestickte Antependium"; Kramer, *A Case Study of the Rupertsberg Antependium*; and Seeberg, "Women as Makers of Church Decoration," 375–384. Seeberg dates the antependium to c. 1220, suggesting that it formed part of the larger project at Rupertsberg of securing Hildegard's canonization.

40. Von Wilckens suggests that the silk could have come from the plunder of Constantinople in 1204. She notes, too, losses to the antependium along the bottom and right side and suggests that pearls once formed part of the ornamentation, based on her observation that certain parts of the antependium (halos, for instance) have excess thread. Von Wilckens, 3.

41. For discussion of the figures showcased on the Rupertsberg antependium, see Von Wilckens, 6–8; Kramer, 35–44; and Seeberg, "Women as Makers of Church Decoration," 377–384.

42. The "group portrait" on the Rupertsberg antependium is reminiscent of the depiction of the canonesses at Hohenbourg, fifty-eight named and two unnamed women, who were featured on the penultimate folios of the *Hortus deliciarum* (fols. 322v–323r). *Hortus deliciarum*, ed. Green, Evans, Bischoff, and Curschmann, II, Pl. 153–154. For discussion, see Griffiths, *Garden of Delights*, 216–217.

43. Von Wilckens, 9.

44. For Medingen, see Riggert, *Die Lüneburger Frauenklöster*, 33–37. See also Appuhn, *Kloster Medingen*.

45. Museum August Kestner, Hannover, W.M. XXII 8. *Krone und Schleier*, no. 480. Henrike Lähnemann explores the iconography of the antependium in light of the intellectual culture

at Medingen: Lähnemann "'An dessen bom wil ik stighen.'" Lähnemann observes that in the Medingen manuscripts nuns are associated with Latin, rather than vernacular, inscriptions (24).

46. Lähnemann, 19–20. For discussion of relations between parish churches and female monasteries (including Medingen), see Röckelein, ed., *Frauenstifte, Frauenklöster und ihre Pfarreien.*

47. Jane L. Carroll argues that tapestries produced by Dominican nuns could further reform within their own communities. Carroll, "Woven Devotions."

48. Lähnemann identifies the inscription as a paraphrase of Song of Songs 7:8: "dixi: ascendam in palmam, adprehendam fructus eius." Lähnemann, 33.

49. Ivo of Chartres, Epist. 142; PL 162: 149. On Matilda as a patron of the church, see Huneycutt, "'Proclaiming her Dignity Abroad.'"

50. "Tu quoque praesens es cum Christus immolatur, cum traditur sepulturae, neutrumque sine tuo celebratur obsequio, cum ibi luminaria praeparas, luminis ubi adesse auctorem et corde credimus et ore confitemur." Hildebert of Lavardin, Epist. I, 9; PL 171: 161.

51. "Nunc autem ei planetam unam transmittimus, supplicantes ut in orationibus vestris nos colligatis, et intuitu dilectionis et devotionis quam ad vos et ecclesiam vestram gerimus et specialiter gerere volumus, officiorum et beneficiorum quae in ea fiunt nos participes faciatis." *Recueil des Historiens des Gaules*, 19, ed. Brial, 322. Continuing, Ingeborg provided detailed instructions for the use of her gift, requesting particularly that the chasuble be worn when the priest celebrated solemn Masses for the feast of the Virgin Mary. On Ingeborg, see Conklin, "Ingeborg of Denmark."

52. Goscelin's description of Edith's needlework appears in the version of the *vita* that he sent to Lanfranc. *Vita s. Edithe*; trans. Wright and Loncar, 66. On the two versions of the *vita*, see Chapter 2, n. 179.

53. For Amalarius of Metz, the priestly garments of Exodus 28 were properly understood as symbols of clerical virtue. Amalarius of Metz, *Opera liturgica omnia*; ed. Hanssens, II, 239–248. On the symbolism of medieval clerical clothing, see Miller, *Clothing the Clergy.*

54. In their visions, women often imagined themselves or other female figures wearing vestments. Christina of Markyate saw herself crowned with a crown on which "hung two white fillets like those of a bishop's mitre." *De S. Theodora*, 52; ed. Talbot, 128; rev. trans. Fanous and Leyser, 54. Elisabeth of Schönau saw the Virgin wearing priestly vestments in a vision, and Hildegard wrote of Pure Knowledge, a female figure, wearing a bishop's pallium. For discussion, see Newman, "Visions and Validation," 174; and Clark, "The Priesthood of the Virgin Mary."

55. Abelard, Epist. 7.15; *The Letter Collection*, 288–289.

56. For a gendered consideration of women's ecclesiastical patronage in late antiquity, see Clark, "Patrons, not Priests." On the liturgical gifts of medieval women, see Mecham, "Breaking Old Habits," 461–464. For textile gifts in particular, see Garver, "Textiles as a Means of Female Religious Participation;" and Seeberg, "Women as Makers of Church Decoration."

57. *Portal zur Geschichte*, Inv.-No. 84.

58. Concerning the cope, or pluvial, see Braun, *Die liturgische Gewandung*, 306–358; for the use of the cope, see 314–317.

59. Heloise, Epist. 6.33; *The Letter Collection*, 258–259. Women's communities were not infrequently left without a priest. At Lippoldsberg, the priest Marcwin resigned in 1136 (having served since 1112), leaving the women without care for two years. The reasons for his resignation are not clear, although the sources refer to "troublesome people" and to Marcwin's own "great infirmity of the flesh." Hotchin, "Women's Reading and Monastic Reform," 146.

60. Griffiths, "The Trouble with Priests"; Griffiths, *Garden of Delights*, 194–212.

61. Ferrante, *To the Glory*, 5.

62. Ferrante, *To the Glory*, 69.

63. As Ferrante commented: "I know what Jerome and Peter Damian and others said about the women they did not approve of, but I am more interested in what they said to the ones they respected and admired and worked with." Ferrante, *To the Glory*, 5–6.

APPENDIX

Note to title: *Beati pauperes; Le Codex Guta-Sintram,* ed. Weis, II, 54.

1. Matt. 5:3.

2. This sentence is an addition to the text of sermon 30.

3. II Cor. 12:9.

4. Jerome, Epist. 22.2; ed. Hilberg, I, CSEL 54, 145.

5. A long section from sermon 30 has been omitted here.

6. Matt. 25:36.

7. Matt. 25:10.

8. Here Abelard is referring to the text of his sermon, Luke 16:9: "Et ego dico vobis facite vobis amicos de mamona iniquitatis ut cum defeceritis recipiant vos in aeterna thabernacula."

BIBLIOGRAPHY

PRIMARY SOURCES

Abelard, Peter and Heloise. *The Letter Collection of Peter Abelard and Heloise*. Ed. David Luscombe, trans. Betty Radice, and rev. David Luscombe. Oxford Medieval Texts. Oxford: Clarendon Press, 2013.

Abelard, Peter. *I sermoni di Abelardo per le monache del Paracleto*. Ed. Paola de Santis. Mediaevalia Lovaniensia Series 1, Studia 31. Leuven: Leuven University Press, 2002.

———. *Introductio ad Theologiam*. PL 178: 979–1114.

———. *Letters of Peter Abelard, Beyond the Personal*. Trans. Jan M. Ziolkowski. Washington, D.C.: Catholic University of America Press, 2008.

———. *Peter Abelard. Letters IX–XIV. An Edition with Introduction*. Ed. Edmé Renno Smits. Groningen: Rijksuniversiteit, 1983.

———. *Sermo 30. De eleemosyna pro sanctimonialibus de Paraclito*. Ed. Aldo Granata, "La dottrina dell'Elemosina nel sermone 'Pro sanctimonialibus de Paraclito' di Abelardo." *Aevum* 47 (1973): 32–59, 54–59.

———. *Sic et non*. PL 178: 1329–1610.

Acta Murensia. Ed. P. Martin Kiem in Franz Ludwig Baumann, Gerold Meyer von Knonau, and P. Martin Kiem, eds., *Die Ältesten Urkunden von Allerheiligen in Schaffhausen Rheinau und Muri*. Quellen zur Schweizer Geschichte, 3. Basel: Schneider, 1883. 3–105.

The Acts of Paul and Thecla: A Critical Introduction and Commentary. Ed. Jeremy W. Barrier. Tübingen: Mohr Siebeck, 2009.

Adrevald of Fleury. *Historia translationis s. Benedicti*. Ed. E. de Certain. *Les miracles de Saint Benoît, écrits par Adrevald Aimoin, André, Raoul Tortaire et Hughes de Saint Marie, moines de Fleury*. Paris: Chez Mme Vᵉ J. Renouard, 1858. 1–14.

Aelred of Rievaulx. *De institutione inclusarum*. Ed. A. Hoste and C. H. Talbot, *Opera omnia*, I: *Opera ascetica*. CCCM 1. Turnhout: Brepols, 1971. 635–682. Trans. Mary Paul Macpherson in *The Works of Aelred of Rievaulx*, I: *Treatises: The Pastoral Prayer*. Cistercian Fathers Series no. 2. Kalamazoo, Mich.: Cistercian Publications, 1971. 41–102.

———. *De Sanctimoniali de Wattun*. PL 195: 789–96.

———. *Sermones I-XLVI*. Ed. Gaetano Raciti. CCCM 2A. Turnhout: Brepols, 1989.

———. *Speculum caritatis*. Ed. A. Hoste and C. H. Talbot, *Opera omnia*, I: *Opera ascetica*. CCCM 1. Turnhout: Brepols, 1971. 1–161. Trans. Elizabeth Connor. *The Mirror of Charity*. Piscataway, NJ: Gorgias Press, 2010.

Der Albani-Psalter= The St. Alban's Psalter= El salterio San Albans. Ed. Jochen Bepler, Peter Kidd, and Jane Geddes. 2 vols. Simbach: Müller & Schindler, 2007–2008.

Alberic of Monte Cassino. "The Homily of Alberic the Deacon on Saint Scholastica." Trans. Thomas F. Coffey in *Diakonia: Studies in Honor of Robert T. Meyer*. Washington, D.C.: Catholic University of America Press, 1986. 289–301.

Alcuin. *Alcuin of York, c. A.D. 732 to 804: His Life and Letters*. Trans. Stephen Allott. York: William Sessions Ltd., 1974.

———. *Carmina*. Ed. Ernst Dümmler. MGH Poetae 1. Berlin: Weidmann, 1881. 160–351.

———. *Epistolae*. Ed. Ernst Dümmler. MGH Epp. 4. Berlin: Weidmann, 1895. 1–481.

Aldhelm. *Carmen de virginitate*. Ed. Rudolf Ehwald. MGH Auct. ant. 15. Berlin: Weidmann, 1919. 325–471. Trans. Michael Lapidge and James L. Rosier in *Aldhelm, The Poetic Works*. Cambridge: D. S. Brewer, 1985. 102–167.

———. *Prosa de virginitate*. Ed. Scott Gwara and Rudolf Ehwald, *Prosa de virginitate: cum glosa latina atque anglosaxonica*, I: *Textus*. CCSL 124A. Turnhout: Brepols, 2001. Trans. Michael Lapidge and Michael Herren in *Aldhelm, the Prose Works*. Cambridge: Cambridge University Press, 1979. 59–132.

Die Ältere Wormser Briefsammlung. Ed. Walther Bulst. MGH Briefe d. dt. Kaiserzeit 3. Weimar: Hermann Böhlaus Nachfolger, 1949.

Amalarius of Metz. *Amalarii episcopi opera liturgica omnia*. Ed. John Michael Hanssens. 3 vols. Studi e Testi 138–140. Vatican City: Biblioteca apostolica vaticana, 1948–1950.

Ambrose of Milan. *De excessu fratris sui Satyri*. PL 16: 1289–1354. Trans. Michèle Bonnot, *Ambroise de Milan: sur la mort de son frère*. Paris: Migne, 2002.

———. *De virginibus*. Ed. and trans. Franco Gori in *Verginità, e, Vedovanza*. Sancti Ambrosii episcopi Mediolanensis Opera 14.1, Opere morali II.I. Milan: Bibliotheca Ambrosiana, 1989. 99–241. Trans. Boniface Ramsey in *Ambrose*. Early Church Fathers 3. London: Routledge, 1997. 73–116.

———. *Expositio Evangelii secundum Lucam*. Ed. Marcus Adriaen. CCSL 14. Turnhout: Brepols, 1957. Trans. Íde M. Ní Riain, *Commentary of Saint Ambrose on the Gospel According to Saint Luke*. Dublin: Halcyon Press, 2001.

Anchoritic Spirituality: Ancrene Wisse and Associated Works. Trans. Anne Savage and Nicholas Watson. New York: Paulist Press, 1991.

Andrew (of Fontevraud). *Supplementum historiae vitae Roberti*. In *Les deux vies de Robert d'Arbrissel, fondateur de Fontevraud: légendes, écrits et témoignages*. Ed. Jacques Dalarun, Geneviève Giordanego, Armelle Le Huërou, Jean Longère, Dominique Poirel, and Bruce L. Venarde. Disciplina monastica 4. Turnhout: Brepols, 2006. 190–300.

Anima mea: prières privées et textes de dévotion du Moyen Age latin: autour des prières ou méditations attribuées à saint Anselme de Cantorbéry (XIe-XIIe siècle). Ed. Jean-François Cottier. Turnhout: Brepols, 2001.

Annales Rodenses. Ed. Georg Pertz. MGH SS 16. Hannover: Hahn, 1859. 688–723.

Annales Sancti Disibodi. Ed. Georg Waitz. MGH SS 17. Hannover: Hahn, 1861. 4–30.

Annalista Saxo. Ed. Georg Waitz. MGH SS 6. Hannover: Hahn, 1844. 542–777.

Anselm of Canterbury. *Letters of Saint Anselm of Canterbury*. Trans. Walter Fröhlich. 3 vols. Cistercian Studies Series 96, 97, and 142. Kalamazoo, Mich.: Cistercian Publications, 1990–94.

———. *Opera omnia*. Ed. F. S. Schmitt. 6 vols. Stuttgart and Bad-Cannstatt: F. Frommann, 1968–1984.

———. *The Prayers and Meditations of St. Anselm*. Trans. Benedicta Ward. Harmondsworth: Penguin, 1973.

The Apostolic Fathers. Trans. Kirsopp Lake. 2 vols. Cambridge, Mass.: Harvard University Press, 1976–1985.

Athanasius of Alexandria. *The Life of Antony.* Ed. and trans. G. J. M. Bartelink, *Vie d'Antoine.* Sources chrétiennes 400. Paris: Cerf, 1994. Trans. Tim Vivian and Apostolos N. Athanassakis, *Life of Antony.* Cistercian Studies Series 202. Kalamazoo, Mich.: Cistercian Publications, 2003.

Augustine of Hippo. *Confessions.* Ed. James J. O'Donnell, *Confessions.* Vol. 1, *Introduction and Text.* Oxford: Clarendon Press, 1992. Trans. R. S. Pine-Coffin, *Confessions.* London: Penguin Books, 1961.

———. *De civitate Dei.* Ed. Bernhard Dombart and Alfons Kalb. CCSL 47–48. Turnhout: Brepols, 1955. Trans. Henry Bettenson, *Concerning the City of God Against the Pagans.* New York: Penguin Books, 1984.

———. *De opera monachorum.* Ed. Joseph Zycha. CSEL 41. Vienna: Tempsky, 1900. 529–596. Trans. Mary Sarah Muldowney in *Treatises on Various Subjects.* Washington, D.C.: Catholic University of America Press, 1952. 327–394.

———. *Epist. 211.* Trans. George Lawless in *Augustine of Hippo and his Monastic Rule.* Oxford: Clarendon Press, 1987. 104–118.

———. *Epistulae.* Ed. Alois Goldbacher. 4 vols. CSEL 34, 44, 57–58. Vienna: F. Tempsky, 1895–1923. Trans. Wilfrid Parsons. *Letters.* 6 vols. Washington, D.C.: Catholic University of America Press, 1951–1989.

Basil of Caesarea. *The Longer Responses.* Trans. Anna M. Silvas in *The Asketikon of St. Basil the Great.* Oxford: Oxford University Press, 2005. 153–269.

Baudonivia. *De vita sanctae Radegundis libri duo.* (Book 2) Ed. Bruno Krusch. MGH SS rer. Merov. 2. Hannover: Hahn, 1888. 377–395. Trans. Jo Ann McNamara and John E. Halborg with E. Gordon Whatley in *Sainted Women of the Dark Ages.* Durham, N.C.: Duke University Press, 1992. 86–105.

Baudri of Bourgueil. *Carmina.* Ed. Jean-Yves Tilliette, *Poèmes.* 2 vols. Paris: Les Belles Lettres, 1998.

———. *Historia magistri Roberti fundatoris Fontis-Ebraudi.* In *Les deux vies de Robert d'Arbrissel, fondateur de Fontevraud: légendes, écrits et témoignages.* Ed. Jacques Dalarun, Geneviève Giordanego, Armelle Le Huërou, Jean Longère, Dominique Poirel, and Bruce L. Venarde. Disciplina monastica 4. Turnhout: Brepols, 2006. 127–187.

Bede. *Historia ecclesiastica.* Ed. and trans. Bertram Colgrave and R. A. B. Mynors, *Bede's Ecclesiastical History of the English People.* Oxford: Clarendon Press, 1969.

———. *In die festo sanctae Scholasticae virginis.* PL 94: 480–489.

Beleth, Johannes. *Summa de ecclesiasticis officiis.* Ed. Heribert Douteil. CCCM 41A. Turnhout: Brepols, 1976.

Bernard of Clairvaux. *On the Song of Songs.* Trans. Kilian Walsh and Irene M. Edmonds. 4 vols. Cistercian Fathers Series 4, 7, 31, 40. Kalamazoo, Mich.: Cistercian Publications, 1971–1980.

———. *Sancti Bernardi Opera.* Ed. J. Leclercq, C. H. Talbot, and H. M. Rochais. 8 vols. Rome: Editiones Cistercienses, 1957–1998.

Bernold of Constance. *Chronicon.* Ed. Ian Stuart Robinson, trans. Ian Stuart Robinson and Helga Robinson-Hammerstein in *Bertholds und Bernolds Chroniken.* Ausgewählte Quellen zur deutschen Geschichte des Mittelalters 14. Darmstadt: Wissenschaftliche Buchgesellschaft, 2002. 279–433.

Bertha of Vilich. *Vita Adelheidis abbatissae Vilicensis.* Ed. Oswald Holder-Egger. MGH SS 15.2. Hannover: Hahn, 1888. 754–763.

Bertharius of Monte Cassino. *Vita s. Scholasticae Virginis.* PL 126: 979–988.

Bible moralisée: Codex Vindobonensis 2554, Vienna, Österreichische Nationalbibliothek. Commentary and trans. Gerald B. Guest. London: Harvey Miller, 1995.

Book of Cerne. The Prayer Book of Aedelualds the Bishop, Commonly Called the Book of Cerne. Ed. A. B. Kuypers. Cambridge: Cambridge University Press, 1902.

The Book of St. Gilbert. Ed. and trans. Raymonde Foreville and Gillian Keir. Oxford: Clarendon Press, 1987.

Caesarius of Arles. *Caesarii Arelatensis Opera*, I: Sermones. Ed. Germain Morin. CCSL 103. Turnhout: Brepols, 1953.

———. *Regula sanctarum virginum.* Ed. Adalbert de Vogüé and Joël Courreau, *Césaire d'Arles, Œuvres monastiques, I: Oeuvres pour les moniales.* Sources chrétiennes 345. Paris: Cerf, 1988. 170–273. Trans. Maria Caritas McCarthy. *The Rule for Nuns of St. Caesarius of Arles: A Translation with a Critical Introduction.* Washington, D.C.: Catholic University of America Press, 1960.

———. *Testamentum.* Ed. and trans. Adalbert de Vogüé and Joël Courreau, *Césaire d'Arles, Œuvres monastiques, II. Oeuvres pour les moines.* Sources chrétiennes 398. Paris: Editions du Cerf, 1994. 379–397. Trans. William E. Klingshirn. *Caesarius of Arles: Life, Testament, Letters.* Liverpool: Liverpool University Press, 1994. 71–76.

———. *Vereor (Epist. 21).* Ed. Adalbert de Vogüé and Joël Courreau, *Césaire d'Arles, Œuvres monastiques, I: Oeuvres pour les moniales.* Sources chrétiennes 345. Paris: Cerf, 1988. 294–337. Trans. William E. Klingshirn. *Caesarius of Arles: Life, Testament, Letters.* Liverpool: Liverpool University Press, 1994. 129–139.

Caesarius of Heisterbach. *Dialogus miraculorum.* Ed. Josephus Strange. 2 vols. Cologne: J. M. Heberle, 1851. Trans. H. von E. Scott and C. C. Swinton Bland, *The Dialogue on Miracles.* 2 vols. London: G. Routledge, 1929.

Capitulare de monasterio S. Crucis Pictavensi (822–824). Ed. Alfred Boretius. MGH Capit. 1. Hannover: Hahn, 1883. 302.

Capitulare ecclestiastica ad Salz data a. 803–804. Ed. Alfred Boretius. MGH Capit. 1. Hannover: Hahn, 1883. 119–120.

Capitulare missorum generale. Ed. Alfred Boretius. MGH Capit. 1. Hannover: Hahn, 1883. 91–99.

Le cartulaire de Marcigny-sur-Loire (1045–1144): Essai de reconstruction d'un manuscrit disparu. Ed. Jean Richard. Dijon: Société des Analecta Burgundica, 1957.

Cassian, John. *De institutis coenobiorum.* Ed. and trans. Jean-Claude Guy, *Institutions cénobitiques.* Sources chrétiennes 109. Paris: Éditions du Cerf, 1965. Rev. and repr. 2001.

Casus monasterii Petrishusensis. Ed. Georg Pertz. MGH SS 20. Hannover: Hahn, 1868. 621–683.

Chaucer. *The Canterbury Tales.* Ed. Larry D. Benson in *The Riverside Chaucer.* 3rd ed. Oxford: Oxford University Press, 1987. 23–328

Chronicon Beccensis Abbatiae. PL 150: 639–690.

Chronicon Lippoldsbergense. Ed. Wilhelm Arndt. MGH SS 20. Hannover: Hahn, 1868. 546–558.

Clement of Alexandria. *Paedagogus.* Ed. and trans. Claude Mondésert and Chantal Matray. *Le Pedagogue*, III. Sources chrétiennes 158. Paris: Éditions du Cerf, 1970.

Le Codex Guta-Sintram: manuscrit 37 de la Bibliothèque du Grand séminaire de Strasbourg. Ed. Béatrice Weis. 2 vols. Lucerne: Editions Fac-similés, 1983.

Conrad of Eberbach. *Exordium magnum cisterciense.* Ed. Bruno Griesser. CCCM 138. Turnhout: Brepols, 1994. Trans. Benedicta Ward. *The Great Beginning of Cîteaux: A Narrative of the Beginning of the Cistercian Order.* Cistercian Fathers Series 72. Collegeville, Minn.: Liturgical Press, 2012.

Die Consuetudines des Augustiner-Chorherrenstiftes Marbach im Elsass (12. Jahrhundert). Ed. Josef Siegwart. Fribourg: Universitätsverlag, 1965.

Damasus. *Epigrammata Damasiana.* Ed. Antonius Ferrua. Rome: Pontificio Istituto di archeologia cristiana, 1942.

De S. Theodora, virgine, quae et Christina dicitur. Ed. and trans. C. H. Talbot, *The Life of Christina of Markyate, A Twelfth Century Recluse.* Oxford: Clarendon Press, 1959; repr. 1998. Trans. C. H. Talbot (rev. Samuel Fanous and Henrietta Leyser), *The Life of Christina of Markyate.* Oxford: Oxford University Press, 2008.

De vita beatae Mariae Magdalenae et sororis ejus sanctae Marthae. PL 112: 1431–1506. Trans. David Mycoff. *The Life of Saint Mary Magdalene and of her Sister Saint Martha: A Medieval Biography.* Cistercian Studies Series 108. Kalamazoo, Mich.: Cistercian Publications, 1989.

Decrees of the Ecumenical Councils. Ed. and trans. Norman P. Tanner. 2 vols. Washington, D.C.: Georgetown University Press, 1990.

Dendle, Peter J. "The Old English 'Life of Malchus' and Two Vernacular Tales from the *Vitas Patrum* in MS Cotton Otho C.i: A Translation (Part 1)." *English Studies* 90 (2009): 505–517.

———. "The Old English 'Life of Malchus' and Two Vernacular Tales from the *Vitas Patrum* in MS Cotton Otho C.i: A Translation (Part 2)." *English Studies* 90 (2009): 631–652.

The Desert Fathers: Sayings of the Early Christian Monks. Trans. Benedicta Ward. London: Penguin Books, 2003.

Les deux vies de Robert d'Arbrissel, fondateur de Fontevraud: légendes, écrits et témoignages. Ed. Jacques Dalarun, Geneviève Giordanego, Armelle Le Huërou, Jean Longère, Dominique Poirel, and Bruce L. Venarde. Disciplina monastica 4. Turnhout: Brepols, 2006.

Donatus. *Regula ad virgines.* Ed. Adalbert de Vogüé, "La règle de Donat pour l'abbesse Gauthstrude." *Benedictina* 25 (1978): 219–313. Trans. Jo Ann McNamara and John Halborg in *The Ordeal of Community.* Toronto: Peregrina, 1990. 32–73.

Donizone. *Vita Mathildis.* Ed. and trans. (Italian and Latin) Paolo Golinelli. *Vita di Matilde di Canossa.* Milan: Jaca Book, 2008.

Eadmer. *Vita sancti Anselmi.* Ed. and trans. R. W. Southern. *The Life of St. Anselm, Archbishop of Canterbury.* London: Thomas Nelson, 1962.

Eberwin of Steinfeld. *Epistola ad S. Bernardum.* PL 182: 676–680.

Einhard. *Vita Karoli Magni.* Ed. O. Holder-Egger. MGH SS rer. Germ. 25. Hannover: Hahn, 1911. Trans. Thomas F. X. Noble in *Charlemagne and Louis the Pious: The Lives by Einhard, Notker, Ermoldus, Thegan, and the Astronomer.* University Park: Pennsylvania State University Press, 2009. 21–50.

Ekbert of Schönau. *Epistola Eckeberti ad cognatas suas de obitu domine Elisabeth.* Ed. F. W. E. Roth. Brünn: Verlag der Studien aus dem Benedictiner- und Cistercienser-Orden, 1884. 263–78. Trans. Anne L. Clark in *Elisabeth of Schönau: The Complete Works.* New York: Paulist Press, 2000. 255–273.

Elisabeth of Schönau. *Die Visionen der hl. Elisabeth und die Schriften der Äbte Ekbert und Emecho von Schönau.* Ed. F. W. E. Roth. Brünn: Verlag der Studien aus dem Benedictiner- und Cistercienser-Orden, 1884. Trans. Anne L. Clark, *Elisabeth of Schönau: The Complete Works.* New York: Paulist Press, 2000.

Emecho of Schönau. *Vita Eckeberti*. Ed. S. Widmann in *Neues Archiv der Gesellschaft für ältere deutsche Geschichtskunde* 11 (1886): 447–454.

Engelmodus of Soissons. *Ad Ratbertum Abbatem*. Ed. Ludwig Traube. MGH Poetae 3. Berlin: Weidmann, 1896. 62–66.

Epiphanius of Salamis. *The Panarion of Epiphanius of Salamis*. Trans. Frank Williams. 2 vols. Leiden: E.J. Brill, 1987–1994.

Eusebius of Caesarea. *Ecclesiastical History*. Trans. J. E. L. Oulton and Kirsopp Lake. 2 vols. Loeb Classical Library 153, 265. Cambridge, Mass.: Harvard University Press, 2014.

Felix. *Vita Sancti Guthlaci*. Ed. and trans. Bertram Colgrave. *Felix's Life of Saint Guthlac*. Cambridge: Cambridge University Press, 1956.

First Corinthians: A New Translation with Introduction and Commentary. Trans. Joseph A. Fitzmyer. New Haven, Conn.: Yale University Press, 2008.

Florentius. *Vita Rusticulae*. Ed. Bruno Krusch. MGH SS rer. Merov. 4. Hannover: Hahn, 1902. 337–351. Trans. Jo Ann McNamara and John E. Halborg with E. Gordon Whatley in *Sainted Women of the Dark Ages*. Durham, N.C.: Duke University Press, 1992. 119–136.

Fructuosus of Braga. *Regula monastica communis*. PL 87: 1109–1127. Trans. Claude W. Barlow. *Iberian Fathers*. The Fathers of the Church, 62, 63, 99. 3 vols. Washington, D.C.: Catholic University of America Press, 1969–1999. II, 176–206.

Fundatio monasterii sanctae Mariae Andernacensis. Ed. Oswald Holder-Egger. MGH SS 15.2. Hannover: Hahn, 1888. 968–970.

Gennadius of Marseilles. *De viris inlustribus*. Ed. Ernest Cushing Richardson, *Texte und Untersuchungen zur Geschichte der altchristlichen Literatur*. 14.1. Leipzig: J. C. Hinrichs, 1896.

Geoffrey Grossus. *Vita Beati Bernardi Fundatoris Congregationis de Tironio*. PL 172: 1363–1446. Trans. Ruth Harwood Cline, *The Life of Blessed Bernard of Tiron*. Washington, D.C.: Catholic University of America Press, 2009.

Geoffrey of Vendôme. *Epistola ad Robertum*. In *Les deux vies de Robert d'Arbrissel, fondateur de Fontevraud: légendes, écrits et témoignages*. Ed. Jacques Dalarun, Geneviève Giordanego, Armelle Le Huërou, Jean Longère, Dominique Poirel, and Bruce L. Venarde. Disciplina monastica 4. Turnhout: Brepols, 2006. 568–577.

——. *Geoffroy de Vendôme. Oeuvres*. Ed. and trans. Geneviève Giordanengo. Turnhout: Brepols, 1996.

Gerald of Wales. *Gemma ecclesiastica*. Ed. J. S. Brewer in J. S. Brewer, James F. Dimock, and George F. Warner, eds., *Giraldi Cambrensis opera*. II. *Gemma ecclesiastica*. London: Longman, 1862. Trans. John J. Hagen. *The Jewel of the Church: A Translation of Gemma ecclesiastica by Giraldus Cambrensis*. Davis Medieval Texts and Studies, 2. Leiden: Brill, 1979.

——. *Itinerarium Kambriae*. Ed. James F. Dimock in J. S. Brewer, James F. Dimock, and George F. Warner, eds., *Giraldi Cambrensis opera*. VI. London: Longman, 1868. 1–152. Trans. Lewis Thorpe, *The Journey Through Wales and The Description of Wales*. Harmondsworth: Penguin, 1978.

Gerhoch of Reichersberg. *Commentarius aureus in psalmos et cantica ferialia*. PL 193: 619–1814.

——. *Epistola Gerhohi ad quasdam sanctimoniales*. In Christina Lutter, *Geschlecht und Wissen, Norm und Praxis, Lesen und Schreiben: Monastische Reformgemeinschaften im 12. Jahrhundert*. Veröffentlichung des Instituts für österreichische Geschichtsforschung, 43. Vienna: Oldenbourg, 2005. 230–234.

Gilbert Crispin. *Vita Herluini*. Ed. Anna Sapir Abulafia and G. R. Evans. *The Works of Gilbert Crispin, Abbot of Westminster*. Auctores Britannici Medii Aevi 8. London: Published for the British Academy by the Oxford University Press, 1986. 185–212. Trans. Sally N. Vaughn in *The Abbey of Bec and the Anglo-Norman State, 1034–1136*. Woodbridge: Boydell Press, 1981. 67–86.

Gilo. *Vita sancti Hugonis abbatis*. Ed. H. E. J. Cowdrey in "Two Studies in Cluniac History 1049–1126." *Studi Gregoriani* 11 (1978): 1–298. 43–109.

Goscelin of St. Bertin. *Liber confortatorius*. Ed. C. H. Talbot, "The *Liber confortatorius* of Goscelin of Saint Bertin." *Studia Anselmiana* 37 (1955): 1–117. Trans. Monika Otter, *The Book of Encouragement and Consolation [Liber confortatorius]: The Letter of Goscelin to the Recluse Eva*. Cambridge: D. S. Brewer, 2004.

———. *Vita beate Sexburge regina*. Ed. and trans. Rosalind C. Love in *The Hagiography of the Female Saints of Ely*. Oxford Medieval Texts. Oxford: Oxford University Press, 2004. 133–189.

———. *Vita et virtutes sanctae Ethelburgae virginis*. Ed. M. L. Colker in "Texts of Jocelyn of Canterbury Which Relate to the History of Barking Abbey." *Studia Monastica* 7 (1965): 383–460. 398–417.

———. *Vita s. Edithae*. Ed. A. Wilmart, "La légende de Ste Édith en prose et vers par le moine Goscelin. I." *Analecta Bollandiana* 56 (1938): 5–101. Trans. Michael Wright and Kathleen Loncar in Stephanie Hollis, ed., *Writing the Wilton Women: Goscelin's Legend of Edith and Liber confortatorius*. Medieval Women: Texts and Contexts 9. Turnhout: Brepols, 2004. 17–67.

———. *Vita sancti Wlsini Episcopi et Confessoris*. Ed. C. H. Talbot, "The Life of St Wulsin of Sherborne by Goscelin." *Revue Bénédictine* 69 (1959): 68–85.

Goswin of Bossut. *Vita Abundi*. Ed. A. M. Frenken, "De vita van Abundus van Hoei." *Cîteaux* 10 (1959): 5–33. Trans. Martinus Cawley in *Send Me God: The Lives of Ida the Compassionate of Nivelles, Nun of La Ramée, Arnulf, Lay Brother of Villers, and Abundus, Monk of Villers*. Turnhout: Brepols, 2003. 209–246.

Gratian. *Decretum*. Ed. Emil Friedberg. *Corpus Iuris canonici, I: Decretum magistri Gratiani*. Leipzig: B. Tauchnitz, 1879. Repr. Graz: Akademische Druck-u. Verlagsanstalt, 1959.

Gregory of Nyssa. *De anima et resurrectione*. Trans. William Moore and Henry Austin Wilson in *Selected Writings and Letters of Gregory, Bishop of Nyssa*. Nicene and Post-Nicene Fathers. 2nd ser. Vol. 5. Ed. Philip Schaff and Henry Wallace. Grand Rapids, Mich.: Eerdmans, 1954. 430–468.

———. *The Life of Macrina*. Ed. and trans. Pierre Maraval, *Vie de sainte Macrine*. Sources chrétiennes 178. Paris: Éditions du Cerf, 1971. Trans. Joan M. Petersen in *Handmaids of the Lord: Contemporary Descriptions of Feminine Asceticism in the First Six Christian Centuries*. Cistercian Studies Series 143. Kalamazoo, Mich.: Cistercian Publications, 1996. 51–86.

Gregory of Tours. *Decem libri Historiarum*. Ed. Bruno Krusch and Wilhelm Levison. MGH SS rer. Merov. 1.1. Hannover: Hahn, 1951. Trans. Lewis Thorpe, *The History of the Franks*. Harmondsworth: Penguin, 1974.

———. *Liber in gloria confessorum*. Ed. Bruno Krusch. MGH SS rer. Merov. 1.2. Hannover: Hahn, 1885. 294–370.

———. *Liber vitae patrum*. Ed. Bruno Krusch. MGH SS rer. Merov. 1.2. Hannover: Hahn, 1885. 211–294. Trans. Edward James. *Gregory of Tours: Life of the Fathers*. 2nd ed. Liverpool: Liverpool University Press, 1991.

Gregory the Great. *Dialogues*. Ed. Adalbert de Vogüé. 3 vols. Sources chrétiennes 251, 260, 265. Paris: Éditions du Cerf, 1978–1980. Trans. Odo John Zimmerman, *Dialogues*. Fathers of the Church 39. Washington, D.C.: The Catholic University of America Press, 1959; repr. 1983.

———. *Moralia in Job*. Ed. Mark Adriaen. CCSL 143, 143A, 143B. 3 vols. Turnhout: Brepols, 1979–1985.

———. *Registrum epistularum*. Ed. Dag Norberg. CCSL 140-140A. 2 vols. Turnhout: Brepols, 1982. Trans. John R.C. Martyn, *The Letters of Gregory the Great*. 3 vols. Toronto: Pontifical Institute of Mediaeval Studies, 2004.

Gregory VII. *Das Register Gregors VII*. Ed. Erich Caspar. 2 vols. MGH Epp. sel. 2.1–2.2. Berlin: Weidmann, 1920–1923.

Guibert de Gembloux. *Guiberti Gemblacensis epistolae: quae in codice B.R. BRUX. 5527–5534 inveniuntur*. Ed. Albert Derolez. CCCM 66, 66A, 2 vols. Turnhout: Brepols. 1988–1989.

Guibert of Nogent. *De virginitate*. PL 156: 579–608.

———. *De vita sua*. Ed. Georges Bourgin, *Guibert de Nogent: histoire de sa vie, 1053–1124*. Paris: A. Picard et fils, 1907. Trans. John F. Benton, *Self and Society in Medieval France: The Memoirs of Abbot Guibert of Nogent*. Toronto: University of Toronto Press in association with the Medieval Academy of America, 1984.

———. *Monodiae*. Ed. Edmond-René Labande. *Autobiographie*. Paris: Belles Lettres, 1981. Trans. Paul J. Archambault. *A Monk's Confession: The Memoirs of Guibert of Nogent*. University Park: Pennsylvania State University Press, 1996.

Guidance for Women in Twelfth-Century Convents. Trans. Vera Morton. Cambridge: D. S. Brewer, 2003.

Guigues de Châtel. *Ad Durbonenses fratres*. Ed. M. Laporte in *Lettres des premiers chartreux: introductions, texte critique, traduction et notes*, I : *S. Bruno. Guigues. S. Anthelme*. Sources chrétiennes 88. Paris: Éditions du Cerf, 1962. 214–219.

Haimo of Auxerre. *In Epistolam I Ad Corinthios*. PL 117: 507–606.

Haimo. *Vita Willihelmi abbatis Hirsaugiensis*. Ed. W. Wattenbach. MGH SS 12. Hannover: Hahn, 1856. 209–225.

Haito of Basel. *Capitula*. Ed. Peter Brommer. MGH Capit. episc. I. Hannover: Hahn, 1984. 203–219.

Heloise and Abelard. *Problemata*. PL 178: 677–730. Trans. Mary Martin McLaughlin with Bonnie Wheeler in *The Letters of Heloise and Abelard: A Translation of Their Collected Correspondence and Related Writings*. New York: Palgrave Macmillan, 2009. 213–267.

Heloise. See Abelard and Heloise.

Herman of Tournai. *De miraculis S. Mariae Laudunensis*. PL 156: 961–1018. Selections trans. Theodore J. Antry and Carol Neel in *Norbert and Early Norbertine Spirituality*. New York: Paulist Press, 2007. 69–84.

———. *Liber de restauratione monasterii Sancti Martini Tornacensis*. Ed. Georg Waitz. MGH SS 14. Hannover: Hahn, 1883. 274–317. Trans. Lynn H. Nelson, *The Restoration of the Monastery of Saint Martin of Tournai*. Washington, D.C.: Catholic University of America Press, 1996.

Herrad of Hohenbourg. *Hortus deliciarum*. Ed. Rosalie Green, Michael Evans, Christine Bischoff, and Michael Curschmann. 2 vols. London: Warburg Institute, 1979.

Hervé de Bourg-Dieu. *Commentaria in Epistolas divi Pauli: In Epistolam I ad Corinthios*. PL 181: 813–1002.

Hieronymus noster. PL 22: 175–184.

Hildebert of Lavardin. *Carmina minora*. Ed. A. Brian Scott. Leipzig: Teubner, 1969.

———. *Epistolae*. PL 171: 135–311.

———. *Vita beate Marie Egiptiace*. Ed. Norbert Klaus Larsen. CCCM 209. Turnhout: Brepols, 2004. Trans. Ronald Pepin and Hugh Feiss in *Saint Mary of Egypt: Three Medieval Lives in Verse*. Cistercian Studies Series 209. Kalamazoo, Mich.: Cistercian Publications, 2005. 73–114.

Hildegard of Bingen. *Epistolae*. Ed. L. Van Acker, *Hildegardis Bingensis Epistolarium*. 3 vols. CCCM 91, 91A, 91B (co-ed. M. Klaes-Hachmöller). Turnhout: Brepols, 1991. Trans. Joseph L. Baird and Radd K. Ehrman, *The Letters of Hildegard of Bingen*, 3 vols. New York: Oxford University Press, 1994–2004.

———. *Explanatio symboli sancti Athanasii*. PL 197: 1065–1082.

———. *Symphonia armonie celestium revelationum*. Ed. and trans. Barbara Newman. *Symphonia: A Critical Edition of the Symphonia armonie celestium revelationum*. 2nd ed. Ithaca, N.Y.: Cornell University Press, 1998.

Hincmar of Reims. *Coronatio Iudithae Karoli II filiae*. Ed. Georg Pertz. MGH LL I. Hannover: Hahn, 1835. 450–451.

Hrabanus Maurus. *Epistola Rabani in Librum Hester*. Ed. Ernest Dümmler. MGH Poetae, 2. Berlin: Weidmann, 1884. 167–168.

———. *Expositio in Librum Esther*. PL 109: 635–670.

Hugh of Cluny. *Scriptum quoddam commonitorium sive deprecatorium ad successores suos pro sanctimonialibus Marciniacensibus*. Ed. H. E. J. Cowdrey in "Two Studies in Cluniac History 1049–1126." *Studi Gregoriani* 11 (1978): 1–298. 170–172.

Hugh of Fleury. *Ex historia ecclesiastica*. Ed. Georg Waitz. MGH SS 9. Hannover: Hahn, 1851. 349–364.

Hymn Collections from the Paraclete. Ed. Chrysogonus Waddell. 2 vols. Cistercian Liturgy Series 8–9. Trappist, Ky: Gethsemani Abbey, 1987–1989.

Idung of Prüfening. *Le moine Idung et ses deux ouvrages: "Argumentum super quatuor questionibus" et "Dialogus duorum monachorum."* Ed. R. B. C. Huygens. Spoleto: Centro Italiano di Studi sull'Alto Medioevo, 1980. Trans. Jeremiah F. O'Sullivan, Joseph Leahey, and Grace Perrigo, *Cistercians and Cluniacs: The Case for Cîteaux*. Kalamazoo, Mich.: Cistercian Publications, 1977.

Institutio sanctimonialium Aquisgranensis. Ed. Albert Werminghoff. MGH Conc. 2.1. Hannover: Hahn, 1906. 421–456.

Inuentio et Miracula sancti Vulfranni. Ed. Dom J. Laporte. Société de l'histoire de Normandie, *Mélanges*, 14. Rouen: Librairie de la Société, 1938.

Irimbert of Admont. *De incendio monasterii sui*. In Christina Lutter, *Geschlecht und Wissen, Norm und Praxis, Lesen und Schreiben: Monastische Reformgemeinschaften im 12. Jahrhundert*. Veröffentlichung des Instituts für österreichische Geschichtsforschung, 43. Vienna: Oldenbourg, 2005. 222–225.

Isidore of Seville. *De fide catholica contra Judaeos*. PL 83: 449–538.

Ivo of Chartres. *Correspondance*. Vol. 1. Ed. and trans. Jean Leclercq. Paris: Belles Lettres, 1949.

Jacobus de Voragine. *Legenda Aurea*. Trans. William Granger Ryan, *The Golden Legend: Readings on the Saints*. Princeton, N.J.: Princeton University Press, 2012.

Jacques de Vitry. *Vita B. Mariae Oigniacensis*. AA SS, June, 4: 636–666. Trans. Margot H. King in *Mary of Oignies: Mother of Salvation*. Ed. Anneke B. Mulder-Bakker. Medieval Women: Texts and Contexts 7. Turnhout: Brepols, 2006. 39–127.

Jerome. *Adversus Jovinianum.* PL 23: 211–338. Trans. W. H. Fremantle, G. Lewis, and W. G. Martley. *Jerome: Letters and Select Works.* Nicene and Post-Nicene Fathers. 2nd ser. Vol. 6. Ed. Philip Schaff and Henry Wallace. Buffalo, N.Y.: Christian Literature Publishing Co., 1893; repr. New York: Cosimo Classics, 2007. 346–416.

———. *Adversus Vigilantium.* Ed. J.-L. Feiertag. CCSL 79C. Turnhout: Brepols, 2005. Trans. W. H. Fremantle, G. Lewis, and W. G. Martley. *Jerome: Letters and Select Works.* Nicene and Post-Nicene Fathers. 2nd ser. Vol. 6. Ed. Philip Schaff and Henry Wallace. Buffalo, N.Y.: Christian Literature Publishing Co., 1893; repr. New York: Cosimo Classics, 2007. 417–423.

———. *Commentariorum in Esaiam.* Ed. Marc Adriaen. 2 vols. CCSL 73, 73A. Turnhout: Brepols, 1963.

———. *Commentariorum in Sophoniam prophetam.* Ed. Marc Adriaen in *Commentarii in prophetas minores.* CCSL 76A. Turnhout: Brepols, 1970. 655–711.

———. *Commentarius in Ecclesiasten.* Ed. Marc Adriaen. In *S. Hieronymi presbyteri opera. Pars I: Opera exegetica I.* CCSL 72. Turnhout: Brepols, 1959. 247–361.

———. *De viris illustribus.* PL 23: 597–716.

———. *Epist.* 52. Ed. and trans. Andrew Cain, *Jerome and the Monastic Clergy: A Commentary on Letter 52 to Nepotian, with Introduction, Text, and Translation.* Leiden: Brill, 2013.

———. *Epitaphium Sanctae Paulae.* Ed. and trans. Andrew Cain, *Jerome's Epitaph on Paula: A Commentary on the* Epitaphium Sanctae Paulae. Oxford Early Christian Texts Series. Oxford: Oxford University Press, 2013.

———. *Jerome: Letters and Select Works.* Trans. W. H. Fremantle, G. Lewis, and W. G. Martley. Nicene and Post-Nicene Fathers. 2nd ser. Vol. 6. Ed. Philip Schaff and Henry Wallace. Buffalo, N.Y.: Christian Literature Publishing Co., 1893; repr. New York: Cosimo Classics, 2007.

———. *Sancti Evsebii Hieronymi Epistulae.* Ed. Isidore Hilberg. CSEL 54–56. 3 vols. in 4. Vienna: F. Tempsky, 1910–1918. Trans. W. H. Fremantle, G. Lewis, and W. G. Martley. *Jerome: Letters and Select Works.* Nicene and Post-Nicene Fathers. 2nd ser. Vol. 6. Ed. Philip Schaff and Henry Wallace. Buffalo, N.Y.: Christian Literature Publishing Co., 1893; repr. New York: Cosimo Classics, 2007. 1–295.

———. *Vita Hilarionis.* Ed. Edgardo Martín Morales and trans. Pierre Leclerc in *Trois vies de moines (Paul, Malchus, Hilarion).* Sources chrétiennes 508. Paris: Cerf, 2007. 212–299.

———. *[Vita Malchi] De Monacho captivo.* Ed. and trans. Christa Gray, *Jerome, Vita Malchi: Introduction, Text, Translation, and Commentary.* Oxford: Oxford University Press, 2015.

Jutta and Hildegard: The Biographical Sources. Ed. and trans. Anna Silvas. Medieval Women: Texts and Contexts 1. Turnhout: Brepols, 1998.

Leander of Seville. *De institutione virginum.* PL 72: 873–894. Trans. Claude W. Barlow in *Iberian Fathers,* 3 vols. The Fathers of the Church, vols. 62, 63, 99. Washington, D.C.: Catholic University of America Press, 1969–1999. I, 183–228.

Libellus de diversis ordinibus et professionibus qui sunt in aecclesia. Ed. and trans. G. Constable and B. Smith. Oxford: Clarendon Press, 1972.

Liber de modo bene vivendi, ad sororem. PL 184: 1199–1306.

Liber pontificalis. Ed. Theodore Mommsen. MGH Gesta pontificum Romanorum 1. Berlin: Weidmann, 1898. Trans. Raymond Davis. *The Book of Pontiffs (Liber pontificalis): The Ancient Biographies of the First Ninety Roman Bishops to A.D. 715.* 3rd ed. Liverpool: Liverpool University Press, 2010.

"The Life of St. Scholastica in the *South English Legendary*." Ed. E. Gordon Whatley with Anne B. Thompson and Robert K. Upchurch in *Saints' Lives in Middle English Collections*. Kalamazoo, Mich.: Medieval Institute Publications for TEAMS, 2004. 199–212.

Mainzer Urkundenbuch. I. Die Urkunden bis zum Tode Erzbischof Adalberts I. (1137). Ed. Manfred Stimming. Darmstadt: Verlag der Hessischen Historischen Kommission, 1932.

Mainzer Urkundenbuch. II. Die Urkunden seit dem Tode Erzbischof Adalberts I. (1137) bis zum Tode Erzbischof Konrads (1200). 2 vols. Ed. Peter Acht. Darmstadt: Verlag der Hessischen Historischen Kommission, 1968–1971.

Maniacoria, Nicolò. *Sancti Eusebii Hieronymi vita*. PL 22: 183–202.

Marbode of Rennes. *Epistola ad Robertum*. In *Les deux vies de Robert d'Arbrissel, fondateur de Fontevraud: légendes, écrits et témoignages*. Ed. Jacques Dalarun, Geneviève Giordanego, Armelle Le Huërou, Jean Longère, Dominique Poirel, and Bruce L. Venarde. Disciplina monastica 4. Turnhout: Brepols, 2006. 526–557.

———. *Liber decem capitulorum*. Ed. Rosario Leotta. Rome: Herder, 1984.

McCracken, George E., and Allen Cabaniss, eds. and trans. *Early Medieval Theology*. Philadelphia: Westminster Press, 1957.

Odilo of Cluny. *Epitaphium Adalheide Imperatricis*. PL 142: 963–992. Trans. Sean Gilsdorf, *Queenship and Sanctity: The Lives of Mathilda and The Epitaph of Adelheid*. Washington, D.C.: Catholic University of America Press, 2004. 128–143.

———. *Sermo 12. De Assumptione Dei genitricis Mariae*. PL 142: 1023–1028.

Origen. *Contra Celsum*. Trans. Henry Chadwick. 2nd ed. Cambridge: Cambridge University Press, 1980.

Ortlieb. *De fundatione monasterii Zwivildensis libri II*. Ed. Ottone Abel. MGH SS 10. Hannover: Hahn, 1852. 64–92.

Osbert of Clare. *The Letters of Osbert of Clare, Prior of Westminster*. Ed. E. W. Williamson. London: Oxford University Press, 1929.

Otto of Freising and Rahewin. *Gesta Friderici I. imperatoris*. Ed. Roger Wilmans. MGH SS 20. Hannover: Hahn, 1868. 338–496.

Pachomian Koinonia. Trans. Armand Veilleux. 3 vols. Cistercian Studies Series 45–47. Kalamazoo, Mich.: Cistercian Publications, 1980–1982.

Palladius. *The Lausiac History*. Trans. Robert T. Meyer. Westminster, Md.: Newman Press, 1965.

The Paraclete Statutes. Institutiones nostrae: Troyes, Bibliothèque municipale, Ms. 802, ff. 89r–90v. Ed. Chrysogonus Waddell. Cistercian Liturgy Series 20. Trappist, Ky.: Gethsemani Abbey, 1987.

Paschasius Radbertus. *Charlemagne's Cousins: Contemporary Lives of Adalard and Wala*. Trans. Allen Cabaniss. Syracuse, N.Y.: Syracuse University Press, 1967.

———. *De assumptione Sanctae Mariae virginis*. Ed. Albert Ripberger. CCCM 56C. Turnhout: Brepols, 1985. 109–162.

———. *De partu virginis*. Ed. E. Ann Matter. CCCM 56C. Turnhout: Brepols, 1985. 47–89.

———. *Expositio in Psalmum XLIV*. Ed. Bede Paulus. CCCM 94. Turnhout: Brepols, 1991.

Passio Sanctarum Perpetuae et Felicitatis. Ed. and trans. Thomas J. Heffernan, *The Passion of Perpetua and Felicity*. New York: Oxford University Press, 2012.

Paul of Bernried. *Vita b. Herlucae. AA SS*, April, 2: 552–557.

———. *Vita Gregorii*. Ed. and trans. I. S. Robinson in *The Papal Reform of the Eleventh Century: Lives of Pope Leo IX and Pope Gregory VII*. Manchester: Manchester University Press, 2004. 262–364.

Paulinus of Milan. *Vita Ambrosii*. PL 14: 27–46. Trans. Boniface Ramsey in *Ambrose. The Early Church Fathers*. New York: Routledge, 1997. 196–218.

Paulinus of Nola. *The Poems of St. Paulinus of Nola*. Trans. P. G. Walsh. New York: Newman Press, 1975.

Peter Damian. *Die Briefe des Petrus Damiani*. Ed. Kurt Reindel. MGH Briefe d. dt. Kaiserzeit. 4 vols. Munich: Monumenta Germaniae Historica, 1983–1993. Trans. Owen J. Blum, *The Letters of Peter Damian*. Fathers of the Church. Mediaeval continuation, 1–3, 5–7. 6 vols. Washington, D.C.: Catholic University of America Press, 1989–2005.

Peter of Blois. *The Later Letters of Peter of Blois*. Ed. Elizabeth Revell. Oxford: Oxford University, 1993.

Peter the Venerable. *In honore sanctae Mariae Magdalenae hymnus*. PL 189: 1019.

————. *The Letters of Peter the Venerable*. Ed. Giles Constable. 2 vols. Cambridge, Mass.: Harvard University Press, 1967.

Plerosque nimirum. PL 22: 201–214.

Possidius. *Vita Augustini*. PL 32: 33–66. Trans. F. R. Hoare in *Soldiers of Christ: Saints and Saints' Lives from Late Antiquity and the Early Middle Ages*. Ed. Thomas F. X. Noble and Thomas Head. University Park: Pennsylvania State University Press, 1995. 31–73.

Protevangelium of James. Ed. Oscar Cullmann in W. Schneemelcher, ed. and R. McL. Wilson, trans., *New Testament Apocrypha*. Vol. 1. Philadelphia: Westminster Press, 1991. 370–388.

Recueil des Historiens des Gaules et de la France. Ed. M.- J.- J. Brial. Vol. 19. Paris: Victor Palmé, 1830.

Reginald of Canterbury. *Vita sancti Malchi*. Ed. Levi Robert Lind, *The Vita sancti Malchi of Reginald of Canterbury: A Critical Edition with Introduction, Apparatus Criticus, Notes, and Indices*. Urbana: University of Illinois Press, 1942.

Reginald of Durham. *Libellus de vita et miraculis S. Godrici, Heremitae de Finchale*. Ed. Joseph Stevenson. Surtees Society 20. London: Nichols, 1847.

La règle du temple. Ed. Henri de Curzon. Paris: Libraire Renouard, 1886; repr. Paris: H. Champion, 1977. Trans. J. M. Upton-Ward. *Rule of the Templars: the French Text of the Rule of the Order of the Knights Templar*. Woodbridge: Boydell Press, 1992.

Regula cujusdam patris. PL 66: 985–994.

Regularis concordia Anglicae nationis monachorum sanctimonialiumque. Ed. and trans. D. T. Symons, *The Monastic Agreement of the Monks and Nuns of the English Nation*. London: Nelson, 1953.

Die Reinhardsbrunner Briefsammlung. Ed. Friedel Peeck. MGH Epp. sel. 5. Weimar: Hermann Böhlaus Nachfolger, 1952.

Robert of Arbrissel. *Sermo Domni Roberti de Abrussello ad Comitissam Britannię*. In *Les deux vies de Robert d'Arbrissel, fondateur de Fontevraud: légendes, écrits et témoignages*. Ed. Jacques Dalarun, Geneviève Giordanego, Armelle Le Huërou, Jean Longère, Dominique Poirel, and Bruce L. Venarde. Disciplina monastica 4. Turnhout: Brepols, 2006. 460–479.

Robert of Ostrevand. *Vita s. Ayberti*. *AA SS,* April, 1: 669–679.

Rudolf of Fulda. *Vita Leobae abbatissae Biscofesheimensis*. Ed. Georg Waitz. MGH SS 15.1. Hannover: Hahn, 1887. 118–131. Trans. C. H. Talbot in *The Anglo-Saxon Missionaries in Germany*. London: Sheed and Ward, 1954. 205–226.

Sacrorum conciliorum, nova et amplissima collectio. Ed. Joannes Dominicus Mansi. 54 vols. Florence, 1759–1798. Paris: H. Welter, 1901–1927 (reprint and continuation); repr. Graz: Akademische Druck- u. Verlagsanstalt, 1960–1962.

Sermo in veneratione sanctae Mariae Magdalenae. PL 133: 714–721.

Sigeboto. *Vita Paulinae*. Ed. J. R. Dieterich. MGH SS 30.2. Leipzig: Hiersemann, 1934. 910–938. Trans. Camilla Badstübner-Kizik, "Übersetzung der Vita Paulinae des Sigeboto und Kommentar." *Studien und Mitteilungen zur Geschichte des Benediktinerordens und seiner Zweige* 109 (1998): 91–184.

Simeon of Durham. *History of the Church of Durham*. Trans. Joseph Stevenson, *The Historical Works of Simeon of Durham, The Church Historians of England*, 3.2. London: Seeleys, 1855. 621–711.

Speculum virginum. Ed. Jutta Seyfarth. CCCM 5. Turnhout: Brepols, 1990.

"*Speculum virginum*: Selected Excerpts." Trans. Barbara Newman in Constant J. Mews, ed., *Listen, Daughter: The* Speculum virginum *and the Formation of Religious Women in the Middle Ages*. New York: Palgrave, 2001. 269–296.

Stephen of Muret. *Regula*. Ed. Jean Becquet in *Scriptores ordinis Grandimontensis*. CCCM 8. Turnhout: Brepols, 1968. 63–99.

Thomas Becket. *The Correspondence of Thomas Becket, Archbishop of Canterbury, 1162–1170*. 2 vols. Ed. and trans. Anne J. Duggan. Oxford: Clarendon Press, 2000.

Thomas of Cantimpré. *Vita Iohannis Cantipratensis*. Ed. R. Godding, "Une oeuvre inédite de Thomas de Cantimpré, la 'Vita Ioannis Cantipratensis.'" *Revue d'histoire ecclésiastique* 76 (1981): 241–316. Trans. Barbara Newman in *Thomas of Cantimpré: The Collected Saints' Lives. Abbot John of Cantimpré, Christina the Astonishing, Margaret of Ypres, and Lutgard of Aywières*. Medieval Women: Texts and Contexts 19. Turnhout: Brepols, 2008. 57–121.

———. *Vita Lutgardis Aquiriensis*. AA SS, June, 3: 234–263. Trans. Margot H. King and Barbara Newman in *Thomas of Cantimpré: The Collected Saints' Lives. Abbot John of Cantimpré, Christina the Astonishing, Margaret of Ypres, and Lutgard of Aywières*. Medieval Women: Texts and Contexts 19. Turnhout: Brepols, 2008. 211–296.

Die Urkunden Friedrichs I. Ed. Heinrich Appelt. MGH DD F I. Hannover: Hahn, 1975.

Urkundenbuch der Klöster der Grafschaft Mansfeld. Ed. Max Krühne. *Geschichtsquellen der Provinz Sachsen* 20. Halle: Otto Hendel, 1888.

Urkundenbuch für die Geschichte des Niederrheins. Ed. Theodor Joseph Lacomblet. 4 vols. Düsseldorf: J. Wolf, 1840–1858.

van Heussen, Hugo Franciscus. *Historia episcopatuum foederati Belgii, utpote metropolitani Ultrajectini, nec non, suffraganeorum Harlemensis, Daventriensis, Leovardiensis, Groningensis, et Middelburgensis*. 2 vols. Antwerp: J. B. Verdussen, 1733.

Venantius Fortunatus. *De vita sanctae Radegundis libri duo*. (Book 1). Ed. Bruno Krusch. MGH SS rer. Merov. 2. Hannover: Hahn, 1888. 364–377. Trans. Jo Ann McNamara and John E. Halborg with E. Gordon Whatley in *Sainted Women of the Dark Ages*. Durham, N.C.: Duke University Press, 1992. 70–86.

———. *Venantius Fortunatus: Personal and Political Poems*. Trans. Judith George. Liverpool: Liverpool University Press, 1995.

Vie de Christina de Markyate. Ed. Paulette L'Hermitte-Leclercq and Anne-Marie Legras. 2 vols. Paris: CNRS, 2007.

Vita Anselmi episcopi Lucensis. Ed. Roger Wilmans. MGH SS 12. Hannover: Hahn, 1856. 1–35.

Vita Burchardi episcopi. Ed. Georg Waitz. MGH SS 4 Hannover: Hahn, 1816. 829–846.

Vita Caesarii. Ed. and trans. G. Morin. Rev. Marie-José Delage with Marc Heijmans, *Vie de Césaire d'Arles*. Sources chrétiennes 536. Paris: Les Éditions du Cerf, 2010. Trans. William E. Klingshirn in *Caesarius of Arles: Life, Testament, Letters*. Liverpool: Liverpool University Press, 1994. 9–65.

Vita domnae Juttae inclusae. Ed. Franz Staab in "Reform und Reformgruppen im Erzbistum Mainz: Vom 'Libellus de Willigisi consuetudinibus' zur 'Vita domnae Juttae inclusae.'" In Stefan Weinfurter, ed., *Reformidee und Reformpolitik im Spätsalisch-Frühstaufischen Reich: Vorträge der Tagung der Gesellschaft für Mittelrheinische Kirchengeschichte vom 11. bis 13. September 1991 in Trier.* Quellen und Abhandlungen zur mittelrheinischen Kirchengeschichte, 68. Mainz: Selbstverlag der Gesellschaft für Mittelrheinische Kirchengeschichte, 1992. 119–187 (172–187). Trans. Anna Silvas in *Jutta and Hildegard: The Biographical Sources.* Medieval Women: Texts and Contexts 1. Turnhout: Brepols, 1998. 65–84.

Vita Genovefae virginis Parisiensis. Ed. Bruno Krusch. MGH SS rer. Merov. 3. Hannover: Hahn, 1896. 204–38. Trans. Jo Ann McNamara and John E. Halborg with E. Gordon Whatley in *Sainted Women of the Dark Ages.* Durham, N.C.: Duke University Press, 1992. 17–37.

Vita Gundulfi. Ed. Rodney Thomson. *The Life of Gundulf, Bishop of Rochester.* Toronto Medieval Latin texts 7. Toronto: Centre for Medieval Studies, 1977.

Vita S. Eckenberti. Ed. Heinrich Boos in *Quellen zur Geschichte der Stadt Worms,* III: *Monumenta Wormatiensia, Annalen und Chroniken.* Berlin: Weidmann, 1893. 129–142. Trans. David S. Bachrach, *The Histories of a Medieval German City, Worms c. 1000–c. 1300: Translation and Commentary.* Farnham: Ashgate, 2014. 61–79.

Vita S. Gaucherii. Ed. J. Becquet, "La vie de saint Gaucher, fondateur des chanoines réguliers d'Aureil en Limousin." *Revue Mabillon* 54 (1964): 25–55.

Vita S. Hiltrudis virginis. AA SS, September, 7: 461–68.

Vita S. Stephani Obazinensis. Ed. Michel Aubrun, *Vie de saint Étienne d'Obazine.* Clermont-Ferrand: Institut d'études du Massif central, 1970. Trans. Hugh Feiss, Maureen M. O'Brien, and Ronald Pepin in *The Lives of Monastic Reformers. 1, Robert of La Chaise-Dieu and Stephen of Obazine.* Cistercian Studies Series 222. Trappist, Ky.: Cistercian Publications, 2010. 129–255.

Vita Sadalbergae abbatissae Laudunensis. Ed. Bruno Krusch. MGH SS rer. Merov. 5. Hannover: Hahn, 1910. 40–66. Trans. Jo Ann McNamara and John E. Halborg with E. Gordon Whatley in *Sainted Women of the Dark Ages.* Durham, N.C.: Duke University Press, 1992. 176–194.

Vita sanctae Balthildis. Ed. Bruno Krusch. MGH SS rer. Merov. 2. Hannover: Hahn, 1888. 475–508. Trans. Paul Fouracre and Richard A. Gerberding in *Late Merovingian France: History and Hagiography, 640–720.* Manchester: Manchester University Press, 1996. 97–132.

Vita sanctae Geretrudis. Ed. Bruno Krusch. MGH SS rer. Merov. 2. Hannover: Hahn, 1888. 447–474. Trans. Jo Ann McNamara and John E. Halborg with E. Gordon Whatley in *Sainted Women of the Dark Ages.* Durham, N.C.: Duke University Press, 1992. 220–234.

Vita sanctae Hildegardis. Ed. Monica Klaes. CCCM 126. Turnhout: Brepols, 1993. Trans. Anna Silvas in *Jutta and Hildegard: The Biographical Sources.* Medieval Women: Texts and Contexts 1. Turnhout: Brepols, 1998. 135–210.

Walafrid Strabo. *Glossa ordinaria: Epistola I Ad Corinthios.* PL 114: 519–551.

Walther of Arrouaise. *Historia translationis reliquiarum Aroasiam. AA SS,* May, 1: 481–488.

The Warenne (Hyde) Chronicle. Ed. and trans. Elisabeth M. C. van Houts and Rosalind C. Love. Oxford: Oxford University Press, 2013.

Westminster Abbey Charters, 1066–c.1214. Ed. Emma Mason. London Record Society Publications 25. London: London Record Society, 1988.

William of St. Thierry. *Vita prima Bernardi.* PL 185: 225–368. Trans. Geoffrey Webb and Adrian Walker, *St. Bernard of Clairvaux.* London: A. R. Mowbray, 1960.

Wolfger of Prüfening. *Vita Theogeri abbatis S. Georgii.* Ed. Philip Jaffé. MGH SS 12. Hannover: Hahn, 1856. 449–479.

Woman Defamed and Woman Defended: An Anthology of Medieval Texts. Ed. Alcuin Blamires, with Karen Pratt and C. W. Marx. Oxford: Clarendon Press, 1992.

Women and Monasticism in Medieval Europe: Sisters and Patrons of the Cistercian Reform. Trans. Constance Berman. TEAMS Document of Practice Series. Kalamazoo, Mich.: Medieval Institute Publications, 2002.

Yardley, Anne B. and Jesse D. Mann, eds. and trans. "The Liturgical Dramas for Holy Week at Barking Abbey." *Medieval Feminist Forum* 49 (2013): 1–39.

RESOURCE WORKS AND MANUSCRIPT CATALOGUES

Fliege, Jutta. *Die Handschriften der ehemaligen Stifts- und Gymnasialbibliothek Quedlinburg in Halle.* Halle: Universitäts- und Landesbibliothek Sachsen-Anhalt, 1982.

Geschrieben und gemalt: Gelehrte Bücher aus Frauenhand. Eine Klosterbibliothek sächsischer Benediktinerinnen des 12. Jahrhunderts. Ausstellungskataloge der Herzog August Bibliothek Nr. 86. Ed. Helmar Härtel. Wiesbaden: Harrassowitz, 2006.

Krone und Schleier: Kunst aus mittelalterlichen Frauenklöstern, Ausstellungskatalog. Ed. Jutta Frings and Jan Gerchow. Kunst- und Ausstellungshalle der Bundesrepublik Deutschland und Ruhrlandmuseum Essen. Munich: Hirmer, 2005.

Lambert, Bernard. *Bibliotheca Hieronymiana Manuscripta.* Instrumenta Patristica IV. 4 vols. in 5. Steenbrugge: Abbatia S. Petri, 1969–1972.

Oxford Latin Dictionary. Ed. P. G. W. Glare. 2 vols. 2nd ed. Oxford: Oxford University Press, 2012.

Rand, Edward Kennard. *A Survey of the Manuscripts of Tours.* 2 vols. Cambridge, Mass.: Medieval Academy of America, 1929.

The Royal Abbey of Saint-Denis in the Time of Abbot Suger (1122–1151). Ed. Sumner McKnight Crosby, Jane Hayward, Charles T. Little, and William D. Wixom. New York: Metropolitan Museum of Art, 1981.

SECONDARY SOURCES

Achelis, Hans. *Virgines subintroductae: ein Beitrag zum VII. Kapitel des I. Korintherbriefs.* Leipzig: J. C. Hinrichs, 1902.

Adkin, Neil. "The Letter of Paula and Eustochium to Marcella: Some Notes." *Maia* 51 (1999): 97–110.

Althoff, Gerd. "Unerkannte Zeugnisse zum Totengedenken der Liudolfinger." *Deutsches Archiv* 32 (1976): 370–404.

Altvater, Fran. "Barren Mother, Dutiful Wife, Church Triumphant: Representations of Hannah in I Kings Illuminations." *Different Visions: A Journal of New Perspectives on Medieval Art* 3 (2011): 1–29.

Amt, Emilie. "The Foundation Legend of Godstow Abbey: A Holy Woman's Life in Anglo-Norman Verse." In Charlotte Newman Goldy and Amy Livingstone, eds., *Writing Medieval Women's Lives.* New York: Palgrave Macmillan, 2012. 13–31.

Andermann, Ulrich. "Zur Erforschung mittelalterlicher Kanonissenstifte. Aspekte zum Problem der weiblichen vita canonica." In Kurt Andermann, ed., *Geistliches Leben und standesgemäßes Auskommen. Adlige Damenstifte in Vergangenheit und Gegenwart.* Tübingen: Bibliotheca-Academica Verlag, 1998. 11–42.

Anderson, Michael Alan. *St. Anne in Renaissance Music: Devotion and Politics.* Cambridge: Cambridge University Press, 2014.

Antin, P. "Jérôme antique et chrétien." *Revue d'Etudes Augustiniennes et Patristiques* (1970): 35–46.

Appleby, David. "'Beautiful on the Cross, Beautiful in his Torments': The Place of the Body in the Thought of Paschasius Radbertus." *Traditio* 60 (2005): 1–46.

Appuhn, Horst. *Kloster Medingen.* Munich: Deutscher Kunstverlag, 1974.

Arnold, John H. "The Labour of Continence: Masculinity and Clerical Virginity." In Anke Bernau, Sarah Salih, and Ruth Evans, eds., *Medieval Virginities.* Cardiff: University of Wales Press, 2003. 102–118.

Badstübner-Kizik, Camilla. *Die Gründungs- und Frühgeschichte des Klosters Paulinzella und die Lebensbeschreibung der Stifterin Paulina: Sigebotos Vita Paulinae als Denkmal hirsauischer Reformliteratur des 12. Jahrhunderts.* Münster: Lit, 1993.

Barré, H. "La Lettre du Pseudo-Jérôme sur l'assomption est-elle antérieure à Paschase Radbert?" *Revue bénédictine* 68 (1958): 203–225.

Barrière, Bernadette. "The Cistercian Convent of Coyroux in the Twelfth and Thirteenth Centuries." *Gesta* 31 (1992): 76–82.

Barrière, Bernadette and Marie-Elizabeth Henneau, eds. *Cîteaux et les femmes.* Grâne: Créaphis, 2001.

Barrow, Julia. "Ideas and Applications of Reform." In Thomas F. X. Noble and Julia M. H. Smith, eds., *The Cambridge History of Christianity, III: Early Medieval Christianities, c.600–c.1100.* Cambridge: Cambridge University Press, 2008. 345–362.

Barstow, Anne Llewellyn. *Married Priests and the Reforming Papacy: The Eleventh-Century Debates.* New York: Mellen, 1982.

Bateson, Mary. "Origin and Early History of Double Monasteries." *Transactions of the Royal Historical Society* n.s. 13 (1899): 137–198.

Bauerreiß, Romuald. "St. Georgen im Schwarzwald, ein Reformmittelpunkt Südostdeutschlands im beginnenden 12. Jahrhundert." *Studien und Mitteilungen zur Geschichte des Benediktinerordens und seine Zweige* 51 (1933): 196–201 and 52 (1934): 47–56.

Beach, Alison I. "Claustration and Collaboration Between the Sexes in the Twelfth-Century Scriptorium." In Sharon Farmer and Barbara H. Rosenwein, eds., *Monks and Nuns, Saints and Outcasts: Religion in Medieval Society.* Ithaca, N.Y.: Cornell University Press, 2000. 57–75.

———. "'Mathild de Niphin' and the Female Scribes of Twelfth-Century Zwiefalten." In Virginia Blanton, Veronica O'Mara, and Patricia Stoop, eds., *Nuns' Literacies in Medieval Europe: The Hull Dialogue.* Medieval Women: Texts and Contexts 26. Turnhout: Brepols, 2013. 33–50.

———. "Voices from a Distant Land: Fragments of a Twelfth-Century Nuns' Letter Collection." *Speculum* 77 (2002): 34–54.

———. *Women as Scribes: Book Production and Monastic Reform in Twelfth-Century Bavaria.* Cambridge: Cambridge University Press, 2004.

Beckett, Katherine Scarfe, "Worcester Sauce: Malchus in Anglo-Saxon England." In Katherine O'Brien O'Keeffe and Andy Orchard, eds., *Latin Learning and English Lore, II: Studies in Anglo-Saxon Literature for Michael Lapidge.* Toronto: University of Toronto Press, 2005. 212–231.

Becquet, Jean. "La Règle de Grandmont." *Bulletin de la Société archéologique et historique du Limousin* 87 (1958): 9–36.

———. "La vie de saint Gaucher, fondateur des chanoines réguliers d'Aureil en Limousin." *Revue Mabillon* 54 (1964): 25–55.

Bedingfield, M. Bradford. *The Dramatic Liturgy of Anglo-Saxon England.* Woodbridge: Boydell, 2002.

Bell, Thomas J. *Peter Abelard After Marriage: The Spiritual Direction of Heloise and her Nuns Through Liturgical Song.* Cistercian Studies Series 211. Kalamazoo, Mich.: Cistercian Publications, 2007.

Benko, Stephen. "The Magnificat: A History of the Controversy." *Journal of Biblical Literature* 86 (1967): 263–275.

Bepler, Jochen and Christian Heitzmann, eds. *Der Albani-Psalter. Stand und Perspektiven der Forschung.* Hildesheim: Olms, 2013.

Berman, Constance H. *The Cistercian Evolution: The Invention of a Religious Order in Twelfth-Century Europe.* Philadelphia: University of Pennsylvania Press, 2000.

———. "Dowries, Private Income, and Anniversary Masses: The Nuns of Saint-Antoine-des-Champs (Paris)." *Proceedings of the Western Society for French History* 20 (1993): 3–12.

———. "How Much Space Did Medieval Nuns Have or Need?" In Sheila McNally, ed., *Shaping Community: The Art and Archaeology of Monasticism.* Oxford: Archaeopress, 2001. 101–109.

———. "Men's Houses, Women's Houses: The Relationship Between the Sexes in Twelfth-Century Monasticism." In Andrew MacLeish, ed., *Medieval Monastery.* Medieval Studies at Minnesota, 2. St. Cloud, Minn.: North Star Press of St. Cloud, 1988. 43–52.

———. "Were There Twelfth-Century Cistercian Nuns?" *Church History* 68 (1999): 824–864.

Berthelier-Ajot, Nadine. "Chelles à l'époque mérovingienne." *Revue du Nord* 68 (1986): 345–360.

Bienvenu, Jean-Marc. *L'étonnant fondateur de Fontevraud, Robert d'Arbrissel.* Paris: Nouvelles Éditions latines, 1981.

———. "Origines et évolution, au XIIe siècle, de la mixité d'un ordre double: Fontevraud." In *Naissance et fonctionnement des réseaux monastiques et canoniaux. Actes du premier colloque international du C.E.R.C.O.M., Saint-Etienne, 16–18 septembre 1985 (C.E.R.C.O.R., Travaux et recherches, 1).* Saint-Etienne: Université Jean Monnet, 1991. 61–79.

Bijsterveld, Arnoud-Jan A. *Do ut des: Gift Giving, Memoria, and Conflict Management in the Medieval Low Countries.* Hilversum: Verloren, 2007.

Birkmeyer, Regine. *Ehetrennung und monastische Konversion im Hochmittelalter.* Berlin: Akademie Verlag, 1998.

Bischoff, Bernhard. "Die Kölner Nonnenhandschriften und das Skriptorium von Chelles." In *Mittelalterliche Studien: Ausgewählte Aufsätze zur Schriftkunde und Literaturgeschichte.* 3 vols. Stuttgart: Hiersemann, 1966–1981. I, 16–34.

Bitel, Lisa M. *Landscape with Two Saints: How Genovefa of Paris and Brigit of Kildare Built Christianity in Barbarian Europe.* Oxford: Oxford University Press, 2009.

Bjork, David A. "On the Dissemination of *Quem quaeritis* and the *Visitatio sepulchri* and the Chronology of Their Early Sources." *Comparative Drama* 14 (1980): 46–69.

Blamires, Alcuin. "*Caput a femina, membra a viris*: Gender Polemic in Abelard's Letter 'On the Authority and Dignity of the Nun's Profession.'" In David Townsend and Andrew

Taylor, eds., *The Tongue of the Fathers: Gender and Ideology in Twelfth-Century Latin.* Philadelphia: University of Pennsylvania Press, 1998. 55–79.

———. *The Case for Women in Medieval Culture.* Oxford: Clarendon Press, 1997.

———. "No Outlet for Incontinence: Heloise and the Question of Consolation." In Bonnie Wheeler, ed., *Listening to Heloise: The Voice of a Twelfth-Century Woman.* New York: St. Martin's Press, 2000. 287–301.

Blumenthal, Uta-Renate. "Pope Gregory VII and the Prohibition of Nicolaitism." In Michael Frassetto, ed., *Medieval Purity and Piety: Essays on Clerical Celibacy and Religious Reform.* New York: Garland, 1998. 239–267.

Bodarwé, Katrinette. *Sanctimoniales litteratae: Schriftlichkeit und Bildung in den ottonischen Frauenkommunitäten Gandersheim, Essen und Quedlinburg.* Münster: Aschendorff, 2004.

———. "Verlorene Zeugnisse einer Frauenfreundschaft. Diemut von Wessobrunn und Herluca von Epfach." In Gabriela Signori, ed., *Meine in Gott geliebte Freundin: Freundschaftsdokumente aus klösterlichen und humanistischen Schreibstuben.* Bielefeld: Verlag für Regionalgeschichte, 1995. 50–59.

Bogumil, Karlotto. *Das Bistum Halberstadt im 12. Jahrhundert. Studien zur Reichs- und Reformpolitik des Bischofs Reinhard und zum Wirken der Augustiner-Chorherren.* Cologne: Böhlau, 1972.

Bom, Myra M. *Women in the Military Orders of the Crusades.* New York: Palgrave Macmillan, 2012.

Bond, Gerald A. *The Loving Subject: Desire, Eloquence, and Power in Romanesque France.* Philadelphia: University of Pennsylvania Press, 1995.

Bönnen, Gerold, Alfred Haverkamp, and Frank G. Hirschmann. "Religiöse Frauengemeinschaften im räumlichen Gefüge der Trierer Kirchenprovinz während des hohen Mittelalters." In Georg Jenal, ed., *Herrschaft, Kirche, Kultur. Beiträge zur Geschichte des Mittelalters. Festschrift für Friedrich Prinz zu seinem 65. Geburtstag.* Monographien zur Geschichte des Mittelalters 37. Stuttgart: Hiersemann, 1993. 369–415.

Boo, Mary Richard and Joan M. Braun. "Emerging from the Shadows: St. Scholastica." In Miriam Schmitt and Linda Kulzer, eds., *Medieval Women Monastics: Wisdom's Wellsprings.* Collegeville, Minn.: Liturgical Press, 1996. 1–11.

Borders, James. "Gender, Performativity, and Allusion in Medieval Services for the Consecration of Virgins." In Jane F. Fulcher, ed., *The Oxford Handbook of the New Cultural History of Music.* Oxford: Oxford University Press, 2011. 17–38.

Boswell, John. *Same-Sex Unions in Premodern Europe.* New York: Villard Books, 1994.

Bourgain, Pascale. "Héloïse, vie et œuvres." *Cahiers de recherches médiévales et humanistes* 23 (2012): 211–222.

Bouter, Nicole, ed. *Les Religieuses dans le cloître et dans le monde des origines à nos jours: actes du deuxième colloque international du C.E.R.C.O.R. Poitiers, 29 septembre–2 octobre 1988.* Saint-Étienne: Publications de l'Université de Saint-Étienne, 1994.

Brakke, David. *Athanasius and the Politics of Asceticism.* Oxford: Clarendon Press, 1995.

———. "The Lady Appears: Materializations of 'Woman' in Early Monastic Literature." *Journal of Medieval and Early Modern Studies* 33 (2003): 387–402.

Braun, Joseph. *Der christliche Altar in seiner geschichtlichen Entwicklung.* 2 vols. Munich: Alte Meister Guenther Koch, 1924.

———. *Die liturgische Gewandung im Occident und Orient: nach Ursprung und Entwicklung, Verwendung und Symbolik.* Freiburg im Breisgau: Herder, 1907.

Brooke, C. N. L. "Gregorian Reform in Action: Clerical Marriage in England, 1050–1200." *Cambridge Historical Journal* 12 (1956): 1–21.

Brower, Jeffrey E. and Kevin Guilfoy, eds. *The Cambridge Companion to Abelard*. Cambridge: Cambridge University Press, 2004.

Brown, Jennifer. "The Chaste Erotics of Marie d'Oignies and Jacques de Vitry." *Journal of the History of Sexuality* 19 (2010): 74–93.

Brown, Peter. *The Body and Society: Men, Women, and Sexual Renunciation in Early Christianity*. Lectures on the History of Religions, n.s., 13. New York: Columbia University Press, 1988.

———. *The Rise of Western Christendom: Triumph and Diversity, A.D. 200–1000*. 2nd ed. Oxford: Blackwell, 2003.

———. *Through the Eye of a Needle: Wealth, the Fall of Rome, and the Making of Christianity in the West, 350–550 A.D.* Princeton, N.J.: Princeton University Press, 2012.

Bugyis, Katie Ann-Marie. "The Author of the *Life* of Christina of Markyate: The Case for Robert de Gorron (d. 1166)." *Journal of Ecclesiastical History*. Forthcoming.

———. "Envisioning Episcopal Exemption: The Life of Christina of Markyate." *Church History* 84 (2015): 32–63.

———. *In Christ's Stead: Benedictine Women's Ministries in England, 900–1225*. Oxford: Oxford University Press, Forthcoming.

———. "Recovering the Histories of Women Religious in England in the Central Middle Ages: Wilton Abbey and Goscelin of Saint-Bertin." *Journal of Medieval History* (2016): 285–303.

Buhlmann, Michael. "Die Essener Äbtissin Hadwig von Wied." *Das Münster am Hellweg* 56 (2003): 41–78.

Bullough, Donald A. *Alcuin: Achievement and Reputation*. Leiden: Brill, 2004.

———. "Charlemagne's 'Men of God': Alcuin, Hildebald, and Arn." In Joanna Story, ed., *Charlemagne: Empire and Society*. Manchester: Manchester University Press, 2005. 136–150.

Burrus, Virginia. "Queer Lives of Saints: Jerome's Hagiography." *Journal of the History of Sexuality* 10 (2001): 442–479.

Burton, Janet. "The 'Chariot of Aminadab' and the Yorkshire Priory of Swine." In Rosemary Horrox and Sarah Rees Jones, eds., *Pragmatic Utopias: Ideals and Communities, 1200–1630*. Cambridge: Cambridge University Press, 2001. 26–42.

Bynum, Caroline Walker. "'Crowned with Many Crowns': Nuns and Their Statues in Late-Medieval Wienhausen." *Catholic Historical Review* 101 (2015): 18–40.

———. *Holy Feast and Holy Fast: The Religious Significance of Food to Medieval Women*. Berkeley: University of California Press, 1987.

Cain, Andrew. "Defending Hedibia and Detecting Eusebius: Jerome's Correspondence with Two Gallic Women (Epp. 120–121)." *Medieval Prosopography* 24 (2003): 15–34.

———. "Jerome's *Epistula CXVII* on the *Subintroductae*: Satire, Apology, and Ascetic Propaganda in Gaul." *Augustinianum* 49 (2009): 119–143.

———. "Jerome's *Epitaphium Paulae*: Hagiography, Pilgrimage, and the Cult of Saint Paula." *Journal of Early Christian Studies* 18 (2010): 105–139.

———. *The Letters of Jerome: Asceticism, Biblical Exegesis, and the Construction of Christian Authority in Late Antiquity*. Oxford: Oxford University Press, 2009.

———. "Rethinking Jerome's Portraits of Holy Women." In Andrew Cain and Josef Lössl, eds., *Jerome of Stridon: His Life, Writings, and Legacy*. Burlington, Vt.: Ashgate, 2009. 47–57.

Campbell, Mary Marshall. "Sanctity and Identity: The Authentication of the Ursuline Relics and Legal Discourse in Elisabeth von Schönau's *Liber Revelationum*." *The Journal of Medieval Religious Cultures* 38 (2012): 159–192.

Canatella, H. M. "Long-Distance Love: The Ideology of Male-Female Spiritual Friendship in Goscelin of Saint Bertin's *Liber confortatorius*." *Journal of the History of Sexuality* 19 (2010): 35–53.

Carrasco, Magdalena Elizabeth. "The Imagery of the Magdalen in Christina of Markyate's Psalter (St. Albans Psalter)." *Gesta* 38 (1999): 67–80.

———. "Spirituality in Context: The Romanesque Illustrated Life of St. Radegund of Poitiers (Poitiers, Bibl. Mun., MS 250)." *The Art Bulletin* 72 (1990): 414–435.

Carroll, Jane L. "Woven Devotions: Reform and Piety in Tapestries by Dominican Nuns." In Jane L. Carroll and Alison G. Stewart, eds., *Saints, Sinners, and Sisters: Gender and Northern Art in Medieval and Early Modern Europe*. Aldershot: Ashgate, 2003. 182–201.

Carruthers, Mary. *The Craft of Thought: Meditation, Rhetoric, and the Making of Images, 400–1200*. Cambridge: Cambridge University Press, 1998.

Cartwright, Jane. *Feminine Sanctity and Spirituality in Medieval Wales*. Cardiff: University of Wales Press, 2008.

Cavallera, Ferdinand. *Saint Jérôme: sa vie et son oeuvre*. Spicilegium sacrum Lovaniense. Etudes et documents. 2 vols. Paris: E. Champion, 1922.

Chiesa, Paolo. "Maniacutia, Nicolò." In *Dizionario biografico degli Italiani*. 69. Rome: Istituto della Enciclopedia Italiana, 2007. 30–32.

Clanchy, M. T. *Abelard: A Medieval Life*. Oxford: Blackwell, 1997.

Clark, Anne L. *Elisabeth of Schönau: A Twelfth-Century Visionary*. Philadelphia: University of Pennsylvania Press, 1992.

———. "Holy Woman or Unworthy Vessel? The Representations of Elisabeth of Schönau." In Catherine M. Mooney, ed., *Gendered Voices: Medieval Saints and Their Interpreters*. Philadelphia: University of Pennsylvania Press, 1999. 35–51.

———. "The Priesthood of the Virgin Mary: Gender Trouble in the Twelfth Century." *Journal of Feminist Studies in Religion*. 18 (2002): 5–24.

———. "Repression or Collaboration? The Case of Elisabeth and Ekbert of Schönau." In Scott L. Waugh and Peter D. Diehl, eds., *Christendom and Its Discontents: Exclusion, Persecution, and Rebellion, 1000–1500*. Cambridge: Cambridge University Press, 1996. 151–167.

Clark, Elizabeth A. "Antifamilial Tendencies in Ancient Christianity." *Journal of the History of Sexuality* 5 (1995): 356–380.

———. "The Celibate Bridegroom and His Virginal Brides: Metaphor and the Marriage of Jesus in Early Christian Ascetic Exegesis." *Church History* 77 (2008): 1–25.

———. "Claims on the Bones of Saint Stephen: The Partisans of Melania and Eudocia." *Church History* 51 (1982): 141–156.

———. *Jerome, Chrysostom, and Friends: Essays and Translations*. New York: E. Mellen Press, 1979.

———. "John Chrysostom and the 'Subintroductae.'" *Church History* 46 (1977): 171–185.

———. "The Lady Vanishes: Dilemmas of a Feminist Historian After the 'Linguistic Turn.'" *Church History* 67 (1998): 1–31.

———. "Patrons, Not Priests: Gender and Power in Late Ancient Christianity." *Gender & History* 2 (1990): 253–273.

———. "Rewriting Early Christian History: Augustine's Representation of Monica." In J. W. Drijvers and J. W. Watt, eds., *Portraits of Spiritual Authority: Religious Power in Early Christianity, Byzantium, and the Christian Orient*. Religions in the Graeco-Roman World 137. Leiden: E. J. Brill, 1999. 3–23.

———. "Sex, Shame, and Rhetoric: En-gendering Early Christian Ethics." *Journal of the American Academy of Religion* 59 (1991): 221–245.

———. "Theory and Practice in Late Ancient Asceticism: Jerome, Chrysostom, and Augustine." *Journal of Feminist Studies in Religion* 5 (1989): 25–46.

Clark, Katherine. "Purgatory, Punishment, and the Discourse on Holy Widowhood in the High and Later Middle Ages." *Journal of the History of Sexuality* 16 (2007): 169–203.

Cline, Ruth Harwood. "*Mutatis Mutandis*: Literary Borrowing from Jerome's Letter to Eustochium and Others in the *Life of Blessed Bernard of Tiron* by Geoffrey Grossus." *Haskins Society Journal* 21 (2009): 125–146.

Coakley, John W. "Afterword: Ordinary Life and the Gendered Imagination." In Fiona J. Griffiths and Julie Hotchin, eds., *Partners in Spirit: Women, Men, and Religious Life in Germany, 1100–1500*. Medieval Women: Texts and Contexts 24. Turnhout: Brepols, 2014. 401–412.

———. "Friars as Confidants of Holy Women in Medieval Dominican Hagiography." In Renate Blumenfeld-Kosinski and Timea Szell, eds., *Images of Sainthood in Medieval Europe*. Ithaca, N.Y.: Cornell University Press, 1991. 222–246.

———. "Friars, Sanctity, and Gender: Mendicant Encounters with Saints, 1250–1325." In Clare A. Lees, ed., *Medieval Masculinities: Regarding Men in the Middle Ages*. Medieval Cultures 7. Minneapolis: University of Minnesota Press, 1994. 91–110.

———. "Gender and the Authority of Friars: The Significance of Holy Women for Thirteenth-Century Franciscans and Dominicans." *Church History* 60 (1991): 445–460.

———. "Thomas of Cantimpré and Female Sanctity." In Rachel Fulton and Bruce W. Holsinger, eds., *History in the Comic Mode: Medieval Communities and the Matter of Person*. New York: Columbia University Press, 2007. 45–55.

———. *Women, Men, and Spiritual Power: Female Saints and Their Male Collaborators*. New York: Columbia University Press, 2006.

Conklin, George. "Ingeborg of Denmark, Queen of France, 1193–1223." In Anne J. Duggan, ed., *Queens and Queenship in Medieval Europe*. Woodbridge: Boydell Press, 1997. 39–52.

Conrads, Peter. *Hieronymus, scriptor et interpres. Zur Ikonographie des Eusebius Hieronymus im frühen und hohen Mittelalter*. Würzburg, 1990.

Constable, Giles. "Aelred of Rievaulx and the Nun of Watton: An Episode in the Early History of the Gilbertine Order." In Derek Baker, ed., *Medieval Women: Dedicated and Presented to Professor Rosalind M. T. Hill on the Occasion of her Seventieth Birthday*. Studies in Church History, Subsidia, 1. Oxford: Blackwell, 1978. 205–226.

———. *Reformation of the Twelfth Century*. Cambridge: Cambridge University Press, 1996.

———. "Religious Communities, 1024–1215." In David Luscombe and Jonathan Riley-Smith, eds., *New Cambridge Medieval History IV: c. 1024 - c. 1198*. Cambridge: Cambridge University Press, 2004. Part 1. 335–367.

———. "Renewal and Reform in Religious Life: Concepts and Realities." In Robert L. Benson and Giles Constable, eds., with Carol D. Lanham, *Renaissance and Renewal in the Twelfth Century*. Toronto: University of Toronto Press and the Medieval Academy of America, 1991. 37–67.

————. *Three Studies in Medieval Religious and Social Thought.* Cambridge: Cambridge University Press, 1995.

Cook, John Granger. "1 Cor 9,5: The Women of the Apostles." *Biblica* 89 (2008): 352–368.

Coomans, Thomas. "Cistercian Nuns and Princely Memorials: Dynastic Burial Churches in the Cistercian Abbeys of the Medieval Low Countries." In Michel Margue, ed., *Sépulture, mort et représentation du pouvoir au Moyen Age.* Luxembourg: Section Historique de l'Institut Grand-Ducal de Luxembourg, 2006. 683–734.

Coon, Lynda L. *Sacred Fictions: Holy Women and Hagiography in Late Antiquity.* Philadelphia: University of Pennsylvania Press, 1997.

Cooper, Kate. "Augustine and Monnica." In Conrad Leyser and Lesley Smith, eds., *Motherhood, Religion, and Society in Medieval Europe, 400–1400: Essays Presented to Henrietta Leyser.* Burlington, Vt.: Ashgate, 2011. 7–20.

Corbet, Patrick. *Les saints ottoniens: Sainteté dynastique, sainteté royale et sainteté féminine autour de l'an Mil.* Sigmaringen: Jan Thorbecke, 1986.

Cowdrey, H. E. J. "Pope Gregory VII and the Chastity of the Clergy." In Michael Frassetto, ed., *Medieval Purity and Piety: Essays on Medieval Clerical Celibacy and Religious Reform,* New York: Garland, 1998. 269–302.

————. *Pope Gregory VII, 1073–1085.* Oxford: Clarendon Press, 1998.

Cullum, P. H. and Katherine J. Lewis, eds. *Religious Men and Masculine Identity in the Middle Ages.* Woodbridge: Boydell & Brewer, 2013.

Curta, Florin. "Merovingian and Carolingian Gift Giving." *Speculum* 81 (2006): 671–699.

Cusack, Carole M. "Hagiography and History: the Legend of Saint Ursula." In Carole M. Cusack and Peter Oldmeadow, eds., *This Immense Panorama: Studies in Honour of Eric J. Sharpe.* Sydney: School of Studies in Religion, University of Sydney, 1999. 89–104.

Cusack, Pearse Aidan. "St. Scholastica: Myth or Real Person?" *The Downside Review* 92 (1974): 145–159.

Dalarun, Jacques. "*Capitula regularia magistri Roberti*: de Fontevraud au Paraclet." *Comptes rendus des séances de l'Académie des Inscriptions et Belles-Lettres* 147 (2003): 1601–1623.

————. *Dieu changea de sexe, pour ainsi dire: la religion faite femme, XIe-XVe siècle.* Paris: Fayard, 2008.

————. *Gouverner c'est servir: essai de démocratie medieval.* Paris: Alma, 2012.

————. "Hagiographe et métaphore. Fonctionnalité des modèles féminins dans l'œuvre d'Hildebert de Lavardin." In Gabriel Bianciotto, Robert Favreau, and Piotr Skubiszewski, eds., *Civilisation Médiévale* I. *Le culte des saints aux IXe-XIIIe siècles: actes du colloque tenu à Poitiers, les 15–16–17 septembre 1993.* Poitiers: Université de Poitiers, 1995. 37–51.

————. "La Madeleine dans l'Ouest de la France au tournant des XIe et XIIe siècles." In Georges Duby, ed., *La Madeleine (VIIIe-XIIIe siècle).* Mélanges de l'École française de Rome. Moyen Âge, 104, 1. Rome: L'Ecole française de Rome, 1992. 71–119.

————. "Nouveaux aperçus sur Abélard, Héloïse et le Paraclet." *Francia* 32 (2005): 19–66.

————. "Les plus anciens statuts de Fontevraud." In Jacques Dalarun, ed., *Robert d'Arbrissel et la vie religieuse dans l'Ouest de la France: Actes du colloque de Fontevraud 13–16 décembre 2001.* Disciplina Monastica 1. Turnhout: Brepols, 2004. 139–172.

————. "Pouvoir et autorité dans l'Ordre double de Fontevraud." In Nicole Bouter, ed., *Les Religieuses dans le cloître et dans le monde des origines à nos jours: Actes du deuxième colloque international du C.E.R.C.O.R., Poitiers, 29 septembre-2 octobre 1988.* Saint-Etienne: Publications de l'Université de Saint-Etienne, 1994. 335–352.

————. "Robert d'Arbrissel et les femmes." *Annales ESC* 39 (1984): 1140–1160.

————. *Robert of Arbrissel: Sex, Sin, and Salvation in the Middle Ages.* Trans. Bruce L. Venarde. [*Robert d'Arbrissel, fondateur de Fontevraud.* Paris: A. Michel, 1986]. Washington, D.C.: Catholic University of America Press, 2006.

Dalarun, Jacques, ed. *Robert d'Arbrissel et la vie religieuse dans l'Ouest de la France: Actes du colloque de Fontevraud 13–16 décembre 2001.* Disciplina Monastica 1. Turnhout: Brepols, 2004.

Davies, Wendy and Paul Fouracre, eds. *The Languages of Gift in the Early Middle Ages.* Cambridge: Cambridge University Press, 2010.

de Fontette, Micheline. *Les Religieuses à l'âge classique du droit canon, recherches sur les structures juridiques des branches féminines des ordres.* Paris, J. Vrin, 1967.

de Jong, Mayke. "Jeremiah, Job, Terence, and Paschasius Radbertus: Political Rhetoric and Biblical Authority in the *Epitaphium Arsenii*." In Jinty Nelson and Damien Kempf, eds., *Reading the Bible in the Middle Ages.* London: Bloomsbury, 2015. 57–76.

de Kegel, Rolf. "Monasterium, quod duplices [. . .] habet conventus: Einblicke in das Doppelkloster Engelberg 1120–1615." In Eva Schlotheuber, Helmut Flachenecker, and Ingrid Gardill, eds., *Nonnen, Kanonissen und Mystikerinnen: Religiöse Frauengemeinschaften in Süddeutschland; Beiträge zur interdisziplinären Tagung vom 21. bis 23. September 2005 in Frauenchiemsee.* Veröffentlichungen des Max-Planck-Instituts für Geschichte, 235. Studien zur Germania Sacra, 31. Göttingen: Vandenhoeck & Ruprecht, 2008. 181–201.

————. "Vom 'ordnungswidrigen Übelstand'? Zum Phänomen der Doppelklöster bei Prämonstratensern und Benediktinern." *Rottenburger Jahrbuch für Kirchengeschichte* 22 (2003): 47–63.

de Labriolle, Pierre. "Le 'mariage spirituel' dans l'antiquité chrétienne." *Revue historique* 137 (1921): 204–225.

de Santis, Paola. *I sermoni di Abelardo per le monache del Paracleto.* Mediaevalia Lovaniensia Series 1, Studia 31. Leuven: Leuven University Press, 2002.

de Vogüé, Adalbert. "The Meeting of Benedict and Scholastica: An Interpretation." *Cistercian Studies* 18 (1983): 167–183.

Depreux, Philippe and Bruno Judic, eds. *Alcuin: De York à Tours. Écriture, pouvoir et réseaux dans l'Europe du haut Moyen Âge.* Annales de Bretagne et des Pays de l'Ouest, 111/3. Rennes: Presses universitaires, 2004.

Derbes, Anne. "The Frescoes of Schwarzrheindorf, Arnold of Wied, and the Second Crusade." In Michael Gervers, ed., *The Second Crusade and the Cistercians.* New York: St. Martin's Press, 1992. 141–154.

Dereine, Charles. "La 'Vita Apostolica' dans l'ordre canonial du IXe au XIe siècles." *Revue Mabillon* 51 (1961): 47–53.

Deutz, Helmut. *Geistliches und geistiges Leben im Regularkanonikerstift Klosterrath im. 12. und 13. Jahrhundert.* Siegburg: Schmitt, 1990.

Deutz, Helmut and Ilse Deutz. "Die Frauen im Regularkanonikerstift Klosterrath: Vom Doppelkloster zu den Frauenprioraten Marienthal und Sinnich." *Geschichte im Bistum Aachen* 7 (2004): 31–54.

Diem, Albrecht. "The Gender of the Religious: Wo/Men and the Invention of Monasticism." In Judith M. Bennett and Ruth Mazo Karras, eds., *Oxford Handbook of Women and Gender in Medieval Europe.* Oxford: Oxford University Press, 2013. 432–446.

————. "New Ideas Expressed in Old Words: The *Regula Donati* on Female Monastic Life and Monastic Spirituality." *Viator* 43 (2012): 1–38.

Ditz, Toby L. "The New Men's History and the Peculiar Absence of Gendered Power: Some Remedies from Early American Gender History." *Gender & History* 16 (2004): 1–35.

Dreger, Moriz. "Der Gösser Ornat im K. K. Österreichischen Museum für Kunst und Industrie." *Kunst und Kunsthandwerk* 12 (1908): 613–653.

Dronke, Peter. "Heloise's *Problemata* and *Letters*: Some Questions of Form and Content." In Rudolf Thomas, ed., *Petrus Abaelardus, 1079–1142: Person, Werk und Wirkung.* Trierer theologische Studien 38. Trier: Paulinus-Verlag, 1980. 53–73.

———. *Medieval Latin and the Rise of European Love-lyric.* 2 vols. 2nd ed. Oxford: Clarendon Press, 1968.

———. *Women Writers of the Middle Ages: A Critical Study of Texts from Perpetua (d. 203) to Marguerite Porete (d. 1310).* Cambridge: Cambridge University Press, 1984.

Dronke, Peter and Giovanni Orlandi. "New Works by Abelard and Heloise?" *Filologia mediolatina* 12 (2005): 123–177.

Dutton, Paul Edward and Herbert L. Kessler. *The Poetry and Paintings of the First Bible of Charles the Bald.* Ann Arbor: University of Michigan Press, 1997.

Edwards, Carolyn Ann. *Noblewomen of Prayer: The Imperial Convents of Regensburg, 1000–1250.* Ph.D. dissertation, University of Notre Dame, 2000.

Edwards, Jennifer C. " 'Man Can be Subject to Woman': Female Monastic Authority in Fifteenth-Century Poitiers." *Gender & History* 25 (2013): 86–106.

Eggert, Barbara. "Textile Strategien der Grenzüberschreitung. Der Gösser Ornat der Äbtissin Kunegunde II. (Amt. 1239–1269)." In Jeffrey F. Hamburger, Carola Jäggi, Susan Marti, and Hedwig Röckelein, eds., *Frauen–Kloster–Kunst. Neue Forschungen zur Kulturgeschichte des Mittelalters.* Turnhout: Brepols, 2007. 281–288.

Ehlers-Kisseler, Ingrid. *Die Anfänge der Prämonstratenser im Erzbistum Köln.* Cologne: Böhlau Verlag, 1997.

El Kholi, Susann. *Lektüre in Frauenkonventen des ostfränkisch-deutschen Reiches vom 8. Jahrhundert bis zur Mitte des 13. Jahrhunderts.* Würzburger Wissenschaftliche Schriften 203. Würzburg: Königshausen and Neumann, 1997.

Elkins, Sharon K. *Holy Women of Twelfth-Century England.* Chapel Hill: University of North Carolina Press, 1988.

Elliott, Dyan. "Alternative Intimacies: Men, Women, and Spiritual Direction in the Twelfth Century." In Samuel Fanous and Henrietta Leyser, eds., *Christina of Markyate: A Twelfth-Century Holy Woman.* London: Routledge, 2005. 160–183.

———. *The Bride of Christ Goes to Hell: Metaphor and Embodiment in the Lives of Pious Women, 200–1500.* Philadelphia: University of Pennsylvania Press, 2012.

———. "Pollution, Illusion, and Masculine Disarray: Nocturnal Emissions and the Sexuality of the Clergy." In Dyan Elliott, *Fallen Bodies: Pollution, Sexuality, and Demonology in the Middle Ages.* Philadelphia: University of Pennsylvania Press, 1999. 14–34.

———. "The Priest's Wife: Female Erasure and the Gregorian Reform." In Dyan Elliott, *Fallen Bodies: Pollution, Sexuality, and Demonology in the Middle Ages.* Philadelphia: University of Pennsylvania Press, 1999. 81–106.

———. *Spiritual Marriage: Sexual Abstinence in Medieval Wedlock.* Princeton, N.J.: Princeton University Press, 1993.

Elm, Kaspar. "Le personnel masculin au service des religieuses au Moyen Âge." In Nicole Bouter, ed., *Les Religieuses dans le cloître et dans le monde des origines à nos jours: Actes du Deuxième Colloque International du C.E.R.C.O.R., Poitiers, 29 septembre-2 octobre 1988.* Saint-Etienne: Publications de l'Université de Saint-Etienne, 1994. 331–334.

Elm, Kaspar, and Michel Parisse, eds. *Doppelklöster und andere Formen der Symbiose männlicher und weiblicher Religiosen im Mittelalter.* Berlin: Duncker und Humblot, 1992.

Elm, Susanna. "Formen des Zusammenlebens männlicher und weiblicher Asketen im östlichen Mittelmeerraum während des vierten Jahrhunderts nach Christus." In Kaspar Elm and Michel Parisse, eds., *Doppelklöster und andere Formen der Symbiose männlicher und weiblicher Religiosen im Mittelalter.* Berlin: Duncker & Humblot, 1992. 13–24.

———. *"Virgins of God": The Making of Asceticism in Late Antiquity.* Oxford: Clarendon Press, 1994.

Engelbrecht, August. "S. Paulas Grab und die alte Geburtskirche und -Grotte zu Bethlehem." *Wiener Studien* 43 (1922/23): 80–86.

Engels, L. J. "*Adtendite a falsis prophetis* (Ms. Colmar 128, ff. 152v/153v). Un texte de Pierre Abélard contre les Cisterciens retrouvé?" In *Corona Gratiarum: Miscellanea patristica, historica et liturgica Eligio Dekkers O. S. B. XII lustra complenti oblata.* 2 vols. Bruges: Sint Pietersabdij, 1975. II: 195–228.

Engh, Line Cecilie. *Gendered Identities in Bernard of Clairvaux's* Sermons on the Song of Songs*: Performing the Bride.* Turnhout: Brepols, 2014.

Esmeijer, Anna C. "The Open Door and the Heavenly Vision: Political and Spiritual Elements in the Programme of Decoration of Schwarzrheindorf." In Karl-Ludwig Selig, ed., *Polyanthea: Essays On Art And Literature In Honor Of William Sebastian Heckscher.* The Hague: Van der Heijden, 1993. 43–56.

Everard, Judith. "The Abbey of Saint-Sulpice-la-Forêt and Royal Patronage in England, c. 1150-1259." *Nottingham Medieval Studies* 47 (2003): 107–139.

Fanous, Samuel and and Henrietta Leyser, eds., *Christina of Markyate: A Twelfth-Century Holy Woman.* London: Routledge, 2005.

Farmer, Sharon. "Persuasive Voices: Clerical Images of Medieval Wives." *Speculum* 61 (1986): 517–543.

Favreau, Robert. "Le culte de Sainte Radegonde à Poitiers au moyen âge." In Nicole Bouter, ed., *Les Religieuses dans le cloître et dans le monde des origines à nos jours: Actes du Deuxième Colloque International du C.E.R.C.O.R., Poitiers, 29 septembre-2 octobre 1988.* Saint-Etienne: Publications de l'Université de Saint-Etienne, 1994. 91–109.

———. "Heurs et malheurs de l'abbaye, XIIe-XVe s." In Yvonne Labande-Mailfert, ed., *Histoire de l'abbaye Sainte-Croix de Poitiers: quatorze siècles de vie monastique.* Poitiers: Société des antiquaires de l'Ouest, 1986. 119–220.

Feichtinger, Barbara. *Apostolae apostolorum: Frauenaskese als Befreiung und Zwang bei Hieronymus.* Frankfurt am Main: P. Lang, 1995.

Felten, Franz J. "Frauenklöster und -stifte im Rheinland im 12. Jahrhundert: Ein Beitrag zur Geschichte der Frauen in der religiösen Bewegung des hohen Mittelalters." In Stefan Weinfurter, ed., *Reformidee und Reformpolitik im Spätsalisch-Frühstaufischen Reich.* Trier: Gesellschaft für Mittelrheinische Kirchengeschichte, 1992. 189–300.

———. "Hildegard von Bingen zwischen Reformaufbruch und Bewahrung des Althergebrachten." In Jean Ferrari and Stephan Grätzel, eds., *Spiritualität im Europa des Mittelalters: 900 Jahre Hildegard von Bingen = L'Europe spirituelle au Moyen Age: 900 ans l'abbaye de Cîteaux.* St. Augustin: Gardez! Verlag, 1998. 123–149.

———. "Norbert von Xanten. Vom Wanderprediger zum Kirchenfürsten." In Kaspar Elm, ed., *Norbert von Xanten. Adliger, Ordensstifter, Kirchenfürst.* Cologne: Wienand, 1984. 59–167.

———. "'Noui esse volunt . . . deserentes bene contritam uiam . . .' Hildegard von Bingen und Reformbewegungen im religiösen Leben ihrer Zeit." In Rainer Berndt, ed., *"Im Angesicht*

Gottes suche der Mensch sich selbst": Hildegard von Bingen (1098–1179). Berlin: Akademie Verlag, 2001. 27–86.

———. "Verbandsbildung von Frauenklöstern. Le Paraclet, Prémy, Fontevraud mit einem Ausblick auf Cluny, Sempringham und Tart." In Hagen Keller and Franz Neiske, eds., *Vom Kloster zum Klosterverband: das Werkzeug der Schriftlichkeit*. Munich: W. Fink Verlag, 1997. 277–341.

———. "Zisterzienserinnen in Deutschland: Beobachtungen und Überlegungen zu Ausbreitung und Ordenszugehörigkeit." In Nicole Bouter, ed., *Unanimité et diversité cisterciennes: filiations—réseaux—relectures du XIIe au XVIIe siècle*. Saint-Étienne: Publications de L'Université de Saint-Étienne, 2000. 345–400.

———. "Der Zisterzienserorden und die Frauen." In Harald Schwillus and Andreas Hölscher, eds., *Weltverachtung und Dynamik*. Studien zu Geschichte, Kunst und Kultur der Zisterzienser, 10. Berlin: Lukas, 2000. 34–135.

Ferrante, Joan M. *To the Glory of Her Sex: Women's Roles in the Composition of Medieval Texts*. Bloomington: Indiana University Press, 1997.

Finn, R. D. *Asceticism in the Graeco-Roman World*. Cambridge: Cambridge University Press, 2009.

Fischer, Bonifatius. "Bibeltext und Bibelreform unter Karl dem Grossen." In Wolfgang Braunfels, ed., *Karl der Grosse: Lebenswerk und Nachleben*, II: *Das geistige Leben*. Ed. Bernhard Bischoff. Düsseldorf: L. Schwann, 1965. 156–216.

Flanagan, Sabina. "'For God Distinguishes the People of Earth as in Heaven': Hildegard of Bingen's Social Ideas." *The Journal of Religious History* 22 (1998): 14–34.

Flynn, William T. "Abelard and Rhetoric: Widows and Virgins at the Paraclete." In Babette S. Hellemans, ed., *Rethinking Abelard: A Collection of Critical Essays*. Leiden: Brill, 2014. 155–186.

———. "*Ductus figuratus et subtilis*: Rhetorical Interventions for Women in Two Twelfth-Century Liturgies." In Mary Carruthers, ed., *Rhetoric Beyond Words: Delight and Persuasion in the Arts of the Middle Ages*. Cambridge: Cambridge University Press, 2010. 250–280.

———. "Letters, Liturgy, and Identity: The Use of the Sequence *Epithalamica* at the Paraclete." In Gunilla Iversen and Nicolas Bell, eds., *Sapientia et Eloquentia: Meaning and Function in Liturgical Poetry, Music, Drama, and Biblical Commentary in the Middle Ages*.Turnhout: Brepols, 2009. 301–348.

Foot, Sarah. *Veiled Women*. 2 vols. Studies in Early Medieval Britain. Aldershot: Ashgate, 2000.

Forey, A. J. "Women and the Military Orders in the Twelfth and Thirteenth Centuries." *Studia Monastica* 29 (1987): 63–92.

Forman, Mary. "Three Songs About St. Scholastica by Aldhelm and Paul the Deacon." *Vox Benedictina* 7 (1990): 229–251.

France, John. "The Iconography of Bernard of Clairvaux and his Sister Humbeline." In Meredith P. Lillich, ed., *Studies in Cistercian Art and Architecture*, VI: *Cistercian Nuns and Their World*. Cistercian Studies Series 194. Kalamazoo, Mich.: Cistercian Publications, 2005. 1–21.

———. "Nuns and the Iconography of Bernard." In *Medieval Images of Saint Bernard of Clairvaux*. Cistercian Studies Series 210. Kalamazoo, Mich.: Cistercian Publications, 2007. 159–176.

Frank, Donald K. "Abelard as Imitator of Christ." *Viator* 1 (1970): 107–13.

Frassetto, Michael, ed. *Medieval Purity and Piety: Essays on Medieval Clerical Celibacy and Religious Reform.* New York: Garland, 1998.

Frauenknecht, Erwin. *Der Verteidigung der Priesterehe in der Reformzeit.* MGH Studien und Texte, 16. Hannover: Hahn, 1997.

Freed, John B. "Urban Development and the 'Cura monialium' in Thirteenth-Century Germany." *Viator* 3 (1972): 311–27.

Freeman, Elizabeth. "Nuns in the Public Sphere: Aelred of Rievaulx's *De Sanctimoniali de Wattun* and the Gendering of Authority." *Comitatus* 27 (1996): 55–80.

———. "Nuns." In Mette Birkedal Bruun, ed., *The Cambridge Companion to the Cistercian Order.* Cambridge: Cambridge University Press, 2013. 100–111.

Frizen, Hildegunde. *Die Geschichte des Klosters Schwarzrheindorf von den Anfängen bis zum Beginn der Neuzeit.* Bonn: Stadt Bonn, 1983.

Fulkerson, Laurel. "*Servitium Amoris*: The Interplay of Dominance, Gender, and Poetry." In Thea S. Thorsen, ed., *The Cambridge Companion to Latin Love Elegy.* Cambridge: Cambridge University Press, 2013. 180–193.

Fulton, Rachel. *From Judgment to Passion: Devotion to Christ and the Virgin Mary, 800–1200.* New York: Columbia University Press, 2002.

———. "*Quae est ista quae ascendit sicut aurora consurgens?*: The Song of Songs as the *Historia* for the Office of the Assumption." *Mediaeval Studies* 60 (1998): 55–122.

Gaehde, Joachim E. "The Turonian Sources of the Bible of San Paolo Fuori Le Mura in Rome." *Frühmittelalterliche Studien* 5 (1971): 359–400.

Ganz, David. *Corbie in the Carolingian Renaissance.* Sigmaringen: Jan Thorbecke, 1990.

———. "The Vatican Vergil and the Jerome Page in the First Bible of Charles the Bald." In John Lowden and Alixe Bovey, eds., *Under the Influence. The Concept of Influence and the Study of Illuminated Manuscripts.* Turnhout: Brepols, 2007. 45–50.

García-Guijarro Ramos, Luis. "The Aragonese Hospitaller Monastery of Sigena: Its Early Stages, 1188-c. 1210." In Anthony Luttrell and Helen J. Nicholson, eds., *Hospitaller Women in the Middle Ages.* Aldershot: Ashgate, 2006. 113–151.

Garrison, Mary. "Les correspondants d'Alcuin." *Annales de Bretagne et des pays de l'Ouest* 111 (2004): 319–331.

———. "The Social World of Alcuin: Nicknames at York and at the Carolingian Court." In L. A. J. R. Houwen and A. A. MacDonald, eds., *Alcuin of York: Scholar at the Carolingian Court: Proceedings of the Third Germania Latina Conference held at the University of Groningen, May 1995.* Groningen: E. Forsten, 1998. 59–79.

Gärtner, Wolfgang. "Das Chorherrenstift Klosterrath in der Kanonikerreform des 12. Jahrhunderts." *Zeitschrift des Aachener Geschichtsvereins* 97 (1991): 33–220.

Garver, Valerie L. "Textiles as a Means of Female Religious Participation in the Carolingian World." In Sari Katajala–Peltomaa and Ville Vuolante, eds., *Ancient and Medieval Religion in Practice.* Helsinki: Acta Instituti Romani Finlandiae, 2013. 133–144.

———. *Women and Aristocratic Culture in the Carolingian World.* Ithaca, N.Y.: Cornell University Press, 2009.

Geddes, Jane. "The St. Albans Psalter: The Abbot and the Anchoress." In Samuel Fanous and Henrietta Leyser, eds., *Christina of Markyate: A Twelfth-Century Holy Woman.* London: Routledge, 2005. 197–216.

———. *The St. Albans Psalter: A Book for Christina of Markyate.* London: The British Library, 2005.

George, Judith W. *Venantius Fortunatus: a Latin Poet in Merovingian Gaul*. Oxford: Clarendon Press, 1991.

Georgi, Wolfgang. *"Legatio virum sapientem requirat*: Zur Rolle der Erzbischöfe von Köln als Königlich-Kaiserliche Gesandte." In Hanna Vollrath and Stefan Weinfurter, eds., *Köln: Stadt und Bistum in Kirche und Reich des Mittelalters: Festschrift für Odilo Engels zum 65. Geburtstag*. Cologne: Böhlau, 1993. 61–124.

Georgianna, Linda. "In Any Corner of Heaven: Heloise's Critique of the Monastic Life." In Bonnie Wheeler, ed., *Listening to Heloise: The Voice of a Twelfth-Century Woman*. New York: St. Martin's Press, 2000. 187–216.

Gibson, Gail McMurray. "The Thread of Life in the Hand of the Virgin." In Julia Bolton Holloway, Constance S. Wright, and Joan Bechtold, eds., *Equally in God's Image: Women in the Middle Ages*. New York: P. Lang, 1990. 46–54.

Gilomen-Schenkel, Elsanne. "Das Doppelkloster–eine verschwiegene Institution. Engelberg und andere Beispiele aus dem Umkreis der Helvetia Sacra." *Studien und Mitteilungen zur Geschichte des Benediktinerordens und seiner Zweige* 101 (1990): 197–211.

———. "Double Monasteries in the South-Western Empire (1100–1230) and Their Women's Communities in Swiss Regions." In Fiona J. Griffiths and Julie Hotchin, eds., *Partners in Spirit: Women, Men, and Religious Life in Germany, 1100–1500*. Medieval Women: Texts and Contexts 24. Turnhout: Brepols, 2014. 47–74.

———. "Engelberg, Interlaken und andere autonome Doppelklöster im Südwesten des Reiches (11.-13. Jh.). Zur Quellenproblematik und zur historiographischen Tradition." In Kaspar Elm and Michel Parisse, eds., *Doppelklöster und andere Formen der Symbiose männlicher und weiblicher Religiosen im Mittelalter*. Berlin: Duncker and Humblot, 1992. 115–33.

———. "Der Guta-Sintram-Codex als Zeugnis eines Doppelklosters." In Jeffrey F. Hamburger, Carola Jäggi, Susan Marti, and Hedwig Röckelein, eds., *Frauen–Kloster–Kunst. Neue Forschungen zur Kulturgeschichte des Mittelalters*. Turnhout: Brepols, 2007. 395–401.

———. "Nekrologien als Quellen für Doppelklöster." In Rudolf Henggeler et al., eds., *Helvetia sacra*. 10 vols in 28 parts (Bern: Francke and others, 1972–2007), 3.1: Elsanne Gilomen-Schenkel, ed., *Frühe Klöster, die Benediktiner und die Benediktinerinnen in der Schweiz* (1986). 75–78.

———. "'Officium paterne providentie' ou 'Supercilium noxie dominationis': Remarques sur les couvents de bénédictines au Sud-Ouest du Saint-Empire." In Nicole Bouter, ed., *Les Religieuses dans le cloître et dans le monde des origines à nos jours: Actes du deuxième colloque international du C.E.R.C.O.R., Poitiers, 29 septembre-2 octobre 1988*. Saint-Etienne: Publications de l'Université de Saint-Etienne, 1994. 367–71.

Gilsdorf, Sean. *The Favor of Friends: Intercession and Aristocratic Politics in Carolingian and Ottonian Europe*. Leiden: Brill, 2014.

———, trans. *Queenship and Sanctity: The Lives of Mathilda and The Epitaph of Adelheid*. Washington, D.C.: Catholic University of America Press, 2004.

Glenn, Jason. "Two Lives of Saint Radegund." In Jason Glenn, ed., *The Middle Ages in Texts and Texture: Reflections on Medieval Sources*. Toronto: University of Toronto Press, 2011. 57–69.

Goering, Joseph Ward. *William de Montibus (c. 1140–1213): The Schools and the Literature of Pastoral Care*. Toronto: Pontifical Institute of Mediaeval Studies, 1992.

Goffart, Walter. "Le Mans, St. Scholastica, and the Literary Tradition of the Translation of St. Benedict." *Revue bénédictine* 77 (1967): 107–141.

Gold, Penny Schine. "The Charters of Le Ronceray d'Angers: Male/Female Interaction in Monastic Business." In Joel T. Rosenthal, ed., *Medieval Women and the Sources of Medieval History*. Athens: University of Georgia Press, 1990. 122–32.

———. *The Lady and the Virgin: Image, Attitude, and Experience in Twelfth-Century France*. Chicago: University of Chicago Press, 1985.

———. "Male/Female Cooperation: The Example of Fontevrault." In John A. Nichols and Lillian Thomas Shank, eds., *Distant Echoes, Medieval Religious Women*, 1. Cistercian Studies Series 71. Kalamazoo, Mich.: Cistercian Publications, 1984. 151–168.

Golding, Brian. "Authority and Discipline at the Paraclete, Fontevraud, and Sempringham." In Gert Melville and Anne Müller, eds., *Mittelalterliche Orden und Klöster im Vergleich: Methodische Ansätze und Perspektiven*. Vita regularis 34. Berlin: Lit, 2007. 87–111.

———. "Bishops and Nuns: Forms of the *cura monialium* in Twelfth- and Thirteenth-Century England." In Janet Burton and Karen Stöber, eds., *Women in the Medieval Monastic World*. Turnhout: Brepols, 2015. 97–121.

———. *Gilbert of Sempringham and the Gilbertine Order, c.1130-c.1300*. Oxford: Clarendon Press, 1995.

———. "Hermits, Monks, and Women in Twelfth-Century France and England: The Experience of Obazine and Sempringham." In Judith Loades, ed., *Monastic Studies: The Continuity of Tradition*. Bangor, Maine: Headstart History, 1990. 127–45.

Granata, Aldo. "La dottrina dell'Elemosina nel sermone 'Pro sanctimonialibus de Paraclito' di Abelardo." *Aevum* 47 (1973): 32–59.

Greven, Joseph. *Die Anfänge der Beginen. Ein Beitrag zur Geschichte der Volksfrömmigkeit und des Ordenswesens im Hochmittelalter*. Münster: Aschendorff, 1912.

Griffiths, Fiona J. "Brides and *Dominae*: Abelard's *Cura monialium* at the Augustinian Monastery of Marbach." *Viator* 34 (2003): 57–88.

——— "The Cross and the *Cura monialium*: Robert of Arbrissel, John the Evangelist, and the Pastoral Care of Women in the Age of Reform." *Speculum* 83 (2008): 303–330.

———. *The* Garden of Delights: *Reform and Renaissance for Women in the Twelfth Century*. Middle Ages Series. Philadelphia: University of Pennsylvania Press: 2007.

———. "'Like the Sister of Aaron': Medieval Religious Women as Makers and Donors of Liturgical Textiles." In Gert Melville and Anne Müller, eds., *Female* Vita religiosa *Between Late Antiquity and the High Middle Ages: Structures, Developments, and Spacial Contexts*. Vita regularis 47. Münster: Lit, 2011. 343–374.

———. "The Mass in Monastic Practice." In Alison I. Beach and Isabelle Cochelin, eds., *Cambridge History of Medieval Western Monasticism*. Cambridge: Cambridge University Press, Forthcoming.

———. "'Men's Duty to Provide for Women's Needs': Abelard, Heloise, and Their Negotiation of the *Cura monialium*." *Journal of Medieval History* 30 (2004): 1–24.

———. "Monks and Nuns at Rupertsberg: Guibert of Gembloux and Hildegard of Bingen." In Fiona J. Griffiths and Julie Hotchin, eds., *Partners in Spirit: Women, Men, and Religious Life in Germany, 1100–1500*. Medieval Women: Texts and Contexts 24. Turnhout: Brepols, 2014. 145–169.

———. "Siblings and the Sexes Within the Medieval Religious Life." *Church History* 77 (2008): 26–53.

———. "The Trouble with Churchmen: Warning against Avarice in the *Garden of Delights*." In Jeffrey F. Hamburger, Carola Jäggi, Susan Marti and Hedwig Röckelein,

eds., *Frauen–Kloster–Kunst. Neue Forschungen zur Kulturgeschichte des Mittelalters.*
Brepols: 2007. 147–154.

———. "Women and Reform in the Central Middle Ages." In Judith M. Bennett and Ruth
Mazo Karras, eds., *Oxford Handbook of Women and Gender in Medieval Europe.* Oxford:
Oxford University Press, 2013. 447–463.

Griffiths, Fiona J. and Julie Hotchin. "Women and Men in the Medieval Religious Landscape."
In Fiona J. Griffiths and Julie Hotchin, eds., *Partners in Spirit: Women, Men, and Religious
Life in Germany, 1100–1500.* Medieval Women: Texts and Contexts 24. Turnhout: Brepols,
2014. 1–45.

Griffiths, Fiona J. and Julie Hotchin, eds. *Partners in Spirit: Women, Men, and Religious Life in
Germany, 1100–1500.* Medieval Women: Texts and Contexts 24. Turnhout: Brepols, 2014.

Grönwoldt, Ruth. "Gestickte Dalmatik aus dem Gösser Ornat." In Reiner Haussherr, ed., *Die
Zeit der Staufer: Geschichte, Kunst, Kultur.* 5 vols. Stuttgart: Württembergisches
Landesmuseum, 1977. I, 632–634 (no. 799).

Grundmann, Herbert. *Religious Movements in the Middle Ages: The Historical Links Between
Heresy, the Mendicant Orders, and the Women's Religious Movement in the Twelfth and
Thirteenth Century, with the Historical Foundations of German Mysticism.* Trans. Steven
Rowan. [*Religiöse Bewegungen im Mittelalter: Untersuchungen über die geschichtlichen
Zusammenhänge zwischen der Ketzerei, den Bettelorden und der religiösen Frauenbewegung
im 12. und 13. Jahrhundert und über die geschichtlichen Grundlagen der deutschen Mystik.*
Berlin: E. Ebering, 1935; new ed. 1961]. Notre Dame, Ind.: University of Notre Dame Press,
1995.

Guest, Gerald B. "'The Darkness and the Obscurity of Sins': Representing Vice in the
Thirteenth-Century *Bibles moralisées.*" In Richard Newhauser, ed., *In the Garden of Evil:
The Vices and Culture in the Middle Ages.* Papers in Mediaeval Studies, 18. Toronto:
Pontifical Institute of Mediaeval Studies Press, 2005. 74–103.

Guillotel, Hubert. "Les premiers temps de l'abbaye de St-Sulpice la Forêt." *Bulletin de la Société
d'Histoire d'Archéologie de Bretagne* (1971–1974): 60–62.

Gussone, Nikolaus "Die Jungfrauenweihe in ottonischer Zeit nach dem Ritus im *Pontifikale
Romano-Germanicum.*" In Jeffrey F. Hamburger, Carola Jäggi, Susan Marti, and Hedwig
Röckelein, eds., *Frauen–Kloster–Kunst. Neue Forschungen zur Kulturgeschichte des
Mittelalters.* Turnhout: Brepols, 2007. 25–41.

Haarländer, Stephanie. "Doppelklöster und ihre Forschungsgeschichte." In Edeltraud Klueting,
ed., *Fromme Frauen—unbequeme Frauen?: Weibliches Religiosentum im Mittelalter.*
Hildesheimer Forschungen 3. Hildesheim: Olms, 2006. 27–44.

———. "'Schlangen unter den Fischen': Männliche und weibliche Religiosen in
Doppelklöstern des hohen Mittelalters." In Sigrid Schmitt, ed., *Frauen und Kirche.*
Mainzer Vorträge, 6. Stuttgart: Steiner, 2002. 55–69

Halpin, Patricia A. *The Religious Experience of Women in Anglo-Saxon England.* Ph.D.
dissertation, Boston College, 2000.

Hamburger, Jeffrey F. "Art, Enclosure, and the Pastoral Care of Nuns." In Jeffrey F. Hamburger,
The Visual and the Visionary: Art and Female Spirituality in Late Medieval Germany. New
York: Zone Books, 1998. 35–109.

———. "Brother, Bride, and *alter Christus*: The Virginal Body of John the Evangelist in
Medieval Art, Theology, and Literature." In Ursula Peters, ed., *Text und Kultur:
Mittelalterliche Literatur 1150–1450.* Stuttgart: Metzler, 2001. 296–327.

———. *St. John the Divine: The Deified Evangelist in Medieval Art and Theology.* Berkeley: University of California Press, 2002.

———. *The Visual and the Visionary: Art and Female Spirituality in Late Medieval Germany.* New York: Zone Books, 1998.

Hamilton, Tracy Chapman. "Queenship and Kinship in the French *Bible moralisée*: The Example of Blanche of Castile and Vienna ÖNB 2554." In Kathleen Nolan, ed., *Capetian Women.* New York: Palgrave Macmillan, 2003. 177–208.

Haney, Kristine. *The St. Albans Psalter: An Anglo-Norman Song of Faith.* New York: Peter Lang, 2002.

Harris, Jennifer A. "Building Heaven on Earth: Cluny as *Locus sanctissimus* in the Eleventh Century." In Susan Boynton and Isabelle Cochelin, eds., *From Dead of Night to End of Day: The Medieval Customs of Cluny=Du cœur de la nuit à la fin du jour: les coutumes clunisiennes au Moyen Âge.* Disciplina monastica 3. Turnhout: Brepols, 2005. 131–151.

Harvey, Paul B., Jr. "Jerome Dedicates his *Vita Hilarionis.*" *Vigiliae Christianae* 59 (2005): 286–297.

Hasdenteufel-Röding, Maria. "Studien zur Gründung von Frauenklöstern im frühen Mittelalter. Ein Beitrag zum religiösen Ideal der Frau und seiner monastischen Umsetzung." Ph.D. dissertation, Freiburg, 1988.

Haverkamp, Alfred. "Tenxwind von Andernach und Hildegard von Bingen: Zwei 'Weltanschauungen' in der Mitte des 12. Jahrhunderts." In Lutz Fenske, Werner Rösener, and Thomas Zotz, ed., *Institutionen, Kultur und Gesellschaft im Mittelalter: Festschrift für Josef Fleckenstein zu seinem 65. Geburtstag.* Sigmaringen: Jan Thorbecke, 1984. 515–548.

Hayward, Rebecca. "Spiritual Friendship and Gender Difference in the *Liber confortatorius.*" In Stephanie Hollis, ed., *Writing the Wilton Women: Goscelin's* Legend of Edith *and* Liber Confortatorius. Medieval Women: Texts and Contexts 9. Turnhout: Brepols, 2004. 341–353.

Head, Thomas. "The Marriages of Christina of Markyate." In Samuel Fanous and Henrietta Leyser, eds., *Christina of Markyate: A Twelfth-Century Holy Woman.* London: Routledge, 2005. 116–137.

Heffernan, Thomas J. *Sacred Biography: Saints and Their Biographers in the Middle Ages.* Oxford: Oxford University Press, 1988.

Heinzer, Felix. "Unequal Twins: Visionary Attitude and Monastic Culture in Elisabeth of Schönau and Hildegard of Bingen." In Beverly Mayne Kienzle, Debra L. Stoudt, and George Ferzoco, eds., *A Companion to Hildegard of Bingen.* Leiden: Brill, 2014. 85–108.

Hellemans, Babette S., ed. *Rethinking Abelard: A Collection of Critical Essays.* Leiden: Brill, 2014.

Hicks, Leonie V. *Religious Life in Normandy 1050–1300. Space, Gender, and Social Pressure.* Woodbridge: Boydell, 2007.

Hill, Joyce. "Making Women Visible: An Adaptation of the *Regularis concordia* in Cambridge, Corpus Christi College MS 201." In Catherine E. Karkov and Nicholas Howe, eds., *Conversion and Colonization in Anglo-Saxon England.* Tempe, Ariz.: ACMRS, 2006. 153–167.

Hillebrandt, Maria, "Stiftungen zum Seelenheil durch Frauen in den Urkunden des Klosters Cluny." In Franz Neiske, Dietrich Poeck, and Mechthild Sandmann, eds., *Vinculum societatis. Joachim Wollasch zum 60. Geburtstag.* Sigmaringendorf: Glock und Lutz, 1991. 58–67.

Hilpisch, Stephanus. *Die Doppelklöster. Entstehung und Organisation.* Beiträge zur Geschichte des alten Mönchtums und des Benediktinerordens, 15. Münster in Westf.: Aschendorff, 1928.

Hindsley, Patrick Leonard. *The Mystics of Engelthal: Writings from a Medieval Monastery*. New York: St. Martin's Press, 1998.

Hinson, E. Glenn. "Women Biblical Scholars in the Late Fourth Century: The Aventine Circle." *Studia Patristica* 33 (1997): 319–324.

Hirbodian, Sigrid. "Pastors and Seducers: The Practice of the *Cura Monialium* in Mendicant Convents in Strasbourg." In Fiona J. Griffiths and Julie Hotchin, eds., *Partners in Spirit: Women, Men, and Religious Life in Germany, 1100–1500*. Medieval Women: Texts and Contexts 24. Turnhout: Brepols, 2014. 303–337.

Hollis, Stephanie. *Anglo-Saxon Women and the Church: Sharing a Common Fate*. Woodbridge: Boydell Press, 1992.

———. "Goscelin's Writings and the Wilton Women." In Stephanie Hollis, ed., *Writing the Wilton Women: Goscelin's* Legend of Edith *and* Liber Confortatorius. Medieval Women: Texts and Contexts 9. Turnhout: Brepols, 2004. 217–244.

———. "St. Edith and the Wilton Community." In Stephanie Hollis, ed., *Writing the Wilton Women: Goscelin's* Legend of Edith *and* Liber Confortatorius. Medieval Women: Texts and Contexts 9. Turnhout: Brepols, 2004. 245–280.

———. "Wilton as a Centre of Learning." In Stephanie Hollis, ed., *Writing the Wilton Women: Goscelin's* Legend of Edith *and* Liber Confortatorius. Medieval Women: Texts and Contexts 9. Turnhout: Brepols, 2004. 307–338.

Hollis, Stephanie, ed. *Writing the Wilton Women: Goscelin's* Legend of Edith *and* Liber Confortatorius. Medieval Women: Texts and Contexts 9. Turnhout: Brepols, 2004.

Hollis, Stephanie and Jocelyn Wogan-Browne. "St. Albans and Women's Monasticism: Lives and Their Foundations in Christina's World." In Samuel Fanous and Henrietta Leyser, eds., *Christina of Markyate: A Twelfth-Century Holy Woman*. London: Routledge, 2005. 25–52.

Hotchin, Julie. "Abbot as Guardian and Cultivator of Virtues: Two Perspectives on the *Cura monialium* in Practice." In Linda Rasmussen, Valerie Spear, and Diane Tillotson, eds., *Our Medieval Heritage: Essays in Honour of John Tillotson for his 60th Birthday*. Cardiff: Merton Priory Press, 2002. 50–64.

———. "Female Religious Life and the *Cura monialium* in Hirsau Monasticism, 1080 to 1150." In Constant J. Mews, ed., *Listen, Daughter: The Speculum Virginum and the Formation of Religious Women in the Middle Ages*. New York: Palgrave, 2001. 59–83.

———. "The Nun's Crown." *Early Modern Women: An Interdisciplinary Journal* 4 (2009): 187–194.

———. "Women's Reading and Monastic Reform in Twelfth-Century Germany: The Library of the Nuns of Lippoldsberg." In Alison I. Beach, ed., *Manuscripts and Monastic Culture: Reform and Renewal in Twelfth-Century Germany*. Medieval Church Studies, 13. Turnhout: Brepols, 2007. 139–189.

Houwen, L. A. J. R. and A. A. MacDonald, eds. *Alcuin of York: Scholar at the Carolingian Court: Proceedings of the Third Germania Latina Conference held at the University of Groningen, May 1995*. Groningen: E. Forsten, 1998.

Huneycutt, Lois L. "Intercession and the High-Medieval Queen: The Esther Topos." In Jennifer Carpenter and Sally-Beth Maclean, eds., *Power of the Weak: Studies on Medieval Women*. Urbana: University of Illinois Press, 1995. 126–146.

———. "'Proclaiming her Dignity Abroad': The Literary and Artistic Network of Matilda of Scotland, Queen of England 1100–1118." In June Hall McCash, ed., *The Cultural Patronage of Medieval Women*. Athens: University of Georgia Press, 1996. 155–174.

Hunt, E. D. *Holy Land Pilgrimage in the Later Roman Empire, A.D. 312–460.* Oxford: Oxford University Press, 1982.

Hunt, Noreen. *Cluny Under Saint Hugh. 1049–1109.* Notre Dame, Ind.: University of Notre Dame Press, 1967.

Hunter, David G. "Asceticism, Priesthood, and Exegesis: 1 Corinthians 7:5 in Jerome and his Contemporaries." In Hans-Ulrich Weidemann, ed., *Asceticism and Exegesis in Early Christianity: The Reception of New Testament Texts in Ancient Ascetic Discourses.* Göttingen: Vandenhoeck and Ruprecht, 2013. 413–427.

———. "The Virgin, the Bride, and the Church: Reading Psalm 45 in Ambrose, Jerome, and Augustine." *Church History* 69 (2000): 281–303.

Huyghebaert, Nicolas. "Les femmes laïques dans la vie religieuse des XIe et XIIe siècles dans la province ecclésiastique de Reims." In *I laici nella societas christiana dei secoli XI e XII: Atti della terza Settimana internazionale di studio.* Mendola, 21–27 agosto 1965. Milan: Vita e pensiero, 1968. 346–389.

Ilgen, Theodor. "Die Weiheinschrift vom Jahre 1151 in der ehemaligen Stiftskirche zu Schwarzrheindorf." *Westdeutsche Zeitschrift für Geschichte und Kunst* 24 (1905): 34–60.

Innes, Matthew. "Keeping it in the Family: Women and Aristocratic Memory, 700–1200." In Elisabeth van Houts, ed., *Medieval Memories: Men, Women, and the Past, 700–1300.* New York: Longman, 2001. 17–35.

Iogna-Prat, Dominique. "La femme dans la perspective pénitentielle des ermites du Bas-Maine (fin XIème début XIIème siècle)." *Revue d'histoire de la spiritualité* 53 (1977): 47–64.

———. "La Madeleine du *Sermo in veneratione sanctae Mariae Magdalenae* attribué à Odon de Cluny." In Georges Duby, ed., *La Madeleine (VIIIe-XIIIe siècle).* Mélanges de l'École française de Rome. Moyen Âge, 104, 1. Rome: L'Ecole française de Rome, 1992. 37–70.

Jacobs, Andrew S. "'Let Him Guard *Pietas*': Early Christian Exegesis and the Ascetic Family." *Journal of Early Christian Studies* 11 (2003): 265–281.

Jaeger, C. Stephen. *Ennobling Love: In Search of a Lost Sensibility.* Philadelphia: University of Pennsylvania Press, 1999.

Jansen, Katherine Ludwig. *The Making of the Magdalen: Preaching and Popular Devotion in the Later Middle Ages.* Princeton, N.J.: Princeton University Press, 2000.

———. "Maria Magdalena: *Apostolorum Apostola.*" In Beverly Mayne Kienzle and Pamela J. Walker, eds., *Women Preachers and Prophets Through Two Millennia of Christianity.* Berkeley: University of California Press, 1998. 57–96.

Johnson, Penelope D. *Equal in Monastic Profession: Religious Women in Medieval France.* Chicago: University of Chicago Press, 1991.

Jolivet, Jean and Henri Habrias, eds. *Pierre Abélard: colloque international de Nantes.* Rennes: Presses universitaires de Rennes, 2003.

Jordan, Erin L. "Gender Concerns: Monks, Nuns, and Patronage of the Cistercian Order in Thirteenth-Century Flanders and Hainaut." *Speculum* 87 (2012): 62–94.

Jungblut, Renate. *Hieronymus: Darstellung und Verehrung eines Kirchenvaters.* Bamberg: K. Urlaub, 1967.

Kaczynski, Bernice M. "The Authority of the Fathers: Patristic Texts in Early Medieval Libraries and Scriptoria." *The Journal of Medieval Latin* 16 (2006): 1–27.

———. "Edition, Translation, and Exegesis: The Carolingians and the Bible." In Richard E. Sullivan, ed., *The Gentle Voices of Teachers: Aspects of Learning in the Carolingian Age.* Columbus: Ohio State University Press, 1995. 171–185.

Kelly, J. N. D. *Jerome: His Life, Writings, and Controversies.* London: Duckworth, 1975.

Kemper, Joachim. "Das benediktinische Doppelkloster Schönau und die Visionen Elisabeths von Schönau." *Archiv für mittelrheinische Kirchengeschichte* 54 (2002): 55–102.

Kerby-Fulton, Kathryn. "Skepticism, Agnosticism, and Belief: The Spectrum of Attitudes Toward Vision in Late Medieval England." In Kathryn Kerby-Fulton, ed., *Women and the Divine in Literature Before 1700: Essays in Memory of Margot Louis.* Victoria: ELS Editions, 2009. 1–17.

Kern, Peter. "Das Bildprogramm der Doppelkirche von Schwarzrheindorf, die Lehre vom vierfachen Schriftsinn und die 'memoria' des Stifters Arnold von Wied." *Deutsche Vierteljahrsschrift für Literaturwissenschaft und Geistesgeschichte* 77 (2003): 353–379.

Kerr, Berenice M. *Religious Life for Women, c.1100–c.1350: Fontevraud in England.* Oxford: Oxford University Press, 1999.

Kessler, Herbert L. *The Illustrated Bibles from Tours.* Princeton, N.J.: Princeton University Press, 1977.

Kienzle, Beverly Mayne. "Penitents and Preachers: The Figure of Saint Peter and his Relationship to Saint Mary Magdalene." In Loredana Lazzari and Anna Maria Valente Bacci, eds., *La figura di San Pietro nelle fonti del medioevo: atti del convegno tenutosi in occasione dello Studiorum universitatum docentium congressus: Viterbo e Roma 5–8 settembre 2000.* Louvain-la-Neuve: Fédération internationale des Instituts d'études médiévales, 2001. 248–272.

Kiff-Hooper, J. A. "Class Books or Works of Art?: Some Observations on the Tenth-Century Manuscripts of Aldhelm's *De Laude Virginitatis.*" In John Taylor, G. A. Loud, and I. N. Wood, eds., *Church and Chronicle in the Middle Ages: Essays Presented to John Taylor.* London: Hambledon Press 1991. 15–26.

Kim, Young Richard. "Jerome and Paulinian, Brothers." *Vigiliae Christianae* 67 (2013): 517–530.

Klapp, Sabine. "Negotiating Autonomy: Canons In Late Medieval *Frauenstifte.*" In Fiona J. Griffiths and Julie Hotchin, eds., *Partners in Spirit: Women, Men, and Religious Life in Germany, 1100–1500.* Medieval Women: Texts and Contexts 24. Turnhout: Brepols, 2014. 367–400.

Klein, Stacy S. *Ruling Women: Queenship and Gender in Anglo-Saxon Literature.* Notre Dame, Ind.: University of Notre Dame Press, 2006.

Kleinjung, Christine. *Frauenklöster als Kommunikationszentren und soziale Räume. Das Beispiel Worms vom 13. bis zum Beginn des 15. Jahrhunderts.* Korb: Didymos Verlag, 2008.

Klingshirn, William E. *Caesarius of Arles: The Making of a Christian Community in Late Antique Gaul.* Cambridge: Cambridge University Press, 1994.

Klueting, Edeltraud. "Die Petersfrauen im Doppelkonvent an St. Peter in Salzburg." In Jeffrey F. Hamburger, Carola Jäggi, Susan Marti, and Hedwig Röckelein, eds., *Frauen–Kloster–Kunst. Neue Forschungen zur Kulturgeschichte des Mittelalters.* Turnhout: Brepols, 2007. 413–420.

Kneller, C. A. "Joh 19, 26–27 bei den Kirchenvätern." *Zeitschrift für katholische Theologie* 40 (1916): 597–612.

Knust, Jennifer Wright. "Early Christian Re-Writing and the History of the *Pericope Adulterae.*" *Journal of Early Christian Studies* 14 (2006): 485–536.

Koebner, Richard. *Venantius Fortunatus: Seine Persönlichkeit und seine Stellung in der geistigen Kultur des Merowinger-Reiches.* Leipzig: B. G. Teubner, 1915.

Koehler, T. "Les principales interprétations traditionnelles de Jn. 19, 25–27, pendant les douze premiers siècles." *Bulletin de la Société française d'études mariales* 16 (1959): 119–155.

Kong, Katherine. *Lettering the Self in Medieval and Early Modern France.* Cambridge: D. S. Brewer, 2010.

Koopmans, Rachel M. "The Conclusion of Christina of Markyate's *Vita.*" *Journal of Ecclesiastical History* 51 (2000): 663–698.

———. "Dining at Markyate with Lady Christina." In Samuel Fanous and Henrietta Leyser, eds., *Christina of Markyate: A Twelfth-Century Holy Woman.* London: Routledge, 2005. 143–159.

Körkel-Hinkfoth, Regine. *Die Parabel von den klugen und törichten Jungfrauen (Mt. 25, 1–13) in der bildenden Kunst und im geistlichen Schauspiel.* New York: P. Lang, 1994.

Koslin, Désirée. "The Robe of Simplicity: Initiation, Robing, and Veiling of Nuns in the Middle Ages." In Stewart Gordon, ed., *Robes and Honor: The Medieval World of Investiture.* New York: Palgrave, 2001. 255–274.

Krahmer, Shawn M. "The Virile Bride of Bernard of Clairvaux." *Church History* 69 (2000): 304–327.

Kramer, Elizabeth Anne. *A Case Study of the Rupertsberg Antependium.* M.A. Thesis, University of Missouri-Columbia, 1999.

Krawiec, Rebecca. " 'From the Womb of the Church': Monastic Families." *Journal of Early Christian Studies* 11 (2003): 283–307.

Krings, Bruno. *Das Prämonstratenserstift Arnstein a.d. Lahn im Mittelalter (1139–1527).* Wiesbaden: Selbstverlag der Historischen Kommission für Nassau, 1990.

———. "Die Prämonstratenser und ihr weiblicher Zweig." In Irene Crusius and Helmut Flachenecker, eds., *Studien zum Prämonstratenserorden.* Göttingen: Vandenhoeck & Ruprecht, 2003. 75–105.

Krumeich, Christa. *Hieronymus und die christlichen feminae clarissimae.* Bonn: R. Habelt, 1993.

———. *Paula von Rom: christliche Mittlerin zwischen Okzident und Orient.* Bonn: Habelt, 2002.

Kuefler, Mathew S. "Castration and Eunuchism in the Middle Ages." In James A. Brundage and Vern L. Bullough, eds., *Handbook of Medieval Sexuality.* New York: Garland, 1996. 279–306.

———. *The Manly Eunuch: Masculinity, Gender Ambiguity, and Christian Ideology in Late Antiquity.* Chicago: University of Chicago Press, 2001.

Kunisch, Johannes. *Konrad III., Arnold von Wied und der Kapellenbau von Schwarzrheindorf.* Düsseldorf: Historischer Verein für den Niederrhein insbesondere das alte Erzbistum Köln, 1966.

Küsters, Urban. "Formen und Modelle religiöser Frauengemeinschaften im Umkreis der Hirsauer Reform des 11. und 12. Jahrhunderts." In Klaus Schreiner, ed., *Hirsau, St. Peter und Paul, 1091–1991.* Vol. II. *Geschichte, Lebens- und Verfassungsformen eines Reformklosters.* Forschungen und Berichte der Archäologie des Mittelalters in Baden-Württemberg 10. Stuttgart: K. Theiss, 1991. 195–220.

———. *Der verschlossene Garten: Volkssprachliche Hohelied-Auslegung und monastische Lebensform im 12. Jahrhundert.* Studia humaniora 2. Düsseldorf: Droste, 1985.

L'Hermite-Leclercq, Paulette. "Incertitudes et contingences aux origines des monastères féminins. L'exemple anglais de Markyate." In Jacques Dalarun, ed., *Robert d'Arbrissel et la vie religieuse dans l'Ouest de la France: Actes du colloque de Fontevraud 13–16 décembre 2001.* Disciplina Monastica 1. Turnhout: Brepols, 2004. 121–137.

Lähnemann, Henrike. "'An dessen bom wil ik stighen'. Die Ikonographie des *Wichmannsburger Antependiums* im Kontext der Medinger Handschriften." *Oxford German Studies* 34 (2005): 19–46.

Laistner, M. L. W. "The Study of St. Jerome in the Early Middle Ages." In Francis X. Murphy, ed., *A Monument to Saint Jerome: Essays on Some Aspects of His Life, Works, and Influence.* New York: Sheed & Ward, 1952. 233–256.

Lambot, C. "L'homélie du Pseudo-Jérôme sur l'assomption et l'évangile de la nativité de Marie d'après une lettre inédite d'Hincmar." *Revue bénédictine* 46 (1934): 265–282.

Laningham, Susan D. "Making a Saint out of a Sibling." In Naomi J. Miller and Naomi Yavneh, eds., *Sibling Relations and Gender in the Early Modern World: Sisters, Brothers, and Others.* Aldershot: Ashgate, 2006. 15–27.

Larrington, Carolyne. *Brothers and Sisters in Medieval European Literature.* Woodbridge: York Medieval Press, 2015.

Laurence, Patrick. *Jérôme et le nouveau modèle féminin: la conversion à la "vie parfaite".* Paris: Institut d'études Augustiniennes, 1997.

Lauwers, Michel. "Les femmes et l'eucharistie dans l'Occident médiéval: interdits, transgressions, devotions." In Nicole Bériou, Beátrice Caseau, and Dominique Rigaux, eds., *Pratiques de l'eucharistie dans les Églises d'Orient et d'Occident (Antiquité et Moyen Age), I: L'institution.* Paris: Institut d'Études Augustiniennes, 2009. 445–476.

———. *La mémoire des ancêtres, le souci des morts. Morts, rites, et société au Moyen Âge (Diocèse de Liège, XIe-XIIIe siècles).* Paris: Beauchesne, 1997.

Lawless, George. *Augustine of Hippo and His Monastic Rule.* Oxford: Clarendon Press, 1987.

Le Goff, Jacques. *The Birth of Purgatory.* Chicago: University of Chicago Press, 1984.

Leclercq, Jean. "'Ad ipsam sophiam Christum': le témoignage monastique d'Abélard." *Revue d'ascétique et de mystique* 46 (1970): 161–181.

———. "Eucharistic Celebrations Without Priests in the Middle Ages." *Worship* 55 (1981): 160–168.

———. "S. Pierre Damien et les femmes." *Studia monastica* 15 (1973): 43–55.

———. "Prières médiévales pour recevoir l'Eucharistie, pour saluer et pour bénir la croix." *Ephemerides liturgicae* 79 (1965): 327–340.

LeMoine, Fannie J. "Jerome's Gift to Women Readers." In Ralph W. Mathisen and Hagith S. Sivan, eds., *Shifting Frontiers in Late Antiquity.* Aldershot: Variorum, 1996. 230–241.

Leopold, Gerhard. "Damenstiftskirche und Wipertikirche in Quedlinburg zur Zeit der ottonischen Herrscher." In Michael Brandt and Arne Eggebrecht, eds., *Bernward von Hildesheim und das Zeitalter der Ottonen: Katalog der Ausstellung, Hildesheim 1993.* 2 vols. Hildesheim: Bernward Verlag, 1993. II, 371–375.

Lester, Anne E. *Creating Cistercian Nuns: The Women's Religious Movement and its Reform in Thirteenth-Century Champagne.* Ithaca, N.Y.: Cornell University Press, 2011.

Lewis, Gertrud Jaron. *By Women, For Women, About Women: The Sister-Books of Fourteenth-Century Germany.* Toronto: Pontifical Institute of Mediaeval Studies, 1996.

Leyser, Conrad. "Augustine in the Latin West, 430-c. 900." In Mark Vessey, ed., *A Companion to Augustine.* Malden, Mass.: Wiley-Blackwell, 2012. 450–464.

———. "Custom, Truth, and Gender in Eleventh-Century Reform." In R. N. Swanson, ed., *Gender and Christian Religion.* Studies in Church History 34. Woodbridge: Boydell Press, 1998. 75–91.

Leyser, Henrietta. "C. 1080–1215: Texts." In Samuel Fanous and Vincent Gillespie, eds., *The Cambridge Companion to Medieval English Mysticism*. Cambridge: Cambridge University Press, 2011. 49–67.

Leyser, Karl J. *Rule and Conflict in an Early Medieval Society: Ottonian Saxony*. London: Edward Arnold, 1979.

Licence, Tom. "History and Hagiography in the Late Eleventh Century: The Life and Work of Herman the Archdeacon, Monk of Bury St. Edmunds." *English Historical Review* 124 (2000): 516–544.

Liebermann, F. "Raginald von Canterbury." *Neues Archiv der Gesellschaft für ältere deutsche Geschichtskunde* 13 (1888): 517–556.

Lifshitz, Felice. "Gender Trouble in Paradise: The Problem of the Liturgical *Virgo*." In Debra Higgs Strickland, ed., *Images of Medieval Sanctity: Essays in Honour of Gary Dickson*. Leiden: Brill, 2007. 25–39.

———. "The Martyr, the Tomb, and the Matron: Constructing the (Masculine) 'Past' as a Female Power Base." In Gerd Althoff, Johannes Fried, and Patrick J. Geary, eds., *Medieval Concepts of the Past: Ritual, Memory, Historiography*. Cambridge: Cambridge University Press, 2002. 311–341.

———. "Priestly Women, Virginal Men: Litanies and Their Discontents." In Lisa M. Bitel and Felice Lifshitz, eds., *Gender and Christianity in Medieval Europe: New Perspectives*. Philadelphia: University of Pennsylvania Press, 2008. 87–102.

———. *Religious Women in Early Carolingian Francia: A Study of Manuscript Transmission and Monastic Culture*. New York: Fordham University Press, 2014.

Linde, Cornelia. *How to Correct the Sacra Scriptura?: Textual Criticism of the Latin Bible Between the Twelfth and Fifteenth Century*. Oxford: Society for the Study of Medieval Languages and Literature, 2012.

Livingstone, Amy. *Out of Love for my Kin: Aristocratic Family Life in the Lands of the Loire, 1000–1200*. Ithaca, N.Y.: Cornell University Press, 2010.

Loewe, Raphael. "The Medieval History of the Latin Vulgate." In G. W. H. Lampe, ed., *The Cambridge History of the Bible*. II. *The West from the Fathers to the Reformation*. Cambridge: Cambridge University Press, 1969. 102–154.

LoPrete, Kimberly A. *Adela of Blois: Countess and Lord (c.1067–1137)*. Dublin: Four Courts Press, 2007.

Luscombe, David E. "From Paris to the Paraclete: The Correspondence of Abelard and Heloise." *Proceedings of the British Academy* 74 (1988): 247–283.

———. "Monasticism in the Lives and Writings of Heloise and Abelard." In Judith Loades, ed., *Monastic Studies: The Continuity of Tradition*. Bangor, Maine: Headstart History, 1990. 1–11.

———. "Pierre Abélard et l'abbaye du Paraclet." In Jean Jolivet and Henri Habrias, eds., *Pierre Abélard: colloque international de Nantes*. Rennes: Presses universitaires de Rennes, 2003. 215–229.

Lutter, Christina. *Geschlecht und Wissen, Norm und Praxis, Lesen und Schreiben: Monastische Reformgemeinschaften im 12. Jahrhundert*. Veröffentlichung des Instituts für österreichische Geschichtsforschung, 43. Vienna: Oldenbourg, 2005.

Lyon, Jonathan R. *Princely Brothers and Sisters: The Sibling Bond in German Politics, 1100–1250*. Ithaca, N.Y.: Cornell University Press, 2013.

MacDonald, Margaret Y. "Was Celsus Right? The Role of Women in the Expansion of Early Christianity." In David L. Balch and Carolyn Osiek, eds., *Early Christian Families in*

Context: An Interdisciplinary Dialogue. Grand Rapids, Mich.: William B. Eerdmans, 2003. 157–184.

Macy, Gary. *The Hidden History of Women's Ordination: Female Clergy in the Medieval West.* Oxford: Oxford University Press, 2008.

Magnani, Eliana. "L'ascétisme domestique féminin (IVe-XIIe siècle)." In Alison I. Beach and Isabelle Cochelin, eds., *Cambridge History of Medieval Western Monasticism*. Cambridge: Cambridge University Press, Forthcoming.

Maier, Marinus. "Ein schwäbisch-bayerischer Freundskreis Gregors VII. nach der Vita Herlucae des Paul v. Bernried." *Studien und Mitteilungen zur Geschichte des Benediktinerordens und seiner Zweige* 74 (1963): 313–332.

Marenbon, John. *Abelard in Four Dimensions: A Twelfth-Century Philosopher in His Context and Ours.* Notre Dame, Ind.: University of Notre Dame Press, 2013.

———. "Life, Milieu, and Intellectual Contexts." In Jeffrey E. Brower and Kevin Guilfoy, eds., *The Cambridge Companion to Abelard*. Cambridge: Cambridge University Press, 2004. 13–44.

———. *The Philosophy of Peter Abelard*. Cambridge: Cambridge University Press, 1997.

Markowski, Michael. "Treatment of Women in Peter of Blois' Letter Collection." In Susan J. Ridyard and Robert G. Benson, eds., *Minorities and Barbarians in Medieval Life and Thought*. Sewanee, Tenn.: University of the South Press, 1996. 63–71.

Marti, Susan. "Double Monasteries in Images? Observations on Book Illumination from Communities in the South-Western Empire." In Fiona J. Griffiths and Julie Hotchin, eds., *Partners in Spirit: Women, Men, and Religious Life in Germany, 1100–1500*. Medieval Women: Texts and Contexts 24. Turnhout: Brepols, 2014. 75–107.

———. "Einleitung: Doppelklöster." In Jeffrey F. Hamburger, Carola Jäggi, Susan Marti, and Hedwig Röckelein, eds., *Frauen–Kloster–Kunst. Neue Forschungen zur Kulturgeschichte des Mittelalters*. Turnhout: Brepols, 2007. 379–382.

———. *Malen, Schreiben und Beten: die spätmittelalterliche Handschriftenproduktion im Doppelkloster Engelberg*. Zürcher Schriften zur Kunst-, Architektur- und Kulturgeschichte 3. Zürich: ZIP, 2002.

Martyn, John R. C. *Gregory and Leander: an Analysis of the Special Friendship Between Pope Gregory the Great and Leander, Archbishop of Seville*. Newcastle upon Tyne: Cambridge Scholars, 2013.

Matter, E. Ann. *The Voice of My Beloved: The Song of Songs in Western Medieval Christianity*. Philadelphia: University of Pennsylvania Press, 1990.

Matthew, Donald. "The Incongruities of the St. Albans Psalter." *Journal of Medieval History* 34 (2008): 396–416.

Mayo, Janet. *A History of Ecclesiastical Dress*. London: B. T. Batsford, 1984.

McDonnell, Ernest W. "The 'Vita Apostolica': Diversity or Dissent." *Church History* 24 (1955): 15–31.

McGovern-Mouron, Anne. " 'Listen to Me, Daughter, Listen to a Faithful Counsel': The *Liber de modo bene vivendi ad sororem*." In Denis Renevey and Christiania Whitehead, eds., *Writing Religious Women: Female Spiritual and Textual Practices in Late Medieval England*. Toronto: University of Toronto Press, 2000. 81–106.

McGuire, Brian Patrick. "Friends and Tales in the Cloister: Oral Sources in Caesarius of Heisterbach's *Dialogus Miraculorum*." *Analecta Cisterciensia* 36 (1980): 167–247.

———. "Holy Women and Monks in the Thirteenth Century: Friendship or Exploitation?" *Vox Benedictina* 6 (1989): 343–373.

————. "Late Medieval Care and Control of Women: Jean Gerson and his Sisters." *Revue d'historique ecclésiastique* 92 (1997): 5–37.

McInerney, Maud Burnett. "Like A Virgin: The Problem of Male Virginity in the *Symphonia*." In Maud Burnett McInerney, ed., *Hildegard of Bingen: A Book of Essays*. New York: Garland, 1998. 133–154.

McKitterick, Rosamond. "Carolingian Bible Production: The Tours Anomaly." In Richard Gameson, ed., *The Early Medieval Bible: Its Production, Decoration and Use*. Cambridge: Cambridge University Press, 1994. 63–77.

————. *Charlemagne: The Formation of a European Identity*. Cambridge: Cambridge University Press, 2008.

————. "Nuns' Scriptoria in England and Francia in the Eighth Century." In Rosamond McKitterick, *Books, Scribes, and Learning in the Frankish Kingdoms, 6th-9th Centuries*. Aldershot: Ashgate, 1994. VII.

————. "Women in the Ottonian Church: An Iconographic Perspective." In W. J. Sheils and Diana Wood, eds., *Women in the Church*. Studies in Church History 27. Oxford: Blackwell, 1990. 79–100.

McLaughlin, Mary Martin. "Abelard as Autobiographer: The Motives and Meaning of his 'Story of Calamities.'" *Speculum* 42 (1967): 463–488.

————. "Heloise the Abbess: The Expansion of the Paraclete." In Bonnie Wheeler, ed., *Listening to Heloise: The Voice of a Twelfth-Century Woman*. New York: St. Martin's Press, 2000. 1–17.

————. "Peter Abelard and the Dignity of Women: Twelfth-Century 'Feminism' in Theory and Practice." In *Pierre Abélard, Pierre le Vénérable. Les courants philosophiques, littéraires et artistiques en Occident au milieu du XIIe siècle*. Colloques internationaux du Centre National de la Recherche Scientifique 546. Paris: Éditions du Centre national de la recherche scientifique, 1975. 287–334.

McLaughlin, Mary Martin with Bonnie Wheeler. "MS T (Troyes Bibliothèque Municipale, MS 802): The Paraclete and the Early History of the Correspondence of Abelard and Heloise." In Mary Martin McLaughlin, trans. and ed., with Bonnie Wheeler, *The Letters of Heloise and Abelard: A Translation of their Collected Correspondence and Related Writings*. New York: Palgrave Macmillan, 2009. 317–325.

McLaughlin, Megan. "The Bishop as Bridegroom: Marital Imagery and Clerical Celibacy in the Eleventh and Early Twelfth Centuries." In Michael Frassetto, ed., *Medieval Purity and Piety. Essays on Medieval Clerical Celibacy and Religious Reform*. New York: Garland, 1998. 209–237.

————. "Gender Paradox and the Otherness of God." *Gender & History* 3 (1991): 147–159.

————. *Sex, Gender, and Episcopal Authority in an Age of Reform, 1000–1122*. Cambridge: Cambridge University Press, 2010.

McNamara, Jo Ann. "Cornelia's Daughters: Paula and Eustochium." *Women's Studies* 11 (1984): 9–27.

————. "The 'Herrenfrage': The Restructuring of the Gender System, 1050–1150." In Clare A. Lees, ed., *Medieval Masculinities: Regarding Men in the Middle Ages*. Medieval Cultures 7. Minneapolis: University of Minnesota Press, 1994. 3–29.

————. *The Ordeal of Community*. Toronto: Peregrina, 1990.

————. *Sisters in Arms: Catholic Nuns Through Two Millennia*. Cambridge, Mass.: Harvard University Press, 1996.

McNamer, Sarah. *Affective Meditation and the Invention of Medieval Compassion*. Philadelphia: University of Pennsylvania Press, 2010.

Mecham, June L. "Breaking Old Habits: Recent Research on Women, Spirituality, and the Arts in the Middle Ages." *History Compass* 4 (2006): 448–480.

Meijns, Brigitte. "Opposition to Clerical Continence and the Gregorian Celibacy Legislation in the Diocese of Thérouanne: *Tractatus pro clericorum conubio* (c.1077–1078)." *Sacris erudiri* 47 (2008): 223–290.

Melve, Leidulf. "The Public Debate on Clerical Marriage in the Late Eleventh Century." *The Journal of Ecclesiastical History* 61 (2010): 688–706.

Meredith, Anthony. "Gregory of Nazianzus and Gregory of Nyssa on Basil." *Studia Patristica* 32 (1997): 163–169.

Mews, Constant J. *Abelard and his Legacy*. Aldershot: Ashgate, 2001.

———. "Guibert of Nogent's *Monodiae* (III, 17) in an Appendage to the *De haeresibus* of Augustine." *Revue des Études Augustiniennes* 33 (1987): 113–127.

———. "Heloise." In Alastair Minnis and Rosalynn Voaden, eds., *Medieval Holy Women in the Christian Tradition, c.1100-c.1500*. Brepols Essays in European Culture 1. Turnhout: Brepols, 2010. 267–289.

———. "Heloise and Liturgical Experience at the Paraclete." *Plainsong and Medieval Music* 11 (2002): 25–35.

———. "Heloise, the Paraclete Liturgy, and Mary Magdalen." In Marc Stewart and David Wulstan, eds. *Poetic and Musical Legacy of Heloise and Abelard: An Anthology of Essays by Various Authors*. Ottawa: Institute of Mediaeval Music, 2003. 100–112.

———. "Hildegard of Bingen and the Hirsau Reform in Germany 1080–1180." In Beverly Mayne Kienzle, Debra L. Stoudt, and George Ferzoco, eds., *A Companion to Hildegard of Bingen*. Leiden: Brill, 2014. 57–83.

———. "Hugh Metel, Heloise, and Peter Abelard: The Letters of an Augustinian Canon and the Challenge of Innovation in Twelfth-Century Lorraine." *Viator* 32 (2001): 59–91.

———. "Un lecteur de Jérôme au XIIe siècle: Pierre Abélard." In Yves-Marie Duval, ed., *Jérôme entre l'Occident et l'Orient. XVIe centenaire du départ de saint Jérôme de Rome et de son installation à Bethléem: actes du Colloque de Chantilly (septembre 1986)*. Paris: Etudes augustiniennes, 1988. 429–444.

———. *The Lost Love Letters of Heloise and Abelard: Perceptions of Dialogue in Twelfth-Century France*. New York: St. Martin's Press, 1999.

———. "Monastic Educational Culture Revisited: The Witness of Zwiefalten and the Hirsau Reform." In George Ferzoco and Carolyn Muessig, eds., *Medieval Monastic Education*. London: Leicester University Press, 2000. 182–197.

———. "Negotiating the Boundaries of Gender in Religious Life: Robert of Arbrissel and Hersende, Abelard and Heloise." *Viator* 37 (2006): 113–148.

———. "Virginity, Theology, and Pedagogy in the *Speculum virginum*." In Constant J. Mews, ed., *Listen, Daughter: The* Speculum virginum *and the Formation of Religious Women in the Middle Ages*. New York: Palgrave, 2001. 15–40.

Mews, Constant J., ed. *Listen, Daughter: The* Speculum virginum *and the Formation of Religious Women in the Middle Ages*. New York: Palgrave, 2001.

Mews, Constant J. and Claire Renkin. "The Legacy of Gregory the Great in the Latin West." In Bronwen Neil and Matthew Dal Santo, eds., *A Companion to Gregory the Great*. Leiden: Brill, 2013. 315–342.

Mews, Constant J. and Micha J. Perry. "Peter Abelard, Heloise, and Jewish Biblical Exegesis in the Twelfth Century." *Journal of Ecclesiastical History* 62 (2011): 3–19.

Milis, Ludo. *L'Ordre des chanoines réguliers d'Arrouaise: son histoire et son organisation, de la fondation de l'abbaye-mère (vers 1090) à la fin des chapitres annuels (1471).* Brugge: De Tempel, 1969.

Miller, Maureen C. *Clothing the Clergy: Virtue and Power in Medieval Europe, c. 800–1200.* Ithaca, N.Y.: Cornell University Press, 2014.

———. "Masculinity, Reform, and Clerical Culture: Narratives of Episcopal Holiness in the Gregorian Era." *Church History* 72 (2003): 25–52.

Monroe, Elizabeth. "Mary Magdalene as a Model of Devotion, Penitence, and Authority in the *Gospels of Henry the Lion and Matilda.*" In Peter V. Loewen and Robin Waugh, eds., *Mary Magdalene in Medieval Culture: Conflicted Roles.* New York: Routledge, 2014. 99–115.

Montgomery, Scott B. *St. Ursula and the Eleven Thousand Virgins of Cologne: Relics, Reliquaries, and the Visual Culture of Group Sanctity in Late Medieval Europe.* New York: Peter Lang, 2010.

Mooney, Catherine M., ed. *Gendered Voices: Medieval Saints and Their Interpreters.* Philadelphia: University of Pennsylvania Press, 1999.

Moore, R. I. "Family, Community, and Cult on the Eve of the Gregorian Reform." *Transactions of the Royal Historical Society* 5th ser. 30 (1980): 49–69.

Moore, Stephen D. "The Song of Songs in the History of Sexuality." *Church History* 69 (2000): 328–349.

Moxnes, Halvor, ed. *Constructing Early Christian Families: Family as Social Reality and Metaphor.* New York: Routledge, 1997.

Muehlberger, Ellen. *Cogitis Me: A Medieval Sermon on the Assumption.* M.A. Thesis, Indiana University, 2001.

Mulder-Bakker, Anneke B. "Ivetta of Huy: *Mater et Magistra.*" In Anneke B. Mulder-Bakker, ed., *Sanctity and Motherhood: Essays on Holy Mothers in the Middle Ages.* New York: Garland, 1995. 225–258.

———. *Lives of the Anchoresses: The Rise of the Urban Recluse in Medieval Europe.* Trans. Myra Heerspink Scholz. Philadelphia: University of Pennsylvania Press, 2005.

———. "Was Mary Magdalen a Magdalen?" In R. I. A. Nip, ed., *Media Latinitas: A Collection of Essays to Mark the Occasion of the Retirement of L. J. Engels.* Turnhout: Brepols, 1996. 269–274.

Mulder-Bakker, Anneke B. and Jocelyn Wogan-Browne, eds. *Household, Women, and Christianities in Late Antiquity and the Middle Ages.* Turnhout: Brepols, 2005.

Müller, Annalena. *Forming and Re-Forming Fontevraud. Monasticism, Geopolitics, and the Querelle des Frères (c. 1100–1643).* Ph.D. dissertation, Yale University, 2014.

Murray, Jacqueline. "Sexual Mutilation and Castration Anxiety: A Medieval Perspective." In Mathew Kuefler, ed., *The Boswell Thesis: Essays on Christianity, Social Tolerance, and Homosexuality.* Chicago: University of Chicago Press, 2006. 254–272.

Muschiol, Gisela. *Famula Dei: zur Liturgie in merowingischen Frauenklöstern.* Münster: Aschendorff, 1994.

———. "Das 'gebrechlichere Geschlecht' und der Gottesdienst. Zum religiösen Alltag in Frauengemeinschaften des Mittelalters." In Günter Berghaus, Thomas Schilp, and Michael Schlagheck, eds., *Herrschaft, Bildung und Gebet: Gründung und Anfänge des Frauenstifts Essen.* Essen: Klartext, 2000. 19–27.

———. "*Hoc dixit Ieronimus.* Monastische Tradition und Normierung im 12. Jahrhundert." In Andreas Holzem, ed., *Normieren–Tradieren–Inszenieren. Das Christentum als Buchreligion.* Darmstadt: Wissenschaftliche Buchgesellschaft, 2003. 109–125.

————. "Liturgie und Klausur: Zu den liturgischen Voraussetzungen von Nonnenemporen." In Irene Crusius, ed., *Studien zum Kanonissenstift*. Göttingen: Vandenhoeck und Ruprecht, 2001. 129–148.

————. "Men, Women, and Liturgical Practice in the Early Medieval West." In Leslie Brubaker and Julia M. H. Smith, eds., *Gender in the Early Medieval World: East and West, 300–900*. Cambridge: Cambridge University Press, 2004. 198–216.

————. "Vorbild und Konkurrenz: Martin von Tours und die heiligen Frauen." *Rottenburger Jahrbuch für Kirchengeschichte* 18 (1999): 77–88.

————. "Zeit und Raum–Liturgie und Ritus in mittelalterlichen Frauenkonventen." In Jutta Frings and Jan Gerchow, eds., *Krone und Schleier: Kunst aus mittelalterlichen Frauenklöstern, Ausstellungskatalog*. Kunst- und Ausstellungshalle der Bundesrepublik Deutschland und Ruhrlandmuseum Essen. Munich: Hirmer, 2005. 41–51.

————. "Zur Typologie weiblicher Heiliger vom frühen Mittelalter bis zur 'Legenda maior.'" In Eckhard Grunewald and Nikolaus Gussone, eds., *Das Bild der heiligen Hedwig in Mittelalter und Neuzeit*. Munich: Oldenbourg, 1996. 39–54.

Müssigbrod, Axel. "Frauenkonversionen in Moissac." *Historisches Jahrbuch* 104 (1984): 113–129.

Naschenweng, Hannes P. "Das Profeßbuch und Necrologium des Benediktinerinnenstiftes Göss 1010–1602." *Studien und Mitteilungen zur Geschichte des Benediktinerordens und seiner Zweige* 108 (1997): 151–229.

Neff, Amy. "The Pain of *Compassio*: Mary's Labor at the Foot of the Cross." *The Art Bulletin* 80 (1998): 254–273.

Nelson, Janet L. "La cour impériale de Charlemagne." In Janet L. Nelson, *Rulers and Ruling Families in Early Medieval Europe: Alfred, Charles the Bald, and Others*. Brookfield, Vt.: Ashgate, 1999. XIV.

————. "Gender and Genre in Women Historians of the Early Middle Ages." In Janet L. Nelson, *The Frankish World, 750–900*. London: Hambledon Press, 1996. 183–197.

————. "Women and the Word in the Earlier Middle Ages." In W. J. Sheils and Diana Wood, eds., *Women in the Church*. Studies in Church History 27. Oxford: Blackwell, 1990. 53–78.

————. "Women at the Court of Charlemagne: A Case of Monstrous Regiment?" In John Carmi Parsons, ed., *Medieval Queenship*. New York: St. Martin's Press, 1993. 43–61.

Newman, Barbara. "Authority, Authenticity, and the Repression of Heloise." In Barbara Newman, *From Virile Woman to WomanChrist: Studies in Medieval Religion and Literature*. Philadelphia: University of Pennsylvania Press, 1995. 46–75.

————. "Divine Power Made Perfect in Weakness: St. Hildegard on the Frail Sex." In Lillian Thomas Shank and John A. Nichols, eds., *Peace Weavers, Medieval Religious Women*, 2. Cistercian Studies Series 72. Kalamazoo, Mich.: Cistercian Publications, 1987. 103–122.

————. "Flaws in the Golden Bowl: Gender and Spiritual Formation in the Twelfth Century." In Barbara Newman, *From Virile Woman to WomanChrist: Studies in Medieval Religion and Literature*. Philadelphia: University of Pennsylvania Press, 1995. 19–45.

————. *Frauenlob's Song of Songs: A Medieval German Poet and his Masterpiece*. University Park: Pennsylvania State University Press, 2006.

————. "Gender." In Julia A. Lamm, ed., *Wiley-Blackwell Companion to Christian Mysticism*. Chichester: Blackwell, 2012. 41–55.

————. "Hildegard and Her Hagiographers: The Remaking of Female Sainthood." In Catherine M. Mooney, ed., *Gendered Voices: Medieval Saints and Their Interpreters*. Philadelpia: University of Pennsylvania Press, 1999. 16–34.

————. "Hildegard of Bingen: Visions and Validation." *Church History* 54 (1985): 163–175.

————. "Liminalities: Literate Women in the Long Twelfth Century." In Thomas F. X. Noble and John van Engen, eds., *European Transformations: The Long Twelfth Century*. Notre Dame, Ind.: University of Notre Dame Press, 2012. 354–402.

————. *Making Love in the Twelfth Century: "Letters of Two Lovers" in Context*. Philadelphia: University of Pennsylvania Press, 2016.

————. "On the Threshold of the Dead: Purgatory, Hell, and Religious Women." In Barbara Newman, *From Virile Woman to WomanChrist: Studies in Medieval Religion and Literature*. Philadelphia: University of Pennsylvania Press, 1995. 108–136.

————. "Preface." In Anne L. Clark, trans., *Elisabeth of Schönau: The Complete Works*. New York: Paulist Press, 2000. xi–xviii.

————. Review of *Affective Meditation and the Invention of Medieval Compassion*, by Sarah McNamer. *Journal of English and Germanic Philology* 110 (2011): 523–526.

————. "'Sibyl of the Rhine': Hildegard's Life and Times." In Barbara Newman, ed., *Voice of the Living Light: Hildegard of Bingen and Her World*. Berkeley: University of California Press, 1998. 1–29.

————. *Sister of Wisdom: St. Hildegard's Theology of the Feminine*. Berkeley: University of California Press, 1987.

————. "Three-Part Invention: The *Vita S. Hildegardis* and Mystical Hagiography." In Charles Burnett and Peter Dronke, eds., *Hildegard of Bingen: The Context of Her Thought and Art*. London: The Warburg Institute, 1998. 189–210.

Newman, Barbara, ed. *Voice of the Living Light: Hildegard of Bingen and Her World*. Berkeley: University of California Press, 1998.

Newman, Martha G. "Real Men and Imaginary Women: Engelhard of Langheim Considers a Woman in Disguise." *Speculum* 78 (2003): 1184–1213.

Nicholson, Helen. "Templar Attitudes Towards Women." *Medieval History* 1 (1991): 74–80.

Nikitsch, Eberhard J. "Wo lebte die heilige Hildegard wirklich? Neue Überlegungen zum ehemaligen Standort der Frauenklause auf dem Disibodenberg." In Rainer Berndt, ed., *"Im Angesicht Gottes suche der Mensch sich selbst": Hildegard von Bingen (1098–1179)*. Berlin: Akademie Verlag, 2001. 147–156.

Nilgen, Ursula. "Psalter der Christina von Markyate (sogennanter Albani-Psalter)." In Michael Brandt, ed., *Der Schatz von St. Godehard*. Hildesheim: Diözesan-Museum, 1988. 152–165.

Nolan, Kathleen. "The Queen's Choice: Eleanor of Aquitaine and the Tombs at Fontevraud." In Bonnie Wheeler and John Carmi Parsons, eds., *Eleanor of Aquitaine: Lord and Lady*. New York: Palgrave Macmillan, 2003. 377–405.

————. *Queens in Stone and Silver: The Creation of a Visual Imagery of Queenship in Capetian France*. New York: Palgrave Macmillan, 2009.

Nolte, Cordula. "Gender and Conversion in the Merovingian Era." In James Muldoon, ed., *Varieties of Religious Conversion in the Middle Ages*. Gainesville: University Press of Florida, 1997. 81–99.

Nyberg, Tore. *Birgittinische Klostergründungen des Mittelalters*. Bibliotheca historica Lundensis, 15. Lund: C. W. K. Gleerup, 1965.

O'Brien O'Keeffe, Katherine. "Edith's Choice." In Katherine O'Brien O'Keeffe and Andy Orchard, eds., *Latin Learning and English Lore: Studies in Anglo-Saxon Literature for Michael Lapidge*. 2 vols. Toronto: University of Toronto Press, 2005. II, 253–274.

———. "Goscelin and the Consecration of Eve." *Anglo-Saxon England* 35 (2006): 251–270.

Oakes, Catherine. *Ora pro nobis: The Virgin as Intercessor in Medieval Art and Devotion.* London: Harvey Miller, 2008.

Odell, Margaret S. "Reading Ezekiel, Seeing Christ: The Ezekiel Cycle in the Church of St. Maria and St. Clemens, Schwarzrheindorf." In Andrew Mein and Paul M. Joyce, eds., *After Ezekiel: Essays on the Reception of a Difficult Prophet.* New York: T & T Clark, 2011. 115–136.

Oliva, Marilyn. "All in the Family? Monastic and Clerical Careers Among Family Members in the Late Middle Ages." *Medieval Prosopography* 20 (1999): 161–171.

———. "The Nun's Priest." In Stephen H. Rigby, ed., *Historians on Chaucer: The 'General Prologue' to the* Canterbury Tales. Oxford: Oxford University Press, 2014. 114–136.

Olsen, Glenn. "The Idea of the *Ecclesia primitiva* in the Writings of the Twelfth Century Canonists." *Traditio* 25 (1969): 61–86.

Ortenberg, Veronica. "Le culte de sainte Marie Madeleine dans l'Angleterre anglo-saxonne." In Georges Duby, ed., *La Madeleine (VIIIe-XIIIe siècle).* Mélanges de l'École française de Rome. Moyen Âge, 104, 1. Rome: L'Ecole française de Rome, 1992. 13–35.

Pappano, Margaret Aziza. "Sister Acts: Conventual Performance and the *Visitatio sepulchri* in England and France." In Teodolinda Barolini, ed., *Medieval Constructions in Gender and Identity: Essays in Honor of Joan M. Ferrante.* Tempe, Ariz.: Arizona Center for Medieval and Renaissance Studies, 2005. 43–67.

Parish, Helen L. *Clerical Celibacy in the West, c.1100–1700.* Burlington, Vt.: Ashgate, 2010.

Parisse, Michel. "Fontevraud, monastère double." In Kaspar Elm and Michel Parisse, eds., *Doppelklöster und andere Formen der Symbiose männlicher und weiblicher Religiosen im Mittelalter.* Berliner historische Studien, 18. Ordensstudien 8. Berlin: Duncker und Humblot, 1992. 135–147.

———. *Les nonnes au Moyen Age.* Le Puy: C. Bonneton, 1983.

———. *Religieux et religieuses en empire du Xe au XIIe siècle.* Paris: Picard, 2011.

Parsons, John Carmi. "Intercessionary Patronage of Queens Margaret and Isabella of France." In R. H. Britnell, M. Prestwich, and R. Frame, eds., *Thirteenth-Century England VI: Proceedings of the Durham Conference 1995.* Woodbridge: Boydell and Brewer, 1997. 145–156.

———. "The Queen's Intercession in Thirteenth-Century England." In Jennifer Carpenter and Sally-Beth MacLean, eds., *Power of the Weak: Studies on Medieval Women*, Chicago: University of Illinois Press, 1995. 147–177.

Peltier, Henri. *Pascase Radbert, abbé de Corbie: contribution à l'étude de la vie monastique et de la pensée chrétienne aux temps carolingiens.* Amiens: L.-H. Duthoit, 1938.

Penn, Michael Philip. *Kissing Christians: Ritual and Community in the Late Ancient Church.* Philadelphia: University of Pennsylvania Press, 2005.

Peyroux, Catherine Rosanna. "Abbess and Cloister: Double Monasteries in the Early Medieval West." Ph.D. dissertation, Princeton University, 1991.

Pierre Abélard - Pierre le Vénérable. Les courants philosophiques, littéraires et artistiques en occident au milieu du XIIe siècle. Abbaye de Cluny 2 au 9 juillet 1972. Colloques Internationaux du Centre National de la Recherche Scientifique, 546. Paris: Éditions du Centre National de la Recherche Scientifique, 1975.

Pollak, Melanie. "The Vienna 'Gösser Ornat' and a Stole and Two Maniples in London." *The Burlington Magazine for Connoisseurs* 73 (1938): 115–121.

Potter, Julie. "The *Vita Gundulfi* in its Historical Context." *Haskins Society Journal* 7 (1995): 89–100.

Powell, Morgan. "Listening to Heloise at the Paraclete: Of Scholarly Diversion and a Woman's 'Conversion.'" In Bonnie Wheeler, ed., *Listening to Heloise: The Voice of a Twelfth-Century Woman*. New York: St. Martin's Press, 2000. 255–286.

———. "Making the Psalter of Christina of Markyate (The St. Albans Psalter)." *Viator* 36 (2005): 293–335.

———. "The Mirror and the Woman: Instruction for Religious Women and the Emergence of Vernacular Poetics, 1120–1250." Ph.D. dissertation, Princeton University, 1997.

———. "The *Speculum virginum* and the Audio-Visual Poetics of Women's Religious Instruction." In Constant J. Mews, ed., *Listen, Daughter: The* Speculum virginum *and the Formation of Religious Women in the Middle Ages*. New York: Palgrave, 2001. 111–135.

———. "The Visual, the Visionary, and her Viewer: Media and Presence in the Psalter of Christina of Markyate (St. Albans Psalter)." *Word & Image* 22 (2006): 340–362.

Ray, Anthony. "Brothers and Sisters in Christ, Brothers and Sisters Indeed: Two Thirteenth-Century Letters of Thomas, Cantor of Villers, to his Sister Alice, Nun of Parc-les-Dames." In Fiona J. Griffiths and Julie Hotchin, eds., *Partners in Spirit: Women, Men, and Religious Life in Germany, 1100–1500*. Medieval Women: Texts and Contexts 24. Turnhout: Brepols, 2014. 213–236.

Rebenich, Stefan. *Hieronymus und sein Kreis: prosopographische und sozialgeschichtliche Untersuchungen*. Stuttgart: F. Steiner, 1992.

Rice, Eugene F. *Saint Jerome in the Renaissance*. Baltimore: Johns Hopkins University Press, 1985.

Riggert, Ida-Christine. *Die Lüneburger Frauenklöster*. Hannover: Hahnsche Buchhandlung, 1996.

Ripberger, Albert. *Der Pseudo-Hieronymus-Brief IX, "Cogitis me": ein erster Marianischer Traktat des Mittelalters von Paschasius Radbert*. Freiburg: Universitätsverlag, 1962.

Robinson, I. S. "*Conversio* and *conversatio* in the *Life* of Herluca of Epfach." In Conor Kostick, ed., *Medieval Italy, Medieval and Early Modern Women: Essays in Honour of Christine Meek*. Dublin: Four Courts Press, 2010. 172–194.

Robl, Werner. *Heloisas Herkunft: Hersindis Mater*. Munich: Olzog, 2001.

Röckelein, Hedwig. "Die Auswirkung der Kanonikerreform des 12. Jahrhunderts auf Kanonissen, Augustinerchorfrauen und Benediktinerinnen." In Franz J. Felten, Annette Kehnel, and Stefan Weinfurter, eds., *Institution und Charisma: Festschrift für Gert Melville zum 65. Geburtstag*. Cologne: Böhlau Verlag, 2009. 55–72.

———. "Frauen im Umkreis der benediktinischen Reformen des 10. bis 12. Jahrhunderts. Gorze, Cluny, Hirsau, St. Blasien, und Siegburg." In Gert Melville and Anne Müller, eds., *Female vita religiosa Between Late Antiquity and the High Middle Ages: Structures, Developments, and Spatial Contexts*. Vita regularis 47. Münster: Lit, 2011. 275–327.

———. "Gründer, Stifter und Heilige - Patrone der Frauenkonvente." In Jutta Frings and Jan Gerchow, eds., *Krone und Schleier: Kunst aus mittelalterlichen Frauenklöstern, Ausstellungskatalog*. Kunst- und Ausstellungshalle der Bundesrepublik Deutschland und Ruhrlandmuseum Essen. Munich: Hirmer, 2005. 67–77.

Röckelein, Hedwig, ed. *Frauenstifte, Frauenklöster und ihre Pfarreien*. Essener Forschungen zum Frauenstift 7. Dortmund: Klartext, 2009.

Roitner, Ingrid. "Das Admonter Frauenkloster im zwölften Jahrhundert: ein Musterkloster des *Ordo Hirsaugiensis*." *Studien und Mitteilungen zur Geschichte des Benediktinerordens und seiner Zweige* 116 (2005): 199–289.

————. "*Sorores inclusae.* Bistumspolitik und Klosterreform im Geist von Cluny/Hirsau in der Diözese Salzburg." *Revue Mabillon* 18 (2007): 73–131.

Rousseau, Philip. "The Pious Household and the Virgin Chorus: Reflections on Gregory of Nyssa's *Life of Macrina.*" *Journal of Early Christian Studies* 13 (2005): 165–186.

Rubin, Mary. *Mother of God: A History of the Virgin Mary.* New Haven, Conn.: Yale University Press, 2009.

Ruys, Juanita Feros. *The Repentant Abelard: Family, Gender, and Ethics in Peter Abelard's* Carmen ad Astralabium *and* Planctus. New York: Palgrave Macmillan, 2014.

Saxer, Victor. *Le culte de Marie Madeleine en Occident: des origines à la fin du moyen âge.* 2 vols. Auxerre: Publications de la Société des Fouilles Archéologiques et des Monuments Historiques de l'Yonne, 1959.

————. "Maria Maddalena." *Bibliotheca Sanctorum*, 8. Rome: Istituto Giovanni XXIII della Pontificia Università Lateranense, 1966. 1078–1104.

Schäfer, Karl Heinrich. *Die Kanonissenstifter im deutschen Mittelalter: ihre Entwicklung und innere Einrichtung im Zusammenhang mit dem altchristlichen Sanktimonialentum.* Stuttgart: F. Enke, 1907; repr. Amsterdam: Schippers, 1965.

Scharer, Anton. "Charlemagne's Daughters." In Stephen Baxter, Catherine Karkov, Janet L. Nelson, and David Pelteret, eds., *Early Medieval Studies in Memory of Patrick Wormald.* Burlington, Vt.: Ashgate, 2009. 269–282.

Scheck, Helene. "Reading Women at the Margins of Quedlinburg Codex 74." In Virginia Blanton, Veronica O'Mara, and Patricia Stoop, eds., *Nuns' Literacies in Medieval Europe: The Hull Dialogue.* Medieval Women: Texts and Contexts 260. Turnhout: Brepols, 2013. 3–18.

Schiller, Gertrud. *Iconography of Christian Art.* Trans. Janet Seligman. [*Ikonographie der christlichen Kunst.* 2nd ed. Gütersloh: Gerd Mohn, 1969]. 2 vols. Greenwich, Conn.: New York Graphic Society, 1971–1972.

Schilp, Thomas. "Der Kanonikerkonvent des (hochadligen) Damenstifts St. Cosmas und Damian in Essen während des Mittelalters." In Irene Crusius, ed., *Studien zum weltlichen Kollegiatstift in Deutschland.* Veröffentlichungen des Max-Planck-Instituts für Geschichte 114. Göttingen: Vandenhoeck & Ruprecht, 1995. 169–231.

————. *Norm und Wirklichkeit religiöser Frauengemeinschaften im Frühmittelalter: Die "Institutio sanctimonialium Aquisgranensis" des Jahres 816 und die Problematik der Verfassung von Frauenkommunitäten.* Göttingen: Vandenhoeck & Ruprecht, 1998.

————. ". . . *sorores et fratres capituli secularis ecclesie Assindensis* . . . : Binnenstrukturen des Frauenstifts Essen im 13. Jahrhundert." In Thomas Schilp, ed., *Reform—Reformation—Säkularisation: Frauenstifte in Krisenzeiten.* Essener Forschungen zum Frauenstift, 3 Essen: Klartext, 2004. 37–65.

————. "Stiftungen zum Totengedenken - Schenkungen für den Schatz." In Birgitta Falk, Thomas Schilp, and Michael Schlagheck, eds., *. . . wie das Gold den Augen leuchtet: Schätze aus dem Essener Frauenstift.* Essen: Klartext, 2007. 39–51.

Schlotheuber, Eva. "Best Clothes and Everyday Attire of Late Medieval Nuns." In Rainer C. Schwinges and Regula Schorta, eds., *Fashion and Clothing in Late Medieval Europe / Mode und Kleidung im Europa des späten Mittelalters.* Basel: Schwabe Verlag 2010. 139–154.

————. "The 'Freedom of their Own Rule' and the Role of the Provost in Women's Monasteries of the Twelfth and Thirteenth Centuries." In Fiona J. Griffiths and Julie Hotchin, eds., *Partners in Spirit: Women, Men, and Religious Life in Germany, 1100–1500.* Medieval Women: Texts and Contexts 24. Turnhout: Brepols, 2014. 109–143.

―――. "Die gelehrten Bräute Christi. Geistesleben und Bücher der Nonnen im Hochmittelalter." In Helwig Schmid-Glintzer, ed., *Die gelehrten Bräute Christi: Geistesleben und Bücher der Nonnen im Mittelalter*. Wolfenbütteler Hefte, 22. Wiesbaden: Harrassowitz, 2008. 39–81.

―――. *Klostereintritt und Bildung: die Lebenswelt der Nonnen im späten Mittelalter*. Tübingen: Mohr Siebeck, 2004.

Schilp, Thomas and Annemarie Stauffer, eds. *Seide im früh- und hochmittelalterlichen Frauenstift: Besitz, Bedeutung, Umnutzung*. Essen: Klartext, 2013.

Schmid, Karl. "Bemerkungen zur Personen- und Memorialforschung nach dem Zeugnis von Abaelard und Heloise." In Dieter Geuenich and Otto Gerhard Oexle, eds., *Memoria in der Gesellschaft des Mittelalters*. Göttingen: Vandenhoeck & Ruprecht, 1994. 74–127.

Schmidt, Paul Gerhard. "Amor in claustro." In Christopher Cannon and Maura Nolan, eds., *Medieval Latin and Middle English Literature: Essays in Honour of Jill Mann*. Woodbridge: D. S. Brewer, 2011. 182–192.

Schnitzer, Rotraut. *Die Vita B. Herlucae Pauls von Bernried: Eine Quelle zur gregorianischen Reform in Süddeutschland*. Bamberg: K. Urlaub, Kleinoffsetdruckerei, 1967.

Schreiber, Georg. "Die Prämonstratenser und der Kult des Hl. Johannes Evangelist." *Zeitschrift für Katholische Theologie* 65 (1941): 1–31.

Schreiner, Klaus. "Mönchtum zwischen asketischem Anspruch und gesellschaftlicher Wirklichkeit." In Hans-Martin Maurer and Franz Quarthal, eds., *Speculum Sueviae: Beiträge zu den historischen Hilfswissenschaften und zur geschichtlichen Landeskunde Südwestdeutschlands: Festschrift für Hansmartin Decker-Hauff zum 65. Geburtstag*. Stuttgart: W. Kohlhammer, 1982. 250–307.

―――. "Seelsorge in Frauenklöstern–Sakramentale Dienste, geistliche Erbauung, ethische Disziplinierung." In Jutta Frings and Jan Gerchow, eds., *Krone und Schleier: Kunst aus mittelalterlichen Frauenklöstern, Ausstellungskatalog*. Kunst- und Ausstellungshalle der Bundesrepublik Deutschland und Ruhrlandmuseum Essen. Munich: Hirmer, 2005. 53–65.

Schuette, Marie and Sigrid Müller-Christensen. *The Art of Embroidery*. Trans. Donald King. [*Das Stickereiwerk*. Tubingen: Ernst Wasmuth, 1963]. London: Thames and Hudson, 1964.

Schulenburg, Jane Tibbetts. *Forgetful of Their Sex: Female Sanctity and Society, ca. 500–1100*. Chicago: University of Chicago Press, 1998.

―――. "Gender, Celibacy, and Proscriptions of Sacred Space: Symbol and Practice." In Virginia Chieffo Raguin and Sarah Stanbury, eds., *Women's Space: Patronage, Place, and Gender in the Medieval Church*. Albany: State University of New York Press, 2005. 185–205.

―――. "Holy Women and the Needle Arts: Piety, Devotion, and Stitching the Sacred, ca. 500–1150." In Katherine Allen Smith and Scott Wells, eds., *Negotiating Community and Difference in Medieval Europe: Gender, Power, Patronage, and the Authority of Religion in Latin Christendom*. Leiden: Brill, 2009. 83–110.

Schulz, Knut. "Das Leben des hl. Eckenbert und die Stiftsgründungen in Frankenthal (um 1125)." In Franz J. Felten and Nikolas Jaspert, eds., *Vita religiosa im Mittelalter: Festschrift für Kaspar Elm zum 70. Geburtstag*. Berlin: Duncker & Humblot, 1999. 141–168.

Seeberg, Stefanie. *Die Illustrationen im Admonter Nonnenbrevier von 1180. Marienkrönung und Nonnenfrömmigkeit: Die Rolle der Brevierillustration in der Entwicklung von Bildthemen im 12. Jahrhundert*. Imagines Medii Aevi 8. Wiesbaden: Reichert, 2002.

―――. "Spuren der Nonnen in den Illustrationen der Admonter Predigthandschriften." In Jeffrey F. Hamburger, Carola Jäggi, Susan Marti, and Hedwig Röckelein, eds.,

Frauen–Kloster–Kunst. Neue Forschungen zur Kulturgeschichte des Mittelalters. Turnhout: Brepols, 2007. 403–412.

———. *Textile Bildwerke im Kirchenraum: Leinenstickereien im Kontext mittelalterlicher Raumausstattungen aus dem Prämonstratenserinnenkloster Altenberg/Lahn.* Petersberg: Michael Imhof, 2014.

———. "Women as Makers of Church Decoration: Illustrated Textiles at the Monasteries of Altenberg/Lahn, Rupertsberg, and Heiningen (13th-14th. C.)." In Therese Martin, ed., *Reassessing the Roles of Women as "Makers" of Medieval Art and Architecture.* 2 vols. Visualising the Middle Ages 7. Leiden: Brill, 2012. I, 355–391.

Semmler, Josef. *Die Klosterreform von Siegburg: ihre Ausbreitung und ihr Reformprogram im 11. und 12. Jahrhundert.* Rheinisches Archiv 53. Bonn: Ludwig Röhrscheid, 1959.

Setzer, Claudia. "Excellent Women: Female Witness to the Resurrection." *Journal of Biblical Literature* 116 (1997): 259–272.

Shadis, Miriam. *Berenguela of Castile (1180–1246) and Political Women in the High Middle Ages.* New York: Palgrave Macmillan, 2009.

Signori, Gabriela. "Anchorites in German-Speaking Regions." In Liz Herbert McAvoy, ed., *Anchoritic Traditions of Medieval Europe.* Woodbridge: Boydell, 2010. 43–61.

———. "Eine Biographie als Freundschaftsbeweis. Paul von Bernried und seine Lebensbeschreibung der seligen Herluca von Epfach." In Gabriela Signori, ed., *Meine in Gott geliebte Freundin: Freundschaftsdokumente aus klösterlichen und humanistischen Schreibstuben.* Bielefeld: Verlag für Regionalgeschichte, 1995. 60–66.

———. "Muriel und die anderen . . . oder Gedichte als Freundschaftspfand." In Gabriela Signori, ed., *Meine in Gott geliebte Freundin: Freundschaftsdokumente aus klösterlichen und humanistischen Schreibstuben.* Bielefeld: Verlag für Regionalgeschichte, 1995. 67–77.

Silvas, Anna M. *The Asketikon of St Basil the Great.* Oxford: Oxford University Press, 2005.

———. *Jutta and Hildegard: The Biographical Sources.* Medieval Women: Texts and Contexts 1. Turnhout: Brepols, 1998.

———. *Macrina the Younger, Philosopher of God.* Medieval Women: Texts and Contexts 22. Turnhout: Brepols, 2008.

Simmons, Loraine N. "The Abbey Church at Fontevraud in the Later Twelfth Century: Anxiety, Authority, and Architecture in Female Spiritual Life." *Gesta* 31 (1992): 99–107.

Simons, Walter. *Cities of Ladies: Beguine Communities in the Medieval Low Countries, 1200–1565.* Philadelphia: University of Pennsylvania Press, 2001.

Sims-Williams, Patrick. *Religion and Literature in Western England, 600–800.* Cambridge: Cambridge University Press, 1990.

Sorrentino, Janet. "'In Houses of Nuns, in Houses of Canons': A Liturgical Dimension to Double Monasteries." *Journal of Medieval History* 28 (2002): 361–372.

Southern, R. W. *Medieval Humanism and Other Studies.* New York, Harper & Row, 1970.

Stein, Frederick Marc. *The Religious Women of Cologne: 1120 - 1320.* Ph.D. dissertation, Yale University, 1977.

Steininger, Christine. *Die ideale christliche Frau: virgo-vidua-nupta. Eine Studie zum Bild der idealen christlichen Frau bei Hieronymus und Pelagius.* St. Ottilien: EOS, 1997.

Sterk, Andrea. *Renouncing the World yet Leading the Church: The Monk-Bishop in Late Antiquity.* Cambridge, Mass.: Harvard University Press, 2004.

Stewart, Columba. *Cassian the Monk.* Oxford: Oxford University Press, 1998.

Stramara, Daniel F. "Double Monasticism in the Greek East, Fourth Through Eighth Centuries." *Journal of Early Christian Studies* 6 (1998): 269–312.

Strohm, Paul. "Queens as Intercessors." In Paul Strohm, *Hochon's Arrow: The Social Imagination of Fourteenth-Century Texts*. Princeton, N.J.: Princeton University Press, 1992. 95–119.

Swanson, R. N. "Angels Incarnate: Clergy and Masculinity from Gregorian Reform to Reformation." In D. M. Hadley, ed., *Masculinity in Medieval Europe*. London: Longman, 1999. 160–177.

Sykes, Katharine. "'Canonici Albi et Moniales': Perceptions of the Twelfth-Century Double House." *The Journal of Ecclesiastical History* 60 (2009): 233–245.

———. *Inventing Sempringham: Gilbert of Sempringham and the Origins of the Role of the Master*. Berlin: Lit, 2011.

Symes, Carol. "The Medieval Archive and the History of Theatre: Assessing the Written and Unwritten Evidence for Premodern Performance." *Theatre Survey* 52 (2011): 29–58.

Taglia, Kathryn Ann. "'On Account of Scandal . . .': Priests, Their Children, and the Ecclesiastical Demand for Celibacy." *Florilegium* 14 (1995–96): 57–70.

Taylor, Larissa Juliet. "Apostle to the Apostles: The Complexity of Medieval Preaching About Mary Magdalene." In Peter V. Loewen and Robin Waugh, eds., *Mary Magdalene in Medieval Culture: Conflicted Roles*. New York: Routledge, 2014. 33–50.

Thibodeaux, Jennifer D. *The Manly Priest: Clerical Celibacy, Masculinity, and Reform in England and Normandy, 1066–1300*. Philadelphia: University of Pennsylvania Press, 2015.

Thibodeaux, Jennifer D., ed. *Negotiating Clerical Identities: Priests, Monks, and Masculinity in the Middle Ages*. Basingstoke: Palgrave Macmillan, 2010.

Thomas, Hugh M. *The Secular Clergy in England, 1066–1216*. Oxford: Oxford University Press, 2014.

Thomas, Rudolf, ed. *Petrus Abaelardus, 1079–1142: Person, Werk und Wirkung*. Trierer theologische Studien 38. Trier: Paulinus-Verlag, 1980.

Tomaschek, Johann. "Carinthischer Sommer 1151. Der Aufenthalt des Bibelkommentators, Nonnen-Seelsorgers und monastischen Theologen Irimbert von Admont im Kloster St. Georgen." In Johannes Sacherer, ed., *1000 Jahre Stift St. Georgen am Längsee. Festschrift. Frauen zwischen benediktinischem Ideal und monastischer Wirklichkeit*. St. Georgen am Längsee: Bildungshaus Stift St. Georgen am Längsee, 2003. 200–223.

Thompson, Sally. *Women Religious: The Founding of English Nunneries After the Norman Conquest*. Oxford: Clarendon Press, 1991.

Thomson, Rodney M. "The St. Albans Psalter: Abbot Geoffrey's Book?" In Jochen Bepler and Christian Heitzmann, eds., *Der Albani-Psalter. Stand und Perspektiven der Forschung*. Hildesheim: Olms, 2013. 57–68.

Tilliette, J.-Y. "Hermès amoureux, ou les métamorphoses de la Chimère. Réflexions sur les *carmina* 200 et 201 de Baudri de Bourgueil." In Georges Duby, ed., *La Madeleine (VIIIe-XIIIe siècle)*. Mélanges de l'École française de Rome. Moyen Âge, 104, 1. Rome: L'Ecole française de Rome, 1992. 121–161.

———. "La vie culturelle dans l'Ouest de la France au temps de Baudri de Bourgueil." In Jacques Dalarun, ed., *Robert d'Arbrissel et la vie religieuse dans l'Ouest de la France: Actes du colloque de Fontevraud 13–16 décembre 2001*. Disciplina Monastica 1. Turnhout: Brepols, 2004. 71–86.

Torjesen, Karen Jo. "The Early Christian *Orans*: An Artistic Representation of Women's Liturgical Prayer and Prophecy." In Beverly Mayne Kienzle and Pamela J. Walker, eds., *Women Preachers and Prophets Through Two Millennia of Christianity*. Berkeley: University of California Press, 1998. 42–56.

Tosti-Croce, Marina Righetti. "La Basilica tra due e trecento." In Carlo Pietrangeli, ed., *Santa Maria Maggiore a Roma*. Florence: Nardini, 1988. 129–169.

Tracy, Larissa, ed. *Castration and Culture in the Middle Ages*. Cambridge: D. S. Brewer, 2013.

Tremp, Ernst. "Chorfrauen im Schatten der Männer: Frühe Doppelklöster der Prämonstratenser in der Westschweiz—eine Spurensicherung." *Zeitschrift für schweizerische Kirchengeschichte* 88 (1994): 79–109.

Trumbower, Jeffrey A. *Rescue for the Dead: The Posthumous Salvation of Non-Christians in Early Christianity*. Oxford: Oxford University Press, 2001.

Turner, Denys. *Eros and Allegory: Medieval Exegesis of the Song of Songs*. Kalamazoo, Mich.: Cistercian Publications, 1995.

Tyler, Elizabeth M. "Crossing Conquests: Polyglot Royal Women and Literary Culture in Eleventh-Century England." In Elizabeth M. Tyler, ed., *Conceptualizing Multilingualism in Medieval England, c.800–c.1250*. Turnhout: Brepols, 2011. 171–196.

Uttenweiler, Justinus. "Zur Stellung des hl. Hieronymus im Mittelalter." *Benediktinische Monatsschrift zur Pflege religiösen und geistigen Lebens* 2 (1920): 522–541.

Vaccari, Alberto. "Le antiche vite di S. Girolamo." In *Miscellanea Geronimiana. Scritti varii pubblicati nel XV centenario dalla morte di San Girolamo*. Rome: Tipografia Poliglotta Vaticana, 1920. 1–18.

Valentine, Susan. "'Inseparable Companions': Mary Magdalene, Abelard, and Heloise." In Katherine Allen Smith and Scott Wells, eds., *Negotiating Community and Difference in Medieval Europe: Gender, Power, Patronage, and the Authority of Religion in Latin Christendom*, Leiden: Brill, 2009. 151–171.

Van Engen, John. "Abbess: 'Mother and Teacher.'" In Barbara Newman, ed., *Voice of the Living Light: Hildegard of Bingen and her World*. Berkeley: University of California Press, 1998. 30–51.

Van Houts, Elisabeth. "Conversations Amongst Monks and Nuns, 1000–1200." In Steven Vanderputten, ed., *Understanding Monastic Practices of Oral Communication (Western Europe, Tenth-Thirteenth Centuries)*. Turnhout: Brepols, 2011. 267–291.

———. "The Fate of the Priests' Sons in Normandy with Special Reference to Serlo of Bayeux." *Haskins Society Journal* 25 (2013): 57–105.

———. *Memory and Gender in Medieval Europe, 900–1200*. Toronto: University of Toronto Press, 1999.

———. "The Women of Bury St. Edmunds." In Tom Licence, ed., *Bury St. Edmunds and the Norman Conquest*. Rochester, N.Y.: The Boydell Press, 2014. 53–73.

Vanuxem, Jacques. "La mort et la sépulture d'Abélard à Saint-Marcel-lez-Chalon." In *Pierre Abélard - Pierre le Vénérable. Les courants philosophiques, littéraires et artistiques en occident au milieu du XIIe siècle. Abbaye de Cluny 2 au 9 juillet 1972*. Colloques Internationaux du Centre National de la Recherche Scientifique, 546. Paris: Éditions du Centre National de la Recherche Scientifique, 1975. 335–340.

Vaughn, Sally N. *St. Anselm and the Handmaidens of God: A Study of Anselm's Correspondence with Women*. Utrecht Studies in Medieval Literacy 7. Turnhout: Brepols, 2002.

Venarde, Bruce L. "Introduction: Robert of Arbrissel's World." In Bruce L. Venarde, trans., *Robert of Arbrissel: A Medieval Religious Life*. Washington, D.C.: Catholic University of America Press, 2003. xv–xxix.

———. "Robert of Arbrissel and his Historians." In Jacques Dalarun, *Robert of Arbrissel: Sex, Sin, and Salvation in the Middle Ages*. Trans. Bruce L. Venarde. [*Robert d'Arbrissel, fondateur de Fontevraud*. Paris: A. Michel, 1986]. Washington, D.C.: Catholic University of America Press, 2006. xvii-xxx.

————. "Robert of Arbrissel and Women's *Vita religiosa*: Looking Back and Ahead." In Gert Melville and Anne Müller, eds., *Female* Vita religiosa *Between Late Antiquity and the High Middle Ages: Structures, Developments, and Spatial Contexts*. Vita regularis 47. Münster: Lit, 2011. 329–340.

————. *Women's Monasticism and Medieval Society: Nunneries in France and England, 890–1215*. Ithaca, N.Y.: Cornell University Press, 1997.

Verbaal, Wim. "Trapping the Future: Abelard's Multi-Layered Image-Building." In Babette Hellemans, ed., *Rethinking Abelard: A Collection of Critical Essays*. Leiden: Brill, 2014. 187–212.

Verbeek, Albert. *Schwarzrheindorf: die Doppelkirche und ihre Wandgemälde*. Düsseldorf: L. Schwann, 1953.

Veyrard-Cosme, Christiane. "Saint Jérôme dans les lettres d'Alcuin: de la source matérielle au modèle spirituel." *Revue des Études Augustiniennes et Patristiques* 49 (2003): 323–351.

Volfing, Annette. *John the Evangelist in Medieval German Writing: Imitating the Inimitable*. Oxford: Oxford University Press, 2001.

Von Moos, Peter. "Abaelard, Heloise und ihr Paraklet: Ein Kloster nach Maß." In Gert Melville and Markus Schürer, eds., *Das Eigene und das Ganze: zum Individuellen im mittelalterlichen Religiosentum*. Münster: Lit, 2002. 563–619.

————. *Hildebert von Lavardin, 1056–1133: Humanitas an der Schwelle des höfischen Zeitalters*. Pariser historische Studien 3. Stuttgart: A. Hiersemann, 1965.

Von Wilckens, Leonie. "Das goldgestickte Antependium aus Kloster Rupertsberg." *Pantheon* 35 (1977): 3–10.

Waddell, Chrysogonus. "Cistercian Influence on the Abbey of the Paraclete? Plotting Data from the Paraclete Book of Burials, Customary, and Necrology." In Terryl N. Kinder, ed., *Perspectives for an Architecture of Solitude: Essays on Cistercians, Art and Architecture in Honor of Peter Fergusson*. Turnhout: Brepols, 2004. 329–340.

————. "'Epithalamica': An Easter Sequence by Peter Abelard." *The Mystical Quarterly* 72 (1986): 239–271.

————. "Heloise and the Abbey of the Paraclete." In Mark Williams, ed., *The Making of Christian Communities in Late Antiquity and the Middle Ages*. London: Anthem Press, 2005. 103–116.

————. "Peter Abelard as Creator of Liturgical Texts." In Rudolf Thomas, ed., *Petrus Abaelardus, 1079–1142: Person, Werk und Wirkung*. Trierer theologische Studien 38. Trier: Paulinus-Verlag, 1980. 267–86.

Waldman, Thomas G. "Abbot Suger and the Nuns of Argenteuil." *Traditio* 41 (1985): 239–272.

Walker, Rose. "Images of Royal and Aristocratic Burial in Northern Spain, c.950-c.1250." In Elisabeth van Houts, ed., *Medieval Memories: Men, Women, and the Past, 700–1300*. New York: Longman, 2001. 150–172.

————. "Leonor of England, Plantagenet Queen of King Alfonso VII of Castile, and her Foundation of the Cistercian Abbey of Las Huelgas. In Imitation of Fontevraud?" *Journal of Medieval History* 31 (2005): 346–368.

Walsh, John. *The Mass and Vestments of the Catholic Church: Liturgical, Doctrinal, Historical, and Archeological*. Chicago: Benziger Bros., 1916.

Walter, Joseph. "Les miniatures du Codex Guta-Sintram de Marbach-Schwarzenthann (1154)." *Archives Alsaciennes d'Histoire de l'Art* 4 (1925): 1–40.

Wansbrough, J. H. "St. Gregory's Intention in the Stories of St. Scholastica and St. Benedict." *Revue bénédictine* 75 (1965): 145–151.

Weis, Béatrice. "Die Nekrologien von Schwarzenthann und Marbach im Elsaß." *Zeitschrift für die Geschichte des Oberrheins* 128 (1980): 51–68.

———. "La prière dans un monastère de femmes en Haute-Alsace au cours du XIIe siècle." In *Naissance et fonctionnement des réseaux monastiques et canoniaux*. Actes du premier colloque international du C.E.R.C.O.R. Saint-Étienne: Université Jean Monnet, 1991. 473–482.

Wemple, Suzanne. *Women in Frankish Society: Marriage and the Cloister, 500 to 900*. Philadelphia: University of Pennsylvania Press, 1981.

Wetter, Evelin. "Von Bräuten und Vikaren Christi–Zur Konstruktion von Ähnlichkeit im sakralen Initiationsakt." In Martin Gaier, Jeanette Kohl, and Alberto Saviello, eds., *Similitudo: Konzepte der Ähnlichkeit in Mittelalter und Früher Neuzeit*. Munich: Fink, 2012. 129–146.

Wheeler, Bonnie, ed. *Listening to Heloise: The Voice of a Twelfth-Century Woman*. New York: St. Martin's Press, 2000.

Wiesen, David S. *St. Jerome as a Satirist: A Study in Christian Latin Thought and Letters*. Ithaca, N.Y.: Cornell University Press, 1964.

Williams, John W. "León: The Iconography of a Capital." In Thomas N. Bisson, ed., *Cultures of Power: Lordship, Status, and Process in Twelfth-Century Europe*. Philadelphia: University of Pennsylvania Press, 1995. 231–258.

Williams, Megan Hale. *The Monk and the Book: Jerome and the Making of Christian Scholarship*. Chicago: University of Chicago Press, 2006.

Wilmart, A. "Nicolas Manjacoria cistercien à Trois-Fontaines." *Revue bénédictine* 33 (1921): 136–143.

Wilms, Beatrix. *Amatrices ecclesiarum: Untersuchung zur Rolle und Funktion der Frauen in der Kirchenreform des 12. Jahrhunderts*. Bochum: N. Brockmeyer, 1987.

Winston-Allen, Anne. *Convent Chronicles: Women Writing About Women and Reform in the Late Middle Ages*. University Park: Pennsylvania State University Press, 2004.

Wischermann, Else Maria. *Marcigny-sur-Loire: Gründungs- und Frühgeschichte des ersten Cluniacenserinnenpriorates, 1055–1150*. Munich: W. Fink, 1986.

Wogan-Browne, Jocelyn. "Dead to the World? Death and the Maiden Revisited in Medieval Women's Convent Culture." In Vera Morton, trans., *Guidance for Women in Twelfth-Century Convents*. Cambridge: D. S. Brewer, 2003. 157–180.

———. "'Our Steward, St. Jerome': Theology and the Anglo-Norman Household." In Anneke B. Mulder-Bakker and Jocelyn Wogan-Browne, eds., *Household, Women, and Christianities in Late Antiquity and the Middle Ages*. Turnhout: Brepols, 2005. 133–165.

Wolbrink, Shelley Amiste. "Necessary Priests and Brothers: Male-Female Co-Operation in the Premonstratensian Women's Monasteries of Füssenich and Meer, 1140–1260." In Fiona J. Griffiths and Julie Hotchin, eds., *Partners in Spirit: Women, Men, and Religious Life in Germany, 1100–1500*. Medieval Women: Texts and Contexts 24. Turnhout: Brepols, 2014. 171–212.

———. "Women in the Premonstratensian Order of Northwestern Germany, 1120–1250." *Catholic Historical Review* 89 (2003): 387–408.

Wollasch, Joachim. "Frauen in der Cluniacensis ecclesia." In Kaspar Elm and Michel Parisse, eds., *Doppelklöster und andere Formen der Symbiose männlicher und weiblicher Religiosen im Mittelalter*. Berlin: Duncker and Humblot, 1992. 97–113.

————. "Parenté noble et monachisme réformateur: Observations sur les 'conversions' à la vie monastique aux XIe et XIIe siècles." *Revue historique* 264 (1980): 3–24.

Wolter, Heinz. *Arnold von Wied, Kanzler Konrads III. und Erzbischof von Köln*. Veröffentlichungen des Kölnischen Geschichtsvereins 32. Cologne: H. Wamper, 1973.

Wood, Charles T. "Fontevraud, Dynasticism, and Eleanor of Aquitaine." In Bonnie Wheeler and John Carmi Parsons, eds., *Eleanor of Aquitaine: Lord and Lady*. New York: Palgrave Macmillan, 2003. 407–422.

Worm, Andrea. "A Gospel Book in Cambridge and the Artistic Relationship Between the Meuse Valley and the Rhineland in the Twelfth Century." In Stella Panayatova, ed., *The Cambridge Illuminations: The Conference Papers*. London: Harvey Miller, 2007. 21–29.

Wulstan, David. "Heloise at Argenteuil and the Paraclete." In Marc Stewart and David Wulstan, eds., *Poetic and Musical Legacy of Heloise and Abelard: An Anthology of Essays by Various Authors*. Ottawa: Institute of Mediaeval Music, 2003. 67–90.

————. "*Novi modulaminis melos*: The Music of Heloise and Abelard." *Plainsong and Medieval Music* 11 (2002): 1–23.

Yarrow, Simon. *Saints and Their Communities. Miracle Stories in Twelfth-Century England*. Oxford: Clarendon Press, 2006.

Yates, Jonathan P. "Weaker Vessels and Hindered Prayers: 1 Peter 3:2 in Jerome and Augustine." *Augustiniana* 54 (2004): 243–259.

Young, Karl. *The Drama of the Medieval Church*. 2 vols. Oxford: The Clarendon Press, 1933.

Zola, Alan G. *Radbertus's Monastic Voice: Ideas about Monasticism at Ninth-Century Corbie*. Ph.D. dissertation, Loyola University Chicago, 2008.

INDEX

Abelard: as abbot of St. Gildas, 34, 150, 225n182; 249n135; and Blamires's medieval "case" for women, 6–7, 42–43; burial at the Paraclete, 150, 173–75; as "exceptional," 33–38; as founder of the Paraclete, 34, 179; and Guibert of Gembloux, 36–37; and Heloise, 136, 149–52, 163, 179–80; influence at Marbach, 105–6, 169–70; and Jerome, 97, 101–2, 109–10; on Jesus's relations with women, 43–44, 60–61, 73; and John the Evangelist, 45–46, 50; and Malchus, 102; and Mary Magdalene, 68, 70; on men's service to women, 25, 57, 127–28, 154, 169–70; as a nun's priest, 3; religious women as *dominae*, 104–5; and Robert of Arbrissel, 35–36; Sermon 30, 104–6, 169–73; and women's constancy at the cross and tomb, 66, 71, 72; and women's prayerfulness, 149–52, 155–56, 167, 170–73. *See also* Guta-Sintram Codex; Heloise; Paraclete
Abigail: intercession of, 152
Abundus, 205n22
Adela of Blois: and Hildebert of Lavardin, 104, 241n16; and Hugh of Fleury, 42–43, 72, 97
Adelheid of Vilich, 243n44
Adelheid, empress, 97
Admont: double monastery, 27; and Gerhoch of Reichersberg, 90; prayers of nuns, 271n118. *See also* Irimbert of Admont
Adrevald of Fleury, 126
Aelfric of Eynsham, 156–57
Aelred of Rievaulx: biblical models for women, 71, 73; choice of priest for women, 203n14; on gifts, 28; and Godric of Finchale, 113; praise for his sister, 131–32; on sexual temptation, 12–13; writing for his sister, 71, 73, 113

Æthelburh of Kent, 151
Agnes of Poitou, 71–72
Agnes, prioress of Nun Appleton, 48
Alb. *See* Edith of Wilton
Alberic of Monte Cassino, 126, 166
Alcuin of York: friendships with women, 84–89; and Jerome, 109, 110; and women's prayers 161–63. *See also* Gisela; Rotrude
Aldhelm of Malmesbury, 83, 126; and Malchus, 240n8; writing for women, 83, 161
Alexander III, Pope, 130
Algasia, 82
Ambrose, saint: interpretation of John 19:27, 46; and sister, Marcellina, 118
Amfrida: noble matron at Bec, 134
Aminadab, Chariot of, 23
Amnon: and Thamar, 138–40
Amtenhausen, 21
Andernach, 21, 133, 233n94, 257n78
Anselm of Lucca, 47
Anselm, archbishop of Canterbury: and clerical celibacy, 81; correspondence with women, 241n18; letter to Robert, 21, 24; on John the Evangelist, 50; on Mary and intercession, 158; and Mary Magdalene, 73, 81; and Matilda of Tuscany, 71; and Reginald of Canterbury, 80–81; and sister Richeza, 133; on wives and intercession, 156; women at Bec, 134. *See also* Bec
Antependium: from Göß, 184, 187, 186 fig. 25; from Rupertsberg, 187–89, 188 fig. 27; Wichmannsburger Antependium (from Medingen), 189–91, 190 fig. 28
Antony, saint, 121
Apostles: depicted on Edith's alb, 183; faithlessness at the cross, 66–67, 70; heretics and the apostolic model, 75–76; involvement with women, 21, 24, 38, 40,

ACKNOWLEDGMENTS

Many friends and colleagues have offered advice and encouragement during the course of my work on this project, helping to shape the book and immeasurably to improve it. It is a pleasure to acknowledge here their kindness, patience, and above all their deep erudition. My heartfelt thanks are due first to Barbara Newman, whose careful reading of the manuscript and judicious comments at a critical juncture gave me renewed energy and a clear sense of the project as a whole. I am deeply grateful to Elisabeth van Houts for her wisdom, mentorship, and friendship. Liesbeth read and commented on an early draft manuscript of this project, offering invaluable advice with characteristic warmth and kindness. Julie Hotchin, Stacy Klein, and Bruce Venarde read chapters at various points, and ultimately also the manuscript in its entirety. Each has engaged deeply and generously not just with this book, but with my research over many years. I am grateful for their extensive knowledge, which they freely share, and for their attentive and critical reading. Tom Noble encouraged this project and its author in many ways, offering a model of scholarly generosity and kindheartedness that is without equal. Among my friends, I particularly wish to thank Helen Jacupke, who has shared her learning and elegance of mind with me, as she has with generations of her students.

While writing this book, I had the good fortune to co-edit a collection of essays with Julie Hotchin on women and men in the religious life in German-speaking lands. I owe a debt of gratitude to the contributors to that project, whose expertise on questions relating to the practice of pastoral care vastly enriched my understanding of nuns' priests. I thank John Coakley, Jennifer Kolpakoff Deane, Elsanne Gilomen-Schenkel, Sigrid Hirbodian, Sabine Klapp, Susan Marti, Anthony Ray, Sara Poor, Wybren Scheepsma, Eva Schlotheuber, and Shelley Amiste Wolbrink. Other colleagues have engaged with the project in its various parts, suggesting improvements and refinements. Conrad Leyser offered valuable comments on an early version of Chapter 4, helping me to clarify and focus my argument. As editors of the *Oxford Handbook of Women and Gender*, Judith Bennett and Ruth Mazo Karras pushed me to sharpen my conclusions on women and reform. Constant Mews has not only written extensively on topics relevant to nuns' priests, prompting my interest, but has also advised and encouraged me in my own research. Constance Berman taught me to see women and men together in monastic reform movements, and to question received narratives. Maureen Miller helped immeasurably in my thinking on women's liturgical textiles, a topic that was initially inspired by her expert study. Gary Macy has advised me, more than once, on questions related to women's liturgical practice. Dyan Elliott has inspired me in countless ways; I gratefully acknowledge my many intellectual debts to her scholarship. Lauren Mancia read several chapters, offering thoughtful advice as well as good friendship. Finally, anonymous reviewers over the years have carefully and thoughtfully considered my draft articles and other projects; it is a pleasure to acknowledge their influence here, and to thank them. They can see, I hope, how valuable their suggestions have been to me.

Several foundations and institutes have supported me during the course of my research; I particularly thank the Alexander von Humboldt Foundation and the National Endowment for the Humanities. With their support, I was fortunate to spend 2007–2008 as a visiting fellow at the Johannes Gutenberg Universität, Mainz. My host, Franz J. Felten, was gracious in welcoming me and unfailingly generous in sharing with me his deep knowledge of female religious life and monasticism. It goes without saying that my research benefited significantly from his counsel. My time in Mainz was made all the more wonderful through the kind friendship of Christine Kleinjung. Invitations to speak at Trier, Eichstätt, and Gandersheim, and at a meeting of the *Arbeitskreis geistliche Frauen im europäischen Mittelalter* in Dhaun gave me the opportunity to present and refine my work on German sources. I am grateful to Alison Beach for including me in the AGFEM "circle," and to Hedwig Röckelein for welcoming me at Gandersheim and sharing her publications with me in the years since. The opportunity to present portions of this work in other seminars and workshops has enriched the project as a whole. I am grateful to readers and audiences at Cambridge, Columbia, Cornell, Ghent, London, Madrid, Notre Dame, Paris, Princeton, Smith College, Stanford University, UC Santa Barbara, the University of Puget Sound, and Yale.

I began writing this book at New York University, and I thank my colleagues there for their rich friendship and support: Karl Appuhn, Zvi Ben-Dor Benite, Linda Gordon, Martha Hodes, Maria Montoya, Molly

Nolan, Kathryn A. Smith, Jane Tylus, Joanna Waley-Cohen, and Barbara Weinstein. Catharine Stimpson deserves my special thanks for her energetic and unfailing enthusiasm for all forms of learning, and her promotion of intellectual enquiry and exchange. In my new academic home at Stanford University, I have been warmly welcomed by a vibrant community of historians and medievalists. I especially thank Paula Findlen, Estelle Freedman, Marisa Galvez, Allyson Hobbs, Jack Rakove, Aron Rodrigue, Kathryn Starkey, Elaine Treharne, Kären Wigan, Caroline Winterer, and Steve Zipperstein. For their guidance at the University of Pennsylvania Press, I am grateful to Ruth Mazo Karras and Jerry Singerman, whose patience with me, and with this project, has been heroic.

My family has provided the deepest, most sustained, and most constant support. My grandparents, Gerald and Kitty Anna Griffiths, have been faithful friends to me, and to all their grandchildren and great-grandchildren, encouraging us always and never faltering in their confidence in our projects. I deeply regret that my much beloved grandmother did not live to see this book in print. My parents, Ian and Christine Griffiths, have supported me in ways that I—now also a parent—am only beginning to understand. They allowed me the freedom of intellectual exploration as I grew up, giving me every opportunity to study and to follow my interests, and sharing enthusiastically in my discoveries. During the years that I have worked on this and other projects, they have patiently and generously encouraged me, welcoming me "home" during working visits to Toronto and caring lovingly for my own children. My sister and brother, Jennifer and Jonathan, are treasured friends—faithful, kind, and wise.

This is a book about men who supported women, and so it seems right to save my deepest thanks for Ronald, who has encouraged me from the moment we first met and who has remained steadfast in his faith in me and in this project. I have learned from him what it is to try my best. Our children—Rupert, Felix, and Augusta—are a constant source of joy, astonishment, and love. I am delighted to dedicate this book to them.